THE DEPTH OF MY FOOTPRINTS

From the hills of Namaila

To the Global Stage

NG'ANDU PETER MAGANDE

MALEENDO & COMPANY

Independent Publishers

ATLANTA, 2018

ISBN-10: 1720954542
ISBN-13: 978-1720954545

MALEENDO & COMPANY
ATLANTA, GA.

www.maleendo.com

Dedication

This written record of my life is dedicated to my mother, Nakanjoli, and my spouse, Joyce for their illustrious mothercraft. I am thankful to my mother Nakanjoli for carrying me and caring for me, especially during the first nine months of my life, when I did not know where and who I was on earth. Even with a heavy load of firewood (*cileye ca nkuni*), a basket (*nsuwo*) full of crops, or a pot (*nongo*) full of water on her head, Nakanjoli still managed to delicately balance her walk in the rocky paths of Namaila so as to protect me from all harm should she stumble and fall.

Nakanjoli gave me a personalized fingerprint that is beyond any crafty forgery. She preserved my early prints, artistically engraved by my feeble fingers and toes on her womb wall beyond the vagaries of climate change. These made me the only one made in the Creator's own image but with my own unique identity.

My mother provided the colostrum that built my immunity against many preying diseases. As I was growing up, even in the absence of diapers in those days, my mother demonstrated the highest level of hygiene by keeping me dry and clean and teaching me the virtues of cleanliness. Nakanjoli carefully selected and fed me the foods that nourished my tender body.

Joyce Mudenda (bina-Choobe) came into my life a few weeks after the demise of Nakanjoli. She was a fitting replacement for my mother. Although, as a working professional, she spent many hours out of our home, she always remembered to prepare for the family's daily needs before going to work. Whenever she was off duty, she occupied herself in cleaning the house and putting the surroundings in order for our comfort.

During my working life, I found my spouse a helpful counsel, always willing to give a second opinion on any matter on which I consulted her. Her enduring patience gave me time to rethink issues and arrive at better decisions. Our conversations on forgiveness taught me how to fight anxiety, anger, fear, and worry.

As I closed my eyes and dozed off, while trying to recall the events that had happened in seventy years of my journey, bina-Choobe was readily available to suggest a more tolerant and diplomatic way of expressing my displeasure at those who had inflicted so much injury to me. Joyce's intercession helped me to absorb all the pain and to stealthily admire the smooth scars that were left on my emotional, mental, physical and spiritual being as mere reminders of my existence amongst humanity.

Foreword

Duing the 1950s, a decade before Zambia's Independence, a five-year-old boy tended cattle and goats and watched over forlorn fields of millet and sorghum in a remote and rugged area of the Zambezi Escarpment in southern Zambia. In his free time, the boy wandered the hills and enjoyed eating a variety of wild fruits and succulent plants and tubers. He played games of self-defence and self-sufficiency with friends his age while learning the art of hunting with a spear and trapping small game, rodents, and birds with flat stones and snares.

He knew every inch of his playground. From the limestone caves (makolyo), whose origins include a dim story that people once hid in them from early slave traders, to the perennial streams, cascading over the escarpment into the arid valley below.

Beautiful as his home was, the boy knew only too well how difficult it was to make a living there. Unlike the plateau to the north and west, and the Zambezi floodplains to the south, the dry soils of the escarpment were thin and unproductive. Life was hard in Namaila.

However, there was a rich variety of wild game in the Namaila hills, such as the aardwolf, aardvark, and pangolin, species of wild animals almost unknown in Zambia. The boy knew about these things intuitively, while at the little Namaila village school, he learnt about a different world with different cultures far removed from his.

The little school succeeded in firing the boy's ambition that would take him beyond his wildest dreams. It is difficult to appreciate the enormous leap the boy made from this humble but magnificent backdrop of the Zambezi Valley to his leadership of an international mission representing the states of a third of the globe. The new challenges demanded of him to improve his arithmetic beyond twenty-two, the familiar number he used when reckoning his family's cattle.

In order to understand and appreciate the roles of the diverse members of the wider community beyond his village, the boy took to playing the intricate game of chess, requiring him to manoeuvre sixteen 'men' through enemy formations on a board of sixty-four squares. The many variants of his childhood traps in the wild were substituted by mental strategies and tactics represented by mathematical notations.

Armed with both traditional and modern skills, the boy matured into a man whose responsibilities took him to all corners of Zambia. His footprints are embossed in the plains of the Chambeshi, Kafue, Luapula, Luangwa and

Zambezi Rivers.

Meanwhile, things have not changed much in the Namaila area of Mazabuka District over decades. Except that people were converted to growing maize instead of millet on the thin ribbons of alluvial soil amongst the hills. But the 'Corridor Disease' wiped out more than half the traditional cattle. Decades of poor rainfall led to enormous pressures on the land. For many of the inhabitants, their circumstances seemed hopeless.

But a boy's fulfilment of a vision of a better life reminded him of his home in the hills of Namaila with an idea of developing the sustainable use of the abundant natural resources. Perhaps new ideas could help the people use the Gumba, a vast woodland, more productively. Land use could be made more efficient and less environmentally destructive to support the sustainable production of wild game and forest products.

The yearning for a better life by the inhabitants of Namaila was but an echo, in the Simukululu hills, of the loud cries of most Zambians. The man's attention was diverted away from dealing with the development issues of Namaila to those of the whole nation of Zambia and other communities far beyond. The call of duty led the man to places far away from the Namaila hills, meeting and interacting freely with strangers in the four corners of the globe.

After steering the seventy-one-member African Caribbean and Pacific (ACP) Group of States into the twenty-first century, Ng'andu was presented a medal by President Matthew Kerekou of Benin as a 'Commander of the Order of the Republic of Benin in recognition of the service rendered to the ACP-EU international community and to the negotiations for the historic twenty-year ACP-EU Cotonou Partnership Agreement'.

By the beginning of the twenty-first century, Ng'andu had become a recognizable figure and voice during international assemblies, including those of the International Monetary Fund and the World Bank. His calm and calculated interventions and contributions on various subjects were always sought after by the conference facilitators and acknowledged warmly by the participants.

Ng'andu's footprints can be found in the Great Hall of the People in China, on the Capitol Hill of the United States of America, in the prestigious Berlaymont Building of the European Union in Belgium, in the Metropolitan Cathedral in Brazil, in St Peter's Basilica of the Vatican City, in the Tegala Gardens of Bandung in Indonesia, in the Hanging Gardens of Babylon, around the legendary Ceiba Tree in front of the El Templete Monument in Cuba, and on the Panmunjom Mountain between North and South Korea.

Nearer to home, Ng'andu left his footprints in the capital cities of many African countries, where he stood beside the giant statues of Mzee Jomo Kenyatta, Nelson Madiba Mandela, Osangefyo Kwame Nkrumah and Emperor Haile Selassie. Members of the African humanity whose heroic acts and personal sacrifices in favour of other human beings are only suited for mythology.

During the first decade of the 21st Century, Ng'andu traversed the globe unwinding the debt web that impeded Zambia's development. His efforts achieved remarkable results for Zambia, whose economy attained annual growth rates of over five per cent.

In 2004, he exhibited a high level of leadership as a spokesperson for recipient countries during the successful negotiations for the overly-subscribed Tenth Replenishment of the African Development Fund of the African Development Bank.

I met youthful Ng'andu during the seventies as we skilfully negotiated for better coffee quotas and prices for our countries during international meetings. In 2005, some twenty-seven years after our first meeting, Ng'andu was available to tactfully navigate around an election impasse whose resolution resulted in my ascendancy to the presidency of the African Development Bank.

Ng'andu Peter Magande was born in 1947 at Mwiinga Cibuyu Village in Namaila area of Mazabuka District in the SouthernProvince of Zambia. He lived in the area until 1958, when he attended boarding schools and later university, away from the village. He started working in the government of Zambia in 1971 until 1994, when he retired at permanent secretary level.

Between 1996 and 2000, he served as secretary general of the African, Caribbean and Pacific Group of states in Brussels, Belgium. Between 2003 and 2008, he was Minister of Finance and National Planning in the Zambian Government under President Levy Patrick Mwanawasa.

Ng'andu's adventurous journey has taken him from being an accomplished shepherd boy in the hills of Namaila to becoming an astute international negotiator resolving economic, political, social, and trade issues amongst nations.

I invite you to follow the footprints of Ng'andu Ciingana Cibiya Peter Magande through the twentieth century to become one of Zambia's foremost public servants and international leaders in the twenty-first century.

Donald Kaberuka
(President of the African Development Bank, 2005-2015)

Prologue

"Do not follow where the path may lead, go instead where there is no path and leave a trail"
Ralph Waldo Emerson

We were having lively discussions with a British Government team in London in 1982 when the leader of our delegation asked that I give a statement on the state of the Zambian economy. After my short intervention, our host openly stated that he did not expect me at such a tender age to be in such an important and high government position. The elderly-looking civil servant further stated that the Director of Treasury in Her Majesty's Government was in his fifties when I was only thirty-five years old.

I remarked that David Stockman, the Budget Director of the United States of America (USA), the largest economy in the world, with a one point four trillion dollar budget at the time, was only eight months older than me. Stockman, who was thirty-six years old, is best remembered for his defence of his first budget by musing that, "None of us really understands what's going on with all these numbers." I took the remark about my age by our host as a compliment and politely thanked our host for his observation.

....

I had just started my civil service career with the Zambian Government in 1971, when an elderly officer took a great liking for me. He would find time to engage me in conversations any time we met. Our conversations were always in the ciBemba language, which I was good at after my tutorials from one of my pen pals. The officer was always praising me for my positive attitude and attributes.

One day, as I met the officer in the corridors, he stopped me and rebuked me for being a cheat. He accused me of claiming to be 'Bemba' when I was not. He admitted that he had not known that I was a Tonga because of my good ciBemba knowledge. I realized then that the officer had mistaken my identity because of my name Ng'andu, which is a clan name for one of the royal Bemba dynasties. I had gained a friend by assumption.

....

I had just disembarked from a plane on a local flight in the middle of the Brazilian Amazon forest in South America when a young black man with a huge radio on his shoulder rushed towards me. While the young man was enjoying the music from his equipment, I saw that seeing me exuded some additional excitement out of him.

"Which part of Nigeria do you come from?" he confidently inquired, as he closed in on me.

"How do you know that I come from Nigeria?" I asked back.

"You look like my people from eastern Nigeria" he answered.

I explained to him that I was from Zambia in Southern Africa.

As we walked towards the terminal building, the young man informed me of his tribe in Nigeria and that he was a student in Brazil taking a course in agriculture. My hosts interrupted our conversation as they ushered me into a car waiting on the tarmac. I had not realized that I was distinguishable by my African appearance from the crowds of the locals out in the Brazilian forests.

....

Having finished delivering a statement on behalf of my country at an annual meeting of an international organization somewhere in Europe, I was approached by a somewhat excited elderly European delegate. He had been requested by the Chairman to make some 'expert' contribution during the conference deliberations, while I had been called upon to do so only as a country representative.

A quick glance at his name tag confirmed that he was a professor; the highest rank at a university.

After exchanging greetings and congratulating me for the eloquent delivery, he confidently asked,

"Doctor, which university in the USA did you attend?"

I answered that I had not been to any Ivy League university and jokingly asked him to make a second guess of where I had my university education. When he mentioned a prestigious British university attended by royalty, I realized that he would never win the guessing game as he was very far off the mark.

I informed him that my *alma maters* were African universities in Zambia and Uganda. I further stated that I was not a doctor of anything. A few more complimentary comments from the professor made me feel proud of my African education. It is not where one gets the knowledge that matters, but rather how one interprets the knowledge acquired in relation to the challenges facing humanity. I regarded the guru's wishes for a prosperous future as a blessing.

'They tried to bury us but did not know we were seeds'

goes a Mexican adage.

After being introduced to some psychology lessons during my university studies, I became a follower of Erik Homburger Erikson, born Erik Salomonsen (15 June 1902 – 12 May 1994), a German-born American developmental psychologist and psychoanalyst known for his theory on the psychosocial development of human beings.

Erik Erikson, in his theory on the psychosocial development of personality, presents the development of personality as an eight stage process. He described the eighth psychosocial stage as one of integrity versus despair. This phase occurs during old age above sixty-five years and is focused on reflecting back on life.

He states that, "As we grow older (65+ yrs) and become senior citizens, we tend to slow down our productivity and explore life as a retired person. It is during this time that we contemplate our accomplishments and are able to develop integrity if we see ourselves as leading a successful life."

Erik Erikson believed that if we see our lives as unproductive, feel guilty about our past, or feel that we did not accomplish our life goals, we become dissatisfied with life and develop despair, often leading to depression and hopelessness.

Erikson goes on to say that the reflection involves looking at one's relationship with mankind and is meant to answer the question, "'Is it Okay to Have Been Me?' Success in this stage will lead to the virtue of wisdom. Wisdom enables a person to look back on their life with a sense of closure and completeness, and also accept death without fear."

....

As I insisted that Zambia's vision covers the period up to 2030, one of the participants wondered why I was so enthusiastic about 2030, when I would not be around to enjoy Zambia's positive developments. I answered that by then I will have incarnated in my grave into calcium phosphate that will fertilise the mango tree planted by my grandchildren, who will enjoy the sweet juicy fruits.

I concluded that I strongly believed that my usefulness was not only in my current form. My answer astonished many participants, but I was happy that it also changed the attitudes of most participants in planning Zambia's future.

....

Towards the end of December 2011, I and Joyce, my spouse of thirty-eight years, decided to retire to the scenic island of Mauritius on a retreat away from the hustle of the hectic life of Zambian politics. We spent time snorkel-diving and seeking the footprints of the long-extinct dodo in the white sands of the Mauritian beaches.

We then left the island and visited the Sun City Resort in South Africa, where we welcomed the New Year with songs that were in tune with the rippling sounds of the artificial waves. During the first week of the New Year, we were in Cape Town. After bathing in the bashing waters of the Atlantic and Indian Oceans competing for space at Cape Agulhas, we climbed the Table Mountain and feasted our eyes on the distant panoramic outline of the southern extremity of the continent of Africa.

The following day, we took a walk to the harbour to book for a ferry ride to the Robben Island. The officer at the museum informed us that this being the busy holiday season, they were fully booked for the next two weeks. He suggested that we book and come back the following week.

I explained that we were senior citizens from Zambia and that being entwined with the history of the prisoners on the island, it was our fervent wish to visit the island during our two days' stay in Cape Town. After a compliment on our youthful looks, the officer offered us the possibility of getting seats, "If you are able to wake up and be here early tomorrow morning."

Punctuality having been one of my hallmarks in my life, we turned up on time and were rewarded by being sold tickets for the first ferry trip to Robben Island. We sailed against the unusual rough ocean currents to the island in the Atlantic Ocean. As the ferry approached the harbour, a flock of seagulls soared overhead to welcome us. When we landed, we were greeted by a flock of penguins that seemed to have mastered a special welcome squawk that reminds one that this is no ordinary place.

After a solemn tour of the desolate island, we were shepherded into this innocent-looking building with narrow corridors. As we gathered outside an unmarked door, the escort dignifiedly introduced himself as a former resident of the island. In a defiant voice, he narrated the emotion-evoking story of the life of Nelson Rolihlahla Mandela (18 July 1918 – 5 December 2013) of which eighteen years were spent in solitary confinement inside tiny Cell 5 of Block B.

Due to waking up early, I forgot to carry a handkerchief and this prompted Joyce to hand over a tissue, which I used to join others in wiping out tears.

The life and deeds of prisoner number 46664 inspired me to recount my footprints on my unfinished journey from the hills of Namaila. Having attained Erickson's age of reflection, I felt the imperative to write about my identity and journey in the hope that someone will find a brave act worth emulating and easily find an answer to the question,

"Is it Okay to Have Been Me?"

Origination Of "The Depth Of My Footprints"

Once I had become familiar with the grazing grounds for our cattle and goats at the age of seven years, Simwaale, my father, decided that it was time for me to take the animals in the bush, alone. On my first day, I took the animals far away from home.

The tranquillity of the bush, while herding the cattle, gave me the opportunity to study. I learnt how to skilfully combine the roles of a shepherd boy and a student by taking my school work with me into the bush, since we had no lights to read at night. I practised my arithmetic by counting the different tree species.

One day, while the animals enjoyed the green vegetation and I got absorbed with my reading under a shade, suddenly, I heard some strange frightening sounds behind a dense thicket on an anthill. I started to round up the animals in readiness for a retreat. I was about to drive the animals away, when my father emerged from behind the thicket. He remarked that he was impressed by my brave reaction of gathering the animals instead of taking flight. My father went on to say that I had passed the most difficulty test in leadership, which encompasses bravery and courage.

Being away in the bush guarding, guiding, and protecting a herd of cattle and goats from predators and stopping them from mischief of eating people's crops, provided the fertile environment for training into responsible adulthood. By the age of nine years, I had accumulated much knowledge on the culture and codes of the value system of my people.

Simwaale often stalked me to ensure my safety and to confirm that I took the animals to the agreed grazing area. The new maize crop, which was very attractive to the cattle and goats, meant that I had to be very alert throughout the day. Any lapse on my part, resulting in the animals straying into a crop field, would invoke a beating by the owner of the maize and by my father for being careless.

One day, after my father caught up with me, I asked him how he was able to locate me in the different areas of the grazing lands. My father revealed that amongst the clues, were my deep footprints, which he carefully read and followed. I then realised that one's path in life is defined by the depth of one's footprints. "*The Depth of My Footprints*" is the narration of my life story in remembrance of the conversation I had with my father on the slopes of the Namaila hills.

Book Reviews

"I would like to say how fascinating I found the book and am amazed at how much could happen to one person. I studied development in politics and learnt much in general about the World Bank, the IMF, and structural adjustment programs. After reading of your insider knowledge and work I am inspired to go back and read more in detail."

-Joanna Booth, *Editor*

"I have gone through your autobiography and I must say I have thoroughly enjoyed myself and come out of it most enlightened. It is a compendium of Zambia's development and gives students of development an insider's view of the various roles different people played in the different aspects of Zambia's economy over time. I have particularly enjoyed your account on Zambia's rural development and some of the challenges you were trying to resolve. Clearly this work is very important and will contribute greatly to future generations to come to grasp with our development history. The narrative is a tapestry of a technocratic, political, and simply an ordinary observer who has experienced these many dimensions first hand. Otherwise, I felt honoured to have been asked to read this."

-Dennis Chiwele, *Development Consultant*

"It is a veritable tour de force. I learnt a lot from it, both at the anecdotal level and in terms of its contribution to history."

-Robert Liebenthal, *Economist*

"The Depth of My Footprints" is an extraordinary story spanning different worlds and changing times. The book reveals what the courage, determination, persistence, obstinacy and occasionally, stubbornness of one economist can achieve. "The Depth of My Footprints" not only provides a complete portrait of the formative and latter years of Ng'andu, but also provides readers with a unique insight into how the remarkable footprints of a young Zambian economist can inspire other economists to emulate the life of an iconic national, regional and global public servant."

-Denis Wood, *Consultant*

NG'ANDU PETER MAGANDE

Contents

NG'ANDU PETER MAGANDE

CHAPTER 1

Genealogy

My mother Nakanjoli (Saliya, Nanchimunya) Mwiinga, the daughter of Mizinga, and my father, Simwaale (Civwanda, Muntuwamoonga, Silas) Magande, the son of Simalambo were first cousins. My paternal grandfather, Simalambo, who was a Headman of Mwiinga-Cibuyu (Cuuwvila) Village, was the eldest brother to my maternal grandmother Mizinga. By Tonga tradition, marriages between first cousins, although permitted, have to be cleansed by holding a special ceremony at which a white hen is slaughtered to invoke the blessings of ancestors long gone.

When I grew up and became curious about myself, I asked Grandmother Mizinga, who willingly informed me about my birth. She said that I was born in a hut with a thatched roof in the early hours of Saturday, 5 July 1947 in Mwiinga Cibuyu Village at Namaila in the Mazabuka District of the Southern Province of Zambia. Being the first born child, I was subject to a thorough inspection and observation by my grandmother, who was a skilled birth attendant. My physical appearance satisfied her that I was a normal baby boy and this was confirmation that my parents' marriage had been sanctified by the cleansing ceremony.

Namaila is a remote and rugged area far from the nearest urban locations of Mazabuka and Magoye towns. The area had no roads except paths for wooden sledges pulled by oxen and paths for walking on. A new bicycle acquired by one of my grandparents was the only most modern transportation equipment. The inhabitants of the area had been driven away into the hills to leave the rich land near the Kafue plains for white settlers, who had retired after fighting in the First World War.

My grandmother informed me further that, I cried louder than many babies did. According to her, this was a good sign of healthy lungs. I told her that even if I had not lived for more than five minutes, my mother should still have claimed the record for giving birth to "a baby with the loudest cry". For it is not how long one lives on earth that matters but what one does even for the shortest period of one's existence on earth.

Mizinga and other elders remembered my birth well as it occurred a few weeks after the demise of my grandfather Cibiya (the pot). The old man had given instructions that he be buried in a sandy area so that he could easily crawl out of the grave once he resurrected. Apparently, his wishes were ignored by the living, who decided to compact his grave with hard soil after his mysterious death in a foreign land.

I was given the name Cibiya, after the man who did not believe in eternal death. Amongst my many given names is Ng'andu, which is my crocodile clan name. In Tonga customs, one may also be called by any of the names of their grandparents as they are regarded as praise names.

As per Tonga tradition, I had a special clay pot (nsambilo) reserved for my cold bathing water until I reached the age of five months. Into the bathing water, which was collected from a venerated pool of the nearest stream, were added all the herbs needed for the proper growth of my physical and mental faculties and protection from infectious diseases and evil spirits. Before bathing, I'd take a few sips of the medicated water. Some of the medicine helped to quickly heal the wound of the umbilical cord. Traditionally, this sacred pot and its contents were the genesis of one's character in adulthood.

My survival in childhood was dependent upon motherly care and plant life. Reference to one not having bathed from such a pot meant that there was a serious omission by the mother and grandmother in the early formation of one's character and physical body. No amount of training in later life would correct the damage from such an act of negligence and omission.

The unfortunate part of this important life-saving ritual was that only the female gender was given the details of what was added to the bathing water. This reinforced the relationship between mother and child, under the saying that, "motherhood is a fact, while fatherhood is a matter of faith".

I had the privilege of lazing around the homes of my grandmother and two grandfathers, Simalambo and Mweemba. I was exposed to the village management systems by Headman Simalambo, who allowed me to sit-in while he was adjudicating cases in the meeting hut (nsaka).

My Family Tree
I am Tonga by tribe, which is matrilineal in blood relationships. This means that kinship is based on the mother or female line. I am therefore more aware of my relatives from my mother's bloodline. I was lucky that by the marriage of my mother and father, who were related, my matrilineal and patrilineal relationships became closer and I knew a lot of the relatives of my both parents.

The inhabitants of Mwiinga Cibuyu Village were related by blood and marriage. This provided a highly dependent and supportive system that cared for everyone. As no one went to bed hungry, these circumstances were regarded as the ultimate in success.

As I sat close to grandfather Matongo (Mweemba Bbokesi), who was Simalambo's young brother, enjoying the coolness of the shade of the huge twenty-five-metre luxuriant Musikili tree in the early fifties, I asked him what made the tree grow so big as compared to the other trees in the vicinity. He replied that trees get their food and water through their roots, which spread around the tree and deep into the ground. Therefore, the health of any tree depends upon the size and the reach of its roots.

Grandfather Matongo explained that the health and behaviour of people also depend on one's family, who provide one's needs in terms of advice and physical needs. In later years, I learnt that some personal characteristics and diseases are inherited through family bloodlines. I, therefore, became interested to know my 'roots' or family tree and I engaged in genealogy.

There is an ancient story often told that the people of my Beetwa clan trekked from the east and settled at Demu near Pemba Township. During the raids by the Makololo (Lozi) tribe under Chief Sebitwane in the nineteenth century, many of the Tonga virgins were abducted and their cattle were taken away westwards and the tightly knit community disintegrated.

The survivors scattered and settled in Gwembe on both sides of the Zambezi Valley, in Cooma, Kalomo, Kazungula, Livingstone, Monze, and the Mazabuka Districts. Still, to these modern times, the Tongas do not live in close-knit large villages, for security reasons. The inhabitants of the six districts and other nearby places share similar names and many traditions.

Sometime in the nineteenth century, Namboozi (Munzya) my great-great-great-grandmother was born. She gave birth to Namweemba my great-great-grandmother, who gave birth to two sons, Hamakowa and Kande, and five daughters: Choobe, Kasamba, Mukanakancimwa, Nanchimunya, and Namboozi.

My great, grandmother Choobe, meaning 'encircling', is rumoured to have escaped from a Makololo slave trek somewhere west of Kalomo Town with her brother. She gave birth to five sons: Simalambo (Ciingana, Sautu), Mpanisi, Mapulawu, Chibuula (Nteeni), and Matongo (Mweemba, Bbokesi; and two daughters Kalinda (Namboozi), and my grandmother Mizinga (Kasamba, Maria, bina-Aaron). Mizinga gave birth to Nakanjoli (Saliya, Namweene), my mother, Namweemba (Kantali, bina-Rhoda), and Uncle Haansaka (Hicaambwa, Mweemba, Aaron). My siblings are Richard Hamainza, Cheelo, Roniah, Peggy, and Danny.

Simalambo, with his second wife, Nkombo, had three sons: Simwaale (Magande, Muntuwamoonga, Chivwanda), Ng'andu (Laimo, Chimwanga), and Pita (Anason, Mudyaki); and three daughters: Chilwalo (Mboozi, bina-Daniel), Nahilika (Mooya), and Kasamba (Kantu, Nsabata, Grace).

Grandfather Matongo had four daughters: Kavumbu (Maria, bina-Benson), Nachikalu (bina-Petrol), Jessie (bina-Boy), and Jane (bina-Hamasiku); and one son, Matiya.

Kalinda had one daughter, Namweemba (Namoonga, binaHachiloli), who was brought up by Matongo from an early age. Namweemba got married to Madenta, the village carpenter, and they had eight children. Bina-Hachiloli and her children relocated to Lubombo near Mazabuka Town and later to the fertile lands of Chief Shaibila in the Mkushi District of Central Province. Bina-

Hachiloli became the matriarch of the family until her demise in 2016.

Aunt Kantali married Fanwell Kachelo Chali (Maison Ntomba) and they had three daughters and five sons. Uncle Aaron and spouse Rhoda (bina-Trade) had eight children and forty-eight grand and great-grandchildren by the beginning of the twenty-first century. I tried many times to assist my uncle to migrate to better pastures, but he resolutely refused, preferring to look after the graves of his ancestors scattered all over Namaila. His reward was the title of Senior Village Headman bestowed on him by Chief Hanjalika in the twenty-first century.

I was fortunate that Grandmother Mizinga, Grandfather Matongo, Father Simwaale, Aunt bina-Hachiloli and Uncle Aaron had long lives and were available and willing to assist me in reconstructing my ancestry.

CHAPTER 2

Flourishing Under Traditional Knowledge

My apprenticeship started early in my life such that by the time I was seven years old, I was capable of guarding a herd of cattle alone in the Namaila forests. I left footprints in the hills, valleys, fields, and even on trees as I climbed to collect various fruits. I memorized the schedules of various activities and the courses to various grazing areas and watering points for the animals as I had not learnt the modern cuneiform writing.

After being made aware of the roots of my ancestry, I was determined to nurture my branch of the family tree. To grow strong roots, it was necessary for me to accumulate as much traditional knowledge on the behaviours of my elders and other members of the village community. I wanted to be properly cultured in the traditions of my relatives and people.

As per local custom, and being of the matrilineal clan, I left my parents after being weaned to live with Mizinga, my widowed maternal grandmother, whom I also called ba-Kaapa. By tradition, she called me her husband and I called her my girlfriend. I and two female cousins shared a mat on the floor of our grandmother's spacious rondavel, where she had a nice bed of fixed stakes. Staying with ba-Kaapa gave me an opportunity to observe her carrying out various chores in and around the hut.

Amongst her many lessons was how to neatly fold our reed mat and the two blankets on one side of the hut every morning. Whoever wanted to sleep early spread the beddings. Any accidental bedwetting, of which mostly I was the culprit, was followed by some soft advice to avoid drinking water just before bedtime.

At her advanced age, Mizinga was a competent storyteller and I enjoyed spending time in the evening with other grandchildren listening to all sorts of fabulous tales (kwaana), fables (kulabika), and wise sayings (twaambyo). Most of the fables and sayings were on morals and the virtues of honesty, kindness, hard work, inclusiveness, and togetherness.

My grandmother was an accomplished cook and she pampered us with her delicious dishes of various fresh and dried vegetables and meats. She even knew how to use the paste of fried groundnuts to tame the bitter medicinal vegetable called ndulwe into a luscious dish. Our reciprocal obligation was to obey all her instructions as they were generated from accumulated Tonga wisdom.

We were also responsible for washing the pots and plates, many of which were made by her from local clay and from hard wood such as from the mubanga tree. After washing them, they were neatly placed on a raised plate rack made of twigs, to dry. The racks were part of the colonial administration's compulsory regulations for maintaining high levels of hygiene in homes.

Ba-Kaapa taught us that we should not take for personal use any item without her permission. In clear terms, nothing belonged to me unless there was an agreement for me to use it. This was long before I read the eighth commandment of the Bible that says, 'Thou shall not steal'.

Ba-Kaapa was a renowned potter, gifted with skills to craft various types of utensils from clay for various uses. She gave lessons to her customers on how to handle the delicate pots and plates she crafted and sold. Apart from observing her at work, we also gained from the lessons to her customers and I do not recall when I last dropped a pot, plate or cup in our home.

Mizinga was an accomplished birth attendant and a counsel for young girls undergoing initiation (kukula). At some point, a young aunt and a cousin were in confinement in my grandmother's house. During the period of confinement, the initiates (bamyooye) were fed with the best foods and smeared with special ochre (musila) and oils from castor (mbono) and khaya nyasica (mululu) seeds extracted by my grandmother. Most often, I was included in the lavish treatment and occasionally, ba-Kaapa rubbed some of the castor oil on me or asked me to take a sip of the oil whenever I had a bowel problem.

After I established contact with Western civilisation at on older age, I learnt that castor oil has anti-inflammatory and anti-bacterial properties. The ricinoleic acid in the oil also helps in inducing easy labour during childbirth. I suspect that my grandmother used the castor oil to assist her to achieve fame in her trade as a birth attendant.

Later in life, I was surprised to find someone completely covered in ochre in a modern sophisticated spa. A tradition in which my grandmother was an expert in the fifties had made others rich. Except for my lack of an innovative mind, I could have made my grandmother wealthy by establishing a beauty spa long before some foreigner plagiarized my ancestor's knowledge.

At times in early childhood, I was among a group of curious youths who were invited by the initiates to watch a special performance called banamacaaca. By some rhythmic tapping of a hollow calabash and the singing of a special song in a totally dark room, we saw shadows of people and domestic animals moving on the walls of the room. This was the equivalent of modern films and has remained one of the mysteries of the Tonga nkolola ceremony.

After some months of confinement, the mooye was released at a lavish party with much singing and dancing. Males jostled to have a glimpse of the beauty with tanned smooth skin, white eyes and long flowing hair. The public display was an announcement that the girl was ready and willing for marriage.

The teachings during confinement included all there was for her to learn on how to be a good wife. No male knew what went on in the house of the female initiates. In fact, it was taboo for a male to get close to a house of an initiate, who was always fully covered in a veil and led around the house by a young girl called kalindizyo. Somehow, the separate secret teachings for young boys and girls, combined well to produce well behaved and resourceful married couples, who constituted peaceful communities.

My grandmother was haunted by some friendly spirits (mizimo) that demanded occasional appeasement. When invoked, she spoke in a strange tongue demanding new clothing and special food. Uncle Aaron, who had just learnt how to ride Matongo's new bicycle was sent to the nearest shop, some thirty kilometres away, to buy new clothing, a blanket, some tea, bread, and sugar for the old lady. I never learnt how to ride a bicycle because the only one in the clan was Matongo's and it was highly prized and only used on important occasions.

On the evening of the appointed day, there was drumming and singing with a special dance performed by ba-Kaapa and other women whose spirits were invoked by the special sounds of the drum. The old lady was adorned in her new dress and rattles (masebelele) around her ankles while shaking a rattle (muyuwa) made of a gourd. The frenzy was followed by feasting. I relished this occasion, not because I believed in its sanctity, but because of the dancing and the rare opportunity of eating some bread and drinking imported tea. Modernity cut short my enjoyment as the old lady had her last performance in 1958.

When I reminded her of the ceremony in the late seventies, she didn't volunteer much about it. She, however, reiterated that the spirits of dead people did sometimes manifest themselves in the behaviour of the living. She explained the significance and value of such beliefs in the society of those olden days. She stated that belief and faith were very important for anything to happen. For her, the spirits were real and appeasing them assured the communities of protection from harm.

In the eighties, ba-Kaapa used to visit us at Chelstone in Lusaka where we had relocated in 1974. To reduce the boredom of 'doing nothing', she'd sit on a reed mat under the shade of the fruit trees while we were at work and greeted anyone passing by on Acacia Avenue. As some passers-by did not respond, one day she asked us why people in Lusaka did not exchange greetings.

I told her that it was not a custom in towns to greet people whom one did not know. She then asked me, "How will you know people whom you do not even care to speak to?" I was beaten by my grandmother's philosophy and humane logic. I wondered why she could not be recruited as a lecturer in Humanism at the President's Citizenship College in Kabwe. With a great sense of guilt, I told her that village traditions are not applicable in towns, even though I knew that my answer was not genuine.

On further reflection, I realized that my many years of modern education at some of the best learning institutions still left some space to be filled by lessons from my humble village teacher of 1953. From that day, I found it difficult to cross paths with other people without greeting them. Luckily, many other traditions and languages have shorter ways of greeting than the elaborate Tonga version, which requires one to enquire on the health or well-being of so many things, including cattle. The easier greetings, such as 'Ni Hao,' in Chinese, 'Habari,' in Swahili and 'Hello,' in English have made it possible for me to faithfully abide by my grandmother's humanistic teaching on exchanging greetings with other human beings.

Due to the proximity of the homesteads of my relatives within the village, I had the opportunity of staying with Simalambo, the Village Headman, and Matongo, his young brother during the day and with Grandmother Mizinga at night. The close relationship between my father and mother gave me an opportunity to benefit from teachings from both my patriarchal and matriarchal connections.

I called Simalambo, my grandfather, 'syaneene'. At syaneene's place, I joined him in the nsaka and listened attentively to the deliberations. When there were no issues for discussion, the old man narrated stories of his hunting expeditions. Some stories were scary, but his ultimate conquest demonstrated his bravely and drew an attentive audience.

Late every afternoon, Kabongomana, the over-one-tonne bull would leave the rest of the herd and come to the nsaka to enjoy a supplementary feed from the hand of Simalambo. The bull was so huge and vicious that a story was told that once it held a pride of marauding lions at bay, protecting the herd of cattle, until the old man arrived on the scene to scare away the lions with his gun. I was introduced to the bull and got acquainted with the huge beast, which enjoyed being stroked by my feeble fingers while licking coarse salt from my palms.

In 1952, Simalambo travelled to Mazabuka Boma, some sixty kilometres away, to buy a new shotgun. He was reported missing after an absence of five weeks from the village. A younger relative, who'd escorted him, reported that the old man had left for home after buying the gun, while he remained with some relatives in town.

After an extensive search, Simalambo's skeleton and the new gun were discovered on a commercial farm in the Kaleya area of Mazabuka Investigations revealed that the old man had been shot dead by a white commercial farmer who suspected him of poaching on the farm. The old man's skeleton and the new gun were retrieved and brought to Namaila for burial.

The funeral of Simalambo was the first one I was allowed to closely witness in my life. I was allowed to witness the funeral proceedings for syaneene so that I could "not have nightmares of him". I was even afforded the opportunity to view his bones before they were buried.

In those times, it was taboo for children to participate in funeral proceedings. Whenever there was a funeral in the village, arrangements were made to camp the children in the distant part of the village, away from the funeral. On their return, the parents brought some gifts for us so that our attention was drawn to the new gifts and not to their trip.

Tonga tradition requires that the first meat eaten by mourners at a funeral must be of the favourite oxen or goat owned by the deceased person. This is normally after two or three days of the funeral gathering during which period, only nsima and vegetables are eaten. Tongas worry if they do not own some livestock to be slaughtered at their funeral. For some reason, pigs are not used in this ritual. Grandfather Simalambo had no worries as he owned many cattle and goats.

The old man's relatives decided to slaughter Kabongomana, the beloved pet of late Simalambo using the new gun. The bull was tethered on the western side of the grave in between two grain bins. Even after three gunshots, the huge bull was still standing. On being hit by the fourth shot, Kabongomana, while bellowing, charged towards the marksman. On reaching the grave, he leapt high into the air and then with a prolonged shrill, he landed on the grave with a loud thud with blood oozing from one of the bullet wounds. Finally, Kabongomana lay still after spilling some blood on his master's grave.

The sounds of the brand new gun and the ferocious bull reverberated in the surrounding hills as if to invite all creatures to my grandfather's funeral. People streamed from all directions. The dogs of the village howled causing frightening orchestrated echoes from the hills. Large swarms of pigeons and doves clustered and flapped their wings in delicate formations above the funeral gathering. In the nearby hills, hundreds of blackbirds perched on tall trees, their presence marked by hushed tones. It was a hallowing and chilling experience, which I will never forget.

Much later when I recounted the events to Uncle Aaron, he was amazed that I could vividly remember the happenings that had occurred when I was only five years old. My grandfather's permanent disappearance taught me that the mystery of birth is correlated to the mystery of death, both of which happen without prior notice.

Syaneene and Kabongomana, my best two friends, succumbed to the power of the gun, but in completely different circumstances. I started building a strong hatred for guns, as they caused the permanent disappearance of those I so dearly loved. I have refused to see the particular gun inherited by Uncle Aaron from Matongo. However, in later life, I bought my own guns as it was a sign of my coming of age. Apart from the few times I went out hunting with trusted friends, my guns are safely tucked away and I have to be reminded to renew the licences every three years as per the law of the land.

The demise of Simalambo resulted in some changes to the administration and physical setup of the Mwiinga Cibuyu Village. Grandfather Matongo succeeded Simalambo as the Village Headman. He also inherited most of the assets including the cattle and the gun from his elder brother. The new headman was a cool tall gentleman, who was interested in the modernity being introduced by the colonizing Europeans.

In his youth, Matongo and some friends had trekked all the way to Kalomo Town in the hope of getting across the Zambezi River to Wankie in Zimbabwe for work in the coal mines. When they ran short of money to continue the journey, the team worked on one of the newly established farms in the Popota area of Choma. Matongo, therefore, encouraged his subjects to adopt the new crops and crop husbandry. The changes in farming methods resulted in increased food security and prosperity for the villagers of Namaila, as they had plenty of small grains and maize.

Within a short period of time, some villagers, including my parents, were producing surplus maize, which they delivered to the nearest crop depot at Nkonkola, about thirty kilometres away. The nearest dip tank was situated close to the crop depot and as per livestock health regulations, we took the cattle for dipping once per month.

Most of Simalambo's children relocated and built new homes in distant places nearer to their fields. Matongo remained in the same old location, where he enjoyed the cool shade of the huge and dense musikili (trichilia emetica) medicinal tree. Uncle Aaron and I moved with Mizinga and her new husband, Haazunga, to a new home on the southern side of the Likoma River. My parents and siblings, together with my paternal grandmother Kasamba, relocated eastwards across the Kakolyo stream.

One day, Uncle Aaron and I were coming from the northern side of the Likoma River, which we found swollen because of heavy rains upstream. My kind uncle decided to carry me on his shoulders as he waded across the river at a point where the current was slow. On reaching the middle of the river, my uncle let go of me and I dropped into the deep water. Since I did not know how to swim, I flapped my hands while gulping a large quantity of water.

My uncle seemed to enjoy the show very close by before he rescued and laid me on the bank of the river. While mumbling something, he hit my bulging tummy with handfuls of wet sand. Suddenly, much of the water in my stomach poured out. He then asked me to put an insect called njebebe, which is agile in water, on my tongue and it bit me. It was strongly believed that the bite of this insect injects some fluid that arouses swimming capability in human beings.

My uncle then explained that he had faked slipping-off into the water. He proclaimed that from thenceforth I would not fear water and that I would never drown. This proclamation helped me as I confidently crossed the Simaila River on the way to and from school.

By some misfortune, my grandmother's new husband passed away late in

1953. His funeral drew thousands of guinea fowls as if they'd come to bid farewell to their tormentor. Haazunga was a good hunter and he provided the family with fowl meat on regular basis. My grandmother decided to relocate back to the northern bank of the Likoma River, where most of the people lived. It was also decided that I should join my parents at their new location as I was a grown-up boy.

Words of wisdom from my parents

Staying with my parents presented new challenges as I took on new responsibilities and had to learn new skills as the eldest child. No more kid-glove treatment such as I'd received from my old girlfriend, Mizinga.

I joined my family in their farming activities. I learnt how to harness the oxen, plough the fields, and sow and harvest the various crops. I do recall a few times when we were in the field by 04.00 hours and, just before dawn, it became pitch-dark forcing us to take a break in the field.

My father was a good planner and organizer. He was a strict disciplinarian and a teacher, demanding the highest levels of obedience, orderliness, and performance. He emphasized the imperative for food security in the home at all times and this required hard work and planning by the head of the family. My father owned some cattle, goats and chickens. We produced cassava, maize, millet, milk, sorghum, and a variety of vegetables. I cannot recall a day when we had no food.

The homestead of well-arranged round houses, grain bins, and livestock kraals was neat and well maintained. During the dry season, we spent time checking and oiling all farming implements, repairing any damaged housing structures, and spreading dried cow dung in the fields.

In spite of his "B" Standard education attained at the new Namaila School, my father taught me how to count, as I had to account for a number of things. My favourite assignment was that of counting the eggs in all chicken nests on a routine basis, without touching them. The myth was that if chicken eggs were touched by a human being, they would not hatch. I enjoyed this assignment because, on this occasion, I was allowed to pick some fresh eggs for the pot. The difficult part was how to remember which nests contained older eggs ready to hatch and which ones had freshly laid eggs.

I devised a method of putting markers on the nests, using charcoal and matching the brooding chickens by the colours of their feathers. I also became adept at adding and subtracting numbers up to twenty-one, the number of days for incubating chicken eggs. My parents were very impressed that there was a proper record of eggs and no more destruction of embryos by picking wrong eggs for the pot.

My father inherited the hunting trait from Simalambo, his father, as he also turned out to be a good hunter. But unlike his father who used a gun, my father used traps and snares. He taught me how to make and set snares and traps for various animals, fish, and birds using ropes, stones, strings, and reed baskets.

As we toured to check the traps, my father showed me various useful plants. He was my encyclopaedia on the names, behaviours, and habitats of various animals, birds, and fish. He explained the uses of the different parts of various animals, birds, fishes and plants. He taught me to respect nature as it provided us with all our needs.

I checked the traps while herding the cattle in the wild. I learnt early in life of the health benefits of such creatures as eel fish and crab from my father who insisted that I take sizable portions of them. I enjoyed a dish of crab meat mixed with flour of fried groundnuts and tomatoes when expertly cooked by ba-Kaapa.

I was always given the privilege of breaking the carapace of cooked crabs and I became an expert. My father explained further that eating brains of some animals could make one develop the habits of the particular animal. I took my father's word as the gospel truth and never challenged his advice for fear of turning into something undesirable!

Once, while on a visit to Washington DC in the USA, some thirty years later, I amazed my hosts and won prizes for my agility at shucking oysters during the National Oyster Day Festival. The value of eel and crab meat was revealed some forty years later, when I read in a medical journal that the meats were major sources of Omega 3 fatty oil and cobalamin (vitamin B12). Both of these foods are important for the development of the brain and general body health. It was only then that I realized and appreciated the efforts exerted by my father for me to have a big brain.

Nakanjoli, my kind and generous mother gave me lessons on many subjects and household chores. Early in life, I learnt of the value of the extended family relationships as my mother kept three of my cousins. She highlighted the need for me to be a role model in behaviour being the eldest child in the home and amongst all my close cousins.

Our mother taught us who to trust and respect in the village. We were told to avoid some people with bad characters. Bad character according to my mother included being rude, lazy, a drunkard, a thief, or someone of abusive nature.

One of the important early lessons that I was given was on the preparation of various foods including porridge and nsima from sorghum and maize flour. My mother supplemented the lessons I received earlier from my grandmother on how to prepare, cook, preserve, and cut various types of meats and vegetables. Often, when our parents were away from our home, I prepared meals for my siblings. Even when Joyce joined me in 1973, she was aware that any complaints on poorly-prepared food would be from my expert knowledge.

Between 1958 and 1971, I spent most of the time at boarding schools and the University of Zambia. I, therefore, had very little time with my mother at the village, in Namaila. In 1971, I was busy settling down in my new job after finishing studies at the university and I could not take any leave. However, my mother used every moment I was with her to give me advice on a number of issues. In June 1972, when I went to the village to say goodbye to the family as I was leaving for Uganda for further studies, my mother escorted me for a long distance.

During our walk, she advised me on many issues including personal relationships and discipline. At the age of twenty-five years, I should have already been raising a family in the village if schooling hadn't occupied that space instead. My mother considered that a pep talk on marriage was necessary. She advised that having been exposed to people from other regions and tribes, my concern should be on the characters and backgrounds of my partners whether in marriage or in personal relationships.

My mother hoped that the wide exposure I had will enable me to choose a spouse with correct virtues of morality, hard work, humility, and kindness. Her farewell message was that even a Ugandan lady would be most welcome in her home as a daughter-in-law. This was the longest and last conversation I had with my mother as she passed-on three days after my return from Uganda in June 1973.

After the death of my mother, my father decided to relocate to Nkonkola to live with his maternal aunts. A few weeks after he had moved, I visited the place to find out how comfortable he was. I was not happy with the house and I proposed that we build a bigger and better house, which I and my family could also use during our visits. He refused, reasoning that he did not want to have a house different from those of other villagers.

I then reasoned that the best thing was to relocate him away from the village. I arranged for him to attend interviews, which he easily passed for a farm on the Magoye Settlement Scheme. Instead of him shifting, he proposed that his cousin Harrison Chuuba, who had attended a farming course at the Kanchomba Farmer Training Institute, should shift to the farm. He convinced me that once Chuuba settled down, he would move and join him. I got a loan and bought twenty heifers and one bull from the Chisamba State Ranch and delivered them to the settlement farm as the property of my father and his clan.

Unfortunately, most of the animals died over a short period of time and Chuuba decided to sell the farm without informing me or my father. Uncle Chuuba relocated to Nkonkola and demanded the house and fields, which he had surrendered to my father. We then asked my father to move to our Choma farm as all his aunts had died by then. My father refused to shift to our farm, arguing that for the farm to operate as a business, no relative should settle on it.

With a great desire and ability to thank my father for all that he had done for me, I was frustrated by his attitude. During one of my visits to the village, I was accompanied by Christopher Mulenga, a close friend of mine, who volunteered to persuade the old man to have a new house constructed. But

Chris's long and friendly conversation did not achieve much as the old man flatly rejected all the proposals. He told Chris that it would be awkward for him alone to have a good house in the whole village.

My father preferred to live like other villagers even after investing so much money and other valuable assets in my education and upbringing. Simwaale passed on in September 2003 and his four siblings shared his assets amongst themselves. I did not inherit any of my father's assets in fulfillment of my 1958 covenant that the education he'd financed was enough inheritance to see me through the rest of my life.

My adolescence
One of the most exciting periods of a boy's life in Namaila was that of herding cattle and learning many survival skills. I joined Pita, my father's youngest brother, in tending the family livestock, although I had no share in them as they belonged to my father's clan by tradition. My father owned a maximum of twenty-two cattle and a few goats, which we counted every day. The number twenty-two is next to twenty-one, the number I used to account for the eggs.

We gathered the cattle belonging to different families, and sometimes even villages, in one place for bullfighting while having our lunch. The loss of a fight by one's bull led to a boxing or wrestling (kamaando) match between the owners of the bulls. The punishment for losing a match often extended to a denial of food, even from one's own parents, for the whole day.

At times, we were made to whip one another while running around an anthill. The faster one ran, the safer he was from the boy behind. Some of the games were played in the nude. Such occasions provided an opportunity for the older boys to enquire into the nature and physical condition of the anatomy of the younger bodies. Any noticeable physiological defect or physical deformity was immediately dealt with by the use of some readily available potent herbs.

Often times, one was directed by the older boys to collect birds' eggs, chicks, or fruits from a tree known to harbour vicious red wasps. As one screamed and scampered from painful wasp stings, this provided amusement for the rest of the team. The belief was that small doses of the wasp poisons made one immune to harmful antigens.

The pain and swelling were instantly toned down by applying the sap of particular medicinal plants. Even the wounds from the whipping games were quickly healed before going home by the application of some herbs such as the plentiful aloe vera. As there were no modern razor blades, very sharp blades of a special grass were used for making an incision on any part of the body when the need arose.

The younger boys were also responsible for collecting the wandering animals, while the older boys spent their time playing games. Due to the new succulent maize plants, which were liked by livestock, sometimes the cattle and goats strayed far from the camp towards the maize fields. One day, while on such an assignment, I saw a long and smooth-looking grey 'pole' rise high in front of me as I walked. I suddenly stood transfixed as the 'pole' towered above me. Surprisingly enough, after a while, the 'pole' dropped to the ground and disappeared into the thicket and I briskly resumed my walk.

Having collected the cattle, I narrated the strange episode to the group, when I reached the camp. One of the older boys immediately identified the 'pole' as a black mamba, one of the world's deadliest snake. He explained that I had been saved from a lethal strike and certain death by my freezing, as the snake does not attack stationary objects. We quickly moved the livestock away to another part of the grazing lands.

The expeditions into the bush were very exciting as there were a lot of related activities. Nutritious food in the form of cow and goat milk was plentiful and readily available. I learnt how to make fire by rubbing dried twigs and we'd roast green maize, pumpkins, sweet potatoes, fish, birds and rodents. These were supplemented by wild fruits and tubers, many of which were medicinal and hunger inhibitors. Among the many fruits were busiika, maabo, mang'ombwa, mafwuuntwa, masuku, mbula, mang'ong'o, matobo, musekese, mucingacinga, ncenje, nyoonyo, nkoloondo, nkuyu, zyiili, and mumbu. Among the succulent tubers were masabe, ndiya, mpeevwu, and sangazi.

Before 1960, there were no exotic fruit trees such as avocado, banana, lemon, mango, orange, guava, and pawpaw in Namaila. The nearest exotic fruit trees were four lemon trees found at Meezi, near Simukululu Mountain. The trees had sprouted from seeds thrown away by cadastral surveyors who'd surveyed and pegged the highest mountain in the region. We enjoyed trekking all the way to Meezi, imitating the surveyors just to pick a dozen juicy lemons.

During the dry season after the crop harvest, the animals were left to wander freely in the fields to enjoy the dried maize stalks and were only collected late in the afternoon. We spent most of the free time on fishing and hunting expeditions. We also organized games such as combo that taught skills of spearing a fast-moving wheel-like tuber with arrows.

We sometimes organized some games imitating family life by the sandy banks of the rivers with girls of our ages, who had not yet been initiated. I often had nobody to partner with, as most of the girls in the village were my relatives. I accepted to play the role of a crowing cock and schemed to shorten my loneliness by maliciously crowing early in order for the couples to wake up.

Herding cattle had a strict disciplinary code, which everyone had to abide by. The code provided for ranking and respect on the basis of age and also the tasks one accomplished. Having a ferocious bull in the herd earned one a lot of respect. I earned respect for my ability to count the animals as they were being separated to be taken to various homes. A few times, I also won some wrestling (kamaando) games against ferocious combatants, which improved my ranking.

Everyone had to abide by the code of secrecy, as the activities and lessons in the bush were strictly for males and were meant to build the body, character, quality, and soul of a man in all respects.

Childhood impressions of village life

Mwiinga-Cibuyu Village is tucked in between the rolling hills at the western end of the Likoma valley on the edges of the Zambezi escarpment. The phasing of the hills into a plateau is the water-shade that divides the water going eastwards to the Zambezi River and that going westwards to the Kafue River. This marks a natural boundary between the Mazabuka District with its fertile farmlands and the desolate and mountainous Gwembe District. The Namaila hills are adorned with steep cliffs and long frightful caves, called makolyo from which the locals extract some gunpowder.

In the 1950s, the village had a large population living in neatly arranged rows of houses, grain bins and livestock kraals. When I was born in 1947, my three close surviving grandparents, namely Simalambo, Matongo (Mweemba, Bbokesi), and Mizinga and their families lived in the same village. I grew up in a large extended family, full of supportive grandparents, aunts, uncles, and cousins. The village was therefore relatively peaceful as the majority of the inhabitants were somewhat related. I cannot recall ever witnessing a serious fight amongst the community members.

Amongst the inhabitants of the village were many artisans capable of making most household tools, utensils, implements, and instruments for various uses. A Chewa trader, John Sakala who visited in a large trading team in 1952 decided to settle and was readily accepted to stay in the village. He added great value to the village as a reputable carpenter who carved and made many wooden articles from the abundant thirty-metre tall mululu (khaya nyasica) trees.

Under the guidance of Grandmother bina-Chiinda, a revered rainmaker and faith-healer in the village, we annually gathered around a sacred hut to pray for rains. Each year, we were blessed and assured of receiving adequate rains that replenished the springs, streams, and rivers with fresh water and encouraged the growth of lush forests. As there was no modern clinic nearby, the forests provided various medicinal plants prescribed by traditional healers in the fight against various illnesses and viral epidemics such as chickenpox.

The village boasted of music experts who composed appropriate songs and skilled dancers who performed at special occasions. As a youth, I learnt how to play many of the musical instruments such as kalumbu, kankobela, and drums and participated in the dances during the various ceremonies. Any shortcomings in my dancing styles were forgiven as I was regarded as 'too educated for village dances'. I later compensated for my youth inadequacies in traditional dancing by being not only an accomplished ballroom dancer, but by being a dancing instructor at Munali Secondary School.

The community members shared the wealth and prosperity of the hills and valleys. These included a supportive traditional family system, a large herd of cattle, goats, and poultry and the natural resources, which included the perennial Likoma River, teeming with all kinds of aquatic life and the plateau (gumba) full of a large variety of trees, grasses, animals, and birds.

The rich alluvial soils in the Likoma valley were fully utilized to grow a wide variety of grains and vegetables. Because of the abundance of sorghum (maila mucheme), the larger area, consisting of five villages in the valley, was named 'Namaila'. The two perennial tributaries of the Likoma River cascading over limestone hills with beautiful waterfalls are called the Kakolyo and Simaila streams.

The natural and domestic resources of Namaila were well preserved through folklore and managed prudently. For example, there was a definite scheme of grazing cattle on a rotational basis, in both the crop fields and grasslands, so that there was no overgrazing in one area. Known medicinal trees were preserved by each person taking only enough of the bark or leaves as required for immediate use. If the treatment prescription required some flowers as ingredients, the flowers were only harvested on the recommendation of a medicine man or woman and by the elders. This ensured the maturing of the flowers into seeds and the germination and promulgation of flesh seedlings.

Fishing was done seasonally between May and July and only in designated streams, rivers, and pools by village groups. Some important wild fruits such as masuku and nkuyu were harvested only by groups of elderly women who knew which ones were ripe and ready for eating. There was no commercial trade in the natural resources of Namaila with the outside world. As a result, money was not a very important asset in my childhood and I never handled any. I do recall trekking some distance to the nearest shops in the farmlands with loads of crops and exchanging these with a variety of goods including clothes.

I recount some of the oral traditions, myths and beliefs, which were part of the natural resource conservation policy and strategy as follows:

- A legend was told of how a hunter who killed a female duiker kept wandering in the forest as he could not find his way home. My father always released any female animal caught in his snares to preserve the animals for reproduction.

- The story was told of the existence of large snakes capable of swallowing a human being in the lush forests at the sources of all streams and creeks. Once in a while, some elder spread a story claiming to have seen a large snake as he strayed in the area. These areas were not trampled upon and this preserved them as river sources.

- It was believed that in the deep waters of some well-shaded pools were long tunnels into the hills with large ghostly fishes with reed plants on their heads. One daring young man who trespassed was nearly swallowed by the quicksand and the incident was attributed to one of the big fishes. These pools were preserved as sacred spawning grounds for fish.

- Smoke from the fire of dried wood of any fruit tree was claimed to make one blind. The fear of getting blind meant that no one cut down a fruit tree or dried logs for firewood.

- The tale of the honey bird leading one to a lion or leopard if one did not leave some honey in the beehive for the bird to eat meant that the bees had some food all the time and continued to make the much-needed honey in the same beehive.

- It was believed that children who ate too many chicken eggs would be barren in their adult life. For fear of being barren, children allowed the eggs to incubate and hatch into chicks, thereby increasing and conserving the chicken flock.

These myths and many more were repeatedly told to the youths by the elders. I learnt the strict rules and discipline of living in this orderly and self-preserving community, while undertaking chores meant for a particular age group. I also accumulated a lot of indigenous knowledge on the culture, economic and social life of my people.

Farming in the area was based on the hand hoe and axes, cow dung manure, foliage manure from the acacia and musangu (faidherbia albida) tree leaves, sorghum, millet, and legumes such as beans, cowpeas, pumpkins, and squashes. The small grains were crushed into flour for cooking into nsima with two flat stones known as zyiyo. One variety of sorghum with sweet stalks was eaten as sugarcane or crushed to get the sweet liquid, which was used to sweeten foods such as musozya.

The newly-introduced maize crop required deep ploughing with expensive equipment pulled by no fewer than two oxen. The steel plough was introduced in the area in 1947 by Cimbolo, a village headman in the area, who bought one after retiring from a farm in the Mazabuka area. Grandfather Simalambo was the third person to own a plough and one of his young brothers became popularly known as Mapulawu, meaning 'many ploughs'.

Due to its wide and long-leaf blades, the maize crop was planted in straight lines with calculated spacing of the rows and seeds. Maize was, therefore, a crop for the rich who had enough oxen and the education to correctly measure the depth and the spacing between the rows and the seeds.

New processing tools such as the pounding mortar (ncili) were introduced and popularized since the stone grinder could not grind the large maize kernels. Preparation of maize flour took a lot of time. To prepare the maize for pounding, one hulled the husks, removed the kernels from the cob and soaked them for some hours. Then, one separated the bran, samp, and grit before pounding the maize into fine white flour.

As cooking nsima from maize flour took a long time, the local people concocted an intermediate recipe by mixing grit and a stock of a local root, called munkoyo to produce a refreshing beverage called cibwantu. This beverage became a popular food item for the busy working community and its preparation was taught to females at an early age. Samp was also cooked into musozya and mixed with groundnut flour (buntele) or sour milk (mabisi).

The excitement that came with the new maize crop quickly died down due to the high production costs, which included expensive chemical fertilisers. The crop was not drought tolerant and could not grow well in the marginal soils of Namaila. Sorghum and other survival crops such as millet disappeared from the area and the name 'Namaila' became an anachronism as the area occasionally was ravaged by famine.

After Zambia's independence in the late sixties and early seventies, there was a strong wave of migration from mountainous Namaila and other parts of Mazabuka and Monze Districts. The people, who had been driven into these unsuitable areas, in order to give way to the white settler farmers along the new line of rail, exercised their freedom of movement to settle elsewhere. Many of the inhabitants of Mwiinga Cibuyu Village relocated to Muchila in the Namwala District and Mukulaikwa in the Mumbwa District in search of fertile lands.

The young people, who attained a reasonable level of education, stayed away from rugged Namaila, their ancestral home. Having spent time in boarding educational institutions and after starting working in urban areas, I visited Namaila only for short periods of time. The lack of a motorable road to my village was a big challenge, as I had to walk a distance of ten kilometres to get to my village. Independence with its modern trappings was somewhat a curse as Namaila lost many of its vibrant citizens and much of its glory.

CHAPTER 3

My Search For Modern Knowledge

The Namaila School, which was situated south of the Chikankata Mission, behind the Mabwetuba Mountain, was started in 1943 after a visit by Shadreck Cheenda, a teacher from Ibbwe Munyama, the then headquarters of the Salvation Army. The establishment of the school, located some fifteen kilometres from our village, provided a rare opportunity for those interested in learning the three R's of 'riting, 'rithmetic, and reading. Simwaale, my father was one of the few who enrolled in the new school. Although he dropped-out in order to get married, his short attendance of the school and his interest made him literate in arithmetic.

The school site perched on a hill became hazardous for young children because of the lack of bridges on all the rivers the pupils crossed. It was therefore decided in 1953 to shift the school westwards to a new location, which was much safer as all pupils had to cross only one river to get to the school.

In the olden days, between May and August of each year, the school teachers toured villages to recruit new pupils, as not many parents were interested in their children going to school to learn the three R's. They felt that traditional knowledge imparted by the community was enough for survival.

In May 1954, when the opportunity for me to sit for the enrolment interviews was presented by Teacher Molly Kazwida during a visit to our village, my father objected. He argued that I was still too young and that I would fail the interview. In fact, he was afraid that there would be no one to herd his cattle and goats. After a short quiz in arithmetic and questions on other subjects, teacher Kazwida insisted that I attend the interviews as, in his own assessment, I was a clever young boy.

I did not accept being a herd boy as my ultimate aspiration. With tears rolling down my cheeks, I pleaded with my mother to lobby my father to allow me to attend the enrolment interviews. After some heavy lobbying, my mother was granted her wish for me to attend the interviews.

Uncle Aaron took me for interviews, by the only bicycle in the village, to the school, which was some fifteen kilometres from our village. Apart from a test in arithmetic, which was easy for me, one other test was to extend one's right arm over the middle of the head. If the middle finger reached the left ear, then one was considered old enough for admission in school.

Teacher Kazwida gave me some hints during his visit to our village on how to achieve this feat by positioning the arm slightly to the back of the head. I remembered this extra tutorial during the interviews and easily passed the test. Some older boys, with longer arms, did not manage and were rejected. I still feel guilty that this is one moment in my life when I passed a difficult test by an examination leakage!

The school calendar, which was greatly influenced by the farming habits of the Tonga tribe, who were the first to make contact with modern agriculture and education, ran from August to June the following year. Opening in August enabled the parents to have money for school fees from sales of their harvested crops. The dry season with low water levels in the streams was also considered the safest time for the young pupils who travelled long distances to school for the first time for the first grade.

In August 1954, I enrolled at Namaila School as Cibiya Magande and started attending school in Sub A at the age of seven years. Namaila School had only four grades of Sub A, Sub B, Standard I and Standard II.

To get to the school on time, I woke up very early in the morning. With a packed meal of either left-over nsima called mbuba, some roast maize or cibwantu, I and other pupils from my village jogged all the way to school. On the way, we washed our faces, hands and legs in the Simaila River. All the pupils had the opportunity to be spruced up during the school drill as there was abundant free water in the rivers they crossed on the way to the school.

I was excited to sit in a classroom and to have the opportunity of interacting with so many strangers from other villages. I had learnt some arithmetic from my father as I had to account for the eggs and livestock. My exhibition of a high ability in arithmetic made me a darling of the teachers, who protected me against bullies.

During the first few weeks of schooling, we wrote in the dust outside the classroom with a finger and later with a stick. Graduation to using white chalk on a slate and onto a pencil and a paper excise book was dependent upon one's handwriting. I quickly managed to recite the alphabet and got my letters straight and graduated to using a slate.

Being the youngest pupils in the class, I and Sandoki Mweemba were abused by the older pupils by being ordered to clean the classroom even when it was not our turn. I recalled that while herding cattle, ranking and respect were earned by the tasks one achieved and not by one's age. I schemed to help Sandoki with his school work and soon we were on top of the class in most tests. This earned us the respect of the teachers, who exempted us from cleaning the classroom under the pretext of being young. This gave us more time to study and do even better.

I enjoyed attending school because it gave me an opportunity to know so many young people from other villages. I soon learnt that there was a much wider space away from Namaila if I took up the challenge. The little school fired my ambition to live beyond my wildest dreams. During the weekends, I joined my family in whatever work was being done that season. The heavy workload was during the farming season when we toiled in the fields as well.

In spite of his initial resistance, my father was very encouraging in my school work as he asked for my performance reports and helped me with the homework. He often reminded me of Cheenda, his former teacher, who greatly impressed him with his mathematical ability.

On one occasion while in Standard One in 1956, my father asked me how I performed in the examinations. I informed him that I got ninety-four per cent in arithmetic and only one pupil who got ninety-six per cent surpassed me. My father got very angry and whipped me hard. He explained that I should never compete or compare myself with other people but with myself, otherwise, I would end up comparing myself with mediocrity.

I reflected deeply on this fatherly advice and found meaning in what my father said. Every one of us was born alone and only comes to know other human beings much later in life. At birth, no one knows other people, not even their own parents. The discovery and exhibition of one's core life values, though late in life, is what makes us achieve our individual greatness.

The benefit that other creatures derive from other peoples' efforts and achievements is only consequential and accidental. As I tended the cattle and goats in the bush, I realized that I was alone and this was a test of my personal competence and capability to fulfill a given assignment. Since there were no other competitors, I had to interpret the instructions, design the processes and procedures and execute the assignment to my own satisfaction and that of my father, the giver of the assignment.

Many years later, I discovered that about the same time when my father was giving me a life-changing lecture on self-assertiveness and self-appraisal out in the Namaila hills in 1957, the literary giant, Ayn Rand, a Russian-born American, had written novels in support of the philosophy of objectivism. I was delighted to realize that my father's philosophy and teachings on life had found common ground with such a world famous philosopher.

My favourite saying by Ayn Rand on rational individualism reads as follows:-

"A creative man is motivated by the desire to achieve, not by the desire to beat others."

For the final examinations in Standard II, we trekked some fifty kilometres to the examination centre at Malala School. I did not find the examinations very challenging. I was elated when the results came out, as I'd got the highest marks in our school. My father was happy when I did not speak of competing with any pupil but with the examiners. Since I and Sandoki earned high marks, we were selected to attend the senior primary school at Chikankata Mission, the new headquarters of the Salvation Army, as boarders.

The news of my good marks elated all my family members and my teachers. However, the problem of financing my further education had to be resolved. At the time, the fee was eighteen British pounds per year, which was a lot of money. I persuaded grandfather Matongo to convene a family meeting to discuss the issue. At a family meeting held under the chairmanship of Grandfather Matongo, it was decided that the two parties, namely the paternal and maternal groups should share equally the responsibility of paying my school fees. Matongo took the responsibility of raising the money on behalf of the maternal group, while my father took responsibility for the paternal group.

One of my aunts, bina-Hachiloli questioned the benefit to be derived by other relatives from my education. She argued that the money to be spent by Matongo on my education will be foregone inheritance by other relatives. She proposed that Matongo should share his assets amongst the relatives now so that those who wished to waste their inheritance on 'unpredictable and unproductive education' of their children could do so.

At that time, there was no relative or clan member who had completed schooling and was working. It was therefore inconceivable that at an age of eleven years I could rise out of Namaila and become a trendsetter for the clan.

The suggestion by bina-Hachiloli could not sway old Matongo, who reminded the gathering that there is always a beginning to everything. To him, my education was to be the beginning of creating a secure future for the clan. He, therefore, offered to support any of the other relatives who wanted to advance their education.

Grandfather Matongo then asked me to make a statement. In my first address to a gathering, I made an undertaking that once I finished schooling and got employment, I would pay the school fees for my siblings and younger relatives. I further stated that I would not inherit anything from any of my grandparents and parents beyond the school fees they would pay for me. Neither would I expect anything in return from my siblings, whom I would support.

Christianity overpowers my paganism

A few weeks after our family meeting, Teacher Molly Kazwida came to our village to inform us that Chikankata School was opening in early August 1958 and that I was expected to travel to the school. He was very happy when he was told that the issue of school fees had been resolved. He gave us the sad news that the relatives of Sandoki, my classmate, had failed to raise the money for his school fees.

Teacher Kazwida promised to escort me and any relative who wished to accompany me, as it was his pride and that of Aaron Mukwamba, the head teacher, that I had qualified to attend Chikankata School. When the trip was due, I could not travel as there was no relative available to escort me. My uncles

Aaron and Pita had gone to seek employment at Siavonga as the construction of the Kariba dam was in progress.

On Saturday, 16 August 1958, Teacher Kazwida visited our village again and offered to take me to Chikankata Mission even without any relative as the school had opened. He proposed that I should travel to the local school early the following morning. I was delighted when my parents accepted his proposal.

I left my village alone on Sunday morning on 17 August 1958 for Namaila School. When I arrived at the school, at about ten in the morning, I found the teacher ready for the trip to Chikankata Mission. Since I had no suitcase or bag, I clutched in one hand some eighteen pounds for school fees and a few pence for my subsistence. In the other hand was a folded pair of shorts and a shirt. I handed over the money to the teacher who carried it.

This was the first time I handled money in my life. Surprisingly, I was not excited about the event as I'd lived comfortably for eleven years in a prosperous but moneyless supportive community. I presume this is why money does not raise a high level of excitement in me. 'Mali taandizwishi moyo.'

We left Namaila about noon for a destination I did not know. The walk to Chikankata Mission over the Mabwetuba Mountain range took many hours. Luckily, part of the route was the same one we'd used when going to the Malala School examination centre. We lodged with a friend of Kazwida at a village near to the mission.

We got to the school on the morning of 18 August 1958. Teacher Kazwida was invited into the office of the school principal, Major Leonard Kirby at 10.00 hours, while I waited on a bench on the veranda of the office. After a long period of waiting, the teacher came out and informed me that the principal was insisting that I should assume a Christian name before I could be enrolled. I informed him that I'd rather go back home than give myself a Christian name for the sake of enrolment. The Salvation Army uses military ranks in its formations.

Teacher Kazwida went back into the principal's office to report my reaction and again stayed for quite some time. When he finally came out, he looked excited and very happy. He informed me that I had been enrolled as the two of them came up with a befitting Christian name. He stated that henceforth I would be known as Peter Magande.

I was angry and burst out into crying and told my teacher that I was not interested in the new name. The teacher pleaded with me but my continued bursts attracted the attention of the principal, who came out to check on what had befallen me. For the first time in my life, I was face-to-face with a white man and I did not know what to expect from him.

After being informed of my objection to the new name and my desire to return to the village, Major Kirby pacified me and calmed me down. He stated that the school authorities would take care of me just like Teacher Kazwida, who was not my relative had looked after me during the long trip from Namaila. He mentioned that he would not allow a bright young boy to be wasted by not being educated just because of a name. He justified the name Peter by explaining its biblical significance and meaning.

After the principal's pep talk, I cooled down and accepted my fate as Christianity had conquered my paganism. I immediately doubted Uncle Aaron's assertion that white people were very bad, especially that he had an encounter only with the district commissioner, who demanded some poll tax. The first white man I met in my life was friendly and wanted me to get educated for some future purpose somewhere, but definitely, not at Namaila.

It was an emotional parting of company with Teacher Molly Kazwida as he had made so much effort to get me into school both at Namaila and Chikankata. But as fate had ordained, after this parting, we never met again as he passed on and my efforts to trace any relative of his over the years failed.

The principal then gave me some utensils and uniform, that included my first pair of long trousers. The school modern attire requiring me to be smart enabled me to acquire my first pair of shoes as well. In spite of not wearing shoes in the thorny bushes of Namaila while herding cattle, I had never had any serious foot injury. I never lost cognizance of the fact that I'd learnt a lot at Namaila School for four years even without shoes. I, therefore, decided to give my own meaning to shoes in my life. At the highest level of my career at fifty years of age, I was more than satisfied with fourteen pairs of shoes.

The principal summoned a prefect who took me to the dormitory where I was shown some space on the floor and where I spread my blanket as my bed. Apart from the floor being made of concrete and therefore very cold when made wet, the floor had been my bed for a long time even at home. The difference was that Uncle Aaron had taught me how to avoid the hard floor by making a mattress from empty hessian bags and dried grass.

I spent the afternoon surveying the school grounds. As nightfall approached, I looked forward to seeing the lights along the streets and in houses. I was amazed that it never got dark as the lights came on immediately the sun disappeared. As I admired the brightness, I wondered why the lights were needed when people were fast asleep during the night.

I was very impressed with Chikankata Mission as it comprised a hospital, a trades' institute, and a primary school. The hospital had a training wing for nurses and medical assistants. At the time, Chikankata Hospital had the largest leprosarium with patients from many parts of Zambia and beyond.

The Mission was located in between two streams that provided water for the community. The surrounding Mapangazya area consisted of a large vibrant farming community that met some of the food needs of both the hospital and our school.

All the new students underwent a comprehensive medical examination at the hospital. During the medical examinations, I was among many pupils who were found with the bilharzia disease, which was prevalent in many rural areas. All the pupils found with various ailments were put on treatment immediately. With a reputable hospital in the vicinity, the school population was healthy and all students were encouraged to participate in physical exercises and some sport.

I settled fast in my new environment in spite of the brutal bullying and mocking, particularly from the pupils in my class who'd arrived earlier at the school. The school had a thriving vegetable garden maintained by junior pupils, which was turned into a battleground for supremacy every Wednesday afternoon. Not much attention was put on stopping my nocturnal enuresis by the school authorities, as it was attributed to the change of the environment and the molestation and it soon stopped.

I was mocked even for my peasantry background as "kana kazwa kumalundu," meaning, 'a child originating from the mountains.' Mountains were regarded as degrading geographical features denoting primitiveness and poverty. Later in life, when I landed at the Geneva International Airport located between the Alps and Jura mountains in Switzerland, I was relieved to learn of the enormous riches and the wealthy citizens of this mountainous country. I resolved to change the misfortunes of the people of Namaila, someday, using the riches hidden in the mountains.

I made a lot of friends who had also done well in their primary school examinations at various schools and had been redirected to Chikankata for senior primary education. My best friend was Geoffrey Hamayobe, a son of Petrol Hamayobe, the bricklayer who'd built the Chikankata Mission Hospital. For his invaluable contribution to the development of Chikankata Mission Hospital, Uncle Hamayobe deserved some permanent recognition, such as the naming of one of the buildings after him. My efforts in this direction with successive Mission administrators have not succeeded.

Sometime in October 1958, Uncle Aaron came to check on me and promised to come back to collect me when schools closed. Unfortunately, he did not arrive when the school closed even after waiting for the whole morning. I, therefore, decided to trek to Namaila alone. It got dark before I had gotten over the Mabwetuba hills into Namaila. Although it was common knowledge that there were some leopards in the forests between Namaila and Chikankata, I was convinced that having been spared by a black mamba, even a leopard would not stop me getting to my destiny. As I was passing by some village in the dark, the dogs barked so fiercely that one of the villagers, Dickson Chibaala Habatumbu, came out of his hut and invited me into his hut.

Even after I'd explained the circumstances for my walking alone in the night, Habatumbu was still angry with me for risking my life. He persuaded me to spend the night at his home, but I insisted that I must get to our village that very day. After a meal, he informed me that my grandmother, Mizinga had died a few days before. I was weeping as we walked in the darkness to my village.

Closer to the village, Habatumbu told me that my grandmother was not dead after all. He was just joking as my mujwama. When I later narrated the story to my grandmother, she just laughed and explained that this was a very ancient valued relationship in Tonga traditions. It allowed the bajwanyina to tease one another even with the most frightening and scary stories. She concluded by saying that ordinarily, elders do not tell lies.

We arrived at my village late in the night and woke up my parents, who were surprised with my arrival. My mujwama admonished them for not collecting me from school. He implored them to ensure that I fulfilled my craving for education as demonstrated by risking my life walking in the dark. Habatumbu then left to return to his village.

This incident must have embarrassed my parents and deflated my father's anger as they were not too concerned with my new name of Peter, which was the name of my father's young brother. I explained the strong religious stance of Chikankata Mission as the headquarters of the Salvation Army.

My parents heard the details of the story of Jesus Christ and the twelve disciples, one of whom was Peter, for the first time. I informed them that the name means a rock or stone in biblical terms and cracked a joke that I intended to be as strong as a rock. My parents and members of the community continued to call me Cibiya, but my official documents bore my new name.

The following year, I arranged with Uncle Aaron that when he comes to pick me from Chikankata, we should pass through Mazabuka Town. I wanted to have the opportunity to see and ride the train for the first time in my life. We made the trip from Chikankata by bus and then had a train ride between Mazabuka and Magoye, a very short distance of a few kilometres. We then trekked eastwards from Magoye to Namaila, a distance of thirty-four kilometres, which is much longer than that between Chikankata and Namaila.

The experience of visiting Mazabuka Town and riding the train was worth it as it raised my social status amongst my peers in the village. I was becoming the envy of my age mates as I was getting way ahead of them in life experiences and knowledge.

Thereafter, I made many trips between Namaila and Chikankata walking alone through the forests of the Mabwetuba Hills. I made a habit of stopping by Habatumbu's residence to brief him on my progress and to assure him that my parents were fulfilling their promise. The old man took a keen interest in my education.

The infrastructure at Chikankata Mission was being expanded to provide for space for the introduction of secondary school classes and also additional medical services. Among the new facilities were additional dormitories, classrooms, laboratories, new wards at the hospital, and a new large dam.

We had an exciting development when the school completed the construction of the first waterborne ablution blocks with showers and flush toilets. I vividly recall the great effort made by the expatriate white teachers to demonstrate the etiquette of bathroom and lavatory use. The two-day demonstrations included how to lift the pan cover, sit on the pan, hang and unroll the toilet paper, flush the cistern, clean, and cover the bowl of the lavatory.

The teachers emphasized that the new equipment with its immaculate white pans and cisterns were very clean and hygienic on their own. One of them even sipped some water from the cistern and dipped his hand into the pan to demonstrate the cleanliness of the system. He stated that the water and the pan will be made dirty only by actions of one of us. They emphasized that each one of us was therefore responsible for cleaning their own mess. We were taught to leave the toilet in the same condition we'd found it.

This reminded me of the wise saying by the philanthropist Mother Teresa (Anjezë Gonxhe Bojaxhiu), which states that:

"If everybody cleaned their doorstep, the whole world would be clean".

We abandoned the pit latrines we'd used up until then and the bathing in the nearby Munyeke Stream. This was a big change for me as we did not even have pit latrines in the village.

The new waterborne sanitary system brought some challenges to many older students who did not want to be associated with cleaning the 'dirty' place. On a Saturday in 1959, a team of older boys failed to carry out their duty as per the roster. When confronted by one of the prefects, they accused me and another young boy, David Ng'andu as the ones who'd failed to clean the ablution block even when it was not our turn to do so.

David and I were summoned to the principal's office. The principal reiterated the imperative for keeping the new facilities clean in order to avoid outbreaks of diseases such as cholera and dysentery. He recited the famous saying by Rabbi Phinehas ben Yair that, "Cleanliness is next to Godliness" and threatened to dismiss us from the school for insubordination.

After checking in our files, he cooled down and stated that he would forgive us because we were very bright students. This incident once more showed the degree of respect the principal had for education and led us to concentrate on our studies while strengthening our friendship.

I have tried to live according to these lessons on hygiene and have managed to keep clean our lavatories and bathrooms even when hosting visitors from the village. The arrangement is that we show the visitors how to use the facilities early in their visit since many are not familiar with these modern facilities. By the way, even some of our visitors from urban areas have to struggle to use some of the modern facilities due to the frequently changing designs of flush mechanisms and handles.

Chikankata School provided carefully formulated and balanced meals. The common diet for the school was of maize porridge for breakfast, then nsima, vegetables, and dried beans for lunch and supper. The kapenta fish, which became common in educational institutions, was not available as it had to be brought from distant Lake Tanganyika in the far north. Every Saturday, the senior students in the Trades Institute and secondary school were treated to a luxurious meal of rice and beef. The beef was from animals slaughtered in the village by the senior students themselves.

The irony was that many senior students exchanged their rice for nsima, as rice was regarded as a snack and not food to satisfy a hungry person. I participated in the nsima-rice barter trade with Dux Halubobya, one of the students in the Trades Institute, who became my long-term associate.

After leaving Chikankata Mission, Halubobya ended up in Canada for training in cooperatives. Upon his return to Zambia, he pioneered the development of the savings cooperative movement by establishing the Credit Union & Savings Association (CUSA) of Zambia under the personal guidance of President Kaunda. Under Halubobya's guidance as general manager, CUSA became a household name in the whole country and helped in building a culture of saving amongst many civil servants. Our paths crossed later in life as we worked in the same ministry, which was responsible for cooperatives and we continued to be close to each other even in old age.

I put a lot of effort in my class work at Chikankata and soon earned the respect of both the teachers and other pupils in my classes. We went through a lot of the usual subjects of biology, chemistry, civics, history, mathematics, and physics.

The lessons on the English language could not cover all that we had to learn. One had to get really interested in order to understand and appreciate the collocation and irregular forms of words such as adverbs, adjectives, nouns, proverbs, and verbs. Some words in English, the so-called 'Queen's language', were very complicated and required a lot of effort to master their spellings and usage. For example, the word 'go', which changes to 'going', 'gone', 'goes' and 'went' and the word 'sing', which becomes 'sings', 'sang', and 'sung'.

I discovered that the English language, like Tonga my native language, also has thousands of idioms and therefore the language was not 'a piece of cake'. After my prized gift of an English dictionary in 1963, my fluency in the English language improved dramatically.

Later in secondary school, the Latin language was introduced. Latin verbs, which have four patterns of conjugation, active and passive voice were even more complicated. With conjugation being affected by person, number, gender, tense, mood, and voice factors, this brought more frustrations and confusion in learning the language. We were assured that once one mastered Latin, they would find English easy as about eighty per cent of the entries in any English dictionary are derived from Latin.

We spent time memorizing and reciting the verses of Civis Romanus the classic textbook for Latin learners, which had so many remarkable stories on the civilization of ancient Rome. Our British teachers did not emphasize the fact that the Latin language was imposed on the British by the conquering

Romans under Emperor Claudius. As we were mere students, we wanted knowledge for passing the examinations and not to engage in ancient politics.

We were taught ciTonga as an academic subject by Teacher Maguswi, but it was punishable for anyone to speak the language within the school premises. Since we knew some items only in Tonga, we sometimes melded Tonga and English words in our speech, but our elderly lady teacher Major Daton could not understand. As it happened, between Latin and English, I strongly believe that a blending of English, Latin, and Tonga words would have produced a rich intercultural language easy to be understood by the members of the local community. After all, English, Latin, and Tonga words use a common alphabet of twenty-six letters, which do not have any diacritical marks.

I was most fascinated by geography, taught by a very gentle and motherly lady, Captain Watkinson. We learnt about all the countries of the world and their peoples, physical features, resources, natural and political divisions, climate, agricultural, and manufactured products. Some of the explorers, such as Vasco da Gama, were covered under geography because of the trade and economic aspects of their expeditions. The knowledge acquired in the geography lessons became handy in my later life as I travelled to various countries of the world.

For the dreaded subject of mathematics, the Mission recruited an American geologist, Dr Arthur Thompson who made the subject less intimidating. I enjoyed mathematics and befriended 'musaama' Arthur Bbuku and a young girl by the name of Irene Kaumba, who were also good at mathematics.

I came to know how the modern numbers are derived from the few symbols using additive and subtractive methods. I learnt that the Hindu-Arabic numeric system was developed by the Persian Muslim Mathematician by the name of Muhammad ibn Musa al-Khwarizmi born around 780 AD in Baghdad.

The hefty American geologist, often seen around picking stones accompanied by a huge Alsatian dog, also introduced American baseball to the school sports programme. As one of his good students in class, I had no choice but to join his baseball game, although I never made it to become a star player. The teaching of mathematics at Chikankata Secondary School laid such a strong foundation that I continued to score distinctions up to university level.

The Trades Institute trained professional artisans in brickwork, carpentry and blacksmithery. The institute's facilities were available to the primary and secondary school pupils. The lessons were given by a very dedicated teacher, Cox Sikumba, who managed to persuade us of the practical value of these skills in real life. Sikumba also took us for physical education and sports.

We made various household items from timber and metal during our lessons. The students of the Trades Institute helped in maintaining the school's infrastructure. I was excited to hold the tools of the various trades such as trowels, levels, craw hammers, welding guns and rods, planes, chisels, saws, and tape measures, which I had never seen before. This grounding in these survival skills at an early age has enabled me to effectively supervise some construction works and carry out maintenance work on our various family properties.

Among the extracurricular activities I actively participated in was drama, in which I always preferred to act the role of one of the three wise men from the east in the nativity play. Once I did offer to take on the role of Jesus Christ in a religious play. But our organizer, Captain Cammody could not allow a human being to assume such a role.

We were indoctrinated to believe that it was blasphemous for a human being to portray Jesus Christ in a play. The role was always played by an unnamed senior teacher, who read the participation of Jesus from behind a curtain. I kept on wandering for many years whether something sinister will happen to anyone who acted as Jesus Christ.

I was therefore mentally liberated when I watched the George Stevens 1965 biblical epic film, The Greatest Story Ever Told in which Max von Sydow convincingly portrayed Jesus Christ and nothing sinister happened to him. With a cast of some of the famous and my favourite actors among them John Wayne, Charlton Heston, Sydney Poitier and Telly Savallas, producer Stevens must have preserved the reverence of the story of Jesus Christ by seeking the advice and prayers of Pope John XXIII before producing the film.

In July 1963, I took a religious course and after baptism and confirmation of my religious name of Peter, I became a Corps Cadet and participated in teaching the Bible readings to younger pupils during Sunday school in the nearby primary schools. This gave me the opportunity to study the Bible from Genesis to Revelations. Religious education (RE) became one of my favourite and easiest subjects. I found the Bible very educational with lessons for all circumstances. I must admit that the teachings of the Bible have assisted me greatly when confronted with many modern-day challenges.

Dancing was not allowed at Chikankata Mission due to its moral sensibilities. Singing, especially of religious songs, was encouraged and I became an active member of the school choir after taking some music lessons.

I joined the Scout Association as a cub and later graduated to a scout. The motto of the movement is "BE PREPARED", which stands for Bravery, Enterprise, Purpose, Resolution, Endurance, Partnership, Assurance, Reformation, Enthusiasm, and Devotion. I enjoyed most of the outdoor camping challenges, such as mountaineering and compass reading as they reinforced the self-sufficiency and survival techniques I'd learnt during my days as a shepherd boy in the Namaila hills.

I continued to do well in class and this greatly pleased my family, who successfully struggled to have money ready for school fees each year. I recall many times when they sold not only the eggs but the chicken as well to raise the required amount. A few times, I remained at the school during the short holidays to do some piece work and earned a little pocket money. However, in

Standard VI, I got a government scholarship for good performance.

The ANC and UNIP formed a coalition Government after the elections in 1962. The firebrand Mungoni Liso, who was parliamentary secretary for education and a member of the ANC, visited our school during the year and gave a fiery speech, in which he assured us that political independence was on the way.

Mungoni Liso prodded us to concentrate on our studies so that we would become the competent manpower that would propel a politically independent Zambia to economic prosperity. He informed us that a Lazarus Cheelo from the Mapangazya area had just completed his degree studies at the University of Rhodesia and Nyasaland in Salisbury (Harare), Southern Rhodesia (Zimbabwe). We were most encouraged by this news of the success of a local boy, who'd graduated from a university.

The new coalition Government introduced a programme of interchanging students amongst the provinces and schools in order to foster national unity. At Chikankata, we received three 'foreign' boys, namely Wisdom Chanda, Isaac Mambwe, and Joseph Mwale from outside the province. The boys were subjected to heavy bullying and mocking, especially since they could not understand nor speak Tonga, the local language. I took a personal interest in trying to protect them as I was interested in the ciBemba language, which I had never heard before.

Joseph Mwale happened to be a son of Dr Siteke Gibson Mwale. At the time, little did I know that Joseph's father's path and mine would cross some forty-two years later. When Dr Mwale was appointed as Zambia's representative to the International Conference on the Great Lakes Region (ICGKR) in 2005, I worked with him to operationalize his office and to establish the Regional Centre for Democracy and Good Governance, later renamed the Levy Mwanawasa Centre for Governance in Lusaka.

Many students came from various schools and denominations in the province. Amongst them was Rueben Kapaale, meaning the 'smart one', who came from the Namwianga Mission of the Church of Christ in Kalomo District. Geoffrey Hamayobe nicknamed the tall handsome boy 'Tallman'. By his noticeable height of over two metres, he could have easily qualified for a position in any basketball team.

Kapaale turned out to be very knowledgeable of not only local political issues but also the American situation. This could have been because of the exposure by the American missionaries who were running the Namwianga Mission. He broke the sad news of the assassination of President Kennedy to the students during lunch, which we abandoned, as we openly wept. He literally recruited most of us into politics and we would be glued to the small radio placed in the dining room at news time. Although much older than me, I spent a lot of time with Kapaale discussing diverse issues.

In December 1963, we sat for examinations after only six months of learning in Form II because the new Government changed the school timetable to follow the Gregorian calendar. This being a final class at the time, there was a lot of apprehension and fear amongst the students on the possibility of failing in view of the shortened learning time. At the end of the school year, I won a prize of an English dictionary as the 'Most Progressive Student in Form II'.

When I went home for holidays, I discussed the matter of my future plans with my parents. As they were unaware of the different professions or careers in the modern world, they could not give me any guidance on careers. I told them that I wanted to be a surveyor and the entry requirement for the course being Form V, I will have to leave Chikankata for some other senior secondary school out of Mazabuka District. They were agreeable to my future plans as I was a pioneer in the family and any career of my choice was welcome.

When I visited Chikankata Secondary School to check for the examination results, I was informed that because of my good scores, the results were referred to the provincial education office for redeployment. I waited for some weeks before word came through the teachers at Namaila School that I had been accepted at the Munali Secondary School in Lusaka. My family and teachers were overjoyed with my achievement and I became a celebrity in the whole of Namaila as Munali was a famous national school.

I went to Chikankata Secondary School to collect my acceptance papers. I was informed that Arthur Bbuku, Geoffrey Hamayobe, Sandford Mweemba, and Rueben Kapaale had also been accepted at Munali. I learnt that Irene Kaumba had done well and was accepted at the girls' national Chipembi Secondary School in Chisamba, Central Province.

I was delighted that my close friends Arthur and Geoffrey had also made it to Munali and we'd continue to be together. I went to lodge at Geoffrey's home for the weekend so that we could plan our first trip out of our homeland.

Munali Secondary School

Geoffrey and I went to buy tickets on Saturday at the Chikankata bus stop near the hospital for our first trip to Lusaka. We spent a bit of time at the shops spreading the news of our feat. While there, we met Lazarus Beviny Cheelo, who was on a weekend visit to his Simutwe Village from Lusaka. He was so happy with the news of our acceptance at Munali Secondary School that he offered us a free lift to Lusaka the following day. We also met an ANC official, who scared us about the volatile political situation in Lusaka. He suggested that we can be assured of safety by having ANC Youth wing cards. We gladly obliged and bought our first political party cards in 1964.

We left Chikankata on Sunday afternoon in Cheelo's motor car. During our conversation on the trip, Cheelo recalled visiting my home at Namaila as an enumerator during the national population census. By the time we were entering Lusaka, it was getting dark. For the first time in my life, I was in the capital city of Northern Rhodesia and was dazed by the bright street lights along the main road.

Cheelo drove through Cairo Road, the central road of Lusaka City, and left us at Munali Secondary School. We were well-received by some senior students and I spent the night in Young House. The school was located some five kilometres east of the city centre, surrounded by beautiful virgin bush like that of Namaila.

Munali Secondary School was the oldest and most prestigious secondary school for black male students in the country. For a long time, Munali and Chipembi were the only schools that provided education up to Form VI and therefore, selection to these national schools was very competitive. Most of the political and civic leaders including KK and most of his first cabinet ministers attended these two schools.

The principal of Munali School at the time, H. Roberts, aka 'Kamwefu' was assisted by a team of dedicated black and white teachers who maintained a clean environment and strict student discipline. Amongst them was Colonel Loftus, the septuagenarian English teacher, who having participated in the Second World War, kept a military grip on classroom discipline. At times he treated us as if we were soldiers in the war front.

David Bailey enjoyed the company of students as boarding master and sports organizer. Ian Salisbury was an enthusiast in commercial subjects and he thoroughly got absorbed when explaining the company balance sheet. The only female teacher was Mrs Josephine Kaunda, who provided a motherly presence in the science laboratories.

Munali Secondary School had adequate infrastructure for both academic and many extracurricular activities, including indoor and outdoor sports. The newest facility was a large swimming pool with Olympic-size diving boards. The surrounding bush and forest, later replaced by Mulungushi Village and Chudleigh Township, was a good course for cross-country races, although many runners were distracted by the juicy guava fruits growing by the stream on the course.

The following Monday after our arrival, we assembled in the school hall for a welcome address and allocation to the various residences. I recall the principal emphasizing the issues of personal discipline and hard work. He reminded us that we were the selected few amongst the many students who sat for Form II country-wide and what distinguished us was our good academic performance. However, we were encouraged to actively participate in sports and other outside school activities.

The dormitories were named after famous historical personalities as follows: Aggrey, Chuma, May, Maybin, Moffat, and Young. The tradition was that students who had relatives before at Munali were assigned to the same dormitories where their relatives had stayed. This clustering of relatives made the dormitories regional and tribal. I did not like this arrangement as it was counter to the intentions of bringing together students from various parts of the country as espoused by the new nationalist Government.

As I had no relative at Munali School before, the boarding master suggested that I go to Moffat House since that is where most students from the Southern Province stayed. I told him that having come this far from my village, I preferred getting a different experience by living with students from other provinces and tribes. I informed him of my beneficial experiences interacting with the family of the 'lost' Chewa carpenter John Sakala at Namaila and the four 'foreign' students at Chikankata Secondary School.

I, therefore, chose Aggrey House, which was at the furthest end of the school compound next to a thicket before the present-day Kaunda Square Township. Although I sensed some apprehension in the boarding master's voice, I stuck by my choice. A prefect escorted me to Aggrey House, where he handed me over to John Nyamadambo, a former student of Chikankata Secondary School to show me around the dormitory.

I was delighted that I belonged to a house named after one of the most peaceful Pan-Africanist who preached co-existence between blacks and whites in Africa, America, and Europe. Aggrey used the black and white keys of the piano as an example of the harmony and peaceful rhythm that different colours can achieve.

Nyamadambo showed me around the four wings of Aggrey House and the common ablution block. Before handing me over to the wing monitor for Wing C, which was to be my residence, he warned me that there would be some bullying and mocking. He explained that the residents of Aggrey House were predominantly from the Eastern and Northern Provinces and that coming from the Southern Province, I would be treated as an intruder.

On the following Tuesday, all Form III students assembled at the Main Hall and we were divided into various classes according to each one's performance in mathematics in Form II. As I had passed with a distinction, I was placed in the 3-A Class.

Surprisingly, I achieved a poor result in mathematics at the end of the first term and was reassigned to the commerce class under teacher Salisbury. I still kept sight of my vision to be a surveyor and studied hard. At the end of the year, I did well and was in the first five positions in most subjects including mathematics.

Later during the year, I was among the few students who were awarded government scholarships for free education up to Form V for good performance in the Form II examinations. My parents and grandparents were very pleased with this achievement as they continued to be relieved of the burden of scouting for money for school fees. Happily, one of the benefits of independence announced before the end of 1964 by the new Zambian government was the policy of free education for all.

We started classes and peace prevailed at my new dormitory for the first few days. On the first Saturday, I went into the ablution block to do some laundry. I found a student from the Eastern Province, who asked me in Nyanja, where I came from and what I wanted there. "Iwe, wachokela kuni and ufuna chiani kuno?"

To me, the question was related to my presence in the ablution block. So I replied in English that I was from Wing C and I wanted to wash some clothes. My answer aroused so much anger in him, such that he held me by the collar of my shirt and smacked me hard shouting that I was a rude boy.

He stated that Aggrey House was not for Tongas and that I should go to Moffat House, where my tribesmen resided. When another student entered the ablution block, my assaulter pretended that nothing was happening between the two of us.

The following day on a Sunday, a similar incident occurred in the same ablution block when I found an elderly student from the Northern Province. This one did not test my knowledge of ciBemba but accused me of lacking respect by going into the toilet when he was there. Surely, how could I have known who else wanted to answer the call of nature! He also had his sport by slapping me and advising me to leave, not only the ablution block, but Aggrey House to Moffat House.

Recalling my strict internship during my days as a shepherd boy at Namaila, I did not report these incidents to the higher authorities, as the issues appeared too localized and were part of my settling down. However, I decided to greet the two older students politely every time I met them and soon I earned their respect.

I participated fully in various sports such as chess, cricket, hockey, lawn tennis, cross country, and ballroom dancing. I joined swimming lessons and by March 1964, I was awarded a proficiency certificate in swimming as one of the best swimmers in the school. I dedicated the certificate to Uncle Aaron who had given me some effective, although unorthodox, lessons in swimming in the Likoma River in 1953.

In chess, I was in both the house and school teams, which dominated the inter-house and inter-school competitions in Lusaka Province. During the absence of Arthur Yoyo, the team captain, I led the Munali School chess team. Later, I took over as the captain of the team and was included in the Lusaka Town chess team.

I enjoyed the new game of cricket played on an oval ground, with its intricate scoring system. However, I soon abandoned the game when Yoyo's high speed spinning ball knocked out three of Lloyd Sichilongo's front teeth during an inter-house competition. At the time, the only cricket protective gear provided by the school was knee pads and hand gloves. I still enjoy watching the Cricket World Cup competitions as I am able to follow the scoring of the runs during the game.

Lawn tennis, although with a rather confusing scoring system, is a more friendly game and is played even by females and the elderly. The game has a toning down scoring system in which a zero score is called 'love', to pacify the player who has no points.

In cross country, Jessie Muleya, the young brother to the legendary Yotham Muleya, also became a national and school champion. It was an exhilarating experience to stand next to Muleya at the start of any race in inter-house and inter-school competitions. Once he was in the lineup, it was a foregone conclusion as to who would lead the Moffat House and Munali School teams to victory.

In 1965, I was elected captain of the Aggrey House cross-country team. Although I could not equal the Muleyas, I always tried to be among the top runners. In 1966, I was in the Aggrey House choir, which scooped the school trophy for melodious singing.

During the 1960s, there was radical political change in most of Africa, due to the growing black nationalism, advocated by the liberation movements. The British Government, which was the world's greatest colonial power could not contain the agitation by the indigenous people and decided to grant independence to its colonies. In February 1960, Harold Macmillan, Prime Minister of Britain, while on a visit to South Africa had stated that, "The wind of change is blowing through this continent, and whether we like it or not, this growth of national consciousness is a political fact. We must all accept it as a fact, and our national policies must take account of it."

In the Central African region, an experiment at regional integration had been tried by forming the Federation of Rhodesia and Nyasaland in 1953. This brought together under one government the territories of Northern Rhodesia, Southern Rhodesia and Nyasaland. The economic motive behind the amalgamation was the abundant copper deposits in Zambia. Zambia, "was the wealthiest of the three and actually contributed more to the overall building of the infrastructure in the Federation." The peoples of the federation enjoyed the joint facilities of a common currency, railway, airline, educational institutions and judiciary.

General elections were held in Northern Rhodesia on 30 October 1962, for members of the Legislative Council. The United Federal Party (UFP) won the majority seats. This posed a problem for both Kaunda of UNIP and Nkumbula of the ANC as neither of them could form a government. Under the urging of the students of Munali Secondary School, the two agreed to form a coalition government under which Kaunda became Minister of Local Government and Social Welfare and Nkumbula was appointed Minister of African Education.

During the Victoria Falls talks of 1963, it was decided that the Federation of Rhodesia and Nyasaland would formally be dissolved in December 1963. Nyasaland was to be granted independence in July 1964, while the independence of Northern Rhodesia would follow at a date to be decided upon through negotiations.

The political situation in the region somewhat cooled down after the dissolution of the Federation of Rhodesia and Nyasaland on 31st December 1963 as demanded by the freedom fighters. Unfortunately, the local tension and rivalry between the ANC and UNIP supporters were growing after the announcement of the election date. The party cadres were getting violent in their efforts to win more members and get campaign funds.

One day, while walking from Munali to Katungu Supermarket at Kabwata, the only big shop in Lusaka owned by Daniel Katungu, a black person, we met some youths in the bush where the current Mass Media is located. They demanded that we show them our party cards. Quick thinking by claiming that we had not bought any party cards since we were students saved us. They advised us to buy UNIP cards as they would not spare us the next time.

When we returned to school, we discussed our encounter and decided to buy UNIP cards as advised. Luckily, we already had ANC cards, which we bought at Chikankata on our first trip to Lusaka. We were aware that the two parties were both fighting for the country's independence and therefore, the party cards were not a big issue to us. I have, since then, paid little respect to the value of political cards.

We agreed on the common strategy of carrying both cards, but in different pockets. The ANC card would be in the left pocket and a small letter 'A' would be marked on the left shoe. The UNIP card being in the right pocket, the right shoe would be marked with a letter 'U'. As the cadres became distinguishable in their party uniforms, it was easy to show them the appropriate card by a quick glance at one's shoes and flashing out the correct card from the pocket. By strictly observing this dress code, most of the students at Munali were able to avoid being beaten up by party cadres.

In the January 1964 elections were held to elect 65 members of the Legislative Council, UNIP won 56 members. KK became the Prime Minister of a new government and led the negotiations for independence. In May 1964, a rally was held at the old airport near Kalingalinga Township to welcome KK and his team from an overseas trip where they had gone to finalise the road map to independence. We walked from Munali to attend the rally in support of a former student of Munali School, who had become the Prime Minister of Zambia. It was at this mammoth rally that the date of 24th October as Independence Day for a new country to be called Zambia was announced.

Many freedom fighters were introduced and they addressed the huge gathering, with promises of better days to come under black rule. The 54-year brave warrior Mama Chikamoneka (Julia Mulenga Nsofwa) got a thunderous applause when she was introduced. So did Rueben Chitandika Kamanga, when he issued his flagship statement that, "If in Ghana and Kenya they did it, why can't we also did it."

A few months later, the Independence Celebrations Organizing Committee announced the programme for preparations for the Independence Day activities. Among the planned activities were calisthenics, involving school children from various schools. I was delighted when our school was included and I was among those, who went through strenuous practices under strict military coaches assisted by Korean instructors.

I feel proud to have been among the thousands of young school children donned in white uniforms, who took part in the formations on Independence Day at the Independence Stadium. I still recall that our group formed the letter 'M' in the word ZAMBIA on the terraces. The few moments after midnight on 24th October 1964 were filled with a thunderous roar as we witnessed the lowering of the Union Jack flag and the hoisting of the Zambian flag.

Independence had arrived and we were proud to sing, "Stand and Sing of Zambia Proud and Free". Indeed we were free to determine our own destiny. I took the opportunity for self-determination to indigenize my name from Peter Magande to Ng'andu Peter Magande. This was officially endorsed on my national registration card, which I acquired in 1965. This is the reason for many Zambians of my generation being known by more than one name.

The landmark occasion of 24th October 1964 separated the ominous past with its racism and oppression from the future of unity and hope for prosperity for all. While Zambians and many other Africans were celebrating the newly-found freedoms, those in countries in Southern Africa entered a tragic phase, when thousands of blacks and whites would die in interracial conflicts. This conflict cut short Zambia's 'honeymoon' and celebrations and diverted national efforts from social and economic development for over two decades.

Sometime in 1965, the newly appointed black Director of Statistics Mpafya Mulenga, one of the first Zambian statisticians, visited Munali Secondary School to give a talk on job prospects in the department. He was also interested in recruiting students to work during the school holidays. In view of my capability in mathematics, I was offered temporary employment during the August school holidays. This was my first paid job and I do not even remember my first salary, although I recall that it was enough for me to live a more comfortable life at school.

During the holidays, I lived in Misisi Compound in a two-room house with Lawson Mweemba, a relative, and his family. We had a pit latrine and a shallow-water well shared by a group of families. Due to limited space in the house, I'd wake up early in the morning and walk to the Central Statistics Office, where I'd spruce myself up for work. I'd then spend the whole day and part of the evening at the offices reading various documents. This widened my knowledge on the state of the newly independent country.

During the weekends, I went to the Palace Cinema near Kamwala Market. Some of the great films of the time were Lawrence of Arabia, The Ten Commandments, and Cleopatra. I also spent time playing draughts in the market, where I earned a little money through bets by defeating well-known draught players.

Before I returned to school, the Mweemba family was allocated a house in the nearby newly completed Kamwala Township and we shifted into one of the modern houses. The director of CSO was highly impressed with my timekeeping and quality of work and he invited me to return to work in the department anytime I wished. I found Mpafya at the CSO when I joined the Civil Service in 1971 and we became very close associates as he kept reminding of my time-keeping habit of 1965.

During the school Easter holidays in March 1966, I was given temporary employment as a veterinary assistant in the Department of Veterinary and Tsetse Control Services. I was posted to the Choma District in the Southern Province and was assigned to the Macha area where I lived with Muntanga, the Veterinary Officer at the Macha Agricultural Camp. The family, which belonged to the Watch Tower Sect, warmly welcomed me and provided for all my needs.

At the time, the department was undertaking a general national cattle vaccination programme. We toured the villages on bicycles to vaccinate the cattle and came back to the camp in the evenings. By coincidence, the department had just acquired modern hypodermic syringes. The programme involving the vaccination of hundreds of cattle was completed in record time due to the use of the modern syringes.

The introduction of the modern equipment was mistakenly attributed to me, due to the agility with which I operated the syringes. The villagers called me 'doctor'. I was on familiar ground with the villagers and their cattle as the environment was similar to that of Namaila.

On the last day of the tour in the Mang'unza area, I suffered from a deathly bout of malaria. I spent the afternoon in a deep sleep under a tree. The attack was so severe that some villagers had to escort us to the camp as I could not even manage to ride my bicycle. Late in the evening, I prepared a 'will' to bequeath my few belongings, as I thought that I was going to die. My host scoffed at my proposal as he was familiar with the hallucinations that accompany serious malaria attacks. I had not suffered from malaria before in my life.

Luckily, the supervising officers in Choma came the following morning for an inspection of the cattle vaccination programme. They found me and Muntanga at the bus stop waiting for a bus to Choma. Realizing the serious nature of my illness and on learning that the programme had been completed successfully, they abandoned their tour and rushed me to Choma Hospital, where I was given a dose of quinine. I recovered within a day and left for my school a few days later. My hosts, the Muntanga family and the Macha community were sad to bid farewell to the 'young veterinary doctor who introduced modern syringes'.

By the time I got to Munali School, my eyes, palms, feet and mouth were all yellow due to the quinine treatment. It seemed that I had been given an overdose of quinine, which gave me some immunity as I did not suffer from malaria during the next thirty-five years up until 2001.

I was doing relatively well with my class work, especially since the major subject of commerce in our class included company balance sheets and international trade, which rely on mathematical calculations. I continued my excellent performance in both mathematics and geography. I found it easy to apply my mathematical ability onto economic systems that include forecasting and calculations of all activities, functions, and institutions involved in transferring goods and services from producers to consumers.

Munali Secondary School and Chipembi Secondary School had a twin relationship that entailed exchanges of weekend visits by senior students of the two schools for social functions such as ballroom dancing and debating events. I was appointed Assistant Food Minister with the responsibility of supervising selected junior students who served as waiters to the host senior students and their visitors. Whenever any one of the hosts was not given a good portion of food, it was not easy for them to openly complain about food in the presence of the visiting ladies.

In the absence of Simon Mulumbi Chushi, the Food Minister, I was the one who was approached privately to seek for a correction of the situation. I then discreetly attended to their requests. This special relationship elevated my status and availed me of the opportunity of interacting at a personal level with most senior students who were in Form VI. Chushi became a lifelong friend and Aned, his newly-found love, warmly welcomed me in their smart home.

Among those who became functional relatives and played significant roles in my later life were Lyson Tembo, the smart Munali School Captain, Benjamin Yoram Mwila aka 'BY', the anchor fullback footballer, Lloyd Sichilongo, the cricketer, Namukolo Mukutu, the scientist, Samuel Mulozi, Daniel Macwani Mike Siwiwalyonda, and Silane Mwenechanya.

In spite of the wide age difference of more than five years, I had the rare privilege of calling most of these seniors by their first names. 'BY', forever affectionately called me "Mune". Being close to the school captain and other leaders of various dormitories and clubs, provided me with an opportunity to learn leadership traits and mannerisms. Apart from the five former students of Chikankata Secondary School, I made long-lasting friendships with new age mates namely, Winston Chikwanda, Joseph Muyangana, Muyoba Macwani, and Wilson Mwandila, with whom we soldiered on together to the University of Zambia in 1967.

In my last year, while in Form V, I was honoured by being appointed Sub-Prefect for Wing D of Aggrey House' occupied by youths in the re-introduced Form I class. This came with the privilege of having a secluded cubicle, which allowed me some quiet time for studying for the final examinations. From being a herd boy, who kept order amongst the itinerant cattle and goats in the Namaila hills, I was now responsible for mentoring and keeping order and discipline amongst a group of young students drawn from all over Zambia.

Having excelled in representing my house in the various sports and activities, I earned respect from my housemates, classmates and student community beyond my school for my achievements and leadership qualities. The special functional relationship I established with the senior and junior students from all over Zambia de-tribalized me, as I realized that I was appreciated and respected more for my service and not for my tribe. I continued to relate with many of them and enjoyed their trust and confidence and that of their families.

I left Munali Secondary School in December 1966 after sitting the Form V examinations. By this time, I had known much of Lusaka Town as I, in the company of friends, spent some time at the 20th Century Cinema in the town centre and at the Palace Cinema in Kamwala. A few times, we visited the famous Kabwata boxing ring to enjoy the bruising matches between tribes.

Before leaving Munali Secondary School, I applied for temporary employment with the Department of Surveys, so that I could work while waiting for the school results. Unfortunately, the available work in the department was at the head office in Kabwe, where I could not find any accommodation. I was then reassigned to the Department of Water Affairs and sent to Mazabuka as a Water Affairs Assistant. In Mazabuka, I lived in a one-roomed rondavel at the Mazabuka Veterinary Research Station, six kilometres from the town centre. I was privileged to be allocated a government bicycle for my local movements.

I enjoyed my work at Mazabuka as it involved touring the rural areas of the Southern Province, planning, designing, and constructing dams and weirs using the newly acquired modern equipment. This gave me an opportunity to put into practice my knowledge of geometry and trigonometry. I became conversant with altimeters, compasses, theodolites, and verniers as the Global Positioning System (GPS) had not yet been invented. After the invention of GPS in 1973 by the USA military, it became easier to provide location and time information anywhere on or near the earth using satellites and the surveyors had an easy job.

I was also assigned the additional administrative responsibility of delivering stores to various stations and paying the monthly wages to all workers of the department in the Choma, Gwembe, Mazabuka, Monze, and Namwala districts. Driver Simuule used to tell me stories of some workers who wondered how a young person at my age could be assigned to carry large sums of money. Such an assignment exposed me to a sensitive responsibility of trust and tested my integrity.

It was not easy to establish relationships with boys of my age at the time, because of the differing levels of education. Many had not managed to go beyond Form II. I used to some time in shops discussing with shop owners and their families. Much of my free time was spent in pubs playing mini soccer, while gulping litres of cocacola and smoking the famous Peter Stuyvesant cigarettes, just because of its 'nice' name. I always had two packets of cigarettes on me and shared them freely with anyone who asked.

My disguised behaviour of frequenting bars and heavy smoking did enable me to get closer to the community. However, I immediately gave up smoking when I was admitted to the University of Zambia in March 1967. Since I had not yet started taking alcoholic drinks, I vowed not to drink until after the last examination at the university after four years.

Lessons from the University of Zambia

To produce the much-needed personnel for national development, a plan was mooted by the Coalition Government of ANC and UNIP in 1963 for the establishment of a university. The idea was supported by a report produced in November 1963 by the Lockwood Commission Enquiry.

In October 1965, His Excellency President Kaunda gave his assent to the University Act Number 66 of 1965. On 17 March 1966, the first intake of 312 students was admitted and the first academic session commenced at the Ridgeway Campus, near the Lusaka Central Hospital, with three Schools of Humanities and Social Sciences, Education and Natural Sciences.

The foundation stone for the University of Zambia on the Great East Road campus was laid on 13 July 1966. A national campaign was mounted inviting the citizens to donate anything of value towards the university. I donated some three pence towards the fund, as I looked forward to being a student of this important seat of knowledge at some future day.

I was very happy when the Form V results came out in early 1967 as I did well in most subjects. Of particular encouragement was my good performance in mathematics and geography, the entry subjects for the surveying course. My boss at work was very pleased and urged me to study surveying as planned.

In early March 1967, I received the message that I had been accepted by the University of Zambia to study for a degree. I travelled to Lusaka to discuss my acceptance and how it related to surveying, my preferred area of study. The UNZA officials encouraged me to get enrolled and promised that by the time of specialization in the second or third year, surveying will have been introduced.

The programme was that all students took a number of common subjects in the first year and then branched off later into subjects of their specialization. On the basis of this understanding, I agreed to enrol in the School of Humanities and Social Sciences.

When we reported for the first term in March 1967, the hostels at the Great East Road Campus were not ready. Accommodation was arranged for all the first year students in the various exhibition halls at the Lusaka Showgrounds. I shared the Tobacco Board of Zambia (TBZ) exhibition hall with another eleven students as our residence.

Our dining room was the Tayali Art Gallery, where we enjoyed lavish three-course meals, which were better than those at the newly opened Intercontinental Hotel. Whenever we had a meal with some meat, we asked for more soup with the meat. The waiters and chefs enjoyed mocking us for not knowing the difference between soup and gravy!

Since most of us were from villages and had attended secondary schools where there was only one course, we gladly opened ourselves to being taught some culinary lessons by the waiters. At least I had learnt some table manners and how to use cutlery at Chikankata Mission and I was happy to add some more knowledge from UNZA, the highest institution of learning.

We were bussed every day to the Ridgeway Campus near the UTH for classes and lunch. A few times when the bus was not available, we covered the distance on foot. Luckily, a few hostels were completed at the main campus before the end of the year and we shifted from the showgrounds into the new hostels. Fidelis Lungu and I occupied room eleven in International Hall No. 5.

At some point during 1967, I was invited to sit for interviews for one of the six ASPAU scholarships offered by the government of the United States of America (USA). I saw an opportunity to fulfil my ambition of becoming a cadastral surveyor. With a specialization in orography, I was going to understand the origins and value of the mountains of Namaila. I went through the interviews with ease and was told to get ready for departure to the USA before September 1967.

Later, the USA Government informed the Zambian Government that the number of scholarships had been reduced from six to three, due to the high cost of the up-scaled involvement of the USA Government in the Vietnam War in Asia. A decision had been made in favour of Caroline Kaunda who was to study dentistry against my surveying.

I gladly accepted the decision as I knew Caroline very well. She was a daughter of Mrs Kaunda, my former science teacher at Munali Secondary School and was a friend of a former classmate. I felt proud when Caroline successfully completed her course and came back to Zambia, and through her reputable dental clinic in Lusaka, she offered an invaluable service to the community.

About the same time, the Zambian Government was offered a few scholarships by the government of the Russian Federation and I was selected to take up one of them. After some extensive research on Communism, I politely turned down the offer and decided to remain at UNZA.

I was doing so well in my favourite subject of geography that at times, I was asked by our lecturer to read my geography essays to the rest of the class. I became confident that at the end of the year, I would be sponsored for a surveying course at an institution outside the country. Sadly, at the end of the 1967 academic year, I got a disgraceful 'D' grade in geography. I did not know the reason for my lecturer to even refuse to discuss the result. All the same, my plans to be a surveyor were shattered.

During the 1967 Christmas holidays, I was consoled by an offer of employment by Barclays Bank Limited to work as a bank clerk. I chose the Chipata Branch in the Eastern Province to explore new territory, especially that, one of my mockers at Munali was from there. Greggie Ng'andu, a former classmate at Chikankata School, who was working in government offered to accommodate me at his house in Kapata Township.

As I waited for a bus to Chipata at the Kamwala bus terminal, I met Solomon Shaba, another former Chikankata schoolmate who was heading to Chipata to visit his relative. We spent two nights at the station before getting seats on one of the United Bus of Zambia (UBZ) buses, which were the only buses in those days. Although I was used to the hills of Namaila, the steep Manenekela cliffs and winding Great East Road at the Luangwa River gave me a scare.

In January 1968, the Zambian government was changing the currency from British Pounds to the new Zambian Kwacha and Ngwee. I was well-received by the branch manager of the bank in Chipata. I was one of the two trusted clerks who were assigned the onerous responsibility of helping the illiterate members of the public to exchange their old money for the new currency. I executed my special responsibility so well and with integrity such that customers sought for my service when they came to the bank.

One day, while having a drink in a local pub, a senior government official asked me why I had chosen to work in Chipata. I excitedly explained that I wanted to know the people of the Eastern Province and their culture. The officer got upset and accused me of taking over jobs from the Easterners. He shouted that the Eastern Province was not for Tongas, since there were no easterners in the Southern Province. As I knew that he was ignorant of John Sakala who peacefully settled at Namaila in 1952, I ignored his intemperate conversation.

I was amazed at the large quantiy of mangoes on the route from Nyimba to Chipata. During the weekends, I'd go out with friends to the areas surrounding Chipata such as Chizongwe Secondary School. To my astonishment, mango and guava trees grew wildly along the streams.

My exemplary behaviour and attitude to customers in Chipata had been relayed and recorded at Barclays Bank head office. When I returned to Lusaka, the bank officer informed me that the bank had opened an account for me at the Mutaba House branch and that part of the balance of my pay and some bonus had been deposited into the account. The account remains open but must be somewhere in a suspense book. The bank management offered me the option of working for the bank during any holidays and to consider joining the bank permanently after my studies.

I returned to UNZA after the December 1967 holidays for my second year and registered for courses in pure mathematics, economics, law, and psychology. My friends used to call this combination of subjects 'queer' and 'awkward'. But I was happy with the combination as I wanted to get a feel of law and psychology, before settling on mathematics and economics.

I decided to apply all my energies to the studies as I had to make up for the geography subject, which I'd failed in the previous year. Occasionally, I composed and contributed poems to the in-house UNZA magazine and also contributed crossword puzzles to the Times of Zambia newspaper for a token fee. I played lawn tennis, mini-soccer, and chess for physical and mental exercises.

In the mathematics course, elementary computer studies were included. At the time, there were only three computers in Zambia, located at UNZA, the mines in Kitwe, and at the Ministry of Finance. The machines were so large that they filled a room of twenty square metres.

In the pure mathematics class, there were five of us and only three students in the class ahead of ours. The senior students were Benjamin (Ben) Mweene, Friday Ndhlovu, and a Tanzanian called Ndelilo, who were very helpful in our studies. Mweene patiently spent a lot of his time getting us through some intriguing mathematical theorems.

Mweene pursued further studies in pure mathematics at the University of Birmingham in the United Kingdom, specializing in algebra. In 1974, he became the first Zambian to get world recognition and was awarded a Doctorate of Philosophy (PhD) degree in mathematics. In his research work on four-dimensional linear groups, he solved a problem that had remained unresolved for fifty years.

Ndhlovu branched off to specialize in economics and on completion of his studies, he went back to the Bank of Zambia as one of the first Zambian economists. Later, he founded the Investrust Bank, which was the first indigenous bank to float shares on the Lusaka Stock Exchange, to widen ownership by the public.

It is gratifying that Mweene and Ndhlovu the first Zambian mathematicians from UNZA have made remarkable contributions to the development of Zambia. In my group, four of the students went into the physical sciences and I was the only one who followed the arts, which is the product of human imagination.

In the economics subject, we started from scratch, but some of the subjects were related to the commerce lessons I had taken during my schooling at Munali Secondary School. I found the lessons in econometrics very fascinating as we had to relate and apply mathematical measures to economic data.

In view of the rapid development of the economics subject during the previous three decades, we were not expected to cover all the important subjects in class. The lecturers referred us to some of the well-known scholars, who'd studied and written extensively on the early thoughts on economics.

Amongst the famous scholars were the classical economists Adam Smith,

Thomas Malthus, Alfred Marshall, and David Ricardo, the mathematical economist Joseph Schumpeter, Robert M. Solow, the Saint Lucian William Arthur Lewis, who specialised in models of economic growth, Maynard Keynes, the father of modern macroeconomics, Paul Anthony Samuelson, father of modern economics, and Walt W. Rostow, the father of the stages of economic growth model.

Once I'd settled on studying economics, it was time to understand this important subject and its various interpretations by different scholars and through different eras. I followed the presentations and definitions by Samuelson, as his 'Economics: An Introductory Analysis' was the official textbook and it was important to be in tune with the lecturers. However, I also found time to read the books by the other scholars.

In the midst of raging critiques of the various economic thoughts, such as Rostow versus Marxism, I could not choose by which economic term to describe myself and my beliefs. I remained neutral preferring to admire all shades of economic theories as having both positive and negative attributes.

By the time I was set to leave the University of Zambia at the end of 1970 , I was very familiar with many economics terms such as classical economics, central economic planning, probability theory and models of economic growth, theory of comparative advantage, supply and demand, free market and the invisible hand, political economy, economic geography and economies of scale, international finance and trade, fiscal and monetary policies, models of economic growth, laissez-faire, multiplier effects, inflation, and the five stages of growth propounded by the various famous economists.

By 1985, when Michael Porter came up with the theory of competitive advantage as a counter to comparative advantage, I was aware of the famous economics qualification of ceteris paribus. In my later life, I found cause to espouse economic development through economic nationalism.

If I had not been discouraged by an expatriate Deputy Secretary to the cabinet, who'd said that I had only a 'flavour of economics' from UNZA and appointed me as administrative officer (Cadet), I would have joined the National Commission for Development Planning in 1972. The diversion to Makerere University to study the new subject of Agricultural Economics reinforced my strong belief in comparative advantage as a follower of David Ricardo. I strongly believed that Zambia's comparative advantage was in agriculture and the country could accelerate its development pace by using its abundant land, water, and cheap labour.

Leo Mdala, one of my classmates in mathematics, was fascinated by physics theories and equations, in particular, those dealing with energy, velocities, and magnetism. He worked on the principle of, like magnetic poles repel each other and unlike poles attract each other. Using toy trains, he came up with the conclusion that head-on collisions by trains could be avoided by attaching magnets with like poles in front of the trains. Once the train engines get closer, they will stop and avoid a head-on collision because of the repulsion of the like poles.

For some reason, Mdala got me close to his ideas. I encouraged him to present his discovery to the Zambian Government for sponsorship to undertake further research as it looked promising for commercial application. Unfortunately, he could not find anyone in the government who was interested in sponsoring further work on this important subject. Mdala went on to study geophysics and worked for the University of Zambia. Within a short period, the Japanese engineers developed the magnetic braking system and ran accident-free bullet trains.

Belatedly, in the twenty-first century, I was determined as Minister of Finance to fund the further development of some of the innovations and inventions. I came up with an Inventors Fund in the 2006 Zambian Government budget. The programme could not achieve much as many Zambian policy makers and civil servants mistook the provision for an 'investors fund'. It was more fashionable to discuss investors who had money and not inventors who had ideas and concepts on solving daily problems.

The lessons in psychology were enjoyable, stimulating, provocative, and informative. In the introduction to the subject, we were taught that psychology was "a scientific study of people, the mind, and behaviour". We then covered subjects such as the intellectual, social, and emotional development of the child. We were introduced to Sigmund Freud's psychoanalytic theory of personality and psychodynamic view of human behaviour and Erik Erikson's psychosocial development of personality and the work of some present-day psychologists.

In cognitive and social psychology, we conducted some experiments in order to try to understand human behaviour and group dynamics. One experiment we did in mystification involved a number of well-dressed UNZA students standing at spaced intervals along Cairo Road from the Kafue Roundabout to the Main Post Office.

At an appointed time, the first student in the south pointed to the sky and shouted, "What is that up there? It is very clear and is moving northwards. Do you see it?" he asked the nearest person to him. The second student some distance away then shouted, "Yes. I see it. It is very big and moving fast. Look. Look there," while drawing the attention of the person next to him and pointing to the sky. By this time, the third student was shouting, most of the people on Cairo Road were 'seeing' something big and moving northwards. But in fact, there was nothing. This was an interesting lesson in social influence and group dynamics.

In law, I found the law of contract most appropriate for business relations. I took a few other short law courses and left the subject to some of my 'learned' friends including Fred Chuunga, Mumba Kapumpa, Reuben Mwape, and Bevin Willombe, who all became prominent practitioners of the legal profession.

At the end of 1968, I took the generous offer by Barclays Bank during the holidays and this time, I chose to work in Livingstone in the Southern Province. I stayed in the Dambwa Township with Solomon Shaba, who was at the time in permanent employment with the Income Tax Department. Solomon had even bought a scooter and he taught me how to ride it. I had no difficulties in passing the driving test.

Back at UNZA for my third year in March 1969, I focussed my studies on economics and mathematics. During the year, there was a crisis within the leadership of the student body. Some students petitioned for the removal of the UNZASU Executive Committee and this was causing instability on campus. Four of us, Patrick Chipungu, Raphael Chenga, Alex Kapenda, and I, all third-year students, offered to form a committee to mediate between the two opposing groups.

As the four of us had not shown any interest in occupying any positions, we were accepted by both the students and administration to undertake this special assignment. However, after some consultations, it was decided that a referendum would be the best way to resolve the matter. We then organized the referendum and the vote was in favour of removing the Executive Committee.

Peace was restored on campus and fresh elections were held for a new Executive Committee. This was the first test of my leadership and arbitration abilities and I feel proud that our efforts achieved a peaceful result for the university community.

Apart from being involved in on-campus politics, I, and a few other students were involved in international politics. We demonstrated at the British High Commission, opposite the University Teaching Hospital (UTH) about the unsatisfactory handling of the Rhodesian UDI issue. On one occasion, the police flushed us out with tear gas from the nearby Oppenheimer College buildings where we sought refuge. We also demonstrated at the French Embassy, opposite the Main Post Office, which was representing the Portuguese Government in the conflict in Angola.

As part of one course in economics, we were required to undertake some research and write special papers in selected subjects. I decided to undertake research on agricultural marketing in Luapula Province as I had not been anywhere further north than ten miles from Lusaka. I was partnered with a classmate, Danny Musenge, whose roots were in that province.

We left Lusaka by bus and spent a night in Mufulira Town with Danny's relatives before proceeding to Mansa through the Pedicle Road in Zaire. This was my first time to be on the Copperbelt and also in a foreign country. At Chembe, I had my first experience of crossing a river by pontoon. The construction of a bridge at Chembe became one of my landmark achievements later in the twenty-first century.

Our research tour took us to Samfwa, Mwansabombwe, Mbereshi, and Kawambwa, interviewing farmers, fishermen, and Government officials. At Samfwa beach on Lake Bangweulu, I admired the only silica sands in Zambia and wondered why there were no lodges or hotels like those in beaches in other countries.

During the tour, I saw a lot of cassava and realized the importance of the crop as a food crop for the local people. Unfortunately, word was going round that one of the freedom fighters had been on tour telling people to stop eating cassava as it was an inferior food. He encouraged the people to adopt maize, which was not grown in the area. Between Chembe and Mansa, there were a lot of orange and lemon trees laden with a lot of fruit, which ended up rotting for lack of a market.

For the first time, I saw well-designed large villages with rows of houses at Mwansabombwe and along the Luapula plains. I appreciated the government's policy of village regrouping as it made it easier to provide modern amenities such as schools, clinics, and piped water. We visited some small patches of banana fields belonging to individuals and the upcoming Mununshi Banana Scheme.

At the end of our research tour in Luapula Province, I decided to take a sightseeing trip to Kasama via Luwingu. Having been to Chipata, Livingstone, and Mansa in the Eastern, Southern and Luapula Provinces, I wanted to experience life in the Northern Province. Although the bus trip from Kasama to Lusaka was long and tiresome, I enjoyed the educational aspect of going through Mpika, Serenje, Mkushi, and Kapiri Mposhi. I became familiar with most of the country from Lusaka to Chipata, to Kasama, to Copperbelt, to Mansa, and to Livingstone.

As per the undertaking made earlier, Barclays Bank employed me again during the 1969 Christmas holidays and I opted to go back to the Livingstone branch. The major attraction was no more the Victoria Falls or Solomon's motor bike, but my newly-found girlfriend, who was taking a course at the Batoka Hospital. Of course, after some serious studying under the sweltering heat of Livingstone, a motor bike trip to the Victoria Falls with Joyce was quite refreshing.

With my practical experience in banking and mathematics skills, the bank branch management entrusted me with the responsibility of assisting other bank tellers to balance their cash drawers at the beginning and end of the workday. This routine was similar to that of balancing the livestock numbers during my youth. At times, I was asked by the branch accountant to escort him to the airport to deliver special mail for the bank's head office in Lusaka

The last year at the university was demanding, as scores in a number of subjects were to determine the final classification of one's degree. By this time, I had recovered in terms of the number of subjects to get a degree, but I needed to consolidate my knowledge of economics. So I took six courses in economics and three courses in mathematics. I also reduced the number of visits to Livingstone to concentrate on studying.

At the end of the university course, in December 1970, I naturally went to Livingstone to await the final university examination results. Barclays Bank management assured me of a permanent job depending upon the results. Just before Christmas, I received a letter dated 21 December 1970 from the Head of Administrative Training at the National Institute of Public Administration (NIPA), Mr P.L. Taylor in which he stated that,

"I have been advised that, subject to your obtaining a satisfactory degree result, Government intends to appoint you to an administrative post in the Civil Service. This Institute is, therefore, arranging a programme of induction training that will enable you to settle down quickly in your new post and equip you to make a positive contribution to the Government developmental programmes."

I was very happy with the results as I passed all the courses and was awarded a Bachelor of Arts degree with credit. I informed the management of Barclays Bank that I could not join the bank, as I was required by the Zambian Civil Service. The trust shown by the bank in giving me responsibilities of handling large amounts of money at the Chipata and Livingstone branches subdued any strong yearning or craving for money. On a visit to the vaults of the Bank of Zambia later in life, I was shown huge stacks of new banknotes. Even then, these did not arouse any instinct of a money-grubber in me.

I'd made long-lasting friendships with many students at Munali Secondary School, who'd qualified to attend the University of Zambia. Because of my frequent change of courses during my first and second years, I came to know many students from schools all over Zambia, who were taking various courses.

Members of my fraternity at UNZA included Cuthbert Chibaye, Patrick Chipungu, Winston Chikwanda, Hanson Kamima, John Kaluzi, Mumba Kapumba, Pepino Kashishi, Ephraim Kaunga, Shadreck Kayumba, Kalunga Lutato, Muyoba Macwani, Leo Mdala, Winner Matongo, Panwell Munatamba, Bradley Muntemba, Danny Musenge, Joseph Muyangana, Wilson Mwandila, Joseph Mwale, and Inyambo Nyumbu.

We mobilized ourselves into a vigilante group called 'monks' to protect the female students against non-students who wished to make friendships with them. The monks would pass time idling at strategic points on the campus looking out for male visitors from outside, whom we termed 'poachers'. Once we saw one, we would shout 'poacher' accompanied by some obscenities. Although we were very protective of our female students, we could not ward them from these 'poachers', who were much older, bigger and richer than us. Some, openly threatened violence when confronted.

Among the many female students whom I associated with in the lecture rooms for various subjects and during extracurricular activities were Emelia Busiku, Tonia Chihana, Angela Hakoola, Angela Chewe, Irene Chintu, Grace

Mumbuna, Mary Nguvu, Peggy Ng'andu, Elizabeth Hakeeta, Barbara Mabula, Dorothy Makubalo, Christine Sakubita, and Macherline Sibanda.

Although we had varying personal interests and were in different faculties, we found time to hang around the campus to discuss our future plans.

Induction of UNZA graduates into the Zambian public service
As instructed, I reported at NIPA on 2 January 1971 and met a number of other graduates to get more briefing on the novel induction course and to sign documents relating to employment in the Civil Service.

One of the important ceremonies we went through was the swearing of the 'Oath of Secrecy', that forbade divulging of information to outsiders. Each one of us promised to keep to ourselves any information that would come our way in the execution of our duties, unless disclosure was required by a court of law or was in the national interest. This was not new to me as I'd learnt to keep so many secrets on the activities in the bush while herding cattle. The difference was that, this time, the level of responsibility had been elevated to the national interest.

The induction course was in three phases spread throughout the whole year. Phase one, of three months duration, was in the classroom and covered introductions to the systems and procedures that are used within the Zambian government management. We were given some background information relating to law, management, and development economics and instructed in special administrative skills relating to government work.

We were taught that a civil servant does not sign correspondence under their personal name but by the designation or title of the position they hold. The procedure of anonymity spreads responsibility to the whole department or ministry and reinforces the principle of collective responsibility.

During phase two, we were posted to provinces to undertake operational assignments. I was posted to the Cabinet Office in Livingstone, the capital of the Southern Province., which I knew very well. The provincial minister was Peter W. Matoka, who was assisted by Permanent Secretary (PS) Ilute Yeta, who became the Litunga IV of Barotseland in 1977. I assumed the duties of Assistant Provincial Development Officer under the supervision of Richard Lichaha, the Provincial Development Officer. I was happy to get back to Livingstone Town where I'd worked earlier in 1969.

During one of my provincial tours, I met Namukolo Mukutu, a former senior schoolmate at Munali Secondary School. Mukutu had just returned from New Zealand where he'd graduated in agriculture and had been posted to Choma to start his civil service career.

My duties included the planning and monitoring of development projects in the province. I wrote detailed tour reports that were submitted to the Provincial Development Committee (PDC) for discussion by the heads of departments.

The trips to Namwala were torturous because of the sand. During one of our tours, W.R.S Stride, the provincial road engineer and I discussed the innovation of mixing sand and cement to spread on the sandy road to harden the surface and a trial application proved effective. During a tour to inspect Munyeke Bridge in the Macha area in 1971, I met some villagers in the Mang'unza area, who recognized me from my earlier work in the veterinary department in 1966.

Being a university graduate, I was given special attention by the Permanent Secretary, who gave me tips on administration while at the office and during our tours. I accompanied the PS to Siampondo Village, the extreme south-western part of the Gwembe District bordering Zimbabwe, to check on the food situation before sending some relief food. At Kalomo Town, we were joined by Joseph Hamatwi, the District Governor and a kapaso (messenger).

When we arrived in Siampondo Village at 1000 hours and found only women at the meeting place. Word was sent to a nearby homestead where there was a beer-drinking session going on. Within a short time, a large number of men, many in a drunken state, gathered at Headman Siampondo's grounds for the meeting. The males did not appreciate the effort made by the government to provide them with relief maize. The village headman even used some insulting language in his comments, stating that the donated maize was used to brew beer as they preferred to eat sorghum.

As it was getting late in the afternoon, we opted to use the shorter route between Siampondo and Kabanga on the plateau instead of going via Sinazongwe to Batoka. At the steep escarpment, the three of us sacrificed the driver and kapaso to drive up the mountain, while we walked for fear of the Landrover rolling backwards.

The governor and I were disappointed with the behaviour of the people. In reaction, the PS advised us that 'development' was a difficult matter and one should be patient when taking new ideas to local communities. He advised that we should first study the social setting and historical background of the people before introducing a new programme or project. This is what was later christened as 'environmental assessment'.

On Saturday 5 June 1971, I returned to the University of Zambia for the graduation ceremony. It was a pleasure to meet my former lecturers and fellow students. On graduation day, I was adorned in my newly-acquired green gown with a golden hood. I recall the pompous walk up the steps onto the rostrum where the chancellor of the university, His Excellency Dr Kenneth David Kaunda and Vice Chancellor Professor Lameck Kazembe Haza Goma were standing. Professor Goma, a renowned scientist was the first indigenous vice chancellor of the university.

It was with a sense of great pride and triumph to kneel and be capped by the chancellor of the university. I set an unbeatable record of being the first university graduate from Namaila. I wished Teacher Kazwida had been present to see the product of his works.

I went back to Livingstone and continued my assignment and everywhere I went, I was showered with messages of congratulations. There was jubilation amongst my relatives and friends when I went to Namaila to show off my new attire and the nicely crafted certificate. In those days, success was enthusiastically shared by even people one was not related to, as one was regarded as a child of the community.

By the end of my attachment to the Southern Province administration, I was fully knowledgeable of the administration systems and procedures of the Zambian Government. The pipe-smoking administrative officer, John C. Mandona and Lichaha took me through all that there was for me to learn. My work exposed me to the economic, social, and political status of the Southern Province.

While on tour of Lake Kariba at Sinazongwe in September 1971, in the company of Alfred Chiponda Assistant District Secretary, I was briefed by the fisheries officers that the waters of the lake were still too fresh to sustain some breeds of fish. Some of the soils, trees, and plants that submerged had not rotted and neutralized and could be poisonous to the fish. At that time, there was no commercial fishing of the famous kapenta (limnothrissa miodon) in the lake.

I became aware that Choma Town, in spite of being centrally located in the province, could not be the capital of Southern Province due to lack of a source of adequate water in the area. Livingstone had become the capital after Kalomo Town in 1907 because of the abundant water in the Zambezi River. I recalled my geography lessons when I learnt that most of the world's major towns were built on the banks of rivers as they provided water for drinking and as a means of cheap transport for local and external trade.

Towards the end of 1971, I was at NIPA, where I joined my colleagues for the final phase of our induction training. This consisted of an intense course in development administration, covering topics in law, economics, management, and administrative skills. We were informed that on satisfactory completion of the course, we would be assigned to various ministries according to our aptitudes, preferences, and the requirements of the civil service.

When asked to indicate my preference, I chose the Ministry of Foreign Affairs as there was a requirement for economists in the missions abroad and I had been interviewed for such a post. I then went to the Cabinet Office to confirm my choice. To my utter shock, the expatriate Deputy Secretary to the Cabinet (Economics) informed me that I could not be an economist because my economics courses at UNZA were shallow. He continued to state that in order to practice the discipline of economics I needed to have a Doctor of Philosophy degree in the subject.

When I got back to NIPA, I informed our lecturer Mrs Turnbull of the humiliation I'd encountered at the Cabinet Office. She advised me that in view of the favourable report from the Permanent Secretary for the Southern Province on my performance during my attachment, I should still consider joining the Zambian Civil Service.

I wrote my first protest letter in the Civil Service to the Secretary to the Cabinet stating that,

"If the Government's policy is to encourage those with little knowledge of a field to improve, then I ask that I be allocated to development planning. If the idea is to continue to import people with PhD in economics and frustrate the Zambian who is interested in this field even giving him no chance to get experience before attempting a PhD, I am at the service of my country'.

The deputy secretary to the cabinet summoned me to his office to discuss what he called my 'rude letter'. During our meeting, I informed him that I intended to stay in the civil service with the hope that I would one day take over his position when he decides to return to his country. I also told him that I will never study for a PhD in economics in my life, but that I will work hard towards becoming one of the reputable economists in the world. It was in fulfillment of my vow that I have not studied for a PhD in economics

When the induction course was over, I was assigned and reported to the Permanent Secretary for the Southern Province in January 1972 and was appointed as an administrative officer (cadet) in the civil service. The title did not bother me much, as I had already set a vision for my professional career to become an accomplished economist.

My first assignment was to supervise the registration of villages in the whole province by a group of UNZA students as per the requirements of the new Registration and Development of Villages Act No. 30 of 1971. This gave me another opportunity to tour the whole province as I delivered food, papers, and other materials to the registration teams. By the end of the registration exercise, I knew the geography of the province and the number and names of many villages in the province.

Many of my associates also joined the Zambian Public Service and provided valuable service in various institutions. While at UNZA, we had forged close relationships and became a united team. The UNZA class of '67, from different regions and tribes, with diverse qualifications were placed across the Zambian public service, where they contributed to the development of an efficient and non-discriminatory public service. I worked closely with a number of them during my public service and I benefitted greatly from their inputs in my work.

Patrick Chipungu went on to do his postgraduate studies overseas, specializing in fish biology and on returning home, he joined the Fisheries Department. He and I planned the translocation of kapenta fish from Lake Tanganyika into Lake Kariba. I recall sitting in my office and receiving telephone calls from Patrick Chipungu's convoy of refrigerated trucks with kapenta fingerlings as they passed through various towns along the route from Mbala to Sinazongwe. By this time, the department had certified the lake's water as safe for aquatic life. This was one of my most exciting moments early in my career.

Elizabeth Hakeeta was the only female economist in the planning division of the Ministry of Rural Development, which I rejoined after my post-graduate studies in 1974. Chintu was the first female officer to rise to the position of deputy director of Budget in the Ministry of Finance. Mabula, Mumbuna, and Nguvu all rose to the position of Permanent Secretary in various ministries. Hambote, Kamima, Kayumba, and Muntemba opted to join the security services, where they rose to the highest positions.

Wilson Mwandila became a familiar smiling face in the female wards of the University Teaching Hospital (UTH) in Lusaka as a caring and renowned gynaecologist. He was in the team of doctors that delivered our twins in 1978. Joseph Muyangana also joined the medical profession. I could not turn down his request to be the best man at his wedding ceremony when he married Margaret Msiska a nurse. The coincidence of both of us having met our partners in hospital wards, Muyangana as a humble doctor and me as a patient, cemented our family relationship.

Ephraim Kaunga joined the Minerals Development Corporation (MINDECO), a parastatal involved in the prospecting and mining of special minerals. I participated in organizing the wedding of Kaunga and escorted him as he led Agness Ndalameta to the altar. Kaunga rose to the position of Permanent Secretary in the Ministry of Finance and Development Planning. As a lecturer at various universities, he greatly contributed to the development of the professional careers of many young people.

Matongo also joined MINDECO and worked in the mining industry for a long time, rising to the position of managing director of the Metal Marketing Corporation (MEMACO). He became a reference on metal markets such as the London Metal Exchange (LME). In later years, Matongo was the managing director of the Reserved Minerals Corporation (RMC), the parastatal company responsible for the mining and marketing of the country's precious emeralds. Matongo carried the emeralds in his hand-luggage for security reasons to the Geneva sales floors in Switzerland without losing even a gram.

John Kaluzi, the physicist, was close to me as we attended mathematics lessons together. Once he tried to convert me to his church by inviting me to services at the Anglican Cathedral in town. While I attended and enjoyed the services, it was not easy for me to abandon my strong belief in the foundational principles of the Salvation Army, which had converted me from paganism to Christianity.

Kaluzi joined the Zambia Electricity Supplies Corporation (ZESCO) and rose to the position of managing director of the power company, where he displayed a rare brand of management and efficiency. The managing director would be at Kariba HydroPower Station in Siavonga by 07.00 hours for an on-the-spot inspection and be back in Lusaka by 10.00 hours for a presentation of his findings to a meeting. During Kaluzi's reign, the ZESCO achieved an unequalled level of efficiency with the capability for officers to arrive at a fault point anywhere in Lusaka within ten minutes.

In 1991, I pleaded with Andrew Kashita, Minister of Energy in the new MMD Government to spare Kaluzi from the random dismissals as he was one of the few, most efficient technicians in Zambia. In spite of my plea, Kaluzi was dismissed for having efficiently managed ZESCO under the Kaunda administration. Within days, Kaluzi was snatched by the power company of Botswana, which he assisted to develop as one of the most efficient power utilities in Africa.

Kalunga Lutato excelled in his studies of the French language and after a short stint at UNZA, as a lecturer he found a job with the United Nations High Commission for Refugees (UNHCR). He served in various countries and was the first Zambian to rise to a high position. In the elevated position, he finally came face-to-face with the armed rebels in the most dangerous conflict spots of Central Africa. Kalunga survived the land mine-infested responsibility and retired honourably in the 21st century.

Discovering the source of the Nile River

In June 1972, I was transferred to the head office of the Ministry of Rural Development (MRD) in Mulungushi House and I shifted to Lusaka, where I stayed at the Longacres Lodge. I was told to immediately prepare for departure to Uganda, to attend a course at Makerere University aka 'The Hill' for a Master of Science (MSc) degree in agricultural economics. A Ford Foundation Scholarship had been arranged for me by Peter Stutley, the planning coordinator.

Timothy Kasapu was the other ministry official nominated to attend the course at Makerere University. Kasapu was much older than me and had worked for the ministry for a long time and was already a Provincial Agricultural Officer based in Kabwe, Central Province.

When I went to Namaila to say my goodbyes, there was a big gathering under the Musikili tree at Headman Matongo's homestead. He proudly announced that I was to be the first member of the clan and family to fly in a plane to Uganda. By coincidence, while we were gathered, a Vickers Viscount plane flew over our village en route to Harare in Zimbabwe. Everyone was excited and wished me luck and that I should return to Namaila after my studies.

As I took my maiden flight on an East African Airways plane to Kampala via Nairobi on 3 July 1972, I recalled the wishes of all my village folk and reflected on my achievements so far. I was content that I was on a pioneering life path as no one of my relatives had ever been to East Africa.

I'd heard of Uganda in my school lessons as the home of the powerful Kabaka, king of the Baganda tribe and as the source of the Nile River, the longest river in the world. I learnt that the Nile River was much longer than our Zambezi River, which flows for 2,560 kilometres before pouring its waters into the Indian Ocean. I was excited and looked forward to visiting the source of the river that meanders through many countries for 6,690 kilometres and which housed the Aswan Dam, one of the largest man-made dams at the time.

I felt greatly honoured to attend one of the renowned universities in Africa, which had been attended by great African leaders including Harry Mwaanga Nkumbula. The two-year Master's programme in agricultural economics was being introduced for the first time at Makerere University for students from Central and Eastern Africa. The aim was to train a cadre of agricultural economists needed in Ethiopia, Kenya, Malawi, Tanzania, Uganda, and Zambia. The agricultural economists should 'be highly skilled in planning and preparation of agricultural development projects, project appraisal, financial assistance request preparation, and analysis of economic growth problems'.

At the Makerere University, Kasapu and I joined a group of eight other postgraduate students drawn from Ethiopia, Kenya, Tanzania, Sudan, and Uganda. All the postgraduate students were accommodated in the new Dag Hammaskjold Hostel. For purposes of sports, meals, and other extracurricular activities, we were allocated to various hostels occupied by undergraduates. I was assigned to Lumumba Hall, named after the revolutionary Congolese politician.

A group of Zambian students taking undergraduate courses in forestry and statistics warmly welcomed us. These included Fanwell Nduna and Jeremiah Banda. The hefty Fanwell Nduna was the chairman of the Zambian Students Association at the university. Nduna faithfully organized successful celebrations of Zambia's independence on The Hill, which brought together many students of other nationalities.

On completion of his studies, Nduna returned home and assisted in the establishment of the ZAFFICO and propelled it to its success. He became a public community leader in Ndola. Banda became the director of the Central Statistical Office and later rose to the position of chief of the demography and social statistics division of the United Nations.

Our coming together every October as a Zambian family and the vociferous singing of the Zambian National Anthem was the envy of many students from East Africa, who could not even exchange greetings across tribes. Zambia was way ahead of most independent African countries in nation-building and unity. Soon, Gatere Mike Gatere, a Kenyan in my class and I found common ground and became close friends.

My stay of eighteen months in Uganda was to be the most adventurous and nightmarish part of my life. The country went through its darkest history under the rule of the despotic General Idi Amin Dada, who staged a successful coup d'etat against President Milton Obote on 25 January 1971. In August 1972, in an act of Pan-Africanism, Amin expelled almost all of Uganda's 80,000 Asians and seized their property, a move which proved immensely popular in Uganda and in most of Africa. However, the euphoria was short-lived as the barbarism applied to the Asians by Idi Amin was internalized and applied to fellow Ugandans, who were savagely brutalized for eight years.

My curiosity on the source of the Nile River was soon satisfied as I and some friends went on a trip to Jinja in eastern Uganda. As we boarded a small boat on Lake Victoria, we were expecting to disembark at some shore. Suddenly, the boat stopped in the middle of the lake. The coxswain pointed at some distance in the lake and drew our attention to a spout of water.

After rising a few metres in the air, the swirling water subsides and starts a westward wave on the surface of the lake. "That is the beginning of the Nile River, the longest flow of water in the world," he explained. This is the only river I have seen, whose source is within a water mass.

The lessons in the agricultural economics programme were not difficult for me. These included economic theory, statistics, econometrics, agricultural production, and marketing, many of which I'd covered in my undergraduate studies at UNZA. My strong background in mathematics was used to explain some econometrics formulae to my classmates, many of whom had done pure agriculture science for their first degrees.

We had a good team of internal and visiting lecturers with considerable experience in the various subjects. Amongst our lecturers were Victor Amman, Hani Afifi, Ian Livingstone, and Matthew Okai, a seasoned civil servant holding the prestigious position of Director of Agriculture in the Ugandan government. The latter taught us that a civil servant must always carry a notebook whenever on tour to record observations, discussions, and events. This was a repetition of my NIPA lessons and I religiously followed the teachings during my working life and this has helped me in recollecting events during my journey of life.

Much of the concern during that era in agriculture in the region was how to improve the marketing of crops and how to remunerate farmers adequately using quasi-governmental institutions. My animal husbandry work in Macha in 1966 and the agricultural marketing research work in Luapula Province put me on top of the class in explaining situational challenges of agricultural development amongst small-scale farmers. We covered subjects on the process of rural change, adoption of new institutions and techniques and the role of farmer organizations, and the mass media.

The lessons in extension and rural sociology brought memories of the tour to Siampondo in 1971 and the advice of the PS on situational analysis and assessment. We learnt the theory of sociology applied to rural social structures, attitudes, community development and social psychology, and their effects on group dynamics and interactions.

In the background course of economic theory, we covered national income and its determinations, relationships between fiscal policy, monetary policy, savings, investment and economic growth, and welfare economics. In agricultural planning and policy formulation, we dealt with issues of project identification, evaluation, implementation, monitoring, and the application of social/benefit cost analysis

One of our assignments was to write comprehensive papers on agricultural marketing. I wrote what I considered to be a good paper highlighting real-life situations in Zambia and some of my personal thoughts. Unfortunately, this did not go down well with Lecturer Livingstone who was regarded as a guru on the subject and had even written a book, which was used as a textbook in the undergraduate courses.

From nowhere, I experienced humiliating episodes of abuse in class and was awarded failing grades in the subject that I knew so well. I reported the matter to Professor JJ Oloya, the head of the department, who summoned the two of us to a meeting. After a parental discussion and advice by the head, I requested that all my papers in the subject be marked by an additional lecturer.

Professor Oloya took on the additional responsibility of checking my agricultural marketing papers. At the end of the course, I scored a decent grade of four out of five points. Professor Oloya reminded me of the incident when he relocated to Zambia due to the deteriorating political situation in Uganda later in the eighties.

One day, Gatere and I decided to witness a session where some seized property in the Wandegeya area near the Makerere University was being distributed by President Amin. As the general entered a butchery, he looked excited to see large chunks of fresh carcasses of beef. He took a big knife and sliced off a piece of meat from a carcass hanging on a hook. Holding high the piece of steak, he turned around and instead of offering the meat, he asked as to who wanted to take over the butchery.

When no one in the frenzied crowd volunteered to take over the butchery, the president pointed at my Kikuyu friend, who was much taller than most of those present and ordered him to the front. The general then shouted, "This is your butchery". Gatere fearfully declined the generous offer, explaining that he was a foreign student at the Makerere University. The second person called out by the president was a man in military uniform, who could not disobey his commander's orders. He meekly moved to the front and received the butcher knife from the general. The butchery closed within three months as the new owner did not even know where to get his fresh supplies of meat.

With the economy run by Ugandan army officers and the president's cronies, local businesses suffered from mismanagement and abuse of power. Production in many factories ground to a halt as unmaintained machinery jammed permanently. By October 1972, commodities such as soap, salt, and sugar were in short supply. Our meals at the Hill constituted of only matooke (plantain porridge).

Some of the students turned into Government agents in exchange for favours such as free houses. Local student leaders disappeared in the night, never to be seen again. Many fled to neighbouring countries, but a good number were eliminated by the regime and their bodies thrown into the rivers and lakes. This barbarism continued for some time with the slaughter of thousands of innocent Ugandans. The pollution of the Ugandan water bodies including lakes with decomposing human bodies led to the suspension of exports of fish from Uganda to the European Union.

Zambians and Tanzanians were suspected of being conspirators against the Amin Government, due to the open and strong opposition of Presidents Kaunda and Nyerere to President Amin. At the height of the insecurity in 1973, when some of us were contemplating abandoning our studies, a meeting was called for all students from Tanzania and Zambia to be addressed by the president at a hotel. We were very scared in view of stories that, sometimes, targeted people were lured to a meeting only to be mowed down by machine guns. The arrival in the hall of the huge two-metre man, with pistols on both hips, accompanied by a platoon of heavily armed and angry-looking soldiers, sent shivers into the audience.

In his address, President Amin castigated our two presidents calling President Julius Nyerere, a coward, old woman and a prostitute, who he loved so much that, "I would have married him if he had been a woman." He called KK, an "imperialist puppet and bootlicker." He encouraged us to work hard at our studies so that on returning to our countries we would topple our presidents as they were pro-European.

After a three-hour rambling speech, President Amin and his heavily armed escorts left. Wondering what was to follow, suddenly the hotel manager announced that we were all to stay on for a party at the invitation of the president. We were happy because we were afraid of venturing into the dark to our residences. We stayed on and spent the night in the hotel, where all kinds of food and drinks were served. Those who could manage continued to drink throughout the night. The meeting made us feel a little secure and we suppressed some of our anxieties, although we had to carry our air tickets and passports all the time.

As a postgraduate student and Zambian civil servant on paid leave under a Ford Foundation scholarship, I had a handsome subsistence allowance, which provided for a comfortable student lifestyle. In 1972, the Zambian Kwacha was very strong at an exchange rate of two US dollars to one Kwacha. Zambian students, found in many African countries, were respected as a wealthy group and often we proudly displayed this affluence.

One evening, two friends and I went for an outing to a posh nightclub in the Bwayise area west of Kampala Town. Gatere, the Kenyan 'butchery owner' was on the floor dancing to some funky rhumba tune, when two well-dressed men sauntered into the dimly lit nightclub.

After surveying the place for a while, one of them shouted, "That's the one," while pointing at my Kenyan friend. Suddenly, four hefty men burst into the club and seized Gatere, dragging him towards the exit. I looked around for our Ugandan colleague, but he was nowhere to be seen. Luckily, the commotion in the nightclub drew him out of the bathroom area, where he had gone. By this time, Gatare had been dragged out of the nightclub.

After informing the Ugandan of what happened, we rushed outside where we found Gatere being bundled into the boot of a Peugeot 504 car. This make of car was associated with the infamous Amin's killer agents. As I tried to pull my friend away, one of the guys shouted, "Just take him also!" After some unsuccessful discussion in English, our Ugandan friend shouted in some strange local language. Suddenly, the four men let go of Gatere and vanished in the dark, while the two men drove off in the Peugeot car, leaving us thoroughly shaken and ruffled. We were so close to being a meal for the man-eating Nile crocodiles.

Our Ugandan friend explained that one of the men might have fancied the beautiful girl who was dancing with Gatere. He stated that these men would have killed our friend and come back to forcibly get the girl. I realized that in a situation of confused state management, many innocent citizens lose their lives at the hands of those who usurp power for personal use. This close shave with death curtailed our ostentatious lifestyle, which had seen us in most leisure places including the legendary and famous Susanna Night Club.

Our change of lifestyle left enough room for studies, which was the core business of our being in Uganda. We also had time to play a lot of games of chess, draughts, Monopoly, Scrabble and lawn tennis, while sipping some Waragi, the famous Ugandan drink. The potent product of banana fermentation and distillation can be designated as a close cousin of Zambia's banned and illicit kacasu.

In Uganda, they did not ban the brewing of the highly intoxicating drink by women in the unplanned shanty compounds. Instead, the innovative Ugandan food scientists found a modern method of purifying the potent concoction into a healthy drink acceptable to the taste buds of Baganda princes. The township women were brought into the lucrative food chain using indigenous knowledge and the local farm produce.

Towards the end of 1972, we were assigned to tour some agricultural areas of Uganda and write detailed papers on the agricultural development situations. To satisfy my insatiable appetite for adventure, I chose to tour the Gulu District in the far north of the country on the border with the Sudan. I chose to tour Gulu because it was the birthplace of Okot p'Bitek, the author of the epic poem 'Song of Lawino', which was one of my favourite poems. The poet advocated for the preservation of the African culture that was being eroded by the adopted mannerisms of the newly educated African elite.

I was paired with Wilson Bagandira, a Ugandan student who also had never been to that part of the country. We arrived in Gulu Town by bus from

Kampala late in the night and spent the night at the bus stop.

We were assisted by the Department of Agriculture to visit most parts of the district. There were similarities between Namaila and Gulu in that sorghum, millet, and legumes were the dominant food crops in both places. My interest was to study the adaptation of the hybrid crop varieties that had been produced by the Makerere University researchers.

Although called 'famine crops', sorghum and millet had been commercialised in low rainfall areas and good yields had been achieved in the Gulu District of Uganda. In Zambia, these local crops had been replaced by maize, a wild plant grown in the Guila Naquitz Cave at Oaxaca in Mexico and domesticated by the native Mayans. The Zambian elites had succumbed to the canning colonialists, who used even taste buds to change our attitudes to our inheritance.

We were at the bus stop getting ready to depart for Kampala after our tour, when word went round that some rebels had entered Uganda at Masaka from Tanzania and were advancing towards Kampala. As Obote's supporters were mostly from the Northern Region of Uganda, the region was immediately put under a government curfew and travel between Gulu and Kampala was banned.

Since we were stranded, my Ugandan colleague approached the District Commissioner (DC) seeking a solution to our predicament. The DC promised to keep us informed of any developments.

After a week of anxiety, we got information that arrangements had been made for 'special strandees' to be escorted by security forces in a convoy of buses to Kampala. When my colleague went to see the DC, he was informed that we were included on the list of the special travellers. Apparently, the Makerere University authorities had contacted the DC to make enquiries as to our safety.

On a designated day, a convoy of buses departed from Gulu Town at sunset with two army vehicles in front as sweepers and another two at the rear. There were so many security roadblocks on the way that this became the most fearful and longest road journey of my life. By God's grace, we arrived safely in Kampala and found the city at peace as the story of the invasion was not true.

Apart from visiting many parts of Uganda, I also had the opportunity to visit many agricultural areas of Kenya in the company of my Kenyan friend during my stay at Makerere University. In Kenya, the independence struggle was focused on land ownership by the indigenous people. The land consolidation law of 1963 spelt out a clear system of land acquisition and management. Private land ownership and cash crop farming were encouraged, accepted and adopted by the people.

The Kenyan Government gradually transferred large tracts of land to Kenyan citizens as part of a land consolidation and resettlement policy. The new, proud landowners applied modern farming methods on their small plots of land and made Kenya a success story in small-scale commercial farming.

We visited Gatere's village in Nyeri in the former White Highlands, which were the backbone of Kenya's agricultural industry. I was amazed at the high productivity of the small-scale farmers, who produced most of the coffee, milk, tea, and the pyrethrum used to manufacture insecticides. Kenya, a country devoid of any minerals was the largest exporter of coffee, tea, and flowers in Africa and became a model of development without minerals.

The realignment of land ownership facilitated the success of intensive nationwide efforts to expand and modernize the farming methods of African smallholders. The tours in both Kenya and Uganda consolidated my personal view that small-scale farming can be commercialised and productive.

CHAPTER 4

Losing My Ancestral Home

While I was away in Uganda for studies at the Makerere University, there was no contact with my family since there were no telephones. I returned to Zambia on 2 June 1973 to conduct research for a dissertation for my course.

As I was settling down at the Longacres Lodge, after my arrival, Ernest Chimuka, an officer at the Ministry of Rural Development came over to inform me that my mother was ill and had been admitted to the Chikankata Hospital. He went on to say that although her condition was serious, they had decided not to inform me earlier while I was in Uganda, as the news would have disturbed me during my crucial final examinations. How more considerate can a human being be!

The following day, I was taken to the Magoye Research Station in Mazabuka, where I was stationed during my research work. I then went to Chikankata Hospital to visit my mother, whom I found in a very serious condition with swollen legs and difficulties in breathing and talking.

With some renewed energy at seeing me, she gripped my hand and welcomed me, saying that she was happy to see me as she had been waiting for me. She continued to say that she did not think that she would live long. She advised that I should take care of my siblings and try to get them educated. I encouraged her by saying that she would not die soon, as we would work hard so that she recovered from her illness.

I was then introduced to the matron who invited me into her side office. She briefed me that my mother's illness was hard to cure as it affected her heart, which had become very weak. She mentioned that they were giving her medicine just to ease the pain and not to cure her. With very little conversation after hearing the devastating news, I thanked her for their efforts and went back to my mother's bedside to bid her farewell.

I then informed my mother of the nurse who wanted to come along with me to see her. After a little description of my long relationship with Joyce Mudenda, my mother wished me luck in my partnership. "Ukamulange kabotu mwana wa bantu," she said in a faint voice. As I was leaving, I surmised that if only Joyce had been the one nursing her, perhaps my mother would have done better with her recovery. This was all wishful thinking.

From Chikankata, I went straight to Livingstone to collect some money from the bank, as I maintained an account there during my absence. I then travelled to Lusaka where a friend organized a second-hand car for me to buy. While in Lusaka, I consulted some medical friends who suggested that I should take my mother to the big hospital in Lusaka. After concluding the car purchase deal, a friend escorted me to Magoye, while I drove the car with "L" number plates.

After a few minutes of our arrival at my house, Mr Siachibizya, the Chief Research Officer (CRO) came over to my house. He asked in a stern tone where I had been. He did not believe my explanation that I had been to Chikankata, Livingstone, and Lusaka in that short period. He stated that they had been frantically looking for me to inform me of my mother's death.

My mother had passed on later that same day I visited her in the hospital. My arrival from Uganda fulfilled her word that she had been waiting for me. The burial took place at Namaila in my absence. My request to the CRO to give Richard Liteta, one of his officers leave to drive me to Namaila in my recently-acquired second-hand car, as I had no license, was granted.

The joy of coming back to Zambia, occupying a big government house and buying a car was dampened by the demise of my dear mother. I was arriving in Namaila in tears of sorrow and not of joy. Even my village folks were thanking Liteta for sacrificing his car and time to take me through the hazardous rocky road to Namaila. They did not know that I had returned from Uganda and that I had become the first person from Namaila to own a motor car.

By the end of the mourning period of seven days, I even had no place to call home as my father decided to relocate to Nkonkola, some twenty kilometres away, to live with his matrilineal aunts. He took with him my two sisters and one brother, while the youngest brother, was taken by aunt bina-Ciingana who lived way out in the Muchila Settlement in the Namwala District. I was not mentioned during the discussions, as it was assumed that I would look after myself with the support of the numerous 'relatives' I had discovered during my travels away from Namaila.

My mother had been a vital branch of the family tree, always available to introduce me to those that came into my life. Her departure left a big gap. On the trip back to Magoye, I fully occupied myself with recollections of the advice that she had given me and convinced myself that I will survive if I faithfully abided by her teachings.

In remembrance of my departed mother, I composed the following poem titled, "The Voice from Below", a week after my mother's burial:

Down, the cold earth do I lie
Humble, like a sheep did I die
Vivid in my memory, are the tears you shed
As I lay for my last moments, under the shade

Lamentably, do I recall, my lavish life on earth
When I gave no thought to the coming of death
Day and night did I live and enjoy, like a prodigal
Giving no consideration, for any earthly goal

Dear son, give thought to everything you do
For life on earth is very short, though good
Though you are like a needle in a heap of hay
There is time while the sun shines to tend the hay

I hear you grumbling about the bad past
But even your generation, will not last
If you continue with your egoistic lust
For things that will one day, turn into dust

Then, as they feign sorrow and dig deep
The grave, in which you finally will sleep
They will wittingly discuss your wealth
That you will leave behind on earth

For down here, there is not enough space
Then you will be as poor as everyone else
And will have left the good earth, as I did
Without a single memorable worthy deed

Let your personal contribution remain behind
As a symbol of your presence, unto mankind
Let their memory of you, be an inspiration
That will encourage them to defeat destitution

My father had no clan land at Namaila and was farming on land belonging to my mother's clan. At the age of twenty-six years, I did not own any property in Namaila or elsewhere in the world. Even the small hut I had constructed earlier in the village had aged and collapsed during my absence. I took nothing from Namaila except the education I had acquired during the previous nineteen years. My umbilical connection with my ancestral home of Namaila was severed by the death of my dear mother in June 1973.

CHAPTER 5

Nurturing My Own Branch Of The Family Tree

At the end of 1968, while I was at the University of Zambia, I was once more employed by Barclays Bank during the holidays and this time, I chose to work in Livingstone. During the Christmas and the 1969 New Year's period, Solomon and I spent time touring the town and having a nice time at various joints. The following day, I had continuous stomach pains, which compelled me to visit the Batoka General Hospital, where I was detained for observations. An enema was done, but there was no sign of anything serious in the stomach and I got discharged after two days.

Among the staff who attended to me at the hospital was a young shy trainee nurse from Choma by the name of Joyce Mudenda (bina-Siila), who fascinated me. As I was discharged early, I lost track of her as the disciplinary code in those days prohibited visits to the nurses' hostels by strangers. After narrating my discovery to Solomon, who had lived longer in Livingstone, he promised to trace her as I had taken note of her name from her name tag.

Solomon's relative, Hezekiah Chibbonta Chilala lived near the hospital with his family of two wives and a number of children. The elder wife was Samaliya Monalisa Choonga, who was a full-time housewife. Chilala, an illustrious accountant in the government, liked cooling from the heat of his work and office by watching films at the local cinema. He converted Solomon and I to this hobby and we often visited his home before or after the film shows.

A few weeks after my hospitalisation, Solomon and I went to pick up Chilala for our usual outing. My eyes seemed to deceive me as I thought that I recognized one of the girls we found at the residence. I was introduced to the two girls by ba-Samaliya. One of the girls was Joyce (bina-Siila) Mudenda, the nurse, who attended to me when I was admitted in the hospital. Ba-Samaliya was a daughter of Mulalu, a brother to Mutoloki, who was Joyce's grandfather. Joyce was a niece of ba-Samaliya, as Anna, Joyce's mother was a daughter of Mutoloki. Joyce's friend was Eileen Masempela, who was in a relationship with Solomon, which culminated in their marrying in 1972.

It seemed that Joyce's aunt found what she was looking for in me, as she gave an elaborate introduction of her tall, but shy niece to me. I suspected that ba-Samaliya later communicated with Joyce's father about me, as my relationship with Joyce blossomed under the guidance of the aunt. However, the formalities for our union were delayed as Joyce had to complete her course and I left for Makerere University in Uganda for further studies.

Auntie Samaliya became our favourite and most dependable member of the family tree. From a mere housewife, she used her limited means to improve her status and the education of her children. She became a reliable officer in the prisons department, where she served for a long time as a correctional officer. Her children were very close to my family and they involved us even in their personal matters such as employment and marriage plans.

One of Auntie Samaliya's children, Chibbonta Chilala decided to migrate to the USA during the nineties. When he came home to bid us farewell, we advised him to look out for opportunities within Zambia before abandoning his country. When Chibbonta Chilala visited his elder sister based in Zambezi town in the North-Western Province, he was lured by the abundant natural resources and opportunities of the area.

Enjoying the warm welcome of the Luvales and Lundas, his tribal cousins, Chibbonta settled down and grew into a pioneering entrepreneur in the province. He established a successful business dealing in honey and rice under the YamBEEji trademark, whose products occupied prominent space on the shelves of the largest supermarkets in Zambia. His missionary role in training small-scale rice farmers exposed his leadership talents that led him to be a founding member and later elected as president of the Zambia Rice Federation.

My mother had given her blessings to my marriage to Joyce, when I visited her in Chikankata Hospital in early June after I arrived from Uganda. During my mother's funeral, I put the matter at the top of my priorities in my discussions with my father, uncles and maternal grandmother, who gave their approval to formalizing my relationship with Joyce. They advised that I should contact Uncle Amon Mazuba, a relative who lived in Mazabuka to follow up the matter with Joyce's relatives.

When Solomon Siamasuku Mudenda, Joyce's father was contacted, he referred the matter to his younger brother, Jacob Mudenda, who lived in Mazabuka Town. By divine coincidence, Amon and Jacob knew each other well as they were both civil servants and they easily concluded the negotiations.

On Friday 15 June 1973, Joyce and I signed our marriage certificate at the Mazabuka Boma in the presence of the Marriage Commissioner, Uncles Jacob Mudenda and Amon Mazuba. The elaborate traditional marriage ceremony was held later at Uncle Jacob's home.

Joyce is the first daughter of Solomon Mudenda of Muchindu Village and Anna Mutoloki of Mutandalike Village, both of Chief Singani in the Choma District. Anna Mutoloki's siblings, born of Mutoloki (Syakanzaba) and Mweembe, were Mukanjezya (bina-Dorika), Johanne Gidwell (Simwaale), and Rhoda. Joyce's maternal grandfather Mutoloki had a second wife and one well-known son was Uncle Bernard, who provided sterling service at the Road

Safety Department of the Zambian government.

Joyce had four young sisters: Pauline, Malita, Emily, and Evelyne. After the demise of Anna Mutoloki at an early age, young Joyce and the siblings were looked after by bina-Stackson, a stepmother, who had six of her own children. In addition, my father-in-law married another three wives who had a large number of children.

I always enjoyed my visits to my in-laws near the Siachitema Mission, as the many children teased me if I could recall their individual names. In the early eighties, I did a good job. But as the number increased, I could only manage to assign them to the four mothers, which in itself was not an easy task. With over thirty brothers and sisters in-law, the family tree grew big with so many branches.

Solomon Mudenda had three siblings: bina-Greener, Jacob and Simakutu, whose name has been inherited by a Health Centre on the Choma-Masuku Road. While I was away in East Africa, Joyce who already had a nursing qualification went back to the Livingstone nurses' training school and completed a course in midwifery. She had to find her own way to Solwezi General Hospital in the North-Western Province, where she was posted. She worked for a short period at Solwezi before resigning from government service to join the mines at Kabwe. After our marriage in 1973, Joyce resigned from her employment with the mines and came to join me in Magoye. She was re-engaged by the Zambian Government and was assigned to work at the Magoye Health Centre.

The pain and loneliness of losing my dear mother in her forties were reduced by the arrival of Joyce in my life. We discussed our family plan and agreed that we would have only four children early and adequately spaced. This was to allow our children to complete schooling before both of us retired from formal employment, which will facilitate proper financial and investment planning in our retirement.

With a wife who, as a nurse and midwife, dealt with family planning, I was confident that the family plan would be implemented without difficulties. However, God's plans are stronger as they are laid out even before one is born as per the book of Jeremiah in the bible. Our elaborate family plan could only partly succeed.

When we relocated to Lusaka in 1974, we stayed in Yarrow Court on Broads Road in Rhodes Park for a few months before moving to Chelstone Township. The semi-detached house at No. 19 Acacia Avenue was much bigger than the flat at Broads Road. Although the yard was small, there were many fruit trees including mango, banana, and mulberry in the yard.

To my surprise, one of our neighbours was Fidelis Kafwimbi, my mocker in Aggrey House at Munali Secondary School in 1964. My mocker was now a workmate as a cooperative officer in the Ministry of Rural Development. We shared a lot in common as we strategized the development of the cooperative movement in Zambia. He now trusted and felt safe with me and often jumped over the short hedge to consult me on various issues, which included his political plans for the 1978 general elections, in which he stood and won.

In the close neighbourhood lived the families of Rodney Mumbi, Rueben Nketani, and Villie Lombanya, all with young children, who played together with our children. Mukutu and his spouse Nxaba (Jane) had also relocated to their plot near the Barn Motel, close enough for frequent exchanges. These neighbours became my functional relatives and we shared a lot together in our lives.

At times, my family was joined at Chelston by Uncle Joseph Kaputa Sikalumba, who was a student of linguistics in France. Joseph's father Sikalumba and Cibiya, my maternal grandfather were brothers. Although Joseph was also 'kana kakumalundu', coming from Meezi, he excelled in his studies. After completing his doctorate studies of the French language, Sikalumba joined the UNZA, where he helped in establishing and developing the Department of Linguistics. He devoted his life in offering specialist and dedicated services to the university community.

As the family visitors were increasing, we devised a workable and reliable system of dealing with them. We agreed that visitors be divided and dealt with according to their gender. I dealt with the males, while Joyce handled all the female visitors.

This arrangement solved the problem of introducing our visitors to the modern bathroom and lavatory facilities within the house. Since both of us had lost our mothers, the burden of hosting relatives was less onerous as the closest relatives were our two elderly teetotallers and highly disciplined fathers, who rarely visited us. Young relatives were allowed to visit us only if their visit was in connection with school matters.

The usual sociological resentment of visitors by urban children due to being shifted from their bedrooms was also resolved by a clear understanding that our children were not to be moved out of their bedrooms to give room to visitors. When necessary, we sacrificed the carpet in the lounge as a visitors' bed when the spare bedroom was occupied. As a result, our children always welcomed any visitor to our home.

As part of our household plan and having settled in our jobs, Joyce and I agreed that we maintain one joint account at a bank, where our two salaries were to be deposited. Later, we opened other accounts for various operations, such as the farm, to which we have been joint signatories. Each one of us has debit cards to the various accounts and is always fully aware of the status of any of the accounts.

Decisions on expenditures are discussed and once agreed upon, either of us signs a cheque to withdraw cash or uses a card to pay a supplier of goods or services. All goods in the house are jointly-owned by the two of us. Whenever we gave away some cattle for gifts, meetings were held on the farm and attended by my father, father-in-law, and Uncle Aaron. This arrangement has been instrumental in creating a harmonious relationship not only between me and my spouse but between our two families.

Our first daughter Choobe, named after my great-grandmother, was born on 21 May 1970 at Choma Hospital. While our second daughter Nakanjoli, named after my mother, was born at the Mazabuka Hospital on 11 June 1974. As per our family plan, Joyce became pregnant in September 1977. In March 1978, we were informed by the medical experts that my spouse was carrying twin embryos and we should expect a breech birth as the embryos were in a sitting position. I had met only one set of twins in my life at Chikankata Mission in the sixties and I looked forward to being a father of twins. In those days, there was no technology to determine the sex of a baby in the womb.

In early June 1978, our anxiety was growing, as to when the twins would be born. I started getting scared of the event, in case there was a need for additional blood after a caesarean operation. I even reduced my outings as Joyce kept on saying, "What if…while you are away?"

Saturday 24 June 1978, started as an ordinary day for the family, except that I had to make breakfast as Joyce's pregnancy was very advanced. At about 0930 hours, I decided to dash into town with a promise to be back soon. At 11.00 hours, when I arrived back home, I was informed that our neighbour, the Mumbis, had rushed Joyce to the UTH as she'd felt some labour pains. I suddenly felt butterflies in my stomach.

I immediately left for the UTH but stopped on the way and took some beer to calm my nerves. On arrival, a nurse met me and led me to the Matron's office. The Matron asked me if I was ready to give some blood. I was about to drop as my knees were very weak when she burst out laughing and I realized that she was a Lozi cousin and was joking. She escorted me to the nursery, where I found the bouncy twins in their cribs while Joyce was resting on a nearby bed. I was relieved that my wife had a normal and smooth delivery as both babies had reversed themselves just before birth. The Matron narrated the fear that grips many men when told to donate blood. I realized then that I was not the only coward.

We named the twins Nchimunya, Namboozi (daughter) and Mutinta, Ciyaama (son). They were born some four years and thirteen days after Nakanjoli. As the mother and babies were in good health, they were discharged within two days. We agreed to share the responsibilities of night care for the babies by each one of us looking after a cot. I had to remind myself of the lessons I had learnt earlier on changing and folding of a diaper and how to prepare and feel the temperature of the milk for the baby bottle. Our family plan, made at Magoye, so far had gone according to schedule with the Creator's support and since we had the four kids, we agreed not to have anymore.

In 1981, Joyce was transferred from Chelstone Clinic to Kanyama Clinic after we had relocated to Northmead. The office driver who lived in Chilenje could not manage to arrive in time to drop her before taking me to the office. I took my spouse to Kanyama Clinic before going to the office on Cairo Road. One morning, while returning from the clinic, I was involved in a road accident near Chibolya Township. After the incident, Joyce was transferred to the Railway Clinic, which was nearer to our home and my office.

Joyce got the children interested in going to church. In 1982, Mother and children started going to the nearby Northmead Assemblies of God Church, where Joyce continued to go for Sunday services even in the twenty-first century.

In August 1983, I was transferred to Kabwe, Central Province as PS where I stayed until 1985. As the third-ranking public officer, it was easy for our children to find school places. Choobe who had attended Chelstone, Silver Rest and Kabulonga Schools in Lusaka was enrolled at Caritas Convent School. Nakanjoli was placed at Neem Tree Primary School, while the twins Nchimunya and Mutinta were at a nursery school.

Mutinta often came home from school and complained of being bored because the teacher was "repeating the same lessons". In spite of our assurances on the wisdom of the teachers, Mutinta's complaints continued. I, therefore, decided to visit the nursery school to discuss the matter with the teachers.

The teachers confided in me that Mutinta was extra intelligent and assimilated information very fast. The nursery supervisor educated me on the term 'gifted child'. She suggested that we should approach the Ministry of Education to find out if there are facilities in the country for a special test for such children. The assessment determines the intelligence quotient (IQ) of an individual, which information is used to focus the child's attention for adult life.

Unfortunately, there were no facilities for such talent identification locally, but arrangements could be made with institutions overseas at our cost. Since we could not afford such an exercise, Mutinta was left to continue learning at the pace of other pupils. At home, he vented his frustrations by dismantling any new toys and preoccupying himself with reassembling them.

In July 1985, I was transferred back to Lusaka to head the Ministry of Agriculture and Water Development. Although I moved to Lusaka immediately after the presidential announcement, it took me time to settle down as the issues of housing and school places for the children could not be sorted out.

Most of the head teachers I approached informed me that there were no vacancies to place our two school-age children. A few of them asked me to check in the new term, some six months away. This meant that both Choobe and Nakanjoli would have to wait to continue their schooling the following year.

One weekend, I travelled to Kabwe, but I was expected to attend a special cabinet meeting on some agricultural matters on the following Monday. I rushed to Lusaka on Monday morning to check on some head teachers before going to the meeting at State House. Unfortunately, I arrived late at the cabinet meeting.

I recall the fear that gripped me as I stood at the back door trying to sneak into the cabinet room. The president noticed me and asked why I was late. I explained that on my return from Kabwe, I had passed through some schools to check on vacancies for one of our children, but was not successful. In reply to a follow-up question on why I went to Kabwe, I explained that I had not been given a house in Lusaka since my transfer and that my family was still living in Kabwe.

The president tried to restrain his emotions but it was evident from his voice that he was very upset. He directed the officers from the Cabinet Office to immediately find a house for us and school places for our children. He wondered as to the kind of treatment the ordinary people were subjected to if children of a permanent secretary, a senior public officer, could not get places in government schools.

Within a few days, we were allocated House No. 393 on Independence Avenue, opposite Maina Soko Military Hospital, a few plots on the eastern side of State House. Choobe got a place at Kamwala Secondary School, where she found a dedicated deputy headteacher, Mrs Majele, who pushed her pupils to their maximum limits. On completion of Form V, Choobe made an unbreakable record by being the first female pupil from Kamwala Secondary School to qualify for admission to the University of Zambia. She pursued studies in economics and graduated with a Bachelor of Arts (BA) degree in 1990.

Choobe, with her spouse Joseph Kisoro of Ugandan ancestry, migrated to South Africa and blessed us with two granddaughters, Amanda (Munkombwe, Komukyeya) and Annabelle (Kabatasingwa, Joyce). Amanda our first granddaughter heeded the calling of her great-great-grandmother and joined the medical field. She attended the prestigious medical school at the reputable Pretoria University in South Africa and graduated in 2014 with exceptionally high grades. Annabelle pursued a degree course in commerce with a major in marketing and graduated in 2017. In addition to having a birth attendant, a midwife, and a medical assistant, the family tree now added a medical doctor.

Nakanjoli was enrolled at Woodlands 'A' Primary School and later qualified to attend Saint Mary's Secondary School within the Woodlands area. After Form V, she attended the Zambia Institute of Management (ZAMIM). Nakanjoli and Adol Mataa her spouse blessed us with three grandsons Mundia, Humphrey, and Adol

Nchimunya and Mutinta, the twins, also enrolled at Woodlands A Primary School, where we had to provide chairs for them to use due to over-crowded classes. Fanwell Mwando, the chauffer surprised us one day when he informed us that Mutinta told him that he wanted to be a spy after completing school. At the time, there were many James Bond films and Hardly Chase novels. But we did not realize that our son had been converted to spying by the messages in these films and books at such a tender age of seven years.

Mutinta moved onto Kabulonga Boys Secondary School, where he served as a vice head-boy (disciplinary). With a flair for mathematics, which was encouraged by teacher Eustakio Kazonga, a genius in mathematics, Mutinta completed his schooling with good grades. He was sponsored by the family and attended Bradley University in Illinois State in the USA, where he studied engineering with a bias for agricultural mechanization. He was a member of a team that designed the first optimizer, a combined tiller for Tillage International, which won the first prize for a new entry at the World Agricultural Expo in Tulare, California, USA.

In addition to his academics, Mutinta assisted in the administration of the university as a student senator and president of both the International Student Organization and the African Student Alliance. He was awarded a Bachelor of Science degree in Mechanical Engineering in 2002. On his return to Zambia, he joined Konkola Copper Mines (KCM) on the Copperbelt. Mutinta's childhood craving for spy work became handy in 2011 as he unraveled the malicious story of a Tanzanian rice trader, who had been sponsored by my political enemies.

Nchimunya left Zambia for the USA in 1995 for further studies at Foxcroft School in Virginia under family sponsorship. She later attended Syracuse University in New York majoring in International Relations. On her return to Zambia, she joined the civil service and was appointed as Second Secretary in the Ministry of Foreign Affairs in June 2003.

However, she did not stay long in Zambia as she left to join her spouse she met at university in the USA. Nchimunya and spouse Hugh Allen-Magande of Jamaican ancestry have blessed us with Zuria (Maleele), a granddaughter and Arieh (Lweendo), a grandson.

Zuria displayed affective and creative traits at the age of six years like her uncle Mutinta had shown at the same age. For example, she emotionally lamented the inadequate attention being given to the vulnerable children in the world! Due to the availability of facilities in the USA, where Zuria is a citizen, she was identified and selected by her teachers to sit for the Gifted Education Student test funded by the State of Georgia under the Georgia Department of Education. She passed and qualified as a Gifted and Talented student (TAG). The IQ level being hereditary, I take pride that I have contributed to Zuria's intelligence streak.

While Mizinga, my grandmother, was happy with our twins born in 1978, she kept protesting and pestering us that it was taboo under Tonga customs to stop one's reproductive life with twins. After some resistance, Joyce and I finally succumbed to custom pressure and grandma's wisdom and did the needful thing. A son was born nine years later, after midnight on 25 June 1987, having missed the birthday of his twin siblings by a few minutes. We named him Simwaale after my father.

As per custom, we decided to take the baby boy to Choma for Aunt Rhoda to give him a maternal clan name. Aunt Rhoda arrived early in the morning at our farm some eleven kilometres from Choma town, as the naming is done at daybreak. On arrival, she asked Joyce to hand over the baby to her. In the process, she mentioned the name Simwaale, which I had given him.

After some words of blessings, Joyce asked the aunt what name she was going to give to the baby. The aunt informed us that she had just given him the name of Simwaale after her elder brother, who lived with her. I told her that I had named the boy Simwaale after my father. We were all very surprised that the name Simwaale, which was not even common, was in both my family in Mazabuka and Joyce's family in Choma. Grandmother Mizinga had at some point speculated that I married a relative from the explanation I gave of Joyce's clan. However, we felt that it was the responsibility of Simwaale, our son to resolve the family connectivity mystery.

Our plan to have children early was partly disrupted by Tonga beliefs. As a consequence, we struggled to raise money as retirees to pay for Simwaale's fees at Saint Andrews School in Eastbourne in the United Kingdom, Lake Road School in Zambia, and later at the Beijing University of Technology in China in the twenty-first century. Simwaale with his partner Hope Mfula have added another branch by the name of Theodore Mutoloki, a grandson born in June 2018.

From the Magoye Health Centre in 1973, Joyce worked as a midwife helping hundreds of mothers at the Chelstone Health Centre, University Teaching Hospital, Kanyama Clinic, Kabwe General Hospital, Lusaka Railway Clinic, Kamwala Clinic, and the Lusaka Civic Centre Clinic from where she retired in 1994.

During this long period of public service, Joyce spread the Magande name amongst many mothers and grandmothers who she joined and assisted in welcoming their offspring into the world as my grandmother Mizinga had done.

On retirement in 1994, Joyce attended a reorientation course organized by the Future Search organization on project evaluation. In March 1994, she attended a workshop in Siavonga on business planning and basic finance for women entrepreneurs. The contents of the course taught by Max Sichula and Dennis Wood gave her a good grounding for her future projects.

As part of the course, she wrote a transport project proposal, which required her to make a number of trips on minibuses between Chelston and the Town Centre as part of market research. I felt an obligation to assist her with the project's cash-flow analysis as this was alien to someone who specialized in dealing with illnesses and dosages of medicines.

Using her retirement benefits and her newly acquired project management skills, Joyce started a small-scale tailoring business with five employees. In 1996, she was among a group of small-scale entrepreneurs who participated at the Berlin Trade Fair in Germany. The Small Industries Development Organization (SIDO) recognized the important role of these entrepreneurs and assisted many with tailoring equipment on hire purchase.

Joyce was among a group of young industrious women, who flew overnight by Zambia Airways to Mauritius to buy clothing material, which they sold to many private shops, especially in the Kamwala shopping area. Her group produced various clothing goods on contract for the Zambia National Wholesale Corporation (ZNWC), which supplied them to the state chain shops throughout the country.

Apart from my first-degree relatives, immediate family members and extended family members, I had the opportunity to meet and know many other people during my journey. Many offered their advice and sometimes material help when I was in dire need. These became part of my extended family.

I was also privileged to be inducted into other families due to my role in cementing their personal relationships as I counseled them during their courtships, weddings, and married lives. During mentoring sessions, I shared my life experiences and lifestyle in the hope that these will be helpful in fostering viable relationships. A number of these relatives remember me during the celebrations of their anniversaries. I mentioned many by name, who shared my battles, moments of triumph and glory and lifted my spirits high when I was down and weak, during my journey.

CHAPTER 6

Academic Lessons To Zambia's Agricultural Development

I arrived in Zambia on 2 June 1973 to undertake research for my dissertation. For my research work, I chose to study some economic aspects of small-scale farming in Zambia to identify the challenges in bringing about an agricultural revolution. I chose the Ngwezi Settlement Scheme in Mazabuka District of Southern Province. The scheme was the oldest, having been established in 1964 as part of the new Zambian government's policy on land consolidation and resettlements.

I was taken to Magoye Research Station on 3 June 1973, where I was to be based while doing my research. Sadly, my mother passed on at Chikankata Mission Hospital just a few days after my arrival in Zambia.

Within the month of June 1973, I lost my mother, bought a car, got allocated a house, and got married. Having settled my family life, housing, and transport issues, I focused on my studies and determined that I should complete my course as soon as possible.

The objectives of the study of the Ngwezi Settlement Scheme were:
(a)   To investigate the sources and levels of farm incomes;
(b)   To determine the factors that contribute towards higher net farm incomes.

I found my research exciting and educative as it entailed having interviews with farmers in the settlement schemes on their farm operations and with managers of various national farming organizations. I was assisted in obtaining reading material by Peter Apedaile and in computerizing and analysing the data by Ephraim Chungwe Kaunga and Benard Beharell of the University of Zambia.

The issues studied, using frequency distributions and multiple regression analysis, were the net farm income in relation to household size, acreage, permanent and casual labour, tractor hire, age, education, and fertiliser cost. Using a linear equation, the effects of the various variables on income over time and at different quantities were revealed. The major influencing variable on productivity turned out to be the personal ownership of land through title deeds. In other words, the relocation from traditional land to the settlement scheme provided opportunities for the farmers to adopt new technologies. My findings confirmed the importance of private land ownership in increasing agricultural production.

I completed my research work and was ready to submit the dissertation when I was informed that my supervisor at Makerere University, Dr Hani Afifi had some problems and the university was trying to assign someone else to supervise me. This issue was resolved towards the end of 1974 and I submitted my thesis to Makerere University for adjudication by a team of examiners appointed by the University Senate. The thesis was found acceptable by all the three examiners and therefore I did not make a personal appearance to defend my thesis.

I was conferred with the degree of Master of Science in Agricultural Economics in 1975, becoming one of the first two black Zambian agricultural economists. Due to the worsening security situation in Uganda during that period, I could not travel for the graduation ceremony and my certificate was brought to Zambia by statistician Banda. The thesis is available at UNZA Research Repository Online under 'Agricultural Sciences'.

My training was so relevant to the programmes of the Zambian government at the time, such that in January 1974, I was appointed to the position of economist. This was before my thesis had been approved by Makerere University. The results of the written examinations and the draft thesis were enough to qualify me for an appointment as an economist. This action seemed to be a fulfillment of my words to the expatriate deputy secretary to the cabinet (economics) in 1971, that I did not need a doctor of philosophy degree to be an economist.

What I needed to be an acclaimed economist was an understanding of "the science of the production and distribution of wealth". After a thorough study of the Ngwezi Settlement Scheme, I fully understood the positive impact of production assets such as land and new technologies of fertilisers on the productivity and wealth-creation by the small-scale farmers. The ordinary people of Munjile and Kataba areas in Chief Hanjalika of Mazabuka District accumulated much wealth by relocating into the scheme just across the road.

At Namaila, I never heard of anyone with a title deed for land, and farming continued to be done on subsistence level under negotiated land ownership. My research confirmed that ownership of land was an enabling instrument for farmers who wanted to adopt and apply new farming technologies.

The Kaleya Smallholder Sugarcane Outgrowers Project
After completing my research work, I was instructed to remain at Magoye while waiting for suitable housing accommodation in Lusaka. In the interim period, I assisted with the planning of new settlement schemes under Family Farms

Limited. The company was headed by Lee Holland, a Canadian University Service Overseas (CUSO) volunteer, who was assisted by George Harris, a CUSO volunteer, Berrings Moonga, and Harris Chibwe.

I helped in interviewing applicants who wished to get settlement farms in the Mazabuka and Monze Districts and this brought me closer to the local communities. Because of the success of the Ngwezi scheme, there was overwhelming demand from many villagers to relocate from the traditional land. This led to establishment of the Mbaya-Musuma, Upper Kaleya, and Silwiili schemes.

I was then challenged by my supervisor, Hank Friso, a Canadian economist in the ministry, to come up with a project that would involve the local people in the lucrative sugarcane growing industry. At the time, sugarcane was being produced only by a corporate company on an expansive estate at Nakambala near Mazabuka Town.

I single-handedly conceptualized and planned the Kaleya Smallholder Sugarcane Outgrowers Scheme, as my maiden project under Hank's supervision. In view of the project being a landmark in my professional economic career, Hank insisted that the project feasibility report should bear my name. I feel honoured that the original report has been preserved and is kept at the offices of the Kaleya Smallholders Company.

During project planning, I had the honour of interviewing the septuagenarian Chief Mwanachingwala, who gave his approval for the project. His Royal Highness (HRH) advised that consideration be given to applicants from outside as his people might not be interested in the laborious growing of sugarcane. The Commonwealth Development Corporation (CDC) accepted a request to fund the development of the project. Although the ministry approved the project, objections were raised by those who argued that the land should be reserved for the traditional cattle keepers under customary land tenure.

To think that keeping cattle in a traditional setting was more beneficial and productive than the commercial growing of sugarcane was the exact opposite of my research findings. This objection was my first encounter with Zambia's obstructive customary land tenure system.

In 1978, Minister Chikwanda requested the president to include the Kaleya Smallholder Outgrowers Scheme, which had stalled since 1974, on the agenda of a special cabinet meeting. This was necessitated by the fact that one of the main objectors of the project was the prime minister. I was honoured and allowed to make a personal appearance and presentation to the cabinet. After my strong and passionate presentation, the project was finally approved by the cabinet for implementation.

I was delighted that the CDC still expressed some interest in funding the project. The project was finally started in 1984, long after I'd left the ministry. Most of the settlers were from the surrounding villages. The Kaleya

Smallholder Sugarcane Outgrowers Scheme is one of the most successful settlement schemes, which has facilitated the creation of millionaire small-scale farmers on less than twenty hectares of titled land.

On 18 September 2007, I accompanied President Levy Patrick Mwanawasa on a visit to Nakambala Sugar Estate to launch the US $160 million expansion project. During the conducted tour, the president was shown and briefed on the smallholder scheme and informed of its remarkable success and my personal involvement in its planning. The president requested the management of the scheme to consider allocating me one of the plots as a symbolic gesture of honour for my role in the initiation of the scheme some thirty-three years before. I have been waiting since 2007 for President Mwanawasa's request to be acted upon.

The agricultural sector in disarray
My family and I moved to Lusaka in June 1974 and I rejoined the planning division of the MRD in Mulungushi House along Independence Avenue. I had no problems getting to work as I had bought a brand new Volkswagen (VW) car from Duly Motors.

Between 1972 and 1980, the MRD had four ministers, namely Reuben Chitandika Kamanga, Elijah Haatukali Kaiba Mudenda, Paul Lusaka, and Alexander Bwalya Chikwanda. The cabinet ministers were assisted by Permanent Secretaries Daniel Hanene Luzongo, Evans E. L. Willima, Jabes Sakala, Hosea Ng'wane, and Andrew Hamaamba.

The planning division was headed by Peter Stutley, Babbar, and Mwape Xavier Mufwaya as planning coordinators. Having joined the planning division in March 1972, I rose through the ranks to head the division as planning coordinator in January 1979.

Out of nine economists in the planning division in 1974, there were only three Zambian economists, namely Elizabeth Hakeeta, Alex Mashebe Mundia, and me. The rest of the staff were expatriates from various countries and the UN system under development assistance programs. Among them were Hank Friso, Adotey Bing, Bill Farmer, and Ravi Verma.

Before Independence in 1964, much of the agricultural activities, based on maize and cattle production, were carried out on land besides the rail line from Kalomo to Kapiri Mposhi. The Mazabuka District produced the bulk of the maize for the country. The maize produced in the Mkushi Block, a purpose-designed scheme for immigrant white settler farmers, was for the mining community on the Copperbelt. There was no commercial maize production in much of the northern and western regions of Zambia, where cassava was the main staple food.

At independence, the country was presented with an agricultural development plan called the UN/ECA/FAO Seers Report in which mechanization and cooperatives were emphasized. The plan drawn without adequate local situational analysis was not appropriate for the new Zambian farmers, most of whom were not familiar with cooperatives and sophisticated equipment such as tractors and oxen-drawn implements.

The new crops and technologies required properly organized land demarcation and conservation. In 1961, an ambitious Mazabuka Regional Plan was conceived and implemented under the supervision of Ignatius Muchangwe, who was the first black District Agricultural Officer. He was assisted by Daniel Hanene Luzongo one of the few graduates in agriculture at independence, having studied at Rhodes University and Cornell University.

Under the Plan, thousands of kilometres of paddocks and contour ridges were constructed on communal lands to separate grazing and cropping lands. Unfortunately, this vital infrastructure was vandalized by the villagers during the freedom struggle. The land conservation plan was abandoned before it reached Namaila, as it was considered to be restrictive in land use by the villagers. However, when schooling became popular and young boys went away to school, the elders who herded the cattle realized the usefulness of the fences. In some areas, this led to the reconstruction of the same fences at the villager's own cost after regretting at having destroyed the earlier free fences.

Mechanization was facilitated by the importation of a large number of tractors by the Zambian Government. The tractors distributed to cooperatives and provincial tractor units for use at subsidized hire charges soon broke down. A directive was given that villagers clear land for tractor ploughing and that they will be paid. Some clever villagers took agricultural and cooperative officers into the Chambeshi Plains, which they claimed to have cleared and demanded to be paid. The villagers were paid for having done nothing, as the natural plains had no trees in the first place.

At times, there were internal divergent views within the Zambian Government as to the best method of introducing modern farming methods and new crops to Zambian farmers. Agriculture as a subset of rural development meant that not enough attention and resources were allocated to the sector. The sector was put in the Ministry of Rural Development. Donors were attracted to the new concept as it involved the 'emancipation of poor Zambian villagers'.

The fashionable term of 'rural development' was not even properly defined and understood. The international development community was still grappling with the definition of 'development', which had been introduced with the independence of many colonies in the sixties. The concept of rural development, which was popularized in the seventies, was defined as being

multi-disciplinary in nature, representing an intersection of agricultural, social, behavioural, and management sciences. It became difficult for many newly independent countries such as Zambia with limited manpower and financial resources to concurrently and effectively attend to so many issues of development in the rural areas.

In the early eighties, Robert Chambers who had worked in Africa for a long time produced his seminal book, Rural Development: Putting the Last First in which he questioned some conventional development ideas and practices. In recognition of the role of the rural poor in defining their poverty, he introduced new concepts such as 'people-centred', 'bottom-up', and 'participatory appraisal'.

The Zambian government in its efforts to focus on agriculture renamed the MRD as the Ministry of Agriculture and Water Development. Unfortunately, the pendulum in thinking had swung too far in the direction of the promulgation of the production and consumption of only maize.

In the Luapula Province, the local people were told by politicians that the local food crops of cassava and sorghum were inferior to maize. It was presumed that the people of Luapula Province would 'develop' by merely changing their diet from cassava to maize. Suddenly the demand for mealie meal rose even amongst communities that did not have any idea of how to grow the crop. Due to the departure of many white farmers, the country was short of nearly all food and industrial agricultural commodities, which had to be imported. The recently independent Zambia was headed for the status of a 'failed state'.

CHAPTER 7

Rebuilding Zambia's Agricultural Sector

The mood of Zambians, who had been pacified by the coming of independence in 1964, was beginning to boil again due to frustrations. Inter-party violence between members of the ANC and UNIP was on the increase. In 1973, the ANC and UNIP agreed to work together under the One-Party Participatory Democracy system and happily, this brought some peace amongst the warring cadres.

Assured of peace, His Excellency the President Dr Kenneth David Kaunda started convening sector meetings to consider an appropriate future development agenda for Zambia. Sometime in 1974, a special cabinet meeting was convened to discuss the state of the nation's agricultural industry. The planning coordinator for our division directed that I attend the special meeting. It was a great honour for me to attend a cabinet meeting at my junior status and young age.

The discussions were thorough and at the end of the meeting, the Minister of Rural Development (MRD) was given specific directives on the way forward in the agricultural sector. The main objective for agricultural development was to become self-sufficient in food and agricultural industrial raw materials within a specified timeframe.

Amongst the directives given were that:

(a)   there shall be enough vegetables produced by the end of 1975 to stop the importation of the same;

(b)   by the end of five years, Zambia will stop the importation of beef;

(c)   within five years, there will be no importation of cooking oil;

(d)   within a period of five years, there will be no importation of sugar;

(e)   within the shortest time possible, all maize and other crops were to be safely secured each year and adequate processing capacity be created;

(f)   efforts will be made to plan and develop agricultural projects in all the provinces of Zambia taking into account local agronomic and climatic conditions.

A few days later, Minister Rueben Chitandika Kamanga chaired a brainstorming session on how to implement the cabinet resolutions with experts from the various departments under his ministry and other stakeholders in the agricultural sector. The Department of Agriculture produced details on the various ecological zones of the country and the crops that were suited for growing by the local people. Each head of department outlined the details of their work plans and the resources, both financial and human, which were required in order to achieve the set goals.

The planning division was to coordinate all the plans and programmes to be implemented by the various departments of the ministry. Being the most senior indigenous economic planner, I was honoured by being appointed the linkman between the policymakers and the project planners, financiers and implementers.

The period between 1974 and 1980 was the turning point for Zambia's agricultural industry. Many projects were initiated and implemented in order to increase the production of agricultural commodities both as food and also as raw materials for many manufacturing industries. Consumption of many commodities was rising rapidly due to increasing incomes of black Zambians, who were getting into paid jobs.

In the area of crops, efforts were made from research to field production and in processing a number of them. In production, the Lima Programme was introduced in order to increase yields of various crops. In the extension area, the Training and Visit (T&V) system, which had succeeded in India, was instituted mainly in the agriculturally-active areas of Eastern, Central, and Southern Provinces.

The ministry produced information on the agro-ecological zones of the country, with information on suitable crops. Booklets were produced on the agronomic suitability of the three zones of the country for specified crops. As the Zambian agricultural scientists and extension specialists were producing literature on new farming technologies, such as hybrid seeds, equipment and chemical fertilisers, the villagers were lagging behind because of high levels of illiteracy in the country.

In 1974, a programme of Functional Literacy, using maize as a core learning subject was introduced in Zambia. Among the farming-loving Tongas, the teaching programme, focusing on elders, was nicknamed Muzenge, meaning 'light', as the classes were held in the evening under candlelight and lanterns. The programme had salutary effects as development goals were linked to literacy objectives around a common activity and the new technologies of hybrid maize and fertlisers.

By the initiative of Prime Minister Mudenda, a new maize milling plant was established in Choma with German Government assistance. The plant produced the famous and sought-after Choma white mealie meal, transported all the way to Lusaka for sale to the elites. The PM's proposal to produce one type of nutritious maize meal was agreed upon by the cabinet.

But like always, the urban bourgeois fought hard and won the battle to continue eating the white maize meal devoid of any food value just because of its white colour. They even euphoniously called the tasteless white maize flour, 'breakfast meal' even when it was consumed for supper! Zambians have continued to admire and eat foods on the basis of their bright colours and not due to the foods' nutritional values. There is a weak link between food and nutrition. A country rich in plentiful nutritious foods such as amaranth (*bbondwe*), which is rich in minerals, proteins, and vitamins, has one of the highest incidence of stunted children in the world.

As per the 1974 Cabinet decision, agricultural projects were located in all the provinces taking into account the traditions of the people and the suitability of the weather and soils. Most of the projects were targeted at the villagers who were encouraged to graduate to small-scale and emergent farmer categories. Development plans, programmes, and projects laid strong emphasis on rural development with a specific aim of expanding the agricultural sector as well as the nascent agro-industries and to reduce regional income inequalities amongst the regions of the country.

From a one-hectare experimental plot in 1963, the Tate and Lyle sugarcane fields at Nakambala Estates in Mazabuka District expanded to 3,600 hectares by 1973 and onto 8,700 hectares in 1980 to reach the cabinet's sugar production target. The expanded cane fields required additional water from the Kafue River for irrigation. I acted as an arbitrator in the negotiations between the Zambia Electricity Supply Company (ZESCO) and the Zambia Sugar Company (ZSC) on the sharing of the waters of the Kafue River between irrigated agriculture and energy generation.

The ZESCO management under Roy Miti argued that the extraction of additional water from the Kafue River for irrigation at Mazabuka would reduce the amount available for electricity generation at the newly completed Kafue Hydroelectric Power Station downstream. To resolve the deadlock, we advised our minister to refer the matter to the cabinet, who finally decided in favour of food (sugar) against energy (electricity).

However, the effectiveness of the synergy of visionary national planning at the time was manifested in the immediate start of the construction of the Itezhi-Tezhi Dam on the Kafue River upstream in Namwala District to conserve more water. By the time the expanded sugarcane fields at Nakambala were ready to take more water for irrigation, additional water was available at the newly-completed dam upstream. The dam did not only satisfy the water needs of agriculture, but later in the 21st century, the dam is used to generate electricity.

One of the tedious duties of the planning division of the MRD was that of setting producer and consumer prices for all agricultural products. This involved calculating production costs of all agricultural products. At the time, as there were no pocket calculators or computers, we had to use cranking machines. Once the figures were known, then uniform prices at both the production and consumption levels to be applied throughout Zambia were determined by the cabinet and announced. The official prices were then monitored by the price control officers in the Ministry of Commerce Trade and Industry.

There were always arguments on prices between the government officials and the farming community, in particular on exotic crops such as wheat, soya beans, Irish potatoes, and tobacco, which were a preserve of the white commercial farmers.

As an economist, I did not fully agree with the policy of setting pan-territorial or uniform prices throughout Zambia. The system ignored the variations in production and trading costs and led to major distortions and imbalances. Although I preferred a pricing system, which took into account the variable production costs in the various parts of the country, I had to implement the government policy. The politicians saw the price levelling as a way of encouraging the production and consumption of new agricultural foods by all Zambians. This ignored traditions and agronomic factors, which resulted in high costs of production and wastage in marketing.

In April 1975, Steven Chiwala, Director of Marketing and Cooperatives led a team of officers for a one-month study tour of the agricultural cooperative movement in Mauritius. Chief Bright Nalubamba, a Cooperative Officer at the time, and I were in the team. This was my first official trip to a foreign country on duty. We toured the whole scenic island interacting with actors in both the agriculture and tourism sectors.

It was a great honour for me to meet the prime minister of Mauritius, Sir Seewoosagur Ramgoolam, who took an active part in the liberation of Mauritius. Twenty-three years later in 1998, I had the honour as secretary general of the ACP Secretariat to pose for photos with the son, Dr Navinchandra Ramgoolam, my agemate, who ascended to the position of prime minister in 1995. Mauritius had by then been completely transformed with modern ICT, textile industries, and highways created from earnings from exports of sugar, textiles, and services.

Mauritius was one of the countries approved as an exporter of sugar to the lucrative European market under the Sugar Protocol of the 1975 ACP-EU Lome Convention. Being a small island, with a limited land area for agriculture, the government decided to uproot the railway lines throughout the island and turn the island into one large sugar plantation. Within a short period, the island nation of 2,040 square kilometres was exporting over 400,000 tonnes of refined sugar per year at preferential prices higher than the world prices.

The knowledge acquired during our trip led to the active revival of the cooperative movement in Zambia and a recommendation to establish the auctioning of vegetables. Another proposal was to rapidly expand sugarcane production to benefit from the Lome Convention to which Zambia was also a member. However, the proposal to upscale sugar production could not be accepted due to a 'shortage of land' in a country of 75 million hectares! Zambia missed a golden opportunity to benefit from the preferential high sugar prices offered under the Lome Convention.

In 1976, I made my first trip to the United States of America (USA) to attend a course in rural project analysis at the Economic Development Institute (EDI) of the World Bank based at the Bank's head office in Washington DC. This was my introduction to the World Bank and its operations. The EDI was described in "The Wall Street Journal" during its founding in the fifties as "the world's newest and most exclusive economics school". In our class, there were twelve of us drawn from all over the world. The lessons took us through the investment process of project analysis, which covered the identification, preparation, appraisal and implementation of development projects.

After rigorous classroom work, during which we worked out exercises and case studies, we went to the Republic of Guyana in South America, for field practice. We actually planned some dairy settlement farms within a few days and presented our project proposals to a workshop of government officials. On our way back to the USA, we toured agricultural projects on the islands of Trinidad and Tobago.

The EDI course, which brought together middle management government officers, armed me with additional tools for national development and project planning. The EDI provided an opportunity for exchange of experiences amongst policymakers and project planners at the global level. At the end of the course, we were awarded certificates by Robert McNamara, President of the World Bank and I became a Fellow of the Economic Development Institute (FEDI) of the World Bank.

The implementation of the cabinet decision to stop the importation of beef within five years demonstrated the immense zeal, capability, and effectiveness of the few planning officers in the ministry during that period. After the directive was given, the ministry formed a Technical Committee, which established a value chain from financing of production to processing of livestock.

The anchorman for the livestock development programme was Namukolo Mukutu, who had been in the last Form VI class in 1964, before Form V became the terminal school class for entry into university. He fondly recollects his role as an usher during the Independence celebrations on 24th October 1964. He studied agriculture, specializing in animal science at the Massey University in New Zealand. With his enviable height, complexion and soft deep voice, he was often mistaken for a Maori prince at the university.

On his return to Zambia in 1971, he joined the Department of Agriculture in Choma, where I met him, before he was transferred to Palabana Training Institute as a lecturer. He then moved onto the ministry headquarters, where he was the first Zambian Chief Animal Husbandry Officer.

For financing the sector, the ministry formed the Cattle Finance Company (CFC) under Silas Muntanga to give loans to farmers, who wished to acquire and rear cattle. In production, the Zambia Agricultural Development Limited (ZADL) was established to produce crops and livestock at farms in Lusaka, Mbala, Mbesuma, Nega Nega, Kalomo, Monze, Naluama, Senanga, Chishinga, and Nanga. Some of the farms, such as the Chisamba and Monze Ranches, were dedicated to producing pedigree bulls and heifers for sale to individual farmers. Joseph Mutelo and Marcelino Busuma Kanungwe provided efficient guidance in the establishment and operations of the Zambia Agricultural Development Limited.

The Western Province, having the second largest cattle population after the Southern Province, had to be dealt with from this comparative advantage. The huge Zambezi plains were suitable for good winter grazing to support a large healthy cattle herd. It was decided that a team of senior officers be sent to engage the people of the province at the highest level on the development of agriculture in general and cattle in particular.

Mulele Mulele, Deputy Director of Agriculture and I were instructed by Minister Chikwanda to travel to Mongu on this assignment. I was excited because I'd worked with Ilute Yeta IV, the Litunga of Barotseland in Southern Province in 1971 and the two of us knew each other well. I'd heard of his abduction from a house of a loyal Lozi friend in Chelstone in 1977 where he had sought refuge as they pursued him to enthrone him as the Litunga. I was keen to see what had become of the reluctant ruler in his new elevated position of king and to share some light moments reminiscing.

We already had good background information in the ministry concerning the status of the Lozi traditional land tenure system in the province. We felt that with an educated retired civil servant as the Litunga, the time was favourable for changing the inhibitive traditional land tenure system. The main purpose of the trip was, therefore, to convince the Litunga and his people to embrace modern methods of farming and in particular of cattle husbandry by introducing the attendant land conservation systems.

At Livingstone, we were joined on the Zambia Airways flight by Prince Inyambo Yeta, the son of the Litunga, who was going home for holidays from university. I seized the opportunity to brief him on our mission and requested him to facilitate a meeting with his father in Lealui. I also asked him to be in attendance in our meetings as he could provide some useful continuity in the future agricultural development of the Western Province. I was made aware of the future plans to install him as the ruler at the Mwandi royal establishment.

An early morning trip by speedboat from Mongu got us to Lealui before noon. The promise by Prince Inyambo Yeta for an early meeting with his father could not circumvent the elaborate Lozi protocol that required even a son to seek permission to see his father! We were made to wait until late in the afternoon to get an audience with the Litunga.

About midday, the Litunga passed by near to us while going to attend a Sunday service at a historic church building close to the palace. I became convinced that if missionary Coillard could convert the Lozis to Christianity, a doctrine based on faith, I could also convince them to adopt modern agricultural practices, which promised visible and physical wealth on earth.

As special guests of the Litunga, we shared some lunch with one of the Indunas. The lunch chat included an apology by the Induna for not serving me the highly proclaimed juicy meat of the hopani. He claimed that the animal had become an endangered species. I proposed to the Induna that the surest way of conserving and continuing to enjoy the delicacy was to domesticate and commercialise the rearing of the hopani and include it in our ambitious livestock project. This would be a good way of using modern methods to enhance traditional lifestyles.

His Majesty Mulena Ilute Yeta IV was a towering man of over two metres in height and a chair to fit his imposing stature looked really formidable on the eastern side of the *Kashandi*. As his entry was announced, we all rose and only sat down after he'd composed himself in the majestic chair. I felt proud to see my former mentor in the high traditional seat of authority and was itching for a productive conversation.

Our visit attracted a large crowd, which overflowed the Kashandi. When the introductions were made, they were in siLozi by an Induna who sat between the Litunga and me. And although my name and title were clearly stated, the Litunga did not seem to have recognized me from our past association. By Lozi tradition, the Litunga did not even acknowledge the presence of Mulele, one of his subjects!

I explained the purpose of our visit and informed the Litunga that the Zambian Government had funds that were to be used for the development of the livestock sector in the country. The project was to include cattle breeding, animal husbandry training, and fencing of pastures and grazing lands. It was the wish of the government to include the Western Province in this national project, which would make Zambia a producer of exportable beef like Botswana next door.

I deliberately mentioned Botswana knowing well that the Litunga had been Zambia's high commissioner to that country and was aware of the pivotal role of cattle in wealth creation in that prosperous and peaceful country. My presentation was interpreted to the Litunga into siLozi by an Induna. Protocol demands that the Litunga must address his visitors in siLozi so that his subjects in attendance can understand the subject being discussed and his reaction.

There was no direct conversation between me and the Litunga in spite of us being about four metres apart and having worked together. I immediately sensed that things had indeed changed as Lozi tradition had taken over my Western-trained mentor.

Addressing me in siLozi as his reply, the Litunga stated, in a stern vice, that the land in Barotseland belonged to all the people and no fencing would ever be allowed. He went on to say that the people and their cattle must have the freedom to move about without obstruction of fences. He directed us to inform whoever had sent us that the people of Barotseland do not want the proposed livestock development project as it would destroy the old traditions of communal land ownership and usage.

The Litunga stated that Barotseland had a working governance system with a team of Indunas, who were responsible for various portfolios. He indicated that the Induna who was interpreting during the meeting was responsible for agriculture and had briefed him on the subject of our trip. He even referred me to what he called the obnoxious land ownership system in the Southern Province, where a few foreigners owned large tracts of land to the disadvantage of the locals who even have no access to some natural water sources due to fences. The attendees kept nodding to indicate approval of everything said by the Litunga.

I then wondered why the Litunga as the Permanent Secretary for the Southern Province did not start a war for equitable sharing of land, as I would have willingly joined the fight. After the crowd had dispersed, the Litunga had a short meeting with us in English. Mulele was then dismissed and I remained for a while during which I was addressed in English and introduced to Lozi rituals, rites and protocols. The Litunga then wished me well during our visit to his land and in my future career.

We left Lealui for Mongu late in the afternoon in a subdued mood. I was frustrated that the Lozi people with an educated chief and an entrenched cattle-rearing tradition will not be included in modernizing their animal husbandry. As we enjoyed the cruise on the meandering but calm Zambezi River, the serenity of the vast Zambezi plains challenged me to indulge in some deep thought on the value of these plains to the ordinary people of the province. I wondered how I would report to my enthusiastic minister that I had failed to convince the Litunga, my former boss, on the benefits of modern methods in cattle farming.

The national livestock development project did not include the Western Province, whose livestock husbandry remained poor. Even the proven high rate of fluke infestation identified at abattoirs through diseased livers failed to convince the local people to believe in modern technology such as vaccines.

In some parts of the country, facilities were created to feed-lot cattle from both commercial and traditional cattle farmers. Under the supervision of George Akafekwa, the services and facilities for the control of cattle diseases were revamped and a regional tsetse fly control project covering Botswana, Zambia, and Zimbabwe funded by the European Economic Community was started.

In September 1978, a historic luncheon was held in the roof-top Makumbi

Restaurant of the Intercontinental Hotel to taste Zambian-produced beef steak. The steak satisfied the taste buds of foreign meat experts who were invited to the luncheon. With a sizable healthy cattle herd, the country was on its way to producing high-quality beef by establishing a state-of-the-art abattoir in Livingstone with EU financial support and to EU standards. The Cold Storage Board under Dominic Chilao got modern equipment for the efficient and hygienic slaughter of livestock in other abattoirs.

We negotiated with the Botswana Government to allow our choice meat to be exported to Europe under the already-known successful brand of the Botswana Meat Commission (BMC). The meat produced at the Livingstone abattoir was to be transported in refrigerated trucks to the BMC meat processing plant at Lobatse for packaging.

A new breed of cattle, the versatile Simmental, a high producer of both meat and milk was imported from Belgium for cross-breeding at the ZADL farm in Lusaka West. Another cattle cross-breeding ranch was established at Batoka in Choma with the financial assistance of the EEC. By 1984, the cattle population in the Southern Province, where cattle keepers embraced modern animal husbandry, had increased due to pedigree bulls nicknamed '*Mukutu, mwana amulozi*'. Annual cattle growth in the country was around 2.8 percent.

Every discussion I attended since 1978 on cattle development in the Western Province ended up with a demand for the cordon line between Angola and Zambia. There is a misconception that the problems of livestock development in the Western Province are caused by diseased cattle moving from Angola. It is true that there was a historical outbreak of rinderpest due to large unchecked movements of cattle from Angola to Zambia in the late twentieth century. With modern technology, such movements can now be effectively monitored using drones and diseases prevented by modern vaccines.

In the twenty-first century, I have had the rare privilege of being close to the youthful His Majesty Mulena Mbumu wa Lubosi Imwiko II, as we worked together at INDECO during the nineties. I have been aware of his keen interest in crop growing and cattle rearing at his farm located in another province. Adapting the Litunga's livestock husbandry in the Western Province would reduce livestock diseases and improve the quality of cattle and beef.

In 2006, I challenged Mundia Sikatana, Minister of Agriculture and Cooperatives with a grant of US $10 million from the Danish Government for cattle development in the Western Province. Most of the funds were as usual used to rehabilitate the cordon line, but the cattle disease burden in the province continues to prohibit the production of quality cattle.

In spite of the hundreds of Zambian veterinarians produced by the Samora Machel Veterinary School at UNZA, named after the Mozambican revolutionary, the cattle disease incidence and burden have proportionally increased. In 2009, Zambia registered incidents of all economic livestock diseases, which have been eliminated or have been brought under effective control in competing neighbouring countries. These have hindered the increase in livestock numbers in Zambia. Zambia's cattle population continues to hover around 3 million, manifesting some deficiency in the training given at UNZA and in the application of animal husbandry in the field.

The modern abattoir constructed in Livingstone under the national livestock development programme was sold during the privatization programme of Chiluba's Administration. The new owners dismantled the plant and used some of the stainless steel tanks for a maize milling plant in Lusaka. The cattle breeding ranches were abandoned and subdivided for allocation of plots to individuals.

The heavy disease burden and lack of modern facilities have prevented the beef industry from meeting quality certifications for export markets. Zambia lost its share of the lucrative EU market under the Beef Protocol of the ACP-EU cooperation. By the beginning of the twenty-first century, Zambians living on 20.3 million hectares of grazing lands were importing tasteless and chemically-treated meat, suspected of being horse meat, from Europe.

One of the important food items from the livestock industry is milk. Following the departure of many expatriate dairy farmers from the country at independence in 1964, the government embarked on a programme of establishing state dairy farms. Five parastatal dairy farms were established at Chipata, Kasama, Mansa, Mongu, and Solwezi.

During the seventies, the government introduced dairy schemes aimed at encouraging indigenous Zambian small-scale farmers to participate in commercial dairy production. The most notable was the Smallholder Dairy Development Project (SDDP), which was funded by a concessional loan from the World Bank. The project was initially to involve farmers in the Mazabuka, Lusaka, and Kabwe Districts.

The arrangement was that the farmers would deliver their small quantities of milk to collection centres where the bulked milk would be picked by the Dairy Produce Board of Zambia. Before long, the project ran into difficulties of delivering fresh milk due to inadequate cooling equipment at the collection centres. Large quantities of milk were being thrown away from the centres. Due to loss of income as the farmers could not sell the soured milk, interest in the project waned.

When I was transferred to the ministry as permanent secretary in July 1985, I found active debate as to the future of the milk production project. After being briefed on the proposal to terminate the project, I suggested that milk could still be sold as soured milk to consumers. I argued that many Zambians had adapted to taking soured milk in view of the intensive campaign by the nutrition experts on its health benefits. I had been brought up in a mabisi eating environment in Tongaland and perhaps my suggestion had some indigenous knowledge and personal motivation.

Arrangements were made for a truck to deliver soured milk to Mulungushi House, the home of the Ministry of Agriculture, for sale. When the program started, buyers of sour milk, mostly civil servants, lined up with containers early in the morning waiting for the delivery van.

While there had been scepticism to my suggestion, soon, the demand for soured milk outstripped the supply within a short period. Soured milk was being sold in various towns covered by the project. The small-scale dairy project was saved and was later extended to include Kabwe, Monze, and Choma Districts.

At some point in the seventies, Zambia was requested to supply goats to the huge Muslim Middle East market. We agreed and invited a team to visit the country to see the goat herds in the Eastern, Central and Southern Provinces. After a tour of a few days, we held a meeting to assess the situation. One of the visitors asked us during the meeting as to when we will show them the goat herds for export! Sadly, this was the end of our export intentions as we were told that the goat population in Zambia of less than five million was too small for the market.

Having failed to convince the Litunga on the need to establish a cattle development project during our visit to Lealui, I proposed to Mulele that at least we could divert our expertise to the production of crops, as these do not require fencing. I daydreamed of vast rice fields and huge plantations of evergreen trees of different fruits including mangoes, guavas, and cashew nuts. The following day, we visited the Ndanda area, situated some distance north of Mongu on the Zambezi River plains.

We had a successful meeting with the local people under the cool shade of a large Lozi mango tree. The people accepted the proposed project to intensify the growing of cashew nuts, mangoes, and rice. We informed them that the Government planned to establish a fruit pulping plant, a cashew nut factory, and a rice mill in Mongu once they produced these crops in large quantities.

As promised, the two factories and a mango pulping plant were established in Mongu and they provided a ready market for the fruits produced by the villagers. The large quantities of mangoes bought from the villagers in the province, who earned some income, were processed into mango juice.

The unit dealing with fruits and vegetables under NAMB was transformed into the Zambia Horticultural Products Limited (ZAMHORT). The new company, under General Manager Simeo Siame, was delegated with the responsibility of purchasing, drying, processing, and packaging of the abundant fruits and vegetables. The company was equipped with new state-of-the-art food processing equipment from Italy. Locally-produced mango and pineapple juices were readily available on the market with some exports to the Middle Eastern countries.

The modern equipment in Lusaka's Buseko industrial area was bought by a foreigner during the Chiluba administration's privatisation era. The trucks taking away the equipment were intercepted at the Chirundu border post by a patriotic Zambian customs officer. The trucks were released on orders of a minister, who reprimanded the officer for frustrating the government's privatisation programme. The government's decision, to allow the removal of the equipment from Zambia, left a big gap in the development of vegetable and fruit production and processing. The irony was that, the equipment was installed in a neighbouring country, which exported tinned fruit juices to Zambia.

Over time, crop production which had improved in the Western Province, also suffered a similar fate as that of cattle. The canals constructed under Japanese assistance for rice growing have not been put to productive use. Fourteen thousand cashew nut trees imported from South America and planted in the western Province in the seventies were not cared for. The mango pulping plant established under ZAMHORT stopped working after being privatized and villagers resumed their cry for a lack of a reliable market for their mango fruits.

Bewildered by the persistently high poverty levels in the 'rich' province, with many eminent people, I was compelled to accompany President Mwanawasa to the Kuomboka Ceremony held on 31 March 2007. I engaged some local people on what was causing the high poverty levels and what possible measures could be taken.

One of the issues they mentioned was the traditional land tenure system. When I referred to this challenge in one of the national planning conferences, I was summoned to appear before the *Kuta* in Mongu to explain my 'damaging' statement. I used my traditional cousin relationship to ignore the summons as my statement was factual. I still challenged some locals to identify a 5,000-hectare piece of land for the establishment of a citrus plantation and processing plant by an identified willing foreign investor. The project located some twenty-seven kilometres from Mongu on the Mongu-Senanga Road ran against the land tenure system.

The increased flower and vegetable production in the eighties, led to the establishment of modern handling and cooling facilities at the Lusaka International Airport under EU financial assistance. These were used to handle vegetables and flowers for export to Europe. In 1984, the facilities were handed over to the newly formed Zambia Exporters Growers Association (ZEGA). Zambia's distinct quality flowers made a great impact on the renowned Amsterdam flower market in the Netherlands.

Another remarkable development was the rapid development of the cotton industry under the newly established Lint Company of Zambia (LINTCO). The Ministry identified the Zambezi and Luangwa Valleys, Chipata, Mazabuka, and Mumbwa areas as the ecologically suited areas for the production of cotton.

A project to increase the production of cotton was prepared with the assistance of Agroprogress, a European consulting firm. The study pointed to the need for effective pest control, which was efficiently promulgated by the extension staff supervised by Mulele Mulele, Chief Crops Officer. Additional research and extension officers were employed. Under the supervision of the illustrious General Manager William Mantanyani, a.k.a. 'Bill' assisted by extension controller Davidson Hanyama, cotton production rapidly increased from three to nine million tons within three years, mostly grown by villagers in the identified areas.

We had earlier abandoned mechanized cotton production in the Mumbwa and Mazabuka areas in preference to production by small-scale farmers. LINTCO established new ginneries at Chipata, Lusaka, Mumbwa, and Gwembe to handle the increased seed cotton production.

Kafue Textiles in Kafue and Mulungushi Textiles in Kabwe were established to process the fast-increasing cotton from the new ginneries. Swarp and Sakiza factories and many small spinning enterprises were established in Livingstone and Ndola Towns to manufacture quality cotton goods for both the local and foreign markets. The 130 vertical industries created thousands of jobs in the production of seed cotton and the manufacture of cloth and garments. By 1980, the Kafue Textiles was producing 25 million metres of cotton cloth, including the famous *chitenge* material, enough for the southern Africa region's requirements.

The famous collarless Kaunda suit, made by the Serioes Company with German modern equipment in Luanshya, was a status symbol for the middle class. I was on a shopping spree in Nairobi, Kenya with a Kenyan friend in the seventies, when I picked a smart-looking collarless suit in the city's cozy boutique. As I advanced towards the cashier, my Kenyan host alerted me that the suit was made in Luanshya in Zambia and I left the suit for him to buy. A few Zambian friends shared similar experiences as high-quality suiting material and men's clothing made in Zambia were readily available in foreign countries in Africa and Europe.

Kenaf production by small-scale farmers was encouraged in the Lukanga Swamps of the Central Province. The processed fiber was used by the Kabwe Industrial Fabrics Limited to manufacture hessian sacks for grain storage.

In the area of irrigation, some ambitious large-scale projects were designed to provide water for intensive crop irrigation on the urging of the prime minister, a plant scientist. The plan was to tap Lake Kariba waters at Siatwinda and get it over the escarpment to Jembo by pipes and release it into the Magoye River near Pemba Town. A series of weirs were to be constructed on the Magoye River from Pemba to Itebe on the Kafue Plains. Land on both sides of the Magoye River was to be properly surveyed, demarcated and allocated on title to individual farmers for irrigated farming.

The other planned irrigation project was to divert the waters of the Lukanga Swamps in Chibombo District by a canal and pipes and release it into the

Keembe River near Mwachisompola. Dams and weirs were to be constructed on the Keembe River down to its confluence with the Kafue River at Sokola. These were futurist projects intended to transform Zambia into a food basket for the region by the effective utilization of water, one of Zambia's abundant natural resources.

The translocation of kapenta fish from Lake Tanganyika into Lake Kariba in 1978 by the Fisheries Department opened opportunities for increased fish production in the country. The ice plant at Kashikishi in the Luapula Province was revamped with the assistance of the Food and Agriculture Organization (FAO). In 1979, the Fisheries Company of Zambia was established to coordinate the production and marketing of fish in the country. However, I recall the minister refusing to approve the holding of a reception for the new company. 'Ba-Mubanga, what are you going to celebrate, when you have not caught even a single fish? Minister Chikwanda asked the new managing director.

In March 1974, I had been promoted to the post of Credit Specialist, with responsibilities of assisting the government financial institutions in their operations. At some point, it was felt that the existing credit institutions giving financial assistance to the agricultural sector were not adequate and appropriate. The Credit Organization of Zambia (COZ), formed just after independence, had been run down by a huge debtor base of uncollectable loans. The Development Bank of Zambia was more inclined to industrial manufacturing projects. I was assigned with the responsibility of studying the current situation and coming up with proposals for an appropriate credit institution.

To assist in arriving at a viable proposition, I studied the whole agricultural credit system in Zambia including the lending schemes run by various commercial banks. At the time, only a few banks had devised special agricultural credit schemes and the most active one was by Barclays Bank Limited. I requested Dennis Wood, who was managing the bank's agricultural credit scheme to assist me in the new assignment.

This brought me closer to Dennis Wood and I soon became curious of his frequent trips to the Copperbelt. One day we were at his home in Chudleigh discussing agricultural credit matters when he answered my curiosity by showing me a picture of a beautiful blonde in a sparkling nurse's white uniform. The young nurse was Monde, who was at the time working at a hospital on the Copperbelt.

When asked for my comment about youthful Monde, I assured Dennis that I greatly benefitted from having Joyce, a nurse, for a spouse. I warned him that he will have to be tolerant enough as other young men will wink at a beautiful girl with royal Lozi blood. Happily, Dennis and Monde tied the knot in 1977. Dennis took my advice and has ignored the judgment in the Anita Hill versus Clarence Thomas case, which criminalized passing compliments on a female's beauty or immaculate dressing as offensive sexual harassment.

After studying many foreign agricultural credit institutions, including the successful Agricole Bank of Egypt, I concluded and recommended that the Zambian agricultural industry required a new effective financial institution. Zambian farmers were subjected to very expensive finance by commercial banks. Much later in the eighties, the Zambia Agricultural Development Bank (ZADB) was formed, as a follow-up, but had a short life as the Lima Bank created in 1986 absorbed all the Government agricultural credit institutions.

In April 1979, Fred Kazunga of the Ministry of Finance, and I accompanied Minister Chikwanda on a whirlwind tour of the USA, Canada, Britain, and Belgium to solicit for funds for agricultural development in Zambia. During the trip, we discussed with officials of the USA State Department, World Bank and Africare in Washington, DC, the Canadian Government and Canadian International Development Agency (CIDA) in Ottawa, the European Union and the Belgium Government in Brussels, and Tate and Lyle Limited in London.

There were some memorable incidents on this trip for my personal reflection. After a busy day of discussions in Washington, DC, we went for dinner. The minister invited some of his friends and His Excellency Ambassador Puteho Ngonda to join us. Amongst the minister's friends who turned up was Vernon Johnson Mwaanga, aka VJ, who was on a private visit to Washington DC.

By the end of the dinner, VJ knew me better from the introduction by his *mushaana*, the minister, and felt comfortable enough to address me as *Oondela*, a typical Tonga term that means, 'my guardian'. After the 1979 meeting in Washington DC, VJ included Joyce and I on the guest list for the lavish parties he threw at his Roma house at the beginning of each year. At one of these parties, VJ introduced us to Hage Geingob, a Namibian freedom fighter, who became the first prime minister and later ascended to the presidency of the Republic of Namibia.

We were booked on a late flight from Washington DC to Toronto in Canada. While waiting for the evening flight, we camped at His Excellency Ambassador Ngonda's residence, where we were well-looked after by the Ambassador's family. This was the beginning of my long and close association with Ambassador Ngonda and his family of Lungowe, Mwiya, Funa, and Mulako Mulala, his sister-in-law.

I became a reliable courier during my numerous trips to and from the USA for messages and gifts to the Ngonda family members in Zambia and vice versa. In return, Mulako availed herself to assist me with my shopping for my family members. Shopping in the seven-storey Hecht's departmental store was intimidating. During my first visit to Washington DC in 1976, I spent my hard-earned dollars in imitating my Arab classmates by buying a lot of gift items, which turned out to be of wrong sizes and this spoilt the Christmas celebrations.

Mulako's assistance ensured my buying clothing and shoes of the correct American sizes for my family. Happily, flights to Zambia were through London, where I made stopovers and enjoyed buying clothing of the familiar English sizes at the crowded Shepherds' Bush Market. Since the Americans refused to adopt the international standard metric system of measurements, one has to be careful when buying clothing and footwear made in the USA.

After our team's meetings in Canada, we were waiting for the flight across the Atlantic Ocean to Europe at Toronto Airport, when a ground hostess informed us that there was no economy class seat for me. She suggested that we top up my ticket to get an upgrade to business class, where seats were available. Minister Chikwanda instead suggested to PS Kazunga that the two of them should downgrade from first to business class and the difference in price be used to cover the needed top up for my ticket. The variations were duly made and I was upgraded to business class without any additional cost.

I wonder as to how many current day Zambian ministers would make such a downgrading decision to the benefit of a junior officer and the government. On the trip, I took up the role of a protocol and technical officer, as Minister Chikwanda argued that he did not need an additional officer just to deal with routine issues of booking hotels and air tickets. In all the countries we visited, I was assisted by embassy staff with protocol duties.

In Brussels, Belgium, the team met officials of the Belgian Government, who offered assistance in livestock development. Our team had very productive discussions with the officers of the EEC, who offered substantial grant financial assistance to unlock Zambia's agricultural sector.

One evening as we were having dinner, I asked for a glass of fruit juice. The meal was delicious with some juicy and tender rump steak, which we were told was from neighbouring Botswana. The price for the meat dish was three times that of a beef dish in the cozy Makumbi Restaurant in Lusaka. When the waiter brought the bill, we were shocked that the price of fruit juice was four times that of alcoholic drinks. The reason given by the restaurant owner was that the fruits, including avocadoes for fruit cocktail were imported from Africa.

On some flights, we were served tasty cashew nuts from some African countries. At the time, the world price for cashew nuts was US $3,000 per tonne against that of copper at US $2,200 per tonne. The minister lamented that a few cashew nut trees would give Zambia more foreign exchange than copper at a much less capital cost.

At a restaurant by the Thames River, the management of Tate and Lyle, the sugar company, gave us a memorable send-off sumptuous lunch, which included an assortment of fresh fruits. Although this was off-season, we were informed that the mangoes for our dessert were in fact from Zambia and the manager encouraged us to develop the fruit-growing industry.

On the home-bound flight, the minister politely directed PS Kazunga to put me in business class as a reward for the work I had done on the trip and also to facilitate my writing the tour report. He jokingly stated that he did not want to lose the valuable information we'd collected should I have an uncomfortable flight.

We had a smooth flight until we ran into a heavy turbulence over the Democratic Republic of Congo (DRC), which caused the huge plane to suddenly drop some twenty metres. The rest of the flight was scary and this has remained my frightful flight through the hundreds of miles of flying. Luckily, we arrived safely in Lusaka and my elaborate tour report on the minister's trip was ready within a few days.

All the foreign governments and institutions we visited were responsive. The minister's trip resulted in the funding of a large number of projects in crop and livestock production and marketing. Where projects were already in the pipeline, funding was made available to start the new projects. In other cases, feasibility studies and research were funded. One would say that the ministry was put into cruising speed to get Zambia's agriculture on the right footing.

An immediate trial export of the delicious Zambian avocadoes to Europe was made. Unfortunately, the fruits were too large to fit in the small glasses used for prawn cocktails. We were wrong to think that the larger the fruits, the more marketable they will be. Instructions were given to immediately start a breeding and selection programme of avocados trees and fruits of the suitable market size. Arrangements were made for the importation of fourteen thousand hybrid cashew nut seedlings from South America for the Western Province.

The components of the critical path for commercial maize growing demanded independent decision-making and timely application of the farming technologies such as fertilisers. The lifestyles on customary land could not accommodate the new technology as the land was communally-owned and utilized. There was, therefore, a demand for titled land by farmers who had acquired new skills and modern technology. By this time, there were no more abandoned large farms for settlement schemes such as the Ngwezi Settlement Scheme.

In order to provide titled land, new areas were identified on traditional land for settlement of hundreds of farmers all over Zambia. One such scheme was the Mumbwa Big Concession of 100,000 hectares, which was surveyed and demarcated by the capable team of Norman Beaumont and Joseph Mutelo of Land Use Services. The target participants in our plans were rural dwellers and small-scale farmers who had the best opportunities to graduate from subsistence to medium-scale farmers.

Only a few farmers settled on the scheme for lack of title deeds and social infrastructures, such as schools and health facilities. Again, efforts to beat the unproductive customary land tenure system failed. Farming has been neglected by the educated Zambians, who feel that the industry is for the uneducated and the retirees. The clarion call of 'Back to the land' by President Kaunda fell on deaf ears as the urban population in Zambia swelled to become a great developmental challenge in the later part of the twentieth century.

In addition to encouraging small-scale farmers, we also encouraged the development and active participation of large-scale commercial farmers in producing special crops. Seeds for most of the new crops could only be efficiently produced by a few experienced and trusted commercial farmers among them Barry Coxe in Mazabuka, D. Hunt of Kabwe, Jones of Kalomo, Scholtze Neil of Chilanga, Puffet in Chilanga, and Green in Choma. Barry Coxe, who had worked with plant breeder Elijah Kaiba Mudenda in the sixties, steered the Zambia Seed Producers' Association for decades. The technical team for maize research was under the supervision of Dusan Ristanovic, who later founded the Maize Research Institute Limited (MRI SEED).

At some point, a diplomat from the Dutch Embassy in Lusaka brought a young man to our offices for an introduction. He explained to the Permanent Secretary that the young man had been an agricultural volunteer in the Northern Province under their country's technical assistance programme to Zambia. Having completed his contract, he now wished to remain in Zambia to engage in farming due to the great potential he saw.

The diplomat stated that financial institutions were demanding a reference letter from our ministry and that a letter signed by the Minister of Agriculture would be an appropriate reference.

The PS instructed me to brief the minister, who approved the request and directed me to draft a letter for him to sign. After an interview with the young man and fully satisfied with his farming ambitions and plans, I drafted a letter, which was duly signed by Minister Chikwanda. The young man, W.K. Lubrinkhof was given a loan by a commercial bank and started his farming career at the successful Mubuyu Farm (New Holland) in the Mazabuka District.

The ministry was to offer a helping hand again when Lubrinkhof wanted to buy the adjacent farm abandoned by a fleeing traitor white farmer, who had been aiding rebel Rhodesian terrorists, who were hunting down the freedom fighters. Mubuyu Farm became a successful producer and exporter of good quality Arabica coffee, which received the international Ulz Kapeh classification, qualifying it to enter the American and Japanese markets. With its various farming operations, which included cultivation and processing of many crops and rearing of fish, the farm created employment for thousands of workers.

As an alternative to individual farmer settlements, an ambitious programme of establishing 10,000-hectare state farms in all the provinces dubbed 'Operation Food Production' was conceived by the government. The programme was contrary to the earlier government policy of 'Production by the masses and not mass production' in order to provide employment opportunities for many individuals.

Officers at the Ministry of Agriculture advised that efforts must continue by providing infrastructure such as titling of land and construction of rural feeder roads for private sector development of agriculture. With Leonard Chivuno, a die-hard socialist director general at the National Commission for National Planning, our advice was ignored. Due to lack of capital and extension staff, the scheme never saw the light of the day.

While these developments were happening in the other parts of the country, there were serious challenges in developing agriculture in the Northern Province. With a large land mass, vast plains, and plentiful water, the province had great potential.

To encourage farming in the region, a new agricultural college was conceived for the area. But the idea met some resistance from those who felt that since farming was not a tradition of the northerners, the college would be underutilized.

We, therefore, planned to include a large number of students from the Southern Province at the new college, who were to be posted as extension officers into the northern region on completion of their courses. In turn, a large number of northerners who were admitted at the Monze College of Agriculture in the Southern Province, were sent to existing commercial farms in the southern region for their attachments.

Finally, the Mpika College of Agriculture was constructed and opened in 1976 with the assistance of the Swedish International Development Agency (SIDA). One unintended positive development, beyond producing agricultural graduates, was that a good number of Tonga graduates decided to settle in the Northern Province to engage in farming instead of being extension officers. They were lured by the abundant land and water resources.

This 'foreign' farming community played an important role in supplying food to the fast-rising population of Mpika Town, which became the Zambian Regional Headquarters of the Tanzania Zambia Railway. They also played a role by practically demonstrating viable modern farming to the local people, who were practising the primitive *chitemene* system. With the urging of Minister Chikwanda, some local Chiefs embraced these 'foreigners' by willingly allocating them the much-needed land. The mixing of students in agricultural training institutions produced nationalists, who were conversant and competent in both ciBemba and ciTonga languages.

The introduction of cattle rearing in the northern region of Zambia posed a more serious challenge as the people were not traditional cattle keepers apart from those on the border in the Mbala and Nakonde areas. State ranches were established and stocked with young animals to provide breeding stock to the farmers.

Unfortunately, the mortality rates were very high, although there were no deadly diseases in the area. We attributed this to the prevalent lumpy-skin disease due to heavy rainfall and to poor management. However, we were puzzled as there were no carcasses of dead animals found on the ranch. The management claimed that the dead cattle were eaten by wild animals. Still, there were no bones found.

While seeking ways of improving management on state ranches, Minister Chikwanda invited George Cornhill, one of his friends from Monze, to establish a model private ranch in the Northern Province. The minister felt that his friend with large herds of cattle in the Southern Province would provide the breeding stock and demonstrate best practice in cattle management. Attracted by the abundant land, Cornhill accepted the invitation and opened a large ranch in Mpika, which was stocked with animals from his ranches in the Southern Province.

Within a short period, the privately-owned ranch had similar problems of high mortality like those of the state ranches. Thorough investigations revealed that the cattle were actually being slaughtered for the pot (*munani*) by the ranch workers. We'd failed to use indigenous knowledge to introduce a farming activity related to the people's culture. Both the state and private ranches failed to achieve the objective of introducing cattle in the region as a wealth-creating asset.

At some point, I led a team of planners from the FAO to check on the suitability of the Chambeshi plains for rice growing. I was amazed with the plentiful surface water abundantly available in the region. A meeting was convened at Mulema, south-east of Kasama, on the banks of the Chambeshi River to discuss our plans. As we were explaining the benefits of growing rice, we were asked how long it took to get income from rice. Having given the answer of four to five months, one villager stood up and after excusing himself, he left the meeting. We all assumed that he was not interested in what we were discussing.

The gentleman came back within one hour with some fish. He immediately asked to intervene in the discussions and asked me if I wanted some fish (*isabi*). After I answered in the affirmative, a deal was made and I paid the fisherman and the fish was delivered to our vehicle. The fisherman then asked us why we wanted them to labour and wait for four months to earn some income from rice, when they could earn money from fish within one hour. We had not planned for development of fishing in the Chambeshi and Luapula rivers as there was no reliable data on fish stocks.

I was not from a rice growing or fishing area. This was one occasion when my university education and loft development ideas met the strongest challenge from indigenous knowledge and traditions. Having no convincing answer to give to the villager, we closed the meeting and the vast open Chambeshi plains have remained 'undeveloped', in my assessment.

On our way to Kasama Town, we stopped to ask a villager why he did not deliver his four bags of maize to the nearest maize depot. He answered that he only grew the maize because of the agricultural extension officers who encouraged him to try the new crop. He expected those who had a use for the maize to buy and collect it from his homestead.

In spite of the challenges in our plans to introduce maize, rice, and cattle production in the Northern Province, we were still determined to introduce some commercial agricultural activity in the area. We envisaged that coffee growing could be a good proposition for commercial small-scale production on the plateau of the Province. Coffee was a perennial tree, which did not require annual planting and costly management. The price of Arabica coffee on the international market was much higher than that of copper.

Together with two project planners from the World Bank, I flew to Kasama in a four-seater plane. I played the role of the co-pilot, since I knew the geography of the area. We got a vehicle from the local agricultural officers and toured the Kateshi and Ngoli areas near Kasama Town and travelled north up to Nseluka. We were happy with what we saw, as there had been a thriving coffee estate at Ngoli in the past and a few scattered plots in the area planted by missionaries. Our conversations with the villagers were encouraging as the villagers appeared willing to engage in the growing of coffee.

It was during this trip that I was introduced to *cikanda*, the Bemba 'polony', produced from some mashed wild tubers. We discussed the possibility of domesticating the cikanda plant, so that it could be grown commercially. Unfortunately, the villagers brought in so many myths about the plant and the traditional way of preparing the cikanda, which discouraged us from further developing our plans. Since then, I have not heard of any efforts made by any Zambian agricultural scientist to domesticate the cikanda plant.

The crop experts continue to spend large sums of money and time on maize, a crop long domesticated in 5000 BC by the natives of South America. Interestingly enough, cikanda has found an assured place on the high tables in most social gatherings such as state banquets, kitchen parties and weddings in Zambia.

In the northern region of Zambia, cassava tubers and the leaves (katapa) were the commonest foods for the majority of the people. Regrettably, the crop had been given a bad name just after Zambia's independence as an inferior food. During the trip, one of the World Bank officers, who was from South America, where cassava was an important food and industrial item, tried to have conversations on the crop with the local people. But the subject did not seem to be of interest to the local people.

I later reported our experiences on cassava during our trip to Minister Chikwanda, who encouraged me to direct the officers in the department of agriculture to include cassava in the crop research programme. The resistance from the officers was intense and as my efforts were not succeeding, I arranged for a meeting between the minister and the director.

I still recall the cynical remark made by Nicholas Mumba, the director of agriculture, during the meeting. Luckily, the minister regarded the offending remark as a joke from a traditional cousin and instructed the director to organise a study tour to Nigeria, where researchers had developed prolific and short-maturing cassava breeds. I learnt of a belated trip much after there were changes of staff in the department of agriculture.

From Kasama, we flew to Nakonde, taking a very low elevation to check on the suitability of the vegetation along the flight route. The expert pilot, who was at our command, did not explain that our action of flying low would consume more jet fuel. After a short local tour and shopping in Nakonde, we took off for Lusaka as it was late in the afternoon.

Somewhere south of Mpika Town, the pilot informed us that he was not sure of the route and we were likely to go astray. He stated that should we use a longer route, we would run out of fuel and crash land. It was, therefore, my responsibility as the co-pilot to suggest how best we could get to Lusaka with the limited time and fuel at our disposal.

Using my scouting compass and map reading skills, I realized that we were somewhere between the Luangwa River and the Great North Road. I advised the pilot to fly in an easterly direction until we reached a big river, which was the Luangwa River. Then we flew southwards over the river until we reached the Luangwa bridge. We then turned westwards and flew over the Great East Road, which led us to Lusaka.

By the time we'd established contact with the Lusaka Control Tower, it was getting dark and it was already past the authorized time for landing. After some explanations and negotiations, we were allowed to land. The aircraft manifest was inspected and found harmless. We bought a lot of beef at Nakonde due to the price advantage. We shared some of the meat with the 'kind' airport control officers and we all happily knocked off.

The team prepared a coffee project that included the financing of the estate and small-scale farmers and the establishment of a factory at Kateshi. The coffee project prepared in 1978 was later implemented with the establishment of the Kateshi Coffee Estate and Factory but without the involvement of the small-scale farmers. The villagers were consigned to the role of lowly paid coffee pickers, which was not our intention when designing the project in 1978. As we had included funds for coffee growers in other parts of Zambia, some commercial farmers on the Copperbelt and in the Southern Province took up coffee growing and made a success of it.

Due to various projects in research and extension, the production of maize increased, necessitating the construction of new maize storage facilities. These were constructed at various depots in the Central Province under EU and CIDA funding. With increased production, the cost of maize marketing by the NAMB was rising and the subsidy becoming untenable.

The minister directed that a comprehensive audit be done to establish the true quantities of maize and the cost of marketing, which included storage. The instruction for the audit exercise included the physical counting of maize bags in selected warehouses.

The audit came up with startling revelations on the amount of theft and fraudulent claims of the subsidy by the staff of the board. At head office, huge payments for transport claims had been made to an officer owning a Fiat 127 saloon car purported to have delivered a number of thirty-tonne loads of maize!

At the newly constructed storage unit at the Mwachisompola depot in Chibombo District, the available stock of maize was less than half of what had been submitted for the subsidy claim. Some senior managers of NAMBoard were dismissed. A recommendation was made for the dissolution of the organization and the transfer of the maize marketing function to the Provincial Marketing Cooperative Unions (PMCUs).

The mismanagement of maize marketing extended to fertiliser, the most important input in modern farming. Large quantities of fertilisers were being transported to the northern region constituting Region I without production of a commensurate quantity of maize. An exercise done revealed that one bag of fertiliser in Region I produced one bag of maize, while one bag of fertiliser in Region II produced more than three bags of maize. Apart from heavy application of fertilisers due to soil acidity, a substantial quantity of the fertiliser sent to Region I was being smuggled out into neighbouring countries.

Due to the excellent relations between President Kaunda and President Tito of Yugoslavia, a tour of three weeks was arranged for Mukutu, Imanga Kaliangile, and I in August 1979 to study the Yugoslav agricultural industry and the cooperative movement. We arrived at Split, the entry point into Yugoslavia, from Rome at about 17.00 hours. From there we took a domestic flight to Belgrade, the capital city. The hustling to get into planes was worse than that at an up-country bus stop.

Finally, we managed to get into a plane at 19.30 hours and got into Belgrade at 20.00 hours. We cleared ourselves in another thirty minutes and waited in the VIP lounge for a Government official. The airport was about to close at 22.00 hours when someone posing as a taxi driver approached us. Since he was one of the few people still at the airport, we accepted his offer and told him the name of the hotel, where we were booked.

On the way, we continued to discuss the poor reception that we were being subjected to by our hosts. The driver kept on fidgeting with the 'radio' or so we thought. By a stray glance at the ceiling of the car, I saw a zip and a microphone pointed at us in the back seat. I alerted Mukutu in vernacular and we decided not to use English in our conversation.

We arrived at the hotel late in the night and our team leader placed the blame on a delayed flight. Brother Mukutu was teaching me some diplomacy, in which it is believed that there are also 'acceptable lies'. More discoveries of listening devices were made during our stay in the country under a communist regime, which relished on eavesdropping on foreigners in order to get some information.

During the trip, we were shown large state farms with impressive crop varieties, fish farms, grapevine fields, and wine-making factories. At a 100-hectare fish farm traversed by a maze of railway lines, we had a four-hour luncheon, during which we tasted nearly twenty brands of locally-made wine.

Towards the end of an enjoyable eight-course meal of fish, the hosts asked us to sign a proposal they had prepared to enter into an agreement on some technical assistance to Zambia. Since we had studied the draft earlier and found it not in the interest of Zambia, Mukutu the team leader refused to sign. The hosts were very surprised that the large quantity of wine we imbibed had not mellowed us.

When we got back home, we made appropriate amendments to the proposed agreement and a strong partnership developed between the Yugoslav and Zambian crop scientists in crop seed propagation. A large number of seed varieties suitable for the various rainfall zones of Zambia were produced at different research stations and by 1980, new improved seed varieties were readily available.

While flying back home, Mukutu proposed that we should continue to enjoy the lavish lifestyle by making our own wine as the technology we saw during the tour was simple. By the following weekend, I attempted making some wine from mulberry fruits from the tree in our yard. After three days, there was no fermentation. A review showed that I had not properly followed the elaborate notes. While we condemned the initial product, it qualified as mulberry jam and my family enjoyed the new product. I tried again, taking more care in following the notes made by the scientist and the result was much better, with an acceptable level of alcohol.

During the next four years, we lived like kings throwing lavish Christmas and New Year's parties, where our guests drowned themselves in home-made wines. We experimented with various indigenous domestic and wild fruits such as masuku and marula.

The wine-making process involves tasting the wine during the racking stages. Perhaps because of my small body, I became allergic to the fungus produced during the fermentation process. I stopped making and drinking wine in 1984. I became alcohol-free as I had stopped drinking beer in December 1980. Being a believer in the Bible, I occasionally obey the advice of Apostle Paul as given to the Corinthians at 1st Timothy Chapter 5 verse 23 with a glass of red wine.

In 1985, Mukutu went commercial and produced quality wine, some of which was served by local hotels as 'house wine' under the Ntandabale brand. He continued to improve his quality and brands with some of the wine finding a ready export market in neighbouring countries. This ingenuity by a patriot was regrettably frustrated by some overzealous tax man, who wanted to get more tax revenue than the total income of a promising small-scale wine industry. Mukutu decided to abandon his promising wine-making cottage industry early in the twenty-first century and turned the winery buildings into a cotton ginnery.

In November 1979, I was in the presidential delegation to the Republic of Iraq. Presidents Kaunda and Saddam Hussein were very close associates. Among the officials in the delegation were Dominic Chela Mulaisho, Leonard Chivuno, Lishomwa Muuka, Akashambatwa Mbikushita Lewanika, Mubanga Chipoya, and Davison Mulela from various sectors of the Zambian economy. I was happy to be in the land of al-Khwarizmi, the famous mathematician, who developed the quadrant. I had the honour and pleasure of meeting President Saddam Hussein during the discussions.

At the time of our visit, the Iraqi Government had made tremendous progress in the provision of free education, subsidized health services and infrastructure. This was made possible by windfall revenues due to the increased oil prices in 1973 from the oil industry, which had been nationalized in 1972. After the '1976 Baghdad Conference for the Eradication of Illiteracy', the Government provided free education to all and by 1982, the country won a UNESCO prize for eradicating illiteracy as school enrolment was 100 per cent. In agriculture, reforms were introduced which provided surveyed farmlands and appropriate irrigation infrastructure to many ordinary citizens.

Our visit was to study the many programmes that benefitted from the oil revenues. We visited a large number of education and health projects within Baghdad City. We toured some very large irrigation projects watered from the Euphrates River, on the way to the biblical city of Babylon. The buildings in the city, although old in appearance were an engineering marvel in design.

On the day of our departure from Bagdad Airport, the plane was about to taxi when President Kaunda realized that Dominic Mulaisho, Special Assistant (Economics), was not on the plane. Suddenly, we saw someone frantically waving while running across the tarmac towards the plane. We were gripped with fear that one of the many armed marksmen surrounding the airport will open fire and gun him down.

When he got to the plane, he looked up at the window where President Kaunda was seated. That is when we realized that it was Mulaisho. The president gave instructions to the crew to retrieve the ramp and they opened for Mulaisho, who climbed into the plane.

Having settled down, Mulaisho was advised by his traditional cousin Lishomwa that, 'If you continue your bad habit of arriving late for events, you will miss the opportunity of entering heaven'. To which Mulaisho retorted, 'I hope that some angel kind enough like H.E. will be available to open the door for me'. This sent us into laughter as the plane took off for Zambia.

In Chama and Lundazi, the extreme north of the Eastern Province, rice was being grown as a subsistence food crop. We, therefore, decided to involve the locals in commercial production. However, we were more careful when interacting with the villagers in view of the Mulema experience. We asked Africare of the USA to partner with the Zambian Government in introducing high-yielding rice varieties.

We visited Lundazi with Africare officials to see if there were other alternative income-generating activities. Since there were no viable income-earning alternatives, the rice project was readily accepted by the small-scale farmers. Although on a relatively small-scale level, the project was successful and continued to produce the famous and tasty Chama rice.

Study tours in the 1970s by Zambian Government officials to different parts of the world enriched the capacity of ministry officers to plan the accelerated development of the country's agricultural industry. We had all the necessary information to design a long-term vision of Zambia's agriculture as the future engine of growth.

Often times, ABC repeated to us former Minister Kamanga's statement made in 1964 that, "If in Kenya and Ghana they did it, why can't we also did it." Although the English by the old man was not correct and was in reference to the freedom struggle, Kenya did excel in the production of flower, tea, coffee, vegetables, and pyrethrum to become a role model of national development without mining in Africa.

By 1980, we had started, revamped and planned a large number of institutions to handle the production, marketing and processing of various crops and livestock products. Apart from crop production and processing companies, new companies to provide locally made and imported farming equipment and credit were established.

These included the African Farming Equipment (AFE) for sale of farm equipment, Batoka Cross-breeding Ranch for cattle breeding, NATCO for tobacco processing, LENCO for manufacturing of farm implements, ZAMSEED for seed production and processing, the Kawambwa Tea Company, the Mununshi banana plantation, the Msekera Research Station and Katete factory for groundnuts.

Other companies and schemes were Rural Air Services for aerial spraying of crops, Zambia Pork Products for pig production and processing, Lundazi, and Chama schemes for rice production.

However, in view of the acute shortage of qualified manpower in Zambia in the seventies, the ministry relied heavily on foreign economists and other professionals from international multilateral and donor organizations such as Agro-progress, ADB, CIDA, EU, FAO, IFAD, MASDAR, SIDA, USAID, and WB to prepare projects. I had the honour and privilege of accompanying these foreign experts into the Zambian countryside on project identification. Many of the foreign technocrats I worked with during this period became close associates of mine for many years after and some featured prominently in my later life.

I had a hand in planning the establishment of many agricultural development projects and companies in Zambia. I took part in the search and selection of the managers for these companies. My involvement sharpened my planning skills and widened my knowledge of Zambia and its enormous agricultural potential. For my professional career development, the challenges during the period 1974 to 1980 tested my professional skills and patriotism. Most of my seniors built and elevated my self-confidence during the numerous trips on which I accompanied them. Many taught me survival skills and manners for the modern world.

Many of my workmates extended unequalled etiquette and lavishly introduced me to those we had the privilege to meet. For example, the ground staff at Toronto Airport must have wondered as to who I was to make a very important person (VIP) give up his comfort in first class to downgrade to a lower class for my comfort. It was the sacrifices of so many such people that my status and professional confidence rose very fast at an early age.

During this period, I was an external examiner for courses at the Natural Resources Development College (NRDC). In 1978, I with a Canadian colleague helped the University of Zambia to design the curriculum of the new agricultural economics courses. Later in 2002, I offered to sponsor an award for the Best Overall Graduating Student in Agricultural Economics in the Bachelor of Agricultural Sciences. It took over two years for the university to answer and approve my generous offer.

I'd planned to create a think tank on agricultural development in Zambia consisting of all the award winners. Without an active tracer programme by the university, it was not possible to locate the award winners once they'd left the university. The Ng'andu Magande Floating Trophy and cash prize was intermittently awarded with the last being on 30 October 2009 to Ms Maureen M. Zulu, as there was no further communication between me and the University of Zambia.

CHAPTER 8

The Politics Of Land Ownership In Zambia

My research on the Magoye Settlement Scheme in 1974 revealed a high correlation between land ownership and crop productivity. My hope was that the Government would use the results to revolutionize agriculture in Zambia. The approval by the Ministry of Agriculture of my maiden project on sugarcane small-scale farming gave me a lot of confidence and encouragement in my work to transform Zambia's agriculture.

Victims of Zambia's land tenure system
I proposed an ambitious land consolidation scheme covering the whole of the Mazabuka District. The proposal was to survey, demarcate, subdivide, and equitably allocate the land and give title deeds to all farmers including small-scale farmers. The project was to be on the same lines as the settlement schemes I'd seen during my tours in East Africa on the Highlands of Kenya and was to reinforce my research findings.

The World Bank provided officers who assisted in preparing the Mixed Farming Development Project (MFDP). After the feasibility study, the officers supported an application for financing to the World Bank and a concessional loan of US $28 million was approved. This was my first contact with the World Bank. Unfortunately, the project could not get cabinet approval for fear of the reaction of the traditional leaders to land titling. This became my second project to suffer from the dual land tenure system under which the traditional leaders have a stronger voice in the utilization of Zambia's most important asset.

A large number of poor people were denied an opportunity to get title deeds for the pieces of land they were using. I still imagine the amount of wealth that the Mazabuka Mixed Farming Development Project, whose major theme was titling customary land, would have generated for the villagers who would have graduated into small-scale farmers.

After the failure of the Mazabuka project, I decided to investigate the relationship between Zambia's independence struggle and land ownership. During my research on small-scale farming, I read much on freedom struggles based on land alienation in many parts of Africa. In a number of countries, the independence struggles were focused on the need to wrestle land from the colonialists, who had settled on the best farmland. In Zambia, the locals were driven some fifty kilometres away from the railway track from Livingstone to Ndola and the land allocated to white settlers. This strip of land has continued to be the most productive area, which produces the largest quantity of Zambia's agricultural commodities.

I discovered that Zambia's independence struggle did not include land ownership, equitable distribution, and secure property rights as major bargaining issues. The freedom fighters anchored their fight on equitable distribution of social services such as schools, hospitals, and housing and the stoppage of the poll tax. In fact, a number of freedom fighters belonged to royal families and therefore could not fight the traditional land tenure system in which they were beneficiaries. The traditional governance systems survived by extracting wealth from the subjects.

On 19 April 1968, His Excellency, the President Dr K.D. Kaunda, gave a landmark speech at Mulungushi Rock of Authority on Zambia's Economic Revolution. He stated that, "The government is also responsible for providing the required structures to encourage development in our farming sector throughout the country. The whole land tenure system must be geared to provide those securities needed to encourage investments to improve the land, required by a modern agriculture. But we must avoid a rigid system, often accompanied by private ownership of the land".

In his long speech, the president mentioned a lot of issues as prerequisites and priorities for rural development. But land, which is Zambia's most valuable economic base asset was mentioned only four times, while land ownership system only once.

Costly commissions of enquiry, such as the Sakala Commission of Enquiry on land distribution in the Southern Province, in general, and Mazabuka District, in particular, were established. With the Commission's conclusion that one family of immigrants, who owned 30,000 hectares of land was using it productively and should not be disturbed, it was obvious that indigenous Zambians had been short-changed on their birthright. Even when the ninety-nine-year leases expire, some corrupt Zambian land officers renew them for another ninety-nine years, giving ownership to land for one hundred ninety eight years, with no consideration for equitable sharing with the indigenous younger generation.

Thirty-eight years after KK's speech, President Mwanawasa stated the following in his speech to the First Session of the Tenth National Assembly on 27 October 2006.

'Mr Speaker, my government is determined to have a Zambia in which there is equitable access to land and security of tenure for the sustainable socio-economic development of the people. During this five-year term of office, a new land policy to address the multitude of constraints will be developed.

Mr Speaker, in view of the fact that almost ninety per cent of the total land area of our country is in customary areas, I wish to implore all our traditional rulers to release part of the land in their respective chiefdoms for investment'.

Sometime in 1978, I requested my Permanent Secretary to allocate me some farmland where I could grow some crops and compare my costs of production with those presented by the farmers. Due to a general lack of interest in farming at the time, there was no senior government official with a large commercial farm. Many preferred to get plots in the semi-urban areas of major towns, where they constructed family homes.

As the Lands Department was under our ministry, I was convinced that my request would be easily accommodated. After a long chuckle, the PS asked, 'Peter, do you really need land at your age? You are too young for such'. At the time, I was thirty-one years old. I was shocked by the PS's reaction, as I was aware that my father who was already fifty-four years of age still had no titled land. I stared at the PS for a while, before I quietly stood up and walked to the door, which I banged behind me.

Most senior politicians and civil servants wanted to settle and had been allocated plots in the Makeni and other semi-urban areas and not in their original villages. The law for getting a mortgage from the Zambia National Building Society (ZNBS) for house construction required one to have a title deed for the land he intended to develop.

The general manager of ZNBS who was a close relative of Simon Chushi, my former schoolmate at Munali Secondary School, encouraged me to apply for a mortgage. But I could not get a mortgage because I had no titled land anywhere in the world.

Since no title deeds were being given for traditional land where villagers lived, the financing from ZNBS excluded the majority of Zambian citizens. This is the reason why the peri-urban areas are inhabited mostly by retired senior public workers and for the lack of modern houses in their Zambian villages.

My application forms for land submitted between 1978 and 2010 have laid in the files buried in thick dust in the Choma, Gwembe Kabwe, Livingstone, Lusaka, Mazabuka and Siavonga Council offices.

When I worked in Mazabuka in 1966, I became close to the Dawoodjee and Ticklay families, who owned large shops in the central business district of the town. Our relationship blossomed when I lived at Magoye in 1974 and later when I visited the town on personal and official duties.

In 1975, Ismail Dawoodjee, a prosperous businessman, decided to sell his properties in the Mazabuka central business district after the June 1975 Watershed Speech by President Kaunda. He offered me his shop and house to buy and offered the butchery to Japhet Choombe, a manager with the Dairy Produce Board. The old man advised me to form a cooperative society with friends in order to widen the ownership of the big shop as per the policy of

KK's administration. I invited some friends and we formed Lukamantano Cooperative Society.

The business plan by the cooperative, a grouping of fourteen educated professionals, highly impressed the old man, such that he decided to offer us to buy all his property in the central business district (CBD) of Mazabuka town. The management of the Zambia National Building Society (ZNBS) showed keen interest to finance the acquisition of the property, on condition that the cooperative society was registered.

The registration of the cooperative society was denied by the Mazabuka District Development Committee (MDDC). The objectors led by Joshua Lumina, a deputy minister then, who lived on Bbata cooperative farm at Turnpike, argued that we were not residents of Mazabuka and that we were too educated to run a cooperative society. The objectors then made a counter offer to buy the property because they were residents of Mazabuka. The offer was rejected by the vendor as he did not consider the applicants capable of managing the property. The opportunity for indigenous local people to own the property in the CBD of Mazabuka was lost due to rivalry among Zambians.

In 1984, while serving in Kabwe as Provincial Permanent Secretary, consideration of my application for a residential plot by the Kabwe Council could not be made because "he will soon be transferred from here and will not build a house. After all, he does not even come from this Province".

In 1995, I applied and attended interviews in Siavonga for a plot where we intended to build a retreat house on the shores of Lake Kariba. The plot was allocated to us by the Siavonga Council. As we were about to submit our building plan, the plot was repossessed because "it was allocated in error as it had already been allocated to someone else".

We discovered that the 'someone else' was a foreign NGO that came to Zambia under the pretext of coming to help poor Zambians. The foreign NGO was now competing with Zambians in acquiring land, one of the most important assets in wealth creation and poverty reduction.

After many visits to Siavonga for discussions with the council officials, we were allocated an alternative plot far away from the shores of Lake Kariba. When we went to inspect the plot, we found a foundation had already been erected by 'someone else'. This time around, the 'someone else' was a relative of an officer of the council.

In September 2010, we were visited at our home in Chilanga by their Royal Highnesses Chiefs Monze, Macha, and Hanjalika. As they were about to leave, Chief Macha took time to survey and admire the modern house surrounded by a neatly kempt garden.

He then asked Chief Hanjalika, my chief, if he had given me some land in my home area. Chief Hanjalika replied that I did not have any, but that I had a commercial farm somewhere in Choma. I then interjected to talk about my frustrations for not getting land in my home area. I talked about the failed

Namaila Community Game Ranch Project and my failure to get land anywhere in the whole Mazabuka District.

"Ba-Mwami, you should have given your subject some land so that a beautiful structure like this one will have been standing in your Chiefdom. It would have added a lot of value to your area," Chief Macha said to Chief Hanjalika.

Some months later, I met Chief Macha at the offices of the Commissioner of Lands in Lusaka, where he had come to collect title deeds for a surveyed piece of land in his chiefdom. He informed me that he was encouraging his subjects to convert traditional land into titled land for security of tenure and proper land use. The chief demonstrated this by constructing a modern piggery on his new titled land.

I am certain that Chief Macha will be so proud when one of his subjects acquires title to a piece of land within the chiefdom and constructs a maize mill to produce and supply livestock feed to him and other farmers. The Chief's trips to Lusaka to buy livestock feed are unnecessary as the chiefdom produces surplus maize, which can easily be processed locally into feed.

I have known a large number of highly educated Zambians whose origins are the typical rural areas of Zambia. The country's land tenure system has not allowed these daughters and sons of Zambia to pay back the rural communities for their early upbringing by settling amongst them. Many of us have opted to settle elsewhere as our ancestral villages cannot accommodate our modern development plans.

My close Lozi associates, among them Situmbeko Musokotwane, Geoffrey Lungwangwa, Mwilola Imakando, Muyoba Macwani, Stephen Muliokela, Namukolo Mukutu, Muyunda Mwanalushi, Oliver Saasa, and Dennis Wood cannot get their development plans through the Lozi traditional system in the Western Province.

It is sad that these educated Lozis have failed to implement meaningful developmental projects for themselves and their ancestral communities. Instead, these members of the Lozi elite have beautiful modern houses and highly productive fenced farmlands with healthy cattle and crops albeit far away from the Western Province.

The people of the Eastern Province have a history of trekking to the mines in South Africa and Southern Rhodesia. After Zambia's independence, they relocated to the new urban areas and established permanent settlements. In remembrance of the abandoned large traditional circular villages they left in the Eastern Province, they have christened the unplanned urban settlements with beautiful names from the province, such as Kamanga, Chawama, Mwaziona, and Mtendere.

Most of these educated urbanites have no plans to go back home as there is no titled land on which to build modern homes. Some have dared to return to their villages after long absences. But with meagre salaries and retirement benefits, they became the subject of a satirical song entitled 'A Phiri Anabwela' sung by Nashil Pitchen Kazemba in the seventies.

A few of my educated Tonga tribesmen, who retired and returned to the Southern Province bought and settled on titled farmlands abandoned along the line of rail by white settlers running away from Zambia's independence. The majority of the Tonga retirees are crammed in the Makeni and Chilanga areas of Lusaka.

My educated friends and associates from the Northern Province are stranded in the urban areas, where they have constructed heavenly mansions. The majority of the rich northern elites have settled in a secluded area, east of Lusaka City on Chieftainess Nkomeshya Mukamambo's land. Overwhelmed by nostalgia for their homeland and to reduce their hidden frustrations, they named their new settlement New Kasama after the capital of the Northern Province. I am not sure if they even got the permission of the BashiluBemba or that of Chieftainess Nkomenshya for their action.

No one of the friends, classmates, or workmates I have mentioned in the story of my life has built a house in their so-called villages in the rural areas. Zambia's rural areas cannot develop when the majority of the educated and enlightened Zambians invest their incomes and skills in urban areas because of the unaccommodating traditional land tenure system.

In December 2012, I took my family to Siavonga for Christmas holidays. Due to lack of accommodation in lodges and hotels, we stayed on a boat anchored on the shores of Lake Kariba. Minister Masebo who met us on the boat during a cruise was shocked to learn that we were staying on the boat and not in our own house. After an explanation of the circumstances for our stay on the boat, the minister asked the council officials to allocate me a plot in the newly demarcated town extension site.

We have not been informed of the decision of the council to the minister's request. I intend to pursue the matter of a substitute stand as promised in 1995, when Stand 894 was taken away without good cause. A number of foreigners who have been allocated plots in Siavonga have constructed lodges. The foreign lodge owners get paid in their countries of origin for boarding and meals, thereby depriving the country of foreign exchange.

In spite of all the titles and designations people give me and the service I have rendered to my motherland, I still cannot be allocated a plot by six district councils, including Mazabuka District where I was born. My family has settled far away from Namaila as I could not find land to establish even a community project. The incident with my PS in 1978 has always resurfaced as I have often seen and heard many frustrated young Zambians who have failed to acquire land in their own country.

I am aware that many Zambians are given plots of land by councils after being pronounced dead by the medical experts. These tiny plots are of no earthly value to a Zambian whose only duty at that point is to contaminate the six feet deep plot with the calcium phosphate from their rotten bones.

Due to the improved education facilities, many Zambians have acquired the skills to engage in modern farming and apply contemporary architecture. Commercial, productive, and technologically advanced agriculture, and modern architecture cannot coexist with traditional undefined land tenure systems in the rural areas of modern Zambia. But the modernity is so unequal that it has left many Zambians far behind.

Legal documents, such as passports and national registration cards for many Zambians bear names of villages and chiefdoms, which have no relevance to the livelihoods of the bearers. The patriotism of many landless Zambians and Zambia's noble motto of 'One Zambia, One Nation' are being compromised by a deficient land tenure system.

An innovative idea I have floated to my bosses has been that every Zambian citizen must be alloted a one-acre plot anywhere in Zambia at the time they acquire a National Registration Card (NRC). The nine digits of the NRC, which are exclusive to Zambian citizens, must be part of the plot number given to an adult Zambian at the age of sixteen years. I am convinced that owning a part of Zambia will arouse a high sense of patriotism amongst the Zambians, which currently is lacking.

In contravention of all presidential wishes over a forty-year period, my offsprings whose great-grandparents were driven out of the rich ancestral lands on the plains of the Kafue River, to make way for white settlers, have continued to eke a living in the barren hills of Namaila. Those who pluck up the courage to migrate to urban areas end up in the sordid unplanned settlements of Chibolya, Kabobola, Makululu, and Malota. I call this 'Zambia's bizarre land tenure system' of which I have been one of the hapless and helpless victims.

The agricultural economist goes farming

During the execution of my duties in the Ministry of Agriculture, I was privileged to visit foreign countries on study tours of agricultural and agro industries. Having visited so many countries, at times I spent a lot of time sharing my experiences with my family. In some of the countries I visited, my hosts took me to their modern homes constructed in their villages or on their farms.

One day in 1981, I was lamenting to my spouse about the amount of free time I had and my frustrations at not having been allowed to take up the employment with the African Development Bank (AfDB) in 1979. Joyce proposed that we look for a farm so that I could use my spare time and put into practice my vast reservoir of knowledge on agriculture. I wondered if this was possible as we had already failed to get land from some district councils and I had no land at Namaila.

The Tobacco Board of Zambia (TBZ) was disengaging from direct production operations to concentrate on the buying and processing of tobacco.

When they advertised some farms for lease, Joyce encouraged me to apply. Joyce and I settled for a farm in the Popota area of Choma District. We took some hours checking the soils in the fields and walking along the streams checking the water availability. I then submitted my application to TBZ with Farm No. 1631 in the Popota Area of Choma as the first choice.

The interviewing panel at the TBZ was chaired by Joseph Mutelo, a senior officer in the Department of Agriculture. Others included Brian Irwin, chairman of the Tobacco Association of Zambia (TAZ), the organization for tobacco farmers. In spite of the precise answers I gave as I had inspected our choice farm, Irwin put it bluntly that he would not recommend me. When pressed by the chairman for his reasons, he said that I only had theoretical knowledge of farming and that I could not manage tobacco, which is a complicated crop.

I felt that Irwin's comment was an affront to my personality. I replied that tobacco growing was as easy as growing oilseed rape, of which we had a thriving crop in our family garden at Chelston. I invited Irwin to pass by and see the vegetable crop. This impolite answer to an impolite remark ended my interview.

During those days, tobacco was not only a 'complicated' crop, but it was a special lucrative crop, grown and traded amongst white farmers and foreign buyers. The crop was the first one to be supported by a loan from the World Bank in the sixties. The crop has a long growing season starting with a nursery and firewood cutting in July, through various growing operations in the field and curing and packaging in specially made barns. The final product is delivered to the Lusaka floors in June of the following year, where the bales are lined up into rows for inspection by buyers who determine the prices for each bale. Normally, there are over 100 grades and a price for each grade of tobacco.

The crop was labour-intensive and due to the continuous operations, it stabilized farm employment. In spite of this, I felt that the comment by the TAZ chairman that I could not grow tobacco was demeaning and I looked forward to a day I would prove him wrong.

The truth of the matter was that my father had taught me how to remove suckers from the tomato and tobacco plants which he grew in the family vegetable garden on the banks of the Likoma River. He then pounded the tobacco leaves and moulded them into balls, which he sold.

Contrary to Irwins objections, I was shortlisted and my name was submitted to the Lands Board at the Ministry of Lands for further interviews. The interviews by the Lands Board were even more difficult as the chairman of the board, Stephen Mwiinga took a hard line with me.

To most of my answers, even when I described the soil types on the farm we'd inspected, the chairman remarked, "Do not be too technical, we know you are educated. Just give us straight answers." I was baffled with the chairman's hostility towards me during the interviews as he already had a large farm. Uncle Fred Mudenda, who became my neighbour played a vital role in my being allocated the farm as he had some incriminating information on the chairman's dealings, which he threatened to disclose to the board.

PS Andrew Hamaamba, Deputy Minister Joshua Lumina, TAZ Chairman Irwin, and Lands Chairman Mwiinga, all influential people in public service felt that I did not deserve to get some titled land in my own country. According to them, I was 'too young', 'too ignorant', 'too technical and educated', or 'not a local resident'.

Finally, I was allocated my priority farm by the Lands Board. Coincidentally, the Choma farm, where grandfather Matongo had worked in his youth, is the same farm my family was given and later bought from the Tobacco Board of Zambia (TBZ). Neighbouring Village Headman Hacoobe, who was introduced to us as Joyce's uncle, confirmed that he'd worked with Matongo on the farm.

I was related to Matongo, while Joyce was related to Hacoobe and we bought a farm where our two grandparents had worked together some sixty years earlier. In Tonga mythology, we call such coincidental happenings as 'callings of the spirits (mizimo)'. Was this coincidence going to be helpful in our farming enterprise?

During the first season in 1982/83, we had no agricultural implements. As a start, we used hand hoes to plant early-maturing maize on the ridges that had been used for tobacco growing during the previous season.

The inhabitants of the neighbouring sprawling village mocked us that we were too young to succeed in using the large farm. They were frustrated that the TBZ, who'd provided them with employment, had ceased farming operations. Luckily, the rains were good during that season and we had a reasonably good maize harvest.

In 1983, while at the Ministry of Finance, I applied for a car loan, which was approved. Instead of using the money to buy a car, I bought a brand new tractor, trailer, and implements from the African Farming Equipment (AFE) company. When I could not present the Blue Book for the car after three months as per standing loan rules, PS Kazunga summoned me to his office.

When asked on what I had used the loan, I admitted that I had bought farming implements instead of a car. I presented the Blue Book for the new tractor to the PS. After explaining my farming ambitions, the PS decided to accelerate the repayment of the loan as a penalty for diverting the car loan. I accepted the punishment because I was confident that I would easily pay off the loan after the crop sales.

During the 1983/84 season, we planted a maize crop on 300 hectares and a small field of sunflowers. In view of the loan, I spent a lot of time at the farm in Choma in order to supervise farm operations. I was at the farm every Friday evening and returned to Lusaka on Sunday evening.

One day, I drove for over four hours from Choma to Lusaka in heavy rain, at night. By the time I arrived home, I was very tired. During the night, our home was visited by uninvited guests, who took the windscreen. By the time we woke up in the morning, there was a pool of water inside the car.

My frequent trips to Choma attracted the attention of the Special Branch, who must have been trailing me. Under the Leadership Code, a set of rules on good governance for civil servants, I was not supposed to engage in any commercial business.

I was summoned to Freedom House, the headquarters of the United National Independence Party (UNIP) by the private secretary to the SG. He informed me that it had come to the attention of the party that I owned a large farm in contravention of the Leadership Code and the SG of the party, Alexander Grey Zulu, wanted to discuss the matter with me.

During the meeting, the SG repeated the allegations and handed over a letter to me. In the letter, I was given two weeks to decide whether to remain in employment and forfeit the property or to resign and continue with my farming. Once again, my farming ambitions were facing another hurdle.

The farm was being leased to me by the Tobacco Board of Zambia, while the new farming equipment had been bought with a loan, which I still had to repay. I was a leasee and a debtor; I did not own any farm as alleged.

I discussed the ultimatum with my family and replied in writing after a day, indicating that I preferred to resign and become a full-time farmer to grow food for the hungry. When I was called back to Freedom House to discuss my reply, I was informed that the decision had been made that I be given a strong warning and be allowed to continue in both employment and farming.

I went to the village to report these happenings to my father. After some family discussions, my younger brother, Richard Hamainza, who had just started his teaching career after completing his course at David Livingstone Teachers' College offered to resign in order to go and run the farm.

While in Kabwe in 1984, as Permanent Secretary for the Central Province, I had the opportunity to tour a number of commercial farms in the Mkushi Farming Block. I admired the excellent tobacco crop on the farms and decided to include the tobacco crop at our Choma farm during the 1984/85 season.

In 1988, I applied to Barclays Bank for a loan to buy adequate farming inputs for growing tobacco for the 1988/89 crop season. We had previously been dependent on loans from the Lima Bank, which were not adequate. Manager Banda of Barclays at the Choma branch visited the farm and together we inspected the fields and the curing facilities, which were in good condition.

I had challenged the chairman of the TAZ in 1982 on how easy tobacco growing was and had gotten a reprieve under the Leadership Code. I felt that it was time to prove my farming capability, if only to satisfy my ego. I was also keen to know the production costs and profitability of the tobacco crop.

We had been experimenting with our own fertiliser and chemical use formula different from those in the Government tobacco-growing manuals.

We had acquired some experience during the previous three seasons and I had a lot of knowledge from my foreign and local tours. The tobacco crop responded well to our experiment and we had a good crop in the fields, which was well-tended by sixty full-time farm workers, most of whom were those who had doubted our capability.

In spite of our farm being only eleven kilometres from the Provincial and District Agriculture offices, no extension officer visited the farm. My brother, Richard, supervised all the farm operations including the curing of the tobacco. When the auction floors opened in May 1989, we were among the first farmers to deliver the early crop. Richard was in attendance on all the days our tobacco was being offered.

On 23 June 1989, I left Zambia for a one-month tour of the USA under the International Visitor Programme (IVP). The tour, sponsored by the USA Government, gave me an opportunity to visit a number of farms producing various crops and livestock, including tobacco, poultry, cattle, and pigs. I visited many agricultural research institutions and colleges and crop processing enterprises such as Monsanto and Sunkist growers, the largest citrus fruit processing and marketing operation in the world.

For one week, I lived with Floyd and Mona Boston in Illinois State, helping the three family members with their farming operations. Their eldest son, Bill Boston a former professor of agricultural economics in West Africa operated a highly mechanized farm of 400 sows and 300 cattle with his wife, one child, and three farm workers on a nearby farm.

I visited many tourist attractions among them were Abraham Lincoln's home and tomb, the Disneyland, the Rocky Mountains, the Kennedy Space Centre, and high-technology industries. I gained an invaluable insight into the roles of federal, state and local governments in regulating, encouraging and supporting the highly developed American agricultural industry through public financial institutions. The tour introduced me to the modern American agricultural industry and fired up my farming ambitions.

When I returned to Zambia, the tobacco selling season was at its peak. One day in August 1989, Richard asked me to visit the auction floors as we were selling the bulk of our crop on that particular day. On arrival at the floors, my brother met and showed me the rows of our bales of tobacco. I was excited and congratulated him for the high grades and prices of our tobacco.

I then saw Brian Irwin, the towering TAZ chairman, who had been my tormentor during the farm interviews in 1982, at the far end of the floors. I went to greet him and to find out his assessment of the quality of the tobacco on offer. He showed me some bales near to where he was standing and mentioned that there was a farmer who had delivered some exceptionally good quality tobacco. Irwin led me to another part of the floors where, while he was admiring some tobacco, he asked me if I knew the owner of the bales. I immediately recognized my TBZ producer's number 394 on the bales.

Instead of answering Irwin's question, I beckoned Richard, who was at the end of the row. I then got the tag from him, which had my TBZ producer's number. When I showed it to Irwin, he could not believe what he was seeing. The number on the tag in my hand was the same as the one on the bales of the tobacco he had been admiring that whole morning.

He asked me if I had employed a Zimbabwean or Israeli farm manager as these were regarded as the best tobacco producers. I informed him that the gentleman standing next to me was my younger brother, Richard, who had produced the tobacco on the floor. Irwin was dumbstruck as I had proved wrong his pessimism expressed at the interviews on my capability to grow quality tobacco.

Our last tobacco sale was on 25 August 1989 and we had a good average price with a good profit. I could not pass on the production data to the staff of the Ministry of Agriculture as no one had shown any interest in visiting our farm.

At the end of the selling period, we were presented with the TAZ trophy and a cash prize of US $ 2,000 as the 'Best Commercial Tobacco Farmer in Zambia for the 1988/9 Season'. I was the first black Zambian farmer to accomplish this feat. I had demonstrated my leadership qualities as a civil servant having risen to the position of Permanent Secretary, and now also as a tobacco farmer.

I flew to Gaborone, Botswana with Siyoto Kunyanda, where I bought two vans, using the dollar prize money and part of the farm income. We drove back the two vehicles to Zambia, via the Kazungula pontoon, making the trip my longest journey as a driver

We held celebrations with relatives, friends, and workers at the farm in Choma and discussed the matter of continuing to grow tobacco; after all, we were experts now. But many family members felt that having won the highest national prize, we should stop the cultivation of tobacco and all other crops and diversify to something else. I personally felt that being a senior Government official, I had an obligation of joining the ongoing global campaign against tobacco consumption by stopping growing the crop.

We agreed to diversify and concentrate our efforts on cattle rearing, which we had started with a herd of twenty-one cattle in 1988. We bought breeding animals from the farm income. In 1991, I got a loan from Lima Bank and bought more breeding cattle from Zambezi Ranching and Cropping Limited. By the beginning of the twenty-first century, we had a sizable herd of cattle of the Boran, Brahman, Bonsmara, and Pinzgauer breeds. We sold steers to abattoirs and the heifers to Heifer International for their 'Passing on the Gift' programme and to the Zambian Government for the 'Cattle Restocking Programme'.

Some of the proceeds from the 1988 crop were used to develop more farm infrastructure for livestock and irrigation. In 1989, we constructed a dam and captured thirty-three million litres of water in the night of 30 December. The dam wall was later increased and now retains 300 million litres of water throughout the year.

Sometime in 1996, the farm was offered to me for sale, after fourteen years of being a tenant. I was overwhelmed with bliss as I finally owned part of my country. With the Ducket, Mudenda, Tsiknakis, and Ohn families as our neighbours, I found the farm a befitting resting place from the hectic office work in Lusaka. These English, Tonga, Greek and Chinese neighbours provided advice on farming and also help to my workers when I was away on national duties. It is my pleasure to record my sincere gratitude to them.

I have thoroughly enjoyed applying my farming skills and agricultural economic theories both in the office and on the farm. Farming has been most fulfilling. The farm in Choma has been our dependable cash cow that has provided for my family's financial needs. The wealth from the farm helped in averting any sinister thoughts of engaging in corrupt practices including those of abuse of office and theft of public money during my thirty-seven years of public service.

CHAPTER 9

Ideals Of The Communism Ideology

In March 1980, I was transferred from the Ministry of Agriculture and Water Development to the Ministry of Defence and promoted to the position of Assistant Head of the Research Bureau of Defence and Security, a unit dealing with Zambia's security systems. The transfer and promotion were meant to stop me from taking up appointments in international organisations.

I embraced the new placement in the closed and vital institution, as a privilege, and I used the opportunity to learn and understand the nation's security structures. Apart from so many other things I came to know, but which I cannot disclose as per the principle of the-need-to-know, I am able to distinguish the different ranks of security officers by the pips on the shoulders of their uniforms. My detailed study of the Zambia National Service, after an extensive tour of the production units, resulted in its restructuring and transfer to a civilian ministry.

In June 1980, the Chairman for Defence and Security, Alexander Zulu led a military delegation for a one-month visit to the Democratic People's Republic of North Korea (DPRK) and the People's Republic of China. The delegation included the top military brass of Zambia, among them, Mibenge, Zyongwe, Moono, Kabwe, Kayumba, Chitoshi, and Colonels Mulenga and Mulele. I was one of the four civilian members of the delegation.

I was excited to have the rare opportunity of chatting with the senior officers of Zambia's defence forces and visiting China, the most populous country in the world. The trip also allowed me to experience communism on its own territory. I had read about Kim Il Sung, and Mao Tsetung, the Presidents of North Korea and China, as modern-day practitioners of Marxism-Leninism.

Having visited Washington and London, the citadels of capitalism, the visit to Pyongyang and later Peking (Beijing) gave me an opportunity to compare the effects of the two warring ideologies on the ordinary people.

The time of our visit was at the height of the Cold War, a neologism used by the political satirist George Orwell (Eric Arthur Blair), the author of 'Animal Farm'. The term was given to the conflict between the believers of capitalism led by the USA and those who believed in communism led by the USSR.

We flew from Lusaka to Bombay by Zambia Airways, the national flag carrier. Our short stay in Bombay was unforgettable for me as I was confronted by a young mother, holding a baby wrapped in a newspaper, asking for money. As I parted with some rupees, I wiped off tears as the sight of such suffering was too much for my conscience to bear.

We then flew to Beijing where we were picked by a military jet from Pyongyang. The plane arrived at the exact appointed time and we took off on time. As we were settling down after take-off, the General next to me drew my attention to the fact the crew did not announce for us to fasten the seat belts during take-off. He observed that the blonde flight hostess continued to move about in the plane even during take-off, which is rarely done. I advised him to call the air hostess and remind her of the omission.

He pressed the call button and the lady came over immediately. His protestations on not being reminded to fasten seat belts were calmed down by the air hostess who replied, "Sir, nothing will happen. This plane was checked and serviced in Pyongyang to pick you from here. So nothing can happen to it. Please enjoy the flight".

This was an amazing introduction to the Communism ideology! Even an air hostess believed that nothing could happen to an aircraft because engineers had worked on it. In other words, man was in control of his own circumstances. At Pyongyang Airport, we were given a colourful welcome with garlands of red flowers presented by smartly dressed young girls. The soldiers on the saluting parade were very impressive and looked like they had been selected for being of the same height, as the white belts made a straight line across the formation.

North Korea had an ideology called the *Juche* Idea expounded by Kim Il Sung, the President and commonly called 'The Great Leader'. The idea, developed from Marxism-Leninism, is premised on self-reliance, independence in politics, and self-defence in the military. The ultimate goal of the ideology was to build strong nationalist feelings in the citizens. It, therefore, challenged each citizen to be the "master of his or her own destiny".

From preliminary contact with the few North Koreans, I concluded that they greatly respected time. During one of my early visits to the USA, I arrived some ten minutes earlier for an appointment. The secretary persuaded me to take a walk as the boss was still busy with another client! She was short of telling me that they had no room for time-wasters. The North Koreans gave us a harsher lesson in time management during our visit.

We visited different parts of North Korea, hosted by various industries and institutions. There were always competent interpreters to explain the various activities, which made our trip enjoyable and fruitful. Everywhere we went, be it in urban or rural areas, we found huge banners with large pictures of a smiling Kim Il Sung, the Great Leader. The hosts informed us that the Great Leader had visited them many times and had stood where they had erected his monument or posters. This was literally everywhere. We could not doubt this story about a leader who had never left his country for over thirty years but had spent time touring the countryside.

One of the high points for a military delegation like ours was to experience the tense atmosphere on the border between North and South Korea at Panmunjom. We were advised that we would be departing from the guest house at 0830 hours. By 0800 hours, the drivers were already revving the engines, a sign that they were ready. By 0815 hours, everybody else was in their vehicle except Chairman Zulu. A few visits to his room by the protocol officers could not achieve much as he was in the middle of a telephone conversation. Finally, the old man appeared at 0910 hours and we felt and sensed the tension amongst our hosts as we were late by forty minutes.

The drive through the city was normal and at a reasonable speed. Once we were in the countryside, the sweeper cars in front took off at very high speed and were leaving the other cars some distance behind. The sweeper cars stopped and the officers had chatted a bit with all the drivers in their local language, which none of us understood. From that point on, all cars had to be close to the sweepers.

I have never experienced being in a car cruising at 280 kilometres per hour. Normally, the two of us and the interpreter in the vehicle chatted and commented on the scenery as we drove along. This time, there was dead silence in the car as the driver looked like a zombie fixed to the steering wheel. As we were going up on the winding road to the observation point at the top of the Panmunjom Mountain, our vehicle swerved at a curve and we had a hairbreadth escape from tumbling thousands of metres down the steep mountain. The driver continued at high speed up the mountain, while I had my heart in my mouth.

As we assembled at the top of the mountain, everyone including Chairman Zulu was talking about the deathly speed we had been subjected to. When openly confronted, the senior Korean escort explained, out of the ear of the Chairman, that we had lost forty minutes in starting off. The lost time had to be recovered on the way. It was against military etiquette for the military people to tell a senior person, even indirectly, that he was at fault. The whole incident soured what could have been a wonderful day at the famous Panmunjom border post.

I had been anxious to see the Military Demarcation Line (MDL), the unique border between North and South Korea that goes through the conference rooms and down the middle of the conference tables where the antagonists meet. The opportunity was spoilt by the manner in which we were delivered to Panmunjom as our stay at the observatory point was cut short.

Later in the evening as we were reviewing the day's events, I seized some lighter moment to explain to Chairman Zulu that his late departure from his room that morning was what nearly cost us our lives on the road. From then on, I became the diplomat to talk to our Chairman when the need arose. Luckily, the matter of punctuality was no more an issue as the Chairman executed his leadership role perfectly.

In Pyongyang, we visited a government kindergarten catering for 300 kids who were taken care of while their parents were at work. We were greatly impressed with the sparkling cleanliness. Even more astonishing was the nimbleness with which the kids dismantled and assembled toy carburettors as part of child play. We were informed that education in the Democratic People's Republic of Korea is universal and state funded. The national literacy rate for citizens of fifteen years of age and older is over ninety-nine per cent.

When we asked for scholarships for Zambian students, the hosts advised us that our candidates must be those who had gotten very good scores in mathematics and science subjects. The Koreans were very advanced in METS (Mathematics, Engineering, Technology and Science), which later became STEM. They indicated that their educational standards were very high and practical, such that by the time a student did eleven years of schooling, he/she must be able to assemble a piece of some utility equipment.

The artistic displays performed for us, which were accompanied by descriptive music pertaining to community activities, were well-rehearsed and well-synchronized. Dancers were adorned in long flowing dresses or loose trousers and shirts. Dancing was by movement of arms and not by wriggling of the waist.

Food was a major challenge from the first day of our arrival in Asia. This was because most of the members of the delegation did not want to eat some of the local foods, such as dog or snake meat. Chairman Zulu vowed that he would be on guard and would never eat dog or snake meat during the whole tour under any circumstances.

One morning, while we were being entertained to some military drills in a big open field, a lactating bitch suddenly ran across the field. In the distance, we could see some kennels. One Korean interpreter shouted repeatedly, "small beef", while pointing at the dog. We had a good laugh when we realized that what we had been relishing as tasty 'small beef' during our meals was, in fact, dog meat. Chairman Zulu was satisfied that it was not snake meat. A few members of the delegation stopped eating 'small beef' or any suspicious-looking meat from that day.

At one dinner, one member suspected that the dish was 'small beef' and asked for another dish. His plate was politely taken away and another plate brought after about twenty minutes. When asked how his meal was, he proudly announced that it was delicious. The interpreter informed us that it was, in fact, the same meat that was cooked and spiced differently. He still could not disclose if it was 'small beef' or not. All he stated was that the goodness of any food is in its preparation, presentation, and nutrients and not in its name or colour.

After these incidences, the questions on what food was being offered reduced, except by the Chairman who wanted to keep his vow. I revelled in tasting any food that was served by our hosts, after all, the saying goes, "When in Rome, do as the Romans do."

Discussing some diversions from the official programme was very tempting for the team, as we wanted to experience the real life of the ordinary people. Once, we were caught off guard as we discussed the irrelevance and unsuitability of a proposed trip. We did not know that a video camera stealthily hidden behind a portrait of the Great Leader was transmitting our conversation to our hosts. Although our conversation was in ciNyanja, the proposed programme was abruptly changed.

Discrete searches behind the portraits of the Great Leader, which were in every room, revealed hidden video cameras. This gave us a ready means to transmit our concerns to our hosts, as we deliberately sat near the portrait of the Great Leader when politely voicing our concerns. At that point, I recalled and narrated my experience of eavesdropping microphones on the trip to communist Yugoslavia in 1979.

We were very impressed with the knowledge of farming by the ordinary Korean villagers, who were organized in cooperatives. Everybody seemed to know the various nutrients of the fertilisers they applied to the various crops and the calendar for applying the same.

Intensive irrigation was encouraged and farmers were equipped with small pumps, which they used to draw water even from the shallow-water reservoirs. A strict land use and conservation policy was applied. The lands with good soils were reserved for grains and vegetables. While all fruit trees were grown on hills 'where other trees grow'.

Our last official engagement was a lavish state dinner of ten courses in a well-decorated ballroom, attended by the Who's Who in the DPRK. The dinner, which started on time, ended as per the programme and this made many of us miss our last course of the dessert, as we all had to leave the banquet hall.

This was the last show of great respect for time and the division of labour among the public functionaries. The dignitaries were at the mercy of the protocol officers as far as timekeeping was concerned. We kept talking about this way of keeping orderliness in state management and hoped that the attitude of Zambians to timekeeping would one day improve.

We left North Korea fully satisfied that we had acquired additional knowledge and skills on how effectively to organize citizens for development. The Juche Idea galvanized the North Korean people to believe that they could conquer any obstacles in the way of their set national goals and vision. The intellectuals, mathematics, science, and technology were respected as strong weapons for the development of the country. Strict timekeeping was part of their tradition.

Our next stop was Beijing in the People's Republic of China. We were delivered to Peking by a military jet, with no one doubting the safety of the flight after experiencing the thoroughness of preparations by the North Koreans. Once in Beijing, our minds were geared to learn about the changes that had taken place since the demise of Mao Tsetung in 1976.

The Chinese Government had introduced a one-child policy in 1979 that compelled married couples to produce only one child. Unfortunately, it was not permissible for foreigners to speak to ordinary Chinese to learn more about their social life and views on such policies. We did not even visit the Mao Mausoleum on Tiananmen Square, constructed from materials from all over China, as there were some renovations being carried out. The poor weather also prevented us from visiting the famous monumental 21,000 kilometres Great Wall of China built in the 14th Century.

During one of our official meetings, Chairman Zulu requested for copies of the Red Book by Chairman Mao. We were informed that the public printing presses were too busy with more important publications and that the famous book was out of print. It seemed like the new breed of younger leaders, trained in the West, wanted to forget the Chairman's teachings.

At another meeting, our delegation recalled the TAZARA Railway and military assistance received and thanked the people of China for this. We requested for continued assistance in spite of the change of the leadership in China. The reply we got was that China could not afford to give aid anymore as they had embarked upon a transformational reform agenda to lift the majority of their people out of poverty. It was made clear that any financial assistance to Zambia in future would be in form of concessional loans.

During our 1980 visit, there was only one shop in Peking called the Friendship Shop where foreigners bought goods using Foreign Exchange Certificates, a special form of currency. It was a criminal offence to change currencies and shop anywhere else. It was also not possible to speak to any local people as our guides were always close by. After a few days in Peking, we left for Nanking in eastern China.

In Nanking, we visited amongst other industries, a large silk-producing enterprise. At the time, the Zambian Government was considering the introduction of silk production in the Zambia National Service Camps and among village cooperatives. A place was identified in Mazabuka District in the Southern Province for training in sericulture. A number of Zambian officials had visited the modern silk factory in Nanking and had been highly impressed and recommended it to other visitors.

It was all excitement as we watched the feeble silkworms munching green mulberry leaves and forming cocoons of a white stuff in which they lived. We learnt that the process involves a female worm laying eggs that are then incubated to produce young worms (larvae). The cocoons and worms are then separated in a process that kills all the worms and the cocoons are processed further to produce strands of silk for weaving into brocades of high-quality fabric.

After a very educational tour, the Chairman turned to the ZNS officers and gave instructions that silk production must become one of the thriving industries in the Service. We were then allowed to ask questions on the whole silk production process. There was general approval that everything was clear.

I timidly raised my hand and my question was, "Since the female moths die immediately after laying 300 eggs and the larvae in the cocoons are also killed during the extraction of the silk from the cocoons, where do you get new females to lay eggs?" The question was unexpected, especially from an economist. After a bit of hesitation, the officer informed us that the new silkworms were genetically produced in a laboratory under strict security and hygienic conditions. This was genetic engineering, which was relatively unknown during that era and was kept as a secret.

Not one of the many Zambians, including Chairman Zulu, who had visited the silk factory before, had been shown the laboratory where these worms were being produced. Silk production was dropped from the ZNS programme and I saved the Zambia National Service from failure and blame in a field in which no Zambian had technical expertise. The technology was far beyond the available genetic engineering capabilities of most countries including Zambia.

We then went on a day's cruise on the Yangtze River, the longest river in Asia. During the cruise, we were informed of advanced plans for a big dam on the river. The construction of the Three Gorges Dam, envisioned in 1919 by Sun Yat-sen began in 1994 and was completed in 2012. The dam became the largest man-made dam in the world with a backflow reservoir of 660 kilometres, the same distance from Kabwe to Livingstone. The huge turbines have the capability of generating 22,500 megawatts (MW) of energy compared to ZESCO's combined capacity of 1752 MW from its seven hydropower stations.

We travelled across to Quangzhou (Canton) in the south eastern region of China. Our only assignment was to visit to a large snake farm on the outskirts of the city before enjoying a fourteen-course farewell luncheon at the Governor's Lodge. The farm produced all types of snakes, which were milked for snake venom sold all over the world for medicinal purposes. We were informed that this particular farm was registered to breed and keep some of the most poisonous snakes in China. After this frightening experience, we headed back to town for our final lunch in China. The host was a septuagenarian military general of the People's Liberation Army.

Traditional Chinese meals usually start with a soup, which one may continue to sip with other subsequent courses. The soup that was served in huge earthen pots looked and tasted like creamy chicken soup with pieces of soft white meat. Our host kept the mood lively on the high table with Chinese stories. Even our inquisitive Chairman Zulu forgot to ask the usual question about the food we were enjoying as the pot was kept full with continuous replenishments with the tasty hot soup.

As the twelfth course was being served, Chairman Zulu tilted the big pot, with the help of a waiter, peeped into the pot and scooped a full ladle of the soup into his plate. He was ready with a soup spoon in his hand when he turned and asked our host.

Chairman: Comrade General, this soup is delicious and the meat very nice. What meat is this?

(*Chairman Zulu held the full soup spoon halfway to his mouth, waiting for the reply*).

General: We call it the Five-Snake Soup because it is made of the five most deadly snakes you saw at the snake farm. The soup is served only to the most distinguished guests like you. I am happy that you are enjoying it.

Chairman: (*Pushing the spoon slowly into his mouth*). I have already taken so much and anyway it is very nice. I might as well finish it. (*He then asked Gen Zyongwe seated on another table*). Gen. Zyongwe, do you know that you have eaten snake meat in the soup?

Gen. Zyongwe: We knew much earlier, Sir. But since it was not in enemy territory, we did not alert you, Sir.

I had never before been in the company of such a hilarious group of military personnel before. The host general became ecstatic while explaining the contribution of the meat and poison of each of the five snakes to human life. Most of them were attributed to contributing to strong masculinity and long life. None of us doubted the sincerity of the explanation from an old man in his seventies who looked so energetic.

Chairman Zulu who vowed never to eat snake meat during the one-month tour of North Korea and China broke his vow on the last day of the tour. A member of our delegation shouted that it took the secret collaboration of the Koreans and Chinese to dupe Chairman Zulu into eating snake meat. The last two courses of our last meal went with a flash as there was so much chattering talk in the ballroom.

We were then driven to the railway station nearby to catch a luxury train to Hong Kong. Before leaving for the 120 kilometres train ride, I spent my last yuan in buying a wine bottle, which had a dead snake inside. I confirmed that the wine was mellow and of correct characteristics as taught by elder Mukutu. I was also assured that the dead snake inside, was from one of the breeds that were in our delicious soup. As a prized souvenir, I carried the bottle in my hand luggage.

After some three-days of frenzied shopping in the modern world famous Kowloon shopping malls of Hong Kong, we left for Bangkok in Thailand on our way to Bombay in India. We became suspicious, when our plane did not land on arrival at Bangkok airport, but continued to circle in the air for some time. Since we arrived at night, we could not even see what was happening on the ground.

Finally, as we were landing, the captain announced that there had been an attempted plane hijack to Cuba, which had been foiled by the military crack squad. Because of the time we spent in the air and the confusion at the airport, our onward flight was rescheduled. We took-off within one hour to Bombay, where we connected with a Zambia Airways flight to Lusaka.

You imagine Joyce's awe-stricken face, as she held a bottle of wine with a snake inside, when unpacking my luggage in our bedroom. I was lucky that the bottle dropped on the soft bed, when she tried to throw it away. Each of my male friends, who attended my birthday party in July of that year, demanded for a sip of the snake wine. As a result, none of us could confirm the veracity of the story by the Chinese sage of the efficacy of the wine. Perhaps the quantity we took was far below the required prescription to cause a required aphrodisiac effect, as portrayed by the old man.

Going through China and North Korea during the eighties gave me an opportunity to learn about the Asian value systems and the state of economic and social development. I was fascinated with the discipline that was exhibited in all activities we were involved, due to the ideologies that fostered national unity, obedience, and self-reliance. I was privileged to accompany senior military officers on the tour of highly secretive countries and to be exposed to many military issues.

I privately thanked President Kaunda for stopping me from leaving Zambia and appointing me in the Ministry of Defence. My responsibilities at the African Development Bank would not have given me an opportunity of travelling through North Korea and China.

The respect for time by both the West and the East was similar. I adopted the same behaviour of strict observance of time. Sometime in the late eighties, a Zambian senior government officer remarked that the strict sense of timekeeping, I developed, will see me rise very high. Towards the end of the 20th Century, while at the ACP, I openly expressed my repugnance with many ambassadors, who claimed to observe ACP time in the middle of Europe, whenever they were late for a meeting.

As prophesied by the Zambian officer, I rose to the respectable position of Minister of Finance and National Planning in July 2003. I upset many colleagues by ignoring them if they arrived late in my meetings. I was spurred on with this behaviour by the Japanese Ambassador, who told me that Zambia could add another two per cent to the rate of growth of the Gross Domestic Product (GDP), if only Zambian officers saved just twenty per cent of the time lost by not being punctual. In spite of my sermons on punctuality, the Zambian economy failed to benefit from an additional two per cent growth due to a habitual lack of respect for time by Zambians.

The mannerisms and procedures of the practitioners of communism in China and North Korea were not very different from those practising capitalism in the West. In both countries, there was great appreciation of the value of science and technology, as a route to transforming national economies. The temerity of the North Korean air hostess was equal to the audacity of American Neil Armstrong, who was the first human being to set foot on the distant moon.

After the visit to the two communist countries, I became convinced of the usefulness of the Zambia National Service, as an instrument for national cohesion, defence, self-confidence, and discipline. I, therefore, felt that I had a role to play in character formation of the young people, who were to come through the Zambia National Service. However, I could not put into practice many of my lessons, as I was transferred and promoted to the position of director of budget at the Ministry of Finance in August 1981.

CHAPTER 10

Inducted As A Custodian Of Public Assets

At the Ministry of Finance, I joined a small team of dedicated officers who were struggling to prepare so many documents on national finances. The ministry had only one computer and no sophisticated adding machines at the time. The officers were the Permanent Secretary Fred Kazunga, Budget Officers Irene Kamanga, Zachea Namooya, Richard Manyika, I. Masumba, I. Mwanambale, J. Chewe W.S. Simutowe, L.P. Mulenga, and Z. Mfune The minister in charge was the Prime Minister, veteran politician Nalumino Mundia, who preferred to call me 'bo-Magande'.

I applied for recruitment of additional officers to beef-up the staff levels in the budget office. Although there was a restriction on fresh recruitments into the civil service, my personal appearance, convinced the secretary to the cabinet Charles Manyema of the need. After interviewing a group of students at the UNZA, I selected eleven, who joined the ministry in 1982.

The operations of the Ministry of Finance are covered by specific laws. The Minister is the only public official in the Government, who is a corporate body, who may sue or be sued under Chapter 349 of the Laws of Zambia. The senior officers of the ministry such as the Secretary to the Treasury and Accountant General are specifically provided for in the Public Finance Act. Some important functions of the government such as loan contraction and appointment of Controlling Officers were a preserve of the Minister of Finance.

The minister was non-resident and could be briefed only at his office at the Cabinet Office when he was not too busy. The PS was not in good health and was often on sick leave. I, therefore, assumed a lot of responsibilities in the management of the ministry. This meant my putting in a few more hours and knocking-off late in the evenings to catch up with the increased workload. In consideration of my personal security and convenience, my family shifted from Chelston to Northmead Township, which was nearer to my office. I was also allocated my first personal-to-holder government vehicle.

Hosting the President
One of the immediate assignments I undertook was to host President Kaunda

at the official opening of the new headquarters building of the Development Bank of Zambia (DBZ) on Katondo Street, opposite the City Library in the Lusaka city centre.

The new bank was seen as a very important financial institution in the government's efforts to create new large industries in the various sectors of the economy. Even in agriculture where the Agricultural Finance Company (AFC) was the specialized financing institution, it was planned that large projects will be financed by the DBZ.

During this era, the World Bank was promoting the creation of development banks in developing countries as special purpose vehicles to undertake the task of preparing viable projects, promoting industrial enterprises, undertaking economic and technical research, conducting surveys, and feasibility studies. Development banks had played a significant role in increasing the pace of industrialization in many developed countries. It was hoped that developing countries could also follow this route to industrialisation.

The ceremony was well attended by officials from foreign development finance institutions including the World Bank. My speech was delivered with a lot of zest as I was knowledgeable of the planned role of the DBZ in supporting Zambia's industrialization. I had read intensively on development banking in preparation for the interviews, which I attended at DBZ in 1978. Although I was offered a job as an economist, I could not take up the offer by a Ministerial decree. As the DBZ function was well-covered by the media, I was instantly introduced to the local private sector and the international financial institutions.

President Kaunda acknowledged publicly that, being a new officer in the job at the Ministry of Finance, he did not expect me to do so well in organizing the function and articulating the role of the new bank. From this early interaction with the bank, I became a respected member of the board, whose advice was sought after and taken seriously. I developed strong relationships with the managing director, Lumbamba Nyambe and his team at the bank.

Budget preparation
The preparation and presentation of the national budget is a constitutional issue, which involves the president of the republic. The Director of Budgets is the officer dedicated to the function of preparing the budget, which is presented to Cabinet for approval. The Minister of Finance then presents the budget to parliament on behalf of the president.

The preparation of the government's annual budget took a lot of time in those days, from July up to the end of the year. In the absence of computers and pocket calculators, numerical work was done by cranking machines. Once ministries presented their requirements, the Budget Office went through all the submissions and trimmed the financial allocations according to available

153

revenues. The budget proposals were presented to Cabinet at a special meeting that was convened at around 20.00 hours.

In those days, prices of essential commodities such as mealie meal, cooking oil, and sugar were announced in the Government annual budgets. The timing of the cabinet meeting in the night was to prevent any leakage of the new revenue measures and prices. It was expected that after the cabinet meeting in the early hours of the morning, the elderly decision makers would be too tired and would go to their homes and sleep. Without cellular phones, they were unable to communicate and alert their relatives and friends on the proposed price increases.

At the conclusion of the cabinet meeting, the Budget Office staff shifted to the government printer, where we spent the rest of the night proofreading and making amendments to the budget as it came out of the printing machines. The high level of loyalty of the Budget Office staff at the time secured the confidential information on the proposed prices and the amendments made and approved by the Cabinet.

My own family and friends had no prior knowledge of the price changes. They knew after the announcement by the Minister of Finance in the budget speech in parliament. Once I was in trouble for not informing my spouse as the price increases on mealie meal were very high and they required a drastic change in the family's expenditure pattern. I told my spouse, who felt that I should have alerted her of the impending increase, that I had sworn at NIPA not to disclose such information to those outside the system.

As is common with most systems dealing with big payrolls, the Budget Office was grappling with the issue of 'ghost' workers. We devised a new system which could easily identify non-existing persons by giving each civil servant an identity number and a code. Regrettably, some members of staff at the paying commercial bank and civil servants who were conniving to create 'ghost' workers were caught and dismissed. To seal the loopholes, the recruitment of civil servants had to be approved initially by the Cabinet Office and then by the Budget Office, where funds for salaries and the numbers were strictly matched and controlled.

In the area of taxation, I used my agricultural background and proposed that the tax rate on agricultural income be reduced to fifteen per cent in order to encourage the development of the sector in an effort to diversify the economy. In support of this strategy, I also proposed the introduction of a Mineral Export Tax (MET) and the creation of an escrow account at the Bank of Zambia to hold the revenues from this source.

As the economy was slowing down, shortages of essential commodities resulted in rising prices. The usual reaction of all governments is to try to cushion the citizens by subsidizing common food items. Under the structural adjustment reforms of the time, removing subsidies was one of the top recommended remedies in any sick economy.

We scrutinized the budget to try to find items whose budget estimates had to be cut. A special audit of the subsidies on mealie meal revealed that coupons were being accessed by even the working class who exchanged them for household goods in shops. We, therefore, recommended the withdrawal of the subsidy in order to reduce the budget deficit. This was my first contact with the rampant abuse of subsidies, which has built my strong dislike for this particular social safety net.

Amongst the many additional duties of the Director of Budgets was that of representing the ministry on the boards of various parastatal financial institutions. I was therefore privileged to attend the meetings of the Boards of Directors of the DBZ, the Zambia State Insurance Corporation (ZSIC), and the Zambia National Commercial Bank.

Learning how to negotiate

Since the Ministry of Finance is responsible for public loan contraction, I was the representative when negotiating loans from international financial institutions. In September 1981, I was a member of a Zambian team that travelled to Washington DC, USA to negotiate for funds from the International Development Association (IDA) of the World Bank for agricultural projects. The team was led by Namukolo Mukutu, an expert in the Ministry of Agriculture, that was the owner of the project.

My role in the team was to make sure that the conditions of the loans conformed to the financial regulations of the Zambian Government. The Legal Officer was Irene Mambilima from the Ministry of Legal Affairs, whose responsibility was to check on the legal provisions of the agreement. Mambilima worked her way through the government's legal system, ascending to the position of Chief Justice of Zambia in February 2015, after a stint as Chairman of the Electoral Commission of Zambia (ECZ), where she supervised the three national elections in 2006, 2008, and 2011.

During the negotiations, we had a bit of a problem because this was the first time that the team members were dealing with the World Bank. In fact, one of the World Bank's project officers took advantage was too negative in his reactions to our presentations. Mukutu and I had attended the course on project appraisal at the Economic Development Institute (EDI) of the World Bank in the seventies.

The two of us were therefore sure of our project analysis and the project's resultant rates of return. In spite of a well-written document and technically supported arguments, the World Bank officer still found something wrong with our presentation. My consultations with a World Bank officer, whom I'd known before revealed that the difficult officer was from a South American coffee growing country, whose coffee crop was destroyed by frost.

The officer must have been detailed by his country to stop Zambia from growing Arabica coffee as Zambia's quality and climate were better. At the time, the international coffee market was highly controlled through a quota system decided by large producers of coffee, who used their cartel powers to bar new entrants into the lucrative industry. With this inside information, we became more aggressive during the negotiations and the coffee project was approved for bank funding.

Mukutu and I decided to assuage the frustrations of the day by relaxing in an exclusive restaurant on Capitol Hill, which is the seat of the USA Congress. As we sauntered into the dim-lit restaurant, dressed to the nines, a waiter rushed to meet us and ushered us into a snug room. A smartly dressed elderly sommelier of fine wine tendered a bulky wine list.

The old man showed a lot of patience as we kept rejecting the wines after testing on account of a variety of reasons. His patience soon ran out as he thought that we were reading the descriptions on the wine list. So, he decided to put us to the test and bet that if we were able to describe a particular wine of his own choice without having read the wine list, he would give us a free bottle of the same wine.

Luckily enough, this was at the peak of our wine-making hobby. Mukutu, the expert, asked for freshly-baked bread as a palate cleanser before tasting the wine in a special wine glass. After a few sips, my elder brother was able to accurately describe the balance of the wine to minute details of acidity, character, flavour, aroma and even the maturity and source of the wine. The expert sommelier lost the bet and he surrendered the second most expensive wine meant for the congressmen, for free!

Having successfully negotiated for funds at the World Bank and showed off our knowledge of wines, we decided to demonstrate our financial muscle by ordering the most expensive sirloin steak on Capitol Hill. By tradition, a good steak goes with a good red wine and in adhering to this protocol, Mukutu ordered the most expensive wine on the Hill. By the time we were leaving the restaurant in the wee hours of the morning, we were seen off by many smiling faces due to the handsome tip we tendered.

In August 1982, I was a member of another government negotiating team that travelled to Rome, Italy to negotiate for funds from the newly created International Fund for Agricultural Development (IFAD). Mukutu was again the delegation leader as the project was for the Ministry of Agriculture. This time, the legal officer was Ms Prisca Nyambe, who became a Puisne Judge of the High Court of Zambia after efficiently serving the Zambian government and the International Criminal Tribunal for Rwanda for many years.

The negotiations at IFAD were easy because I knew some of the officers of the organization. I had earlier on, taken an active part in discussions on the creation of the organization while I was at the Ministry of Agriculture. I also knew the first president of the organization as I was on the team that presented Zambia's support for his candidature. I got on so well with him that he, at some point, invited me to join the organization, but I could not take the offer.

However, our visit to Italy was socially ill-timed, as the month of August can be described as one long holiday for the Italians. It is a common trend for everybody in Italy to leave the cities for the countryside and the seas due to the scorching heat. We found Rome deserted and every evening we spent a lot of time hunting for an open restaurant. Once we'd found one, we'd concentrate on enjoying our hard-to-find meals and did not scrutinize the bills.

One evening when we decided to inspect the bill, we discovered that it had been inflated by nearly fifty per cent. The proprietor, who behaved in a friendly manner, claimed that the fault could have been caused by lack of technicians at the central processing centre as most of them had gone on holiday. We lost a substantial amount as we had already been in Rome for some days.

As we were checking out of the hotel owned by a Christian organization, we painstakingly went through our bills to the discomfort of the lady at the reception, who was attired in religious regalia. To our surprise, all the bills for the three of us were inflated by the inclusion of services that we'd never ordered. If we had not been diligent and trusted the worker due to her religious appearances, we could have lost a lot of money paying for 'air'.

This being my first trip to Rome, I took the opportunity to visit the Vatican City, the seat of the Roman Catholic Church and home of the Pope. During this visit, we also toured the historical Colosseum, remembered as the entertainment arena for fights between gladiators and beasts. The honour of attending mass inside St. Peters Basilica, the holiest church and the burial site of Peter one of the twelve disciples of Jesus Christ, only came much later in life. My service to humanity was rewarded by a ticket that provided me a seat close to the Altar, where the Pope sits.

In October 1981, I was a member of a Zambian team, led by General Kingsley Chinkuli, Minister of Power, Transport, and Communications, that travelled to Harare, Zimbabwe to negotiate the break-up and equitable sharing of the assets of the Central African Power Corporation (CAPCO) and the joint railway system. The delegation of the new Zimbabwean Government was led by Simba Makoni, Minister of Finance, who'd lived in Zambia for some time during the liberation wars.

The major issue was the arrears of US $71 million accumulated on power supplied to Rhodesia during the period of the Unilateral Declaration of Independence (UDI) by the rebel Government of Prime Minister Ian Smith. The rebel Government refused to pay for power supplied by the jointly owned Kariba Hydropower Station. We, therefore, expected a sympathetic hearing and a quick resolution of the matter from the new Zimbabwean Government and in particular from the youthful Minister of Finance, who was aware of Zambia's sacrifices in the liberation struggle.

Instead, the officials of the new government of independent Zimbabwe refused to cooperate. They argued that it was not their responsibility to pay for the power used by the Government of rebel Ian Smith, their enemy. Our counterargument that, the Zambian Government could not switch off the power to the country, as the majority to suffer would have been the black Zimbabweans, was not accepted by the Zimbabwean delegation. I recall that our negotiations abruptly ended on a Friday afternoon as our hosts were rushing to their new farms for the weekend.

Our delegation leader, a four-star decorated military man could not accept defeat. He conceived an ingenious plan to resolve the matter peacefully without further negotiations. Chinkuli recommended to the Zambian cabinet that any further joint venture with the Zimbabwean Government in power-generation on the Zambezi River should be tied to the pre-payment of the arrears. The adoption of the recommendation by the cabinet of Kenneth Kaunda was made in a highly charged atmosphere due to non-cooperation by the new government, which came into being with Zambia's help. The non-payment of the US $71 million arrears has delayed the development of the Batoka Gorge Hydropower Station near the Victoria Falls for over three decades as subsequent Zambian administrations stood by the 1981 Cabinet decision.

In spite of the challenges experienced on some of the assignments, they gave me some grounding in negotiating with Governments and also with multilateral financial institutions and I became conversant with their loan conditions.

CHAPTER 11

My Role In Zambia's Industrialization

In August 1983, I was promoted to the second highest civil service position of Permanent Secretary, with the main responsibility of supervising the operations of ministries. I was then among the group of young Permanent Secretaries in the service. The highest civil service position of secretary to the cabinet eluded me during my twenty-three years of service.

Dominic Mulaisho later confided in me on the protracted debate by Cabinet on the recommendation to promote a young officer. As the discussion dragged on, he requested to make a contribution. Being a philosopher, he used the analogy of a tomato farmer, who after tending a good crop, one day he finds one small tomato has turned red indicating ripeness.

The question he posed was, "Will the farmer leave the small ripe tomato on the plant so as to wait for the big green ones to get red and ready?" The answer was that the small ripe tomato had to be harvested and cooked as it was ready. The recommendation to promote me was adopted unanimously by Cabinet.

My first posting was at the Ministry of Commerce, Trade, and Industry (MCTI). At the MCTI, I took over from Kabuka Nyirenda, a veteran civil servant, who put me through a thorough hand-over ceremony. The minister was Clement Mwananshiku who was later succeeded by Leonard Subulwa. Among the officers I found were Joseph Mayovu, undersecretary, and Anderson Zikonda, director of the standards department, who became executive director of the African Regional Intellectual Property Organization (ARIPO). The ministry was responsible for price control and the industrialization of the country through public and private participation.

Due to the many new responsibilities under the ministry, there was a lot of pressure on its few officers. I applied to the Cabinet Office for recruitment of additional officers. Our application went through Cabinet Office and my lobbying with the Director of Budget Danny Musenge won the day. In one go in 1983, the MCTI recruited thirteen new university graduate economists for the various departments.

The Small Industries Development Organization (SIDO) Act and the Village Industries Service (VIS) Act had just been passed and staff recruitment was underway. For the position of Director of SIDO, I discussed with the preferred candidate Dr Chiselebwe Chishimba Ng'andwe, a lecturer at UNZA and then finalized his appointment. Mrs Mapoma took office as the chairman of the Village Industries Service.

Zambia had applied for membership to the Sugar Protocol of the Lome Convention and the International Coffee Organization (ICO). The discussions on the applications revived my memories of my planning days at the MRD and I had answers to all the questions asked about the two crops. I led the delegations to the annual meetings in London and Brussels and successfully defended the applications. Zambia became eligible for allocation of specified quantities of coffee and sugar for export under the international special market access arrangements.

At earlier meetings of the Inter-African Coffee Organization (IACO) in Abidjan, Cote Ivoire, during the seventies, I met Donald Kaberuka of Rwanda, with whom I struck some cordial relationship that blossomed in the twenty-first century.

On the regional scene, the Treaty establishing the Preferential Trade Area (PTA) for Eastern and Southern Africa came into force in September 1982. Having offered to host the institution, Zambia had to find suitable office space and finalize all protocols on staff and hosting responsibilities.

The delay in finalizing the protocols was due to our demands to secure a large number of posts for Zambian nationals. Even after enlisting the assistance of veteran UN staffer, South African Baxter Nomvete, the only senior position given to Zambia was that of Director of Finance and Administration, which was taken up by Francis Walusiku, a former deputy secretary to the cabinet.

Foreign Exchange Ministerial Allocations Committee
One of the delicate assignments of the MCTI at the time was that of allocating the scarce foreign exchange (forex) to applicants from the various sectors of the economy, except mining. The responsibility was for the Foreign Exchange Ministerial Allocations Committee (FEMAC) of eight members, all from the public service, for which I was the chairman.

The Ministry received applications from those wishing to be allocated forex for payments for imported goods and services. The staff of the Ministry sifted through thousands of applications and then made recommendations to the Committee, indicating the sector, purpose and the amount to be allocated.

Before each sitting of FEMAC, the Ministry would receive an indication of the available forex from the BOZ as advised by the forex earning organizations, such as the mines, for distribution amongst the approved applicants. Often times, the available forex was only ten per cent of demand.

What caused more pressure was that the members of FEMAC were all public officers who did not know many of the applicants from the private sector. I became aware that at times the allocations were on basis of guesswork.

There was also a feeling that the public sector was getting an unjustifiably higher proportion of the forex mostly for consumer goods.

Some of the successful applicants had no businesses and they ended up re-selling the foreign exchange to the genuine importers. This activity created a lucrative secondary or black market for foreign exchange with cost implications on the genuine importers and consumers of imported goods.

I recommended to the Secretary to the Cabinet, Evans Willima that the FEMAC membership should include representatives of the private sector through their umbrella body, the Zambia Industrial and Commercial Association (ZINCOM). I argued that the representatives would assist in the detailed assessment of the applications as they knew the active players in the various sectors of the economy. While waiting for a reply from the SC, I briefed both Dominic Mulaisho at State House and Vernon J. Mwaanga, Chairman of ZINCOM, who both heartily welcomed my proposal.

The Secretary to the Cabinet, who was totally opposed to my proposal, rebuked me during my meeting with him for proposing the involvement of the private sector in a highly sensitive function of the government. I was frightened by his threat and thoroughly disappointed with the tone of the conversation as I'd known Willima at the MRD when he'd been my permanent secretary. At the time, he had shown a lot of confidence in me, treated me very well, and respected my professional advice. This time around, he threatened that he would recommend to the president that I do not get confirmed in my acting appointment as permanent secretary for showing such anti-government behaviour.

Fortunately, my proposal was leaked and published in one of the dailies during the weekend of the Zambia International Trade Fair in 1983 and it received overwhelming support from the private sector. The secretary to the cabinet succumbed to the public's positive reaction by approving my proposal.

The private sector nominated members to FEMAC and immediately, the number of applications for foreign exchange reduced significantly. The applications from the private sector were subdivided into sectors and initially vetted by the sector committees of ZINCOM before being considered by the FEMAC. This was one of the most meaningful collaborations between the public and private sectors in the economy.

Many deserving private companies, whose operations had been constrained by lack of foreign exchange for a long time, welcomed the new arrangement. Amongst the successful happy bidders were a group of women entrepreneurs who had started exporting locally made goods, two food canning companies that imported new modern equipment, a chemical company, a company running double-decker buses that eased transport problems in Lusaka City and a company importing irrigation equipment.

I visited most of the companies that were allocated foreign exchange to appreciate their operations. I came to know the owners and managers, with whom I cultivated long-lasting personal relationships. Apart from Arthur Bbuku, whom I had been with at Chikankata and Munali Schools, new associates, running important industries included Mrs Catherine Mwanamwambwa, Mrs Katongo Maine, Chad Kaunda, Ashok Oza, Pat Puta, and Amon Sibande

The new system, which was more transparent and inclusive, had its own enemies, the black dealers, who thrived on false applications and the selling of foreign exchange on the black market. They were not happy as their life-line had been cut off. I was accused of owning shares in so many companies that became vibrant due to the new foreign exchange allocations system.

The other outcome of the involvement of ZINCOM was an allegation that I had secretly approved an allocation of US $2 million foreign exchange to Zambia Safaris Limited, a tourism company in which VJ was a partner. How could I have secretly allocated so much foreign exchange to one company when I had just opened up the system to the involvement of so many other stakeholders?

While pondering on an appropriate response to these malicious allegations, the Director of the Anti-Corruption Commission (ACC), His Lordship Justice Brian Doyle summoned me to his office. He disclosed that investigations into the US $2 million allegation had been going on for some time. He informed me that the investigations were closed as there was no evidence on the allegations.

He then showed me a bulky file, which contained investigations on many allegations against me. He stated that so far all the allegations against me had been found to be false. He encouraged me to continue being upright in my work.

Due to the heavy demand on my time at the MCTI, I had a written down schedule, which was religious followed by my Personal Secretary, Mary Mukuwa. This enabled me to meet many customers. By the time I left the Ministry, I was happy that I had known personally not less than eighty per cent of the captains of the Zambian industry and that my personal decisions had assisted them to contribute to the development of the country.

Of particular interest to me was the establishment of many agro-processing companies producing such items as canned fruit juices, canned meat, and livestock feeds. The economy was being diversified away from mining and primary agricultural commodity production.

I became convinced that with more financial support and political will, our local entrepreneurs were capable of manufacturing a lot of goods for both the local and foreign markets. I have kept this faith and this is what has made me use any given opportunity as a public offer to support local companies. The development of the internet has provided an opportunity for budding entrepreneurs to acquire information and appropriate equipment or designs from anywhere in the world.

With the encouragement of the Director General of the ACC, we became very strict with the allocation of foreign exchange, insisting that all applications must follow the laid down procedure. An application by National Holdings Limited, a UNIP Party company managed by Petronela Chisanga, nee Kawandami was not considered due to not submitting the detailed documents on time and this did not go down well with Humphrey Mulemba the secretary general of UNIP.

He was incensed when Mary Mukuwa, my personal assistant, did not recognize his voice on the telephone and made him wait for me to finish a discussion with some businessmen before passing over the call to me. My apology was unacceptable to the SG of the Party, for what he termed my rudeness and insubordination to the Acting Head of State. The SG slammed the telephone receiver and later publicly displayed his anger by refusing to shake hands at the airport when we received President Kaunda from his foreign trip.

I now had poor relations with the two most senior public officers. These were the secretary general of the party and the secretary to the cabinet. Luckily, my appointing authority was the president and the two could only make recommendations to my appointing authority. Our differences were caused by my wanting to institute a transparent and rational system of allocating the country's foreign exchange.

A few days later, I was summoned by Prime Minister Nalumino Mundia, who enquired on what had transpired between Mulemba and me, as he had recommended my dismissal from employment. After I explained the telephone incident, the PM revealed that the president had instead decided to transfer me to Kabwe as PS for the Central Province. He advised me to obey any instructions that may be issued on the transfer, as he believed that I will be back in Lusaka soon.

In March 1984, I was transferred from the Ministry of Commerce, Trade and Industry to Kabwe, Central Province, in the same capacity of permanent secretary. Although there was apprehension that I will refuse the transfer, I moved to Kabwe immediately as directed by the head of state. I imagined that this will give me an opportunity to learn how to operate at provincial level at a senior level., since I had worked in the Southern Province earlier in the seventies.

As head of the civil service in the province, I was also responsible for party matters such as organizing the site for a UNIP convention at the Mulungushi Rock of Authority, near Kabwe. Joshua Mumpashya, Member of the Central Committee and Musole Kanyungulu, Provincial Political Secretary and I had to receive the UNIP Secretary General, when he visited Kabwe to check on the preparations for the convention. To my embarrassment, he withdrew his hand once he had greeted the two officials at the helipad, where we went to meet him.

I had a useful and educative stay in the province, which included extensive tours of the Serenje, Kapiri Mposhi, Mkushi, and Kabwe Districts. The opportunity of touring the Kabwe underground mine gave me a sense of the hazardous work the miners have to do. I visited a number of farmers in the Mkushi Farming Block and in the ZCCM settlement scheme in the Kabwe District. I did not only admire the excellent tobacco crops in the Mkushi Block, but I decided to grow some tobacco at our Choma farm during the 1984/85 season.

I toured the Mulungushi Textiles and the Zambia Railways Headquarters including the company's ultra-modern workshop, capable of forging any kind of industrial piece of equipment. I encouraged ZR management to advertise their engineering capability to the public, especially the large farming community in the province. We asked ZR management to submit regular reports to the office of the MCC on their operations. The Managing Director, Emmanuel M. Hachipuka, welcomed this invitation and kept our office up to date with information on the operations of the Zambia Railways.

In 1985, it was the turn of the Kabwe Golf Club to organize a tournament, which was on the national golf calendar. The club requested the assistance of our office in inviting President Kaunda to grace the occasion. As a keen golfer, the president accepted the invitation and travelled to Kabwe for the tournament.

As we were waiting for the game to start, the president asked for my handicap. I jokingly replied that I was on handicap 36, which is the starters' grade. I had not even started playing golf. In the midst of laughter in the club room, the president stated that he will not transfer me from Kabwe until I had attained handicap 18 and become a bogey golfer. That is when I realized that the president's visit to Kabwe was not only for golf but was meant to get an assessment of my performance in running the province.

Taking industrialization to rural areas

In keeping with the close relations I had fostered while at the Ministry of Finance, Lumbamba Nyambe, Managing Director of DBZ, kept me abreast of developments in his institution. He reported that the Bank had made a lot of progress in identifying viable projects in the various parts of the country.

However, the Bank's efforts to identify local partners by advertising in the newspapers had not achieved much progress. There were very few Zambians who were thinking of going into large-scale industries at the time. The MD asked our ministry to help in identifying potential Zambian investors, who could partner with the Bank.

In 1982, while I was Director of Budget at the Ministry of Finance and a member of the DBZ Board, I had urged the DBZ to apply a discriminatory policy of favouring indigenous Zambians in loan approvals. Once, I successfully prevailed on the board to reject a loan application by some resident

Zambians for a hotel in a rural area of Zambia.

As early as 1982, I knew the powers of the Minister of Finance over all the parastatals. The request by the MD of DBZ to find local people was, therefore, a personal challenge to me for my earlier uncompromising stand on supporting indigenous Zambians.

One of the projects identified was the mining of agricultural lime at Chivuna, some twenty kilometres from Mazabuka Town. The Bank hired a geological company that carried out some exploration work, which revealed a deposit of over 50 million tonnes of lime. Another project was for timber logging and furniture manufacturing in the Luapula Province.

Samples of the limestone sent to laboratories in Germany and USA indicated a very high content of magnesium oxide (MgO) of twenty-one per cent and calcium oxide of forty-nine per cent, making the lime most suitable for agricultural and industrial purposes. The use of lime enriches the soils for crop farming after many years of applying chemical fertilisers.

I took the MD's challenge and asked Daniel Mapiki Simooloka, a businessman in Monze, to form an organization as a vehicle for the mining of the lime. Chivuna Lime Project Limited was formed and registered on 6th September 1985 under the umbrella of the Monze Ranching, Dairy, and Mining Cooperative Society.

Simooloka became chairman of the new company. Mr Lazarus Beviny Cheelo, the Simutwe university graduate, who'd given Geoffrey and me a free lift to Munali Secondary School in 1964, was appointed the managing director. I used some bit of influence to get Cheelo appointed as my part payment for his benevolent act of 1964.

Due to complicated land ownership in rural areas, plot 3940, the project's land was held under a Tenancy-in-Common. Membership of the tenancy included Chief Hanjalika (John Hamweenzu Matambo), G. P. Chiboola, J. Jabala, V. Michelo and the chairman.

The DBZ advanced a loan, which was used to pay for equipment in 1989 from Dr H. Marx, a Germany engineering company. With the involvement of the Minister of Finance, Gibson Chigaga and the Zambia Cooperative Federation Limited, the USAID chipped in with a handsome grant to the company in 1990 for site preparation and construction of infrastructure.

The USAID when approving the request to finance the project demanded an enlarged membership of the cooperative to accommodate the local people. They also indicated a willingness to give more money to import additional modern mining equipment once the site infrastructure had been completed. Bennie Mwiinga and I paid the membership fees for all the new members, most of whom were villagers in the Chivuna area.

I negotiated for storage of the project's machinery, including laboratory equipment, at the Nakambala offices of the Zambia Sugar Company, while waiting for completion of the construction works, which were being done by

Messrs Minestone Limited. In view of the slow progress, one of the potential large customers for the lime, ZCCM Limited got interested in taking over and developing the lime mining operations at Chivuna.

When I learnt of a plan by ZCCM of constructing a railway line from Chivuna to Magoye, I got excited and persuaded the cooperative members to work jointly with the ZCCM. But the chairman of the cooperative could not be moved. He instead sought the personal intervention of President Kaunda to stop the takeover of the mine by ZCCM. The strong belief in cooperatives at the time invoked the sympathy of President Kaunda who persuaded ZCCM to back off.

In November 1993, the Minister of Agriculture, Food and Fisheries, Simon B. Zukas expressed his support for the project by asking Dean Mung'omba at the National Commission for Development Planning to seek donor financial assistance.

In spite of my urging, the company management failed to account for the released funds in the manner agreed with the USAID and the Ministry of Finance. The DBZ loan could not be serviced. Minestone, who were owed large amounts of money, seized the equipment, which they sold elsewhere. Financial assistance dried up and in spite of the presidential support, the project could not progress. After the failure of this viable project and Lukamantano Cooperative Society in 1975, my support and enthusiasm for cooperatives waned.

The huge lime deposit, which is registered by the SADC Secretariat as having a capacity to supply agricultural lime to the whole region, lies unexploited. The project for timber production, which was identified in the Luapula Province could also not be developed due to lack of capable local partners.

Member of the Tariff Commission Enquiry

Zambia's industrialization after independence was based on import substitution, whose major principle is the high protection of local industries. The goal was to produce many of the imported commodities in the country with minimum consideration for comparative advantage. While there were local raw materials to process agricultural commodities, other products required imported raw materials. As the country ran out of foreign exchange in the eighties, the production of these goods was adversely affected. The shortages caused distortions in the pricing of most goods, especially consumables, in the economy. Government's policy of price control was impossible to apply.

In June 1986, President Kaunda appointed me a member of a Tariff Commission Enquiry to collect the public's opinion on the state of the country's tariffs. The nineteen-member commission under Chairman Mark Chona and Secretary Mumba Kapumba included John Hudson of ZNFU,

Japhter Nkunika of the Customs Department, Lazarus Bwalya of the Taxes Department, Mrs Grace Silangwa of INDECO, Clement Mambwe, Situmbeko Musokotwane, Andrew Kashita, Edwin Koloko of ZCCM, and Martin Sakala of the Bank of Zambia.

The Commission toured the whole country over a period of thirty days, holding public hearings in all the eight provincial centres. This gave me the opportunity to intimately know the members of our Commission, most of whom I closely worked with later in life. I had the privilege of visiting many of the places I had been to earlier while on various other assignments. I found the Commission's work useful and have used the data gained on this assignment in my public service and consultancy assignments.

CHAPTER 12

Rewarded By The Food And Agriculture Organization

In June 1985, I was transferred back to Lusaka to head the Ministry of Agriculture and Water Development. The ministry's operations were familiar to me as I'd worked there as a planner for eight years between 1972 and 1980.

The Minister at MAWD was General Kingsley Chinkuli, former and first Zambian Commander of the Zambia Army. Having gone to a famous Military Academy in UK, the Minister was particular on everyone obeying all his instructions. My stint at the Ministry of Defence and the experience of working with many bosses of different dispositions helped me to relate to the General's military instructions. The Minister was assisted by two Deputy Ministers, namely Daniel Munkombwe and Gilbert Zimba.

Apart from supervising the ministry's planning operations in 1975, I was in the Zambian team, which campaigned for Lebanese Edouard Saouma for the position of director general of the FAO of the United Nations. Following his election, the new DG offered Zambia a position of Assistant Director General. The ministry identified Daniel Hanene Luzongo who was accepted by the FAO but was stopped from taking up the appointment by presidential decree. At the time, I was too junior and young to vie for such a high international job.

Ten years later in 1985, I led the Zambian delegation to the annual meeting of the FAO in Rome. I read out a supportive country statement in which I recalled the many positive developments that had taken place under the initiatives of Director General Saouma. Among them were the establishment of independent offices of the FAO in member states, the establishment of World Food Day, the creation of the FAO Technical Cooperation Programme, and his dedication and support to third world countries. With Zambia having benefitted from these initiatives, I, therefore, joined the other delegates of developing countries in supporting his re-election for another term.

Immediately after delivery of the statement, I was invited to the office of an Assistant Director General. Our conversation on Zambian agriculture included a lot of questions on my personal profile. I wondered if I was being considered for an appointment in the organization. Having missed the opportunity in the seventies, due to age consideration, I was willing to accept the offer if made. My host ended our conversation by thanking me for the detailed brief on Zambia's agricultural industry.

A few months later, His Excellency S.A.T Wadda, FAO Resident Representative to Zambia delivered an invitation from the FAO Director General for me to visit any country of my choice in the world to be fully funded by the FAO. He explained that the minimum period of the visit should be thirty days. I accepted the invitation, but Cabinet Office indicated that at my level, I could not be released for a period of thirty days. However, after some negotiations with the secretary to the cabinet, I was allowed to undertake the trip for the full period.

Having already visited many parts of the world, I chose Brazil in South America as my preferred destination. Brazil the largest country covering forty-seven per cent of the continent attracted my curiosity. I had visited Guyana in South America in 1976 on a study tour as a student at the World Bank's Economic Development Institute and I was desirous of seeing the larger part of the South American continent.

The trip, which I made in April and May 1986, covered all the regions of Brazil from the north to the south and included stopovers in Salvador, Recife, Petrolina, Brasilia, Londrina, Sao Paolo and Rio de Janeiro. I visited a number of agricultural research stations and some large agricultural production and equipment manufacturing establishments.

I was fascinated and highly impressed by the research work in the production and utilization of cassava, soya beans, and sugarcane crops. Brazil was way ahead in the use of fuel from sugarcane and cassava. Cassava had also a special place in the diet of the Brazilian people as a source of carbohydrates. I was amazed that cassava was readily available in all eating establishments, including first-class hotels. Cassava flour was freely sprinkled on meals even by those who did not consume sugar or salt.

During my stopover in Brasilia, the capital of Brazil, I met some Zambian students. These were Gerald Wakumelo, Duncan Chaloba, Leon Mboloma, and Steve Mwamba, who organized a get-together for me. After learning of some of their problems, I discussed these by telephone with genial Nalumino Mundia, the Zambian Ambassador responsible for Brazil but based in the USA.

Brasilia, the capital, is well-designed with innovative and imaginative architecture. The city was planned by Lucio Costa and the buildings designed by a team under the renowned architect Oscar Niemeyer, who took part designing the United Nations Headquarters building in New York in the early 1950s.

The satellite townships, where most of the population of Brasilia live, are located some twenty kilometres away from the city centre. All social amenities such as education and health facilities are available in the townships. The people come into the city mostly by efficient public transport only for business, either in government offices or private companies. Brasilia City is the only twentieth-century city that was declared a UNESCO World Heritage Site. I had the privilege of touring the magnificent hyperboloid Cathedral of Brasilia.

While visiting a successful and wealthy fruit farmer on two acres of land, I plucked an enticing guava fruit from a tree. The farmer assured me that I could establish a guava plantation in Zambia from the seeds of the one fruit after eating it. As advised, I dried and carried the seeds. At the Heathrow Airport I shocked a customs officer when he realized that I'd gone through the red light just to declare a few fruit seeds wrapped in a piece of paper. After lecturing him about the strict plant importation control measures in place in Zambia at the time, the officer allowed me to carry the seeds through the airport.

At the Lusaka International Airport, the customs officer allowed me to carry the seeds only after talking to an agricultural officer. I gave the seeds to Tex Habeenzu, a former schoolmate and an expert horticulturist at Mount Makulu Research Station. Habeenzu produced healthy seedlings that we used to establish a flourishing orchard of guava trees at our Choma farm.

While on a visit in the Makeni area, a friend boasted of some juicy quavas in his garden. He reluctantly disclosed that he got the seedlings from Habeenzu. We had a nice laugh, when I told him that he had been given seedlings from my batch. The ever-green five hundred trees producing juicy fruits are a living symbol of practical technology transfer from Brazil to Zambia.

We tried to sell the quavas in Choma Town, but the Zambians' taste buds are averse to eating fruits. Our offer to the community of Njase Girls Secondary School to harvest free quavas every weekend was only honoured on three weekends. We were informed that, the students regarded harvesting quavas, as a demeaning hobby. During the years of flush fruits, we allow a troop of baboons, which makes an annual pilgrimage to the farm, to help us in reducing the wastage.

My tour to Brazil gave me the added impetus to supervise the planning and establishment of large estates for the production of cassava and sugarcane. The Brazilians had developed the technology for the production of ethanol from these crops and popularized their use in vehicles and industrial machines, thereby reducing the cost of industrialization.

I did not stay long at MAWD after my return from Brazil as I was transferred to the National Commission for Development Planning in July 1986. Having worked in ministries dealing with agriculture, commerce, finance, industry, local government, security, trade, I was entrusted with the responsibility of overseeing the country's planning system. This was an exciting experience and opened my thinking to conceptualizing synergies amongst the Zambian government structures and programmes.

CHAPTER 13

The Revival Of An Effective Agricultural Credit System

With the Zambian economy going into a slumber in the mid-eighties, there was no room for ambitious new infrastructure projects. The relations between the Zambian Government and the international donor community were strained due to differences on the implementation of policy reforms. The Zambian Government felt that attention should again be redirected to the development of the agricultural sector as the mining sector had failed the country.

At a press conference held on 27 November 1986, President Kaunda announced a proposal to rationalize all agricultural credit institutions and create an agricultural bank to be known as Lima Bank. Recalling that I had recommended the creation of a new agricultural credit institution in 1978, and perhaps to test my conviction on the recommendations I had made earlier, President Kaunda appointed me the pioneering managing director of the Lima Bank.

In the afternoon, I was summoned by Prime Minister Kebby Musokotwane to his office. After a few pleasantries and congratulations, the Prime Minister briefed me on the importance of the bank in view of the government's plans to revamp the agricultural sector. He informed me that he had confidence in me and that he will be available for any consultations. I had expected more about the new bank, but the Prime Minister did not give much on the new institution.

When I got home that evening, I was questioned by my family about my new job at a non-existent organization. I assured them that I'd helped to create the new Zambia Agricultural Development Bank (ZADB) at the Ministry of Agriculture and Water Development and establishing Lima Bank would not be a big problem.

I recollect making some notes on the new bank that very evening on the kitchen table while bouncing off some of my ideas with Joyce, as she prepared our supper. The new bank was to assist farmers to efficiently grow more food and I had to strategize how this would be done in the appropriate setting of the kitchen.

I visited the Ministry of Agriculture to get briefed by senior officials but I was met with a hostile reception and directed to the Ministry of Finance for advice since Lima Bank was a financial institution. The reception at the Ministry of Finance was no better than that which I'd received at the other ministry.

For over one month, I had no office, no staff and no finances to operationalize the new bank and nobody seemed to care. I suspect that the President was being told that all was well. I was operating from our house as if I was starting a private institution for personal gain. Later in December 1986, I was given two offices by Managing Director Amon Chibiya of the ZADB in Society House on Cairo Road, within the floors used by his institution. The Ministry of Cooperatives under Minister Justin Mukando and Permanent Secretary Yuyi Libakeni was also housed in the same building, which had four elevators.

I immediately realized and felt the infinite powers of managers of parastatal organizations as one elevator was reserved for the sole use of the managing director of the Zambia National Building Society. Not even a minister could use it even if it was the only one in working order. At Mulungushi House, where Mukando, Libakeni, and I had worked, four ministers and hundreds of officers shared two elevators.

The rude comments I heard while in the other three elevators invoked my intervention. My friendly conversation with the concerned managing director resulted in the abandonment of the assumed powers over a public property and saved the officer from insults by the aggrieved passengers.

Just before Christmas in 1986, I was given a cheque by the permanent secretary at the Ministry of Finance for the operations of the Lima Bank. Since the new bank had no bank account, the cheque of one million Kwacha was in my name. I kept it at home during the long Christmas holidays and deposited it into our family account the following week.

Early in 1987, Mumba Kapumpa assisted me to finalize the Articles of Association, while I worked on the conditions of service, audit, and credit control systems and regulations. In March 1987, the board of directors for the Lima Bank under Chairman Kapasa Makasa was appointed. I and my Personal Assistant Sherry Simubali relocated from Society House to the AFC offices in Kulima House along Cha Cha Cha Road.

When reporting to the board on the progress made so far in finalizing the various documents for the operationalization of the Bank, I recommended the use of experts to come up with acceptable personnel procedures. We then engaged the Copper Industries Service Bureau (CISB) of ZCCM to undertake a thorough job evaluation and the consultant's proposals formed part of the important documents in the operations of the Bank.

At the end of April, the Government released a K50 million cheque in the name of the Lima Bank, which had no bank account. I asked the permanent secretary about my counter-signatory when opening a new account as there were no other officers of the bank. He replied that since he had solved my problem of lack of money, other issues, including that of where to keep the money, were my responsibility to resolve.

It took me some days to negotiate with the MD of ZADB to allow his Chief Accountant to be a co-signatory. I was finally greatly relieved having deposited the cheque in a new account in one of the commercial banks for safety. I then retired the one million kwacha that I had received earlier.

In mid-1987, the AFC was dissolved and Lima Bank took over all the assets and liabilities of both the AFC and ZADB. Amongst the assets was a large number of members of staff and a huge stock of bad debts as AFC had relaxed its lending procedures in consonance with the socialist policies that had developed in other economic areas.

Many of the delinquent borrowers of the AFC were those who wrongly believed that the loans were not to be repaid as they were independence gifts. They were debtors to the COZ, which had been formed immediately after independence. The new bank implemented strict lending rules and debt collection measures, such as confiscation of valuable assets including cattle from cattle-keeping defaulters.

I directed the Lima Bank officials at the Kalomo branch to confiscate cattle from a well-known village headman and to release them only after he'd paid the total outstanding loan. This approach sent a clear message to debtors and changed the behaviour of the borrowers. At the end of the 1988/89 season, the Bank's loan recovery rate improved significantly to over eighty-five per cent.

The AfDB was even prepared to give a line of credit to the Bank because "Lima Bank Limited has a strong leadership which is doing a commendable job in laying the foundation for the evolution of a well-organized and viable financial institution." Unfortunately, the Ministry of Finance did not approve the loan.

In 1989, Lima Bank acquired a computer from Woodgate Holdings Limited. A thorough orientation on its proper operation and use were given by Misiteli Ngwenya and Ernest Zebron staff of the seller. Many officers and I took a keen interest in learning the use of the computer and were able to keep accurate data on the operations of the bank. This increased the resource envelope for the loan portfolio of the bank as all recovered money was put into the revolving loan fund.

I attended a seminar on, "New Financial Instruments for Development" at George Washington University in the USA, sponsored by the US Agency for International Development (USAID). With additional tools acquired, I introduced new management systems in the bank. As a result, the bank's annual loan recovery rates went up to above ninety-five per cent.

The good loan recovery rates excited the Lima Bank management, who allocated more funds for lending. Special schemes for lending for beekeeping, irrigation, timber logging, and artisanal fishing were introduced in selected and suitable areas of the country. The programme included the identification of manufacturers or importers of various equipments such as saws, ploughs, hammer mills, scotch carts, beehives, boat engines, fishnets, and banana boats, which were required by our clients in the rural areas.

Approved loans were paid directly to the suppliers, while our clients just collected the implements by the presentation of Local Purchase Orders (LPOs), without handling any money. These schemes saw a resurgence of economic activities in areas such as Kabompo, Kaoma, Sinazongwe, and Samfwa. The performance assessments for staff were on the basis of their lending levels for the activities suited to their areas. Slowly, there was some diversification away from cropping in the economic activities in many rural areas.

The Kaleya Engineering Limited, owned by Boart (Zambia) Limited of Anglo American Limited was identified as the supplier of oxen implements to Lima Bank clients. Nkwazi Net Company of Kafue was the supplier of nets and boats, while Marine Services of Lusaka supplied boat engines. The arrangement worked very well and many small-scale farmers were equipped through loans from Lima Bank. The bank paid the suppliers for bulk delivery of the equipment to the branch nearest to the customers.

My managers and I created close relationships with the owners and those managing all the companies. We could contact them at short notice and get our requirements. I became personally acquainted with Piet Siwale of Boart, Siyoto Kunyanda of Marine Services, Peter Munthali of Nkwazi Net Manufacturing, and Ashok Oza of Saro Engineering Limited.

One aspect of farming, which I still felt had not been adequately attended to, was irrigated agriculture. I was aware that special programmes had been designed in the past in order to finance irrigated farming, in particular for special crops such as flowers and vegetables. However, the earlier financing schemes by the Zambian Government and financial institutions benefitted mostly the expatriate commercial farmers in the semi-urban areas.

It was clear that once these farmers had made their money, they diversified into other enterprises or left the country. This time around, Lima Bank management, against the Board's resistance, was keen to try some Zambian farmers with the latest centre pivot irrigation technology.

Louis Chilala was a renowned and prosperous farmer close to Mazabuka Town having successfully applied the loans he got from commercial banks. One of his sons, Costain Chilala, abandoned studies at UNZA in preference to becoming a full-time farmer in the Mkushi Block. The old man affectionately talked about his son who loved farming and who had taken after him.

During one of my farm tours, my team was hosted by budding farmer Chilala. He had begun to develop some irrigation farming drawing water from the nearby Lunsemfwa River. He was already showing the same traits of successful farming as his father. I, therefore, picked Costain Chilala as a suitable guinea pig for my vision in large-scale irrigated farming.

I had seen and admired large irrigation farms in Brazil, Iraq, and the USA during my tours and had planned irrigation projects of various sizes while in government. I was convinced that Zambia's future was in agriculture and in particular in irrigated farming.

President Kaunda kept lamenting about the millions of litres of water that mocked at him as they flowed away to the oceans. I was determined to banish the shame of the Head of State. With my involvement, we had already trapped billions of litres of water at Mazabuka and at Mpongwe for the irrigation of thousands of hectares of sugarcane, soya beans and flowers.

I summoned Chilala to my office and introduced my plan to him. He was initially reluctant to commit himself to a large loan at the time. I explained to him about the easy-to-use modern centre pivot irrigation technology and assured him that with the waters of the perennial Lunsenfwa River, he would succeed.

After some months of persuasion and hesitation, Chilala agreed to append his signature to a loan application form, which had been filled in by the branch manager for our new Mkushi Branch, on my instructions. Chilala's loan application, for two centre pivots, was deferred twice by the board due to strong objections from two board members.

Lawrence Bwalya representing ZIMCO Limited was one of the board members who felt that the loan was being recommended on personal and tribal basis as Chilala and I were Tongas. Although I got offended with this accusation, I decided not to give up. My appeal to senior officers at ZIMCO was favourably considered and the application approved.

In spite of loan funds being readily available, Chilala had to overcome a series of obstacles in order to get the project off the ground. At some point, he camped in Lusaka for days just to get an appointment with a public officer who was responsible for issuing water permits. While millions of litres of water were cascading over the Muchinga Escarpment and 'mocking' President Kaunda, approving a permit to farmer Chilala to extract water for irrigation was proving near impossible. While I had appreciated the ZESCO objection to allow extraction of additional water at Nakambala, I could not understand the resistance to grant a permit to farmer Chilala. After visiting the equipment suppliers in the USA, Chilala realized the ease of operating the modern technology and he became resolute and more determined to implement the project.

Finally, the two centre pivots were installed and with the new irrigation technology, Chilala was set on the path to becoming a successful commercial farmer. By 2006, Chilala had installed forty-two centre pivots at his Chimsoro Farms. The 'tribal' ZIMCO Board member was not available to visit Chimsoro

Farms to see the fruits of my Tonga experiment.

Chimsoro Farms cultivated the second largest irrigated fields after the Nakambala Sugar Estates, for which I also helped to get additional water from the Kafue River in the seventies. Maize yields of over six tonnes (120 bags) per hectare and wheat yields of eight tonnes per hectare by Chimsoro Farms beat even those achieved at crop research stations. Chimsoro Farms produced ten per cent of Zambia's grain requirements. This meant that Zambia needed only ten farmers of Chilala's proficiency and size for the country's grain needs to be met. This has been my vision.

Costain Chilala was decorated with a Medal of Distinguished Service by the president of the Republic of Zambia for his contribution to the country's food security in October 2002. As he walked with pomp on the grounds of State House, I could see that he was relishing the deserved thunderous ovation. Although I was not invited to the ceremony and watched television from our lounge, less than one kilometre away from State House, I felt proud to have been a designer and creator of an indigenous Zambian farming hero.

Apart from Chilala, other farmers were assisted under the Lima Bank Irrigation Fund. Many specialized in growing exotic flowers and vegetables. A group of female entrepreneurs, among them Mrs Catherine Mwanamwambwa and Mrs Katongo Maine, whom I knew when I was at the MCTI, were engaged in growing vegetables and flowers for export.

With financial support from a loan fund at the DBZ, the number of Zambian farmers practicing irrigated farming in the semi-urban areas increased and both floriculture and vegetable farming thrived in Zambia.

The responsibilities at Lima Bank brought me closer to the ordinary people in the agricultural sector from all corners of Zambia. I had another opportunity to visit the various parts of the country to discuss real and local issues. I revisited some of the projects I'd initiated while at the MRD in the seventies. I was a recognizable figure even in the rural areas of the country.

With my added skills in financial institutions, I assisted many Zambians to establish commercial banks and consultancy firms in various professions. As a development bank, the Lima Bank supported newly created or established commercial banks by maintaining active accounts in these banks. Amongst them were Capital Bank and Finance Bank, which were established and owned by local businessmen whom I knew very well.

Internationally, I was a consultant to the FAO on agricultural credit, to the World Bank on the futuristic report on "Sustainable Growth with Equity in Sub-Saharan Africa – A Long-Term Perspective", and to the International Food Policy Research Institute (IFPRI). Assignments I carried out for these multilateral institutions gave me the opportunity to understand their development policies and strategies implemented at the global level.

In February 1991, I received an unexpected visitor at my office at Lima Bank. My personal assistant, Shirley Simubali, informed me that Mr Mulemba had come to see me. I asked her which Mulemba, recalling my sad encounter with Humphrey Mulemba in 1983 when he was secretary general of the ruling party and I was at MCTI. She informed me that it was Humphrey Mulemba and I still asked her, "Which one?"

Simubali then came into the office to confirm that it was the former SG of UNIP and she asked me if I had a problem seeing him. I told her to allow him to come in. The few minutes before his entry into my office were some of my tortuous in my life because I did not know what had brought him to my office. As he entered, he shouted, "Peter, how are you?" while extending his hand for a handshake. I was delighted that the hand that had been withdrawn from me for the previous eight years was now readily available for me to shake.

We discussed agriculture in Zambia and the great potential awaiting a supporting environment. He praised me for the work I was doing at the Lima Bank. Mulemba then turned to politics and informed me of his role in the new Movement for Multiparty Democracy (MMD He stated that the MMD would like me to join the incoming administration. He indicated that they had discussed my placement at either the Bank of Zambia or the Ministry of Finance. In reply, I assured him that I was ready and willing to work in any suitable capacity for the sake of my country.

After Mulemba left, I took time to explain to Simubali my past relationship with him and why I had been apprehensive about his visit. I then briefed her on the purpose of his visit. She encouraged me to accept the offer as my technical skills could be useful to the country, even under a new political party. A few days later, Flavia Musakanya dropped in and delivered a message similar to the one by Mulemba. I had also known her while at MCTI, but under some pleasant circumstances as an enterprising business lady.

The visits to my office by two prominent members of the new MMD Party must have become common knowledge in government circles. A district governor from the Eastern Province visited State House and reported that Lima Bank had given out a lot of loans to opposition farmers. He recommended that I be dismissed as managing director.

Simubali informed me that she had heard a story that I was likely to be dismissed from Lima Bank for supporting the new opposition. While I had supplied some information, I was concerned that such an action would dent the good reputation, which I had labored to build for twenty years in the public service. I was not overly worried about losing a job as our Choma farm was doing well and I was prepared to relocate to the farm.

CHAPTER 14

The Dawn Of Change In Zambia's Governance

As the slogan, 'it pays to belong to UNIP' became a channel of getting more public resources for personal use, humanism, a noble ideology, which had been promulgated by President Kaunda in order to develop an equitable way of sharing the country's wealth could not take root. The management of parastatal organisations showed great ambivalence, accommodating both those who favoured socialism and the supporters of capitalism.

The increased loan approvals by the Lima Bank, which I was managing, were attributed to my alleged support for the opposition and not seen as a way of enriching the poor farmers. Some UNIP leaders even recommended my dismissal for giving out loans to farmers from public funds.

President Kaunda did not fire me. Instead, he transferred me on 22 March 1991 to the Industrial Development Corporation Limited (INDECO) to assume the position of Executive Director (Agri-business). I was responsible for supervising the chief executive officers of twelve quasi-government agriculture and agro-processing companies. I joined the team of Lawrence Bwalya, Evaristo Kasunga, Dennis Lwiindi, Maxwell Mwila, Shimukowa Shalaulwa, and Stanley Tamele under Mwene Mwinga, the managing director.

In the letter of transfer, the President was gracious enough to thank me for "the services you have rendered in setting up the Lima Bank and steering it through its first years of existence". He revealed that INDECO was going through a difficult time and that the changed economic policies would usher in a period of greater competition. Amongst the major new policies were the privatization of some parastatals and the liberalisation of the economy.

Sometime in the eighties, the Zambian Government invited UNIDO and UNCTAD to help survey the availability of raw materials for processing in the various parts of the country. The survey, supervised by Akashambatwa Mbikusita-Lewanika, Director of Projects in INDECO Limited, identified various raw materials in each district of the country. Just as the agronomic study of 1974 was the reference for crop and livestock production plans, the INDECO industrial raw material survey was used to establish various industries in the country. It was such judicious planning that all parts of Zambia had some local industry using local raw materials and to engage the local community.

In view of the growing inefficiencies in the management of the parastatal companies, a study was initiated in 1990 to come up with a reform agenda. The UNIP National Convention of March 1990 resolved to implement privatisation of non-strategic state companies. Mwene Mwinga, a member of the Central Committee of UNIP was appointed as Chairman of a 'Task Force on Privatisation', formed in September 1990 to recommend modalities for privatisation.

INDECO Limited was renting out some of the surplus office space in INDECO House to private companies. One of INDECO's tenants on the seventh floor was Productivity Computer Systems Limited, owned and operated by Robert 'Bob' Sichinga, who was in the business of selling Compaq computers.

I had been fascinated by the new computer technology that was fast spreading across the globe. The computerization of the Lima Bank made me appreciate the benefits of the real-time application of computer technology to operational challenges. I, therefore, acquired a Compaq Prolinea 4/25E personal computer from Sichinga's company for personal use and made great efforts to learn how to use it.

In the process of discussing personal business, Sichinga and I concluded our conversations with the topical issue of the economic and political situation in the country. We shared some notes on a number of development issues and how the situation could be remedied. Some of the notes ended up at the MMD Party Secretariat and were incorporated in the MMD Party Manifesto.

Due to the coming in of a new government with a stronger bias towards economic liberalisation and privatisation, the focus of the reform study was reviewed in 1991. The study considered the future roles and the appropriate restructuring of ZIMCO and its subholding companies within a liberalised economy, taking into account the on-going privatisation programme.

In July 1992, Privatisation Act No. 21 was passed to create the Zambia Privatisation Agency (ZPA). Members of the ZPA were appointed and John M. Mwanakatwe was elected Chairman in August 1992. In April 1993, ZIMCO was transformed into an investment holding company and I was transferred from the Zambia National Commercial Bank and appointed the group investment director (GID) responsible for the agribusiness directorate.

My assignment at INDECO Limited and ZIMCO consolidated my knowledge of the Zambian economy having been a provincial development planner, agricultural planner and farmer, public finance manager, industrial policy formulator, security advisor, regional public administrator, development banker, and now executive business manager. I was conversant with both the public and private sectors of the Zambian economy. With the high prospects of a new administration under a democratic environment, my earlier belief in the capability of Zambia's entrepreneurs was rekindled.

Many young people took advantage of the liberalized environment by being suppliers to the parastatal manufacturing companies. As the supervisor of many parastatal manufacturing companies, at times I had to intervene in order to resolve contractual problems. This gave me the opportunity to know many private suppliers. I took the opportunity to familiarize myself with the operations of the various companies through frequent country-wide visits to witness industrialization at work.

The revival and challenges of multi-party system in Zambia

In 1973, under an agreement signed between President Kaunda and Harry Nkumbula in Choma, Zambia became a one-party state, with UNIP the only registered legal party. The pact brought some peace amongst party cadres, who had engaged in violent confrontations. In enjoyment of the democratic rights that came with the country's independence in 1964, Zambians continued to vote for the president and the members of parliament during the One-Party Participatory Democracy period.

Regrettably, one-party states cultivate cults of personalities under which leaders are revered as demigods by the followers. In Zambia, Kenneth Kaunda, the only presidential candidate was pitted against an animal instead of a human being. In later elections, we had a choice between KK and a frog or a hyena. With so many hyenas in the numerous game parks in Zambia, it was inconceivable as to which hyena would have occupied State House if KK had lost the elections.

As populations increased, many socialist governments, including that of Zambia, failed to satisfactorily apply the socialist/communist principle of, "From each according to his ability, to each according to his needs". Production and productivity were getting less as the state was not allowing citizens to fully exploit their personal abilities. In many socialist countries, intellectuals and innovators were persecuted and management of the state enterprises was placed in the hands of party cadres.

In Zambia, UNIP's monopoly and poor governance, food shortages, and a general economic decline led to the sudden rise of a vibrant opposition movement. The economic situation deteriorated fast after the failure of the 1987 'Growth from Our Own Resources' development plan. The Zambian Government turned to the international community for assistance to revive the collapsed economy. With harsher conditions imposed by the BrettonWoods Institutions and donor community, it was not possible for the Zambian Government to continue with socialist economic management.

By the end of 1989, there were world-wide demonstrations against the socialist and communist establishments in preference to nationalism and liberalism. This movement galvanized a spirit of courageous defiance to one-party rule all over the world.

Due to the agitation within UNIP, the Fifth National Convention of the Party was held in March 1990 at the Mulungushi Conference Centre, to review and consider the rising tide of resistance to the one-party state and the democratization of party management. This turned out to be a good opportunity for the 'Young Turks' to express themselves on the topical political issues. The fighting spirits of the young turks and others opposed to KK's rule were fired up by the visit of Nelson Mandela a.k.a. 'Madiba' on 27 February 1990, after his release from twenty-seven years of imprisonment.

Amongst the UNIP rebels were Alexander Chikwanda, Vernon Mwaanga, Sikota Wina, and Fredrick Hapunda, who issued a written statement at the March 1990 convention on the unsatisfactory state of the management of both the Party and the Government. They openly called for the reform of the organization of UNIP and the abandonment of the one-party system. I was privileged to be briefed on some economic aspects of the written manifesto before it was delivered at the convention.

After presenting their views, the group stormed out of the convention as there seemed to be no consideration to acknowledge or accommodate their recommendations. This was an open internal rebellion within the UNIP and was unprecedented. However, these progressive voices were met by strong resistance and violence fanned by those who shouted, "Kumuulu Lesa, Pansi Kaunda", meaning "In heaven God, on earth Kaunda". The zealots of the One-Party system regarded KK as equivalent to God on earth.

On 19 June 1990, Prime Minister Malimba Masheke announced the removal of subsidies on maize meal, one of the conditions under the IMF program. The ensuing high food prices led to riots in Lusaka City Centre instigated by students from the University of Zambia. The proclaimed free health and education systems had broken down due to a lack of adequate resources.

In spite of the high prices for ordinary commodities, many were not readily available and one had to be on the lookout for any queue in town. Many people, especially from rural areas joined queues in the hope that they were for some rare commodity. After spending hours in the queue, they'd sadly discover that the queue was for the viewing of a corpse. As per Zambian funeral traditions, they filed past the dead bodies of strangers and made another trip the following day to hunt for the evasive essential commodities.

The privileged UNIP youths usually invaded the state shops as early as 04.00 hours in the morning. Aided by frightened shop managers, they bought all the essential commodities. They then sold these just outside the shops at very high prices in spite of the Government price control policy. I was fortunate to have a friend, who owned a grocery store in town. He alerted me whenever he managed to get some essential commodities for his shop.

Whenever an opportunity arose for me to make a foreign trip, I came back with additional tablets of soap and packets of sugar to share with customs officers at the airport and family friends. Socialism, which we extolled in our economics lessons at UNZA and the peaceful one-party state, had failed and life was not easy for the ordinary Zambians.

The Economics Association of Zambia (EAZ) used to hold monthly meetings open to members and the general public at the Pamodzi Hotel. I was a prominent member of the EAZ having participated in its evolution from 1981 when it was called the Economics Club housed at the UNZA Economics Department. I participated fully in the discussions sharing valuable information I had accumulated from the various organizations I had managed in the economy during twenty years of public service. The discussions at these monthly meetings always veered onto the state of the economy and the failure of socialist policies.

At a meeting held in early June 1990 at the Pamodzi Hotel, the discussions and mood were defiant and highly charged. A rumour filtered through that state agents were organizing to disrupt the meeting and arrest the attendants. We decided to move our meeting out into the car park to continue the discussions so that it would be easy for us to scamper when confronted.

It was at that meeting that a decision was made to invite selected Zambians to a special meeting to form an opposition movement. Akashambatwa Mbikusita-Lewanika, Chairman of the EAZ, invoked by the gene of his fearless father Godwin Mbikusita-Lewanika, the founding president of the African National Congress, sacrificed to convene such a meeting. He offered to contact prominent citizens to invite them to the meeting to be held in Livingstone Town in the Southern Province.

The EAZ organizers of the meeting of the opposition activists had difficulties in raising funds, especially since at the time, it was risky for any businessman to be seen to be associated with the emerging opposition groups. While agonizing on the financing of the meeting, Theo and Mutumba Bull, the proprietors of the Garden House Motel along the Mumbwa Road offered their premises as a venue.

The impact of the 1990 attempted coup d'etat
On 1 July 1990, Lt. Luchembe Mwamba with others organized a coup d'etat to seize governmental power by military force while President Kaunda was on the Copperbelt to open the International Trade Fair in Ndola. Hundreds of jubilant young people marched past our house on Independence Avenue going eastwards to State House, a few plots away. Some of the demonstrators were on bus carriers waving tree branches and singing, "Kaunda alala, alala".

I recalled my personal and frightful experiences of life under the military regime of Idi Amin in Uganda in the seventies. The horrific and gross violation of human rights was indescribable as it did not spare even the best and most humble human being. I hoped that Zambia would not fall into the hands of the military personnel whose performance assessment is based on the number of 'enemies' one killed in combat. Many coup d'etat experienced in Africa at the time were bloody and barbaric with the use of various savage methods of eliminating the perceived opponents.

Our residence being close to state house, a number of friends telephoned me in the night to inquire on our safety. I assured them that we were safe and in describing the confused situation, I also advised them not to venture out of their houses. Coups d'etat are associated with chaos and looting. At dawn, groups of people were returning from the direction of state house in a subdued mood. We concluded that the military takeover had been thwarted.

After midday, an announcement was made on Radio Zambia by Grey Zulu, SG of UNIP, that Mwamba and the other plotters had been arrested. Unfortunately, this was followed by a week of violence during which even the UNZA was closed as the students were at the forefront of the riots.

During the week, President Kaunda succumbed to the mounting pressure and announced that there would be a national referendum later in the year on the central political issue. The people were to decide on whether Zambia should continue as a One-Party Participatory Democracy or change back to a democracy of many political parties.

The birth and evolution of the Movement for Multiparty Democracy
On 20 July 1990, some 130 people attended a meeting held at the Garden Motel. The issue of the chairmanship of the meeting, and consequently of the new organization, took time to resolve. A number of prominent citizens, among them John Mwanakatwe, a former cabinet minister and Robinson Nabulyato a former Speaker of the National Assembly were requested to chair the meeting but declined.

Finally, Arthur Wina, a former cabinet minister and a businessman accepted the onerous task of steering the new organization through the turbulent times. The Movement for Multiparty Democracy (MMD was formally launched. Amongst the attendees, who ended up in the Interim Organizing Committe were Ephraim Chibwe, Fredrick Chiluba, Andrew Kashita, Humphrey Mulemba, Vernon Mwaanga, Levy Mwanawasa, Baldwin Nkumbula, Ludwig Sondashi, and Sikota Wina.

The MMD, an alliance of civil society organizations, among them the EAZ, LAZ, PAZA, UNZASU, ZACCI, and ZCTU had the sole purpose of agitating for an end to the one-party political system. With mounting pressure, President Kaunda improved his offer to full general elections and set them for the following year, thereby cutting short his term.

I counted myself amongst the group of professionals, who were dissatisfied and ignored as I was regarded as 'not pure UNIP'. In my professional area, I saw the economy sliding into serious difficulties. But then, the UNIP District Governors had the last word on the distribution of the nation's wealth amongst the citizens. Sadly, the governors' unorthodox method was leading to large disparities amongst the citizens and disaffection for the Government.

In January 1991, the Movement was registered as a political party. The deteriorating economic situation in the country assisted the MMD Party to rapidly gain widespread popularity among the populace. A well-articulated manifesto, written by some of the best brains in the country, was presented to the people. The major thrust being the reform of the national economic and political management system, with democracy and privatization as the main strategies.

At the First Extraordinary Congress of the UNIP held at the Mulungushi Rock of Authority between 3 and 6 August 1991, President Kaunda stated that:

"Comrades, it must be understood that the basic political reform we have set out to undertake is to give our Nation a clear, firm and workable formula to allow the people of Zambia to change their governments as and when they decide to do so smoothly, peacefully and in a democratic manner through the ballot box".

I was privileged to have a number of senior officers in the various wings of Government with whom I shared information on the evolving political situation in the country. For example, the top officers of the Special Branch had been with me at UNZA and we often met at various functions and exchanged notes. The mood in the country was that of removing UNIP and KK from power, although my associates in the security wings were reassuring KK that all was well and that he would win the elections.

The elections of 31 October 1991 were peaceful and resulted in a resounding victory for the MMD Party with Fredrick Titus Jacob Chiluba, aka "FTJ" defeating KK for the position of President of the Republic of Zambia.

On 2 November 1991, KK appeared on national television and delivered a passionate farewell speech wishing the new Government success in doing what he might have failed to do. He informed us that he would leave for his retirement home at Shambalakale farm in the Northern Province. For an African leader who had forfeited part of his mandate and called for early elections, KK's words touched many of us who had been scared of violence from UNIP cadres. The transition and peaceful change of guards earned Zambia and Kaunda the greatest respect and admiration from the international community.

Regrettably, Kaunda suffered great humiliation and indignity at the hands of Chiluba, a few years after the peaceful change. KK was even arrested by more than sixty policemen dressed in battle fatigues and armed with assault rifles on the Christmas Day of 1997 under the orders of a born-again Christian President. He was taken to Mukobeko State Prison in Kabwe, where he went on a hunger strike. It took the personal intervention of Mwalimu Nyerere, former President of Tanzania to save a frail-looking and bearded KK from the vengeful President Chiluba.

KK, one of the few living gallant freedom fighters, continued to be marginalized and harassed by the Zambian Government until President Mwanawasa ascended to the presidency in 2001. The new president did not only restore the protocols due to KK as a former Head of State but he also conferred a state honour of the Order of the Eagle of Zambia on Tuesday 14 January 2003 and built a retirement home for the former president.

CHAPTER 15

My Reflections On Kenneth Kaunda's Rule

In 1991, Zambia's political landscape changed as Zambians voted to have a new political party in power with new managers. By this time, I had worked for twenty years in the Zambian public service. I benefitted greatly from the policies of the UNIP Administrations under KK. For most of my schooling, my school fees were paid by the Government through competitive scholarships and later under the policy of free education for all.

This was the greatest gift to me from those who fought for Zambia's independence. Shielded from the urban areas of Zambia by the remoteness of Namaila, I did not personally suffer the inconveniences caused by the bad behaviour of the white racists before independence.

Raised in mountainous Namaila, my lessons at the small primary school opened opportunities for me to aspire to travel to distant lands. As I climbed to the top of the highest mountain and looked at the distant horizon, I set my ambitions beyond those of the Namaila community. Through the learning and working environments, I was exposed to different cultures and was challenged to interact and offer my ideas for our common goals.

I had personal contact with President Kaunda on numerous occasions, while executing various Government duties. I admired his acute memory of remembering people's names as he habitually mentioned people's names. He related closely with me and at any of our many meetings, he enquired about my family with the question, 'Bali buti bamaama?' meaning, 'How is my mother?' referring to my wife. KK fondly addressed me as, 'Mwanaamudaala', which is a respectable Tonga way of recognizing the role played by one's father in their upbringing. The other person who used this term in addressing me was Chikwanda, whenever he did not want to call me by the clan name of Ng'andu, which was close to his royal blood.

I worked in KK's administration from 1965 to 1991 in many different Ministries and parastatals, where I gained valuable skills and expertise. I applied the experiences of working in the Zambian Government in global responsibilities. I was required to visit most of Zambia and many foreign countries to exchange conversations on development issues.

I anxiously followed and at times enjoyed the benefits and comforts of some of the remarkable innovations of the twentieth century, such as those in information and communications. In the area of information technology, we were lucky that the colonialists introduced television in 1961 in Kitwe as an extension of the station in Zimbabwe.

Although the Kitwe station catered for the white miners, it made it easy to open another station in Lusaka in 1965, a year after gaining independence. I recall the famous Flintstones, an animated cartoon series, which provided a relaxing atmosphere after some difficult assignments at UNZA.

During the century, tremendous strides were made in the fields of communications and transportation technology. Railway passenger movement benefitted from the introduction of the speed trains travelling at over 300 kilometres per hour. The invention of the intermodal freight container, used on both water and land, made a major contribution to the movement of goods thereby fuelling globalization.

The rapid development of civil aviation was facilitated by the end of the Second World War, which resulted in the conversion of redundant military aircraft to civil use. With already large planes in service, attention was drawn to developing faster planes with the capability of cutting flying times.

On an official trip to Washington DC, USA, I literary starved and used the savings to top up my official business ticket for a Concorde plane flight to London by British Airways. The Concorde was the fastest plane capable of cruising at twice the speed of sound.

As I walked towards the check-in counters at Dulles International Airport, a young man in a smart BA strip approached me and in impeccable English asked, "Mr Magande, I presume?" It was obvious to me that he'd seen my picture somewhere and had been practicing his etiquette for my reception.

The protocol at the check-in desk and in the departure lounge was beyond my imagination. Taking off at the speed of 275 km/h, the Concorde plane displayed its uniqueness. The Captain added more anxiety when he announced that the flight to London, which normally took over seven hours with other planes would take less than four hours.

As I took another sip from a glass of chilled scented tomato juice, the Captain announced the change from sonic booming to pulsating throbs of the turbojet engines as they propelled the sleek plane past the supersonic speed. The Captain enthusiastically invited us to relax and enjoy a once in a lifetime experience.

I held steady the plate of Sevruga caviar on my small table before peeping out and in the distance, I saw the curve of the earth beneath the beautiful indigo blue sky. For the brunch, which was served at a cruising speed of 2,180 kilometres per hour and an altitude of 56,000 feet above sea level, I enjoyed with relish some lamb fillet with mustard and herb crust, spinach, and sea salt roasted new potatoes.

I recalled the Vickers Viscount that flew at 300 km/h past our meeting as we discussed my school fees with grandfather Matongo in 1958. Everyone was excited when the old man stated that I was to be the first member of the clan to fly in a plane. At the time, none of us gathered under the big Musikili tree could prophesy that the education I was clamouring for would one day make me a member of the elite group of 2.5 million passengers that had flown at supersonic speed.

Because of my education, I progressed in life at supersonic speed from a shepherd boy to an international public servant and cabinet minister.

Being one of the few indigenous Zambian university graduates at the time, I was given challenging responsibilities, which provided me with the opportunity to express my talents and expose my ability to innovate. During this period, Zambia went through different phases in its development and I fully participated in planning many development projects throughout the country.

I will admit that the mixing of external politics and economics at some point in the history of Zambia caused the steep decline in the country's fortunes. For example, the contribution to the liberation of southern African countries was at a huge cost to the Zambians. Being a political issue, there were no written down commitments as to how Zambia was to benefit from the independent countries.

Apart from independent Namibians, who offered placements of Zambians in their new administration, the other beneficiaries of this costly sacrifice often forget the contribution of Zambians to their liberation. Even when the matter of compensation to Zambia of the US $14 Billion assessed in lost infrastructure was discussed in regional meetings or at the United Nations, support from the beneficiaries has been weak.

Much of the early success of Zambia was due to patriotism exhibited by incorruptible political leaders and the followers, who came together as a united force. They felt that Zambia's wealth belonged to all Zambians under the motto of 'One Zambia, One Nation', coined by one of the freedom fighters.

Many of the first generation Zambian politicians and technocrats, did not enrich themselves through corrupt practices in public offices. I remember being advised to respect public property to an extent whereby, we had to account for even pens, pencils and note books we were given to use on the tours. KK's rule reinforced much of my childhood lessons from my relatives on integrity, humility and empathy.

Institutions such as the Anti-Corruption Commission, SITET and the Drug Enforcement Commission were created in order to control excesses in behaviour of the citizens in general and public officers in particular. I will admit that some of my colleagues found themselves victims of false allegations. But on the whole, those of us who were accused were given the opportunity to answer any charges and exculpate ourselves.

Up until the late eighties, Zambian politics was clean and issue-based as politicians stood and won elections in constituencies far away from their ethnic origins. Political campaign messages were never based on nor emphasized the geographical origins or the ethnicity of a candidate. I adore KK and his cohort for adopting the motto of One Zambia, One Nation, which laid a strong foundation for national unity, that made Zambians of the time, role models in intertribal coexistence.

President Kaunda and his family did not lead an opulent lifestyle like some other African and latter-day Zambian leaders. For example, President Kaunda was admitted into UTH for his annual medical checkups. The president's children were in local educational institutions, except Panji Kaunda, who attended one of the elite military academies in Britain with other Zambians.

It was a pleasure to engage in brotherly casual chats, with fellow-student Waza Kaunda, in the corridors of the University of Zambia. He struggled like everyone else to get his answers correct in the human biology examinations before qualifying as a medical doctor. Seeing him beside their beds in the UTH, many patients recovered from their ailments as Waza aptly applied the therapist's empathic understanding derived from his father's philosophy of humanism.

While KK and most of his team showed great humility, some UNIP young zealots became too greedy and used their positions and power to terrorize other citizens. To maintain their vantage positions, they eulogized and idolized KK and shouted slogans even those against humanism. I have not had the opportunity to ask President Kaunda, a staunch Christian, how he'd felt when UNIP cadres were chanting and equating him to God.

A few heads of parastatal organizations assumed extra powers and adopted foreign lifestyles. However, they rarely exhibited any nepotism when employing workers as this was mostly done through interviews by the company's administrative personnel. These 'well-connected' Zambians claimed that they were working on instructions from the president when their actions became objectionable. These statements on the omnipotence of President Kaunda elevated him to a level of a dictator and made him the main target of the movement to change Zambia's management.

My personal reason for joining the movement to change the UNIP Government under KK was to have my voice heard when deciding the destiny of my country. I cherish the freedom to express myself on any issue; a right my father emphasized when tutoring me for life survival. The opportunity of advising the cabinet on policies was obstructed by a few who felt that their voices and opinions were more important than those of other citizens.

I hold a strong belief that, if President Kaunda allowed open debate on the state of the nation and presented a reform programme and a leadership succession plan to his rule at the Fifth Convention of UNIP in March 1990, Zambia would have taken a different and perhaps a more progressive path towards the twenty-first century.

CHAPTER 16

Failure To Fit In The New Administration

With so many interest groups to accommodate, it took some time for President Chiluba to complete the formation of his new administration in November 1991. Many of my associates visited Government House on Leopards Hill Road, opposite the Chrismar Hotel, where President Chiluba was camped, to solicit and lobby for jobs. A good number of them were appointed to various positions in both the government and the parastatal institutions.

When finally completed, the FTJ Cabinet of twenty-three included fourteen young ministers with doctor of philosophy degrees in various academic disciplines. Akashambatwa Mbikusita-Lewanika and Baldwin Nkumbula, the sons of the fathers of the independence struggle, were amongst those appointed to ministerial positions.

The youthful ministers were joined by old timers who included Michael Chilufya Sata, Guy Scott, Simon Zukas, Ludwig Sondashi, Andrew Kashita, Humphrey Mulemba, General Godfrey Miyanda, General Christon Tembo, and Emmanuel Kasonde. This team gave high hopes to the Zambian people that the country would be led on the right path to develop rapidly and banish the widespread poverty.

President Chiluba whipped up the emotions of the suffering Zambians with his eloquent speeches during the campaigns and at his swearing-in ceremony.

At his first press conference, he demonstrated and publicly stated his resolve to be a working president by standing throughout the long press conference. At the second press conference after ninety days, when asked why the working president was sitting for most of the time, replied that, "I did not know how sweet this chair was," while pointing to his seat. The presidential joke was not in good taste for the majority poor Zambians, who were still waiting for rewards for their sacrifice.

My intimate conversations with most of the new ministers and after observing their enthusiasm and mannerisms, generated personal misgivings on the capability of the new team to carry out a shared vision for Zambia. In fact, as I discussed the change of guards with many of the younger ministers, I openly prophesied that Zambia's economic and social development would stagnate and only be revived after a decade.

In November 1991, I was asked by Mrs Flavia Musakanya to get to Government House to see Valentine Musakanya. Chiluba had asked Musakanya, the first head of the civil service after Zambia's independence, to help in setting up a working public service as he was very knowledgeable of public administration. As I drove to my assignment, Flavia Musakanya reminded me of our earlier conversations at Lima Bank and persuaded me to accept one of the two posts she had mentioned to me. At Government House, I met an officer who asked who I was and whom I wanted to see. When I told him my name and that I wanted to see Valentine Musakanya, the officer asked me to follow him.

As he opened a door to a room, I came face-to-face with President Chiluba, who warmly gestured that I take a seat opposite him. I had met him only once in Livingstone in the seventies when he was attending a trade union conference. After a few pleasantries, he offered me a job as managing director of the Zambia National Commercial Bank. This was totally different from the positions I had discussed with some of the MMD founding members.

At the mention of the bank, I twitched, forcing the president to explain that this would be only for six months as he would review my appointment and give me a more senior appointment. He directed me to report to the Government House the following morning to be taken to the bank. Some of the people I consulted on the matter, late that night, doubted the genuineness of the consultations they'd had with the president and advised me to turn down the appointment.

As I did not know President Chiluba well, I was prepared to trust his word. The following day, I did as instructed and went to Government House, where I found Lawrence Bwalya who had been my workmate at the INDECO head office. We were picked up in one car by the Inspector General (IG) of Police, Nzunga Syakalima for a drive to Cairo Road, the central business district of Lusaka City.

On our way, the IG diverted to his office and while he left us in the car, I asked Bwalya to which institution he was being taken. He totally surprised me by answering in a disinterested voice that he did not know. I wondered why someone who had been my workmate at INDECO was not prepared to have a conversation on our strange happenstance, since I had no powers to overturn his stroke of fortune.

The Inspector General of Police and Bwalya left me in the vehicle as they went into ZIMCO House. After a short while, the IG came back and informed me that Bwalya was the new Director General of ZIMCO. We then drove across to the ZANACO head office, which was within the same square.

At the reception, we asked for the floor number of the office of the MD as both of us had never been to the new building. We got into the executive lift up to the executive floor. The IG informed the MD's personal assistant that we wanted to see the MD. She went into the office to alert the MD of our presence and came back to usher us into the office.

Mr Friday Chakanga Ndlovu, the MD for ZANACO, who seemed surprised to see us, beckoned us to take seats, a distance away from his desk. I guessed that this was for him to finish off whatever he was working on before engaging us in conversation. I took a seat while the IG moved towards the MD's desk and after a salute, he informed Ndlovu that I was the new MD and told him to leave the office immediately.

Ndlovu was asked for the keys to the office and company car. As I had by then been asked by the IG to move nearer to the executive desk, I received the bunch of keys. He was then told to wait in the office of the secretary. As he walked out, I recalled my time with him as my senior at UNZA in the sixties when we shared headaches over some mathematical equations. At the time, neither of us had imagined that we would be pitted against each other as pawns in a game of political supremacy between KK and FTJ.

In the civil service, to which I had belonged for a long time, civil servants dealt with one another with civility and gave each other time to prepare handing-over notes for the system to continue smoothly. It was only at the political level that the changes were effected immediately after the president's announcements.

Elijah Mudenda, a former Prime Minister and my trusted mentor confided in me on how he was stranded when he was dropped. Another outgoing Prime Minister was abandoned at Mulungushi Conference Centre by the official escort.

I learnt that at INDECO Head Office, the MD was told to leave the office by an unknown man in a security uniform without anyone to take over. Using his own initiative, the MD summoned one of his executive directors to rush to the MD's office to take over the office. Instead of being thankful to the ousted MD for handing over the office to him, the new MD exhibited great antagonism towards his benefactor.

After I settled down in the office, I summoned the personal secretary to introduce myself to her and to give her a bit of explanation as to the course of events. After being shown around the large office and the adjoining boardroom, I summoned the company secretary (CS), George Mwambazi, to my office. I repeated the story of what had happened and directed him to ensure that all the bank's assets were guarded and secured.

I then requested the personal secretary to summon all the directors into my office. Their quick response in coming to my office gave me the impression that everyone was already aware of the happenings in the building. The management team consisted of Timothy Daka, Winston Chikwanda, my former classmate, Lloyd Chongo, William Holman, Tom Kapapa, George Mwambazi, and E. P. Xavier.

As a follow-up to the Matero Reforms announced by the Zambian

Government in 1968, negotiations were held with the owners of commercial banks. When the foreign owners of the banks rejected the idea of joint ownership, the Zambian Government decided to establish the Zambia National Commercial Bank in 1969. The twenty-nine indigenous Zambians who had established a private bank called the Commercial Bank of Zambia in 1968 agreed to partner with the Government with a two per cent shareholding in ZANACO.

With the strong support of the Zambian Government, the majority shareholder, the bank grew to become the largest commercial bank in Zambia. At the time of my joining the bank in 1991, ZANACO had a total asset base of K18.6 billion and thirty-eight branches in Zambia and one branch in London, United Kingdom with a total of 3,000 employees.

In my address to the senior staff, I gave a short history of my work experience including the fact that I had worked for short periods in another commercial bank as a clerk in the sixties. I encouraged everyone to be free to bring out any new ideas and that I looked forward to working cordially with every member of staff.

A new five-member board of directors chaired by Lawrence Bwalya, Director General of ZIMCO, was appointed and it included Batwell Kapota, a commercial farmer in Kabwe, George Sokota, an accomplished accountant at Deloitte and Touche, and James Mtonga, permanent secretary at the Ministry of Finance.

The senior management team was reconstituted and was made up of Chikwanda, Stanely Chinungo, Chongo, Holman, Kapapa, Mrs Orlean Moyo, Mwambazi, and Xavier.

With my experience in project planning, public finance, and development banking, I found the work at the largest commercial bank exciting but relatively easy. Huge sums of money were made on daily basis as customers who brought their money for safe-keeping were charged interest. In the lending portfolio, the Zambian Government was a captive borrower with over fifty per cent of the bank's lending portfolio held in government treasury bills.

Under the UNIP administration, government ministries and parastatals were instructed to maintain accounts with the people's bank and the funds were invested in short-term financial instruments. This gave the bank a comparative advantage, although the bank's commitment to the important agricultural sector was only ten per cent of total exposure.

The austerity measures and the monetary and fiscal reforms in the economy implemented by the new MMD Government had an adverse impact on bank activities. In 1990, the inflation rate rose to 122.4 per cent, while the Kwacha depreciated by 73.6 per cent against the dollar. The Treasury Bills base rate rose to 139 per cent. The measures, in turn, reduced the available funds for lending to the economic actors. In 1991, the Gross Domestic Product (GDP) decreased by 1.8 per cent.

During my tenure of office, ZANACO achieved some milestones such as the pioneering establishment of automated teller machines (ATMs) in Zambia's banking industry, the ZANACO Savers Account and an Export Revolving Fund. The bank's profit before taxation went up from K1,884 million for the year ended March 1992 to K4,072 million for the financial year ended March 1994.

In my capacity as managing director, I was elected chairman of the Zambia Bankers' Employers Association, responsible for coordination of the collective activities of commercial banks. I chaired the meetings of the managers of all banks. During this period, bank employees went on a strike in spite of pleas from various bank management officials.

I presided over a meeting of the Association that decided to dismiss all the disobedient workers who'd ignored managements' instructions to end the strike. This action restored the banking industry's credibility and discipline. I do not recall any strike by bank employees during the rest of the twentieth century.

I actively participated in the promulgation of new investment and banking regulations that resulted in the enactment of the Investment Act, the Banking and Financial Services Act, and the Securities Act that gave birth to the Lusaka Stock Exchange.

The period spent at ZANACO had its own life-changing moments. There was no review of my stay at ZANACO after six months as earlier intimated by President Chiluba. I was not even written a letter of appointment by the president. I was not given an audience to brief the president, my appointing authority on the operations of the bank or any senior member of the MMD administration.

The accounts of ZANACO for the year 1992 caused a misunderstanding with the majority shareholder due to the large profit attained during the year. The accounts were not approved on the objection of the chairman of the board of directors, who was not happy with the high profitability of the bank.

Bwalya accused me of manipulating the accounts in order to post a large profit. The chairman refused to accept the explanations that the exchange gains propped up the profit-after-taxation from K990 million in 1991 to K1,884 million in 1992. No amount of explaining could satisfy the board chairman, who twice postponed the approval of the accounts by the Board.

The matter was only resolved after I asked Sokota, a board member and one of Zambia's highly qualified accountants to explain the accounts to the chairman. Although the staff and the twenty-nine private shareholders were happy with the good outturn, the behaviour of the chairman, representing the majority shareholder, the government, could not be explained rationally.

In March 1992, while serving in an acting capacity as managing director of ZANACO, I received a letter from the secretary to the cabinet conveying a message that I was being retired from the civil service in the national interest with effect from 29 February 1992. Even though I was on secondment to the parastatal sector, I was among a large number of Permanent Secretaries who were laid off by the new MMD Government. In the "national interest" means that one is inimical to the interests of the country and therefore should not be assigned any national duties.

The following month in April 1992, I was confirmed as managing director. The confirmation letter signed by the DG of ZIMCO Limited ended with, "Please, allow me to congratulate you on this well-deserved appointment". How could someone who is inimical to the nation be congratulated for holding a high office in a public financial institution?

I decided to challenge the decision in order to clear my name. Belatedly, a favourable decision was conveyed to me by the new secretary to the cabinet, Aldridge Adamson in March 1995. The effective retirement date was changed to 31 March 1994.

On many occasions, members of the public came to my office asking for unsecured loans claiming to be members of the ruling MMD Party. Some made it clear that they had to be compensated for their financial support to the MMD. While many stopped after my explanations, two of them reported to the Minister of Finance, who arranged a supper for me and the 'customer', where I was politely directed to look at the request. Even after numerous requests, the gentleman refused to submit a project proposal and the bank's stand not to give him a loan was blamed on me personally.

The bank was undertaking a number of initiatives in line with the policies of the new government. As some of the plans and measures were far-reaching and involved large numbers of staff, for example, the early retirement package, my management felt that it was necessary to keep the chairman fully informed.

The management prepared a comprehensive paper for presentation to a meeting of the board on 9 April 1992. As per routine, I booked to brief the ZIMO Director General at 1430 hours on 8 April 1992 at his office in ZIMCO House. Unfortunately, I found that he had gone to another meeting with instructions that I should wait for him. Since my office was just across the road, I informed his secretary that I would rush back when the boss returned.

When I was told of the DG's return at 1630 hours, I rushed and was at his office within five minutes, as the offices were close by. When I entered his office, I found the Finance Director of ZIMCO with him. The immediate issue raised by the DG was why I had decided not to wait for him as instructed. I explained that in view of the board meeting the following day, there were a lot of documents to go through and I could only do that while waiting for the meeting with him. Bwalya remarked that as Chairman of the ZANACO Board, he decided what was important and I should have waited at his office as per his instructions.

I immediately sensed the highest level of hostility whose origins I did not know. All I could do was to apologize. I was then asked for the subject of our meeting, even though I had given that when making the appointment. I indicated that the restructuring and staff placement proposals were the urgent issues for the board's consideration. I then started leading the two officers through the documents.

Even before I had finished my brief, the DG started making comments on personnel placements. He commented that some of the staff proposed for promotion did not have the requisite experience and that they should be placed on probation. He also wondered why there were so many females being recommended for promotion, an issue which was adequately explained in the board papers.

The DG then asked me why there were so many officers proposed for promotion from one tribe. Before I could even seek a clarification as to which tribe, he shouted, "I will not tolerate tribalists at the bank and these proposals indicate that you are a tribalist". I was so shocked that suddenly I felt a chill go through my whole body and I started perspiring profusely. Sensing the tension in the room, the finance director asked the DG that we adjourn the meeting and that he would brief him before the meeting the following day.

I walked out of the DG's office without uttering a word. The finance director caught up with me at the escalators and escorted me halfway to my office. When I got to my office, I told my personal assistant what had happened at the office of the Zimco Director General and I left for home.

As I was having my supper, Joyce who sat with me at the table asked what had happened at the office. My spouse with over twenty years of nursing practice had noticed something abnormal as I was eating. After I explained the whole episode of my meeting with the DG of ZIMCO, Joyce collected some medicine, which she asked me to immediately take.

The following morning, my wife advised that I go to see a doctor. We went to the UTH where I was attended to by the managing director, Dr Eddie Limbambala, who examined me and informed me that my blood pressure (BP) reading was 180 over 130. The doctor stated that considering the time when the incident happened, I was lucky that I was out of danger of a stroke. This is a condition that became common vocabulary in my life due to its fatal consequences as it claimed some of my close associates and one of my bosses.

The doctor then narrated different situations that trigger high blood pressure and this included work situations. I explained what had happened at work the previous day. He said that it was the shock of what was said about me, which caused the fatal reaction. He gave me some medication and instructed me to take some bed rest immediately.

I instructed the board secretary to ask the chairman to postpone the meeting and this was done. In the meantime, I asked the Board Secretary Mwambazi to indicate the tribes of each of the officers recommended for promotion. I had personally recruited more than forty fresh university graduates at the Ministries of Rural Development, Finance, and Commerce and at Lima Bank between 1978 and 1987. I never asked any of the candidates for their tribe or province of origin. I was more interested in the qualifications and characters of the candidates.

By the promulgation of the national motto of 'One Zambia, One Nation', the freedom fighters managed to de-tribalize many Zambians and I counted myself amongst those converted to a united nation. I, therefore, wondered when the DG of such a huge conglomerate with thousands of workers found time to look at the tribes of all the officers and the value of such an exercise.

During the management discussions, the board secretary explained the difficulties he encountered in getting correct information on tribes of officers as some names were common in different provinces. He also mentioned that it was not professional and normal personnel procedure in Zambia at the time to ask the officers for their tribes. I was aware that the only arm of Government that had the prerogative to inquire about one's tribe was the Zambia Police because some criminal activities are prevalent in particular cultures.

We were informed that the name Zimba was common in Eastern, Luapula and Southern Provinces. The name Mulenga was found in the Northern and Southern Provinces and that of Mwale was found in the Eastern and Northern Provinces. This showed that names in Zambia did not denote one's origins or tribe. I was convinced that DG Bwalya could not be correct on the tribes of the officers recommended for promotion in the bank.

Armed with this vital information, I brought up the subject in the board meeting. As I was about to make my presentation, Chairman Bwalya interrupted me by saying that the matter would not be discussed as it was not necessary. I wondered how the information which had caused a lifelong illness on me could not be necessary. What had been the aim of bringing up the issue of the tribes of the officers in our meeting at the DG's office?

Happily, for the recommended officers and the bank, the board approved my proposals. The officers were promoted and ZANACO continued to perform exceptionally well, claiming the number one spot in the country's banking sector.

I wish to record my thanks to Joyce, my spouse, and to Edwin Limbambala, who quickly diagnosed and identified the illness and gave me treatment within the first twenty-four hours of getting the high blood pressure. Our family physician Dr Duff Kopakopa of Premium Medical Services, Lusaka has patiently counseled me on how to manage the illness since 1992. When in Brussels between 1996 and 2000, Dr Vincenzo Costagliola of Medicis Medical Center, Brussels ably attended to my health issues, including the hypertension, which could have been exacerbated by the strenuous responsibility of balancing the interests of eighty-six member states. I am eternally grateful to all of them.

One of the major policies of the new administration of the MMD party in 1991, was to liberalize the economy by giving more space to private individuals to engage in the various operations of the economy. While agriculture was already highly privatized in terms of production, the government was still involved in the marketing and processing through government-supported institutions.

My involvement with the modern agricultural sector from being a farmer and planner in the seventies to a supervisor of processing companies under INDECO, gave me a clear understanding of the challenges of the sector. In 1986, three thousand bags of our maize, which we had sold to a government institution from our Choma farm, were soaked by the rains and rotted at a depot near our farm.

My protestations on the wastage were dismissed with the comment that since I had already been paid, I should not worry as the maize was not mine. We immediately abandoned maize growing and switched to producing tobacco. I had been advocating for privatized marketing of the agricultural commodities for a long time due to negligence by parastatal managements.

Many of the commodity suppliers, who engaged the INDECO processing companies I supervised, welcomed the policy of the new government, although there were some contractual hitches I had to resolve. At the same time, some of the operators and companies encouraged me to start a commodity marketing company.

Being a strong advocate of private marketing and my curiosity on privatization of the economy under the new environment led me to register Luba Chemicals Limited (Luba) in 1992, with the objective of engaging in the selling of agricultural inputs and purchasing of crops. I was keen to prove the viability of the business into which I had induced others to enter. The company's head office was located in CUSA House on Cairo Road and was manned by two people.

I chose the Chitanda area in western Chibombo District as our company's area of operation. I recruited Kola Habachela, a cousin residing in the same area as the local agent, whose responsibility was to select and supervise the participating farmers. To create a relationship with the farmers, in 1993, the first year of operating, the company engaged only in buying maize from the farmers on cash basis.

Selection of participating farmers for the first season was restricted to married farmers who owned farming implements and established homesteads. The ones who had sold more maize to Luba were preferred. The contract signed by the participating farmers, promising that they will deliver three bags of maize for every bag of fertilizer at harvest time, was the only security. Part of the agreement stipulated that the farmer will only sell surplus maize after reserving his family's food needs.

During the second season, I used my own money to buy the required inputs, which the company delivered to the farmers' homes at no cost and on time. I was aware that yields in ecological zone two could be as high as fifty bags per hectare. This meant that a good farmer who borrowed eight bags of fertilizer for a hectare of maize, could reap over fifty bags of maize, out of which he surrendered only twenty-four bags to our company.

Due to the strict and timely supervision by the agent, who was empowered with a motorbike, the yields were very high and all the farmers delivered the contract bags to the local depot at the agent's home. Having earlier supervised some milling companies, I had no difficulties in selling the maize to the millers based in Lusaka. In the second year, the company got a loan from a commercial bank and increased the number of clients, some of whom got loans for implements.

A few farmers turned out to be untrustworthy and tried to cheat. At one homestead, I had to draw out my revolver from the holster after a debtor farmer displayed aggressive and suspicious behaviour. We supervised the shelling of his maize and left only enough for his family needs but made him sign application forms for the following season.

By 1994, our small company with only three fulltime employees was handling a marketing operation in the agricultural sector of thousands of bags of fertilizers and maize. We had created good working relationships with the farmers, banks and processing companies. I proved that involvement in the value chain was profitable and could uplift the small-scale farmers. I was also happy that the workers of Luba Chemicals achieved improvements in their lives. One of the workers bought a van and the other acquired a hammer mill.

While the new MMD Administration wanted to institute an active privatization policy in crop marketing, it was not sure that the private sector was ready to undertake efficient marketing of crops, and in particular of maize, the staple crop. In May 1992, while serving at ZANACO, I was appointed by the Secretary to the Treasury, Professor Benjamin Mweene to chair a ten-person Committee "to advise the new Zambian Government on long-term strategies for the involvement of the private sector in the agricultural sector under a liberalized economy".

A committee constituting of J.M. Chirwa, O. Chibowa, W.J.S Hudson, M.M. Mutanuka, M.F. McPherson, M. Banda, B. Nonde, and JJ Shawa was appointed. All the members were senior executives of the government, agricultural and farmers' organizations, a cooperative movement, commercial banks, and the Bank of Zambia.

The committee was vested with the responsibility of proposing ways of creating an orderly disengagement by the government from crop marketing. For this to be attained, an institutional arrangement to support effective crop marketing was proposed. Such an arrangement was to include financing, legal, and institutional mechanisms that would attract the private sector to fully participate and take over crop marketing.

Putting together the rich reservoir of experience and knowledge amongst the members, the committee produced a detailed report on various aspects of agricultural development and crop marketing in particular. The committee did not feel that the immediate opening up and the liberalization of the marketing of all crops in the whole country was the best approach.

At that time, the country was experiencing shortages of maize mainly due to drought. Diversification of national food sources from maize to other crops was also considered. The committee recommended the establishment of a Food Reserve Agency (FRA) whose responsibility was to maintain a strategic reserve of food for national security. Another recommendation was that the withdrawal of the government from crop marketing should be gradual, in a planned manner, in phases, and over time. Phase one should allow the private sector to buy maize and other crops within fifty kilometres from the urban areas, while the FRA would buy beyond this limit.

We proposed that individual maize consumers and millers in urban areas such as Lusaka City should buy maize from nearby producing areas such as Chongwe, Chibombo, and Mwembeshi for grinding at private milling plants. Once the private sector, which included the consumers and millers, had established effective marketing chains within this area, then the FRA would move further away into the distant rural areas.

The FRA was to build and maintain grain storage facilities for the security reserves and to lease to the farmers, consumers, and millers. Some farmers were interested in holding maize in secure storage at a fee until prices improved. Such an arrangement would improve the incomes of farmers and smoothen their income earning throughout the year.

The committee's detailed report, which was presented to Guy Scot, Minister of Agriculture and Emmanuel Kasonde, Minister of Finance, was not acted upon by the government. In view of the huge amounts of money and volumes of grain involved, there is a huge wastage of both grain and public funds. The loser is the farmer who is paid low producer prices to meet the hidden costs of maintaining an inefficient marketing system that benefits the consumer.

The suffering of Farmer Chindindiindi was demonstrative of the lack of a proper support system to farmers by the Chiluba Government and the high cost of the poor marketing of crops in Zambia. If the recommendations of the Magande Report on Crop Marketing of 1992 had been adopted and implemented, the nation would not be losing so much food.

Farmer Chindindindi had been growing maize and wheat crops in the Chilanga area close to Lusaka since the sixties. In 1991, the Zambia National Commercial Bank approved a medium-term loan for new equipment, which included a 250-horsepower tractor and a combine harvester. He was also advanced an overdraft for inputs and operating costs.

With new equipment, he planted his winter wheat crop on time and had the best crop of his farming career on his 2,500 acres farm. The assessment was that the income from the crop would pay off the whole loan at once. In those days, farmers signed forward marketing contracts with agro-processing companies for marketing of special crops such as wheat and soya beans.

Just as the farmer was getting ready to harvest his irrigated wheat crop, the MMD Government announced the liberalisation of crop marketing. This opened the way for milling companies to buy their raw material needs from the cheapest sources and the National Milling Company decided to import wheat and abandoned the local farmers.

Chindindiindi harvested 14,000 bags of wheat, which he could not sell on the open market at competitive prices. He kept the wheat in storage in the belief that the government would intervene to get him a good price from the milling companies. Unfortunately, there was no help forthcoming and the wheat rotted in his warehouse leaving a huge unpaid loan.

As the seasonal loan was overdue, the new ZANACO management decided to repossess the farm, which had been pledged as security. The farmer sought my assistance. Feeling guilty that it was my management that had given him the loans, I approached the ZANACO Managing Director to discuss other ways of recovering the loans.

In a meeting with James Ngoma, the MD and his staff, I proposed that they allow the old man to subdivide the farm and sell plots, so that the proceeds would go towards liquidating his indebtedness. I emphasized that this approach had worked well during my tenure at Lima Bank, as it was inhumane to evict old people from land on which they had lived for most of their lives. At Lima Bank, we called it, 'the human way of debt restructuring', which benefitted many debtors, while the bank fully recovered the outstanding loans.

My proposal was considered and approved by the bank. Many people bought plots on the surveyed land and the total outstanding loan was repaid. I was most satisfied to see that old Chindindiindi and his family continued to live peacefully on a small remainder of the farm until the old man's demise at the ripe age of ninety years.

In April 1993, the Zambia National Commerciall Bank gave an advance to the Football Association of Zambia (FAZ) for the national team's trip to Mozambique. While the team was away, the FAZ Chairman Michael Mwape came to see me and asked for some further financial assistance for the team's trip to West Africa. I demanded that they must first pay back the money they'd borrowed before we could consider another advance. From his passionate and detailed explanation, there was not enough time, as the team was just passing through Zambia on their way to West Africa.

As an ardent supporter of the national football team and as I had consulted my chairman on the first request, which was approved, I approved another advance. The team connected through Lusaka where more players and officials including the FAZ Chairman joined on the journey to Senegal via Gabon by a Zambia Air Force military plane.

A few days later on 27 April 1993, I left for the USA at the invitation of the

NCR Corporation, the suppliers of computers to our bank. On our first day, we had to leave Washington DC very early in the morning for a visit to one of the computer warehousing facilities. As we were having our early breakfast, one of our hosts came over to me and whispered that the plane carrying the Zambia National Team had crashed in West Africa. He continued to say that from the reports received, all on board perished.

I could not hold back my tears as I dropped my utensils and started sobbing publicly. We abandoned our breakfast and I retired to my room with a sense of guilt. I concluded that it was our bank's financial assistance that enabled the team to undertake the fateful journey. I vividly recalled my conversation with the FAZ Chairman as he'd pleaded with me that without our financial support the team would not make it to Senegal for the match. He was not aware that even with our bank's assistance, the match was not going to be played.

We cancelled the day's tour programme and the delegation remained at the hotel in mourning for the sporting heroes. Our three weeks' trip, both in the USA and Scotland was a sorrowful one as we had to contend with so many questions about the accident from so many people who spoke highly of the departed players everywhere we went.

On my return to Zambia, I brought the matter of the FAZ advance to our board with a recommendation to have the amounts for the two trips written off. The situation was that the cash drowned with the footballers and no one alive was to be held accountable. The board accepted my recommendation, although the chairman made some comments apportioning some blame on my management.

Sometime in 1993, our bank was asked to advance a loan to the Zambian Government for the salvaging of the ZAF plane off the coast of Gabon. As I was aware that the Zambian Government had no capacity to undertake such a task, I requested a copy of a contract signed with an organization that was competent in salvaging operations. I insisted on such documentation in view of the large amount requested for the loan. When no such documentation was presented, I declined to take the matter to the Board. This raised a lot of resentment against me within Government circles.

I learnt later that the huge loan was approved by the ZANACO Board a few weeks after I had left the bank. During a visit to the accident site in Gabon in 1997, I was informed that no salvaging work was ever undertaken by the Zambian Government and the plane wreckage was still in the deep ocean.

The report on the plane accident has not been released to the chagrin of the living relatives of the accident victims. Consultations on the compensation to the thirty affected families were protracted and only concluded and the families paid in 2004 after I became Minister of Finance.

Perhaps as a way of fixing me, some Government ministries and departments, that were customers of ZANACO, were directed by senior Government officers to divert their deposits to private commercial banks. As part of liberalisation, government ministers refused to bank their ministry's public funds with the people's bank. They preferred to deal with private banks where they negotiated and got higher interest rates, which found their way into their personal accounts. This action was irregular and corrupt according to the financial regulations we followed in 1981 when I was Director of Budget.

In order to compete in the new environment, my staff and I had to sniff around in Government departments to know which ones had received funds from the Ministry of Finance. We thought we were lucky at one point when we heard that a named Ministry had received a cheque for a very large amount of money meant for payment of arrears to its employees. I asked one of our senior officers to follow up the matter and get the deposit into ZANACO.

When the officer was told that she was too junior to discuss the matter of the cheque with the minister, I decided to speak directly to the minister, as he was the one to make a decision on where to deposit the public funds. In our telephone conversation, the minister confirmed that he had the cheque and would deposit it in the bank that gave him the highest interest rate. He stated that our bank's highest rate was not good enough and therefore he could not deposit the cheque with us. I, therefore, gave up as the rate I offered was the highest according to my mandate.

I learnt later that the cheque was deposited into a foreign bank under a time-deposit arrangement under the minister's name. Requests to the Treasury to intervene fell on deaf ears as I was told that liberalisation was also applicable to the banking sector and therefore it was our responsibility to fight for customers in the open market.

Having been a custodian of public funds at the Ministry of Finance during the eighties, I found this arrangement repulsive, out of order, and a flagrant abuse of office. After a lot of debate in the public media, the case ended up with the anti-corruption organs, who established some wrong-doing after investigations. However, no action was taken against the Minister as "the penalty of K50.00 for such an offence is too small to waste government money on prosecuting the case," according to the Attorney General.

Regrettably, by this decision of the Attorney General not to prosecute a clear case of abuse of office, the floodgates of abuse of public office and property were wide open. We started seeing government vehicles in wedding convoys of children of senior government officials, a practice which had never been seen under the previous administration. Privatization and liberalization became personalization even of government property.

One evening in May 1993, I attended a reception for delegates to an international conference organized by the Ministry of Local Government and Housing at the Pamodzi Hotel. Deputy Minister Valentine Kayope was the host and was at the entrance receiving the guests.

Minister Sata was also arriving as I was approaching the host. As Kayope and I were in a conversation, Sata asked Kayope if he knew me. Kayope replied that he knew me very well as I'd found him at the MRD when I joined the Ministry. He added that I'd performed very well during my youth.

Michael Sata told Valentine Kayope that I was the managing director of the Government Bank, who was refusing to give money to the people who funded the MMD campaign. He stated that I had even turned down requests from government ministers, as if the money belonged to me. He then boisterously shouted, "Iwe mwaiche, uleemona," meaning, 'young man you will see,' Thereby drawing the attention of the other guests, who were waiting to shake hands with the Minister Kayope. When one of them asked me about the conversation that delayed the entrance protocols, I lied, as I could not tell a foreigner that I was being threatened by a government minister.

I did not enjoy my favourite apple juice drink at the reception and left early for home, wondering as to what fate was at my doorstep. At that time, I had not been given an audience by my appointing authority nor any senior MMD government official.

A few weeks later I was transferred to the ZIMCO head office, by a letter written by the Director General of ZIMCO. My priviledge of being a presidential appointee which I enjoyed since 1982 was no more. I occupied the position of Group Investment Director (GID) for all agricultural and agro-processing parastatal companies. I was now under the direct supervision of Lawrence Bwalya, Director General of ZIMCO, with whom I had already had poor working relations at Lima Bank and at ZANACO.

My salary in the higher position was frozen because it was deemed to be far in excess of what the other Group Investment Directors were earning. The salary was to remain at the same level until the gap in salary differential with other GIDs was wiped out or narrowed to a reasonable level. I was not allocated a company car on personal-to-holder basis. Meanwhile, I was directed by the DG to return the vehicle I had used at ZANACO.

I refused to be a mere observer during the negotiations between the potential buyers of the parastatal companies and the specially-constituted teams under the Zambia Privatization Agency (ZPA). Being fully knowledgeable of the operations and financial status of most companies, I felt that I should use the knowledge to achieve better deals for the Government. My supervisor found time to give me a pep talk and admonished me for perceived non-cooperation with some potential private buyers of the companies under my division.

After all that I did to conceptualize, create, operationalize, and develop many of the parastatal institutions during my twenty-three years of public service, I was frustrated with the Chiluba Administration's 'no sacred cow' privatization programme. Some companies were strategic in the economy and I could not see any good reason for privatizing or liquidating them. Others were viable and were offering a commendable service to the Zambian communities. While I tolerated the gross personal mistreatment, I could not accept the suppression of my strongly held principles on national development.

By a letter of 6th May 1994, the secretary to the cabinet conveyed a decision of the president to retire me with effect from 5th March 1992 with instructions for me to continue working as a permamnet employee of ZIMCO, even when I had never applied for a job with ZIMCO. I therefore, decided to resign from public service, after twenty-three and a half years of service and gave a notice of 31st May 1994 as my last working day.

My request to buy a second-hand vehicle on retirement, as provided for in the general conditions of service for senior public workers, was rejected by the Director General of ZIMCO. In defiance, I parked the vehicle at home, while waiting for my appeal against the decision and left for a new job in Europe.

Instead of calling me for discussions, my former employer hired Messrs Chifumu Banda and Associates, a law firm that demanded the vehicle with threats of taking the matter to court. Luckily, a new board under Chairman Shalaula Shimukowa was appointed before the court hearing of the case and the board offered the vehicle to me to buy.

I used the period between 6 May and 31 May 1994 to scout for a job. The Ministry of Agriculture, Food, and Fisheries (MAFF) had just started a private sector development project funded by the AfDB and the Zambian Government. They advertised for the position of Project Coordinator and I was lucky to be accepted and appointed. I reported for duties on 1 June 1994 on a three years' Technical Assistance contract funded by the African Development Fund of the ADB.

In my new position, I shared an office in Mulungushi House with Ballard Zulu an economist, songwriter, and singer from the planning division of the ministry.

The Zambia Agricultural Marketing and Processing Infrastructure Project (ZAMPIP) worth US $48 million was in line with the recommendations of the Magande Committee of 1992. The project was to develop the capacity of the private sector and facilitate its effective and efficient involvement in the production, marketing and processing of agricultural inputs and produce under the liberalized environment.

My role was to coordinate the many institutions participating in the various components of the project. The institutions involved included commercial banks; MAFF; the Ministry of Works and Supply; the Ministry of Finance; the Ministry of Commerce, Trade and, Industry; and the Bank of Zambia.

The credit component for the private sector did not move well because the commercial banks refused to take the money for lending at cheaper rates than their own funds. Even the offer of a high handling fee did not entice them to get involved. By the end of the project, a sizable amount was still in a special account at the Bank of Zambia.

Some rural roads were rehabilitated under the project and storage infrastructure was built in the agriculturally active areas of the Central and Southern Provinces. Funds for marketing by the private sector were under the control of the Department of Cooperatives and Marketing.

Most of the short-term loans were not recovered as many borrowers were cronies of the new leadership of the political system. Even an animated debate in parliament did not move the powerful defaulters to repay the loans as many of them were the same members of parliament. This reminded me of the failure of the COZ and the African Fund for Improvement of Farming (AFIF) in the seventies due to powerful and connected defaulters.

The project, which had a noble objective of enabling the private sector to actively participate in agricultural marketing failed. This is one of the reasons for the government's continued involvement in the purchasing and distribution of agricultural inputs and produce.

CHAPTER 17

"Cuundu Caitwa 1996"

After the 1962 elections, Harry Mwaanga Nkumbula the leader of the African National Congress (ANC) with his few elected Members of the Legislative Council, held the balance of power between poor UNIP under Kenneth Kaunda and the wealthy United Federal Party (UFP) of the white settlers. Each of the leaders of the UNIP and UFP approached the old man separately to form a coalition government. Nkumbula opted to join Kaunda instead of accepting the offer of the wealthy white settlers. It was this one act of patriotism by Nkumbula that gave birth to self-rule and led to an independent Zambia in 1964.

Zambia was headed for inter-party chaos between the ANC and UNIP supporters in the early seventies. Nkumbula accepted the proposal for the ANC, with a strong dominance in the Southern Province, to amalgamate with UNIP into a one-party state in 1973. The new political dispensation achieved a high level of peaceful coexistence amongst the party cadres in the country. When the One-Party State failed to deliver inclusive development, the people of the Southern Province joined other progressive Zambians to fight for multiparty democracy and economic liberalisation.

The Southern Province overwhelmingly supported the MMD in 1991 by voting for Chiluba as president and all the MMD candidates for the nineteen constituencies. By the end of 1994, the MMD had lost the vice president and many other founding members, who had formed new political parties. It was decided to hold a meeting in 1996 in order to guide the people of the Southern Province as to what position to take in view of the proliferation of political parties. I was an active member of the Ngoma Yamaano Cultural Association at the time and was actively involved in arranging meetings of the association.

In my interactions with politicians from the Southern Province, I sensed that there was some uncertainty as to the political direction the people of the province were to take. There were also frustrations due to lack of development in the province. The Mazabuka to Monze stretch of the Great North Road was in a deplorable condition resulting in road accidents. There were no more appointments of people from the southern Province in the government and parastatals. I was a victim, as four nominations by ministers for me to chair parastatals were rejected. A few radicals were advocating for the formation of a political party in the province.

On 17 February 1996, a meeting of all politically-minded Tongas was convened at Monze to strategize on the political stance of the Southern Province in view of the general elections later in the year. Southern Province is affectionately called Cuundu by Tongas and this meeting was the first of its kind in independent Zambia. We dubbed it Cuundu Caitwa.

I took the responsibility of inviting both Vernon Mwaanga and Anderson Mazoka to the meeting in their capacities as political and technical leaders from the province. Both were cited as being among the Tongas, who were not interested in taking the political leadership of the province and of Zambia.

I was delighted when they both agreed to attend the meeting, as I wanted them to hear the undertones on the country's political situation. I accepted the condition that I drive them to the Monze meeting. This allowed my two elder brothers to engage in some reflective conversation on the topical issues confronting the nation in general and the Southern Province in particular, in a relaxed mood. Andy and VJ were from different backgrounds and took different roles in the development of the country.

VJ rose from the youth wing of the freedom movement and even won elections as a Member of Parliament for Roan Constituency on the Copperbelt. During his youth, he, therefore, regarded the whole of Zambia as his political base. I got closer to VJ, as he continued to call me Oondela and to invite me and Joyce to his New Year's parties at home since our 1978 meeting in Washington DC, USA.

I also met VJ a few times at the offices of Curray Limited on Cairo Road, when he took the risk of offering his office as a meeting place during the formative stages of the MMD. He assigned himself the role of a 'king maker' in the politics of Zambia.

Andy emerged from the post-Independence technocrats, who gave up the trappings of the developed world after their studies to return home and offer patriotic service. He had a brush with negative regionalism when he was hounded out of Zambia Railways on some allegations. He joined the Anglo American Corporation (AAC) at Boart Zambia Limited in Ndola. By the time I met him for the first time in 1988, he was Chief Executive Officer of AAC in Central Africa.

In spite of the Zambia Railways sad incident, Andy was regarded as a balanced Zambian, without tribal inclinations by his juniors of all tribes. I had cultivated a very close relationship and we spent time discussing development projects and economic matters in general and those pertaining to the Southern Province in particular.

I had the rare privilege of listening to the intense conversation between the two during the more than four hours' drive to and from Monze. The discussions between VJ and Andy, to which I played the devil's advocate, gave me a glimpse of Zambia's future from both the political and economic perspectives.

208

I told VJ that the days of committed nationalists, when he stood for elections on the Copperbelt were slipping away. I reminded the two of the tribal, call them, regional disturbances that had surfaced in Eastern, Northern, and Western Provinces since independence. The *Umozi ku maawa* cessation movement in the Eastern Province was even supported by President Kamuzu Banda, who claimed that the boundary between Malawi and Zambia was the Luangwa River. He even boasted that Zambia was afterall being ruled by his people. This caused tension between the two countries, and in a personal protest, I stopped drinking Tanganda Tea imported from Malawi. The agitation by the Bembas was more daring and damaging because it was led by a senior founding member of UNIP and the new nationalist government. Republican Vice President Simon Kapwepwe openly complained that 'his' people were being side-lined and persecuted in the new government. He resigned from the government and UNIP in August 1971 and formed the United Progressive Party (UPP) to fight for space for his people.

At the time, I had just completed my university studies and was working in Livingstone. A Bemba friend expressed sadness at the tribal utterances and development. Being aware that Kapwepwe is the one who coined the name of Zambia for our independent country, we did not understand who were Kapwepwe's people. Kapwepwe had enjoyed the company of the Lozis during his incarceration in Mongu. Were these not his people as a vice president of Zambia? Everyone, who claimed to be a Zambian, under the motto of "One Zambia One Nation", coined by John Njapau, was trying to find space in an independent Zambia. In my view, this was the beginning of regionalism that has fanned tribalism in Zambia, which has made some tribes to claim that they cannot be ruled by other tribes. During the 2001 election campaign a loyal Bemba publicly proclaimed that his tribe was created to rule and not to be ruled by others.

I forewarned my passengers of impending hostility against them at the cuundu caitwa meeting. The people of the Southern Province felt that there was no politician, who was courageous enough to fight for them. They wanted a politician who was capable of using Kapwepwe's language. I advised my elder brothers not to react in a confrontational manner. I was happy when VJ showed his high sense of diplomacy by calmly participating in the meeting, in spite of the provocative remarks made against him by some participants.

In the midst of great agitation to form a new political party, I advised the participants, that in view of the short time to the October 1996 general elections, no politician from the province should form a new political party. I suggested that instead, people must be left to support parties of their choices during the elections. I proposed that the province should start preparing for the 2001 elections by identifying possible presidential candidates since President Chiluba will not be eligible to stand for the third time as per the provisions of the Republican Constitution. I hoped that one of my two passengers will accept nomination under the MMD Party, as both were eminently qualified, according to my assessment.

Having won the fight for multiparty democracy in 1991, Zambians were free to associate with anyone and meet without any name-calling at the time. At the well-attended Monze meeting, officers from the Zambia Police were in attendance only to keep peace. On my return to Lusaka, I found time to brief some of my non-Tonga friends on some of the issues discussed at the Monze meeting and no one took offence.

Grandfather Matongo's homestead and the Musikili tree under whose shade important decisions on my education were made.

Below: Grandfather Bbokesi Mweemba Matongo, who sacrificed all for my education.

Above: Grandmother bina-Aaron, Mizinga kept me at weaning age and assisted me to build my first house.

Above: With my father (Simwaale), mother (Nakanjoli),
brothers, sisters and cousins at Namaila in 1971.

Receiving my graduation
credentials from President
Kenneth Kaunda, Chancellor
of the University of Zambia,
Lusaka 1971.

Above: At Munali Secondary
School, 1966

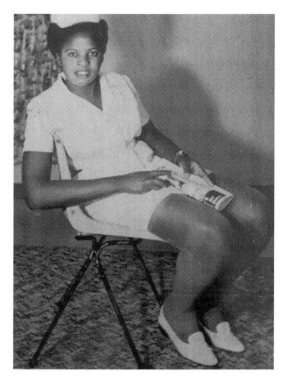

Right: Joyce Mudenda, in the sparkling white nurses' uniform that attracted me at Batoka Hospital in Livingstone Town in 1969!

Below: Solomon Mudenda, my father-in-law with Joyce's step mothers at their homestead at Siachitema, Choma

Above: Simwaale, Nchimunya, Nakanjoli, Choobe, Mutinta, Ng'andu, Joyce

Left: Between Simwaale my father and Simwaale my son

Below: My fathers house, which he refused to be modernized.

Below: With Solomon Shaba, a faithful friend at Dambwa Township in Livingstone Town, 1968.

Below:With Geoffrey Hamayobe, my first friend out of Namaila area at Chikankata Primary School.

Below:North Korea 1980

Above: In 1966, I assumed a leadership role as supervisor of a wing of a dormitory occupied by young pupils at Munali Secondary School.
Below: On board two next to Arthur Yoyo at a Chess game against Prince Phillip Secondary School. Chess was my favorite pastime.

Left: The orchard of 500 tress that has been estbalished at Tubumbe Estates at Popota from one guava fruit I carried with me from Brazil to Zambia in 1986

Below: In the field of the trophy-winning virginia tobacco crop at our Tubumbe Estates, Popota, Choma 1989.

Above: Teaching the workers how to look after and use the tractor at Tubumbe Estates.

Below: Tubumbe Estates has adequate water throughout the year supplied from a dam.A herd of Bonsmara cattle at Tubumbe Estates, Popota

Above: A herd of Bonsmara cattle at Tubumbe Estates, Popota

Above: Mrs Joyce Magande with Zambian Embassy and fair staff at the Berlin Trade Fair, Berlin Germany, 1996.

Above: My Beautiful wife Mrs Joyce Mudenda Magande 1999

Left: Dressed for the Kuomboka Ceremony Gala Night of the Lozi tribe at a hotel in Lusaka on 6th February 2010.

Above: Entering Parliament building to present the 2006 national budget.

Right: Mrs Joyce Magande with cousin Mrs Grace Choombe on the campaign trail in the Chilanga Constituency in 2006.

Above: With my family at Woodlands Lusaka 1993

Below: With my family and uncle Joseph Sikalumba
at Chelstone Township Lusaka 1980.

Left: President Mwanawasa knew how to enlighten the frightening moods at his State House press conferences. Here, my good friend Bates Namuyamba could not resist appreciating a joke directed at him.

Below: Exchanging notes with the Bank of Zambia Governor Caleb Fundanga.

Above: Enjoying a joke by Brig General Godfrey Miyanda.

During the 2006 election petition, I was ably represented by Steven Malama, State Counsel, one of Zambia's best constitutional legal minds.

Left: With Lord Plumb of EU and Willa Mung'omba during celebrations of the Queen's day 2004..

Right: Exchanging valuable information with Sindiso Ngwenya, Secretary General of the Common Market for Eastern and Southern Africa. Close by is AU Commissioner for Economics, Mkwezalamba

Left: With my former Munali school captain Ambassador Lyson Tembo and his wife at the Zambian embassy in Moscow, Russia in 2004.

Right: With Mrs Joyce Mudenda Magande

Left: With Emmanuel Kasonde, my predecessor and Hon Mulenga, Minister of Education at Parliament after budget presentation, 2004.

Right: With senior citizens Mulenga, Me, Ntalasha, Kapulu, Chipango and Kamba at the National Constitutional Commission meeting at Mulungushi Centre, Lusaka 2010.

Left: ACP-EU officials with President Eyadema of Togo, Lord Plump at Lome, Togo.

Right: With Ugandan delegates Ezra Suruma, Emmanuel Mutebile and John Twinomusongizo at the 1993 ADB annual meetings.

Left:Arthur Bbuku congratulating me for presenting the national budget.

Right: Taking-over the Ministry of Agriculture as permanent secretary from Namukolo Mukutu as the minister, General Chinkuli witnesses the occasion in 1985. Francis Mbewe and Inyambo Nyumbu were interested in what was happening.

Left: With Vernon J 'Oondela' Mwaanga

Right:With Dr and Mrs Bwalya Ng'andu and Mrs Magande 2005

Left: Joyce Magande at the gates of office of the Prime Minister in Fiji Islands 1998

Below: In Brussels, winter in Belgium.1997

Above: White House, Washington DC, USA 1989

Right: Arrival in Brussels, Belgium 1997

Below: Carrying the 2004 Budget accompanied by Dr. Amanda Kisoro our first granddaughter.

Above: Our home in Chilanga, Lusaka

Above: With Mrs Magande, Simwaale, Dr & Mrs Sikalumba 2004

Left:Namukolo Mukutu says he is amazed that I have assimilated most of what he taught me over a period of thirty-five years of our friendship. This was when I got an ovation for presenting my first national budget. 2004

Right: A gift from President Patasse of Central African Republic

Above:Visiting Kigali Genocide Mueum, Kigali, Rwanda 2018

Above: Admiring a gift of an eagle in flight with Mrs Magande as I was conferred with the Fellowship of the Zambia Institute of Banking and Financial Services in 2006, Lusaka.

Above:Visiting Kennedy Space Center NASA, USA

Right: Nakanjoli kitchen party with Grandma Samalia Chilala and aunt Emily Simunchembu

226

Left: With Vice President Prof Saitoti of Kenya 1999

Below: With Mr Speaker Amusaa Mwanamwambwa 2006

Below: At ACP Secretariat, Brussels, Belgium 1996

Below: With the Bostons at their farm in Illinois, USA 1989

Above: With Gerry Muuka and Ephraim Kaunga at a Workshop in Kitwe on Structural Adjustment Programmes (SAP) July 1994

Left:Welcoming President Bingu wa Mutharika of Malawi

Right: With Rajkeswur Purryag, ACP Chairman of the Council of Ministers, Oudrago, ACP Chairman of the Committee of Ambassadors and Carl Greenidge, ACP Deputy Secretary General at the ACP Secretariat, Brussels Belgium, 1996.

Left:With President Nujoma of Nambia, 1987

Right: Presenting a report with my co-consultant Smith to the UNDP team led by Mrs Olubanke Akerele-King in Lusaka Zambia, 2002.

Above: H E President Levy Mwanawasa, State Counsel
introduces me as his 'compass' while campaigning for me
in the Chilanga Constituency in September 2006.

Below: Welcoming President Mwanawasa to the 2007 Kuomboka
ceremony of the Lozi tribe at Limulunga, Mongu. Others in the
picture are Mrs Mwanawasa, Ministers Pande and Namugala
and the Ngambela.

Above: What a way to say a last farewell by my elder brother Anderson Kambela Mazoka at a wedding on 27 August 2005 at Chamba Valley in Lusaka.

Below:"Here is a copy I have signed for Your Excellency's attention" I said to President Levy Mwanawasa.

Above: Joyce and I enjoying the company of H.E President Kenneth Kaunda during the commemoration of Africa Freedom Day, Lusaka.

Below:Absorbing political and economic strategies from two eminent Africans, Dr Kenneth Kaunda, freedom fighter and former president of Zambia and Dr Donald Kaberuka, president of the African Development Bank during the opening of the ADB office on 31 July 2008 in Lusaka, Zambia.

Above : Second ACP Summit in Santa Domingo, Dominican Republic November 1999. On my right is President Lionel Fernandez Reyna, the host and next to him is President Omar Bongo of Gabon, the outgoing ACP Chairman.

Below: 2nd ACP Summit in Santa Domingo with President Fernadez Reyna Dominican Republic 1999

Above: With President Ketumile Masire of Botswaana 1996

Above: Swearing-in at State House, Lusaka,Zambia 2006

Below: With Hon Chikwanda and fellow former Ministers of
Finance, 2012

70 years plus 340 days of age,
Mabuyu Gardens June 2018
The collection of Ng'andu Peter Magande

CHAPTER 18

Persuaded To Forsake My Beloved Zambia

In March 1996, I received a surprise telephone call from Lt. General Christon Tembo, Minister of Foreign Affairs asking me to drop by his office for some consultations. During our meeting, the Minister informed me that the position of secretary general of the African Caribbean and Pacific (ACP) Group of States in Brussels, Belgium had been vacant for nearly eighteen months.

The Minister explained that the Group had held a series of elections and neither of the two candidates from Gabon and Zimbabwe could get the mandatory two-thirds majority votes. The ACP Council of Ministers, therefore, decided to ask the Southern Africa Development Community to find a suitable candidate. The SADC Summit had, in turn, asked Zambia to propose one of its nationals for consideration by the SADC Council of Ministers, which would, in turn, submit the name to the ACP Committee of Ambassadors (CoA) for approval.

The Minister went on to disclose that so far four Zambians had been considered by the Zambian Cabinet and submitted to the SADC Ministers and the ACP CoA. Unfortunately, all had been found unsuitable. The Minister requested me to submit my CV for onward transmission to the CoA in Brussels.

I knew that the job would be easy for me as I was familiar with the ACP Group. I'd been dealing with the ACP-EU Lome Convention since 1976 at various ministries. Under the Lome Convention, the Partnership Agreement signed in 1975, the European member countries extended favourable financial and trade facilities to the ACP Group member countries that included Zambia.

In the 1970s, I was a member of the teams that negotiated for funds from the EU to support a number of Zambia's agricultural projects and for preferential market access into the European member states for beef and sugar. Zambia also qualified for financial support under the STABEX in cases of short-term fluctuations in earnings from exports of agricultural commodities and minerals.

As per my ritual, I requested the Minister to give me time to make consultations on the matter. In view of my poor relationship with the MMD

Government at the time, many my family members and friends advised me to turn down the offer. Two days later, I informed the Minister that I did not feel comfortable to be nominated by the MMD Government for such a lofty international job. I further stated that I was preparing to put myself as a candidate for the Magoye Constituency in Mazabuka District.

The Minister informed me that he had worked very hard to get the approval for my nomination from higher authorities. He further advised that going away from Zambia, at that moment in time, might be the most advisable thing for me to do. I again asked for more time to consider the issue. My plan was to keep quiet until the lapse of the deadline for nominations, which was on Friday.

On Thursday morning, the Private Secretary to the Minister telephoned me to remind me that the deadline for the nomination was the following day. She asked that I should deliver the CV by the end of the working day. As I did not deliver the CV to the Secretary, the Minister himself telephoned me early on Friday morning asking me if I was deciding to let down my country as the deadline was 12.00 hours on that day.

The tone of the General during our conversation, which was spiced with some vernacular, sounded like there were some personal security issues involved. After being denied appointments in Zambia, why was I now being given this chance to leave mother Zambia? Had my political ambitions and movements had offended the higher authorities?

I somehow felt that I was lucky that I was being advised by a senior military man on a personal security issue. I quickly put my CV on diskette since I had become computer literate then and delivered it to General Tembo's office where I left it with his Secretary at 10.00 hours.

By 16.00 hours, the Minister informed me that the CV had been received and dispatched to all ACP member states by the ACP Secretariat. When I asked him if a team had been constituted to help me with the campaign, the Minister assured me that there would be no campaigning as the CoA was to decide on the basis of my qualifications and experience.

In May 1996, I was informed of my acceptance by the ACP Committee of Ambassadors as the only candidate to be considered by the Council of Ministers at their meeting in Apia, Western Samoa, somewhere in the Pacific Ocean. General Tembo informed me that I was expected to present myself to the Ministers at their meeting for adoption.

I went to consult Syamukayumbu Syamujaye, Minister of Commerce, Trade and Industry, who was responsible for ACP matters, on travel arrangements to Samoa in the Far East. He congratulated me and informed me that I had to foot the bill for my trip to Apia. Although I had the capacity to meet the costs of the trip, I requested the Government who nominated me to show its commitment by sharing the cost. After some negotiations, the Minister was given authority for his Ministry to meet part of the costs for my accompanying him to the ACP Council meeting.

We reached Apia in the early morning of 23 June 1996 after many hours of flying via Harare and Sydney. I was beginning to know places that I'd never dreamt of during my youth at Namaila. Luckily, my geography lessons had left an imprint of the whole world in my head. On 26 June 1996, I was elected as the new secretary general of the ACP Group by acclamation by the ACP council of ministers under the chairmanship of Zephirin Diabre, Minister of Finance and Economic Planning of Burkina Faso.

I was the first national of a country from the Southern Africa region to lead the ACP Group of seventy-one states formed in 1975. My tenure of office was to run for only three-and-a-half years, up to February 2000, which was the balance of the usual five-year term. The honour that was being bestowed on Zambia by my election was not acknowledged. I do not even recall any local media coverage of my appointment into a position responsible for the development of countries spread throughout the world.

In spite of arriving home on 5 July 1996, which was my forty-ninth birthday, I restrained myself from celebrating. On 8th July, my request to cut short my contract as Planning Coordinator of ZAMPIP to take up my new position based in Brussels was granted by the Permanent Secretary of MAFF.

I tried to make an appointment to brief and say goodbye to the president, my Nominating Authority, but this was proving difficult. On 15 July 1996, I wrote a farewell letter to President Chiluba, which I intended to drop at State House on my way to the airport. As we were about to drive off to the airport with protocol officers from the Ministry of Foreign Affairs, a telephone call came through informing me that President Chiluba was ready to see me.

I rushed to State House leaving the escort officers at our house and met the President for less than ten minutes as I had to catch my flight to Europe. In that short time, it was not possible to have any meaningful discussions. This was my second and last one-on-one audience with President Chiluba.

CHAPTER 19

A Call To International Assignments

When I arrived in Brussels on 16 July 1996, I was met by the Zambian Ambassador to the Benelux countries, His Excellency Isaiah Chabala and some embassy staff. There was no staff from the ACP Secretariat in spite of having sent a telex message giving details of my flight. The following day when I reported for work, the Deputy Secretary General, Carl Greenidge explained that he did not receive my telex message concerning my travel arrangements. There were no internet or cellular telephone communication facilities in those days.

Greenidge, a citizen of the Republic of Guyana in the Caribbean was Acting Secretary General during the eighteen months when there was an election impasse. The Caribbean region had canvassed for his confirmation in the high office. The African member states were opposed as the Caribbean and Guyana in particular had produced the pioneering secretary general of the ACP, Sir Shridaf Raphal in 1975. I fully understood Greenidge's frustrations at his not being confirmed and I asked for his cooperation, as I was not at fault. I directed my attention to studying and understanding the origins, objectives, procedures and goals of the ACP Group and the 21-year ACP-EU cooperation.

I came back to pick up my family towards the end of December 1996. We left Lusaka on 4 January 1997 and arrived in Brussels in the middle of a cold winter of temperatures of minus ten degrees. We were received at the airport by Ambassador Chabala and staff and officers of the ACP Secretariat. I then decreed that no officers should spend time escorting me to the airport or receiving me whenever I arrived from a foreign trip.

Daylight was at its shortest and I left for work in the darkness and arrived back at the hotel when it was already dark. As this was the first time for my family to experience the cold northern hemisphere weather, Joyce, Mutinta, and nine-year-old Simwaale were disconsolate.

After a few days' stay in the hotel, we moved to the permanent residence in Waterloo Canton, some distance away from the ACP offices. Soon, the children left for overseas institutions in USA and UK as they could not manage to adequately pick up French, the common language in Belgium. Flemish, the other official language was even more complicated.

The official residence of the Zambian Ambassador to Belgium was also located in Waterloo Canton, about two kilometres from our home. Chriticles Mwansa, who was working for the World Customs Organization (WCO), lived in the same area with his family. Mwansa took advantage of our intimacy to seek advice when he was called for interviews for a higher position in the Zambia Revenue Authority (ZRA). I was pleased that my advice put him on the path to the top position of Commissioner General, which he occupied later in the twenty-first century.

I found myself in one of the busiest public offices in the world. The ACP-EU grouping with eighty-six countries was the second largest intergovernmental organization after the United Nations System under Ghanaian Secretary General Kofi Annan, at the time.

Visiting the three regions meant that I was away nearly half of each month. Joyce was left alone in a new environment with a serious language problem as she did not even have a smattering of French. Mrs Chabala, the wife of Ambassador Chabala and Mrs Magande became close associates since they were most of the time left at the residences.

The ACP Secretariat is a multilingual institution catering for the interests of member countries in Africa, the Caribbean and Pacific regions in their relationship with the European Union. This made a big change from my previous work as a consultant. The compensation was adequate as my new monthly salary was US $8,500 in addition to so many allowances. However, I looked forward to touring the many countries across the globe as the greatest learning opportunity and benefit.

The Secretariat had eighty-four members of staff recruited from thirty-two countries across the Group membership. Among them were Ms Patricia Zebron and Brenda Montah from Zambia. I kept the personal assistant, Madiene Keita-Gaye from Mali, whom I found in the office of the secretary general. The working languages for the institution were English and French. Portuguese was later added as the third official working language.

In February 1996, I had enrolled for French lessons at the Alliance Francaise de Lusaka in preparation for my active private consultancy life. The little knowledge of French I acquired became useful as I was able to understand and speak some French. By the time I left the Secretariat in 2000, I was able to communicate in the French language. Unfortunately, this ability was soon lost after my return to Zambia as French made way for my native Tonga and other Zambian local languages.

The Council of Ministers appoints the secretary general (SG) on rotational basis amongst the three regions, as the principal authority at the ACP Secretariat, taking into account merit, competence, and integrity. The SG is appointed for a five-year term and is the Secretariat's designated representative. Although as already mentioned, in special circumstances, the term of tenure is made shorter, like what happened to mine.

As my tenure of office at the ACP Secretariat was to overlap into the twenty-first century, the Council of Ministers assigned me to develop new systems that would be appropriate for the new Millennium. I was directed to work out a new structure befitting the exigencies of the evolving international relations.

When I arrived at the ACP Secretariat in July 1996, the Lome IV Convention signed in 1990 had not yet come into force due to non-ratification by some ACP and EU member states. The Headquarters Agreement signed in 1975 between the ACP Secretariat and the Belgian Government had not yet been ratified by the Belgian Government.

I met the Belgian Minister for International Cooperation to whom I reiterated the status of his country in the ACP-EU cooperation as a host and founder member of the EEC in 1948. The Minister lectured me about the intricate Belgian dual-cabinet system, one Flemish and the other French and promised to follow up on the issue.

Without the required ratification of the various protocols, the provisions of the Lome Convention could not apply. These became the main urgent assignments I had to deal with. Others were:

i) the clarification of the status of South Africa in the ACP Group, as it had signed a separate special agreement for support from Europe;

ii) the convening of the first Summit of the ACP Group to agree on negotiating issues and give a clear mandate to the negotiators; and

iii) the constituting of negotiating teams for the successor agreement to the Lome Convention.

The ACP Secretariat was responsible for the coordination of all intergovernmental development cooperation activities between fifteen European Union (EU) members and seventy-one African, Caribbean, and Pacific (ACP) states in liaison with the European Commission and the Secretariats of the EU Council of Ministers, and the EU Parliament.

The ACP Secretariat organized and serviced the meetings of the ACP and ACP-EU Committees of Ambassadors, the ACP-EU Joint Assembly of 142 Members of Parliament, the ACP and ACP-EU Councils of Ministers, covering the portfolios of Finance and Planning, Trade, Foreign Affairs and Development Cooperation/Aid, and the meetings of technical experts from governments, NGOs and civil society.

I was fortunate that at the time of assuming office, the EU Commissioner for ACP-EU relations was Professor Joao de Deus Pinheiro, a Portuguese with so much understanding of the development challenges of the developing countries. The Commissioner had spent five years lecturing at the University of Lourenzo Marques in Mozambique in the early seventies. With the affable Englishman Phillip Lowe as Director General for Development, and fatherly Flemming Bjornekaer as Secretary General, it was easy to resolve many administrative and development issues.

Sometime in 1998, I negotiated and convinced the EU Commission to provide funds for the construction of the SADC Headquarters in Gaborone, Botswana. I felt that the office building would be a fitting repayment to SADC for having supported my candidature. Unfortunately, the offer by the EU was rejected by the SADC Summit held in Mauritius, on grounds that the organisation did not want to be dependent on foreigners. The huge modern head office of the African Union AU), an anti-imperialism organisation, based in Addis Ababa, Ethiopia, was built and donated to the Africans by the Chinese Government.

The Lome IV Convention was coming to an end in February 2000 and there was active debate amongst the European Union members on whether to negotiate for another agreement. There was great anxiety amongst the ACP states on the likelihood of not having a successor agreement as a good number of them were dependent on trade facilities and grant finances for their development programmes.

In November 1995, at the conclusion of the review of the Lome IV Convention, the ACP Council of Ministers decided that a Summit of ACP Heads of State and Government was imperative in order to put the ACP-EU cooperation in a political perspective before the start of negotiations for a new agreement.

As the supervisor of the ACP Secretariat, I had the rare opportunity of playing the role of a roving ambassador amongst the various interest groups. I met and advised the Heads of State and Government leaders throughout the three regions of the ACP Group. In return, I received wise counsel from many of them on various issues including the governance of their countries.

I made an early visit to Southern Africa in October 1996 to thank the member Governments for my appointment and to discuss the status of South Africa in the ACP. At the time, South Africa had a separate agreement with the EU. I was warmly welcomed in Botswana, Namibia and South Africa, being the first SG of the ACP Group from the SADC region.

I met President Ketumile Masire of Botswana and Prime Minister Hage Geingob of Namibia, both promised to support me in my new assignment at the ACP Secretariat. Minister Lieutenant-General Mompati Merafhe of Botswana and Minister Hidipo Hamutenya of Namibia diligently fulfilled the presidential promises in their contributions as members of the ACP Council of Ministers. They joined the debates to protect and defend me whenever they sensed that I was being unfairly criticized and on a regional basis.

I had useful discussions in South Africa with a team of officers in the Office of the Presidency. They indicated that South Africa was desirous of joining the ACP Group. The ACP Secretariat was honoured to play host to Thabo Mbeki, Deputy President of South Africa in November 1996, when he visited Brussels for consultations with the EU on the Trade, Development and Cooperation Agreement (TDCA). In April 1997, South Africa became a qualified member

NG'ANDU PETER MAGANDE

of the Lome Convention adding another voice from my region.

When preparing for the 1997 Summit of the ACP Heads of State and Government, I visited Gabon and discussed the hosting arrangements with President Omar Bongo. Being the first ACP Summit without any precedent, the host-to-be was apprehensive about the capacity of the ACP Secretariat to organize such a big meeting. I assured President Bongo that all would go well.

I then visited Zimbabwe to invite President Robert Gabriel Mugabe to preside over the Summit as his country held the chairmanship of the ACP Council of Ministers. I also visited Togo to invite President Gnassingbe Eyadema, who hosted the signing ceremony for the Lome I Convention some twenty-one years earlier in February 1975.

As a founding member of the ACP Group, I asked President Eyadema for his views on the progress of the Group's integration mission. In his candid manner, he stated that regional integration would continue to be a pipe dream as many African leaders were not prepared to make their countries subservient to regional integration bodies. He went on to say that very few Heads of States and Governments took for discussion to their Cabinets the speeches they read and the resolutions they agreed to at these meetings. According to President Eyadema, many leaders do not even own or understand the nice speeches they read at the meetings as these were prepared by ministers seeking patronage from their bosses.

I made a number of visits to the various ACP regions to invite Government leaders and heads of regional organizations to attend the first-ever ACP Summit. The Summit was held in Libreville, Gabon, in West Africa on 6 and 7 November 1997 and was well attended by Heads of Governments from the three regions. President Mugabe presided over the opening formalities and gracefully handed over the chairmanship to President Bongo of Gabon.

Zambian President Chiluba could not attend the ACP Summit held in November 1997 due to serious instability in Zambia after the contentious 1996 general elections and the deteriorating economic conditions. Public service workers, including medical staff, were on strike and this led to the dismissal of 200 medical doctors, a record in Zambia's history. On 27 October 1997, there was an attempted military coup d'etat against the Zambian Government.

A large contingent of Zambian media personnel who had travelled to cover the ACP summit had to urgently return to Zambia. Amongst them was Ben Kangwa from the Zambia National Broadcasting Services, who had a long interview with me in Gabon to showcase Zambia's leadership of such an important intergovernmental body. The interview, when screened back home was not in good taste with the country's political leadership and Kangwa faced difficulties in his job.

The Summit reviewed the political, economic, and social situations in ACP countries, the Intra-ACP cooperation, the relationship between the ACP and the European Union, and the relationship between the ACP countries and the wider international community. The Heads of States came up with the Libreville Declaration in which they reaffirmed their political commitment to the principles and objectives of the Georgetown Agreement of 1975, which had led to the establishment of the ACP Group.

The rapidly changing international environment posed some daunting challenges for the ACP Group. The Heads of State and Government laid out the measures envisaged to maintain and strengthen the ACP Group for active participation and integration in the globalizing economy. The Heads dedicated themselves to a number of initiatives and actions and invited the partner European Union and the international community to support them.

President Eyadema had reminded me during our meeting before the Summit that the European Union only achieved closer integration under a strong and politically-minded Commissioner Jacques Lucien Delors. The remarkable contribution to the attainment of the united Europe by the French economist/politician was recognized by declaring him an Honorary Citizen of Europe.

I thought that President Eyadema's message was very clear on what I was expected to achieve in my new position. I, therefore, delivered a strong political speech at the ACP Summit in the hope of getting support in implementing meaningful initiatives on integration during my tenure. Sadly, when I tried to push some radical ideas through the Committee of Ambassadors, I received a tongue-lashing even from Ambassadors of 'small' ACP member countries, under the pretext of their countries' sovereignty. I soon realised that some ambassadors who had served at the United Nations and the African Union could not distinguish between the raison d'etre of the political bodies from that of the ACP Group.

Namaila remembered

Having settled in my job at the ACP Secretariat in Brussels, my mind started wandering back home and I felt a need to assist in the establishment of an appropriate project for the benefit of the Namaila community. I was aware that Mwiinga Cibuyu, my rich childhood village had lost much of its prosperity a few years after Zambia's independence.

Farming, in particular of maize, had failed because of the poor soils of the area and the persistent drought. As a result, many of the inhabitants had migrated in search of richer soils. Younger people who had obtained higher education beyond Namaila School had settled or got employed in other parts of Zambia.

Livestock keeping had also not been profitable as the outbreak of diseases decimated the cattle numbers. I personally had replenished my uncle's herd a few times, but this was not a sustainable long-term solution as they also soon succumbed to the diseases due to poor management.

After explaining my predicament to development experts, they advised that game ranching could be the best alternative for the rugged terrain of Namaila.

In 1998, I wrote to His Royal Highness (HRH) Chief Hanjalika (Philip Malambo) introducing my idea and soliciting for his support. I had known the chief in the eighties when he worked at a chemical company, where I used to buy agricultural chemicals. After his installment as my chief, he challenged me to come up with viable development projects for my home area.

In my letter, I gave the geographical details of the area I proposed for the project. These were the familiar grounds I traversed many times in my youth while herding my relative's cattle. My thoughts had moved away from the Magoye Settlement abandoned by my uncle, the CBD of Mazabuka of 1975 and Chivuna Lime project of 1984 to the Namaila area where my ancestors were buried and I was born. I thought then that the previous projects failed because I had involved people who did not know my poor background and how eager I was to banish poverty during my generation.

I asked HRH to get the consent of the Village Headmen for the feasibility study to be conducted. This was what my former PS in Livingstone had taught me in 1971. The Chief held a series of meetings with his subjects in the Namaila area to introduce and explain the game ranch project concept. He was assisted by Mulamfu Simuyuni, who at the time was managing a game ranch on a private commercial farm within the Mazabuka district.

The conclusion of these meetings was an acceptance by the community for the carrying out of a feasibility study. The Village Headmen also accepted that should the feasibility study come out positive, they would willingly assist in the development and operations of a community game ranch. I insisted that declarations of community support written in ci-Tonga be signed by each Village Headman in the presence of His Royal Highness the chief and this was done.

Chief Hanjalika informed me that the community of Namaila was willing to support my idea. I then approached the Centre for the Development of Industry (CDI) for the financing of the technical feasibility study. I contacted Mr Richard Jeffrey, a wildlife expert who worked out a comprehensive budget for the study. The CDI agreed to meet part of the cost of the study and requested that the promoters take up a third of the cost estimated at US $35,000. As I was the only promoter, I accepted the arrangement and willingly made my contribution, which was much more than I paid for the cooperative members of the Chivuna lime project in 1989.

I requested Cosmas Michelo and Mulamfu Simuyuni to facilitate and coordinate the carrying out of the feasibility study by arranging field trips and meetings with the local leaders. Richard Jeffery was engaged as the Consultant/Team Leader and he assembled a team of appropriate experts to undertake the feasibility study.

Visits were made to Namaila by the experts in January and February 1999, during which discussions were held with the local community of the area to get their understanding of the project. The visit on 8 February 1999 was an aerial reconnaissance of two hours using a Cessna light aircraft from Jeffery's aviation company. The low-flying plane attracted a lot of attention from the local people, especially the young ones who had never seen a plane in their lives.

The team, after taking into consideration all the factors, concluded that a game ranch under a joint venture between the community, Government and private investors could be established in the 'Gumba' area of Namaila. The study identified the possibilities of various tourism activities such as hunting, mountain hiking, eco-tourism, and bird-watching. The attractions of Namaila include the limestone caves of archaeological and historical significance.

The consultants recommended the establishment of a Safari Lodge on the Game Ranch and camping facility to encourage 'weekenders' from nearby Lusaka City. It takes only twenty minutes to fly to Namaila from Lusaka City airport. Jeffery was interested in providing flights for tourists into the game ranch from Lusaka City. The study proposed a detailed business plan with an estimated investment of US $2 million over a ten-year period.

I was excited when I read the report and its positive conclusion as at long last, I would reconnect with my childhood and pay back to the Namaila community for encouraging me to get educated. I dispatched copies of the report to Chief Hanjalika with a request that he holds further meetings with the community to explain the findings of the study team.

Through a series of communications, the Chief assured me that the community had accepted the proposed project and will be waiting for its implementation. I arranged for a group of Village Headmen to visit a private game ranch in Choma close to our cattle ranch to see how wild animals were being managed on a commercial farm. In view of the failure of the Lukamantano and Chivuna cooperatives, I proposed to operate the game ranch under a community trust.

Towards the end of 1999, while I was packing to come back home, I discussed the game ranch project with my associates in Brussels. Many were keen to get involved, either in developing one of the activities or organizing tour groups to visit the game ranch. Some had heard of the game rancher in Zimbabwe who specialized in taming elephants for elephant-back safaris. Such approaches to tourism development were very inspiring. I, therefore, planned to get fully engaged in developing the game ranch at Namaila in addition to developing our family farm in Choma.

I arrived in Zambia from Belgium in March 2000 and I immediately went to see Chief Hanjalika to get a full brief on the happenings in the country and in his Chiefdom. He made some comments on the deteriorating economic situation in his Chiefdom due to drought and animal diseases.

HRH informed me that the game ranch project had been warmly received by the majority of the people of Namaila. However, one Village Headman in the Meezi area, where grandfather Sikalumba had lived, raised an objection. He was concerned that the project would introduce dangerous animals such as lions and that the game fence would block the road to the primary school. There was no proposal to introduce lions or other harmful animals and the project provided for a safe fenced passage through the ranch.

When I visited Namaila, I was informed by Uncle Aaron that the headman was a retiree who had assumed the position of headman in a village in Meezi. He had told the community that I just wanted to take over the communal land for personal use. In spite of my uncle's explanation to the headman and people that I already owned a big farm in Choma the fears generated by a newcomer to the area did not die.

In the twenty-first century, one villager was denying me the opportunity to invest and develop a community project in my place of birth at Namaila. From Kaleya sugarcane scheme in 1974, through the urban Lukamantano cooperative in 1975, Chivuna lime in 1984 to the Namaila community game ranch in 2000, my plans to develop my local community had met various obstacles.

I, therefore, decided that it was time to stop being paternalistic about my home area and move on. I informed Chief Hanjalika that I was abandoning the community game project. This also meant that I would not have any more dealings with my place of birth as I did not own any land at Namaila or in the Mazabuka District.

The abandoned ambassador at work

Within two years of my being at the ACP secretariat, my relationship with the Zambian Government authorities soured. No Cabinet Ministers attended any of the ACP meetings. The junior Ministers who were delegated to attend did not even acknowledge the presence of a Zambian SG at the ACP Secretariat in their speeches nor pay any courtesy calls on me.

Luckily, some SADC countries that had lobbied for my appointment continued to support me in view of the innovations I'd introduced which led to efficient operations of the Secretariat. The only Zambian Cabinet Ministers who paid courtesy calls on me during my long stay were VJ, Minister of Foreign Affairs, and Enock Kavindele, Minister of Commerce, Trade, and Industry. The two were on other assignments in Brussels when they dropped in at the ACP Secretariat.

President Chiluba made a number of trips to Brussels between 1998 and 2000 to consult his African trade union colleagues who'd helped him to attain his political ambitions. I came to know them well as they were part of the influential African Diaspora in Brussels. They persuaded the President to give me an audience, but he flatly refused to be associated with me and the ACP Group.

A number of ACP Heads of State and Government, including His Majesty

King Mswati of Swaziland, Flight Lt. Jerry Rawlings of Ghana, and President Mathieu Kerekou of Benin, paid courtesy calls on the ACP Secretariat while visiting Brussels. Many other Heads of State and Governments gave me audience during the ACP Summits and in their countries. President Chiluba did not attend the two ACP Summits held in Gabon and in the Dominican Republic. He could not accommodate me for meetings even as I passed through Zambia on my tours to the region.

On Saturday, 11 July 1998, at a reception in his honour at the residence of the Zambian Ambassador to Belgium, the President even directed me to give up a seat next to him for a Belgian. In his short speech, the President directed that no other Zambian in Brussels should be addressed as His Excellency apart from the Zambian Ambassador. I was the only other Zambian in Brussels in a high international public office who was addressed as His Excellency as demanded by diplomatic etiquette.

On 1 June 1998, the Lome IV Convention came into force after attaining the threshold signatures for ratification. The Secretariat worked closely with ACP countries to prepare projects for the utilization of the fourteen billion Euros still unutilized under the Eighth European Development Fund. The ACP Negotiating mandate, structures, and the formats for the impending negotiations were approved by the Council of Ministers during its sixty-eighth session prior to the launch of the negotiations on 30 September 1998.

The decisions of the first Summit included a directive to the Council of Ministers to involve all stakeholders in the negotiations. The Secretariat designed and embarked on a novel elaborate and extensive consultative format involving experts from governments, regional institutions, NGOs, and the private sector. During these meetings, held both at the ACP Secretariat in Brussels and in various capitals, I met and established personal relationships with hundreds of politicians and development activists.

The ACP Council of Ministers had also given a directive for the Committee of Ambassadors to undertake tours to all European Union states to solicit for support on some aspects of the future agreement. This gave me the rare opportunity of visiting most of the EU member countries and interacting with Heads of State and Government, parliamentarians, leaders of civil society, and captains of industry.

In the area of debt, the Summit mandated the Ministers of Finance of ACP countries to formulate strategies aimed , inter alia, at securing the speedy implementation of the initiatives on debt, ensuring the urgent adoption of a more comprehensive set of measures pertaining to debt, cancellation of the debt of the least developed countries, ensuring closer cooperation, and coordination among ACP countries on monetary and financial matters and examining the implications for ACP countries of the planned EU single monetary currency.

The Ministers of Finance and officials held their meetings in June 1998 in

Brussels to consider the matters of debt, coordination, and cooperation. The Ministers directed that we have a separate meeting of the National and Regional Authorizing Officers to consider the financing arrangements under a future ACP-EU cooperation agreement.

During their meetings, the Ministers of Finance called on all international financial institutions, bilateral and commercial creditors to fulfill their obligations under the Heavily Indebted Poor Countries (HIPC) Initiative and to support measures to improve its eligibility conditions so as to allow the ACP States to focus on other impediments to growth and poverty alleviation. They reiterated that the solidarity and cohesiveness of the ACP Group should be enhanced by the establishment of an appropriate forum to examine the debt problem and share experiences and exchange experts and information.

On ACP-EU future relations, the Ministers indicated that the complexity of cooperation highlights the need to re-examine in a more comprehensive manner, the role, structure, and functioning of the EU Delegations in ACP countries, and of ACP National Authorizing Officers.

The ACP Secretariat negotiated and attained observer status at the International Monetary Fund (IMF), World Bank, ACCT (Francophonie), United Nations Conference on Trade and Development (UNCTAD), World Trade Organization (WTO), United Nations General Assembly, and all regional economic communities (RECs) in the three regions of the ACP. It was a great honour and privilege for me to lead the ACP Secretariat delegations to the meetings of these intergovernmental institutions.

The relationships gave me an opportunity to visit Geneva, New York, and Washington DC. I was afforded personal audiences with the leaders of these global organizations and benefitted greatly from our exchange of views on various subjects. As the Chief Executive Officer of the second largest intergovernmental organization, I was always given space to address the meetings to give official and personal perspectives on a number of security, social, political, and economic issues.

The follow-up to the decisions of the Ministers of Finance involved the Secretariat attending meetings of the AfDB, the World Bank, and the IMF during which issues of debt, regional cooperation and integration, and structural adjustment reforms were addressed.

I attended the 1999 IMF/World Bank Annual Meetings in Washington, DC; during which the Heavily Indebted Poor Countries (HIPC) Initiative, including its comprehensive review, was discussed. After holding a number of regional meetings within the ACP Group, I became conversant with the debt initiative and appreciated the challenges faced by many debtor countries, including Zambia, to reach the threshold for debt write-off.

I held discussions with the Vice Presidents of the World Bank and with the Deputy Managing Director of the IMF who promised close cooperation in a number of areas. At the request of the ACP Secretariat, the World Bank established an International Task Force (ITF) on Commodity Risk Management in Developing Countries to look into problems of country vulnerability to commodity price fluctuations and instability.

Under the observer status, the ACP Secretariat was provided with adequate facilities such as well-equipped office accommodation and the right to attend all meetings and seminars. Such facilities greatly enhanced the coordination of the regional financial institutions and member countries by the ACP Secretariat during and after the IMF/World Bank meetings. I met and came to know personally the Ministers of Finance of most ACP countries. However, I never had a meeting with the Zambian delegation at any of these gatherings. The wide contacts and relationships I made while at the ACP facilitated my carrying out duties as Minister of Finance and National Planning later in the twenty-first century.

In view of the large volume of documents we prepared and shipped to the numerous organizations and meetings all over the world, I organized for funds from the European Commission for the full computerization of the Secretariat with internet connectivity. By 1998, the Secretariat stopped carrying heavy metal trunks full of personal computers and documents to the various meetings in the ACP regions, as laptops and diskettes became the fashion.

I also guided the Secretariat in taking a leading role in the development of virtual internet communities. We had in place a very good administrative database application that was developed in-house and which provided management with timely reports and enabled the officers to work independently of one another. I was among a few privileged public executives, who owned an Ericsson GH688 cellphone, the latest communication technology launched in 1966, which made it possible for me to communicate from many locations in the world.

Denied a second term of service at the ACP
Six months before the end of my contract in February 2000, the Committee of Ambassadors activated the procedures of recruiting a Secretary General by inviting member states to make nominations. However, many ambassadors informed me that should I be supported by my country for a second term, they will recommend to their governments to support me for a new contract.

In June 1999, I wrote a report to the Zambian Minister of Commerce, Trade, and Industry, responsible for ACP matters, on the procedures for selecting an SG. I reported on my performance at the ACP Secretariat and requested that the matter of renewing my contract be brought before President Chiluba.

As the time was running out, the Committee of Ambassadors approached the Zambian Ambassador inquiring on the position of the Zambian Government on my contract. But they drew a blank as he could not offer an official opinion.

President Bongo of Gabon was prepared to campaign for me as a repayment to me for holding the first ACP Summit in his country. This was because the hosting of the ACP Summit had made the President and his party win the national elections that followed the Summit. President Bongo even sent Jean Ping, his Minister of Foreign Affairs, who became the chairman of the Commission of the African Union, as a special envoy to Lusaka to deliver a message to President Chiluba.

In August 1999, while attending the Summit in Maputo, Mozambique, I joined the other Zambians in welcoming President Chiluba at the airport. The President expressed surprise at my presence in the lineup at the airport. The Minister of Foreign Affairs informed me that the matter of my contract had been discussed with the President and a decision was to be taken soon. However, one of the Deputy Ministers who was in the delegation confided in me that there was no possibility of my contract being renewed due to the hostility towards me by some senior Zambian Government officials.

The Second Summit of the ACP Heads of State and Governments
The successful holding of the first Summit in 1998 and the resultant initiatives encouraged the Heads of State and Government to call for a second Summit in order to usher the ACP-EU cooperation into the twenty-first century. I was once more honoured and called upon to supervise the arrangements for another ACP Summit.

While the ACP Group had agreed in 1997 to hold the 2nd Summit of the ACP Heads of State and Government in December 1999 in the Dominican Republic in the Caribbean, the Summit had to be brought forward to the end of November 1999 on advice of airlines that planned to reduce flights towards the end of December 1999 for fear of something happening, due to the Y2K computer problem. Y2K was the common abbreviation for the year 2000 software problem also named the Millennium Bug, which was associated with the popular roll-over of the millennium at midnight on 31st December 1999.

The Summit was held between 22 and 26 November 1999 in Santo Domingo. A private dinner I had with the youthful President Lionel Fernandez Reyna of the Dominican Republic provided me with a rare opportunity to learn and appreciate what visionary statesmanship is all about. The president had made the provision of a computer to every school pupil as the top priority of his mission during his term of office. The president expressed his optimism for a smooth transition into the 21st century, as a lot of work had been done to forestall any computer hitches.

During the meetings, many Heads of State and Government paid glowing tribute to my work at the ACP Secretariat during my three-and-a-half years' service, when I played the roles of Chief Convener, Negotiator, Advisor, and Supervisor of the negotiations between the ACP Group of seventy-one states and the fifteen European Union members. The negotiations culminated in a twenty-year partnership agreement for future cooperation with a development aid package of 13.5 billion Euros for the first five years.

My own government did not appreciate the services I had provided to the international community. In fact, I had to lobby an official in the Zambian delegation to include a sentence in the Minister's speech on the work I had done at the ACP Secretariat. Fortuitously, I met millions of political refugees driven out of their countries by poor governance on my global travels, who gave me appropriate advice on how to handle such situations.

The reply by President Chiluba to President Bongo's approach concerning my contract must have been a clear 'No' as it encouraged the latter to nominate one of his nationals for the position of SG. The Santo Domingo Summit endorsed Jean-Robert Goulongana, Gabonese Ambassador to Brussels as the new ACP SG of the ACP Group.

I accepted an invitation by President Bongo to the lavish party he proudly hosted to celebrate the election of his compatriot. I was surprised when he did not only thank me for the achievements I had accomplished, but he also proposed a toast to my prosperous future.

The following was my farewell speech to the ACP Group delivered at the Summit in Santo Domingo, the Dominican Republic on 26 November 1999.

"Your Excellencies,
Heads of State and Government,

I am most grateful for the opportunity Your Excellencies gave me to be at the helm of this important organization during this exciting period. The period is exciting as there are so many epoch-making happenings within the Group and outside.

I assumed the post as a compromise candidate after a period of eighteen months of inconclusive elections. I was therefore in a most favourable situation as none of the staff members had campaigned for or against me. I have decided not to seek re-election so that there is continuing unity in the Group. My decision has been vindicated by the early decision of the ACP Council of Ministers to elect a new Secretary General.

Your Excellencies,

My assignments during the short period at the ACP Secretariat have been onerous. In 1996, the revised Lome IV Convention had not yet been ratified and this was delaying the drawing of funds under the Eighth European Development Fund. I worked on this issue and gladly, by June 1998, all ACP and EU member states had completed this political process and the Lome Four Convention became effective.

The next assignment was to organize the first Summit of the ACP Heads of State and Government. I was put at the deep end of the pool as there was no precedent to such a heavy responsibility. As a former swimming champion who learnt swimming by being dropped into a river by a demanding uncle, I wholeheartedly welcomed the challenge.

The ACP Libreville Summit and Declaration will occupy a prominent page in my memoirs. After having a historic declaration, I realized that I had opened a 'can of worms' as each paragraph contained Presidential instructions, which as a former obedient civil servant I had to obey. The instructions included:

(i) The preparations for the negotiations for a successor agreement. This was at the time when the ACP Group was not even sure that there would be a future agreement with the European Union;

(ii) The review of the institutions of the Group to attune them to the twenty-first century;

(iii) The launching of the ACP Group in the international arena and the creation of strategic alliances;

(iv) The possibility of another ACP Summit before the end of the Twentieth Century.

Your Excellencies,

In your instructions on future negotiations, you indicated that we should consult all stakeholders before engaging in negotiations. As per your instructions, the Secretariat embarked on the most exhaustive and extensive consultations in the history of the ACP-EU cooperation. I will not bore Your Excellencies with the number of meetings we held in the ACP countries and regions and in Brussels at the ACP House.

I wish to sincerely thank the Ministers who clearly demonstrated their commitment to the Group by attending the consultations. We also invited many experts from the many regional institutions, the NGOs, and the private sector. I wish to thank them most sincerely as we produced a truly representative ACP negotiating mandate.

Negotiations are currently on and should lead to the conclusion of a new ACP-EU cooperation agreement. I am hoping that this will indeed happen before 29 February 2000 when I leave. I will use all my ingenuity and remaining energies in the next three months to make sure this does indeed happen.

Your Excellencies,

I am leaving the ACP Secretariat when the ACP has made other friends apart from the all-weather European Union. The ACP has acquired observer status in many international organizations. I have signed Memoranda of Understanding with many other international organizations. This public relations work was most fulfilling as it means that the ACP Group will be where other decisions on subjects of concern to the Group are made.

Your Excellencies,

My duties afforded me the opportunity to visit your countries. Many of you heartily welcomed me. You did not only open your palaces for meals with your families and friends but you also opened your hearts as you shared your frustrations, hopes, and expectations on running your countries. These stately conversations will ring loud in my head, for they assisted me in having a wider view of world affairs. They helped me crystallize the purpose for my being on earth and sharpened my vision for humanity.

You honoured me by giving me noble assignments. I had to organize two Summits in a space of two years. I hope that I lived up to your expectations. Any shortcomings could be attributed to my being only human. I look forward to future conversations with all of you. We now have the internet in Zambia and I hope we will be able to continue our relationships through this modern facility".

CHAPTER 20

The Challenges Of Being An International Diplomat

I have given details of the work I undertook while at the ACP Secretariat and one could be tempted to conclude that all was plain-sailing during the forty-two months of my service. Unfortunately, such a lofty job, with opportunities of criss-crossing the world and meeting prominent citizens and world leaders is accompanied by misadventures, dangers, humiliation, intrigues, and frustrations caused by Mother Nature and fellow human beings. I highlight a few of these life-changing and at times nail-biting experiences.

Bangui peace rattled by snipers
One of the major roles of the ACP Group was that of conflict resolution in member states using the ACP-EU Joint Parliamentary Assembly consisting of Members of Parliament from the ACP and EU member states. The arrangement was that the Secretariat made a preliminary visit to the country in conflict followed by a team of Members of Parliament, who presented their tour report to the Joint Parliamentary Assembly.

In the 1990s, the Central African Republic (CAR), a beneficiary of ACP-EU cooperation, experienced a series of military mutinies against democratically elected President Ange-Felix Patasse. I was delegated by the ACP Council of Ministers to visit the country for discussions with the Government to assess the situation. On a flight from Abidjan, Cote d'Ivoire to Bangui, I met Anicet Georges Dologuele, who had been recalled from the IMF and had been appointed as Minister of Finance. Our flight time to Bangui was used up to productively discuss a lot of developmental issues.

On arrival at Bangui M'Poko Airport at 1900 hours, we were met at the plane and driven to the VIP lounge by heavily armed men. After completing arrival formalities, we were led to a waiting convoy of vehicles. I suddenly realized how tense the situation was as the convoy consisted of camouflaged military vehicles. The new Minister I'd met on the plane did not mention anything about the security situation in his country during our conversation as he was not aware, having been away from home for a long time.

We weaved our way to Oubangui Hotel on the banks of the Ubangi River, through rubble and military roadblocks manned by heavily armed soldiers. At the hotel, we found more soldiers. My escort, a senior Government officer took time to brief me on the security situation in the country. He explained that the rebels were on the other side of the river and at times, they did fire rockets across the river. He assured us that President Patasse had given instructions for my total safety and a platoon of soldiers was deployed to guard my delegation of two.

I must have shown some fear as at one point, he asked me if nobody had briefed me on the security situation before embarking on my goodwill mission. I was not aware that Bangui had been described as, "one of the most dangerous cities in the world" in a 1996 international travel alert. After the escort officer left, I ordered some room service and retired for the night.

The following morning, a Minister came to pick us up from the hotel for the appointment with the President. The heavily armed convoy drew a lot of attention as we drove through town to the President's residence. President Patasse demonstrated his humility by refusing to occupy the imperial palace constructed and occupied by ousted Emperor Jean-Bedel Bokassa. The new President lived in his family house.

President Patasse explained his country's difficult situation. He expressed great appreciation for my personal sacrifice to visit his country during a volatile period. I judged the President as a humble man, who was genuinely keen to develop his country. As a crop scientist, the President had contributed to the development of some crop varieties, which were named after him. His country was doing well after the removal of Emperor Bokassa. Unfortunately, regional politics and conflict between the southerners and northerners in the country, fanned by divided loyalties amongst the military had taken centre stage.

My visit and our discussions centred on the role that the ACP Group could play in resolving the current situation with the rebels. I promised to convey his message to the ACP Group.

In the evening, we decided to have our meal in the hotel's restaurant. As I and my accompanying officer were eating, the General Manager rushed in and asked us to immediately leave for our rooms. I heard some gunshots from the direction of the river. The General Manager whispered that the rebels had tried to cross and were intercepted by Government soldiers. There was a commotion in the hotel and by the time we got to the second floor, where our rooms were, the corridor was full of soldiers, all to secure our personal safety.

My Senegalese accompanying officer, hypothesized that the rebels might have gotten wind of my visit and wanted to embarrass the Government by harming us. The ACP Group was highly respected in the West African region, especially amongst the French-speaking countries for the benefits they had derived since its founding in 1975. The rebels might have thought that the capture of the SG of the ACP Group would make headlines and improve their political bargaining position.

We spent the following day sightseeing and buying a few souvenirs. In the evening, we were guests of the family of Gregoire Willybiro and his Zambian wife, Annie Silumesi. Due to the frightening events of the previous night and our flight the following day, the gathering dispersed early. However, the evening was spent productively as I was briefed by some senior public workers on the state of the country. I was informed that in the CAR, all civil servants grow their own food and do not use their salaries for buying food. That is how they survived during the long periods of conflict when they were not paid salaries for over one year.

My escort Minister came the following morning to accompany me to the airport. While waiting for our departure, the minister received a telephone call. After a short conversation, he passed over the receiver to me. I was surprised that it was President Patasse who was enquiring on our safety. I assured the President that we were safe and would be taking off at any time. My memories of this scary visit to Bangui and the humble scientific President are revived by the gift of a carving of a leaf given to me by the President, which adorns our lounge.

A sip of Yaqona (Kava) calms down the storm of Fiji

On a flight between Australia and Fiji going for a Ministerial Meeting on Sugar on 13 June 1998, the Chief Pilot gave a warning that we would be going through some turbulent weather. Having been on numerous flights before when the captain's warning did not materialize, except once over the Congo, I continued reading while relaxed in the wide-bodied plane. Suddenly, the huge plane started swerving violently. Articles such as spoons and cups were being tossed all over the cabin.

Visibility was less than twenty metres and many passengers started praying loudly. We had entered into a heavy thunderstorm. By the grace of God, we landed safely at Nadi Airport on a submerged runway in heavy pouring rain. The Meeting was held at a beautiful lodge on an island joined by a bridge to the mainland.

As the storm continued for some days, some jutting rocks disappeared into the ocean causing a lot of anxiety amongst most us who were from Africa. The bridge was submerged while the heavy rains continued pouring. The weather people announced that the ocean level was rising and could affect the resort island where we were lodging.

I had taken Joyce along with me on the trip on what was supposed to be another honeymoon but the weather was spoiling our outing as the stress levels rose very high. The tension was only toned down by the traditional yaqona drinking ceremony given in my honour as a special guest on my first visit to Fiji.

The yaqona or kava drink is an intoxicating beverage made from the aromatic roots of kava or piper methysticum of the pepper family. The drink was the right recipe as it has effects of calming anxiety, stress and restlessness and treating insomnia. A beautiful wooden bowl called tanoa used during the ceremonies adorns our living room as a reminder of our visit to Fiji.

The locals explained that the heavy rainfall and high tides were normal and that we should not worry too much. Joyce and I thereafter greatly appreciate the vagaries of nature and the vulnerability of the people of the island nations and the reason for their specific mention in the ACP-EU Lome Convention.

Saved by oxygen therapy

I was on a flight to West Africa and while reading some documents, I started feeling dizzy. I called the cabin crew and explained the strange feeling. By the time a passenger doctor arrived at my seat, I had passed out and they had to revive me with some oxygen. After I had come round, I was advised to keep the oxygen face mask on for the duration of the long night flight to Gabon. I was scared that it was claustrophobia. Luckily, I was informed that there was poor ventilation in the corner of the cabin where I was seated as the plane was an old one belonging to an African aviation company. Since then, I prefer to sit in the aisle seats.

Zambia equated to Heaven on Earth

Having completed my mission to Cote d'Ivoire, I decided to pass by Mali to see the land from where a number of the illegal immigrants to Zambia nicknamed senesene originate. During the stopover in Bamako, proceeding passengers were advised to remain on the plane. Due to my curiosity, I asked a hostess if I could be allowed to visit the terminal building to have a feel of Mali. The air hostess instead asked me for my country of origin. When I mentioned Zambia, she refused to allow me to disembark.

I tried to reason with her by explaining who I was, but she could not give in to my request. I thought that perhaps she had heard of the hostility some Zambians had for the senesene and feared that I could be a victim of reprisal. Instead, she explained that the ground temperature was 45 degrees on that day and that not being used to such high temperatures, I could collapse. Lusaka's highest temperature is below 35 degrees.

Once back in Brussels, I narrated my experience to His Excellency the Ambassador of Mali, who had encouraged me to make a stopover in Bamako. I complained that the flight crew deprived me of the opportunity to touch Malian soil due to high temperatures. The Ambassador lamented that "Secretary General, for some of you, when you pray to God that you go to heaven, you mean something out of this world. But for some of us, being in Zambia, your country, means that God has answered our prayers and has taken us to heaven."

I could not believe what I was hearing, except that my eyes which were seeing the sad expression on the Ambassador's face gave in and tears rolled down my cheeks as I imagined how desolate other people's circumstances are.

I have continued to shed tears every time I recollect and relate this conversation with a senior African diplomat.

Senegalese 'Door of no return'

In February 1999, the ACP and EU Ministers went to Dakar in Senegal for their continued negotiations. It was believed that different environments provided a different negotiating atmosphere as the negotiators would experience at first-hand the living standards in beneficiary countries. During the visit, we were invited to take an excursion to Goree Island some two kilometres at sea from the port of Dakar.

On the island was a very lively escort who explained the historical significance of the island as a slave loading port. As we went through some dark dungeons, I felt my humanity challenged by the harsh treatment meted out to the slaves by the slave traders. The tour route culminates at the ignominious 'Door of No Return'. Once a slave reached the other side of that door, their fate into slavery was sealed and they could not return.

We were informed that more than half of the slaves loaded into ships never made it to their destinations in the Americas. They died of starvation and overcrowding. Many others were thrown into the sea for various reasons, including for being too weak or not being submissive to the lust demands of their masters. The imagination of the barbaric treatment meted to these innocent human beings overwhelmed me and I was one of the many visitors who wept in public.

Turned into a drug dealer

At the end of every ACP meeting in member countries, the ACP Secretariat staff stayed behind for another day or more to assist delegates from other countries with their return travel arrangements. Negotiations between the ACP and EU shifted to Dakar, Senegal in February 1999. The Zambian delegation led by a Deputy Minister left Dakar immediately after the discussions. I did not even have the chance to meet any member of the Zambian delegation.

As I was preparing to depart for Brussels at the end of the meetings, I was hanging around in the lobby of the hotel seeing-off delegates leaving at about 18.00 hours when I met the Zambian Ambassador to Brussels. He informed me that he would be travelling the following day but was not sure of the routing, which might mean a longer flight.

He mentioned that he had a small parcel and requested me to take it to his wife in Brussels. When I enquired as to the contents, he said that it was some medicine for his wife brought from Zambia. My wife and I were aware of the health condition of the Ambassador's wife as we lived within the same canton. The Ambassador gave me a paper bag, which contained the Economist Magazine, some ACP documents and a small well-wrapped brown parcel.

Although I had already packed and could have carried the small parcel and papers in my hand luggage, I decided to put the parcel in the big suitcase. However, my sixth sense commanded me to unwrap the parcel. As I did so, I was suddenly overpowered by a strong smell that engulfed the room and sent me to the floor. I rose up and rushed to switch on the air-conditioning and opened all the windows. I then rewrapped the parcel wondering what kind of a strong drug was in the parcel.

After composing myself, I telephoned the Ambassador and asked if he knew the contents of the parcel he had given me to take to his wife. He answered that he did not know, but that he was told by the officer who'd carried it from Zambia that it was medicine for his wife's ailment. I then informed him that I had opened the parcel and it contained some very strong-smelling drug. I told him that I was returning the parcel and that we should meet in the lobby.

I used the staircase for fear that if there were other people in the elevator, they might smell the drug and report to security personnel and I would get arrested. For the period I was getting down the staircase, I was a drug carrier by design of my own Government. I found the Ambassador in the lobby and he innocently and calmly took the paper bag without any comment.

A few minutes later, I left for the airport for a night flight via Amsterdam Airport Schiphol, one of the airports with an efficient drug surveillance system. Joyce was devastated when I narrated the incident to her and she advised that I should never carry any parcel for anyone regardless of how dignified they may look. Since that incident, I have refused to carry even small envelopes for other people unless they open them in my presence to confirm that they are not laced with drugs.

On reflection, it is anyone's guess as to what could have happened to me had I carried the Ambassador's medicinal parcel to Amsterdam on Friday 12 February 1999. The certainty was that I would have been arrested as a drug peddler.

I thank my God that He protected me against the evil intentions. In spite of my pleadings, the Zambian Ambassador to Belgium never revealed to me the name of the Zambian Government officer who gave him the drugs. However, on my return to Zambia, I came to know the Government officers who were behind the plot to implicate me in drug dealing. My own Government did not want me to return home as a free man but to languish in a foreign prison.

CHAPTER 21

Leaving The 20th Century With Honours

On 29 February 2000, I bade farewell to the ACP Secretariat and my family vacated the official residence in Waterloo for Europa Hotel to facilitate the packing of our goods. I received a lot of people at the hotel who encouraged me to stay on and get a job in Europe or elsewhere. Some, who knew of my relations with the Zambian Government and had followed the happenings back home, were apprehensive of the type of welcome and treatment that I would receive. Some, who originated from unstable countries, even expressed concern for my personal safety and assisted me to acquire appropriate protective clothing.

Two members of staff of the ACP Secretariat, Kenneth Kumampley and Valerie Adodo visited us twice at the hotel and we had prayers together. On their last visit on Sunday, 5 March 2000, Kumampley asked me to which church I belonged and at which church I had been attending services in Brussels. I told him that I was baptized under the Salvation Army in 1958. But that I had stopped being a regular churchgoer in 1968 and had not been to any church in Brussels during my three years' stay.

Kumampley expressed utter surprise, stating that my character and behaviour was not that of a person who did not go to church. I thanked him for his positive assessment and he promised to continue praying for me to maintain my character.

When I went to say 'goodbye' to the Zambian Ambassador at the Embassy on 2 March 2000, we had a long discussion covering a number of issues. I enquired as to the reasons for the Zambian Government not supporting the renewal of my contract. He indicated that he had not been able to discuss the matter with the authorities in Lusaka. I mentioned the Dakar drug parcel incident and encouraged him to reflect on it and asked him to be kind enough to give me details when he'd gathered enough information.

I had a wonderful time in Brussels, the diplomatic capital of Europe. With so many foreigners from all over the world, it was easy to interact and share experiences of living in a huge cosmopolitan city. We spent weekends visiting shopping malls within Belgium and at times we ventured into the neighbouring countries of France and Germany. As members of the Benelux community, we did not require travel formalities when crossing borders of the six founding members of the European Union.

In June 2000, I was invited by the ACP Secretariat and the Government of the Republic of Benin to travel to Cotonou in West Africa to witness the signing of the new twenty-year ACP-EU Agreement by the eighty-six member states. In spite of my broken left leg still being in a plaster of Paris after a flimsy accident on our lawns, I could not miss such a momentous occasion. I left Lusaka for Cotonou via South Africa on 20 June 2000.

At the colorful ceremony held on 23 June 2000, the seventy-one ACP States and fifteen Members of the European Union signed the Cotonou ACP-EU Partnership Agreement in the glow of nearly one billion beneficiaries of the unique north-south relationship. Under the guidance of the co-chairman of the Council of Ministers, Prime Minister Anicet Georges Dologuele of the Central African Republic, speakers herald the agreement as a new era of cooperation.

The agreement was named after the capital city of Benin. As the Secretary General of the ACP Group during the period of negotiations, I contributed to the realization of the special agreement, which was described as "a culmination of a long process of eighteen months of negotiations between the EU and the ACP".

The choice of Benin as a host country was most appropriate in view of the prominence given to political dialogue amongst the partners in the new agreement. The meeting was to honour President Kerekou, 'the father of democracy', who'd become the first sub-Saharan African strongman to accept multiparty elections and gave up power when he lost the elections to the opposition in March 1991. His decision to peacefully cede power set off a wave of untangling the undemocratic one-party rule across Africa. The strong wind of change started in Benin, reached Zambia within six months, and on 2 August 1991, the Zambian Constitution was amended to provide for multiparty politics.

I was decorated by President Mathieu Kerekou of Benin with the insignia of "Commander of the Order of the Republic of Benin (COB) in recognition of the service rendered to the ACP-EU international community and to the negotiations for the historic twenty-year ACP-EU Cotonou Partnership Agreement". The occasion was one of the happiest moments in my life as it marked the pinnacle of success in my public service career of twenty-nine years. Earlier in 1997, I was recognized by the International Who's Who of Professionals, the ultimate global professional directory as an "Honoured Member for 1997" in testament to my professional, academic, and civic achievements. With a 'Distinguished Leadership Award' by the American Biographical Institute for "outstanding contribution to contemporary society", I left the twentieth century behind with visible footprints for posterity to follow.

CHAPTER 22

Learning To Survive In A Hostile Home Environment

My assignment at the ACP Secretariat came to a close at the end of February 2000 after a stay of three-and-a-half years. The Zambian Ambassador and his spouse came to the Brussels Airport to see us off to Lusaka on the evening of Wednesday, 8 March 2000. The Ambassador informed us that he had spoken to officials in Lusaka and they had assured him that there would be some senior Zambian Government officers to meet us on arrival at the Airport. When Joyce and I arrived at the Lusaka International Airport the following morning, the Zambian Government officers were not available to meet and get us through the arrival formalities.

I did not want to disbelieve the Ambassador but concluded that even he was not being told the truth by his own bosses that they did not want me back in Zambia. I, therefore, did the clearance with the help of some friends and relatives and managed to get through both immigration and customs formalities after about one hour of trotting between offices. We left the airport for town and stopped over at the newly constructed Manda Hill Mall.

We later proceeded to our house on Independence Avenue in the Woodlands area of Lusaka City. The house had been offered to us in 1997 for a hefty K140 million when the Chiluba Administration was implementing a house ownership scheme for sitting tenants. As we had lived in the house for eleven years, we qualified to buy the house. Our appeal to have the exorbitant price reduced only got us a reduction of K6 million.

We finally paid K134 million only to learn that the next highest-priced Government house on Independence Avenue was a double storey mansion, which was sold to a tenant of three years for only K19 million. In some townships, many houses were sold to tenants for as little as ten thousand Kwacha following an on-the-spot valuation by President Chiluba himself.

I tried to get an appointment to see the Minister of Foreign Affairs to report my return from the ACP Secretariat, where the Zambian Government and SADC had sent me. When it became impossible to see the Minister, I transferred my request to the office of Vice President Lt. General Tembo, who was instrumental in my going to the ACP Secretariat when he was at the Ministry of Foreign Affairs. He had since been promoted after the 1996 elections. Even the Vice President's office could not give me an appointment.

Finally, I approached the staff at State House to secure an appointment with President Chiluba as I was desirous of reporting my return to someone in the Zambian Government. For the three-year duration of my assignment at the ACP Secretariat, I did not manage to have an audience with President Chiluba in Zambia or elsewhere in the world. My efforts through this channel also did not succeed.

Our goods, including a motor vehicle, arrived in containers in June 2000 from Brussels and we sought clearance for them. Most of the goods were quickly cleared, but we had to apply to the Ministry of Foreign Affairs for the clearance of the vehicle as I was a returning diplomat. It took the Permanent Secretary Ngosa Simbyakula at the Ministry six months to reply to my letter of June 2000. In his letter of December 2000, PS Ngosa Simbyakula informed me that the Ministry could not get involved in the clearance of our vehicle as I had gone to the ACP Secretariat in my personal capacity. While I was convinced that the correct situation was reflected in the correspondence of 1996, it was not possible to get access to the files as they were kept by the senior officers.

In the meantime, the officers at the Zambia Revenue Authority confirmed that I was entitled to have my vehicle cleared by the Zambian Government through the Ministry of Foreign Affairs. They authorized me to continue using the car with diplomatic number plates until the matter was resolved. The car was cleared in June 2003 after rumours were rife that President Mwanawasa might appoint me into his administration.

As the Chiluba Government had rejected me, I decided to look in another direction for a path to my future. I recalled a story I'd heard on my travels to distant lands of a wealthy man, who after eating the sweet mango fruit he bought at the market, he decided to throw away the hard unpalatable pit onto the top of a rubbish dump. Some weeks later, the warm and damp compost nourished the seed which produced a lush seedling. One of the garbage collectors dug it up with some of the rich compost and took it home where he planted it in his garden. A few years later, the family of the garbage collector was enjoying the luscious mangoes in the community and the wealthy man was the loser.

My own Government tried to bury me by throwing me into the international community. But I accumulated unsurpassed knowledge and inimitable skills, which I decided to put at the service of other governments and organizations.

I set up a one-room office in our house with a personal computer and internet connectivity. With the technology of the twenty-first century, I was able to communicate with the rest of the world from the comfort of our home. Using my worldwide connections, I soon found work with international organizations advising them on various development issues.

I could not win any consultancy work with the Zambian Government even after attending interviews conducted by my former junior officers on subjects which I knew very well. During the interviews at the Ministry of Finance for a consultant to accompany the Zambian government delegation to the Monterrey Conference in Mexico in March 2002, I was even abused by a panelist. I lodged an official complaint with senior officers of the ministry, but nothing was done.

The rejection by my own Government was painful and this was exacerbated by the loss of many associates who passed on during my absence. The list was long but it included Bennie Mwiinga, Christopher Mulenga, Josephine Walubita Nyirongo (our lawyer), Ronald Penza, Alfayo Hambayi, John Shimaponda, and Dean Mung'omba. A large number of patriotic managers, whom I worked with and supervised in the parastatal organizations located from Luanshya to Livingstone had also passed on. For me, this was Zambia's darkest period when the country lost many of its most aggressive and promising leaders and innovative upcoming entrepreneurs.

I became a regular lecturer at the Macroeconomic and Financial Management Institute for Eastern and Southern Africa (MEFMI) in Harare, Zimbabwe on subjects of regional integration, the World Trade Organization (WTO), and the ACP-EU Cotonou Agreement. This gave me an opportunity to understand the economies of the eight member countries of the region by interacting with the students, who were serving public officers in finance and planning ministries. I facilitated, attended and lectured to numerous workshops in Zambia and the region on trade, regional integration, and the ACP-EU agreement.

When we arrived back home in March 2000, Zambia's economy was on its knees. The hopes of a quick economic revival after the change of parties, administrations, and ideology in 1991 had evaporated. Maize meal, the staple food was being sold by the roadside in one-kilogram packages called 'Pamela' in a country of forty-two million hectares of arable land. I once more became one of the agitators for a change of Government, while a number of young Zambians formed new opposition political parties.

CHAPTER 23

The Anderson Kambela Mazoka Connection

Lima Bank under my management was in partnership with many private companies among them the Kaleya Engineering Limited of Boart in supplying ox-drawn equipment to small-scale farmers. In 1988, I learnt that Boart was selling their oxen-drawn equipment manufacturing facility at Kaleya in Mazabuka District. Lima Bank staff visited the factory and proposed that Lima Bank organizes a group of farmers to form a public company to buy the factory from a loan from the bank. We strategized that I should approach the high authorities in Boart to present our proposal.

When I contacted Siwale, General Manager of Boart, he advised that I speak to his superiors at the Anglo American Corporation (AAC) offices about our offer. I then telephoned Anderson Kambela Mazoka aka 'Andy', the Chief Executive Officer of AAC and briefed him on the issue of Kaleya Engineering Limited. When I asked for an appointment to see him at his office, he instead told me that he wished to visit me at my office. I obliged him his wish as it was a privilege to be visited by the most powerful private sector chief executive officer in Zambia.

Andy came over to my office on Wednesday 31 August 1988 and this was the first meeting in our lives. I briefed him on our idea of farmers buying his company, which manufactured ox-implements at Kaleya. I informed him that I had sounded out my idea with Fitzpatrick Chuula, MP for Magoye Constituency in which the factory was located and he supported the idea. I had also briefed Kapasa Makasa, our board chairman, who'd also given his approval.

Andy confirmed the plan to sell-off the factory as part of the rationalization strategy by AAC. He promised to consider our request, as it was not a big issue according to him. He stated that his preference was for local people to buy and own the company.

Having finished the business for our meeting, Andy switched onto politics and asked me if I was standing in the Magoye Constituency during the 1988 October General Elections. When I stated that I was not standing, he then requested me to support Ben Wycliff Mwiinga, a newcomer, as Chuula, the incumbent MP was standing in the newly created Moomba Constituency. He mentioned that Mwiinga had discussed his intentions to stand, but indicated that I must be approached on the matter.

On Friday, 16 September 1988, Mwiinga visited me at home with a request that I accompany him on a tour of the Magoye Constituency on Saturday, the following day. I obliged as I was now aware of the bigger picture as discussed with Andy. We had a successful trip as we met a lot of people to whom I introduced Mwiinga as their 'new Member of Parliament'. During the trip, I also left a trophy at Saint Joseph's Secondary School at Chivuna as my donation for the school's sports programme.

My father was delighted to see us as he had been approached by so many people enquiring on possibilities of my standing in the elections. Since I had not briefed him, he did not know what to tell the people. Luckily, Chief Hanjalika was holding meetings in the Nkonkola area. We went to one of his meetings at Hanzala School, where I introduced the 'new MP' for the area to him. His Royal Highness (HRH) was appreciative of my initiative to undertake such an exercise and promised to support my candidate.

The following Sunday, I gave a detailed brief of our trip to Andy at his Kabulonga residence. My elder brother, as I began to call him, He was thankful of my having undertaken the first assignment he'd delegated to me.

Mwiinga was elected the MP for Magoye Constituency during the October 1988 general elections. He was MP for Magoye Constituency for only three years as President Kaunda voluntarily cut short his reign and called for snap general elections in 1991 after the re-introduction of multiparty democracy. Mwiinga then shifted and stood in the new MazabukaCentral Constituency where he again won.

Andy was older than me by four years and hailed from Monze District, while I was from Mazabuka District. He attended schools in Monze and Malole, while I went to schools in Mazabuka and Lusaka. He did his university education in the USA at the Union College, where he graduated in 1969 with a degree in mechanical engineering.

For his thesis, Mazoka designed and built a wind tunnel in ten weeks. Andy's wind tunnel became a students' reference project for thirty years. I attended UNZA in Lusaka and Makerere University in Kampala in East Africa. The thesis for my second degree in agricultural economics was on the economics of small-scale farmer settlements in the Mazabuka District in Zambia.

Andy spent most of his working life in Kabwe at Zambia Railways, rising to the high position as the first Zambian Managing Director. He then joined the Anglo American Corporation (AAC) at Boart in Ndola and rose to become Chief Executive Officer of AAC in Central Africa. He knew a lot about the corporate world even beyond Zambia's borders.

I spent most of my working life in Lusaka in six ministries and four parastatal organizations, where I rose to the positions of permanent secretary, managing director and group executive director. My work in the public service gave me the opportunity to know a lot of people both in the civil service and in the private sector. I toured all the provinces of Zambia on project planning and supervision. My work also exposed me to multilateral international organizations, such as the UN System and to officers of various foreign governments with diplomatic relations with Zambia.

Andy and I had a common interest in farming, having been brought up in Tongaland, the entry point of modern farming in Zambia. We spent weekends on each other's farms in Choma and Kabwe. We strategized on how we could develop our farms and share new technology with other farmers. We envisioned my farm in Choma as a cattle breeding ranch with a capacity of selling thousands of young stock to the small-scale farmers. We planned the establishment of private abattoirs and meat processing factories in cattle-rearing areas of the Southern Province as part of vertical integration.

Between 1988 and 1996, Mazoka and I became very close friends, although I kept on reminding him that being older, I looked to him for some mentoring. He retorted by saying that he was happy to have such a clever young brother who was a subject of discussions by many people due to his public service. Although we rarely discussed much of our past lives, we found enough time in our early meetings to exchange valuable personal information.

Andy had a small room for socializing close to his office in the AAC Building on Independence Avenue. He called the room 'the mentoring room'. Sometime in the eighties, he invited me to his office and after some serious discussions in the office, he took me to the mentoring room, where he introduced me to a group of enterprising young men and women. The group of young people all in the private sector and being mentored by Andy included Hakainde Hichilema, a.k.a HH. I soon discovered that the group was imbued with Andy's management skills.

Andy, HH and I held meetings strategizing on how to exploit the agricultural potential of the country. In fact, Andy and HH later went into partnership in owning some companies. I became the sounding board on Government policies and regulations as I was knowledgeable of government systems and operations. I could not participate in ownership because I was a public officer bound by the rules of the Leadership Code.

Andy was an ardent hunter and fisherman. He initiated me into big game hunting as we spent fearful nights in the Nkala and Bbilili Game Management Areas. I easily transformed my sharp skills at bird shooting learnt in my youth to big game hunting. The dependency on each other in the face of a charging wounded male lion or in pitch darkness bonded a strong brotherhood between the two of us. We became each brother's keeper. But I could not fathom the value of making a torturous trip all the way to Senanga in the Western Province just to catch a few fish, a hobby Andy faithfully fulfilled each year.

To kill the frightening nights in the bush, I narrated stories about my hunter grandfather Simalambo. Andy had little history about his ancestors. He was carving out his own history with his personal exploits. He used every opportunity that arose to make a name for himself. For example, when his uncle was posted to work in the Northern Province, this opened a window for Andy to become the school captain of Malole Secondary School, where he learnt and became fluent in the ciBemba language and culture, the knowledge that became valuable later in his life.

The time spent in the secluded environments of the bush and the farms gave us the opportunity to discuss issues beyond our hobbies and families. I became familiar with the detailed operations of the mining industry in Zambia. During one outing to my farm, we had a long discussion until well after midnight on the best mode of privatizing the mines.

We only went to bed after I convinced my elder brother that unbundling the mines was a more acceptable mode of privatization that could spread ownership and risk, as well as encourage competition amongst the various mine owners. I envisaged that such an arrangement would give an opportunity for some enterprising Zambians to band together and buy one of the mines.

Our families got closer when Joyce and Mutinta Christine Mazoka recollected that they had both attended Namwianga Secondary School in Kalomo District in the sixties. The two ladies found a lot of common subjects for their conversations, while Andy and I were absorbed in discussions on some topical national issues.

At times, like when planning the house at Malende, the foursome sat together and shared ideas on various aspects of the design of the house. The house plan included a spare self-contained bedroom reserved for Joyce and I, should we decide to spend a weekend away from the noisy City. At the time, I saw us enjoying cowboy horse rides on our farm in Choma after our retirement.

The two ladies plotted a surprise lavish fiftieth birthday party for Andy, which I was fully aware of. Andy only came to know of his party when he arrived at the venue. He was indeed surprised that I'd kept such an event as a secret to myself for so long. I suspected that this exhibition of some of my inner character built Andy's trust of and confidence in me as he could rely on me to keep any shared information.

In 1995, our daughter Nchimunya was accepted by Foxcroft School in Virginia, USA to do her high school studies after doing well in the TOEFL tests. Joyce and I escorted her to school and then, we continued our trip onto the famous tourist island of Maui in Hawaii for a belated honeymoon.

We were enjoying ourselves basking on the white sands of the Pacific Ocean when I received a telephone call from Andy, who sounded agitated. He reported that 100 herds of cattle had been taken away from our Choma farm by bailiffs in the company of armed policemen. They claimed to have been sent by the management of Lima Bank, who alleged that I'd failed to repay the loan I'd acquired from the Bank in 1991. I explained to my elder brother that there was no truth to the allegation as we had been making timely loan repayments.

All the same, Andy offered to pay the outstanding amount to have the animals returned to the farm. I told him that as a disease control measure, no animal which left the farm should be taken back onto the farm. Ngenda Sipalo, Legal Counsel for Lima Bank denied ever having issued any seizure instructions. By this time, the animals were already at the kraals at Choma abattoir ready for auctioning. Unfortunately, the local people, who knew me well, could not buy the animals from my farm seized under unclear circumstances.

The police revealed to us that they were working on instructions from some senior Government officers who'd hatched the devilish scheme to tarnish my name. At that time, I was working as a private consultant having left government service in 1994. Our lawyers Acquar Chambers took legal action against the bank. The loan was repaid to Lima Bank according to the agreed schedule. Although the case took long, we were finally compensated in 2003 by Lima Bank (In Liquidation) for wrongful seizure of our property.

In July 1996, I left Zambia for Belgium where I'd got a job as the SG of the ACP Group. Having found suitable accommodation in Waterloo Canton, I came back to Lusaka in December 1996 to pick up my family whom I had left behind. In view of our wide network of friends, Joyce and I decided to hold a farewell party to signal our departure from Zambia, as we were expected to be away for a minimum of three-and-a-half years. The Mazokas agreed to host the event at their new Malende home east of Lusaka City so that the occasion served as a housewarming party for their new residence.

The party, which was held on 28 December 1996, was attended by a large number of prominent people, most of whom I'd come to know during my thirty-two years' stay in Lusaka. I appealed to those present to cultivate their inter-personal relationships in spite of my absence. I revealed that if it were not for the national duty of representing Zambia in the international fora, I'd wanted to stand in the elections in the Magoye Constituency. I promised that I would be keenly observing the political situation back home.

In March 1998, Andy and I were invited by the CDC to participate in a high-level international workshop held at Oxford University in the United Kingdom on investing in Africa. The guest speaker was President Kaguta Museveni of Uganda and I had the privilege of sitting next to him during the welcoming dinner. This gave me the opportunity to continue our conversation of April 1997, when he had come to address the ACP-EU Joint Assembly in Luxembourg on African politics. I had a productive conversation with one of Africa's forthright politicians.

Andy addressed the workshop from the perspective of an investor in Africa. In his speech, he emphasized that there was a welcoming investment climate in Africa for those who take time to understand the local environment. My speech was on the political environment in the ACP countries in Africa and the relevance and potential of the preferential agreements with Europe.

I revealed that in spite of over two decades of concessional funds and preferential treatment by Europe, many African countries failed to achieve any meaningful development. Many governments could not honour supply contracts for commodities best suited for production in their countries. Zambia failed to supply beef and sugar under the commodity protocols. This indicated that something else was deficient and I concluded that the missing link between resources and development in many African countries was good governance and leaders of integrity.

During the workshop, I met a vibrant young Zambian student who introduced herself as Dambisa Moyo studying for a PhD degree in economics. I encouraged her to study hard so that on completion of her studies, she would return home and assist in developing her country. Moyo completed her studies and instead of coming home, she became a renowned global economist in the twenty-first century with her seminal book, "Dead Aid, 2009", which shook the international development aid community.

In his review of Moyo's book, Kofi Annan, former United Nations Secretary General stated that, "Dambisa Moyo makes a compelling case for a new approach in Africa. Her message is that, 'Africa's time is now'. It is time for Africans to assume full control over their economic and political destiny. Africans should grasp the many means and opportunities available to them for improving the quality of life".

After the official events in the evening, Andy and I sat in my room discussing topical issues pertaining to Zambia until the early hours of the following morning. On parting, we agreed that Andy should visit me in Brussels for further discussions.

Later during 1998, Andy came to Brussels to visit us accompanied by a high-ranking official of the Zambian High Commission in London. The three of us had a lively discussion in my house on the deteriorating state of the Zambian economy. The two visitors briefed me that things were getting worse both politically and economically as the MMD Party had lost many of its credible leaders, who'd resigned from the Government.

Andy stated that he had decided not to join any of the new parties in the hope that Chiluba would take some of the advice he'd given him on how to improve the governance of the country. The families of Andy and FTJ had lived in Kansenji Township in Ndola for some time. Andy mentioned that it would be woeful to see the Zambians lose hope while there were many Zambians who could help to efficiently manage the country's affairs.

Andy stated that having been in the private sector for so long, he did not know many people that he could bring together in a political party. He said that he was prepared to give advice on technical and management issues and asked me to abandon my job and return to Zambia to engage in active politics.

I gave an extensive brief to my elder brother on the responsibilities of the

SG of the ACP Group and the immense benefits that would accrue to me personally and to my country from the international exposure. I retorted that being my elder, he should go first and I would take over after he had retired. I assured him of my total support should he venture into politics.

We concluded that the MMD Party had a saleable manifesto. After all, both of us had made contributions to the rich MMD manifesto, which had given so much hope to the Zambians during the 1991 election campaigns. All that was required was a team of credible Zambians of integrity to implement the lofty policies of the MMD Party.

We strategized that Andy should stand for a position in the MMD at a lower level and move up gradually. I reminded Andy of the conclusion made at the Cuundu meeting in 1996 that we must prepare for the 2001 elections. The young man in our midst seemed to enjoy our lively conversation.

As per our strategy, Andy stood and was elected treasurer for Bauleni Ward, in which Malende, his residence, is situated. Andy reported to me that he was summoned to State House after the elections. In the meeting with President Chiluba and Michael Chilufya Sata, the Secretary General of the MMD, Andy was informed that he would not be allowed to use the MMD as the ladder for his future political ambitions. On that account, he was directed to resign from his new junior party position.

Andy reported that the meeting was so unfriendly that he had to abandon his car and hired a taxi to take him home. He further reported that some remarks not allowing certain tribes to rule Zambia were made during the meeting. When Andy refused to resign, the elections were nullified by the SG of the MMD, who directed that fresh ward elections be held.

During the subsequent elections, Andy was elected to the same position, but in absentia, as he was out of the country. The Bauleni Ward Executive Committee was this time accused of committing a serious offence of insubordination and was dissolved.

It became obvious to Andy and I that our conversation in my house at Waterloo in Brussels was reported in detail to President Chiluba. It also became clear that there was a conspiracy within the ruling MMD Party to bar some citizens from aspiring to high public offices on tribal grounds.

It was after the frustrations of not being allowed to continue in the MMD Party that Andy decided to look for an alternative route to getting to the top leadership of Zambia. I advised against starting a new party as the registration could be denied or inordinately delayed by the MMD Government. Like had happened in the past with a number of political parties, Andy was appointed President of the United Party for National Development (UPND) in 1998.

The UPND was formed by a group of professional Zambians from various parts of the country and they welcomed Andy as a professional technocrat and not as a politician. In his messages, he addressed issues affecting all parts of Zambia and all Zambians. Andy never uttered words such as 'my people' or 'wako ni wako' like other politicians who advocated for tribal special treatment and favours.

I was thrilled when I heard this development as I knew some of the founding members as patriotic and sober Zambians of integrity. I immediately dispatched the guest list of our farewell party to my elder brother. I advised Andy to contact many of the people on the list to help him sell his vision to the Zambians through the UPND. I briefed some of my associates in Zambia on the new political programme and they were excited and offered to assist.

In October 1998, while on a trip to the Southern Africa region, I passed by Lusaka and bought my membership card No. 34 from the UPND Secretariat at the temporal offices in the Lusaka Showgrounds.

I was of the belief that the political dispensation that had been won in 1991, with the fighting spirit of many Zambians including Chiluba, which allowed the co-existence of many political parties, also opened up for individuals to choose what party to belong to. I'd forgotten that Chiluba had admitted after ninety days of being in office in 1991 that he had realized how sweet the presidential seat was.

As a consequence, the political atmosphere under Chiluba's leadership deteriorated, especially towards the 1996 general elections as he had to fend off the many admirers of the sweet seat. Zambia was once more headed towards the 'big man' syndrome that had nurtured the one-party state for eighteen years and which many noble Zambians worked so hard to remove.

The UPND party members and supporters were greatly encouraged when the UPND got its first Member of Parliament, Griffiths Nang'omba who won the 30 November 1999 by-election in the Mazabuka Central Constituency following the demise of Bennie Mwiinga, the MMD Member of Parliament. The win by a Lozi in a constituency in Tongaland demonstrated the non-tribal character of the Tongas and the UPND.

Andy and his spouse came to our house on Tuesday 14 March 2000 to welcome us back to Zambia after we returned from Belgium. Since we had not bought any furniture by this time, the four of us shared space on the ledge in the empty lounge. This was how modest Andy was. We wished one another good tidings in the twenty-first century as we had not met since the beginning of the new Millennium. During our long conversation, we covered a number of subjects, including the state of our families, farms, and the Zambian economy and politics.

On 13 April 2000, Hakainde Hichilema came over to brief me on a number of development projects. HH and I shared a lot of information on business development ideas including directorships in companies, lime and chalk mining, cattle feedlots, and abattoirs. While I was away in Europe, HH and I kept an active conversation on many project ideas.

On Saturday, 15 April 2000, Costain Chilala and spouse dropped in from their Chimsoro Farms in Mkushi. He briefed me on the progress of the irrigation programme. We shared plans on the production of export crops under irrigation, forming a joint farming company and on the utilization of our Chilanga plots, which we acquired in 1994.

Having already joined the UPND in 1998, I became an active member of Mazoka's 'kitchen cabinet' and became intensely involved in the operations of the UPND. Although I had no official title or position in the party's management structure, being a close friend, I had the liberty to engage Mazoka even on the most sensitive issues with proposals for a meaningful manifesto. Knowing most Zambians who worked in both public and private sectors, I was active in recruiting many influential 'silent' supporters. I even helped in composing his inclusive 'Shadow Cabinet'. With my connections in Europe and elsewhere, I had a rich reservoir of advisors and I solicited advice from the various cooperating partners on the way forward.

On 16 April 2000, the UPND officially launched its manifesto. This was a very important day as Mazoka explained the capability and vision of the leadership of the party. The Manifesto showed a clear path to a peaceful country of prosperous citizens.

We then planned an extensive tour of the country by Mazoka to sell himself and the newly-launched UPND Manifesto. The tours were going smoothly until on the night of 13 September 2000, when Mazoka was involved in a freak road accident around Serenje Town on his way from the Northern Province. We realized how scared and desperate the political opponents were getting and we took special precautions.

While the politics was going on, I continued with my professional work. I spent some time in Malawi on a consultancy project on Malawi and the ACP-EU agreement. For most of October and November 2001, I toured the rural areas of Eastern, North-Western and Southern Provinces on consultancy work under Kane Consult Limited evaluating the operations of the US $300 million five-year Agricultural Sector Investment Program (ASIP).

Apart from collecting information on development in general and economic activities in particular, I had the opportunity to engage in some political discussions with local communities. These consultancy studies required the convening of workshops for stakeholders, mostly Government ministries and the donor community. I became conversant with the Poverty Reduction Strategy Paper (PRSP), one of the country's main development planning documents produced in 2000. I was, therefore, able to advise Andy on economic matters and the political barometer, which seemed ripe and in favour of him and the UPND.

I was not surprised by the huge crowd that turned out at the High Court to escort Mazoka during the nomination on 29 November 2001. We were happy that the people embraced the message of hope by the UPND presidential candidate.

On Thursday, 13 December 2001, we travelled to Mapangazya for a rally.

The rally was held a few kilometres away from Malala School, where I had sat for my Standard II examinations in 1958. The attendance was large and overwhelming. Mazoka gave me the platform to address the rally after introducing me as, "my friend and young brother".

Being in the shadows of the Mabwetuba Hills, my local environment, I outlined most of the UPND's economic plans, emphasizing the role of agriculture in national development. I gave a brief of my past involvement in national planning and the many projects I had worked on in the Mazabuka District. Before the large crowd, I promised to assist President Mazoka to develop the country and asked the people to vote for him.

We then rushed back to Lusaka as Mazoka had an appointment for a television interview. I, with an associate, sat with Mazoka at his Malende home going through all possible issues that were likely to be raised. As he was leaving for the studios, I advised that he should insist on changing the chair they usually use as it was not suitable for the purpose.

At the studios, he asked for a change of chairs and the one he used allowed him to portray a relaxed and poised dignity. We did not need to hire expensive foreign image builders as Andy already had good manners, character, and a presentable image. He was called, *Mwana Mubotu* meaning 'good child' because of his affable personality.

The television interview on Thursday, 13 December 2001, was a turning point for the UPND presidential candidate, as his message gave hope to the suffering Zambians. Mazoka, in a presidential posture, gave a winning show by eloquently elucidating the plans of the UPND in the various sectors of the economy.

After Joyce and I had cast our votes at the Community Hall at State House on Thursday, 27 December 2001, we spent the rest of the day at home, but with our ears glued to the radio for news on the election results. Our home was more or less another Control Centre for the UPND. We were kept busy throughout the period of voting and after. By Friday evening, the results from fifty per cent of the constituencies had been announced and Mazoka was leading in the presidential race.

In the early hours of Saturday, 29 December 2001, it was announced that voting in some of the remote constituencies including Chiengi Constituency in Luapula Province on the border with the DRC had not been completed due to a shortage of ballot papers. The chairman of the ECZ, Judge Bobby Bwalya announced that they had decided to deliver more ballot papers by Zambia Air Force and to extend the voting period.

As soon as we learnt of this development, we suspected that some foul play was being hatched by the ruling MMD party. Unfortunately, due to the long distance to Chiengi, we could not organize observers to be present as the additional ballot papers were being off-loaded from the ZAF planes. No foreign observers had also gone to these far-flung areas. We were now banking on the fact that the number of voters in these outlying constituencies was small and they would not overturn the overwhelming votes amassed by the UPND candidate in the urban areas.

We spent a lot of time consulting with the observer missions from the SADC, EU, Carter Center, and Coalition 2001 Centre, which deployed hundreds of observers in the country. By early Saturday morning, the observers informed us that Mazoka had won the presidential race. We organized a press conference at the Mulungushi Conference Centre to make the announcement.

Concurrently, the MMD announced from their Ibex Hill Command Centre that Mwanawasa, their candidate, had won. This caused immediate confusion to the whole process. The UPND cadres, who had invaded the Manda Hill Shopping Mall to celebrate Mazoka's win, started rioting. Mazoka went onto public media to appeal to the supporters not to be destructive as "any damaged property will have to be repaired by our new government".

In northern Zambia, people were still voting using freshly delivered ballot papers some two days after the polls had closed. For the first time in its history, the government-owned Times of Zambia newspaper published two editions on Saturday 29 December 2001, with conflicting voter figures and this added more confusion to the whole situation.

Between 29 December 2001 morning and Tuesday 1 January 2002 afternoon, so much happened, including a meeting at Malende amongst some opposition parties to discuss the formation of a coalition government.

On Monday 31 December 2001, six opposition parties lodged a petition with Chief Justice Matthew Ngulube on the manner of conducting the whole election process. The case was allocated to Judge Peter Chitengi, who asked for time to study the matter. As the High Court adjourned about mid-morning on Tuesday, the crowd of restless and highly charged opposition party supporters at the High Court premises had swelled to about 10,000.

Security concerns for President Mazoka at the High Court meeting were raised as we were gathered at my house. The intense discussions concluded that Hakainde Hichilema and I should get Andy safely out of the High Court premises. The two of us were considered the most apolitical to undertake such a mission in a highly charged political environment.

As we were driving to the High Court, we decided that using the back door was much safer. We negotiated our way through the police officers who were stationed at the back gate near the INDECO Flats. A mere mention of the name Mazoka was enough for us to get the sympathy of the security officers. Hakainde Hichilema went into the High Court building, while I remained in the vehicle, ready to drive off.

Immediately the court adjourned, Hakainde Hichilema came back with Andy and some senior UPND officials. Andy gave instructions to the officials to allow for some time before telling the supporters gathered on the High Court grounds of his departure. We then whisked Mazoka through the back gate and took him to a safe place.

In the evening, Mazoka held a press briefing at Malende and indicated that the UPND would not accept the results of the elections, should they favour the MMD. He further stated that the voting, which was still going on in some of the remote parts of the country, was facilitating the rigging of the elections.

On Wednesday 2 January 2002, Judge Chitengi rejected the plea of the opposition parties. He ruled that the inauguration of the new president could be delayed as results for most of the constituencies had been received.

The margin of 33,997 votes between Mwanawasa and Mazoka was the narrowest between two presidential candidates since Independence in 1964. This showed that the voters had difficulties in choosing between Mazoka and Mwanawasa.

Due to the many anomalies of the 2001 general elections, the request for postponement of the swearing-in ceremony was transformed into a full petition of the results of the presidential vote. In the meantime, President Mwanawasa continued to rule as the de facto President of Zambia. We had no other avenues to fight the new government apart from waiting for the decision of the courts. I was directed to keep abreast of all happenings on the economic matters, as this was the area that we expected to derail the new president and government.

During the opening of parliament in February 2002, the president reiterated the need for accountability, zero tolerance for corruption, and good governance to promote the rule of law. Parliament failed to elect a new speaker, signalling a further deterioration in relations between the opposition parties and the governing MMD party.

The UPND with the largest number of opposition MPs was asked to nominate a candidate for the position. After consultations, favour finally fell on Fredrick Hapunda, one of the early rebels and a former Minister of Defence in KK's administration. I was assigned to find him and brief him on the new developments.

When I went to his home on Ibex Hill, I was informed that he was in Siavonga at his Kariba Lakeside lodge. While we were making arrangements to contact him, we were informed that he'd left Siavonga and was on his way to Lusaka. I briefed Hapunda, who accepted the challenge and agreed to have his name submitted as a candidate. During the elections held on 6 February 2002, the outgoing Speaker, Amusaa K. Mwanamwambwa got eighty votes against Fredrick S. Hapunda who got seventy-seven votes as some UPND members of Parliament were lured to vote for the candidate of the ruling party.

After President Mwanawasa appointed the cabinet and addressed parliament, an economic bombshell fell on his new administration. At the end of January 2002, the Anglo American Corporation (AAC) announced that it was pulling out of the Zambian mining scene due to low copper prices of around sixty-one cents per pound.

Mazoka, who had been at the helm of AAC for eighteen years, was aware of the dire consequences of such a drastic move. The projection was that the KCM mines would be out of business within a year if no new money was provided. Many in the opposition were celebrating that the Mwanawasa administration would soon collapse under the weight of the social instability that would result from massive unemployment.

Some UPND zealots and opposition members even publicly attributed the AAC's pull out to Mazoka's influence on his former employer. Those of us close to and who knew Mazoka well felt uncomfortable as this was giving a bad picture of the patriot who wanted to salvage Zambians from the mismanagement by the Chiluba regime.

The managers of AAC helped in some way by denying any connections with the political situation in Zambia. The chairman of AAC stated that "The problems we are suffering predate the elections…We are obviously acutely aware of the social and economic impact of the closure of these mines on the Zambian copper belt."

I re-activated my long-established relations with the World Bank to get more information on the effects of this action by the AAC. In early March 2002, I received a draft copy of the World Bank/IMF report after their fact-finding mission to Zambia. The report was alarming. It gave graphic details of the levels of unemployment of miners and those under the subcontractors. It was stated in the report that within nine months, the Copperbelt region was likely to be under social turmoil and ungovernable with a serious breakdown of law and order.

In sharing the IMF/WB Mission's findings with Mazoka, I reminded him of our conversation at my farm in the nineties when I proposed the unbundling of the mines as the best mode of privatization. Such a method would have spread the risk of failure in the industry to the many investors. The sale to AAC was like putting 'all one's eggs in one basket'.

We concluded that the impending national catastrophe would have long-term negative effects on the people, such that it would be very difficult for any administration, including that of the UPND, to quickly repair the damage.

After some intense consultations, including a trip to South Africa, Mazoka informed me that he was going to help and would not allow Zambia to collapse. I suspected, although he never admitted, that some emissary had delivered an SOS message from President Mwanawasa. Mazoka started a series of interviews with various local and foreign news media stating that,

"I would like to assure would-be investors that we intend to sort out our political differences and bring Zambia into line with other acceptable countries for investment.

If we let Konkola die, then we have a very serious problem for the economic situation of this country.

The first is that as a businessman, I recognize that in a company like Anglo, the managers act on behalf of the shareholders. Their mandate is to make profits and that position demands that if they see any danger or threat to the assets of the investors, they must react in the most prudent manner. That is one hat. The other I wear as a Zambian citizen. The mining industry is one of the most important economic sectors of the country, and without it, we will face serious problems. It employs the largest number of private workers and if we do not look after that investment, we'll be in big trouble.

It would really spell doom for Zambia. Konkola Deep Mine is the only mining project of substance that will replace the ageing mines on the Copper Belt".

Although there was no admission by the new government of the positive impact of these statements from UPND President Mazoka, his words were taken seriously by the mining community in view of his experience as AAC boss for nearly two decades.

Since I was assigned the task of collecting information on the economic sectors and with my connections as a former chairman of the Economic Association of Zambia (EAZ), I kept myself busy by attending meetings called by various organizations. I held frequent meetings with President Mazoka to review the happenings in the country.

As soon as the issue of the mines seemed to have been resolved, a serious shortage of maize due to drought and poor attention to agriculture by the Chiluba Administration, arose. In May 2002, President Mwanawasa declared a national emergency and appealed for international food aid. The food shortage threatened more than 2.5 million Zambians with starvation.

The pull-out of AAC from the mines and the food shortages attracted my attention as the two sectors were very important to the economic and social lives of Zambians. The UPND had wooed the people with its down-to-earth manifesto and their continued support could only be maintained by the party leadership being abreast with current issues and offering viable solutions.

At the beginning of March 2002, I was nominated by the EAZ to be in a delegation of the Energy Regulation Board (ERB) on a tour of energy providers and regulators in the USA. We arrived in Miami, Florida on 6 March 2002, a few days after the whole western United States had suffered an unexplained power black-out.

In Miami, we attended an Energy Regulators' Conference for North and South America. We visited the National Association of Regulatory Commissioners (NARUC) where we got a full briefing on the separation of production, transmission and distribution functions. In Washington DC, we met the officials of the Departments of Agriculture and Energy.

We visited the Edison Electric Institute (EEI) whose members provided electricity to 220 million consumers, operated in all fifty states, and directly employed more than 500,000 workers. We travelled by road from Miami through the states of Georgia, Tennessee, Kentucky, West Virginia,

Washington DC, and Pennsylvania, reaching New York on 15tMarch 2002.

The trip to the USA reinforced the professional view held at the time that the separation of the Zambian energy sector into three companies dealing with production, transmission and distribution would improve efficiency. The delegation made recommendations to this effect and the EAZ took the responsibility of championing the new proposal in various fora.

At the time, the Kariba North Bank was under a separate company, which produced energy and sold to ZESCO. The relationship between the two companies was strained as ZESCO had a huge bill of outstanding payments for energy supplied by the generating company. While the general mood in professional circles was for separation of responsibilities, ZESCO was vigorously lobbying some politicians to take over the Kariba North Bank.

On our return from the USA, I found that the political situation was still unsettled. In the UPND camp, there was a view that the president of our party should be a Member of Parliament. This was considered to be a way of providing a platform for the UPND to continue articulating its likeable manifesto. But others felt that the presence of the party president in parliament would intimidate the other ordinary UPND Members of Parliament.

David Matongo, MP for the Pemba Constituency offered to step down and cause a by-election under which Andy was to stand as the UPND candidate. However, after intense consultations, the idea was dropped, but we had to consider a system of how the MPs would interact with the party policymakers outside parliament. The proposed model of MPs holding monthly meetings with the NEC members was rejected by the MPs. A lack of a structured relationship between the party's policymakers and the elected representatives continued to cause conflicting views on a number of issues between the two groups.

In April 2002, I was on the committee that organized the wedding ceremony for Chiko, Mazoka's first daughter, and Toti, an African-American. The wedding reception held at Malende was attended by the cream of Zambia's personalities in both the business and political spheres. It was a hilarious occasion as Chikwanda, my former boss at the MRD was the venerable Guest of Honour. I played the venerated role of the family spokesman.

The year 2002 was a difficult one for the new Mwanawasa administration in both economic and political terms. The anti-corruption fight, which included the removal of the immunity of former President Chiluba by Parliament in July 2002 and the arrest in April 2002 of Sata, aroused the most divisive tribal hostility against Mwanawasa by the Bemba-speaking politicians. Sata, now a leader of an opposition party, waged a relentless battle alleging that Mwanawasa was tribalistic, nepotic, and anti-Bemba. In June 2008, Mwanawasa summed up the attacks by stating that, "Sata maliciously made my job difficult to govern this country'.

Mazoka was being enticed, by those who were fighting Mwanawasa, to form a coalition government. Meetings were held 'under the tree' at his Malende home with some opposition leaders, including B.Y. and former President Chiluba. They were hopeful that the court petition would end in their favour.

During one meeting, an opposition leader openly told the gathering that he would not accept Mazoka to be his leader. Recalling the meeting at State House in 1998 amongst Chiluba, Mazoka, and Sata and the tribal sentiments expressed then, I organized a strong opposition to any alliance and we managed to convince Mazoka to refuse to have any further dealings with the tribally-minded opposition leader.

On Tuesday 3 June 2003, Andy invited me to accompany him on a visit to his Taba Farms in Kabwe and I willingly obliged and even offered to drive. Taba Farm had a special place in Andy's life as it had been his refuge when he'd suddenly resigned from Zambia Railways in the seventies. 'Taba' means to support someone or something from falling.

Andy was developing a modern centre pivot irrigation project at the farm with a large water reservoir in the middle of the fields. We perched on one of the dykes like solitary water birds, out of earshot of any other person or creature except the hidden musical crickets. I sensed that the 1998 Brussels incident, when we'd trusted a third person as we'd planned our political careers in Zambia's political arena, had been a great lesson to my elder brother. This time around, he could not trust anyone except me with his thoughts on his and Zambia's political future.

During our conversation, we observed that there were serious problems in the country caused by the unstable economic and political situation. There were incessant tribal attacks on President Mwanawasa even after he had appointed ministers from opposition parties and other tribes. As attention was being directed to political bickering, the economy was floundering and the tribal divisions could destroy the unity of Zambia.

Andy confirmed that he had been approached by President Mwanawasa with an offer to form a coalition government as the closest loser in the 2001 elections. In spite of advice that being in government would be more helpful to the UPND's cause and help in healing the disappointment of many UPND supporters on the 'stolen' 2001 elections, Andy had rejected Mwanawasa's offer.

He informed me that he was under great pressure from various quarters to allow me to join the Mwanawasa Government and assist with the economic management of the country. He stated that he would not object if I personally felt comfortable as I was not in the management team of the UPND. I replied that I was willing to act as a consultant, especially that I did not know Mwanawasa.

I informed Andy that since I had no political ambitions, I would not join the management team of the MMD Party and would leave the government once the economic situation had improved. Andy stated that should the economy rebound due to my involvement, he foresaw a changed role for me in Zambia's political future and that he would not mind under which political party this happened.

Andy encouraged me to meet President Mwanawasa and listen to his story. He stated that he foresaw a turnaround of the economy under a good economic manager and that President Mwanawasa, being a lawyer, would listen to my advice on economic matters. It was clear to me that Andy was conveying a message to me from President Mwanawasa, whom I did not know.

I met President Mwanawasa on Sunday 8 June 2003 and he offered me the job of Minister of Finance and National Planning but I requested for time to consult.

The following day, I sought the advice of Mwene Mwinga, one of my close friends on the Sunday happenings. He advised that I should accept President Mwanawasa's offer but that I should brief President Mazoka before meeting the Republican President again. He offered to accompany me to Malende, the residence of the Mazokas. When we got to Malende, we only found Mrs Mazoka, who informed us that President Mazoka was somewhere between Kasempa and Mumbwa Towns from his tour of the North-Western Province.

I went ahead to break the news of President Mwanawasa s offer to Mrs Mazoka. Her reaction was instant and unfriendly. I realized that Andy had not informed his spouse of the events of the past few days including our meeting. Our efforts to speak to Andy on the phone failed and we left Malende with a promise that I would continue to try to reach him.

Andy and I had a long discussion at my home on Tuesday 10 June 2003. I informed him that I had not accepted the offer as I felt the need to consult him before making a final decision. We analysed various scenarios and concluded that I should accept the offer of appointment as Minister in the Mwanawasa administration. Andy repeated that Zambia had to be saved. He also said that this might give me another route should I decide to be active in the Zambian political arena in future.

He promised that he would reciprocate my trust in him and the sense of secrecy by not issuing a public statement on my appointment if and whenever it was made. I was appointed Minister of Finance and National Planning on 3 July 2003. Many people thought that I had betrayed Andy and expected him to take a strong stand on my appointment and publicly denounce me. My elder brother kept his promise to me and never publicly uttered any disparaging remarks against my appointment.

On Tuesday, 12 August 2003, I was informed of Andy's admission at the CFB Hospital along Addis Ababa Road in Lusaka. In view of his critical state, private arrangements were made for his immediate evacuation on Thursday afternoon to a South African hospital.

On 11 September 2003, while leading a delegation to Brunei for the

Commonwealth Ministers of Finance and to Dubai for the IMF/World Bank Group Annual Meetings, I decided to check on Andy at the hospital. After all, I had made a small contribution towards his evacuation. The Zambian Embassy staff in South Africa informed me that a staff member, who had been evacuated from the Zambian Embassy in Addis Ababa, Ethiopia, was also admitted to the same hospital.

When we got to the hospital, I saw Mrs Mazoka in the corridor and enquired on Andy's condition and told her that I wished to see him. She stated that she had to consult the doctor. I then went to see the sick officer from our Addis Ababa Embassy, who was by then in a stable condition as her illness had been identified.

When I went back to check with Mrs Mazoka, she informed me that the doctor advised that no one should see the patient at that time. I then proceeded to the doctor's room to plead with the doctor for permission to see my friend and mentor. I found a senior nurse who informed me that Andy's relatives had advised that I should not be allowed to see him. In spite of my plea that I was a close friend, the nurse stated that they had to respect the wishes of the relatives as per medical ethics.

I then went back to say goodbye to Mrs Mazoka, who I assumed had given the instructions to the hospital staff. I gave her an envelope and tearfully left the hospital without seeing Andy. The envelope, with its contents of a small donation, was hand-carried to Zambia by a friend of Mrs Mazoka and handed back to me many months later. Joyce and I decided to keep the envelope as part of the Mazoka memorabilia.

The accompanying Embassy staff later confided in me that no Zambian Government official had been allowed to see Andy since his hospitalization. Since they were aware of my close association with him, the staff thought that I was going to be allowed to see him. I continued my trip to Brunei while reflecting on the power of politics to divide families. In this case, politics by supporters created a wedge between an unconscious Mazoka and me.

Between June 2003 and August 2005, I and Andy did not meet. On 27 August 2005, Joyce and I attended a wedding ceremony held at the ZAF Mess for Mazila, daughter of Dr and Mrs Mwene Mwinga, who married Elisha Mwale. Amongst many other invited guests were Mr and Mrs Mazoka.

Since we were seated at different tables, Andy and his wife came over to our table to greet us. As he firmly gripped my hand while placing the other on my shoulder, he shouted, in his usual praise manner, 'Kalombwana kaku-Nkonkola' meaning 'the boy of Nkonkola'. I and Joyce then exchanged hearty pleasantries with Andy and Mutinta. This was the last time that Andy and I met and had a conversation as Andy passed-on at a hospital in South Africa on 24th May 2006.

After the Freedom Day honours' ceremony on 25 May, a special meeting of Cabinet was convened to get details of Andy's death, arrangements for the transportation of the remains from South Africa and the burial. There was a need for a government officer to liaise with Andy's family on the arrangements. When I offered to play this role, President Mwanawasa objected to my proposal.

The Cabinet then settled for Vernon Mwaanga to liaise with Andy's relatives in the belief that he would be treated with some respect by the mourners as an elder and close associate of late Andy. To everyone's shock, VJ was badly beaten and his ear injured by UPND cadres when he went to Malende to check on the funeral arrangements. I never understood the reason for beating up VJ at Andy's house.

At this point, a number of Cabinet Ministers were so upset and proposed that the Government stops being involved in the funeral arrangements. However, President Mwanawasa retorted that hooliganism by a few unruly citizens should not prevent his administration from giving a befitting funeral to one of Zambia's illustrious sons.

Andy's remains arrived on Saturday, 27 May 2006, from South Africa and he was buried on the grounds of Malende on Monday, 29 May 2005, which was declared an Official Day of mourning by President Mwanawasa. Joyce and I did not attend the burial of my elder brother at Malende on advice that I could be harmed.

I consoled myself with the thought that Andy was no more at Malende and all those gathered at Malende will never have the kind of mentoring I had from him during the eighteen years of my association with him.

In fact, none of them was there when Andy and I met for the first time in 1988 and shared our life experiences, missions, and visions. None of them was there when we took turns to keep vigil in the pitch darkness of the dangerous forests of Bbilili Game Management Area for the safety of each other.

None was there when I safely conveyed Andy and VJ from Lusaka to Monze in 1996 for a meeting of the Ngoma Yamaanu Cultural Association while listening attentively to their conversation on Zambia's future.

None was there when Andy and I strategized on our involvement in Zambia's future in the lounge of my house in Waterloo Canton in Belgium. The third person during that discussion migrated to a European country after the 2001 elections.

None of them was there when Andy and I had shared experiences well past midnight in the students' hostel at Oxford University as resource persons to an international audience on investments and development in Africa.

None of them was there when we designed the Malende residence and the gardens, paying special attention to the shape of the roof and the location of the various trees and shrubs to give maximum shade and comfort to the visitors including those gathered for Andy's funeral.

None was there when Andy and I pondered on a befitting reply to the call for national duty by President Levy Mwanawasawhile perched on the concrete walls of the irrigation canal at Taba Farms in Kabwe. Our thoughtful reaction and patriotic reply to President Mwanawasa's request ensured Zambia's economic survival and propelled the Zambians towards a future of hope and prosperity.

I was certain that most of the mourners would soon leave Malende, without knowing Andy and remembering him only by the unknown mourner who wailed loudest during his funeral. Of course, VJ would have enduring memories of Andy, which were to be rekindled by the damage to his eardrums by some UPND zealots.

With deep reflections on the invaluable intimate interactions I'd had with Andy, I found inner peace within myself. I had no urge to fight anyone of those gathered around Andy's lifeless body at Malende. In a prayerful mood, I said, '*Kalyookezye mwana mubotu*', meaning 'Go and Rest Good Child'.

CHAPTER 24

President Mwanawasa Assesses My Capability

On 20th November 2001, I was visited at home by Their Excellences Jack Kalala and Ian Sikazwe, who introduced themselves as part of the campaign team for Levy Patrick Mwanawasa, the MMD Presidential candidate. I knew Sikazwe from our days as permanent secretaries in the eighties when we were neighbours on Independence Avenue, but I had not met Kalala before.

The two emissaries asked for my stance in politics and invited me to join the Mwanawasa campaign team. I explained that I wanted to remain in private practice as I had missed an opportunity to engage in mainstream politics in 1996 when I was made to leave the country for the job at the Secretariat of the African Caribbean and Pacific (ACP) Group of States in Belgium. I informed them that I was assisting the UPND President Mazoka with his campaign.

I stated that the MMD Party would not win the elections in view of the immense suffering the Zambians were going through. I also told them that even if Mwanawasa won the elections, he would be a puppet of Chiluba, his benefactor, who had woken him up in the night to stand for elections at the MMD NEC meeting. Chiluba had declared that he would remain party president even after leaving the Republican office.

Kalala stated that even if MMD did not win, Mwanawasa would win the confidence of the voters because of his high integrity. The two promised to come back after the elections to invite me to join the Mwanawasa MMD administration. They claimed that Mwanawasa has a clear personal vision for Zambia's future and would need competent Zambians like me to work with. Since I did not know Mwanawasa, I jokingly stated that we would see who was cleaner and with more integrity between Mazoka and Mwanawasa.

I was not aware then that Kalala persuaded Mwanawasa to get back into politics in 1998, the same year in which I also persuaded and convinced Andy to join politics. Zambian politics during the following few years became a battle between the two reluctant politicians of integrity. The clean politics exhibited by the two provided an enabling environment for my effective participation in Zambia's development.

On the afternoon when I was with Andy at Taba Farms, on 3 June 2003,

Moses Banda, the economic advisor to the president, telephoned my home and left a message that he wished to speak to me. Both of us being very active members of the Economics Association of Zambia, I thought that Banda wanted to discuss some topical issue on the economy as there was no animosity amongst professionals.

On 5 June 2003, Banda came to our house early in the morning to inform me that President Mwanawasa wished to see me over the weekend. Banda reminded me of our first encounter in the late seventies when I had been the head of the Planning division at the Ministry of Rural Development (MRD).

He said that he joined the planning division after graduating from UNZA then, due to the trust he had in me. We also worked together for a short period at ZANACO in the nineties. He stated that I should now reciprocate his trust as he had known me for this long time and that he vouched for my integrity to the president, who did not know me at all.

On the morning of 8 June 2003, Bates Namuyamba, Minister of Transport and Communications and a long-time friend, telephoned to thank me for agreeing to join the Mwanawasa Administration. During our conversation, the minister mentioned that he was aware and happy that my party's President Mazoka, had given his blessings to my joining the MMD Administration.

I realized that the president had consulted many other people on his intentions to appoint me. My meeting with President Mwanawasa on the afternoon of Sunday 8 June 2003 was in a cordial environment over a glass of fruit juice. I requested for time to consider the president's offer of appointing me as Minister of Finance and National Planning.

I was in the bad books of the MMD Party since my days at ZANACO in the nineties, when they had accused me of being too mean and strict on giving the bank's money. Relations had deteriorated further after I'd joined the UPND in 1998. Being close to UPND President Mazoka, I assisted him in presenting a message of hope during the 2001 general elections and this angered many MMD supporters.

My family was surprised by the turn of events but were delighted with the news when I reported on my meeting with the president. No one of us had expected the offer to be that of Minister of Finance and National Planning. They all encouraged me to accept the offer.

Before my nomination as a Member of Parliament and appointment as Minister of Finance and National Planning on 3 July 2003, I went through rigorous testing by President Mwanawasa, to establish my suitability and commitment. The design of the test luckily also assisted me to judge the sincerity and intentions of the one who was testing me.

On Wednesday, 11 June 2003, I received a letter from the Secretary to the Cabinet, appointing me a consultant to the Zambian Government team that had gone to Washington DC. The team led by Dipak Patel, Minister of Commerce, Trade, and Industry included Mundia Sikatana, Minister of

Agriculture and Water Development, Situmbeko Musokotwane a.k.a. 'Situ', Acting Secretary to the Treasury and Denny Kalyalya, Deputy Governor of the Bank of Zambia. I left Lusaka on Friday, 13 June, and joined the team the following day.

I had met Patel in 1994 when I was at ZIMCO Limited and he was then Minister of Commerce, Trade, and Industry in the Chiluba administration. Executive Director Shalaulwa Shimukowa, who was responsible for the trading companies and I went to the Minister's office to present a proposal on some aspects of the privatization programme. Our proposal was to divide the huge spaces in the state shops into cubicles and rent them out to Zambian small-scale entrepreneurs, was turned down with scorn.

We were told that our proposal was too socialistic, patronizing to Zambians, and against the MMD's privatization policy. Consequently, the empty halls were sold to foreign investors. I came to learn much later that in fact, the foreign supermarkets that bought the state shops and became fashionable in Zambia, charge a slotting fee or slotting allowance in order for commodity suppliers to have their product placed on the supermarkets' shelves. In simple language, they rent out shelf space to commodity suppliers.

I had met Situ before as a member of the Tariff Commission of Enquiry in 1986. In 1998, I found Situ in Mbabane, Swaziland, where he was an advisor to the Central Bank of Swaziland. Situ's family hosted me for a dinner at their residence during which we had very productive discussions on Zambia's economic situation. I had not met Mundia Sikatana in any official capacity, although I had heard of him in connection with the numerous litigations by the MMD during its struggles to survive.

A large budget deficit was recorded during the first quarter of 2003 and the Zambian Government had failed to observe many of the benchmarks under the Poverty Reduction Growth Facility (PRGF) programme of the IMF. Consequently, the PRGF was suspended in March 2003.

The ministerial delegation held very useful discussions with desk officers responsible for Zambia at both the IMF and the World Bank. The officers explained in detail what was required to be done in order to get Zambia's relationship with the Bretton Woods institutions back in good standing.

In the absence of a substantive minister at the Ministry of Finance and National Planning, the IMF officials were skeptical about the possibility of keeping the promises that were being made by the team. This was evident in the undiplomatic manner we were being addressed. Although I knew a number of the IMF and World Bank officers with whom we had discussions, I was content with being an observer from the back row as I was introduced as a consultant.

Our delegation concluded its consultations and was getting ready to return to Zambia on 18 June, when I received a telephone call from Lusaka directing me to stay on in Washington DC and await the arrival of President

Mwanawasa.

I used the waiting period to consult officials of the IMF and World Bank on issues that could improve Zambia's relations with the Bretton Woods institutions. I also consulted many of my close associates on the offer of an appointment made by President Mwanawasa. Mohamed Muhsin, a vice president of the World Bank from Sri Lanka, responsible for ICT encouraged me to accept the appointment. I knew Muhsin for some time as he was the financial director of the Zambia Industrial and Mining Corporation Limited conglomerate in the eighties.

Muhsin advised me that it would be imprudent to refuse a calling for national duty by a Head of State. He mentioned that he had been a presidential advisor for a long time and it is an onerous but honourable assignment. We listed a number of issues to be included in a detailed ninety days' Plan of Work, which I prepared and presented to my boss. Muhsin assured me of the support of the World Bank and advised me to consult the World Bank country officers as they had the best experience, which I could apply in guiding the Zambian economy.

I received detailed briefings from Louis Kasekende, the Ugandan Executive Director at the World Bank on the triggers and slippages of Structural Adjustment Programmes (SAPs) and how to adjust. He advised that in view of the inability of the government to meet the conditions of SAPs, I should look at the possibility of reverting to project funding. Due to the slippages, Zambia had been downgraded to a low case under the Country Policy and Institutional Assessment (CPIA). Abraham Mwenda, his Zambian Special Advisor, also gave some good tips on the operations of the Bank. Mwenda later became the managing director of the Development Bank of Zambia.

At the IMF, I had discussions with Beninese Abdoulaye Bio-Tchane, the director of the Africa Department who promised to fully cooperate with me. The executive director for Africa, Ismaila Usman and the team responsible for Zambia under David Andrews expressed willingness to visit Zambia to work out measures to control the budget deficit.

On my return to Lusaka, I had to rush to the village to check on my 79-year old sick father. I found him on his deathbed with most relatives having already arrived at the village. On Thursday 3 July 2003, while I was at the village, an announcement was made in Lusaka on my nomination as Member of Parliament and appointment as Minister of Finance and National Planning by President Mwanawasa.

I had not listened to any radio news while at the village and was not aware of the developments. I started off for Lusaka about noon and made a stopover in Mazabuka Town for a chat with the first UPND Member of Parliament, Griffiths Nang'omba. A tyre puncture a few kilometres between Mazabuka and Kafue further delayed our arrival in Lusaka to 19.00 hours.

I was informed of my appointment by my wife, who stated that an officer from State House had been to the house with a message for me. When informed that I had gone to the village, a message was relayed to Mazabuka Police to locate me and bring me to Lusaka. The police arrived at Nachintyambwa Village around 23.00 hours in pitch darkness.

My village folk were so scared that initially, they denied that I had been there during the past few days. They feared that being an active member of the opposition UPND, the police might have been sent to arrest me. However, they cooperated when they were informed of my appointment and they told the officers that I had left for Lusaka that afternoon.

At 1100 hours on Friday, 4 July 2003, I was sworn-in at State House. Immediately after the swearing-in ceremony, I went to the ministry and addressed the management team of two deputy ministers, the acting secretary to the treasury and the heads of departments. I invited each one to work closely with me. Noticing some unease on the faces of the ones who had mistreated me as I had sought consultancy work from the ministry, I assured the gathering that I had not gone there to dismiss any one of them.

I explained to the officers that I was familiar with the operations of the Ministry of Finance and National Planning from my previous work experience in the early eighties. In 1986, I was the Permanent Secretary for the National Commission for Development Planning. As national planner at NCDP, I superintended over the production and coordination of the national development programmes of all the ministries and in all sectors of the Zambian economy.

I stated further that, I supervised the Government's budget and coordinated bilateral relations with all foreign governments and multilateral donor organizations. I also had the rare opportunity of interacting with representatives from all governments and international organizations that had offices in Zambia. I therefore planned to utilise my vast experience in bilateral and multilateral diplomacy when dealing with the country's cooperating partners.

However, I boasted of my thirty years of service in public institutions and informed the officers that I had exhibited a very high level of personal integrity and did not condone corruption and abuse of public resources or office. I publicly declared that I will be a model supervisor in public service and that, "I personally will be clean in my delivery of national duties and will not take for personal use even one ngwee of public money".

By 1230 hours, I was at the Pamodzi Hotel chairing a ministerial workshop on the World Bank's Country Assessment Strategy (CAS) for Zambia, co-chaired by the World Bank Director for Zambia, whom I met in Washington DC earlier in June. The World Bank officials revealed that most projects supported by their institution had stalled leaving large sums unutilized in the banks. They stated that the relations between Zambia and the World Bank had not been properly handled, with lapses on loan repayments even when money was available in the government account at the Bank of Zambia.

With so much data provided in the workshop papers, it was easy for me to appreciate the economic problems of the country. Soon I was sharing strategies and plans with Ohene Nyanin, the Ghanaian World Bank Country Representative, whom I'd met earlier when both of us were in the Diaspora in America and Europe.

In the evening, I played host to the CAS workshop participants at a reception, which was oversubscribed by curious attendants who were eager to see and talk to me. I met a lot of people who sympathized with me in view of the enormity of the task at hand. I was warned to be careful with my social life as some citizens, who would be hurt by the measures to correct the economic situation, could take desperate retaliatory actions against me.

As I picked a glass of fruit juice from a tray held by a young lady, a concerned citizen, Bwalya Ng'andu, who was aware of the dire economic situation, suggested that I consider engaging a food taster for my personal security. I then recalled the advice given to me by a leader of Fiji Island in the Pacific Ocean, who warned me to be extra careful in my eating habits, as I bade farewell to him in 2000.

One of my fellow ministers in a foreign country had their relative kidnapped by those who felt that the anti-corruption crusade was closing on them. I take this opportunity to apologize to all those I offended by not accepting their friendly offers of food or drinks. They should know that my impropriety was for a good national cause and for personal preservation.

My first day as minister was a busy but fruitful one as I met many officials from both the Zambian Government and the donor community, who mattered most in my new assignment.

CHAPTER 25

Reactions To My Appointment As Minister Of Finance

The Zambia Congress of Trade Unions (ZCTU), through its Secretary General Sylvester Tembo in welcoming me, advised that I should use my immense experience as a public servant at both the local and international levels to improve the operations of the Ministry of Finance.

H.E. Ambassador Martin Brennan of the USA commended President Mwanawasa for my appointment and hoped that I would quickly resolve the problem of the budget overrun.

On Saturday, 5 July 2003, which was my 56 birthday, I gave an extensive interview to journalists from the Times of Zambia in which I unfolded my vision for the economy. Through the president's appointment letter, the CAS meetings and the comments by various notable public figures, I was made aware of the various issues I had to deal with. The Times of Zambia wrote extensively on my interview and gave some background of my past work experience.

The trip to Washington DC and my meetings there gave me a direct line of communication to the relevant officers of the IMF and World Bank, the most influential and important financial institutions in the world. Much of Zambia's foreign debt of US $7.2 billion was owed to the IMF, World Bank, and the AfDB.

The Daily Mail of 8 July 2003 stated that;

"It had to take Mr Mwanawasa more than a month to appoint Mr Magande whose CV is quite impressive and one just hopes he is the man we have been waiting for to inspire the team at the Ministry of Finance for the country to pull through economically. He has a good CV and he needs to be given chance to prove his worth".

The Times of Zambia edition of 10 July 2003 reported that;

"The USA Ambassador Martin Brennan said the appointment of Mr Magande had been welcomed by many stakeholders and this indicated that he was the right person for the job and hoped that he would improve the economy. The budget overrun has to be tackled immediately as this is a crisis that will affect the nation and the international donors have to be involved if the country has to solve this problem".

While most media houses gave me and my team a chance, in contrast, the Post newspaper took an antagonistic approach. Apart from the newspaper's witheringly and scornful editorials, they encouraged readers' letters that bordered on personal slander, even questioning my citizenship, professional qualifications and work experience.

In a two-column article entitled, "Magande's appointment" of Friday, 4 July 2003, the Post stated that,

"The announcement of the appointment of Peter Magande as the new Minister of Finance is not shocking because the rumour has been doing rounds for too long. But it is sad because we have tried to understand and answer the questions: Why Magande? What success stories does he carry with him that make him fit for the job he has been given? Who is he to be able to provide leadership on the economic front at such a troubled time? We have no answers to these questions, but one thing we know is that he is opposition UPND President Anderson Mazoka's very close associate. This is probably what explains his appointment. Can things surely be reduced to this level – a competition for weak souls?"

In reply to the Post's negative messages, I sent a messenger to deliver my curriculum vitae (CV) to the newspaper's offices, but this was not even acknowledged. I also contacted two shareholders of the Post, who were my friends seeking their intervention on my behalf. But they informed me that they could not intervene in the matter. I was greatly consoled when Mazoka reminded me that the people, who were writing the adverse articles at the Post, were much younger than me and were still in school when I was already in responsible public positions and they did not know me.

I could not prove the claims made that the Post's harsh editorials were actually written by a cabinet minister who felt snubbed by the president who did not appoint him to the position I was given. Other speculations were that the editorials were the work of UPND officials who were opposed to my decision to "save the crumbling Mwanawasa administration, which was at the brink of collapse". With my record as advisor to the UPND president, many UPND members knew that I would deliver in my new position.

It was becoming evident that I had opponents within the MMD and also in the opposition parties. Since part of my assignment was to eliminate the budget deficit by prudent financial management, many civil servants also saw me as an obstacle towards achieving their personal expenditure plans.

Having concluded that some of the critics were uninformed young people and others were envious of my appointment, I decided to focus my energies on fulfilling the mandate given to me by the Appointing Authority. This required me to show some tact, firmness, consistency, and creativity, and at times some aggressiveness.

As I searched for where to find support, I strategized that dialogue with all stakeholders would be the most effective tool in getting these various constituencies to understand my mission and vision. The goal was to enhance transparency, accountability, and ownership of the planning, implementation, and monitoring of the development effort.

In between the large number of meetings with selected officers within the Government, I accommodated the private sector. Within a short period of time, I met so many representatives of private sector institutions, many of whom I had met during my previous thirty-two years of public service.

The most vocal opposition to my appointment in the Mwanawasa MMD Administration came from my Tonga tribesmen. They alleged that I had betrayed my brother Andy for 'thirty pieces of silver'. They did not know that Andy had approved and blessed my move to save our mother Zambia. I did not need the pieces of silver since as a private consultant, I was already earning not less than US $ 500 per day on my contracts, my family lived in our own house on Independence Avenue and we owned a thriving farm in Choma.

I did not even discuss my salary and other conditions of service of my new job with my Appointing Authority before reporting for work. I only knew the minister's monthly salary and allowances in September 2003, after I received my first pay slip for working for three months. My spouse even asked me if what I received was an allowance for some impending tour. My motivating factor when accepting the request by President Mwanawasa to serve in his administration, was to apply the vast experience I had accumulated and defeat the daunting economic problems of Zambia at the time.

During the Heroes and Unity Holidays of July 2003, I attended the Lwiindi Ceremony of the Tonga-speaking people in Monze and took the opportunity to speak to some provincial officials of the UPND. Some of my tribesmen went as far as labeling me a traitor for accepting to work in President Mwanawasa's administration. I decided to ignore the Tonga new definition of a traitor.

I was aware that Mainza Chona and Harry Mwaanga Nkumbula, two of Zambia's great nationalists, had also earned this derogatory title for furthering nationalistic visions by working together with President Kaunda before and after Zambia's independence. Without Nkumbula's capitulation and willingness to form a coalition government of his ANC and Kaunda's UNIP in 1962, Zambia's self-rule would have been delayed. Without Nkumbula signing the Choma Declaration, which ushered in the One-Party State, many innocent Zambians would have died in unnecessary inter-party violence.

In Parliament, I received mixed reactions and I was cautious not to offend anyone in my contributions. As the Government side started praising me for my technical explanations and answers to numerous questions, the UPND boasted of having loaned me to the incapable MMD. I was carving out a group of dedicated followers from both sides of the House.

CHAPTER 26

The Challenge Of Change At The Ministry Of Finance

Z ambia's major problem at the time was a lack of balance between revenues and expenditures, leading to a huge budget deficit. Poor financial management resulted in the Government spending money, which it did not have. Such action increased the domestic and foreign debts, which were already very large. Lack of adherence to agreed budget execution benchmarks eroded the confidence of cooperating partners, who were reluctant to provide additional development assistance. Much of the expenditure was on non-capital items with personnel emoluments for public workers claiming about forty per cent of the government discretionary budget.

Contriving a Winning Strategy
As I settled down at the Ministry of Finance and National Planning, I realized that there was little consultation and coordination amongst the officers within the Ministry and with those in the vital related institutions. What was required was for me to mould a team of committed Zambian technocrats within the departments of the Ministry, who were to assist me in getting to the Zambian stakeholders to make them understand the country's woes, our plans, my mission, and the national vision.

I needed the inputs of the Bank of Zambia (BoZ), Zambia Revenue Authority (ZRA), Zambia National Tender Board and the Central Statistical Office (CSO). With my distinctive experience at the seventy-one member ACP Group, this was one job I took on with a personal conviction that I was capable of contributing significantly to solving Zambia's economic problems.

The following constituted the executive team at the Ministry and in the related departments:-
- Hon. Felix Mutati, MP, Deputy Minister (DM)
- Hon. Mbita Chitala, MP, Deputy Minister (DM)
- Dr Situmbeko Musokotwane, Acting Secretary to the Treasury (A/ST)
- Mr Leonard Nkata, Permanent Secretary, Financial Management & Administration (FMA)
- Mr Richard Chizyuka, Permanent Secretary, Budget & Economic Affairs (BEA)

- Mr Chitundu N. Mwango, Accountant General (AG)
- Dr Caleb Fundanga, Governor, Bank of Zambia (BoZ)
- Mr Berlin Msiska, Commissioner General, Zambia Revenue Authority (ZRA)
- Mr David Diangamo, Director, Central Statistical Office (CSO).
- Dr Kabeta B. Muleya, Director, Zambia National Tender Board (ZNTB).

During my five-and-a-half-years stay at the Ministry, there were a number of transfers out of the Ministry and departments of some of my juniors. Amongst those transferred were Mutati, Chitala, Musokotwane, Nkhata, Chizyuka, Diangamo, Mwango, Msiska, and Muleya. Those who came into the Ministry included Kapambwe Simbao (DM), Jonas Syakafuswa (DM), Evans Chibiliti (ST), Wamundila Lewanika (PS), Chriticles Mwansa (ZRA), Kapitolo (ZNTB), and Buleti Nsemukila (CSO). The position of Accountant General was occupied by Mike Goma in 2004.

The vital position of Secretary to the Treasury was vacant. Situmbeko Musokotwane was under an EU–funded contract as advisor to the Ministry of Finance in Zambia on the preparations of the Poverty Reduction Strategy Paper (PRSP). A request by President Mwanawasa to the EU, before I joined the Ministry, to have Situ appointed into a line management civil service position was not approved. Not even my intervention with the friendly EU Delegate changed the EU's decision. Situ did not accept being appointed on much inferior civil service conditions and we were about to lose him.

My request to Governor Fundanga to appoint and fund Situ under any advisory position in the Bank was accommodated by the Bank. Situ was then seconded to the civil service and appointed as Secretary to the Treasury in August 2003.

During my earlier work as director of budget in 1981, I realized that it was important for the senior officials of the Ministry of Finance to keep warm relations with the Special Advisor (Economics) at State House. In 1981, while at the Budget office, I enjoyed cordial relations with the advisor Dominic Mulaisho. This time, I was fortunate that Moses Banda, the Special Advisor (Economics) was the one who head-hunted me and we started working closely together even before I was appointed.

The Special Advisor (Economics) was a vital link for me to the president. Whenever I had a strong view, which I wanted to be adopted by the president on any vital issue, I made a draft reply to myself. And then negotiated with the economic advisor to finalize the letter and put it on the President's desk for his consideration and signature. By the time I received the president's answer, I would already have worked out an implementation process. Fortunately for me, the many issues that went through this subtle fast track did succeed.

I made it clear during my first meeting with the senior officers in July 2003 that I will introduce some changes in the operations of the ministry and I expected maximum cooperation from all the officers.

I demanded the highest levels of professionalism and active participation. All officers were to make inputs in all documents emanating from their departments ending up on my desk. I provided written feedback on most of the proposals. Junior officers were given the opportunity to originate proposals on technical issues handled in their departments. They were also given the opportunities to attend internal, local, and foreign meetings as part of their apprenticeships.

My meetings with visitors were attended by desk officers or subject officers and by my Deputy Ministers if they so wished. To facilitate such an arrangement, my appointments in my diary were notified to the secretaries of my DMs, the day before the meetings. Such advance notice included the subject for discussion with the visitor. The DMs then gave notice as to whether or not they were attending the meeting. The DMs and officers who attended were encouraged to actively participate by giving their opinions during the meetings.

I applied my experience as a seasoned long-serving civil servant to delegate and share work with the two DMs. The two were fully engaged in the operations of the Ministry. Subjects were apportioned to them and they were fully accountable to me for the execution of their portfolios. They were responsible for the day-to-day supervision of the heads of the departments handling the subjects under them.

My two deputies attended both local and foreign meetings on the allocated subjects and submitted reports and briefs to me, which we discussed. One of the DMs took full advantage of my open door system and soon he learnt a lot about public service procedures and various technical subjects, which he coordinated, such as regional integration and trade.

My management style raised the morale, professionalism, proficiency, and efficiency of the majority of the officers. For most young professionals, they saw me as an ally in bringing out innovations in the processes and systems in the operations of the Ministry. I restrained myself from recommending the removal or transfer of officers from the Ministry even those with allegations against them. This was with my strong belief that my integrity and leadership style would attract some to change their past bad habits and many did change.

I was alerted of an officer who was known to leak information on IMF issues to a leader of an opposition party and I was advised to have the officer transferred. I resisted the advice, as I knew that my style of management, which included frequent briefings to the public on operations of the Ministry, will soon make her side job irrelevant. Much of the information became readily available through press briefs or on the IMF website. In frustration, the officer, who had no secrets to leak, opted to leave the Ministry and she was granted her wishes.

Of course, on some serious issues, I did take drastic action. For example, I recommended the transfer of an officer who'd kept a letter of an offer of a grant of twenty million pounds by a donor for over two months in her drawer. In another instance, I recommended the dismissal of an officer who had withdrawn a large amount of dollars from a project account for personal use. The stern action against these officers gave early notice that I would not retain or entertain corrupt or ineffective officers in the Ministry.

In May 2004, President Mwanawasa sent me a copy of a letter written to him by one of my junior officers. In the letter, the officer alleged that there was lopsided development in the country due to tribalism in the sharing of the top key positions in the Ministry of Finance and National Planning. The officer singled out the Southern Province as having been given a higher allocation in the 2004 budget due to my personal influence.

Members of Parliament from the northern region of Zambia embraced the tribal allegation during their budget debates in Parliament, even when they could not prove their assertions from the official reports presented to Parliament. I felt hurt with these insinuations just like when the Director General of ZIMCO accused me of tribalism in 1993. Luckily, my blood pressure was under control at the time.

At Uncle Webbs, a social joint, a group of Bembas took pleasure in taunting Tongas. Someone, I had regarded as a friend, stirred commotion when he publicly declared that Mwanawasa must be removed from office because he is now promoting even Tongas to run the Ministry of Finance. He continued to say, "This ci-Magande has no brains to run the Ministry of Finance". I wondered why throughout my public service, the people who accused me of being tribal and incapable were from the Northern Province.

At the time of the allegation on unbalanced development, I had been in the Ministry for only ten months and the 2004 budget had been approved some 40 days earlier. No funds for capital projects from the 2004 budget had been disbursed to any province.

In my reply to the allegations, I gave the president details of the budgeting process and the role of ministers in the exercise. I informed him that before my appointment, there had been four successive Ministers of Finance from the northern region and my two deputy ministers were from the same region. I concluded that if ministers have powers of influencing the allocation of public funds, then the northern region, which had enjoyed the benefits of a succession of ministers must be very developed.

The President accepted my recommendation to immediately remove the officer as the allegations were false, divisive and malicious and the officer's language was toxic.

The office of the Minister of Finance and National Planning was serviced by the following officers:-

Mr. Chileshe Kandeta	-	Public Relations Officer
Mr. Musiwa Muyatwa	-	Protocol Officer
Mr. Kaputo Mayani	-	Driver

Mr. Conrad Haabukali	-	Driver
Mr. Bryson Phiri	-	Driver
Ms. Josephine Nsama	-	Office Assistant
Ms. Christine Mulando	-	Office Assistant
Ms. Hilda Mwandawande	-	Secretary
Mrs. Gertrude Mubanga	-	Secretary
Ms. Mary Grace Zulu	-	Secretary
Mrs. Brigid C. Siakalenge	-	Personal Secretary

As has been my principle during my public service, I retained all the officers I found in the minister's office, with a conviction of converting them to my work beliefs, ethics and system. Under the coordination of Brigid, the team provided diligent service to my office both locally and when on foreign tours. Due to the effective preparations, I was always on time for my numerous appointments, flights and travel plans, many of which were through some of the busiest airports in the world. At all times, the team executed their job with maximum conscientiousness and according to our agreed procedures and programs.

Brigid did a splendid job while working with me, even when confronted with risky situations such as when she opened a letter addressed to me, which was laced with a white powder suspected to be ricin poison. On a trip from St Kitts and Nevis to Washington DC, she was subjected to an intense interrogation at Miami Airport for carrying the delegation's imprest. Even when there were many visitors wishing to see me, Brigid meticulous screened and booked them as nobody was to be refused an audience with me. However, anyone late by more than ten minutes forfeited their opportunity to see me and had their appointment rescheduled.

I was delighted when many of my former junior officers were retained and promoted by successive administrations. These included Musokotwane who was promoted to Cabinet Minister and Ministers Mutati and Simbao who were retained by President Banda in his new Cabinet in 2008.

The Patriotic Front Government of President Sata, which came to power in 2011, promoted Felix Nkulukusa, James Mulungushi, Pamela Chibonga and Agnes Musunga to the position of Permanent Secretary. Dennis Chisenda was appointed Director General of the Zambia Procurement Authority (ZPA).

Successive Ministers at the Ministry of Finance retained my former Personal Secretary, Brigid Siakalenge, who continued to provide effective and proper management of the office of the Minister of Finance and National Planning.

Apart from dealing with fiscal policy and human resources issues, at times I dealt with mundane administrative issues such as the cleanliness of the offices. I proposed that the Ministry outsources the work of cleaning the offices instead of relying on our officers. Within a short period, the old maroon carpets on the two executive floors looked bright and sparkling clean. This attracted the attention of a visiting fellow Cabinet Minister, who accused me in his Parliamentary debate on the 2004 budget of squandering public resources on new furniture for my offices!

I set high standards in personal hygiene, honesty, morality, and integrity and luckily, I was emulated by most of the officers. In fact, not one of my immediate subordinates in all the departments of the Ministry was arrested for impropriety such as theft of public property or abuse of public office during and after my five-and-a-half years at the Ministry of Finance and National Planning.

Coordination of Fiscal and Monetary Policies
The Bank of Zambia has an important role in the management of money supply in the economy. On 25 July 2003, Governor Caleb Fundanga arranged an introductory meeting at the Bank of Zambia with the Chief Executive Officers and the chairmen of all financial institutions operating in Zambia. I informed them that having been a banker, I was aware of the developmental role of banks and other financial institutions. I informed them that I expected maximum support in evolving appropriate fiscal and monetary policies and bank customer products.

I signaled my love for innovations and boasted of the ZANACO management under my supervision in the early nineties having introduced the first Automated Teller Machine (ATM) in Zambia's banking industry. I urged the banks to quickly develop an integrated ATM system so that customers could draw money from any ATM regardless of their bank in order to reduce the cost of doing business. I had experienced and benefitted from such a system in Europe during my three-year stay.

The financial institutions reacted positively and came up with new products and spread their operations by opening new offices. I felt honoured to participate in the ceremonies to open new offices at Arcades shopping mall, Matero, Kalingalinga and Kamwala townships in an effort to get the banking services closer to the people.

In a meeting with the governor of the Bank of Zambia, we discussed a number of issues concerning the appropriate fiscal and monetary policies and how we would relate to each other. At that time, there was active international debate on the need for the autonomy of the central banks.

I felt uncomfortable to allow independent operations of the central bank as the fiscal and monetary activities were still closely interrelated but inadequately coordinated. Zambia was still grappling with a hurriedly announced market economy after so many years of a centrally planned socialist command economy. Government operations were inclined towards sector policy instruments with no integrated long-term planning.

I was also aware that there were not enough regulations for an independent monetary authority to be effective. The huge national debt and large budget deficit would not allow the monetary authority enough space to determine aggregate output of the economy through increased expenditure.

I was able to hold onto my views even when I was visited and lobbied on the matter by Tito Mboweni, the governor of the Reserve Bank of South Africa, who was the Chairman of the SADC Committee of Governors of the Central Banks. However, I fully agreed on implementing measures towards the targets of the SADC Macroeconomic Convergence, which included a single digit inflation rate and five per cent budget deficit by 2008.

I discussed with Governor Fundanga the benchmarks on which to judge the success of the Bank of Zambia's team among which was the inflation rate and general monetary stability. Lower inflation would facilitate cheaper financing for industry. I proposed that we could, therefore, adopt the principle of inflation rate targeting as one of the criteria when appointing or reviewing the contract of service of the governor of the central bank.

After discussing the merits and demerits of such a measure, we agreed that for the time being, we should work to bringing the rate of inflation to a single digit after which, we could review the situation. I promised not to interfere with the operations of the Bank of Zambia, but that I would seek explanations on monetary issues should they inhibit macroeconomic activities.

I was fortunate that Fundanga had also worked in the Zambian Government and the international financial environment. He understood fully the complementary roles of his office and mine and that of the fiscal and monetary policies in national development. The Bank Governor was an expert on economic theories having been a lecturer at the University of Zambia. He put the theories into practice when he worked at the AfDB, Ministry of Finance, National Commission for Development Planning, and Cabinet Office. By coincidence, Situ and Caleb both attended university in Germany.

Using the Monetary Policy Advisory Committee, the Bank of Zambia tamed the inflation to a single digit rate of 8.2 per cent by 2006, just two years after my discussions with Governor Fundanga. This was the lowest inflation rate in thirty years. In the same year, the Government achieved a budget deficit of 1.5 per cent of Gross Domestic Product (GDP), the lowest in a decade.

The two low macroeconomic parameters led to an annual GDP growth rate of 5.8 per cent. On both inflation rate and budget deficit, Zambia was ahead of the target date of 2008 set by SADC. Fiscal and monetary policies and capital market instruments were on target to achieving macroeconomic stability.

Apart from taking measures to tame the rampaging inflation, the Bank of Zambia was active in the foreign exchange market. While allowing the market the freedom to operate, the Bank started building up the country's reserves for a 'rainy day' in view of the volatility of the commodity market in which Zambia sold its mineral resources.

The major disruption did not come from the known macroeconomic parameters, but from a governance issue. In June 2008, President Mwanawasa suffered a stroke and was hospitalized in France. This caused a lot of uncertainty in the market as to the ability of the financial system to manage the economic parameters and the ensuing reactions.

On Friday, 4 July 2008, a false story circulated in the media emanating from South Africa that President Mwanawasa had passed away in France. I contacted the Bank of Zambia and requested that an officer should monitor the exchange rate from morning to late afternoon.

By 1730 hours when I checked with the Deputy Governor, as the Governor was out of the country, the sad news had registered a huge negative impact on the Kwacha. The local currency had lost thirteen per cent of its parity with the US dollar within hours. The anxiety on the health of President Mwanawasa was beginning to undo our hard-earned macroeconomic stability achievements and I could not allow this.

The actors in the monetary sector met with the Central Bank. Governor Fundanga and I discussed and agreed that we come out and calm the capital markets. We both gave interviews to the reputable global news media Reuters. We stated that President Mwanawasa had established systems and procedures that would not break easily because of his ill health. We told the whole world that President Mwanawasa gave space to his juniors to implement government policies and these juniors were available to continue the good work in his absence.

Governor Fundanga announced that Zambia had foreign reserves of five months import cover. We vowed to continue with prudent fiscal and monetary management. It also transpired that the death story was not true, although the President was still in a coma. Our efforts paid dividends as the Kwacha stabilized around K3.20 per US dollar.

Economic macroeconomic parameters do not always react to numbers such as the amount of revenues or foreign currency. They sometimes are influenced by the trustworthiness of the financial managers and the leaders of the nations. "When Alan Greenspan (of the USA Federal Reserve Board) cleared his throat, the world economy trembled," according to Raymond Seitz of the Sunday Telegraph. Although, Fundanga and I, had not reached the reverence level of Greenspan, who stayed in his position for nineteen years, our collective management of the fiscal and monetary policies, and the corrective actions taken, had a stabilizing effect on the Zambian economy.

Revamping public revenue collection systems
The Zambia Revenue Authority (ZRA) is the major tool for collecting revenue for the Zambian Government. In the late 1990s, revenue collected was only thirteen per cent of the GDP, a very low figure by any standard. The 2003 budget deficit was partly caused by the inability of the ZRA to collect adequate revenues for use by the government.

By the time of my second arrival at the Ministry of Finance in 2003, President Mwanawasa had already started some re-organization of the authority by appointing Berlin Msiska as the first Zambian Commissioner General. In 2007, Berlin was replaced by Chriticles Mwansa, who was recalled from the World Customs Organization (WCO) in Brussels.

I became acquainted with modern equipment for customs border operations during my work at the ACP Secretariat. In my introductory address to the ZRA management in August 2003, I promised to facilitate any modernization they planned. I prodded them to acquire new technology and institute new systems in order to improve revenue collections from taxable economic operators. The new equipment for border clearance was to reduce false declarations by cross-border traders. Luckily, modernization and simplification of customs and border procedures was part of the global ASYCUDA program under the Kyoto Convention of the World Trade Organization (WTO) to which Zambia was an active member.

To actualize my dream, a team of officers from ZRA and the Ministry undertook a tour of some countries in the region to observe the use of scanners at borders. The scanners, with the capability of detecting types of goods in a container, were one of the latest technologies in traffic inspection at country borders.

On the team's recommendation, tender procedures were put in place to acquire two scanners as an initial program.

While efforts were being made to acquire the equipment, we realized the need for improvements in the administration of the authority. In 2006, we requested assistance from the IMF in conducting a diagnostic study of the organization. The study led to the institution of modernization reforms that included re-organization of departments and computerization.

Funding from the USA Millennium Challenge Account through the Threshold project was used to implement these reforms as ZRA was one of the target institutions. The objective of the anti-corruption programme was aimed at preventing corruption in targeted government institutions, improving public service delivery to the private sector, and improving border management of trade.

In order to improve service delivery to customers, the ZRA refurbished the Client Service Centre, a one-stop shop for all dealings with ZRA. The centre was opened by President Levy Mwanawasa joined by U.S. Ambassador to Zambia Carmen M. Martinez and visiting Deputy Chief Executive Officer of the Millennium Challenge Corporation Rodney Bent on 27 March 2007. The ZRA was the first public institution to establish an integrity committee.

On Friday, 6 June 2008, I commissioned the Non-Intrusive Mobile equipment for the Zambia Revenue Authority at the Chirundu Border Post. The equipment was the first of its kind in Zambia and propelled the country into the modern customs world. The technology greatly improved revenue collection as it reduced smuggling and false declarations of goods at the border.

The Zambian tax authorities had for a long time been struggling on the best way to handle the informal sector. In 1982, when I was director of budget, we introduced a tax clearance certificate for any operating business that required a renewal of a business licence from a government institution. This improved compliance by many taxpayers. However, the law was repealed in the 2001 budget without a replacement law. With the encouragement of the Vendors' Desk at State House under the Chiluba Administration, economic activities shifted from established and licensed premises onto the streets.

Large sums of money circulated in the hands of businesses that did not contribute to the revenues of the government. While the GDP was increasing, government revenues and its ability to provide public goods and services, such as roads and medicines, were declining.

Because most small businesses gave the excuse of not being able to maintain proper books of accounts for tax purposes, we decided in 2004 to remove this requirement. I was fortunate that the proposal to introduce a three per cent presumptive tax for small businesses with an income threshold was overwhelmingly accepted. This new tax raised substantial revenues from those patriotic citizens who volunteer to register as taxpayers.

Zambia is the only country I know of in the world where to pay tax to the government is voluntary and yet since time immemorial, "a tax is a contribution to state revenue compulsorily levied on individuals, property or businesses".

The street vendors have no documents to show their status in commerce to any agent of the government. The vegetable street vendors squatting on the pavement of other traders make more income than the owners of the pavement who sell vegetables inside the shop. The anomaly is that the taxmen and licensing officers wiggle through these business people on the pavement in order to get into the shop to demand tax or a licence from the shopkeeper whose customers have been hijacked at the entrance of the shop.

Travel Expenditure Control

At the press conference held on 15 June 2004, President Mwanawasa made some reshuffles. The major one was the replacement of Leslie Mbula as Secretary to the Cabinet with Joshua Kanganja, a lawyer. I visited the new SC to convey my congratulations and to brief him on my expectations for full cooperation from him as a former classmate at UNZA. We had taken some law courses together during our undergraduate studies at UNZA in the sixties. Following a full brief on the HIPC Initiative, I requested the Secretary to the Cabinet to impose strict discipline on all civil servants in budget execution and financial management.

President Mwanawasa gave the new Secretary to the Cabinet and me the responsibility of vetting the lists of delegates for all foreign travel by all public workers as a cost-saving measure. Appendix A of Form 48 (1996) had to be filled in by both ministers and civil servants. The form required data on the budget allocation, amount spent and the balance, the cost of the trip, the purpose and reason for not being represented by the staff of the resident or nearest Zambian Mission.

If the travel budget was exhausted, the concerned ministry requested for a variation within their ministry. Approval for such variation requests were not often made as the budget was an activity-based one and no item approved by parliament was allowed to lose money to travel.

The desk officers in the Ministry of Finance responsible for the ministries prepared reports on the outcomes of any meeting held outside Zambia for my information. I then prepared a brief to the president for his information. At times, President Mwanawasa asked me for clarification when my report was at variance with that of the portfolio minister.

The new foreign travel procedures also applied to those accompanying the President on state visits and to various summits. Often times, President Mwanawasa used his red pen to reduce what the two of us considered to be a reasonable list to less than half. When that happened, we sat with the Secretary to the Cabinet to reassign the duties of those to travel.

No civil servant knew as to who, amongst the three of us had removed their name from the travelling party. The President also directed that all officers travelling with him must attend the pre-departure briefing meetings at State House. This was to enable everyone on the trip to be acquainted with the Zambian position on all the subjects for discussion at the summits.

I recall an incident on a foreign trip, when President Mwanawasa directed that an officer already in a foreign country should return home even before the opening of the Summit, as he had not seen him at the briefing meeting at State House in Lusaka. On another trip, President Mwanawasa felt that there was no need for three economists in the delegation stating that, "after all, Minister, you know the summit subjects very well and you can adequately brief me".

Once, I was tongue-tied when, during a briefing meeting just before the start of a summit, President Mwanawasa asked me why there were so many security officers to a summit dealing with economic matters. For every presidential foreign trip, we compared the costs of using the presidential plane against taking a commercial flight. Luckily, President Mwanawasa undertook a limited number of foreign trips each year and these were known and budgeted for in advance.

We institutionalized the reporting of each presidential foreign visit to Parliament with details of issues discussed, outcomes and the cost. Ministers were instructed to present written reports on return from their trips to the president and the Cabinet. By this time, I would have already submitted a brief prepared by our ministry.

Reforming the Public Finance Act

By July 2004, the Ministry of Finance and National Planning had put in place all possible and appropriate instruments for the efficient and prudent management of the public finances. While studying the various pieces of legislation on public financial management, I was not happy that the Public Finance Act delegated the responsibility of appointing controlling officers to the Minister of Finance, who is a politician.

The controlling officers were civil servants under the disciplinary control of the Secretary to the Cabinet. The Minister of Finance, as a politician, has no disciplinary control on the civil servants. Controlling officers are in charge of public funds and the ministers have a limited role in controlling the application of these funds. In fact, the Auditor General audits the work of civil servants and not the ministers. As a minister could not discipline a civil servant, the whole arrangement weakened financial control and accountability.

In my consultation with the Minister of Legal Affairs, I urged him that we make amendments to the law by removing the responsibility of appointing the controlling officers from the Minister of Finance. I proposed that instead, the Secretary to the Treasury, the most senior civil servant in the Ministry of Finance, be the chief controlling officer, with the responsibility of appointing and controlling the controlling officers in the various ministries and grant-aided institutions.

A new Public Finance Act was passed by Parliament in July 2004 reposing the powers of appointing controlling officers in the Secretary to the Treasury. The chief controlling officer and his appointees, the controlling officers, are jointly accountable to the Public Accounts Committee (PAC) of Parliament. I followed this new arrangement by removing the Minister of Finance from the membership of the PAC.

The new Finance Act provided for stronger sanctions and penalties, enforced existing regulations and withholding of cash releases to non-complying ministries and the publication on a quarterly basis of the projected and actual cash allocations to line ministries.

Many Members of Parliament were surprised that I'd proposed the removal of legislation that gave me powers to appoint the officers who handle public funds. For me, I was more concerned with accountability and financial discipline with clear lines of command and authority amongst public workers dealing with public funds.

I became preoccupied with a lot of meetings discussing various reforms in the management of government resources. As a way of opening up government planning to the public and formalizing their participation, we established Sector Advisory Groups (SAGs) for each Ministry. We held a conference for all members of the SAGs and donors at the Pamodzi Hotel on 29th October 2004, to explain the purpose of the Groups.

With a new Public Finance Act, I was certain that the work of the

Accountant General and the internal auditors in the ministries would be made easier. The next stage was to strengthen the Office of the Auditor General to be able to carry out forensic audits for value for money. On 9 November 2004, we held discussions with the visiting Auditors General from the Netherlands, Norway, and the United Kingdom, who had agreed to assist in the strengthening of the Office of the Auditor General of Zambia. Apart from funding from the donors, my ministry honoured its budget allocation for counterpart funding. The Auditor General's office expanded in both personnel numbers and office decentralization into the provinces.

Consolidating Public Procurement and Supply Systems
On the assumption of the office of Minister at the Ministry of Finance in 2003, I was urged to process the enactment of legislation that would apply to the profession of procurement and supplies. Earlier in the eighties, I had been involved in legislation that rationalized the accountancy profession in Zambia. This time, I worked closely with Mwape A. Mutakila and Misheck N. Kaoma, both who were fellows of the chartered institute of purchasing and supply (CIPS, UK) with the later being the president of the Zambia chapter. Under the leadership of the two fellows, the Zambian members of the institute advocated for the establishment of an indigenous local institute.

It was my great feeling to see the happy faces of the procurement professionals on the day of the launch of the Zambia Institute of Purchasing and Supply (ZIPS). The legal recognition of the local institute by the government under Act No. 15 changed the behaviour of the procurement professionals. The ZIPS law was later followed by a new procurement law that created the Zambia Procurement and Purchasing Authority (ZPPA).

The ZIPS law reinforced the processes in the supply chain for goods and services. There was a provision for mandatory recruitment and placement in the procurement and supply functions of officers with practicing licences issued by the ZIPS. The law regulated the operations of procurement professionals and consolidated sanctions and penalties for erring members and employers. The new law contributed greatly to improving accountability and transparency in procurement, as membership of all procurement committees in both public and private institutions included officers, who gave quality advice when considering tenders for procurement and supply of goods and services.

First Generation Financial Management Reforms
As a condition for accessing the Heavily Indebted Poor Countries (HIPC) Initiative, Zambia prepared a Poverty Reduction Strategy Paper (PRSP) in 2000 in which the country's intentions on reviving the ailing economy were spelt out. I was well-versed with the PRS approach, which had been introduced in 1999 by the International Monetary Fund and the World Bank when dealing

with low-income countries.

I had attended the 1999 annual meetings of the IMF and World Bank at which the initiative was extensively discussed. Most major aid donors and lenders also adopted the approach. The PRSP process had five core principles, which included result and partnership orientation, long-term perspective, and comprehensiveness.

During the implementation of the PRSP, a number of economic management tools were introduced to aid the achievement of the intended objectives. Many of the economic management tools introduced were in the area of economic governance. The tools were to assist in combating corrupt practices, which were rampant at the time in many public institutions.

Many donors, amongst them the DFID, EU, IMF, Ireland, NORAD, and the World Bank were supporting various initiatives by the Zambian Government. A decision had also been made to create a Planning and Economic Management Department (PEMD) at the Ministry of Finance.

In 2002, I was engaged as the coordinating consultant of the four teams of thematic consulting specialists who identified and prepared projects to operationalize the 2nd Country Cooperation Framework (CCF) 2002-2006 for the Ministry of Finance and National Planning and the United Nations Development Programme (UNDP).

Part of my terms of reference read,

"To lead the process of project development and ensure that the established benchmarks for each stage of the process including the expected stakeholder consultation process are achieved. Serve as the main liaison official with the Ministry of Finance and National Planning, all government and national institutions serving as implementing and coordinating agencies, concerned government departments, UNDP, bilateral and multilateral organizations, NGOs and CBO and all other stakeholders ensuring that all are aware of the status of implementation".

By the conclusion of our consultancy work, I was very knowledgeable of the main actors in Zambia's development efforts. In 2003, the Zambian Government initiated 'first generation' budget reforms when formulating the 2004 Budget. This entailed moving to Activity Based Budgeting (ABB), where funding was to specific programmes and activities of Ministries, Provinces, and Spending Agencies (MPSAs). Further, the annual budget formulation process began to be undertaken in a more strategic and medium-term context by producing a Green Paper containing a rolling three-year Medium-Term Expenditure Framework (MTEF).

Amongst the other tools were the Public Expenditure Management and Financial Accountability (PEMFA) Reforms and the Integrated Financial Management Information System (IFMIS). These tools of economic planning and financial management had the objective of developing clear linkages amongst resource mobilization and allocation, disbursement, utilization, and outcomes. They assisted in the fight against corruption and wastage of public resources by internalizing the ownership of development through transparency and accountability of the public finance managers.

Many of the tools were popularized by the IMF and adopted by many donors to assist in their support programmes to the developing countries. In Zambia, lack of astute implementation of these tools led to poor national budgeting and a mismatch between revenue and expenditure, which led to the famous overrun or budget deficit of 2003.

Being desirous of eliminating the budget overrun incurred in early 2003, I was, therefore, determined to put the various tools in operation to aid the efforts in prudent financial management. The MTEF and ABB were operationalized and used when preparing the 2004 and 2005 budgets, while the PEMFA was adopted in January 2005 and IFMIS was introduced in 2006.

Zambia's huge foreign debt had to be serviced and this meant diverting the country's revenues from development programs. This, in turn, resulted in a lack of funds for spending on local programs in social services such as medicines and capital infrastructure. The additional expenditures on the new allowances for civil servants were to be met from additional borrowing, thereby ballooning the budget deficit. Getting debt forgiveness was a priority as it would release substantial amounts of resources for local programs.

One of the principles of the PRSP was the involvement of all stakeholders including trade unions and other nongovernmental organizations (NGOs) in its preparation and implementation. During the deliberations on various budget issues, we held meetings with the Trade Unions under the chairmanship of Cabinet Office. We brought to their attention the difficulties of continuing to increase salaries for civil servants in the face of a serious shortfall in revenues.

On Friday, 15 August 2003, the Ministry presented to the Cabinet the first draft MTEF for the 2004 to 2006 period. This was a detailed proposal on revenue sources and expenditures over a three-year period, which was open for public discussion. As part of the reforms of the budgeting process, spending agencies used the ABB to link budget allocations to service delivery and outputs. This reform made the budgeting process more transparent.

In view of the novelty of the budgeting process, Cabinet took some time to discuss the MTEF and the proposed Letter of Intent (LoI) to the IMF. The LoI describes the policies that any Government intends to implement in the context of its request for financial support from the IMF.

In September 2003, the Ministry of Finance and National Planning issued a seminal document on budget preparation. A brief version of the document is reproduced here:-

A process of budgeting called the Medium-Term Expenditure Framework (MTEF) has been agreed upon by the Cabinet.

This new process helps to improve the allocation of the estimated revenue on various expenditure categories over a three-year period.

The process evolves out of making projections on revenues from various sources and allocating these resources according to agreed priorities.

Before allocating the revenues through the budgeting process, there is need to provide a general macroeconomic framework in which macroeconomic parameters are projected or estimated.

These parameters which need to be projected or estimated include:

- Government policy objectives as provided in the Poverty Reduction Strategy Paper (PRSP) and the Transitional National Development Plan (TNDP).

Macroeconomic targets or broad goals on:
- gross domestic product growth rate
- inflation rate
- fiscal deficit
- foreign reserves quantity
- current account deficit
- domestic and foreign debt amounts
- strategies for developing the various sectors of the economy.

The core business of any government is to provide services and infrastructure and not to produce goods.

In the framework paper are indicated the policies of Government, targets of revenue, strategies and global allocations to the various expenditure categories.

Ministry officials have been trained on the MTEF and Activity Based Budgeting (ABB). It is therefore hoped that next year's budget and future ones will be more focused by indicating the activities to be undertaken in order to attain clearly identified outcomes and outputs.

Under the approved budgeting process, we intend to hold meetings with the stakeholders so that they make an input into the programs and projects which they will own and help in implementing.

The proposed budgets will be extensively discussed and the final draft presented to Cabinet for consideration before presentation to Parliament".

In October 2003, the first Green Paper outlining the macroeconomic framework for the budget was produced. In it were presented projections of various economic parameters including economic growth, inflation rate, exchange rate, balance-of-payments, domestic, and foreign debt service payments.

During the same month, I was a participant at the 6th National Convention (National Indaba) convened by President Mwanawasa at the Mulungushi Conference Centre in Lusaka. The main purpose of this national event was to collectively consider the economic problems the country was facing and come up with shared solutions.

In spite of the presidential call to national duty to all citizens and a lot of persuasion, the major political opposition parties, namely the PF and UPND did not attend the National Convention. They did not want to share their ideas or to hear the ideas of other citizens. However, this did not reduce the enthusiasm of those who attended especially from the private sector. After all, this was the first time that such an opportunity had been provided for collective reflection on the Nation's problems since the First Republic. I recall that former President Kaunda used to convene such national fora during his reign.

Most valuable conclusions were arrived at by the various sector groups and these were compiled into a booklet. President Mwanawasa gave instructions in writing to each minister to implement sector-specific recommendations pertaining to their portfolio by incorporating them in the 2004 budget.

The country's development process was formalized with a clear roadmap to include a Green Paper, Annual Budget, MTEF, National Plan, and a Vision. The Ministry with the assistance of UNDP had started an exercise of producing a Vision 2025, which we changed to Vision 2030. Templates on the various documents were produced for easy follow-ups by the citizens. All officials in the Ministry of Finance and National Planning had to make efforts to understand the various parameters in the documents for them to be able to explain to the stakeholders.

The period between July and December 2003 gave me a rare opportunity to comprehend Zambia's economic and social status and its challenges. I was privileged and became aware of some of the reasons that led to:-

- The MMD Zambian government borrowing a huge amount of US $650 million in 1995;
- The Zambian Government and the mining investors signing the Development Agreements in the 1990s, with extremely liberal concessions;
- The Zambian Government undertaking privatization at giveaway prices;
- Zambia being admitted to membership of the club of poor countries under the IMF/World Bank's Heavily Indebted Poor Countries' (HIPC) Initiative in December 2000;
- The increasing poverty among Zambians between 1992 and 1998 under the new government of the MMD Party;
- Zambia's national budget being supported by donors up to forty-two per cent.

Privatization of the Zambia National Commercial Bank
In 1993, while I was managing the Zambia National Commercial Bank, I received information from one of the minority shareholders of the bank that some ministers in the MMD Administration were conniving to buy ZANACO Bank under the pretext that it was loss-making. I confronted the Minister of Finance, Ronald Penza and asked him if there was any truth to the rumour. He

answered by asking me why I should be concerned if that were to happen. I explained that I did not want to get a bad name that I'd failed to manage the bank.

I immediately connected this scheme to the problems my management had with the chairman of the board on the 1992 accounts. It seemed that I had been expected to participate in running down the highly profitable bank so that it would fetch a low price.

As I became convinced that there was a manoeuvre to sell ZANACO shares, I proposed to my management that we create a fund in which all the employees were to contribute some money on a monthly basis. The fund was to be used to buy shares when the Bank's shares were put on sale. Information came my way that the Minister of Finance, Penza was not happy when he heard of my plans of establishing a fund for the staff.

The Zambia National Commercial Bank was finally tranched for privatization in 1998 by the Chiluba Administration during my absence. This was some five years after I was removed from the bank. The main reason given for privatizing the bank was that the bank's balance sheet was very poor due to bad debts.

The negotiations on the privatization of ZANACO were protracted due to changing circumstances. At one point, the exercise was connected to a deal on a bungled fuel procurement deal by the Zambian Government. At some other time, the privatization was connected to one of the foreign commercial banks operating in Zambia, which was alleged to be using an outside bank as a front. Then, the issue of the valuation of the bank arose and took time to be resolved by the Zambia Privatization Agency.

At the time I was appointed minister in July 2003, the privatization of ZANACO was one of the conditions for the foreign debt write-off under the Heavily Indebted Poor Countries (HIPC) Initiative agreed to by the Chiluba Administration in December 2000.

Recalling the manoeuvre of 1993 when a few Government officials wanted to buy the bank, I insisted that only 49 per cent of the bank's shares should be sold to the strategic partner. I suggested that out of the remaining shares, the Government will retain twenty-five per cent while some of the shares could be offered to the staff and to the local private investors.

When I insisted on concluding the sale as it was a condition of the HIPC Initiative, there were strong objections from the Patriotic Front. Michael Sata, president of the PF, who was a member of the Chiluba Administration, now turned around and vehemently opposed the privatization. At the same time, the PF leader was openly advocating for the sale of shares of parastatals to the workers.

When I heard that the PF planned a demonstration to march to my office, I welcomed the move as this was going to be an opportunity for me to address the PF cadres. However, the Minister of Home Affairs advised the president not to approve the demonstration for fear of violence. After my pleas, the president allowed the demonstration to go ahead, with a warning that I would be personally held responsible for any security lapses.

The demonstrators led by Sata marched from the Kabwe roundabout of the Cairo Road to the ZANACO Head Office in the south near the Kafue roundabout. From there, the PF cadres and street kids, led by Guy Scott the vice president of the PF, marched through Independence Avenue to our ministry on Chimanga Road and presented a petition to me.

I enthusiastically explained the Mwanawasa Administration's development programmes and how the privatization of ZANACO was related to the HIPC Initiative to the demonstrators. I explained that should the Patriotic Front win elections even in the distant future, they will find a healthy national balance sheet with little debt. This would mean more Government revenues and a favourable environment to borrow funds for spending on projects. The demonstrators who were peaceful throughout dispersed with a clear understanding of the government's intentions and the future national benefits.

The part-privatization of ZANACO was one of the most successful as it increased the number of Zambians with shares in the bank, from twenty-nine to 3,361 out of which 707 were bank employees. The Rabo Bank of the Netherlands, which bought forty-nine per cent of the shares, was a renowned international bank, especially for financing agriculture. No branch of the ZANACO Bank was closed as earlier feared.

As per my prediction, due to the success of the HIPC Initiative programme, the PF Government, which was formed in 2011, inherited a country with little debt. This facilitated the use of domestic Government revenues and borrowed money for development of physical infrastructures such as roads and school buildings.

Paradoxically, the PF administration established a Commission of Enquiry chaired by lawyer Sebastian Zulu in 2012 to investigate "the fraudulent privatization of the Bank". Although I spent over two hours with the Commission as a witness, their report has never been made public. I still do not know how the bank was fraudulently privatized and by whom as the ZPA negotiating team was led by Dominic Mulaisho, one of Zambia's most upright citizens.

CHAPTER 27

Initiating Economic Austerity, 2004 National Budget

In my appointment letter, President Mwanawasa stated that;

"It will not be an excuse to say that your officials misled this Government when you could have been in the position to correct them and to provide leadership."

I, therefore, took personal charge and led the preparations of the 2004 budget and attended as many consultation meetings as I could. I had become aware of the difficulties my predecessor Emanuel G. Kasonde had in explaining the 2003 budget to Parliament once it had been presented. When the numbers could not add-up, the budget was thrown out by Parliament and all the blame was placed on the minister.

The escalating budget deficit in the first quarter of 2003 was also blamed on the Minister, although much of it was due to the flawed negotiations by some civil servants with the public service unions. I was therefore on maximum alert, especially since my ambiguous party allegiance made me vulnerable to criticism from so many quarters. I was not a passive listener but was an active participant guiding the budget discussions.

At some stage, the officers submitted a draft Yellow Book of hundreds of pages of numbers for the 2004 budget. They proposed that we meet after two days to give me ample time to go through the voluminous document. I counter proposed that we meet the following day. I went through the whole draft and retired to bed at 0200 hours. At 0600 hours, I took my morning tonic swim in the family pool and I was as fresh as a daisy.

To the surprise of the officers, who attended the afternoon meeting, I presented a list of errors up to the last page. The errors included spelling mistakes and wrong additions and subtractions. This single incident was an indicator to my officers of my capacity to read every word and figure in any document they submitted to me regardless of its bulkiness. It was from this belief in my capacity that the officers raised their level of alertness and contributions and together we created a winning team.

With the vast amount of knowledge accumulated, I participated in drafting the Presidential Speech delivered on Friday, 16 January 2004, at the official opening of the Third Session of the Ninth National Assembly. In his speech,

President Mwanawasa covered a number of important developments and institutions in state governance. Amongst these was the appointment of the first female clerk of the National Assembly, Mrs Doris Katai Mwiinga who supervised radical parliamentary reforms that included the participation of the stakeholders and the establishment of Parliament Radio and constituency offices.

The President emphasized the importance of decentralization and hence the establishment of a Decentralization Secretariat, repositioning of the post of District Commissioner, recreation of the House of Chiefs, establishment of the Police Public Complaints Authority, restructuring and decentralization of the Office of the Auditor General, enhancement of the Drug Enforcement Commission and the Human Rights Commission, the pursuit of the policy of zero tolerance to corruption, progress on the work of the Task Force on Corruption, and the decentralization of the Anti-Corruption Commission.

In the area of the economy, the President reported the positive and negative results of 2003, which included the implementation of sound fiscal and monetary policies, key structural reforms such as the Debt Policy and Strategy, and economic diversification program. The President explained the harmful effects of fiscal deficits, which had been caused by poor budget execution. He pointed out that the mismatch between revenue and unplanned expenditure led to suppression of priority programs such as those in the education and health sectors. He reported that failure to observe financial prudence had resulted in the cancellation of the PRGF, non-attainment of the HIPC Completion Point, and the withholding of donor support.

The 2004 National Budget was prepared under extensive consultations at pre-budget fora with various stakeholders, both from within the Government and nongovernmental organizations. Having worked in the Ministry of Defence, I was trusted by the security wings, who also agreed to extensively discuss their budgets with me. Submissions from ministries had to accommodate the recommendations of the October 6th National Convention. The budget proposals had to conform to the new ABB format. In meetings with the public service unions, the problems of the ghost workers and the negative impact on the budget resource sharing between consumption and capital expenditures were highlighted.

Having received the presidential instructions through his parliamentary speech, we completed the drafting of the 2004 Budget proposals, which we presented to the Cabinet on 19 January 2004. We also started discussing and developing various systems and programs to improve financial management.

While the budget is framed by the budget officers and Ministries, the Introduction and Conclusion parts of any budget speech are a personal responsibility of the Minister of Finance and should reflect the vision of the Minister. The theme of the budget gives a general direction as to the purpose of the various policies, programs, and projects in the Yellow Book as agreed between the Ministry of Finance and the implementing ministries and agencies.

I delivered the 2004 Budget speech with verve on the afternoon of Friday, 6 February 2004, to an anxious Parliament presided over by the Honourable Mr Speaker Amusaa Mwanamwambwa.

I followed the rules as advised, except that I frequently sipped some water to soften my voice and keep it clear during the over–two-hours' speech. I had learnt this much earlier during one of my sessions on image building and public speaking. Luckily, the mannerism drew the attention of some Members of Parliament, who kept making running commentaries every time I took a sip, thereby helping in keeping everyone in the House fully attentive.

The 'Strangers' Gallery' was packed with visitors, many of whom had participated in the consultations on the country's economic and social future. They were eager to know if their needs and aspirations had been taken into account in the final budget speech. The following were the 'Introduction' and 'Conclusions' parts of the Budget Speech, whose theme was, 'Austerity for Posterity'.

INTRODUCTION

Mr Speaker, the Budget for 2004 is anchored on the premise that the empowerment of the Zambian people must be the only reason for all our development endeavours. This will secure sustained and broad-based development, which will create wealth, reduce poverty and raise living standards of all the citizens. Government, therefore, recognizes that it must constantly evaluate its performance, identify the shortcomings, and re-dedicate itself to ensuring the realization of the full potential of the Nation's greatest asset: the Zambian people.

With this premise in mind, in the 2004 Budget, the Government has focused expenditures on areas that will directly involve and benefit the people and curb waste within the public sector. Only by observing prudence in expenditure can the limited resources be directed at priority investments, which will reduce poverty and create wealth. Thus, the theme of the 2004 Budget is "Austerity for Posterity" by which, I mean, the observance of fiscal prudence and postponement of needless present consumption in order to secure our future sustained prosperity.

CONCLUSION

Mr Speaker, I have not increased the Value Added Tax (VAT) above the current rate of 17.5 per cent, but have instead increased the Pay As You Earn tax threshold. This is to allow the few working citizens some more take-home pay. But for how long shall the development of our country depend upon fewer than 500,000 citizens in formal employment? Each one of us must make a contribution to the well-being of our country. The harmonization of much of the tax regime during this year is, therefore, to make it fair and equitable.

Mr Speaker, the 2004 Budget will require thirty-six per cent financing by our cooperating partners in a year when Zambia shall be celebrating forty years of her independence. We are all aware of the famous tribe that wandered in the wilderness for forty years looking only to God for manna from heaven. In Zambia, all too often, we have collected 'masuku' and mushrooms without regard to how they came to be.

Mr Speaker, I call upon each one of the Honourable Members and every Zambian citizen to declare that we have had enough share of wandering in the wilderness. Now is the time to break with the past. Now is the time to act to redeem Mother Zambia from the shame of being one of the poorest countries but immensely endowed with natural resources and beauty. Zambia, our motherland, must not continue to bleed and weep from loss of her daughters and sons, due to diseases, ignorance, hunger, and migration.

Mr Speaker, how many of us do visualize forty years from now, proclaiming that, "Yes, I was there in the year of our Lord 2004, and am proud to have been part of the winning team"? Such foresight is a tribute of men and women of vision, willing to challenge the unknown future, with courage and determination. As I look around this august House and beyond, I see many patriotic Zambians with these valiant qualities, willing and ready to make history by sacrificing present illusory comforts for posterity.

Mr Speaker, the Government's first act of austerity is my Ministry's inability to finance the usual cocktail party at the end of my budget address this afternoon. This is a clear indication that from now onwards, it will not be business as usual".

As I concluded my address, there was an instantaneous and rapturous applause by Members of Parliament on both sides of the Chamber. They were joined by the visitors in the 'Strangers' Gallery, who gave me a standing ovation. Mr Speaker, a strict disciplinarian seemed to ignore the break of the Parliamentary rule that does not allow the visitors to participate in the proceedings of the House.

The clerk later confided in me that the Speaker restrained himself from admonishing the cheering visitors because the behaviour was historic in the life of the Zambian Parliament, as no Minister of Finance had ever received such a supportive public response.

The opposition UPND wanted to steal the limelight from me by preparing what they called 'an alternative budget' in the absence of the Party's President. When Mazoka returned from his hospitalization in South Africa, he was made to go straight from the airport to the Freedom Statue to address a huge mass rally. In his comments, he stated that the 2004 Budget was so bad as if it had been prepared by an eight-year-old child. However, the idea of having an opposition's alternative budget quickly fizzled away and everyone's attention focused on the government's 2004 austerity budget.

Interaction with stakeholders through professional bodies
After the presentation of the budget address on a Friday afternoon, professional organizations arranged functions at which the budget details were discussed with the professional fraternities in a more open environment. In the evening of Friday, 6 February 2004, I attended a budget dinner organized by the Zambia Institute of Chartered Accountants (ZICA), at which there was a lively exchange of views on the various budget measures.

The following morning, I was at a budget breakfast by 0700 hours organized by the Economics Association of Zambia (EAZ). Perhaps my having been Chairman of the Association in the sixties intimidated those who might have wanted to ask difficult questions. Otherwise, the discussion was friendly and many supported the measures, such as the wage freeze, that were in the 2004 Budget.

On Sunday morning, I was on Television Zambia in an interview with Frank Mutubila and Dennis Wood, two renowned budget analysts. At 1430 hours I was a participant at a meeting at State House between President Mwanawasa and the trade unions.

On 27 February 2004, I was a guest of honour at the annual ball of the Zambia Financial and Banking Services Association (ZFBSA).

In 2004, the Government's focus was on fiscal prudence and austerity by avoiding wastage and directing resources to priority areas as a prerequisite for securing the new PRGF and reaching the 'completion point' of the HIPC Initiative. The focus had to be accompanied by not-so-popular actions to be taken during the year, which included a freeze on salaries of civil servants. The salaries for the ministers were instead reduced by thirty per cent by presidential decree. Due to the hostility to President Mwanawasa at the time, even these plausible efforts in financial expenditure control were not applauded nor acknowledged.

I received many letters congratulating me for a well-prepared and well-presented budget. Unfortunately, the opposition Members of Parliament were strategizing to use the same tactic that had derailed my predecessor. The trade unions were also getting ready for a showdown on the wage issue even after getting a personal explanation of the difficult financial situation from the president.

Winning the trust of the opposition parties in Parliament
On Saturday, 14 February 2004, the President invited a few cabinet ministers at the State Lodge to discuss how to handle the opposition to the budget arising from both the opposition parties and the trade unions. My proposal to engage the opposition was supported and I was given the mandate to meet anyone for face-to-face discussions.

When I sought the advice of the parliamentary staff, I was informed that it was up to the executive to decide how to discuss any contentious issues with the opposition within parliamentary rules. However, they advised that it would be preferable to establish a committee that would officially report the conclusions of such discussions to the Committee on Estimates.

I, therefore, accepted to meet a select group of opposition members to thoroughly scrutinize the whole budget and agree on amendments should the need arise. The general view from my cabinet colleagues was that such an approach would fail and the Government would once again be embarrassed by having to adjust the budget. I assured them that being a former director of budget, I knew which issues were emotive and how to handle them and that the debacle of 2003 would not be repeated.

At our first meeting, the opposition parties submitted forty-two proposed amendments with a proposed large additional expenditure budget. The opposition then got better organized and appointed Ms Edith Nawakwi, FDD Member of Parliament for Munali Constituency and former Minister of Finance as the group leader to coordinate their input. I met President Mwanawasa with my proposed replies on the long list. He gave me the go-ahead to discuss with the opposition team. At the end of the second consultative meeting, the list of amendments had been reduced to fifteen items.

With further negotiations and consultations, the list came down to twelve amendments. The ad-hoc committee mandated me with the responsibility of introducing all the amendments as we discussed each Ministry's estimates in the House. The opposition team agreed that those who were involved in the negotiations would debate first after I had presented the proposed amendments. This agreement surprised many of my opponents including some of my cabinet colleagues and the UPND members who were spoiling for a showdown with their 'rebel member'.

Due to the exhaustive consultations with the stakeholders, the 2004 Budget was approved in record time by Parliament. To buttress and facilitate the new consultative process between the Ministry of Finance and the Parliamentary Estimates Committee, a team of private budget experts was appointed by the National Assembly. With the advice of the team, which was headed by Lloyd Sichilongo, a former school mate and director of budget, the Parliamentary Estimates Committee was focused during our consultations. The subsequent national budgets I presented were discussed in a professional manner under a friendly atmosphere by the House and approved in record time.

Trade unions boycott interaction with my ministry

Having won the support of my fellow Parliamentarians on many budget provisions in the 2004 budget, I was ready and well-armed to meet the trade unions to polish out employment issues such as the wage freeze and conditions of service. I was banking on the warm and encouraging welcome remarks by the Secretary General of ZCTU as a basis for our future cooperation.

I arranged a meeting with the trade unions for Saturday, 3 April 2004. My team arrived at 0900 hours and waited until 1200 hours without the union side forming a quorum. The unions had agreed to boycott meeting the Government team over the budget. The following week, I informed the unions that I was still prepared to attend a meeting as long as they called me after they'd organized themselves and had formed a quorum at a venue of their choice.

Unfortunately, some leaders of the Zambia Union of Financial and Allied Workers (ZUFIAW) did not forgive me for the dismissal of their striking members when I was Chairman of the Zambia Bankers Employers' Association in 1993. They were aware of my strong negotiating skills. Now they had an opportunity to snub me by advising the leaders of the Civil Servants Workers Union (CSWU) not to cooperate with me. One of the ZUFIAW senior officials even boycotted all functions organized and hosted by my Ministry, in spite of the union being in the financial sector that fell under my Ministry's portfolio.

In July 2013, I attended a church service for a departed friend at Saint Ignatius Roman Catholic church in Lusaka. The ushers directed me to a bench where other former government officials were seated. Right in front of me on the next bench was the ZUFIAW official who had vowed never to meet me. As the presiding priest pronounced the 'Rite of Peace', during which the congregants shake hands, the ZUFIAW official turned round and behold, my hand was extended waiting for a handshake. Witnessed by so many people in the house of God, the ZUFIAW official shook my hand and we exchanged messages wishing each other peace. I thanked my departed friend for his death, which led to the reconciliation between me and the ZUFIAW official.

As the expenditures on wages had led to the 2003 budget deficit, I took a hard stance and decided not to compromise on the wage freeze issue. I and the unions never met for all the period of my service at the Ministry of Finance.

Another group of stakeholders, who were difficult to work with, were the non-governmental organisations (NGO's), most of which had been formed after the new political dispensation in 1991. My interest in my ministry working together with the NGO's dealing with poverty met with some resistance. My particular concern was the duplication of programmes. I wanted us to define poverty and identify the affected individuals, so that we have focussed intervention measures.

While the workshops were well-attended, the discussion results were disappointing as much time was spent on blaming the government for the high poverty levels. Leaders of some NGO's arrived at conferences held at five-star hotels in the latest four-wheel drive motor vehicles. The participants whose attendance perks included a breakfast, lunch of sirloin steak, and a five-figure attendance allowance, refused to be coordinated or regulated by the government.

We could not agree on the designation of poor people as this included retired workers with blocks of rented out rooms in Kanyama and Chawama

Townships, and earning substantial incomes. These were regarded as poor because of the location of their properties in Kanyama and Chawama Townships, which were started as unplanned settlements in the sixties. Most of the population of Lusaka City was regarded as poor since much of the city constitutes of such townships.

The definition of poverty was blurred by the greedy, who wanted to get more and more. Some leaders of well-known NGO's turned down invitations to workshops and instead, sent junior officials on account of the per diem to be paid being too low. I got the impression that some conference resolutions on poor people included the participants, who came to the meetings in luxury vehicles defined as grants by foreign donors.

The attitude of the trade unions deprived the workers of an opportunity of getting their ideas being incorporated in innovative public finance management systems conceived by the Mwanawasa administration. The unions never contributed meaningfully to any of the plans and programs that got Zambia out of its economic problems onto an impressive growth trajectory. However, because of the mode of open dialogue espoused by President Mwanawasa, my Ministry received maximum cooperation and valuable contributions from the business, donor, and some cooperating NGO's.

In spite of the hostile behaviour of the trade unions and some NGO's, the year 2004 ended on a positive note with cooperating partners committing to give financial support to the Public Expenditure Management and Financial Accountability Reforms (PEMFAR). The reforms had the main objective of improving transparency, accountability, ownership, and the tracking of financial resources in all ministries.

The financing agreement between the Zambian Government and eleven cooperating partners was signed on 8 December 2004. The extensive reforms covering all ministries and the other new systems developed during the year helped in improving financial management and curbing the rampant wastage of public resources.

CHAPTER 28

Dismantling The Government's Domestic Debt

A part from the well-known external debt of US $7.2 billion owed to non-residents, the Zambian Government had accumulated a huge domestic debt to suppliers of various goods and services. A good number of suppliers were victims of corruption as there was no laid down system on who got paid and when. Many waited for long periods before being paid. We decided to introduce a new system for procurement of government goods and services. For the new system to work, we had to clear the huge payments arrears owed before introducing the new system.

We established a Local Debt Dismantling Committee, with instructions that the Committee should strictly follow the well-known principle of First-In-First-Out (FIFO) and that monthly payments must be made in all categories of suppliers and creditors. I instructed the officers to negotiate with all the contractors for special debt repayment conditions. Any contractor who agreed to write-off the huge accumulated interest amounts was paid the total outstanding principal immediately.

I emphasized that I would not tolerate any corrupt practices or political victimization of any genuine supplier who was owed some money. During my stay at the Ministry of Finance, no supplier was identified by nor discriminated on the basis of their political affiliation. On the day-to-day operations and supervision, the portfolio was under one of my DMs, with instructions to report any problems to me.

At some point, the MMD Secretariat tried to influence us to discriminate the suppliers in favour of MMD members. I reported my resistance to these approaches to President Mwanawasa, who intervened with a stern warning to the MMD Secretariat not to interfere in my work. The new procedure introduced some transparency and brought some relief to many suppliers who had been waiting for years to be paid.

Those who were used to corruptly collecting cheques every Friday afternoon for nothing were disappointed and they publicly voiced their dislike of me in minibuses as they passed by our ministry on Chimanga Road. Those who could not continue to enjoy the results of corrupt practices claimed that I was a foreigner who did not deserve the appointment. A niece of mine who was in a minibus as a conversation raged about my nationality came to my rescue and shamed those who claimed to know me by explaining who I was.

The issue of my nationality having been settled, the corrupt accused me of being a branch of President Mwanawasa's family tree and that I only got the job by favour on a family basis. I was neither related to the President nor a foreigner. President Mwanawasa removed the jinx that prevented the Tongas from being appointed Ministers of Finance since 1969 when Elijah Kaiba Mudenda was removed from the Ministry.

As dealings with the Zambian Government had been personalized, many suppliers felt that they had to see me in person to explain their problems as they had waited for a long time. A young man from Mansa arranged for a meeting with me. In the presence of the subject officer, he narrated his story concerning a debt for supplying vegetables to the Prisons' Department, which invoked sympathy from me. However, when I asked for details of his farm and residence so that our officers would visit him, he became jittery as he had no farm that had produced any vegetables.

My threat of an immediate arrest was met by pleas for forgiveness. This was clear proof that claims were made by and payments made to dubious suppliers who had not supplied any goods or services. In Uganda, they termed such transactions as 'paying for air', even when everyone knows that air is a precious free gift from God.

One case that drew my immediate attention was that of Ruth Chabala and 29 Others vs The Attorney General. This was the case of compensation to the surviving relatives of the victims of the 1993 Gabon air crash. Various individuals, including the relatives and lawyers of the litigators, visited my office to complain about the delayed payments after the court judgment in their favour. The tragic event was still fresh in my memory because I had approved the travel imprest for the football team as an advance when I was Managing Director of ZANACO in 1993.

The Attorney General informed me that funds released for compensation were not enough to pay all the claimants at once. Perhaps due to the careless application of laws, the claims for compensation were rising at a fast rate. I issued instructions that payment on the ten-year-old case must be included in the 2004 budget and be on the priority list. Consequently, the payment was made to the lawyers through the Ministry of Legal Affairs just before the 40th Independence Anniversary celebrations.

Out of the action to pay the relatives of the late footballers, my enemies found a case against me. They reported to President Mwanawasa that I had approved an unexplained huge payment to a UPND lawyer. I explained to the President that the payment was for the Gabon air crash case that had dragged on for a long time. We, therefore, decided to make a substantial provision in the 2004 budget in order to close the sad chapter involving our national football team.

I further produced evidence showing that the lawyer was selected by the claimants and dealt with the Ministry long before I had arrived on the scene. It was a coincidence that he belonged to my former party. The payment had nothing to do with the political affiliation of the lawyer. President Mwanawasa was surprised with my explanation, which proved the malice of the allegation. He even thanked me for having paid the compensation to put to rest the case. He intimated that he would inquire on why the report on the plane accident had not been released.

Sometime in May 2004, James Banda, a former schoolmate at Munali Secondary School mentioned that the old man Rupiah Bwezani Banda, a.k.a. RB wished to see me. After explaining the reason for the visit, I gladly obliged. On the afternoon of Wednesday, 16 June 2004, I received RB, whom I had not met for over twenty years. I knew the old man as a UNIP politician and we had both worked in the Ministry of Rural Development in the seventies. In spite of a presidential press conference the previous day, during which some major reshuffles were made by President Mwanawasa, the two of us did not have much to discuss as we had lost touch with each other during the long lapse of time and we were not political activists.

This time around, RB was seeking assistance as a representative of a Dutch company that had problems with payments for supplying hospital equipment to the Zambian Government. The company had a long-standing contract but after fulfilling its obligation, payment had not been forthcoming. The desk officer in attendance recalled some earlier discussions of the matter. She explained that the equipment was part of the ambitious programme by the Zambian government to equip all hospitals with modern theatre equipment. The debt had increased to a substantial amount and some of the medical equipment was beginning to break down for lack of spare parts.

RB narrated the origins of the relationship between the foreign company and the Zambian Government. He explained that his representation fees were the only current sure source of income for his family's livelihood. I promised to look into the matter and advised RB to check with me in a month's time. Because of RB's political membership in the opposition UNIP, his visit to my office and my warm welcome to him became a subject of great interest and discussion in the Ministry.

By the time RB made his second visit, some payment had been made by the debt committee. The old man was most appreciative of the action taken by the Ministry. He advised the young officer, who was in attendance, to learn from my work ethics of keeping promises and of not to discriminate one Zambian from another on any basis. He hinted that he was being side-lined because of being a staunch UNIP member. He stated that my behaviour was a sign of a great leader and he wished me success in my future endeavours.

After RB left, the young officer stated that I was extremely lucky to have a much older person speak so highly of me. I shared some history on RB and informed her that I was a junior officer when RB was in positions of influence. The officer said that RB would find a way to thank me for what I had done as he looked desperate during our first meeting.

I advised the officer that it is honourable to look after old people who had provided services to the nation in the past. I challenged her with an assurance that if she executed her work diligently, I would unreservedly speak favourably of her in spite of her tender age.

Many members and leaders of the opposition PF and UPND parties felt free to meet me at my office at the Ministry head office and at parliament buildings. The Minister of Finance is the only minister who has an office at Parliament buildings to facilitate his work schedules. The new procurement and billing system did achieve some measure of success and many creditors expressed their gratitude.

Many of my visitors at the ministry headquarters were attracted to a picture frame hanging on the wall with the inscription reading, "I shall pass through this world but once. Any good therefore that I can do or any kindness that I can show to any fellow creature, let me do it now. Let me not defer or neglect it, for I shall not pass this way again." I was highly inspired when, as part of their parting comments, many loudly read the saying attributed to quaker missionary Stephen Grellet (2 November 1773 – 16 November 1855), which had so much meaning in my life.

CHAPTER 29

The IMF Cheerleader's 2005 Budget

After returning from a foreign trip on 18 December 2004, I embarked on the finalization of the 2005 budget. On Tuesday, 21 December 2004, we held a joint meeting of cabinet ministers and officials at which we discussed the MTEF and the 2005 budget proposals. During the discussions, the President advised the cabinet ministers to fully involve their juniors as there were a lot of new policies, programmes, and procedures that were being introduced.

He warned that cabinet ministers will be held responsible if their deputies debated in Parliament like opposition members as all Government Ministers must be conversant with agreed Government reforms and policies. He encouraged the ministers to consult me on financial issues in the budgets of their ministries before making their parliamentary budget statements.

On 30 December 2004, I was a guest on the Government Forum radio program. I took the opportunity to discuss most of the budget policy proposals but without giving away specific numbers. With so many instruments at our disposal and many participating stakeholders, the preparation of the annual budget was much easier. The SAGs whose membership included civil society, the private sector, academics, and cooperating partners played a vital role in formulating sector budgets.

Between 10 and 13 January 2005, the Cabinet considered the detailed budget proposals and the President's speech to Parliament, which was officially opened on Friday 14 January 2005. On Saturday, 15 January 2005, the Cabinet convened to finalize the budget and synchronize it with the President's speech delivered the day before. At thirty minutes past midnight on Sunday morning, the Cabinet approved the 2005 budget.

I presented the 2005 Budget on Friday, 28 January 2005. The budget invited the Zambians to wait a little under the theme, 'Steadfastness for Accelerated and Broad-based Growth'. The goal of the Government was to continue with the viable economic policies that would provide a stable macroeconomic environment for private sector investment. This would, in turn, promote broad-based growth, national unity, economic and political stability.

The budget presentation was followed by a series of functions by professional organizations including the EAZ and ZICA. During the discussions with the professionals, there was appreciation on the fiscal prudence and accountability in the management of public resources. The total budget for poverty reduction programs had been released in 2004 compared to fifty per cent released in 2003.

Financial analysts were cheered that the country was back on track with the HIPC Initiative and on its way to the Completion Point that would see a huge reduction in Zambia's foreign debt. This had required me, and Ministry officials, to make endless trips to negotiate debt relief with the creditors even in some hostile weather conditions such as cold Moscow.

During the previous year, a number of programs and initiatives such as the Private Sector Development Initiative (PSDI), credit reference service, Financial Sector Development Plan (FSDP), and the Action Plan for the PEMFAR had been approved. Export earnings from metals reached the highest level since the mid-1970s. Non-traditional export earnings rose to 30.6 per cent of total exports as a result of efforts at diversification.

In the agricultural sector, production by small-scale farmers had risen due to the continuing Fertiliser Input Support Program (FISP), Food Security Pack, and the increase in the number of beneficiaries. In the manufacturing sector, import duties on many raw materials had been reduced. At the personal tax level, the top rate for income tax was reduced from 40 to 37.5 per cent and the threshold increased. For the first time in history, returning Zambians from working overseas were allowed a vehicle as personal effects. To encourage technology adoption, customs duty on mobile phone handsets was reduced.

While the budget speech covered all the above and many more programmes, projects, and policies in detail, it was strange to see the Post Newspaper devoting the whole of its Page 6 on Saturday 29 January 2005 to make a detailed commentary on the budget and calling it, "Magande's budget disaster – a sick joke".

Finance Minister Peter Magande's budget, heralds the biggest crisis for the MMD since coming to power in 1991. The disastrous budget pushes Mwanawasa's government to the brink of ruin with horrific blunders, appalling analysis and arrogant stupidity that can only be blamed on the Minister of Finance himself.

Amidst the pomp and ceremony that surrounds the occasion of the annual budget, Magande proudly unveiled plans that will bring suffering and poverty to all. Members of parliament, observers and analysts were left wondering whether the grinning Minister of Finance had any idea of the disgraceful mess he was happily announcing, or whether his self-satisfaction at his high-flying job had overtaken any technical, professional or moral capacity he might have previously possessed.

On the innovative successful negotiations and consultations with the opposition parties in Parliament on the 2004 budget, the Post wrote,

Last year, Magande was like a *salaula* trader, negotiating budget amendments with his former UPND colleagues – that is how the presidential travel budget was reduced – this year it might be worse – there may be chaos.

In spite of this criticism, the Post went on to state that,

This budget designed by your self-proclaimed International Monetary Fund (IMF) cheerleader gets us nowhere.

I was excited that the Post identified me with a leadership role in the revival of Zambia's economy as a cheerleader. I embraced the responsibility of encouraging other citizens to support President Mwanawasa's economic plan.

The author of the Post editorial was not aware of the role of President Mwanawasa and the new Minister of Finance and National Planning in the design and evolution of the various reforms on public finance management.

The 2005 budget was approved by the Cabinet before I left for Japan in mid-January and no officials were adjusting figures in my absence. The discussions and approval of the national budget were no more a midnight issue as happened during President Kaunda's reign when I was the Director of Budget.

The Medium-Term Expenditure Framework (MTEF) was a three-year rolling budget and the stakeholders had information on projected revenues and expenditures two years in advance.

The consultations between the Government and opposition parties on the budget outside the Chamber were to facilitate detailed discussions and to map out a common vision and goals out of the government expenditures. The Mwanawasa Administration had no hidden agenda in allocating public funds to various projects and wanted the opposition parties, the taxpayers, and ordinary Zambians to know all the details.

Under the agreed disclosure arrangement with the IMF, during the preparation of the PRSP, which was prepared with the involvement of stakeholders, member Governments approved the publication of all documents submitted to the IMF on its website. The transparency reforms were decided by the shareholders of the IMF, who included Zambia. Correspondence between Zambia and the IMF, including the conclusions of the Article IV Consultations and the LoIs were readily available on the website of the IMF for any stakeholder to read and comment upon.

The budget was one of the development instruments in which the stakeholders were involved through the SAGs. Regrettably, the Patriotic Front Party of Michael Sata refused to be involved in any Government programs and did not know much of what was going on in state governance.

In spite of the invitation by the Post to the civil society to attend meetings of the Parliamentary Committee to make submissions, very few observers turned up as many had already participated fully in the budget preparations. The 2005 budget was therefore approved by Parliament without much confrontation between the Government and the opposition parties.

The Patriotic Front Party, which refused to participate in planning meetings, paid dearly when they formed a government in 2011, leading to an admission by their Secretary General that they had not known the state of the country's social and economic condition when campaigning. Their many promises made during their campaigns were without background information.

New projects and programmes started under the personal instructions of President Sata were not in tandem with the medium and long-term national plans that evolved with stakeholders' participation under President Mwanawasa. After the demise of President Sata and without coherent written down plans, Zambia's economy went out of balance and soon started sliding down.

CHAPTER 30

Unshackling Zambia From Its Foreign Debt

My major immediate preoccupation in 2003 was to get a program with the International Monetary Fund (IMF), which would open the donors' doors for continued foreign financial assistance. A successful program with the IMF was also one of the conditions for qualifying to the Completion Point of the Heavily Indebted Poor Countries (HIPC) Initiative at which point Zambia would get massive debt write-off.

Fufilling the HIPC Initiative Conditionalities
Zambia reached the Decision Point of the enhanced HIPC Initiative in December 2000. This was after the Zambian Government convinced the AfDB, IMF, World Bank, and the international community that Zambia was so poor and indebted that it could never service its external debt obligations. The accumulated debt since 1964 had reached US $6.5 billion by 2000 and rose to US $7.2 billion by 2003.

The high external debt was unsustainable and could not be resolved by traditional Paris Club mechanisms such as debt rescheduling. In any case, the larger amount of Zambia's external debt was owed to multilateral creditors such as the IMF, who did not participate in debt relief under the Paris Club.

The Chiluba administration agreed to implement a set of measures over a three-year period in order to reach the floating HIPC Completion Point and receive full and irrevocable debt relief by December 2003. The Zambian Government willingly accepted the special conditions as outlined in the Decision Point Document for the Initiative, dated 20 November 2000. The fifteen key structural reforms/objectives termed 'HIPC triggers' were in the following areas:-

(a)   Poverty Reduction

Zambia must adopt a Poverty Reduction Strategy Paper (PRSP), prepared through a participatory process, and make satisfactory progress with implementing and monitoring the PRSP for at least one year based on an annual report.

(b)   Social Policy

Combating HIV/AIDS - Zambia must:

(i)   Fully staff the secretariat of the HIV/AIDS/STD/TB Council; and
(ii)   Integrate HIV/AIDS awareness and prevention programmes in the pre-service and in-service programmes of at least ten key ministries.

Education Sector Reform - Zambia must:

(i)   Increase the share of education in the discretionary budget from 18.5% in 1999 to at least 20.5%;
(ii)   Raise the starting compensation for teachers in rural areas above the poverty line for a household, as defined by Central Statistics Office (CSO); and
(iii)   Prepare an action plan for increasing student retention in Northern, Luapula, Eastern, North-Western, and Western Provinces.

Health Sector Reform - Zambia must:
(i)   Implement a scaled-up action plan for malaria;
(ii)   Re-organize to make fully transparent and efficient the procedures and mechanisms for the procurement of drugs;
(iii)   Ensure the timely release of complete, detailed, annual health expenditure data; and
(iv)   Ensure actual cash releases to District Health Management Boards are at least eighty per cent of the amount budgeted.

(c)   Macroeconomic and Structural Reform

(i)   Maintain a stable macroeconomic environment, evidenced by satisfactory performance under a programme supported by a PRGF arrangement;
(ii)   Implement an Integrated Financial Management Information System (IFMIS) on a pilot basis in at least three ministries and conduct a review of the pilot programme;
(iii)   Prepare and implement a Medium-Term Expenditure Framework (MTEF) that is approved by the Cabinet;
(iv)   Restructure and issue international bidding documents for the sale of the majority [controlling] interest in ZESCO; and
(v)   Issue international bidding documents for the sale of the majority [controlling] interest in ZANACO.

The Chiluba Administration, which committed to the conditions in

December 2000, had failed to fulfil many of the above fifteen benchmarks. Presumably, in 2001 the administration's attention was focused on preparations for the general elections due later in the year. After the resignation of most of the senior members of his administration, President Chiluba was preoccupied with political engineering for survival rather than fixing the broken-down Zambian economy.

The new Mwanawasa Administration that came into power in January 2002 after the general elections immediately embarked on renegotiating some of the conditions, while promising to adhere to the others. The condition of selling a controlling interest in ZESCO was altered in early 2003 at Zambia's request to requiring the commercialization of the company instead. The request to vary the condition on ZANACO was not agreed to by the IMF as it was directly connected to financial management, a matter that fell under the responsibilities of the organization. There was evidence of mismanagement of ZANACO due to interference by the Zambian Government.

The 2003 budget was presented by Kasonde under gloomy economic and political conditions caused by the drought and withdrawal of Anglo American Corporation (AAC) from Zambia's mining industry. The budget estimate was that the donors would provide 42.7 per cent of the required funds. In spite of the Minister's optimism, due to some slippages in the management of the macroeconomic area, the economic programme went off track in early 2003. This led to the cancellation of the Poverty Reduction and Growth Facility (PRGF), a financing support programme, by the IMF in March 2003.

As agreed during President Mwanawasa's visit to Washington DC in June 2003, an IMF mission arrived in Zambia in mid-July 2003 to assist in designing a new Staff Monitored Program (SMP). The SMP was a temporary measure before the country could again qualify for a PRGF and the HIPC Initiative.

Although I was a freshman, I led the Ministry's team into the negotiations with the IMF for the standby programme. The major aspect of the negotiations was to convince the IMF staff of the synergies of the proposed policies and expenditure programmes towards macroeconomic stability. By 27 July 2003, the IMF team was satisfied with our draft LoI, which came out of intense Cabinet discussions, as a number of Cabinet Ministers were clamouring for 'business as usual'. The LoI contained a number of policies and programmes to be followed by the Zambian Government during the period of the SMP.

During the SMP period, reviews on Government performance were conducted every three months. We waged a vigorous campaign for everyone to understand the implications of not adhering to the conditions and not getting debt relief. I dealt with pockets of resistance to the austerity measures by some Ministers and senior civil servants by discreetly seeking President Mwanawasa s intervention.

The measures for adhering to prudent fiscal management were spelt out in the 2004 national budget presented to Parliament on 6 February 2004 under the theme, 'Austerity for Posterity'. Among the unpopular belt-tightening measures was a six-month freeze of public employees' wages, which were pegged at 7.8 per cent of GDP. Additionally, about 495,000 workers were expected to shoulder the burden of an income tax hike of up to forty per cent.

Public workers staged a major strike against the high taxes and wage cap. The Zambia Congress of Trade Unions claimed at the time that ninety per cent of public sector workers heeded the strike call. I kept on wondering if the civil servants did not care about the sick who could not receive even the simplest treatment of the commonest medicines. Ministers were dispatched to the provinces to explain the dire economic situation and the tax rises.

In March 2004, President Mwanawasa stated that the government was determined to reach the HIPC completion point, noting that debt servicing was "crippling" the country. He said even the financial assistance that the country received from the donor community was immediately paid back to the creditors. In accounting terms, there was a negative flow of development assistance in favour of the donors.

President Mwanawasa gave full support to the measures that were being implemented as I presented frequent briefs on the various monetary and fiscal actions taken. By June 2004, after one year of quarterly reviews, we managed to adhere to all the benchmarks under the SMP and we then negotiated to get back on a new PRGF.

On 14 June 2004, the IMF approved a new PRGF with a one-year duration in which the country had to reach the floating Completion Point of the HIPC Initiative. We were not accorded the usual three-year period given to attain the floating Completion Point as Zambia had already failed since January 2001. The 2004 budget had already spelt out the austerity measures to be implemented during the year towards macroeconomic stability.

On the HIPC triggers, a lot of work was done concurrently with the SMP conditionalities as follows:

1.   The Poverty Reduction Strategy Paper (PRSP) that was prepared through a participatory process was being implemented in 2004 through the adequate release of funds for the Poverty Reduction Programmes. In the first quarter of 2004, K120 billion was released out of an annual budget of K521 billion;

2.   The HIV/AIDS/STD/TB Council was established and the professional posts outlined in the original structure for the council were filled. In addition, a strategic plan for the Council was prepared and this included the expanding of the scope of the council by taking its operations down to the district level;

3.   Integrated HIV/AIDS awareness and prevention programmes were

introduced in the pre-service and in-service programmes in the Ministries of Health; Education; Agriculture and Cooperatives; Tourism & Natural Resources; Science Technology & Vocational Training; Commerce Trade & Industry; Home Affairs; Youth, Sport & Child Development; Community Development of Social Services; and Finance & National Planning;

4.   The share of education in the discretionary budget was increased to 21.5% in the 2004 Budget, which was one percentage point above the HIPC Completion Point target;

5.   The starting compensation salaries for teachers in rural areas were increased to above the poverty line for a household, as defined by CSO;

6.   An action plan for increasing student retention in Northern, Luapula, Eastern, North-Western, and Western Provinces was prepared;

7.   A scaled-up action plan for malaria was implemented by increasing the accessibility of insecticide-treated nets through coupons to pregnant mothers and removal of taxes, testing household spraying control methods on the Copperbelt, and switching the malaria drug policy from chloroquine to coartem, the new drug;

8.   Re-organization to make fully transparent and efficient the procedures and mechanisms for the procurement of drugs by tendering functions of the Medical Stores Limited to Crown Agents;

9.   Ensured the timely release of complete, detailed, annual health expenditure data by preparing and presenting this data at the bi-annual consultative meetings with the donors to the health sector reforms by the Health Sector Income and Expenditure Committee;

10.   Ensured actual cash releases to District Health Management Boards of at least eighty per cent of the amount budgeted. In 2003, the actual cash releases were eighty-four per cent and in the first quarter of 2004 they had exceeded ninety-nine per cent;

11.   Initiated the implementation of an Integrated Financial Management Information System (IFMIS) by evaluating the tender for the software for the system, with the award of the tender pending a "no objection" decision from the World Bank for the favoured supplier;

12.   Prepared and published a Green Paper indicating the macroeconomic and fiscal frameworks for 2004-2006 as a preliminary

document to the publication of the Medium-Term Expenditure Framework (MTEF) that was scheduled for publication in June/July 2004, once approved by Cabinet;

13.   Made significant progress in implementing the strategy to fully commercialise ZESCO by completing the 'entry conditions' of the strategy that was formulated with the support and participation of the World Bank;

14.   Issued international bidding documents for the sale of a controlling interest in ZANACO. However, as the preferred bidder was linking the transaction to other financing facilities it has with the Government, the ZPA Board approved commencement of parallel negotiations with the reserve bidder.

I did not feel that the HIPC conditionalities were onerous in any way, as they were what the Zambian Government was expected to do in order to deliver effective and efficient services to the Zambian people. It was the responsibility of the Zambian Government to tame the rampaging HIV/AIDS and I did not understand why the government failed to recruit staff for the HIV/AIDS Council. A joint IMF/World Bank mission visited Zambia to assess performance against these benchmarks in the second half of 2004.

Due to the time difference between Lusaka and Washington DC, sometimes, I stayed awake until late in the night to await telephone calls from the country directors at the two institutions. On the night of Wednesday 6 April 2005, I received confirmation that the World Bank Board had approved Zambia's satisfactory execution of the benchmarks in fulfillment of the HIPC Initiative.

I then telephoned President Mwanawasa, waking him up, to pass on the good news. After all, we agreed that I would keep him fully informed all the time. These were tense moments as any recurring slippage would have plunged Zambia into an untold economic crisis.

The IMF Board gave its approval two days later on Friday, 8 April 2005. This approval of Zambia's attainment of the Completion Point meant that over half of Zambia's foreign debt of US $7.2 billion was to be written off as agreed earlier in December 2000.

To keep the stakeholders fully informed of the good news, I held a press briefing on Saturday afternoon at our Ministry. I was at Radio Zambia on Sunday morning and on Television Zambia in the afternoon. I expected that such historic good economic news would make the headlines of the public media, especially those that had been so critical of my appointment. Alas, this was not to be. Juicy political stories and sports continued to make the headlines for news on radio, television and newspapers. My consolation and encouragement was the large number of messages I received from ordinary

Zambians and foreigners on the landmark achievement.

We held a celebratory party for Ministry officers at the legendary Garden Motel, the birthplace of multipartyism. The choice of venue was deliberate as I reminded the celebrators that it was there that Zambia's future political direction had been mapped in July 1991. I invited them to spread the good news on the country's changed economic situation and encourage everyone to take part in the development efforts.

Sharing the HIPC experiences with peers
In April 2005, I led a delegation to Washington DC for the Spring Meetings of the IMF/World Bank Group. During the meetings, the officers of the two institutions acknowledged the achievement by Zambia of attaining the elusive Completion Point due to prudent economic management.

The African Union organized a meeting in Dakar Senegal in May 2005 for African Ministers of Finance to discuss the debt problem and how to raise development funds within Africa. President Abdoulaye Wade of Senegal was very candid in his opening remarks and reminded us that Africa had enough resources if only they were shared equitably amongst the Africans. He gave an example of the enormous oil reserves in some neighbouring African country, which was not being shared with his country.

He argued that the country boundaries in Africa were a creation of the colonialists and it was weak colonialists who got poor countries for colonies. Before the Scramble for Africa Berlin Conference of 1884, the natural resources belonged to the undivided Africa and all the African people.

I contributed to the issue of debt by narrating what Zambia had gone through in order to attain the Completion Point of the HIPC Initiative. I explained that many of the attached conditionalities were in fact to the benefit of the Zambian Government and people. For example, the strengthening of the HIV/AIDS Council was in the interest of Zambians afflicted by the pandemic. This was not to benefit the BWIs Institutions in any way. All that happened because the Zambian Government had failed to identify the priority issues that affected the ordinary Zambians.

Some African Ministers argued that debtor developing countries should not be compelled to undertake harsh measures before being forgiven their debts. However, President Wade retorted that African leaders who borrowed and misused the loans must be made accountable to their people. He explained that even when loans are used for projects such as school buildings, these are for political campaigns as they can be seen by the voters.

The President stated that schools are just heaps of bricks covered with roofing sheets but not provided with trained teachers, adequate equipment and facilities to produce educated citizens. The Senegalese President went on to say that most of the good roads constructed from loans were for the comfort of the politicians and the elite, who owned expensive imported cars.

I was once more requested to participate during the September 2005 IMF Ministerial press conference. In my presentation, I stated that the IMF programmes and facilities were transitory and that we all must work hard to wean our countries from these programmes.

I mentioned that Zambians looked forward to the savings from the debt relief, which will be applied to the health and education sectors, wealth, and job creation programmes. The IMF programmes should be seen as part of the exit strategy of any country from poverty and the financial discipline exhibited during the implementation of the PRGF should be entrenched as a permanent part of normal financial operations of any government.

In April 2006 I attended a meeting of the ACP Finance Ministers on the HIPC Initiative at the ACP Secretariat in Brussels, Belgium. At the meeting, I was once more asked to brief my colleagues on the Initiative and the conditions that Zambia fulfilled in order to get to the Completion Point. I emphasized that the program was anchored on disciplined fiscal management, which sometimes is resented by even fellow ministers.

I went further to explain that the program requires political will from the Head of State and technical competence and cooperation from the other ministers and officers. I mentioned that sometimes, officers have to be sacrificed if they stand in the way when implementing the harsh austerity measures. A proposal by some ministers from middle-income countries to be supported for inclusion under the HIPC Initiative was not supported. It was argued that these countries can raise adequate resources internally from their growing economies, but they fail to put in place effective tax systems.

Face-to-face with the Paris Club Creditors
On the evening of Saturday, 10 May 2005, my delegation left Dakar for Paris, France to confront the creditor countries of the Paris Club on Zambia's debt. I was briefed by my officials that normally the Paris Club wrote-off or rescheduled only seventy-five per cent of a country's debt and that the speech they had prepared for me was in line with this tradition. Zambia had been to the Paris Club three times during the nineties but its debt continued to rise.

I told the officers, who included Ronald Simwinga, who had attended many Paris Club meetings, that I intended to amend the speech to my taste to include compelling reasons for Zambia to get a 100 per cent debt write-off. I stayed up late that night to rewrite the speech. I included some historical perspectives on Zambia's debt including the cost of the liberation wars. I emphasized the need for funds to improve health and education facilities for the poor people in Zambia. Due to the servicing of the huge debt, the Chiluba Administration had been unable to construct social infrastructure and to provide social services for ten years.

During our breakfast, I rehearsed the new speech with my officers in the manner I intended to deliver it to the members of the Paris Club. The officers admitted that the speech had changed and did contain persuasive arguments for a better deal. By the time we entered the meeting room at 0830 hours on Wednesday, 11 May 2005, I was fully prepared to make the maximum impact.

Mrs Odille Renard Basso of the French Ministry of Finance and Treasury and the Co-President of the Paris Club chaired our meeting. Delegates in attendance were from the eleven creditor members of the Paris Club and observers from the IMF, Spain, UNCTAD, and the World Bank.

Each of the delegation had a copy of my statement and followed as I read it. After I had delivered the statement, a few complimentary comments were made by the Chairperson who proposed an adjournment to the afternoon, which was overwhelmingly supported. We were informed that the Paris Club members wished to consider our appeal and would come with an answer after lunch.

My officers informed me that this was un-procedural, as normally a reply was given immediately after the debtor's statement. I teased them that I am used to breaking records and that something unusual was about to happen during our negotiations.

Although we had been made to wait a little longer, my delegation remained jovial and had a good lunch awaiting some news on our request. The meeting resumed at about 1500 hours, way after lunch time and was expected to continue into the following day. The Chairperson and a few delegates made some positive comments on the achievement of the Mwanawasa Administration in attaining the Completion Point of the HIPC Initiative in a record time.

The Chairperson then announced that our request had been considered and on the basis of our statement, the Paris Club members had decided to write-off US $1.8 billion of Zambia's US $1.92 billion debt owed to the members. The cancelled debt was 94 per cent, which left a balance of US $124 million or six per cent. In addition, fifty per cent of all amounts due between 2005 and 2011 would also be written off. This was unprecedented in the history of the Paris Club and this amazed my officers.

The chairman and other creditors stated that the contents and my convincing manner of delivering the country statement had persuaded them to conclude such a generous debt write-off agreement for Zambia. I was overwhelmed and gave a very short acceptance speech to thank the Chairperson and delegates for their most favourable consideration to Zambia's development plans.

As our assignment had been accomplished in one day, we had all the time to do some sightseeing in the City of Paris. I accompanied the officers in climbing France's cultural icon, the 324-metre Eiffel Tower. Although I had visited Paris and toured the Tower many times before, I had not managed to find space and time to reach the top in view of the large number of tourists.

This time, I managed to get to the top of the tower. Atop the tower, I marvelled at 'The hateful shadow of the hateful column of bolted sheet metal' developed by Gustave Eiffel, whose childhood was supported by a loving grandmother and a mother running a charcoal business. The 'remarkable piece of structural art' was the most visited tourist attraction in France, receiving over five million visitors per annum. Frenchman Eiffel had earlier built the Statue of Liberty designed by sculptor Frederic Bartholdi in France, which was donated to the USA by the people of France and stands at the entrance to the New York harbour.

Good tidings from the G20 at Gleneagles, Scotland
On 7 July 2005, while on a presidential delegation to London, I learnt that the G8 leaders of the developed countries, meeting at Gleneagles in Scotland, had decided to support the HIPC Initiative with a new initiative called the Multilateral Debt Relief Initiative (MDRI). Sadly the good news was spoilt early that day by the terrorist bomb attacks in London, which claimed a number of innocent lives.

The G8 proposed a full cancellation of debts owed to the International Development Association (IDA) of the World Bank, the International Monetary Fund, and the African Development Fund (AfDF) of the AfDB by the developing debtor countries that had completed the program under the HIPC Initiative.

Zambia having completed its HIPC Initiative program in April 2005 was eligible for more debt relief under the MDRI. A quick calculation showed that Zambia's foreign debt, most of which was owed to IDA, IMF, and AfDF, would be reduced by over ninety-five per cent.

I shared this information with the Zambian High Commissioner to the UK, His Excellency Anderson Chibwa as I waited in his office for my flight to Lusaka. We were both excited in the midst of the gloom caused by the bomb attacks. I must have had the most peaceful and deepest sleep on the long flight to Lusaka that night. Luckily, the modern planes with advanced navigation technology have the ability to withstand even heavy thunderstorms and we did not have any violent plunge like that of the Zambia Airways 1979 flight over the stormy Congo skies.

Zambia's liberation from the HIPC Club
The group of donors who met in Kampala in 2004 and in Copenhagen on replenishment of the African Development Fund of the AfDB, had to consider their earlier recommendations in relation to the new MDR Initiative. As a representative of the Southern Africa beneficiary countries, I attended the meeting held between 7 and 9 December 2005 in Washington DC. At the meeting, the donors considered the formula to be used in writing-off the debts, taking into account eligibility, cut-off date, threshold, and date of implementation.

I left Washington DC on Saturday, 10 December 2005, and connected with another group of ministry officials in London for a trip to Moscow, Russia, for bilateral debt negotiations. We were in Moscow between 12 and 15 December. We managed to get some assurance that Zambia's debt would be presented to the Russian Parliament by the end of the year. The weather was harsh with temperatures of minus fifteen degrees.

While in Moscow, I received a telephone call from a Zambian youth seeking an appointment. When I informed him that I was in Moscow, he said that I must be enjoying flying all over the world. I informed him that all passengers, in a flying plane have to be seated and firmly anchored by safety belts and that the temperature in Moscow was minus fifteen degrees. I then asked if he would enjoy being fastened for such long periods of time and staying in such cold weather.

After exclaiming, "That is very cold", he then asked, "By the way ba-minister, is it true that you are paid ten per cent by the creditors when you successfully negotiate a debt write-off for Zambia?" He explained that one of his friends had told him that I would be a very rich former minister by the time I was through with the negotiations on Zambia's huge external debt.

When I returned to Zambia, I met the young man and explained to him about my assignment as it related to Zambia's external debt. I even disclosed my salary, which was in no way fixed on the basis of my efforts on Zambia's external debt. With a clear understanding that I was not a debt collector paid a commission, the young man grew to be one of my strongest admirers. But I still wonder as to how many Zambians think that I became rich by negotiating the write-off of Zambia's huge debt with the creditors!

The end of 2005 was spent at home discussing local issues and signing agreements with ambassadors of creditor countries on debt cancellation and support to the 2006 budget. Agreements were signed with the ambassadors of Belgium, France, the Netherlands, and Norway. The latter two were interested in giving financial support to the 2006 elections.

On Friday, 30 December 2005, the last working day of the year, I signed a debt cancellation agreement with the new American Ambassador to Zambia, Her Excellency Ms Carmen Martinez for the debt of US $280.50 million. I was surprised that the debt schedule included an amount negotiated by our team led by Daniel Luzongo for importing wheat under the PL 480 One Entitlement in 1978!

During 2005, the country attained the Completion Point of the HIPC Initiative and received substantial debt relief. Zambia's foreign debt, which had accumulated to US $7.2 billion since 1958 when the first loan was acquired by Zambia (Northern Rhodesia) for the Kariba Hydroelectric Power Station, was disappearing without much fanfare. Annual foreign debt service fell from an average of US $300 million to around US $80 million per year. President Mwanawasa nicknamed me 'Mr HIPC' in recognition of my role in negotiating the debt write-offs with the various creditors and since Zambia was no more a Heavily Indebted Poor Country (HIPC), although it still had a lot of poor citizens.

Zambia's balance sheet was getting cleaner, thereby creating an opportunity for the country to apply its local resources and revenue to wealth generating projects and vital social services and economic infrastructure. I was excited as I saw space to fit in innovative plans for the future development of the country. To chart the way forward on the utilization of the savings, we held workshops and seminars with stakeholders to share information on some of the financial instruments such as the IFMIS and MTEF and the Employment and Labour Policies.

The table below shows Zambia's external debt from 2004 to 2010 as a percentage of the Gross Domestic Product (GDP).

YEAR	2004	2005	2006	2007	2008	2009	2010
Total Government External Debt							
	7,250	4,651	0.972	1,104.65	1,188.55	1,544.52	1,766.16
Total External Public debt as % of GDP							
	130.2	50.95	11.12	9.20	10.55	11.14	10.93

The IMF report on Zambia's HIPC Initiative achievement stated that,

"Zambia has qualified for IMF debt relief because of its overall satisfactory recent macroeconomic performance, progress in poverty reduction, and improvements in public expenditure management. Zambia has enjoyed sustained robust growth, a striking turnaround in economic performance that has been underpinned by a marked improvement in public finances. Although still too high, inflation has moderated and gross international reserves are relatively low.

By pursuing politically difficult spending restraint in 2004, the government was able to sharply reduce its borrowing and halt an unsustainable rise in domestic debt. This, in turn, brought lower interest rates and increased the private sector's access to domestic credit.

The government has established a sound record of implementing its poverty reduction strategy. While public expenditure management systems have been improved, their planned further strengthening is crucial. Performance in these areas provides assurance that resources made available under the Multilateral Debt Relief Initiative will be used effectively"

CHAPTER 31

Mwanawasa's Compass For Zambia's Economic Future

With a clean national balance sheet, the Mwanawasa Administration was determined to raise the economic growth rate to over six per cent in order to reduce the stubborn poverty levels, which were above fifty per cent. To position development in a medium-term framework, it was decided to prepare a Fifth National Development Plan (FNDP) to cover a five-year period. The 2006 budget was to mark the beginning of the implementation of the Plan.

On Tuesday, 31 January 2006, the Business Post speculated that,

"As finance minister Ng'andu Magande sharpens his mouth to present the 2006 National Budget this Friday, it must be clear that people have high expectations. From the discussions we have had with representatives of various industries, this year's budget should be a starting point for a new economic dispensation. It is a new dispensation because the attainment of the Completion Point under the HIPC Initiative has marked a new beginning for Zambia. Most foreign governments have renewed their friendship with Zambia, most of them offering full debt cancellation. With actions such as these, as well as the encouraging economic numbers, Magande's job will be a relatively easier one".

Within two years, the pejorative editorials by the Post were substituted by an admission that Zambia was on the threshold of a new beginning. Within thirty months of the active participation of the 'IMF cheerleader' in the management of the public finances and assets of Zambia, positive results were showing. Indeed, my job was becoming easy to execute, because obstacles had been cleared.

As a follow-up to the President's policy speech in January, I presented the 2006 Budget on Friday 3 February 2006 with the theme, 'From Sacrifice to Equitable Wealth Creation'. In the budget, a number of incentives, innovative initiatives, and projects and programmes were announced.

The 2006 Budget Speech concluded that:

"Mr Speaker, the year 2006 must set a stage for the Zambian economy to move to a higher level of sustained growth and development in the wake of massive debt forgiveness. In our resolve to move this country forward and to create wealth, thereby defeating poverty, we need to pull all our efforts together.

Sir, may I re-reiterate that developing this country is the sole responsibility of the Zambian people. The Government has taken the lead with definitive key policy initiatives and I challenge the private sector and all Zambians to do the rest. I have faith in my fellow countrymen and women because they have the skill, innovation, entrepreneurial spirit, and the appetite to move the Zambian economy to the next level of development".

In 2004, I had proposed the abandonment of the traditional Export Processing Zones (EPZs) in view of Zambia's geographical location far away from all international seaports. In any case, Zambia's potential market of over 200 million consumers was within reach at all its eight borders. One of the major new initiatives towards effective and competitive industrialization was the establishment of Multi-Facility Economic Zones (MFEZ) under the Japanese Triangle of Hope concept and the Chinese assistance programme.

In the area of trade, value chain analyses for priority sectors were programmed. For easing investment processes, the Zambia Development Agency (ZDA) was established as a 'one-stop-shop' to bring together the operations of five statutory bodies involved in investments, industry, and trade.

To reduce the cost of doing business, an ambitious infrastructure development program was planned and initiated. New hydropower stations were to be constructed and fuel tanks for reserves were to be constructed in strategic locations all over the country. In the road sector, financial resource management was separated from physical planning and the execution of roadworks. This saw the effective operationalization of the Road Development Agency (RDA) and the Road Fund Agency (RFA) as independent units. In the ICT sector, the customs duty of fifteen per cent on computer parts was removed.

The percentage of the budgets for education and health went up to 26.9 per cent and 18 per cent of the discretionary budget respectively. The Government created the Youth Empowerment Fund, the Youth Constituency Development Fund, and the Inventors' Fund to operationalize the innovations identified through the Junior Engineers and Technicians and Scientists (JETS) over decades.

In the housing sector, the manufacture of cheap cement was encouraged by the President laying the foundation stone for the extension of the Chilanga Cement Works in January 2006. At the function, he announced that the Government was considering reducing customs duty on machinery for manufacturing of cement and roofing sheets. Customs duty on these imports was in fact suspended in the 2006 budget.

In recognition of their role and participation in national development, the stakeholders proposed that the Fifth National Development Plan and Vision be specifically mentioned in the new Zambian Constitution. They argued that such a provision would rule out Zambia being governed without a development plan as had happened between 1991 and 2002.

Instead of a mention of the specific plan, the consensus settled on having a provision in the new Constitution, which would compel the government of the day to prepare an annual budget in conformity with medium and long-term development plans. The draft constitution made a provision under 'Legislation on Budgeting and Planning' for national development planning.

In the Foreword to the FNDP, President Mwanawasa stated that,

"The absence of planning tends to force us to concentrate on short-term needs representing narrow sectional interests thus denying the country the opportunity to attain broad-based socio-economic development.

The re-introduction of national planning in 2002 and the creation of Sector Advisory Groups (SAGs) and the proposed strengthening of district and provincial planning divisions will guide the planning and implementation process. Development planning is essential in providing clear definitions and articulations of national, provincial, and district priorities. The FNDP has ensured that sectoral strategic plans are well coordinated and are inter-linked

I wish to thank all Zambians for contributing effectively to the preparation process of the FNDP. Government will continue to consult citizens in key areas involving planning and implementation processes so that their inputs are taken into account".

On Wednesday, 26 July 2006, while hundreds of citizens were attending the consultative meeting, President Mwanawasa dissolved Parliament and consequently the Cabinet. He was signaling that politics must be divorced from the consultative development planning processes. His argument was that Zambia must anchor its long-term development on continuity of development programmes implemented by an effective civil service and efficient private sector. On the same day, the President announced 28 September 2006 as the date for the presidential and parliamentary elections.

The optimism in the Nation at the beginning of 2006 after the debt write-off had translated into reality during the year in both the political and economic areas. The 2006 elections were judged as the most peaceful, well-organized, free, fair, and transparent by many local and foreign observers. The election period reported only one case of a skirmish in the whole country. Zambians proved to be a peaceful people if shepherded by a good and capable leader of which President Mwanawasa was one.

The voter turn-out of seventy-one per cent was the highest since the advent of multiparty democracy in 1991. This was credited to the efficiency of the ECZ under the first female Chairperson, Her Lordship Justice Mrs Irene Mambilima and to the discipline of the members of the ruling MMD Party under President Mwanawasa. No opposition party petitioned the presidential elections.

On Monday, 9 October 2006, President Mwanawasa announced the new Cabinet at a Press Conference at State House. I was re-appointed as Minister of Finance and National Planning. In the short letter of appointment, the President wrote;

"I have re-appointed you Minister of Finance and National Planning because I am certain that you are the man we need for the job of economic emancipation. This term is particularly expected to be more challenging but we must work together to meet the weather".

I reported for work at the Ministry on Wednesday, 11 October 2006 after having been sworn-in on the day before. I was fully briefed by the Heads of Departments on the status of operations in the Ministry. All operations had continued as planned and the staff was busy preparing the 2007 Green Paper. My anxiety about a budget overrun was settled when I was informed that preliminary data indicated that there had been no over-expenditure on the budget for the elections. Clearly, this was a record performance in public finance management in the history of the country.

On Friday 27th October 2006, President Mwanawasa officially opened Parliament. In his visionary speech, the President welcomed and congratulated the elected Members of Parliament and thanked the voters for voting for him. The President stated the following:-

"I am greatly humbled by their confidence and trust in my leadership and that of the Movement for Multiparty Democracy (MMD).

I thank all Zambians, who despite the heated electioneering, the elections were held under a peaceful atmosphere thereby demonstrating Zambia's determination to uphold her proud and consistent record as an oasis of peace. This signifies the maturity of our emerging democracy and our unity in diversity.

As I said in my inauguration speech, I would like to leave behind a legacy of the rule of law, self-sufficiency in food production, increased employment, economic empowerment, and stability in our socio-economic policies.

Consequently, my administration will continue to foster transparency and accountability in the running of public affairs. My administration will continue the fight against corruption because this ensures that public resources are protected for the benefit of all Zambians.

In the next five years, my administration will continue with implementation of prudent macroeconomic policies, so as to consolidate macroeconomic stability. Our goal is to achieve higher and sustained economic growth of at least seven per cent per annum. The focus in my second term will, therefore, be to broaden and accelerate economic growth. The people of Zambia now want results and a translation of the macroeconomic achievements into an uplifting of their standard of living".

In the economic area, it seemed that many captains of industry had found time to read and fully embrace the 2006 budget in which they were called upon "to move the Zambian economy to the next level of development". They went into their boardrooms to answer and translate the plea by President Mwanawasa and me for entrepreneurship and innovation.

The year 2006 set an enabling stage for the Zambian economy to move to higher levels of sustained growth in the wake of massive debt forgiveness. But it was necessary to ensure that the growth process was local and benefitted more local people by integrating them in the economic activities.

It was evident that my instructions, nicknamed the cheerleader by the Post newspaper, had been followed diligently by all the players and spectators who were enjoying the game. Occasional visits to State House for intimate conversations with President Mwanawasa, the Commander-in-Chief, who had publicly called me a 'compass' for his ship in September 2006, confirmed that he too was relishing the evolution of Zambia's development status. Amongst the many landmarks of the year 2006 were the following:

- Zambia held the most peaceful, fair, free and transparent general elections since 1991

- Completion of the preparation of the Fifth National Development Plan (FNDP) and Vision 2030

o Expressions of the self-confidence by the Zambians and a desire to lay a clear roadmap as a rallying point for all development efforts during the next twenty-five years.

o The futuristic theme of the FNDP was, "Broad-based wealth and job creation through citizenry participation and technological advancement".

- Single digit inflation rate of 8.2 per cent, the lowest in a period of thirty years since 1975

- Domestic borrowing (budget deficit) of 1.5 per cent of GDP, the lowest since 2000

- Current account deficit of 2.5 per cent from 11.8 per cent in 2005

- National foreign debt of US $635 million down from US $7200 million

- Annual foreign debt service down to US $33.9 million from US $374.8 million

- Copper prices to a historical high of US $3.05 per lb. ($6770 per tonne)

- Total export earnings up to US $3.9 billion from US $2.2 billion in 2005

- Non-Traditional Export (NTE) earnings of US $754.9 million from US $576.7 million in 2005

- Maize production of 1,400,000 metric tonnes from 866,000 tonnes in 2005

- Mining sector growth rate of 11.8 per cent from 7.9 per cent in 2005

- Energy sector growth rate of 11.3 per cent from 5.4 per cent in 2005

- External trade balance of US $1176 million from US $10 million in 2005

- Treasury Bills average yield rate at 9.8 per cent from 16.7 per cent in 2005

- Composite yield rate of 12.6 per cent from 23 per cent in 2005

- Capital market capitalization of 52 per cent from 11 per cent in 2005

- Customs duty on computer parts removed

- Carbon tax on motor vehicles introduced

- Three per cent presumptive tax for SMEs introduced

- Planning and Economic Management Division established

- Commercial bank's capitalization increased from K2 billion to K12 billion

- Corporate tax rate for banks reduced from forty-five to forty per cent

- Microfinance Regulations approved

- Credit Reference Bureau agency granted a licence

- Direct Budget Support (DBS) by donors approved and agreements signed

- Zambia Development Agency (ZDA), a 'one-stop shop' established

- Multi-Facility Economic Zones (MFEZ) planned and identified at Chambeshi and Lusaka South

- Citizens' Economic Empowerment Commission (CEEC) and Fund

established

- Youth Empowerment Fund created

- Youth Constituency Development Fund created

- Gender Ministry created

- Zambia acceded to the AU African Peer Review Mechanism

- Education: 7100 teachers recruited

- Health: five hospitals: Chadiza, Mumbwa, Kapiri, Samfwa and Shang'ombo started

> Abolition of user fees in health facilities in rural areas
> Establishment of a Drug Supply Fund
> PMTC services on HIV transmission extended to all districts
- Rural Finance Program to expand services of NATSAVE initiated.

It was not always smooth sailing when debating some of the new proposals in the Ministry and in the Cabinet. I recall the protracted discussions on the bill to create the Citizens' Economic Empowerment Commission. I was among a few cabinet ministers who advocated for the definition of Zambian citizen to include the word 'indigenous'. President Mwanawasa and the Minister of Legal Affairs argued that there can be no other definition apart from the one in the constitution.

We then requested for a caucus of the MMD Members of Parliament at State House to resolve the issue. In spite of our heavy lobbying with the other MMD members the matter was referred to Parliament. Finally the bill was passed by a slim majority without the word indigenous in it. However I was happy that at last there was a special purpose vehicle for assisting Zambians with the technical advice and finances.

There was strong resistance to reducing the corporate tax rate for commercial banks in view of their unwillingness to reduce interest rates on their lending. As a former banker, I was convinced that too much liquidity with the banks would compel them to reduce interest rates and introduce new products.

By the time of the general elections in October 2006, the Ministry of Finance and National Planning had collected most of the data and compiled a preliminary annual report in readiness for a new administration. At a function to bid farewell and in anticipation of my not going back to the Ministry of Finance and National Planning after the 2006 elections, I issued the following statement:

"Never in the forty-two years' history of Zambia has there been such a low level of foreign debt, single digit inflation, below twenty per cent interest rates, low deficit financing, high copper prices of over US $8000 per tonne, a strong Kwacha and a financially disciplined Government all at the same time. Therefore, there is need for the Government and other participants in the economy to efficiently and efficaciously manage the change by creating new and viable relationships.

There is need to cooperate and accommodate the aspirations of all those alive, who sacrificed to bring about the current most conducive macroeconomic environment in the history of Zambia. Inequitable sharing of the benefits of these gains with glaring disparities amongst the inhabitants could lead to conflict and instability. The current Zambian Government, which led the Nation to this enviable macroeconomic situation, solicits the cooperation of all the participants in the economy as it seeks to create new relationships and inter-linkages for equitable wealth creation and sharing".

The national budget was being produced in a transparent medium-term micro-fiscal framework with the involvement of the Cabinet, Parliament and ordinary stakeholders through the SAGs. The various budget processes such as ABB and financial controls such as IFMIS that were introduced were achieving financial discipline, equitable allocation of public resources and technical efficiency, which resulted in the credibility and predictability of the national budget.

The Zambian economy achieved so many milestones and I was among the architects of the country's clearly laid down future development trajectory. The year was a turning point for me personally and for the country.

CHAPTER 32

Designing Youth Empowerment Programmes

During the period of economic hardships towards the end of the 20th Century, lack of school places and employment in Zambia led to social problems amongst the youth. Very young people took to the streets in urban areas to beg for money. An investigation revealed that most of them were sent by their unemployed parents or guardians to beg in the streets.

Under the earlier programme, the street kids were taken to Kanakantapa Settlement Scheme in Chongwe to engage in farming. Many of them deserted after a short stay as they were not interested in farming. President Mwanawasa decided to revive the programme started under KK's administration to round up these unskilled and unemployed youths and to take them for special programmes.

This time, it was decided to take them to Chiwoko Zambia National Service Camp in Katete District in the Eastern Province for training in various skills. The younger ones were taken to homes for the homeless run by nongovernmental organizations (NGOs). Within a short period of time, Zambia had no kids begging on its streets. To buttress these efforts and programs, a law to punish parents who sent their children in the street was enacted.

In 2004, a group of 114 were enrolled and 94 graduated in 2006. In May 2007, a total of 434 youths were enrolled and many of them successfully completed their skills training programme. They had covered amongst others, the subjects of agriculture, bricklaying, automotive mechanics, music, metalwork, carpentry, cultural awareness, and survival skills.

In January 2005, while accompanying the First Family on a State Visit to Japan, I briefed President Mwanawasa that the problem of youth unemployment was becoming a topical and critical issue and could derail and overshadow all other development achievements. The problem was commonly referred to as a 'time bomb'.

When we returned to Zambia, I instructed the Secretary to the Treasury to solicit for visionary proposals from young people under what we called 'Vision 2030' through a public advertisement. An advertisement placed in the media inviting plans from anyone below the age of forty years drew thousands of brilliant proposals from youths across the country. The new programme was to extend beyond the street kids by embracing all youths in developing entrepreneurship.

On 12 April 2005, I led a delegation to Washington DC for the Spring Meetings of the IMF/World Bank Group. During the meetings, the two institutions made sure to mention the achievement by Zambia of attaining the elusive Completion Point due to prudent economic management. We were informed that the World Bank wished to include Zambia's efforts in a special report on youth empowerment.

During our visit, Her Excellency Ambassador Inonge Mbikusita-Lewanika introduced me to a group of American private businessmen called Friends of Zambia. In our discussions, they informed us that they wanted to get involved in a Large-Scale Youth Investment Strategy to create employment opportunities for the youth.

This project was to provide the youth with financial resources, training, and business development services required for them to set up micro-enterprises and small to medium-sized businesses. The proposed vehicle to be used to implement the youth investment strategy was to raise funds through private debt conversion. I was excited and invited them to visit Zambia for further discussions.

The Friends of Zambia and officials of ImagineNations visited Zambia for detailed discussions. The Youth Fund to raise funds through debt conversion aimed a target of US $100 million. The ambitious fund supported by the Friends of Zambia, ImagineNations, the African Development Foundation and the Nike foundation was registered in Zambia. In 2006, the Ministry of Sport, Youth, and Child Development, which had participated in discussing the project since 2005, withdrew from the project. They argued that there was no need for the involvement of private investors in youth programs as the Youth Development Fund in the national budget was adequate.

I was aware of the shortcomings of the government's Youth Development Fund as I had assisted in reviving it. I was therefore very disappointed with the decision of the sector Ministry to reject a partnership in youth empowerment, an area which is responsive to public-private partnership as it requires a lot of imagination and innovation. I and Rick Little of ImagineNations sought the intervention of the Secretary to the Cabinet in the matter. Unfortunately, he could not override the officials of the Ministry of Sports and Youth. Zambia lost an opportunity to comprehensively fund and deal with the problem of youth unemployment with additional grant money.

On 8 September 2005, I led a delegation to India for the India-Zambia Joint Economic Commission meeting. During the flight, I was introduced to Naveen Kapur, an Indian businessman. Kapur's company had been involved in some projects that were being implemented using the line of credit acquired by President Mwanawasa from the Indian Government during his state visit in early 2003 just before I joined the Government.

The line of credit had been used to purchase vehicles for some government security departments, including the Zambia Police. Proposals had been made to use the balance of the funds for the education and agriculture sectors, although specific projects had not yet been developed.

I had a useful conversation with Kapur, who informed me that their company manufactured a variety of equipment, suited to small-scale entrepreneurs. I suggested that we procure some tools for our graduates from the trades' institutes to be given as seed capital. Kapur confirmed that they could carry out such a project as they had done one elsewhere in Africa. I recalled how agitated the Minister of Agriculture and Cooperatives was after his visit to India on the effectiveness of simple hand-operated equipment in rural development.

The Indian Government was agreeable to the use of the balance of the line of credit for the youth empowerment and small-scale farmers. I easily convinced the Minister of Agriculture that the government buys hand-operated agro-processing equipment for village cottage industries such as rice milling and cashew nut processing in the Western Province. The cashew nut industry remained underdeveloped in the province due to lack of simple appropriate equipment for cracking the hard nuts.

Kapur and officials from the Ministry of Agriculture headquarters visited the Western Province and prepared a project proposal. However, a senior civil servant in the Ministry shot down the project arguing that what the villagers required was automated processing equipment.

In the speech to open Parliament for the 2006 session, President Mwanawasa stated that:

By the available demographic data, over fifty per cent of Zambia's population constitutes of mainly young people below the age of thirty years. This is the future generation that has to be actively engaged in the development of the country as they are the ones that will need a prosperous country. In recognition of this fact, the Government has initiated programmes to impart life-survival skills to the youth. As part of the Government's new thrust to deal with youth problems and unemployment, the following programmes will be implemented by my Government:-

- amend the syllabus in schools to make it relevant to the country's environment and development plans by imparting appropriate knowledge in the areas of agriculture and mining to the pupils;

-

- establish a Youth Empowerment Fund to provide seed money for youth projects that will be the backbone of Zambia's future industrialization;

-

- graduating students from our technical colleges will be provided with appropriate toolkits for them to be immediately ready to engage in their chosen vocations;

- establish a special dedicated fund to be known as a Youth Inventors' Fund to provide financing to young Zambian inventors who have inventions and innovations that require commercial development.

-

Mr Speaker

I am confident that the programmes I have outlined will bring hope to our future generation and galvanize them into a productive force for the development of our country. I must alert those who intend to benefit from these initiatives that competition will be high and therefore all our youths must aim to be the best in the areas of their interest.

The Youth Empowerment and Inventors' Funds were established and funding was provided in the 2006 national budget. All the graduates of Government Trades Institutes in Zambia in 2007 were given free toolkits for their trades. President Mwanawasa presided over a special national graduation ceremony held at the Lusaka Business and Vocational College and announced that the free toolkits programme was a way of the youths benefitting from savings from the HIPC Initiative.

The plan was to continue giving free toolkits to all graduates of both public and private training institutes as from 2008. The trained and empowered youths were to be assisted to form public companies in their towns under the guidance and supervision of the local trades training colleges.

These companies were to be funded by the Citizens' Economic Empowerment Commission (CEEC) to develop their capacities to undertake major public works. With adequate skilled members and capital, the companies would then be given preference for any work on government infrastructure such as schools and health facilities. Such an arrangement would reduce the cost of constructing and maintaining public infrastructure while absorbing the trained youths in meaningful national development.

Through my interaction with the Governor of the Bank of Zambia, I was made aware of some funds that had not been utilized by the ZAMPI Project in the nineties, when the project had been terminated. The funds were deposited in a special account at the Bank of Zambia. After explaining the youth empowerment concept, the funds were made available to the ambitious youth programme.

In June 2007, I was on President Mwanawasa's delegation to Ghana for an AU Summit. During our stay in Accra, I had the opportunity of discussing with my counterpart the use of HIPC savings. He informed me that at Completion Point in December 2004, it was decided to indicate the amount of savings in each future budget. The identified amounts were then allocated to specific projects that permanently bore the name of 'HIPC Project'. The priority was given to projects that benefitted large communities.

One innovative HIPC project was concerned with hygiene amongst school-going children. Unemployed youths were selected, trained, and loaned hair-cutting and grooming equipment. Each loanee was allocated a particular school, whose pupils he/she was responsible for grooming their hair at a nominal fee. The project created employment for hundreds of youths with steady incomes and also kept the school pupils kempt.

I recalled the contemptuous comments that greeted my proposal in 2006 that the Government empowers selected street kids with wheelbarrows on a loan basis from the HIPC savings. I sought the assistance of the Lusaka City Council Town Clerk to get me the details on the youths that facilitated the daily vibrant trade and transportation in the city. We discovered that the active street youths were hiring the wheelbarrows on daily basis from some enterprising executive director working for a bank. I was convinced that owning a wheelbarrow would raise the morale of the youths and make them more productive.

I discussed with the management of the new steel plant at Kafue a possibility of them selling steel to youths at a special low price. We agreed that some youths be assisted to develop a special wheelbarrow and cart for the cross-town transport business. While the Kafue Steel Plant owners and the youths welcomed my plans, many Government officials scoffed at my down-to-earth ideas.

I recall the enthusiasm with which President Mwanawasa introduced to the Cabinet at a lunch the new hand-washing basin with a tap on stands invented by a young man in 2005. He proudly declared that this hygienic hand-washing equipment would help the nation in the fight against cholera. I then proposed to the Ministry of Commerce Trade and Industry to assist the inventor to patent the tool and support the establishment of a manufacturing plant.

I proposed to the Honours' Committee chaired by the Vice President that the villager who had established a power generating unit from scrap metal to supply electricity to his village in Mporokoso District be honoured. I was among the excited crowd that gave a standing ovation to the ingenious innovator on the grounds of State House as President Mwanawasa decorated him with a national medal. I was always on the lookout for youths who exhibited rare talents.

Following the visit of President Mwanawasa to China, I proposed that the Government initiates some viable innovative programmes to identify, mentor, and finance enterprising young people who would develop new businesses and create employment and wealth. The President was agreeable to my proposal and directed that my Ministry must come up with some plans.

I came up with a proposal whereby Zambian youths were to be sponsored on trips to China to observe the work ethics of the Chinese. Everyone who had been to China had marvelled at the work ethics of the Chinese and the consequential phenomenal development achieved by china within thirty years.

I requested Mable Mung'omba, the Director General of the newly created CEEC to liaise with Sebastian Kopulande of the China-Zambia Business Association (ZCBA), formed in September 2004, in organizing the educational tours. The ZCBA had been organizing tours for existing entrepreneurs. I was convinced that young Zambians who would be inspired after observing the Chinese at work, would be the vanguards of a CEEC youth entrepreneur empowerment programme in partnership with existing entrepreneurs who would provide guidance and mentorship.

I discussed with President Mwanawasa a draft proposal to resuscitate a reformed National Service in 2010, focusing on leadership skills. This was to include the involvement of the character-forming NGOs such as the Scouts and Girl Guides Movement, the church and the disciplined retired military personnel, with whom I had some fruitful discussions. By 2008, the Mwanawasa Administration laid down the foundation for a robust youth empowerment programme that was to create thousands of opportunities for youth employment. A well-endowed Youth Empowerment Fund with resources from various sources was created.

Regrettably, the well-laid-out ambitious youth empowerment scheme did not continue after the demise of President Mwanawasa and my departure from the Cabinet in 2008. This has led to thousands of educated and trained young people roaming the streets of every town in Zambia with no capital, tools, employment, nor livelihoods.

CHAPTER 33

Rebuilding Zambia's International Image

At the conclusion of the discussions by the Ministerial team to the IMF in June 2003, I remained behind and joined President Mwanawasa on his visit to Washington DC between 22 and 24 June 2003. The President's visit was to mend the broken relations with the Bretton Woods Institutions and the USA Government. The President held discussions with the officials of the IMF, World Bank and the USA Government on various subjects. During the last meeting with the President of the World Bank, President Mwanawasa introduced me as the incoming Minister of Finance and National Planning.

In my letter of appointment dated 3 July 2003, the President directed that "It is particularly important that you should keep the World Bank and the International Monetary Fund as well as the European Union and other cooperating partners fully engaged so that we derive the maximum benefit from our association with them".

During my personal briefings with President Mwanawasa, many other international organizations such as, COMESA, the Commonwealth, SADC, and the UN System were added to the list of the organizations I had to create harmonious relations with. I was also instructed to keep warm bilateral relations with individual donor countries.

Zambia had been a beneficiary of political support, technical assistance, grants, and concessional loans from most of these countries, global development, financial, and governance institutions since the sixties. Some of them such as COMESA and SADC had been formed with Zambia's advocacy and promotion of regional integration. Donor support in the 2003 budget was estimated at forty-two per cent and therefore cooperation with the donors was crucial.

I found space to meet ambassadors of the donor countries. Between 14 and 30 July 2003, I met ten ambassadors of the donor countries and all of them promised to transmit our requests to their capitals. I also gave an assurance that things would be done differently and that they should be ready to give advice as I would involve and engage them in seeking the way forward for the Zambian economy.

This assignment involving foreign governments and institutions was the easiest for me as I dealt with the donor community as Permanent Secretary for the National Commission for Development Planning in 1986. I dealt with the donors in the various sector ministries that I supervised. At the close of the 20th Century I was a global diplomat at the ACP, where as the Secretary General, I interacted with the fifteen EU ministers responsible for development cooperation on behalf of the seventy-one ACP countries.

In 1980, I was a member of a government delegation on a tour of the People's Republic of China and North Korea. I visited the USA many times since my first visit in 1976 when I attended a course in project analysis at the EDI of the World Bank. In 1984, I hosted H.E. Nicholas Platt, USA Ambassador to Zambia in Kabwe during his tour of the Central Province. In reciprocity, the USA Government sponsored me for a one-month tour of the USA in 1989 under the International Visitor Programme (IVP). Since then I have had close association with the staff of the American Embassy and USAID in Lusaka.

Relations with the Bretton Woods Institutions
Zambia joined the International Monetary Fund (IMF), one of the institutions of the United Nations (UN) system, in September 1965. Relations between the Zambian Government and the IMF and World Bank (Breton Woods Institutions) soured in the eighties when the Zambian Government refused to abide by the conditions of the Structural Adjustment Programmes (SAPs). The Government decided in May 1987 to limit its foreign loan repayments to only ten per cent of the outstanding debt.

The Zambian Government was imitating the Mexican Government, which had defaulted on repayment of its sovereign debt in 1982. This led to a staggering debt of US $6.2 billion by 1991 when the UNIP Government was replaced by the MMD Party Government.

The new MMD Administration under President Chiluba created an environment for cooperation with the IMF. This led to a new SAP with the liberalisation of the economy and privatization as the major conditions. In 1994, the Chiluba Administration borrowed heavily around US $680 million from the IMF under the new SAP and used the money to repay some of the outstanding arrears.

While it was easy for the Chiluba regime to announce general structural reforms and policies, such as price and exchange rate deregulation, the government did not keep pace with the demands on governance. According to Malcolm MacPherson, "From early 1995, the pace and direction of reform changed. Policy dialogue and openness gave way to belligerence and confrontation. Cooperation between the government and the donor community was abandoned".

Towards the end of the 20th Century, President Chiluba's macroeconomic management once more slipped and poverty levels rose. Poor financial and political governance led to a loss of trust in the MMD government by the international community. The Zambian people lost faith in President Chiluba and stopped him from standing for a third term. In the 2001 general elections, Levy Patrick Mwanawasa was presented as the MMD Party candidate and he was elected Republican President.

An assessment made in early 2003, showed that the Zambian Government was poor at fulfilling promises it had made under SAP and the HIPC Initiative. President Mwanawasa promised to implement the benchmarks and a new deadline of the end of 2004 for reaching the Completion Point was agreed upon.

Without donor support, there was limited revenue to fund the national budget. A large budget deficit had been recorded during the first quarter of 2003. Due to the Zambian Government having failed to observe many of the fifteen benchmarks, the PRGF with the IMF was cancelled in March 2003.

A three-year track record of fiscal discipline and a PRGF were among the benchmarks for the attainment of the HIPC Completion Point and debt relief. With the poor performance on most benchmarks, Zambia could therefore not qualify for debt forgiveness under the HIPC Initiative in 2003 and continued to service the debt of over US \$7 billion.

I had established and enjoyed strong personal relations with the country representatives of the two Bretton Woods Institutions in Zambia since 1976 when I became a fellow of the EDI. I shared many moments of reflections on Zambia's development with Sarchar A. Khan, Uche Mbanefo, Kingsley Amoako, Lawrence Clarke, and Kapil Kapooron the World Bank's assistance to Zambia.

In 1988, I assisted John Mupanga Mwanakatwe to produce Zambia's input into the 1989 World Bank's Study on "Sub-Saharan Africa – from Crisis to Sustainable Growth With Equity – A Long-Term Perspective". In 2003, I co-opted Joseph Kakozaand Ohene Owusu Nyanin, the current IMF and World Bank Country Representatives, respectively into our review meetings. After all, they were the main judges of Zambia's performance in economic management.

My trip to Washington DC in June 2003 and my meetings there enabled me to reactivate and establish easy lines of communication to the officers of the IMF and World Bank, the two most influential and important financial institutions in the world. I received a letter from James D. Wolfensohn, President of the World Bank on my appointment stating that "Congratulations on your appointment and thank you for your willingness to take on this additional responsibility", signaling the Bank management's willingness to cooperate.

The IMF Mission that visited Zambia in June 2003 insisted that they be allowed to meet the NGO community without the presence of any Government officers, a request I resisted, but finally approved. Unfortunately, the media reports quoting those who attended the meeting were critical of the IMF.

The desire by the IMF team to interact directly on national issues with the NGOs outside the government structure had backfired. This was the last time the IMF officials tried to dictate the format of their discussions in Zambia. From then on, they allowed me to take control of the processes and to repair the damaged relations.

Zambia reached the Decision Point for the enhanced HIPC Initiative in December 2000. This was after the Zambian Government had convinced the ADB, IMF, World Bank, and the international community that Zambia was so poor and indebted that it could not repay its foreign debts. The accumulated debt had risen to US $7.2 billion by 2003, with a debt service of nearly US $400 million per year.

By 27 July 2003, the IMF team was satisfied with our draft LoI, which was a result of intense Cabinet discussions. Zambia was put on a Staff Monitoring Programme, which required performance assessments every three months.

The most critical benchmark to observe to ensure that Zambia reached the HIPC Initiative Completion Point by the end of 2004 was to maintain a stable macroeconomic environment, evidenced by satisfactory performance under a programme supported by a PRGF arrangement.

Due to the high level of coordination and cooperation amongst the stakeholders, we easily met the conditions of the SMP and qualified for a new PRGF.

After an assessment early in 2005, we received confirmation in April that the World Bank and IMF Boards had approved Zambia's satisfactory execution of the benchmarks in fulfillment of the HIPC Initiative. The performance restored Zambia's respectability in the international financial community.

Having realized how far the country had veered off the development path, I advised President Mwanawasa to concentrate on economic matters and to reduce the time spent on political issues. I also requested the World Bank to upscale funding on workshops for journalists on financial and economic reporting, so that the Zambians were correctly informed of the many developments in the economy.

During the April 2005 Spring Meetings of the IMF/World Bank Group, my delegation had discussions with Gobind Nankani, VP for Africa at the World Bank and Peter Ngumbullu, Executive Director at the IMF.

On Wednesday 27 July 2005, the Deputy Managing Director (DMD) of the IMF, Takatoshi Kato arrived in Zambia for an official visit. In the afternoon, he paid a courtesy call on President Mwanawasa. On 28 July, I accompanied the DMD to a breakfast meeting with the donors and to other meetings with the economic ministers, chairpersons of parliamentary committees and the members of civil society. We then visited Kwasha Mukwenu, a women's club in Matero Township. The DMD visited some rural projects in Mazabuka the following day, before holding a press briefing on his trip.

At all these open meetings, the participants were free to express themselves on any economic issues in the presence of the officials of my Ministry. The DMD mentioned that in the IMF's assessment, Zambia was back on the right track. He hoped that prudent fiscal policy and economic management would be entrenched for the country to benefit from debt relief and reduce the high levels of poverty. The DMD proved that there was indeed participatory management of the State's economic affairs as promised by President Mwanawasa during his 2003 discussions at the IMF Head Office.

During the 2005 Annual Meetings of the IMF/World Bank in September, we met the senior management of both the IMF and World Bank. In all the special committees we attended, we were invited to give briefs on the HIPC programme and got a lot of praise for prudent financial management and unprecedented economic performance. Zambia was once more visible in the international financial arena.

I was among the five African Ministers of Finance who met with the Secretary of the Treasury of the USA Government, who encouraged us to continue our fiscal discipline and prudent financial management.

Gobind Nankani, WB Vice President informed us that because of the achievement, Zambia was upgraded to middle case status under the IDA. This meant that the country would get more concessional funding. He requested that we host the 2006 World Bank Regional Consultations to be attended by over one hundred Bank officers based in Africa. We accepted to host the meeting as it was a great mark of recognition by the World Bank.

In between the meetings, we found the time and negotiated a loan from the Arab Bank for Economic Development in Africa (BADEA) for feeder roads in the Copperbelt Province and township water supplies in the Central Province. We also negotiated an International Development Association (IDA) credit for malaria control. We held discussions with officers from the Friends of Zambia and MCA and participated in workshops for the youth and civil society, in which Zambia had a strong representation.

I was in Washington DC in December 2005 as a representative of the beneficiaries of the African Development Fund (AfDF) to consider the application of the new MDRI. At a working lunch with Francesco Caramazza and David Andrews, the IMF officers responsible for Zambia, we analyzed Zambia's situation using the agreed new formula. This showed that Zambia's debt would be reduced from US $7.2 billion to US $502 million if all Paris Club members honoured the agreement of May 2005.

The officers informed me that because of the prudent fiscal and monetary management by the Zambian Government, the IMF Managing Director Mr Rato also wished to visit Zambia for an on-the-spot appreciation of the situation. We scheduled the visit of the Managing Director for March 2006.

The World Bank Vice President for the Africa Region, Nankani arrived in the country on Wednesday, 1 February 2006 in time to witness the presentation of the budget on 3 February. He paid a courtesy call on the President and also attended some of the budget discussion meetings by the professional bodies.

My work at these meetings was less onerous as the economy was showing an upward trend in growth and this was positively impacting the middle class. The World Bank 2006 Consultations for Africa were successfully held in Lusaka. The last visit of a senior World Bank official to Zambia was on 10 February 1992 by Lewis Preston, the President. I was then among the few selected Zambians who had taken part in lunch discussions on the state of the Zambian economy with the dignitary at the Lilayi Lodge.

On Wednesday, 15 March 2006, Mr Rodrigo de Rato, Managing Director (MD) of the International Monetary Fund arrived in Zambia. Rato's visit coincided with a roundtable of finance ministers, parliamentarians, civil society representatives and journalists from Ethiopia, Ghana, Malawi, Mozambique, Tanzania, Uganda, and Zambia, which I chaired. The focus of the roundtable discussions were the challenges that these countries would face in making use of donor resources, especially after the 100 per cent debt relief extended by the Fund under the MRDI.

It was a great honour for me as the host to take the MD of the IMF to State House for a courtesy call on President Mwanawasa. Our engagement with the IMF had matured and had been accorded due recognition. It was most encouraging to hear the MD report to the President that Zambia had pursued a strategy of promoting macroeconomic stability and good public sector management, which had resulted in sound growth of the financial and private sectors.

The MD went further to say that the IMF gladly supported these efforts due to the evidence of determination by the financial managers to achieve the Millennium Development Goals. The MD visited the Kasisi Orphanage in Chongwe District to appreciate some of the problems in the social sector.

While in Washington DC for the 2006 Spring Meetings in April, our delegation was kept busy with engagements with the IMF and World Bank officials and other participating countries. We had meetings with the MD of the IMF, the Vice President of the World Bank, and the Deputy Assistant Secretary of the Treasury in the USA Government.

It became routine for me to hold meetings with the senior officials of the Bretton Woods Institutions. These occasions facilitated my receiving appropriate advice on public finance management issues. The visits to Zambia by the MD of the IMF and the Vice President of the World Bank signalled the re-establishment of the highest level of cooperation between the Zambian Government and the managers of the Bretton Woods Institutions.

In fact, the IMF management's trust of the Zambian Government reached such a high level that decisions by the Executive Board of the IMF on issues concerning Zambia were made on the basis of the 'lapse of time' procedure. This procedure reduces the cost of governors' decision-making process as members cast votes on issues by individual communication to the secretary of the board without holding a formal meeting.

Zambia fails to benefit from regional integration

The Zambian Government under President Kenneth Kaunda had been a strong advocate of regional integration and cooperation since Independence in 1964. KK strongly believed that the countries of the southern Africa region would enjoy the fruits of independence and assist those still fighting only through collective and collaborative efforts.

In pursuance of this policy, the Zambian Government was active in the conceptualization, establishment and operationalization of the regional economic units of the Southern Africa Development Coordination Conference (SADCC) and the Preferential Trade Area (PTA) for Eastern and Southern Africa as springboards for partnership during and after the liberation wars. President Kaunda galvanized the Zambians to take calculated risks, which cost the country billions of dollars and many lives of Zambians.

The PTA, based in Zambia, became the Common Market for Eastern and Southern Africa (COMESA) in 1994. In 1992, SADCC, based in Botswana, was transformed into the Southern Africa Development Community (SADC) with a different set of objectives elaborated in the Windhoek Declaration. Development of adequate hard infrastructure was emphasized by both COMESA and SADC as the logical means to improving production and regional trade. I was a member of the Zambian teams of technicians that gave support to the politicians as they elaborated upon the aims of the various regional integration organizations in the seventies.

The theme of the 1992 SADCC Annual Conference of 'Towards Economic Integration' provided a policy framework for 'SADCC to become an effective instrument of economic transformation and integration'. Some eight years later, the organization had not achieved much towards economic independence and integration.

I prepared a comprehensive brief on the strategic operations of the EU as a regional integrated unit to present to the 1999 SADC Summit. Having been nominated by SADC, I regarded it my obligation to brief my sponsoring organization on my assignment. In spite of the acknowledgement by the Summit that "the basis for cooperation between the ACP and EU countries since 1975 comes to an end in February 2000, and that negotiations are in progress", I was not given space to address the SADC Summit on the EU operations, the EU-ACP negotiations, or on my personal achievements at the ACP Secretariat.

For over three years I supervised the relations between the ACP States and the EU, the most successful regional integration effort in the world. I hosted and advised senior officials of the Regional Economic Units whenever they visited Brussels for discussions and negotiations with the EU. I expected that the SADC being a beneficiary of substantial EU technical assistance had moved a long way towards fulfilling the Windhoek Declaration.

The democratization of South Africa in 1994 seemed to have reduced the vibrancy of the SADC. As the decentralization of sector responsibilities to member countries did not work, a decision was made to centralize the secretariat staff at the headquarters in Botswana. Apart from the change of name to Southern Africa Development Community and the proclamation of twenty-seven protocols, no visible infrastructure had been developed.

Having been in the technical committees during the early life of SADC, it was now a privilege for me to be a member of the Council of Ministers, which supervises the Secretariat. In early August 2003, I attended a meeting of SADC Ministers of Finance in Gaborone, Botswana. I had productive private discussions with Mr Trevor Manuel, Minister of Finance for South Africa, on Zambia's relationship with the BrettonWoods Institutions. South Africa as a member of the Development Committee of the IMF had influence in making some of the decisions on countries in the region. I asked the Minister to intercede on behalf of Zambia during discussions in the closed-door committee meetings.

During the ministerial meeting in Gaborone, I was reminded of the SADC macroeconomic convergence benchmarks and the SADC Trade Protocol and that Zambia had not taken action to implement these instruments of integration. I had completed a consultancy study on the relations between the African Union (AU) and the Regional Economic Communities (RECs). SADC was one of the nine RECs spread all over Africa working towards the African Common Market through regional economic integration. During my consultancy, I took time to read a lot of literature on all the RECs and the African Union.

It is a common understanding that regional integration requires the convergence of macroeconomic benchmarks of inflation, budget deficits, public debt, current account, and GDP growth. Zambia's macroeconomic parameters were far from those of the integration targets and the country was behind in the implementation of tariff reduction on items on Schedule 'B' of the Trade Protocol.

In the 2004 budget, action was taken to reduce tariffs towards the SADC Customs Union in 2012. By 2006, Zambia was on the way to meeting most of the targets on the Macroeconomic Convergence Parameters. However, I was not happy with the performance of SADC in the area of infrastructure. My push to make the Kazungula Bridge, an essential link in regional trade, a SADC project did not succeed and the vital project was overly delayed.

By 2007, I threatened to stop attending SADC Ministers' meetings as there was no evidence of a willingness to implement any infrastructure projects beneficial to Zambia. Zambia was singularly bearing the high cost of repairing roads that were being run down by the increased traffic of inter-regional trade amongst the COMESA and SADC member states.

Zambia did not receive any funds under the trade and integration compensation mechanisms established by the two regional bodies during my tenure of office at the Ministry of Finance. Dual membership to COMESA and SADC was a cost to Zambia as both became more interested in soft infrastructure issues of trade processes and procedures, instead of hard infrastructure. In spite of the necessity for infrastructure in regional integration, COMESA only established an underfunded Infrastructure Fund in 2008.

One of the founding objectives of SADC was economic integration and socio-economic cooperation. The initial structure of the secretariat with decentralized country sector responsibilities was to implement spatial production and encourage trade liberalisation within the region. COMESA and SADC would continue to be works-in-progress in terms of trade liberalisation and economic integration unless the secretariats have constitutional powers to override members' political powers and sovereignty. Most of the members in the two regional bodies have been independent for relatively short periods. It will take a long time for them to cede power to the secretariats as they still want to enjoy some rights under the subsidiarity principle.

In spite of President Kaunda spending a lot of time and Zambian human and financial resources in midwifing many intergovernmental political and economic organizations, Zambians cannot count on any tangible benefits. While the few of us who led international organisations such as the ADB, ACP, ARIPO, and the International Conference on the Great Lakes Region (ICGLR) displayed exemplary management skills, it has not been easy to get Zambians in senior positions in the regional integration units. Negotiations for more positions were made more difficulty, at times, by President Kaunda, who was most accommodating to the demands of other member countries in the region.

Once, Zambia had to give up the right to provide a governor on the board of an international organisation to a country, which had less than one percent of shares against Zambia's five percent. While the president's patronizing attitude was good politics, it was not beneficial to the country and it weakened the institutions as some managements did not provide experienced, strong and effective leadership.

The Commonwealth and MEFMI Relations with Zambia

The Commonwealth is a voluntary institution that brings together the United Kingdom and its former colonies to share experiences in social and economic management. The ZIBAC Forum provided an opportunity for the Zambian public and private officials to learn about what was happening in the other countries of the Commonwealth. While at the ACP Secretariat, I shared ideas with the former Commonwealth Secretary General Chief Emeka Anyaoku, who commissioned a high-powered team that produced an informative report on Post-Lome IV arrangements.

At the request of President Mwanawasa and with the support from the United Kingdom Department for International Development (DFID) and other donors, the Commonwealth Business Council provided assistance for the establishment and operations of the Zambia International Business Advisory Council (ZIBAC).

The Council was set up to provide international business perspectives on policies and practical measures to help strengthen and smoothen the investment climate and business environment in Zambia.

In September 2003, I attended the 2nd Zambia International Business Advisory Council meeting in Livingstone, Southern Province. In fact, for this particular meeting, the Government Ministers and private sector leaders travelled together in one bus from Lusaka to Livingstone. This provided for open discussions on a number of subjects all the way to Livingstone Town.

Being knowledgeable of the countryside, I played the role of a travel guide, pointing out landmarks on the route, including projects such as Kaleya Outgrowers' Scheme, Magoye Settlement Scheme, and Batoka Ranch, which I had participated in planning during my youth. The attractions included the Munali Pass, the 16,000-hectare Nakambala Sugar Estates, the Choma Museum, and the Kalomo Mound. I was delighted that many leaders appreciated and became aware of the many tourist attractions between Lusaka and Livingstone.

On 11 September 2003, I led a delegation to Dubai for the IMF/World Bank Group Annual Meetings. On the way, we attended the Commonwealth Ministers of Finance meeting in Brunei. During the meeting, I and the new Minister of Finance for Nigeria, Mrs Ngozi Okonjo-Iweala, a former senior executive of the World Bank, brought some fresh thinking and contributions on a number of issues.

As a new member of the club, I had a lot to learn from some of the long-serving ministers. However, it was the newcomers who made the greatest impact at the African Finance Ministers' Press Conference during the Dubai IMF/World Bank Meetings. I presume that since we were new, we were not inhibited by protocol and expressed our views on various issues in a candid manner.

A new Malawian Minister of Finance, Goodall Gondwe, a former head of the IMF Africa Department was appointed in 2004. Gondwe was the Acting President of the ADB in 1980, who corresponded with Chikwanda on my recruitment by the ADB. We became very close associates and shared many ideas and programmes. Gondwe adopted Zambia's fertiliser support programme and perfected it, making Malawi a model country in food security, which won the Malawian President an international medal.

364

In 2005, Gondwe, Ngozi and I were joined by Kwadwo Baah-Wiredu, Minister of Finance for Ghana as the indomitable quartet that became the voice of Sub-Saharan Africa. The foursome influenced many decisions made in the global financial debates on Sub-Saharan African countries for five years. Among the topical issues we effectively coordinated were those of debt and donor support.

I became an effective contributor during the debates of the Commonwealth Finance Ministers meetings. During the 2004 meetings held in St. Kitts and Nevis in the Caribbean in September 2004, I moved a Vote of Thanks to Prime Minister Denzil Douglas' opening speech.

I chaired the Macroeconomic and Financial Management Institute of Eastern and Southern African (MEFMI) Finance Ministers' Forum during my tenure as minister. Before joining the Zambian Government, when I was a regular lecturer at the MEFMI in Harare, Zimbabwe, I became familiar with the Institute's mission in capacity building for staff of financial and monetary organizations. I used the prior knowledge to advise the institution on its operations and policies.

In 2005 I attended the MEFMI Finance Ministers' Forum and the Commonwealth Finance Ministers' Annual Meetings in Bridgetown, Barbados. The meetings for the two organizations were usually held concurrently and back-to-back with the annual meetings of the IMF and World Bank to save money.

On arrival in Bridgetown, I was informed that I will be a discussant on a presentation by Professor Jeffrey Sachs during the Conference on the implementation of the Millennium Development Goals (MDGs). Sachs a renowned development economist was at the time Advisor to the UN Secretary General Kofi Annan.

The Commonwealth Finance Ministers discussed the progress on the implementation of the MDGs. The climax was the presentation by Prof Sachs, which unfortunately had to be done through teleconference as poor weather in the region prohibited all flights. My concise intervention on the debate on MDGs, trade and aid injected a lot of new insights and optimism. Professor Sachs was also an optimist who advocated that with additional finances, good management, and proper focus, the MDGs could be attained by many countries within the timeline. I was greatly honoured to share an international platform to discuss the MDGs with one of the gurus on development.

The ministers' deliberations focused on challenges for Africa on migration, remittances, and development. The overall conclusion was that African Governments must create an enabling environment for their nationals in the diaspora to migrate back or send their surplus funds for investments in their countries. We admitted that so far, Africa was on the losing end as most educated Africans preferred to work in developed countries instead of returning home after their studies. Lack of educated Africans, who could improve the management systems exacerbated the poor environment.

At the time, Zambia had a serious problem with migration of health personnel to Europe and the matter had been presented at a World Health Organization (WHO) conference. A project proposal was prepared suggesting that the beneficiary developed countries should assist in expanding Zambian training facilities for health personnel. Many participants at the Commonwealth meeting showed great interest in the Zambian project proposal.

During the MEFMI Forum, Zambia was elected Chair of the MEFMI based in Harare, Zimbabwe for a period of twelve months. Coincidentally, Ephraim Chungwe Kaunga, Director of Programs from Zambia was appointed to act as the Executive Director for the Institute in view of the departure of the previous head whose contract had expired.

In September 2005, during the deliberations of the Commonwealth HIPC Forum, I explained Zambia's journey through the fifteen benchmarks up to the Completion Point and the future plans on the usage of the savings from the debt write-off. At the conclusion of the meeting, Zambia was elected Chair of the Commonwealth HIPC Forum and we were asked to host the following year's Forum meeting. The 2006 HIPC Forum meeting was successfully held in Livingstone, Zambia between 7 and 12 April 2006.

By 2006, Zambia had established good relations with the Commonwealth and MEFMI Secretariats and was honoured by leading the two organizations during the same period. The Ministry of Finance and National Planning seconded an officer to the Commonwealth Secretariat on request and Zambia benefitted from the offer of legal assistance during the vulture fund case. I was pleased when Caleb Fundanga, former governor of the Bank of Zambia and a member of my economic team, was appointed Executive Director of MEFMI in 2014, providing an opportunity to continue flying Zambia's flag high.

Resolving an election impasse at the African Export and Import Bank
In August 2004, I attended the Annual General Meeting of the African Export and Import Bank (Afrexim Bank) in Abidjan, Cote d'Ivoire. My main assignment was to hand over the chairmanship of the Bank, which Zambia assumed at the 2003 Annual Meetings held in Zambia in May 2003 just before I was appointed Minister.

At the Abidjan meeting, a serious governance issue on the appointment of a new president arose and I was called upon to resolve the impasse before relinquishing the Chairmanship.

Although all recruitment procedures had been followed, Egypt the host country of the Bank insisted that their candidate was not treated fairly. However, the governors stuck to the unwritten equity rule that the hosting country shall not also provide the president of the institution. This was made at the inception of the bank in order to allow for the sharing of the benefits of the institution and hence cement cooperation amongst the shareholders.

After a protracted debate concluded late in the night, the matter was resolved. Jean-Louis Ekra, the candidate who scored the highest points during the interviews was adopted as the new president of the Bank. I then handed over the Chairmanship of the Bank to my counterpart from Cote d'Ivoire. The new president was later sworn-in and took over from the founding president, Christopher Chuka Edordu. Ekra, ably steered the Bank on a successful path for ten years until September 2015, when he gracefully retired.

During the celebrations of the 20th anniversary of the Bank in June 2013 in Addis Ababa, Ethiopia, I was among the eminent persons who were invited to the joyous occasion by president Ekra. The invitation to me was in recognition of "the stellar role you played in providing tremendous support in your capacity as Chairman of the General Meeting at the height of the shareholder dispute of the Bank".

I was requested to share with the audience my experiences and assessment of the Bank's performance in the context of the vision of its founding fathers and opine on the future prospects of the Bank. My presentation made the young people aware of the vision and pioneering effort of the founding fathers of the bank.

I was privileged to share the podium with His Excellency General Olusegun Obasanjo, former President of Nigeria, who reminded me of his visit to Zambia in 2003. Other luminaries were Ode Ojowu, a technocrat in the Nigerian Ministry of Finance in 1993, Babacar Ndiaye, founder of the Afrexim Bank and former President of the AfDB, who had conceptualized the bank. Christopher Chuka Edordu, pioneer President of the Bank and current Chairman of the Board wrote in my copy of the 20th Anniversary book that, 'Many thanks for your role in the Bank'.

Following on the warm relations between the Afrexim Bank and Zambia, the country hosted the 22nd Annual General Meetings in June 2015 in Lusaka Zambia at which President Ekra bade farewell.

"The choice of Zambia as host country for this year's Annual General Meeting is not by accident. It was based on the strong working relationship which exists between Afrexim Bank and Zambia. Afrexim Bank greatly values its partnership with Zambia and the Government of Zambia's continued support for the Bank's operations and activities in this country", stated the outgoing President Ekra during the 22nd Annual General Meeting hosted by Zambia in June 2014. I did not attend the meeting in Lusaka, as I was not invited by the host Zambian authorities.

Department for International Development of the UK Government
While I was at the ACP Secretariat towards the end of the 20th Century, I worked closely with Briton Philip Lowe, Director General for Development in the European Commission. The Director General introduced me to the staff

of the Department for International Development (DFID) of the United Kingdom, amongst them the Secretary of State, The Right Honourable Clare Short and Director Mark Lowcock

The United Kingdom had been an influential member of the ACP-EU community since joining the grouping in 1973 along with a large number of its former colonies. In July 1999, Clare Short presented a report at the ACP Secretariat on the role of the new European Commission in international development in support of a post-Lome IV agreement. A new Commission had just been appointed after the resignation of the previous one due to perceived corruption. The DFID played a supportive role to the ACP Group, leading to the successful conclusion of the ACP-EU negotiations.

Since the UK was one of the three largest aid donors to Zambia, I made early contacts with Hellen Mealins, Head of the DFID office in Zambia to discuss a wide range of developmental issues including public sector reforms. In September 2004, the British High Commission arranged a tour for me of relevant institutions in Her Majesty's Government in London on my way to the Caribbean for the Commonwealth Finance Ministers' Meeting. I had discussions with Honourable Hilary Benn, the Secretary of State for International Development and with Honourable Christopher Mullin at the Foreign and Commonwealth Office.

I also held discussions with the officials at the Bank of England, the Treasury, and the National Audit Office (NAO). The discussions at the NAO were very educative as they included systems and procedures for the auditing of security institutions including the military. Zambia's security wings had not been subjected to audits for a long time.

I took the opportunity to discuss the possibility of a novel project on public service reform. My feeling was that we needed a programme that could focus on re-orienting the civil service to a specific mission with clear codes of conduct and identifiable goals. My idea was further discussed during the meetings of the Zambia International Business Advisory Council (ZIBAC).

Lord Simon Cairns, the Co-Chairman of ZIBAC and Lord Andrew Turnbull, a former Secretary to the Cabinet of the United Kingdom Government, who served in Zambia as an ODI Fellow in 1968, were assigned to help in further developing the project. The proposal was incorporated in the Triangle of Hope (ToH) under Civil Service Reorientation for Efficiency and Integrity. This was under a ToH Committee chaired by Jack Kalala, Special Assistant to the President for Project Monitoring and Implementation.

Later in 2007, I signed a partnership agreement with the DIFD, whose major thrust was financial support to Zambia's Parliament. The main objective of the support was to create a Representative, Responsive, Efficient, Effective, Accountable, Accessible and Linked (REAL) Parliament.

Denmark promises to open up Zambia's western corridor

A few weeks after my arrival at the Ministry of Finance and National Planning, I was visited by the outgoing Danish Ambassador to Zambia on 24 July 2003 to bid me farewell. The ambassador explained his country's assistance to Zambia, most of which was concentrated in the Western Province. He informed me of his frustrations on the failure of many of the projects funded by Denmark to reduce poverty of the Zambians.

I was concerned to hear the depressing story from an ambassador of a developed country that was among the few generous providers of development aid that long surpassed the threshold of 0.7 per cent of Gross National Income (GNI) set by the United Nations. The fact that Zambia was not making good use of the grant funds from Denmark was not encouraging. I informed the ambassador of the 1978 efforts and assured him that I was also very interested in tackling the high poverty levels in the Western Province since it had great potential in agricultural development.

There and then, the Danish ambassador offered US $10 million for any project in cattle production in the Western Province. The 'farewell gift' was transferred to the Ministry of Finance and National Planning before the ambassador left Zambia.

I discussed the use of the money with Mundia Sikatana, the Minister of Agriculture, who was excited about the prospects of increasing the cattle herd in his home province. I then contacted George Akafekwa, retired expert veterinarian, whom I introduced to the Minister. As a cattle farmer, I had heard of many stories of misapplication and misappropriation of donor funds meant for livestock development in Zambia and I wanted the private sector to get involved in the project.

The planned cattle development project included the reconstruction of the legendary cordon line between Angola and Zambia. The civil servants rejected the idea of involving the private veterinarians. The project implementation became a subject of an audit query as the bush seemed to have regenerated fast making the cordon line invisible to the auditors! I then appreciated and shared the frustrations of the former Danish Ambassador.

In December 2004, Denmark hosted and chaired the negotiations for the Tenth Replenishment of the African Development Fund (AfDF) between the ADF Deputies and a team of African Finance Ministers.

The discussions under the Chairmanship of Sven Sandstorm, a former MD of the World Bank, were very successful. My interventions as a spokesperson for the beneficiaries were assisted by the guidance of the Chairman, whom I knew way back when he was at the World Bank.

The honour of being a spokesperson was spiced up by the privilege of sitting next to Ole Moesby, the Undersecretary for Multilateral Development. I used the rare opportunity to learn as much as possible on the 'How' of development in a developed mixed economy applying the flexicurity model of development, which combines a flexible labour market allowing easy hiring and firing, generous social safety net and an active labour-market policy with rights and obligations for the unemployed.

I established warm relations with the new Danish Ambassador to Zambia, Orla Bakdal as I assured him of strict accountability for all Danish development aid. Our discussions resulted in the offer of substantial funding for projects in various sectors of the Zambian economy.

In March 2007, the Danish Minister for Development Cooperation, Ulla Pedersen Tornaes visited Zambia. At the end of the Minister's visit, we were informed that Denmark was prepared to provide funds for the construction of a modern bituminous road and bridges from Kasempa in the North-Western Province through Kaoma, Mongu, and Senanga to Katima Mulilo in south-Western Province. The road was to facilitate the easy and quick transportation of minerals from the new mines in the North-Western Province and reduce the load on the old road from the Copperbelt to the southern border.

The Danish Ambassador reflected on the Minister's trip in a letter to me as follows: "The analyses and information you shared with her were very fruitful and constructive. Several times during my Minister's continued stay in Zambia, she referred to her conversation with you. Once again, thank you for contributing to making my Minister's visit to Zambia a huge success. I trust that it has contributed to strengthening our good bilateral relations even further".

Circling the Cuban Ceiba tree for good luck

Cuba made overtures to join the African Caribbean and Pacific Group of States when I was the Secretary General in 1999. I was privileged to meet Cuban senior officials with whom I discussed the economic and social status of the country before I supported the request and made a recommendation to the Committee of Ambassadors. Cuba was admitted into the ACP Group on 14 December 2000, a few months after I left the ACP Secretariat.

On Monday, 17 April 2006, I led a Zambian delegation to Cuba for the Joint Economic Commission meeting. Our delegation was taken on an extensive tour of various industries, research, and training institutions. We were surprised and impressed with the island's high level of development against the background of long-standing sanctions imposed after the 1961 missile crisis by the USA. Our bilateral discussions focused on technical assistance in the agricultural and health sectors in which Cuba had a world reputation.

Cuba had eliminated malaria through biological control. The malaria-carrying Anopheles mosquito had been made impotent and was unable to produce the parasite that causes malaria. I signed a Memorandum of Understanding requesting research on malaria and the resumption of the supply of medical personnel to Zambia.

During our stay in Havana, we were taken to a number of historical tourist attractions. I joined a long queue of curious tourists to walk three times around the legendary ceiba tree while mentioning three wishes and making an offering. Since the wishes are not written in advance, I do not even remember any one of them, except that I have a belief that some have been fulfilled. After all in Hebrews 11 verse 1, it is written that 'Faith is the substance of things hoped for, the evidence of things not seen'.

Our next stopover was Washington DC in the USA for the Spring Meetings of the IMF/World Bank. We could not fly directly to the USA and we were advised by the Cuban Customs officers not to carry anything made in Cuba into the USA because of the USA embargo. Any items made in Cuba were confiscated by the USA customs service. We overloaded one officer who took a flight that did not pass through the USA with our souvenirs, which included the famous Cuban Cohiba cigars.

European Union Relations with Zambia

During the seventies, I worked closely with Charles Brooks of the EEC office in Zambia and the country benefitted greatly from grant funding for a number of agricultural projects. Having served as Secretary General of the ACP Group in Brussels, Belgium during the last decade of the 20th Century, I found it easy to establish a cordial working relationship with the Delegation of the EU in Zambia.

After my return to Zambia in 2000, the EU Delegation Office under Jochen Krebs extended the protocol I had enjoyed in Brussels as a high profile diplomat by inviting me to meetings and social functions, where I interacted with the diplomatic community.

I benefitted greatly from information from the EU on the political situation in Zambia. During the 2001 general elections, I was in close contact with the EU Observer Mission on behalf of the UPND.

As a private consultant, I was a facilitator at workshops discussing the ACP-EU Cooperation under the Cotonou Agreement. During one of the workshops on Public-Private Dialogue/Institutional Reform and Capacity Building, I was critical of lack of private/public dialogue. The resolution of the workshop on this matter led to the formation of institutions and formal structures for dialogue between the Zambian Government and the Zambian private sector.

As Minister of Finance, I became the National Authorizing Officer responsible for supervising the preparation and implementation of the National Indicative Programme (NIP) and the Country Strategy Paper (CSP) supported financially by the EU. The responsibility included making funding requests to the EU for all the sectors. Through the earlier consultancies, I was already aware of the selection of the transport sector as the country's focal sector for the 380 million Euros under the 10th European Development Fund (EDF).

Applying my immense knowledge of the ACP/EU procedures, I made early requests for funding of projects in the focal sector under the Zambia-EC Country Strategy Paper. In 2003 and 2004, President Mwanawasa commissioned the Monze-Zimba Road and the Kabwe-Kapiri Mposhi Road both funded by the EU. Our request to use the balance of the money on the Kabwe road for the Zimba-Livingstone Road was granted and the road was worked upon. The EU gave Zambia a grant to extend the Livingstone Airport from 2.3 to 3.0 kilometres in order for it to accept bigger aircraft.

Due to the improved democratic and public finance management systems, respect for human rights and gender, reduced levels of corruption and good governance in general, the EU allocated an additional amount of ninety-six million Euros as an 'incentive tranche' to the Zambian Government in 2007.

I enjoyed close personal relationships with Their Excellencies, EU Delegates Jochen Krebs, Henry Sprietsma, and Derrick Fee and translated this into a benefit for Zambia. The EU was the first Cooperating Partner to adopt the Direct Budget Support (DBS), which made it the 'leader' donor under the JASZ. The Netherlands, United Kingdom (DFID), and World Bank soon followed suit.

The DBS form of aid funding is highly dependent upon the trust and confidence of the donor in the integrity of the managers of public finance in the recipient country. The Ministry officials had demonstrated a capacity to adhere to the tough and numerous performance indicators and targets, which were assessed at regular intervals.

The United Nations System

The choice of 24 October as Zambia's Independence day signalled the strong belief by Kenneth Kaunda in the principles of the United Nations (UN). The UN was formed on 24th October 1945, while Zambia was born on 24 October 1964. The UN system was a very important Cooperating Partner in a number of projects in the social sectors and governance issues of the country.

My consultancy work with the UNDP in 2001 and 2002 on the UNDAF and the UNDP Country Programme under the first Country Cooperation Framework (CCF) provided me with the opportunity to know the structure and operations of the UN System and its support programmes in Zambia. I established close and cordial working relations with Mrs Olubanke King-Akerele, UN Resident Coordinator and UNDP Country Resident Representative, who was a passionate advocate of self-empowerment and leadership.

King-Akerele became the Minister of Commerce and Industry and later Foreign Affairs once her war-torn country Liberia achieved peace under a democratically elected government led by Ellen Johnson Sirleaf, the first elected female Head of State in Africa. Due to her concern for Africa's emergent and future leadership, King-Akerele created a board game called

'Growing Africa's Leadership'.

The adoption by the UNDP of the Human Development Index (HDI) devised by Mahbubul Haq, the Pakistan economist in 1990, shifted emphasis from national income accounting to people-centred policies. The Human Development Indices capture life expectancy, education, and income per capita as the most important aspects of human achievement and development.

The Zambian Government subjected itself to an annual assessment and prepared a Zambia National Human Development Report (ZNHDR) in collaboration with the UNDP and other stakeholders. The report helped in refocusing public financial resources towards human development priorities.

The UNDP helped to galvanize the cooperating partners to offer effective support to the Zambian National Assembly and to the electoral systems and processes. The country managed to implement a multi-sectoral response to HIV and AIDS with the continued support of the UNDP and its partners in capacity development.

Aeneas Chuma, the Zimbabwean UNDP Coordinator during the latter part of my term at the Ministry of Finance and National Planning became a friend and confidant with whom I shared a lot of ideas on governance issues. During this period, we saw much change in the aid architecture and in the renewal of the mission of the United Nations' presence in Zambia. Chuma used his diplomatic skills to achieve synergy amongst the development partners.

On 10 March 2004, I met the Administrator of the United Nations Development Program (UNDP), Mark Malloch Brown, the third highest-ranking official in the United Nations System, over a breakfast in Lusaka. Brown was the lead participant in the team that devised the UN's Millennium Development Goals (MDGs) of 2000.

During his visit to Zambia, the Administrator was accompanied by Roland Msiska, UNDP Director for the Southern Africa Capacity Initiative as I had intimated my desire to discuss ICT as a capacity facilitation tool for improved education. I was accompanied by Allan Mulenga, Minister of Education to the breakfast discussions.

Our discussions with the Administrator were focused on improving Zambia's education system by introducing and popularizing e-learning using information technology (IT). E-learning is an IT tool available to educators to make the curriculum for any subject any time and at any place. The program supplements existing classroom work and the mix can vary depending upon the environment.

The problems of lack of teachers in rural Zambian schools such as Siangombo and Namaila Schools resulted in inadequate preparations of the pupils who ended up failing in the examinations. Teachers posted to these remote schools abandoned the schools for lack of social facilities. I believed that the problem could be resolved by the use of solar power for computers for teaching and for social services by a few highly skilled and motivated teachers.

The Administrator was keen to assist the country to implement a pilot project in a few selected schools in remote rural areas of Zambia. Unfortunately, the Minister of Education was not a disciple of ICT. To my utter shame, he told our guest that many of my development ideas, including the one on e-learning, were for the 23rd Century and not for the present as he himself was still grappling to understand the innovations of the 19th Century!

The school computerization programme, which would have seen the introduction of computer tools in most of the Zambian schools by 2008, did not take-off as the Ministry of Education did not follow-up our discussions with the UNDP Administrator. All the same, I was glad that I had succeeded in getting to Zambia the number two official of the United Nations dealing with development issues. Brown was appointed Minister in 2007 by British Prime Minister Gordon Brown. In 2008, he represented the British Government at the funeral of late President Mwanawasa and found time to visit my office for some intimate conversation.

International Fund for Agricultural Development

As a farmer, I was interested in the UN organization's dealings with the agricultural issues, in particular, those impacting on small-scale farmers. In 2000, I was a member of a team of consultants under Kane Consult Limited that undertook a post evaluation of the US $300 million Agricultural Sector Investment Project (ASIP). From our findings, it was obvious that the project had not attained the intended goals. Due to the poor results, the donor community decided to boycott funding of the agricultural sector in Zambia ommunity decided to boycott funding of the agricultural sector in Zambia. I used the World Bank officers to lobby the other donors to resume financing of the sector.

Investigations revealed that the International Fund for Agricultural Development (IFAD), a specialized UN organization based in Rome, had just completed writing its Country Strategic Opportunities Paper (CSOP) for the period 2004 to 2007.

I was familiar with the institution as I had taken part in discussions on its establishment and special mandate in the seventies. In 1981, I took part in negotiating the first loan from IFAD to Zambia for the Eastern Province Agricultural Development Project. It was therefore easy for me to engage in meaningful discussions on the role of IFAD in Zambia.

Our discussions at the Ministry of Finance and National Planning were directed at finding a productive role for IFAD in developing accessible rural financial services. During the review of the CSOP completed in October 2004, we identified the National Savings and Credit Bank (NATSAVE) as a participant on behalf of the Government under the Rural Finance Expansion Project (RFEP) implemented between 2004 and 2010. The IFAD committed a concessional loan of US $13.8 million to facilitate the computerization and expansion of the bank's branch network.

I feel proud that the RFEP Project has been successfully executed by the Project Unit based in the Ministry of Finance under the leadership of Mike Mbulo. The project has facilitated the provision of banking services by NATSAVE in the remote rural areas of Zambia such as Chama, Kaputa, Kazungula, Mporokoso, Mpongwe, Petauke, and Zambezi through the bank's expanded branch network.

Zambia's relations with cooperating partners had substantially improved, three years after I had occupied the office of Minister of Finance and National Planning. I had fully engaged the various cooperating partners to the benefit of the country whose reputation had been restored. I was trusted by many administrators of partner development offices such that I could request for release of budgeted donor funds by telephone and the funds were transferred to the Government's general account at the Bank of Zambia within hours.

CHAPTER 34

Harmonization With The Cooperating Partners

My last seven months as Minister of Finance and National Planning before the 2006 general elections were a busy time, but with less stressful work. The budget over-run and foreign debt issues had been decisively dealt with and were behind us. The officers at the Ministry of Finance and National Planning were trusted public servants providing public services and goods in a transparent and accountable manner. The economy had attained macroeconomic stability and was moving in rhythm with the policies that had been collectively and consultatively agreed upon with the majority stakeholders.

By April 2005, we had established trusted good relations with bilateral and multilateral cooperating partners. This led to the signing of a large number of aid agreements with foreign governments and international financial organizations for funding of many projects in all sectors. During the previous year, I had hosted ministers and senior officers from the AU, Finland, IMF, USA, DFID, World Bank, JICA, SIDA, and the PTA Bank, who praised and encouraged us to continue on the path of fiscal prudent management.

One of the problems of donor aid was that there was a lack of coordination amongst the donor countries. Most often, each donor chose which sector and sometimes even the geographical area of Zambia to direct their aid. This made aid ineffective and led to complaints by the aid recipients, who sometimes spent more time on meetings with donors than on project implementation.

At a meeting of donors in Rome, Italy, in 2003, it was decided that an effort be made at harmonizing aid under the coordination by the recipient countries. Zambia was selected as one of the few participants in the Aid Harmonization-In-Practice (HIP) Initiative. A Memorandum of Understanding (MOU) between the Republic of Zambia (GRZ) and its development partners was signed in April 2004.

With a macro level focus, the HIP Initiative aimed at getting development partners and the Ministry of Finance and National Planning to agree on actions, practices, and targets for harmonization around processes such as the Poverty Reduction Programme and the Medium-Term Expenditure Framework (MTEF).

The development of an Aid Policy and Strategy document emerged from the Wider Harmonization in Practice (WHIP) Initiative as one of the outputs described in the MoU of the Harmonization Framework.

The Aid Policy was the product of a series of consultations within the Government and with many stakeholders, including the country's cooperating partners. The main goal in developing the Aid Policy was to ensure that Zambia had a systematic and coordinated approach for soliciting and managing aid.

The policy recognized that, to the extent that external resources become part of Zambia's own funds, the strategies for aid management are fundamentally the same as for managing domestic resources. A number of reforms were proposed to enhance the systems and structures that manage local resources. The degree to which the Zambian Government can effectively receive and account for aid is, to a large extent, dependent on the country's ability to manage its domestically generated resources. Cooperating partners, in turn, collaborate to improve predictability of funding and alignment with Zambia's own financial management systems.

The MoU on HIP was drawn up as a follow-up to the resolutions of the Monterrey Consensus (2002), the Rome Declaration on Harmonization (2003), and the Strategic Partnership with Africa (SPA).

The MoU set out the different financing modalities, the conditions, and review processes between the Ministry and development partners. The composition and terms of reference of key consultative groups were clearly laid out in the document. The MoU highlighted the principles, processes and procedures that aimed to enhance aid effectiveness through Aid Harmonization and Coordination as follows:

• The principles refer to ideals of promoting, through the leadership of the Government of the Republic of Zambia (GRZ), the strengthening of government decision-making and the alignment of donors' development efforts to national policies and implementation procedures.

• The processes refer to initial and intermediate stages of developing national strategies and policies such as reforms, reviews, and capacity building processes, which constitute the framework within which aid coordination and harmonization can take place.

• The procedures spell out how to implement the various processes resulting in national policies such as the Zambia Aid Policy.

In developing Zambia's Aid Policy and Strategy, we relied on the findings of a commissioned extensive research work done by Professor Oliver Saasa in which he concluded that "the objective of developing an aid policy for a country is to ensure that a country has a clear, systematic, and well-coordinated approach to solicit for, and acquire, utilize, manage, report, monitor, and evaluate assistance from development cooperating partners. Clear policies on development cooperation would serve as a practical and useful tool to both government-based operational staff that utilize aid as well as donors themselves that would be made aware of the country's objectives for, and intended use of, external resources".

Our interaction with the Cooperating Partners when trying to resolve Zambia's huge debt and high poverty levels exposed the country's weakness in planning. The outstanding debt had been contracted for a number of projects and programmes in various sectors with no commonality in terms of their long-term objectives. Many lenders and donors did not know how the projects they financed were related to what other donors were supporting. A question that kept creeping into our discussions with the donors was, 'What will you do differently, once the huge debt is written off?'

Luckily, President Mwanawasa had already answered the question by reviving national planning in 2002, as soon as he took office. The answer to the donors' question was that "the Zambian Government intended to plan its development agenda and coordinate donor support." We then invited the donor community to provide development assistance within the Government's plans. We conceived the Joint Assistance Strategy for Zambia (JASZ) in 2006 as an instrument for harmonizing the assistance from the many Cooperating Partners amongst themselves and with Zambia's development plans.

The Government's development agenda was articulated in the three related planning instruments, defining the long, medium and short-term development objectives, namely, the National Vision 2030, the Fifth National Development Plan 2006 –2010 (FNDP), and the rolling Medium-Term Expenditure Framework 2006 – 2008 (MTEF). The long-term development planning objectives were articulated in the National Vision 2030, where the country aimed "to become a prosperous middle-income country by the year 2030."

The FNDP, which constituted the Government's Medium-Term Strategy, represented the first building block for achieving the Vision's objectives. Its theme was 'Broad-based Wealth and Job Creation through Citizenry Participation and Technological Advancement', with the strategic focus on 'Economic Infrastructure and Human Resources Development'. The MTEF (MTEF) articulated the short-term macroeconomic framework during the period 2006-2008, aiming at sustaining and building on the gains achieved in the recent years. The framework helps in balancing the requirements of ongoing projects with available revenues and therefore programming incremental development.

After presenting the various instruments, the donors arrived at a consensus that the existing planning instruments provided a comprehensive framework for addressing poverty and promoting sustainable development. They provided a platform on which they could support the Government's development agenda. The instruments also provided an acceptable basis for aligning Cooperating Partners' development assistance to the country's systems. The Joint Assistance Strategy for Zambia (JASZ) was, therefore, the Cooperating Partners' joint response to the national development agenda. It also provided a joint medium-term national instrument to manage development cooperation with the Government.

The JASZ was buttressed by a MoU signed by a large number of Cooperating Partners on Direct Budget Support (DBS) and the Zambia Aid Policy and Strategy in 2006. Budget support involves policy dialogue, financial transfers to the national treasury of the partner country, performance assessment, and capacity building, based on partnership and mutual accountability. It is a means of delivering better aid and achieving sustainable development objectives by fostering a partner country's ownership of development policies and reforms.

The PRBS policy dialogue was linked to the annual High-Level Policy Dialogue (HLPD) meetings between the government and the Group of Cooperating Partners (CPG) that were signatories to the Joint Assistance Strategy (JASZ) and chaired by me. The CPG was subdivided into two sub-groups, namely, the Heads of Cooperation (HoC) and the Heads of Mission (HoM). The HoC led by a Troika focused on operational multisectoral issues including strategic developmental policy matters and met monthly with the Secretary to the Treasury.

Some cooperating partners, while submitting to the principles of the JASZ, wanted to provide development assistance on a parallel basis outside the Direct Budget Support mechanism. I agreed to such arrangements, knowing well that the Ministry had by then the capacity to synchronize and coordinate the various projects and programmes within the principle of 'division of labour' under JASZ and the coordinated national plans. Among the cooperating partners that wished to have stand-alone programmes were the AfDB, China, Japan, and the USA, whose detailed individual support programmes were elaborated in separate documents.

Nourishing the relations between the ADB and Zambia
My relationship with the AfDB dates back to the seventies when I worked with some of the bank's staff on preparing projects for funding support by the bank. In view of my acquired experience and skills in project evaluation, some of the foreign experts I worked with in the Ministry of Agriculture enticed me to join their organizations. I refused many job offers until in 1979 when the Head of the Agricultural Projects Department of the AfDB, Kwaku Morris Nyahe lured me into joining the African Development Bank.

The Ministry of Finance supported my application to the ADB and tasked Undersecretary Rodger Sakwanda to hand-carry my application forms to Abidjan, Cote D'Ivoire. I was invited for interviews. Having earlier been stopped from leaving the civil service, I planned to discretely attend the interviews in Abidjan.

I applied for three days' leave from 3 to 5 October 1979, which was easily approved and left Lusaka on the evening of 2 October 1979 by UTA. I sat for the interviews and left Abidjan for Lusaka on Thursday evening. The plan worked well as I was back in Lusaka by Friday, 5 October 1979 and reported for duty the following Monday. Only the Undersecretary (Administration) Silumelume Mubukwanu and my family knew of the trip.

In December 1979, I received a letter of appointment to the position of Agro-Economist at the Headquarters of the ADB in Abidjan. The attractive remuneration package included various allowances plus a monthly salary of US $1,578. I started negotiating for release on an unpaid leave of two years. By mid-January 1980, the air tickets for me and my family arrived and we planned to leave by the end of the month.

Because of packing over the weekend, I arrived a bit late at the office on Monday 28 January 1979. I found a message that I should call at the office of the PS immediately. I was expectant that the PS might have received a favourable reply from Cabinet Office on my request for unpaid leave.

After exchanging usual greetings, the Permanent Secretary handed me a copy of a letter dated 24 January 1980 addressed to Evans I. L. Willima, Secretary to the Cabinet, which I immediately recognized as coming from the office of the President.

In part, President Kaunda's letter read, "I understand that this officer is being encouraged to join the UNDP on a secondment basis… I have been following the activities of this officer and find him very helpful, particularly in the promotion of the Lima Programme…I want Mr Magande moved immediately to the Ministry of Defence as Deputy Director of the Research Bureau in the Ministry of Defence. While there, I would want him to assist not only in the research but also coordinate the planning activities of all production units under the Ministry of Defence…"

I was devastated as my chances of working in an international organisation were blocked by the head of state. The PS advised me to ask the Minister to intercede on my behalf. He said that in the meantime, I should stop making preparations for departure.

I went about my work for the day as if nothing serious had happened. After work, I collected Joyce from the UTH but did not break out the bad news until we reached home in Chelstone. She was very disappointed but commented that we were lucky that we had not advertised any of our goods on that very day. I informed her that I would be asking the Minister to try to persuade President Kaunda to rescind his decision.

When I briefed Minister Chikwanda later during the week, he was also very upset and informed me that he would find time to discuss the matter with the President. The Minister then asked Goodall Gondwe, Interim President of ADB for a postponement of my reporting and this was granted. In spite of the concerted efforts by my Minister, President Kaunda did not rescind his decision.

While the Minister and I were battling for my release to join the ADB, the

Zambian Government was going all over Africa campaigning vigorously for Willa Mung'omba, aka 'Willa' for the position of President of the same ADB. The campaign, which was headed by Rodger Sakwanda, was successful and Mung'omba became the first Zambian President of the ADB in 1980 for a term of five years.

I reported for work on 17 March 1980 at the Office of the Chairman for Defence and Security. In May 1980, I confirmed my inability to take up the offer of appointment at the African Development Bank. My family and I were consoled that, "to every dark cloud, there is a silver lining." As we gave in, we felt that recognition by the Head of State could be a forerunner for a better future.

After settling in his new job, Mung'omba canvassed for the 1982 ADB Annual Meetings to be held in Zambia. As I was then at the host Ministry of Finance as Director of Budget, I helped in organizing the successful annual meetings. It was at this meeting that a landmark decision to open up the shareholding in the ADB to non-regionals or non-African countries was made. This led to a stronger regional bank as new richer members put in more capital.

Willa attempted to get me released by President Kaunda to join him at the AfDB as a staff member. In spite of his efforts not succeeding, Willa developed a special relationship with me and highly respected me. Instead of starting as a junior staff member in the Bank in 1980, I skipped many steps and became the Governor for Zambia on the Board of the Bank with powers of influencing important decisions in the operations of the Bank.

I capitalised on the close relationship with Mung'omba by including him in the team of elders I often consulted in my challenging job as Minister of Finance and National Planning in the 21st Century. As a former president of the ADB, Mung'omba attended the Bank's annual meetings and we used these occasions, far away from home, to reflect on various national economic issues.

The first meeting I attended in my new capacity as governor was the ADB 2004 Annual Meetings and the 40th Anniversary Celebrations of the Group in Kampala, Uganda in May 2004. It was a great pleasure to visit Makerere University, my Alma Mater, which I had attended in the seventies. As I had been associated with the ADB since 1978, I was asked to make contributions during discussions in the various committees.

The Zambian delegation had a successful tour as Zambia was appointed the Rapporteur and I eloquently read the conclusions of the main meeting. Zambia was also nominated as a representative of the Southern Africa recipient countries on the negotiations for the African Development Fund (ADF) Tenth replenishment.

During our meeting with Omar Kabbaj, ADB President, we got a commitment for the Bank to open a country office in Lusaka. Zambia was also put on the list of possible locations of the ADB headquarters should a final decision be made not to return to Cote d'Ivoire. We also had discussions with the Organization of Petroleum Exporting Countries' (OPEC) Fund and got an additional loan for the Mongu/Kalabo road.

The team of African Finance Ministers appointed at the Kampala ADB meeting to negotiate the ADF-X replenishments held the first meeting with donors in Copenhagen, Denmark in mid-December 2004. At the meeting, I was elected the spokesperson for all the recipient countries.

I managed to once more apply my negotiating and diplomatic skills as the spokesperson for the recipient countries. By the end of the negotiations, the pledges made by the ADF Deputies were forty-three per cent more than those made for the ADF IX replenishments.

Having successfully concluded negotiations with the Paris Club on 11 May 2005, I and some officers left Paris and a happy Ambassador Ian Sikazwe, for London en route to Abuja, Nigeria for the 2005 Annual meetings of the ADB Group. The ADB meetings were special and important as the governors were to elect a new president of the Bank.

The meetings were preceded by an Economic Commission for Africa (ECA) Conference and an ADB Symposium. I had by this time won a large following amongst my fellow ministers and also the officials from the banking sector and finance ministries, such that my interventions at the meetings were greeted with thunderous ovations.

I had a meeting with Standard & Poors, a rating agency, who were interested in rating Zambia after the HIPC Initiative accomplishment. I signed a financing agreement with the ADB for the Lake Tanganyika Regional Development Programme.

The governors reconstituted themselves into an electorate for the position of president of the Bank. I had instructions to vote for Donald Kaberukaof Rwanda as President Kagame had made a personal visit to Zambia to seek President Mwanawasa's support for his national. By coincidence, Kaberuka had been known to me personally since the 1970s when we were both junior economists in our respective governments. My dilemma was that I knew candidates Amoako, Kaberuka, and Ogunjobi intimately.

By the third vote, three candidates had dropped out. The fourth vote resulted in a stalemate between Donald Kaberuka and Olabisi Ogunjobi, aka OO, the Nigerian young economist whom I had met at the ADB headquarters in 1979 when I went for job interviews. OO had taken me to dinner, which was spent reminiscing about the gone past including the interviews and his visits to Zambia in the eighties.

As per the Bank's voting rules, the voting was postponed to the next meeting of the governors, which was convened within two months. The extraordinary meeting was convened at the Temporary Relocation Agency (TRA) of the Bank in Tunis on 21 July 2005. I presented a strong message from President Mwanawasa and SADC on the region's expectations on the new ADB boss.

The voice of Zambia's Governor influenced most voters in favour of Donald Kaberuka, a former Minister of Finance of Rwanda who became the seventh president of the ADB Group. Donald Kaberuka provided sterling leadership that made the AfDB a premier regional financial institution during his ten years' reign.

While in Tunis, I had very fruitful discussions with the Zambian Bank staff at a dinner hosted by Andrew Mwaba and his family. Others in attendance were Charles Lufumpa and Rex Situmbeko and their spouses. I promised that I would lobby the new president for promotion and recruitment of more Zambians.

The new president of the Bank, once he settled down, did write to me that, "I want in particular to acknowledge your personal efforts to ensure that we quickly arrived at a conclusion that saw our bank emerge strengthened and partnership re-invigorated. This outcome would not have been possible without your personal commitment and the tireless efforts you invested".

I was privy to presidential correspondence in which Zambia's pivotal role in the elections was acknowledged by the President of Rwanda who wrote to thank President Mwanawasa "for your government's commitment in supporting our candidate, which permitted this outcome".

Donald visited Zambia and opened the ADB Country Office on 31 July 2008 fulfilling a promise he had made just after his election. The auspicious occasion was graced by Dr Kaunda, Mark Chona, and Willa Mung'omba, who was the Guest of Honour. I reminded KK of the events of 1980 when he stopped me from joining the AfDB and the old man just laughed.

President Kaunda stopped me from joining the ADB as a junior professional staff member in 1980. My befitting reward for my obedience and patience and for being a victim of the presidential prerogative was the honour of being a governor for Zambia on the board of the AfDB in 2003.

The ADB under President Kaberuka, with whom I had close personal relations, fully supported Zambia's development effort. The new office in Lusaka facilitated quick decision-making on issues concerning financing of projects.

Re-energizing the China-Zambia relations

Amongst the cooperating partners, that I was instructed to create a special relationship with, was the Government of the People's Republic of China (PRC). At the beginning of the 21st Century, China became the third fastest growing economy in the world after implementing a series of reforms for over three decades.

With the end of the Cold War, the American business community took advantage of the opening up of the nearly two billion consumer population of China by relocating many of their manufacturing industries to special Multi-Facility Economic Zones (MFEZ) in China offering very attractive incentives.

Within a short period, China's economy, growing at more than ten per cent per annum, became the second largest to that of the USA.

Although a fierce battle raged for some time in the USA on what was called outsourcing and 'exporting of jobs', soon the relocation of industries was accepted as good business. It was cheaper to use American advanced technology with Chinese labour in China to manufacture consumer goods for the American market.

Since China's resurgence as an economic powerhouse during the period between 1978 and 2005, there were a lot of questions raised through the Western media and in open debates on China's role in Africa. Arguments were raised that China's engagement in Africa is exploitative and in self-interest.

I had the opportunity to take part in these debates at meetings of the African regional integration units, the European Union, the AfDB, International Monetary Fund (IMF), World Bank, and other various international fora. In the development finance market and after the HIPC Initiative, China was accused of free-riding, that is increasing its lending to post-HIPC countries by taking advantage of the fiscal and balance-of-payments space created by the debt relief.

It was true that China made a strong presence in Africa in its quest to acquire raw materials needed for its blossoming manufacturing industries. China was a newcomer in Zambia's mining industry. The first Chinese mining company to buy a mine was China Non-Ferrous Mining Corporation (CNFM) in 1998.

Since 1916, some 16 million tonnes of Zambia's copper were taken out of the country by companies from the West and South Africa with no noticeable contribution to developments in the country's infrastructure. Zambia's protestations in various fora did not achieve anything as the multinationals were supported by their governments, which benefitted from the official and elicit income flows. The paternalistic attitude of the West had little to show for the hundred years of colonialism and mining in Zambia.

As a new member of the community of 'developed countries', China was an important partner in Zambia's development efforts. In my strategic position as Chief Economic Advisor to the President of Zambia and to economic participants in the Zambian economy, it was imperative that I have a clear understanding of China's intentions in Zambia and in Africa in general.

I had read many books on socialism and communism, the two ideologies of the East during my student days. I was also one of the lucky Africans to visit China in the eighties just after the demise of Mao Tsetung. I was in a position to recall China's developments over a thirty-year period.

My understanding was that Zambia's relationship with China dated back to the sixties when China supported the liberation wars waged by blacks against the white racist regimes. At the time, China was isolated by the powerful members of the United Nations and its agencies because of their abhorrence of China's human rights record in its governance system. Although not directly involved in the Cold War, China was also viewed by the West as an enemy because of its support of the socialism and communism ideologies.

Kenneth Kaunda of Zambia argued vehemently that unless China was admitted as a member of the United Nations family, it was going to be difficult to engage it in meaningful dialogue on its internal affairs. In return, China supported Zambia in its wars against racism in the region by way of military equipment and training. Zambia was used by China and other countries in the East as a vehicle for supporting the liberation movements.

At the height of the liberation wars in the seventies, Zambia's developed trade routes to the outside world through the west and south were blocked. The World Bank, British and Canadian consultants produced a report on the possibility of opening new routes through East Africa. The study identified the potential for a railway line through Tanzania to the port of Dar as Salaam and recommended for financial support to construct the rail line.

Due to tacit support of the racist regimes by most Western countries, the railway line project was declared uneconomic and was not supported. Kaunda then approached Mwalimu Nyerere for support to request the Chinese Government to construct the railway line as a joint project between Tanzania and Zambia.

Nyerere, who was a strong supporter of the liberation movement and Pan-Africanism supported Kaunda's idea and approached the Chinese Government during his visit in February 1965. President Mao Zedong granted the request and on 6 September 1967, an agreement amongst China, Tanzania, and Zambia was signed in Beijing, China.

The Chinese Government provided a turnkey project and its citizens to construct the longest railway line in Africa between Kapiri Mposhi in Zambia and the port of Dar as Salaam in Tanzania. The construction took five years between 1970 and 1975, with the involvement of 50,000 Chinese workers and Tanzanian and Zambian workers. Once completed, the project provided protection for Zambia's foreign trade routes through a friendly country.

Since the sixties, China and Zambia have enjoyed friendly and very productive relations in most areas of development. Many Zambians have gone to China for training, not only in railway engineering but in many other fields.

I arrived back home on 28 October 2003 from a trip to Russia, where we went to negotiate for a debt write-off. I was busy with the preparations of the 2004 budget when I was directed to accompany the President on a State Visit to the Peoples' Republic of China. I was eager to visit China after my last trip some twenty-three years earlier.

President Mwanawasa emphasized that I had to make the trip as there were a number of financial agreements to be signed in Beijing and only the Minister of Finance could sign. I was comforted by this stance by the President, early in my assignment, as it meant that no public officer would commit the Zambian

Government to some obscure financial deal without my approval. At that time, Zambia was going through trying moments in financial management and the involvement of the Head of State was paramount in inculcating fiscal discipline amongst all public workers, including Ministers.

Among the protocols signed during the trip under the watchful eyes of Presidents Mwanawasa and Hu Jintao of China were those covering the involvement of the Sino Hydropower Company in the development of the Itezhi-tezhi and Kariba North Bank Power stations.

During the official luncheon, I was privileged to sit in between two high-ranking members of the Chinese Communist Party Committee and Government. One was an old man in his seventies and the other a young man in his forties. I reminded the septuagenarian of the fourteen-course meal that had been laid out for us during our visit to China in 1980 and asked if they still enjoyed such lavish lifestyles.

The old man explained that the country had gone through a revolution and transformation in thinking and expenditure. The reforms started in 1978 led to some behavioral changes with the Chinese Government being more judicious in the use of resources. He further went on to say that the blend between his old generation and the young highly-educated Chinese was very effective in achieving the momentous development being witnessed.

When reminded of the comment on the Red Book, he stated that the book had been reintroduced as a textbook in schools because it contained some important teachings of Chinese traditions and culture, which were needed to guide even a modern society. While the one-child policy had been relaxed, many young couples adopted a policy of small families. Many parents invested heavily in the upbringing and education of their only child and this resulted in a highly healthy and educated young generation.

Our banquet, set in a colorfully decorated grand hall, was a five-course meal, consisting of some tasty local foods from the countryside. Under the reformed land law, the small-scale farmers owned plots of land carved from large state farms, which had once belonged to collective communes. Side by side on the tables were sets of sparkling steel cutlery and beautifully carved bamboo chopsticks. Democracy had permeated even into the dining rooms as we had a choice as to which eating utensils to use. I demonstrated my skills, which I had acquired in 1980 at using chopsticks to the amazement of the hosts and other Zambian delegates.

While the serving ladies were adorned in the Chinese traditional qipao, with slits high up the waist, all the Chinese males in the hall were in black suits and tie. They had abandoned the traditional Mao suits. The food, dress, eating utensils, and music demonstrated the fusion of the old and modern China, which was taking its own development route to become the fastest growing economy in the world under the Communist Party of China. The dividing line was that while the West believed in the existence of God, the majority of the

Chinese people believed in atheism.

Since initiating market reforms in 1978, China shifted to a hybrid planned but market-based economy and experienced rapid economic and social development. GDP was growing at a record pace of more than ten per cent, lifting more than 500 million people out of poverty. The China I had seen in 1980 had completely changed and developed with mostly foreign investment in manufacturing. Although most of the manufactured goods were for foreign markets, the foreign investors created thousands of jobs while China's population of 1.3 billion provided a ready local market.

The raw materials going into the manufacturing factories in China were from developing countries such as Zambia, which have abundant minerals. I, therefore, envisioned a changed and developed Zambia within thirty years if we applied lessons learnt from such foreign visits.

I left Beijing immediately after signing the various agreements to rush home to finalize the 2004 budget. At some connecting airports, I negotiated my inclusion on flights as I did not have prior bookings. While at the ACP Secretariat, at times, I was on flights of twenty hours criss-crossing the globe. I, therefore, developed a habit of carrying a lot of documents for reading during the flights. On my way back from China, I had the opportunity to catch up on all the briefs on the 2004 budget.

During my long stopover in Hong Kong, I spent some time discussing the airport's developments with some airport officials. It was a marvel to see how the ocean was being pushed away and runways created by dumping thousands of tons of imported gravel transported by huge barges from distant lands.

On 16 November 2004, I was at State House for talks between President Mwanawasa and a delegation from the Communist Party of China. The talks culminated in the signing of an agreement that provided a soft loan for the rehabilitation of the TAZARA. I signed for Zambia, while the Tanzanian Minister of Transport signed on behalf of his country.

On 3 February 2007, a high-powered Chinese delegation led by President Hu Jintao arrived in Zambia for a three-day state visit as part of a historic African tour. This was the first time for Zambia to host a Chinese President, in spite of the very warm and long-standing fraternal relations between China and Zambia fostered by KK.

The milestone visit, which was welcomed by most Zambians, was marred by the antagonistic behaviour of the leader of the Patriotic Front, Michael Sata. He seemed to have forgotten all the assistance extended by China to Zambia under the UNIP government in which he was one of the leaders. Sata threatened to organize the miners to not only demonstrate but to also sabotage the mines during the visit of President Hu to the Copperbelt.

He further ordered that no PF members, including civic leaders, should take part in any State functions organized for the visitors. At the time, the PF controlled the Lusaka City Council and the councils on the Copperbelt.

Everyone in the Mwanawasa Administration and many citizens were surprised with this behaviour as no politician had behaved in such a manner before.

Protocol demands that the Mayor of Lusaka City, the capital of Zambia, must receive all dignitaries who visit the city. The Mayoress, Ms Susan Sikazwe and Chawama Ward Councillor, Musonda Mwaume, both of the PF, decided to join the government team in welcoming President Hu at the KKIA.

True to his word, PF President Sata called a press briefing where he publicly attacked the Chinese and denounced and announced the dismissal of the Mayor and her deputy, even before the visitors left. This was the most embarrassing moment for President Mwanawasa. As someone who was very close to the President during the bilateral talks and State banquet, I sensed his frustration and anger, but I advised him not to take any action against Sata.

Due to security concerns, President Hu's trip to the Copperbelt to unveil the Chambishi MFEZ was cancelled. Instead, we arranged a ceremony on Sunday 4 February 2007 at the Mulungushi International Conference Centre where President Mwanawasa and President Hu unveiled the Chambishi Zambia–China Economic and Trade Cooperation Zone. The Zone was to be a landmark development project by President Mwanawasa's administration with industries that were to create nearly 60,000 jobs. During the talks, President Hu announced an estimated investment of US $800 million in the mining industry over the next three years by Chinese companies.

After the official talks, I was honoured with the responsibility of signing a number of protocols and agreements covering financing of projects in the various sectors of the economy. The accord was to strengthen political and economic collaboration and cultural interaction. A concessional loan of US $100.15 million was granted to Zambia to cover earth-moving and irrigation equipment, grain silos, water and sanitation projects, and the uncompleted Government Office Complex. The area of trade was strengthened by a Special Preferential Tariff Agreement that opened the huge Chinese market by increasing the number of exports from Zambia to China on zero tariffs from 190 to 442.

A grant of an unspecified amount was also promised to cover the costs of one large hospital, an agricultural technology demonstration centre, anti-Malaria disease research hospital, two rural schools, and a modern sports stadium. The Chinese Government also agreed to consider the financing of projects under ZAMTEL and ZESCO through its parastatal Export and Import Bank (EXIM) of China.

On 22 February 2007, I addressed a letter to the President of the EXIM Bank of China, Li Ruogu, to initiate negotiations for the concessional loans. Soon I knew most of the Chinese bank and government officials engaged in negotiating the financing and supervision of the projects accepted by the Chinese Government.

On Monday, 25 February 2008, President Mwanawasa was visited by the

Chinese Minister for Commerce, who was sent to discuss some of the projects agreed upon during President Hu's visit. During the discussions, it was brought to our attention that due to financial constraints, the Chinese Government had decided to convert the grant for the Ndola stadium into a soft loan.

In a sharp reaction, the President informed the Chinese Minister to cancel the project as he could not approve a loan for a leisure project. It was only after the Secretary to the Treasury and I confirmed that the soft loan would be adequately profiled that the President accepted to proceed with the social project. However, he directed that the earth-moving equipment, which was also covered by a soft loan, must be delivered before the fourth quarter of the year.

I made frequent calls to the Chinese Ambassador to facilitate the early delivery of the earth-moving equipment by Messrs CATIC Limited of China. We had to make special arrangements with the Tanzanian Government to move the equipment on their roads in spite of it being above the allowable load weight.

During the negotiations with the Eximbank of China and CATIC Limited, the suppliers of the earth-moving equipment, we agreed on a new mode of utilization to make the equipment last longer. Similar equipment bought in 1995 had not been properly utilized. The new arrangement was to divide the equipment into only four units, which would move from province to province. The equipment was to start making gravel roads from Lusaka as they were being delivered to various destinations and directions.

In our discussions, CATIC Limited agreed to establish a central spare parts storage centre in Zambia for all the equipment supplied to the countries of the Eastern, Central, and Southern Africa. After five years, the company was to establish a factory to manufacture some of the less-sophisticated spare parts in Zambia.

In May 2007, I was amongst over 2000 delegates to the annual meetings of the African Development Bank Group in Shanghai, China. The city I had visited in 1980, then characterized by rice fields, was now a big city dominated by skyscrapers. My driver could not even locate the hotel we had stayed in, twenty-seven years earlier.

China was one of the non-regional shareholders of the regional bank and the meetings were the first to be held outside the African continent. Having had very fruitful relations with the ADB since 1978, I was requested to be one of the discussants on the presentation on Africa-China relations and its impact on Africa's development. With my two extensive trips to China spaced apart by twenty-seven years of reforms in China, I was able to relate my debates to the phenomenal developments that had been achieved since my first visit.

During the discussions, the Chinese Ministers and senior officials explained that China had been excluded from the African continent's development arena for a long time. They were surprised that the West, which had been in Africa for centuries extracting the continent's natural resources, was now accusing China of exploitative relations. They also reminded us that the country had only recently started participating in global organizations such as the World Trade Organization (WTO) and the International Labour Organization (ILO). The onus was on African governments to teach the Chinese companies the rules of the game such as labour laws as they invested in Africa.

For Zambia, its relations with China have been beneficial starting from the early days of Zambia's independence in the sixties. The TAZARA was an epoch-making project that saved Zambia from humiliation by the racist regimes in the south after the southern routes were closed. Under President Mwanawasa, large investments were made and agreed upon by Chinese private companies in the mining and agricultural industries. The Chinese Government provided concessional loans and grants for social infrastructure, most of which was constructed by Chinese companies, long after President Mwanawasa was no more.

The modern Levy Mwanawasa Stadium in Ndola, the Chambishi MFEZ in Kitwe, the Levy Mwanawasa Hospital in Lusaka, the Government Office Complex in Lusaka, and the extension of the Kariba North Bank Power Station stand as testimony of the many benefits to Zambia under the China-Zambia cooperation. China had become a dependable development partner not only to Zambia but to many other African countries.

The Triangle of Hope: The anchor for Zambia's Cooperation with Japan
The Japanese Government had offered technical assistance to Zambia for a long time under the Japanese International Cooperation Agency (JICA). The assistance was on a bilateral basis and not under the multilateral Overseas Development Assistance (ODA) umbrella. Japan was one of the donor countries that had agreed to write-off Zambia's loans early under the HIPC.

In my early engagement with the Japanese Ambassador, I was informed that the Japanese Government was keen to continue its development assistance to Zambia. However, I was reminded that some projects did not have trickle-down impact to the poor Zambians. Massive assistance in the agricultural sector had resulted in the production of thousands of veterinarians, but Zambia's livestock industry continued to underperform in terms of disease control and breeding.

The ambassador urged me to start thinking of new programmes and projects that would have a positive impact on the lives of the ordinary Zambians. By 2003, the Japanese Government was investigating new ways of extending further effective assistance to developing countries including Zambia.

While many workers were planning for the end of 2004 parties, I was getting ready to join the deputies of the African Development Fund (ADF) at the negotiations for the Tenth Replenishment of the Fund in Copenhagen,

Denmark, as the representative of Southern Africa. The trip turned out to be the most memorable in my working career and opened a historic chapter in the relations between Japan and Zambia.

I arrived on time at the Lusaka International Airport for a 1430 hours flight on 14 December 2004 to South Africa on my way to Denmark. I had settled in my seat on the plane when, a youthful-looking Japanese man rushed into the plane and came to sit in the empty seat next to me. After exchanging casual greetings as is my custom, the gentleman opened his handbag and took out a document before depositing the bag in the baggage hold above. He was in a hurry to read the document he had brought on board with him.

Out of curiosity, I noticed that the document was a speech I had delivered to the donor community at a breakfast meeting the previous day. I took out one of my business cards and without being invited, I placed the card on the speech my neighbour had begun to read. After realizing that the name on the speech and the card was the same, he turned to me and shouted, 'No'. I shouted back, 'Yes'. He then extended his hand for a handshake, which I accepted.

The Japanese man introduced himself as Hiroyuki Moronaga, an official of the Japan International Cooperation Agency (JICA). He explained that as they were discussing Zambia's development prospects with some Japanese diplomats in Lusaka, one of them had referred to a speech I had delivered to the donor community.

He was advised to get a copy of the speech before flying out and this was the reason for his late arrival at the airport. He then stated that since the author of the speech was sitting next to him, he would rather listen to me than read my speech. I concurred with his reasoning and we started a lively conversation long before the plane took off.

Moronaga informed me that the Japanese Government had decided to identify three African countries in the categories of 'inland', 'coastal', and 'island' to apply the development model they had used in Asia. Through JICA, they had hired a Malaysian Consultant, whose responsibility was to tour Africa and identify the three countries with the best characteristics and environment for massive Japanese development assistance.

JICA would then help the three countries to draw medium-term development plans. Using successful development experiences of East Asia, the Japanese Government would explore alternative and possible approaches to make aid work more efficiently and effectively. The objective of the Japanese Government was to demonstrate the effectiveness and applicability of its aid delivery mechanism model used in Asian countries as opposed to the model used by the West in African countries. The goal was to create successful models of economic development in Africa under the South-South Cooperation.

When I enquired how far the country identification exercise had gone, Moronaga informed me that their final trip had been to East Africa a few days before. When they were about to leave for South Africa to present their final report at a JICA regional meeting, they were informed of the postponement of the meeting. He then suggested to the consultant that they make a detour and spend the interim period in Zambia visiting a friend.

He informed me that, all the same, they had an enjoyable stay in Zambia, as they did not do a lot of work since Zambia was not among the countries to be assessed. They were now on their way to report and make final recommendations to the JICA Africa regional office in South Africa.

In reaction to my curious questions about the whole program and why Zambia was not a candidate for the investigation, Moronaga suggested that I discuss with the Malaysian Consultant, although they already had completed their exercise. He then swapped seats with the consultant who came to sit next to me.

The consultant introduced himself as Dato Jegasothy Jegathesan, a.k.a. JJ, a former Deputy Director General of the Malaysian Industrial Development Authority (MIDA), who worked with the authority for thirty years. Jegathesan was one of the architects of the Malaysian economic miracle under Prime Minister Mahathir Mohamad. He was now a private consultant and with his thirty years' hands-on experience, he had been hired by the JICA for this special assignment.

I immediately recognized the voice as the one that I had heard at a World Bank seminar in Washington, DC in March 1996. The landmark seminar on "The challenges and strategic options of integrating Africa into the global economy" brought together ministers, civil servants, and the private sector. I attended the seminar with minister Ronald Penza, Jacob Mwanza and David Matongo. Jegasothy Jegathesan admitted that it was him, who had been at the seminar. As a resource person, he had given a lecture on the Malaysian development model. He was utterly surprised and impressed with my memory as I reminded him of the many jokes, similes, wise sayings, and advice he gave eight years earlier.

Jegasothy Jegathesan gave me details of the proposed program by the Japanese Government and the countries he had visited. The Japanese Government was desirous of investing as much money as would be needed in the three selected African countries to enhance the environment for the promotion and diversification of industries. When Jegasothy Jegathesan mentioned the identified 'inland country', which I knew very well, I asked why Zambia could not be considered as a better candidate.

Jegasothy Jegathesan informed me that during their short stay in Zambia, he had wanted to discuss with the officials at the Ministry of Commerce, Trade, and Industry about Zambia's industrialization program, but was told that the Minister was out of the country. He stated that he was very lucky to meet and speak to the Chief Planner for Zambia., as he called me. He then asked me to brief him on Zambia's development plans. I seized the opportunity to sell my country with elaborate explanations of Zambia's natural endowment and potential and the proposed plans to exploit the abundant human and natural resources. For most of the flight, we were engaged in an intense exchange of views comparing Japanese development assistance to the Asian countries with that of the Western countries to Africa.

We discussed the World Bank's Report of 1993 coined 'The East Asian Miracle: Economic Growth and Public Policy' that tried to identify and explain the phenomenal development of the high performing Asian economies, which included Japan. We were aware of the role of Japanese subsequent development assistance that resulted in significant economic success for some countries of the region that were termed the 'The Asian Tigers'.

To the contrary, billions of dollars poured by the West in Africa have not shown much development. Millions of Africans, trained under the Western countries' benevolence migrated to the West to provide the much-needed manpower and to enjoy the comforts of these developed countries. Although many Westerners had spent their precious time trying to stop the slave trade of African labourers, the modern-day educated Africans were enticed to voluntarily leave their countries for the West. While the slave trade provided the West with African untrained cheap labour, in modern times, Africa provides highly trained cheap workers to the West.

We lamented the fact that Africa has become famous for its poor people in shanty communities and the wildlife in game parks awaiting marauding foreign tourists. In Zambia, some of the best lands suited for crop farming, which were turned into cattle ranches have now been converted into game ranches. With modern financial payments instruments, entry fees to these game ranches and lodges are paid in the capitals of the rich countries. This behaviour accentuates the economic leakage effect of tourism, thereby reducing its developmental impact on developing countries.

By the time we were fastening seat belts for landing at OR Tambo International Airport in South Africa, I had made a strong case for Zambia to be included in the Japanese modernization scheme. As we were parting, Jegasothy Jegathesan declared, "Because of you, I will strongly recommend that Zambia be on standby for the program".

I told him, "I trust that you will facilitate Zambia becoming the 'Roaring Lion of Africa".

As I perused the notes for my presentations to the ADF-X meeting in Denmark, on my onward flight, my mind constantly digressed to the conversation I had with Jegasothy Jegathesan. I imagined what Zambia would look like in twenty years' time, with nicely planned townships, country roads and bridges designed and built with Japanese technology.

I imagined tall buildings on Cairo Road in Lusaka resembling the world's tallest twin towers of Kuala Lumpur. I started dreaming of a train zooming past the maize fields of Chisamba at 300 kilometres per hour. I envisioned Zambia as a centre of excellence in ICT, education, and health tourism. Such infrastructure was possible as Japanese development assistance already achieved such successes in some Asian countries.

I arrived back home with great satisfaction on the results of our trip to Denmark. I briefed President Mwanawasa on both the JICA programme and the ADF-X replenishment negotiations. He congratulated our team on the successful ADF negotiations and showed keen interest in my discussions with the JICA search team.

A few days later, the Japanese Ambassador Masaaki Miyashita visited my office to inform me that from the brief he had received, I had made a positive impression on the JICA Mission. The team concluded that Zambia possessed positive attributes to accommodate massive Japanese assistance. He told me that my request to have Zambia included on the new Japanese Government development assistance initiative in Africa was forwarded to the higher authorities in Tokyo. He advised that I should adequately brief President Mwanawasa so that he makes a formal request to the Japanese Prime Minister during the State visit to Japan in January 2005.

In our preparatory meetings for the trip to Japan, many Government officials emphasized the need for Japanese assistance in the area of technology transfer for small scale industries. I had not been to Japan before and I was keen to see the results of Japanese high technology and the prosperity that I read of in many books. I looked forward to travelling on the high-speed train (bullet train) on the railway constructed in the sixties between Tokyo and Osaka, funded partly with a loan of US $80 million from the World Bank.

In the afternoon of Sunday, 16 January 2005, I left for Japan to accompany President Mwanawasa on a State Visit. During our preliminary meetings in Japan, we discussed Japan's development assistance to Zambia and the debt write-off. As per our request to see small-scale enterprises, the delegation was taken on a tour of the Ota Techno Wing, which houses a number of small-scale industries.

In one room of about sixteen square metres, we found an elderly man with two young men and four robot machines. The elderly man was the father of the two young men. They were a small-scale family business assembling a special component of the robots used in the assembling of Honda cars. The robot component made by the family enterprise weighed about thirty kilograms and was about twenty centimetres long.

During the debriefing meeting after the tour, President Mwanawasa was asked by a Japanese Government official if what we saw was the kind of technology he wanted for the Zambian small-scale entrepreneurs. The President stated that what we had seen was too sophisticated for the Zambian environment. In the ensuing discussions, many ideas were floated but all were far from the sophisticated computer engineering we had witnessed.

The official discussions presided over by Prime Minister Junichiro Koizumi centred on debt cancellation and education infrastructure. At the conclusion of the talks, I was once more privileged to sign debt cancellation agreements with Ambassador Miyashita, witnessed by the Japanese Prime Minister and President Mwanawasa. The agreement covered debts of US $688.8 million or approximately K3.2 trillion and wiped-off all debts owed by Zambia to Japan.

President Mwanawasa did raise the matter of small-scale industries and the new Japanese development assistance initiative under JICA with the Prime Minister. He was advised to meet Ms Sadako Ogata, the Director General of the Japanese International Cooperation Agency for more detailed discussions.

The President delegated me with the responsibility of contacting Sadako Ogata for a meeting. I requested Ambassador Miyashita to assist me to make the necessary arrangements, knowing that he and I had discussed the special project. I had met Sadako Ogata in the nineties while I was at the ACP Secretariat when she was the UN High Commissioner for Refugees. I used my prior knowledge of her to brief and advise President Mwanawasa on the likely tone of his conversation with her.

President Mwanawasa had a very productive meeting with Sadako Ogata. When he mentioned the Japan aid delivery programme, the DG stated that JICA was keen to work with the Zambian Government. I and the Japanese Ambassador to Zambia were instructed to arrange for a visit to Zambia of some JICA officials.

Chief Cabinet Secretary Hiroyuki Hosoda hosted a dinner for the Zambian delegation. In keeping with old Japanese traditions, we squatted on the floor with bare feet, while adorned in very expensive kimonos. The modernity of shining silver cutlery was mixed with traditional chopsticks.

The delegation had the honour of having lunch at the Imperial Palace with His Imperial Royal Highness Crown Prince Naruhito. For the first time in my life, I sat next to the Japanese Crown Prince. I had conversations with royalty elsewhere before. I was amazed by the prince's simplicity, warmth, and knowledge of world geography.

The President's delegation had the privilege of attending a special tournament of Sumo, the traditional Japanese wrestling, which was declared a national sport in 1909. To accompany its critical editorial on the president's visit to Japan, the Post showed a comical cartoon of President Mwanawasa as a Japanese *rikishi* in a *mawashi*.

I had my wish fulfilled when our delegation took a ride on the Shinkansen (bullet train) to Aichi-Nagoya, the site of the Japan Expo 2005, whose theme was Nature's Wisdom. Among the attractions, some of which were already ready, were human-like robots, 3D rides, virtual reality shows, and futuristic means of transportation. Beyond the bullet train, a driverless train had been developed.

The seminar on 'Zambia's Potential' organized by the General Manager of the Japan External Trade Association (JETA) Kiyoshi Yamado, was not very successful. Most of the participants did not know much about Zambia and were frustrated when they learnt of Zambia's small population, which could not provide a viable market for their huge manufacturing industries.

As a follow-up to the discussions between President Mwanawasa and Sadako Ogata, JICA dispatched a mission in March 2005 to discuss how to synergize the Japanese assistance program with Zambia's development plans.

Since I was already a convert to the technical assistance project, I asked the President to have an audience with the JICA Mission for a detailed presentation. As per his principle of inclusiveness, President Mwanawasa decided instead that the JICA Mission should make a presentation to the full Cabinet for a collective appreciation of the proposal. Jegasothy Jegathesan made a power-point presentation with many references to the development endeavours of Malaysia, which had been transformed from a producer of raw rubber, to a manufacturing economy.

After a lively discussion, the Cabinet accepted the JICA concept. President Mwanawasa displayed unprecedented political will and gave full support to the proposal. The strong political will and support from the President were critical to effective implementation of the Japanese aid programme. The program under which the Japanese Government was prepared to finance technology transfer from any part of Asia to Zambia was termed the Strategic Action Initiatives for Economic Development (SAIED) on Trade and Investment Promotion, a.k.a the Triangle of Hope (ToH).

On 21 December 2005 during the signing of the final debt relief agreement with Japan in Lusaka, I said, "Your Excellency, I wish to take this opportunity to applaud the Japanese Government for considering assisting Zambia in its long-term development vision. The programme called the Triangle of Hope to be fused into the Fifth National Development Plan will see Zambia take a giant step as the 'Roaring Lion of Africa' tearing the crust of underdevelopment that has characterised most of the African continent.

Zambia is a country on the move and the path to future prosperity is clearly laid for all to travel on. The Zambian Government is fully committed to this programme as the support of the Japanese Government in this endeavour will assure us of success."

The ToH concept, with its three pillars, is assisted by the Quadrant Strategy. The strategy of twelve task forces consisted of seventy members from the government and the private sector who were appointed by President Mwanawasa. The task forces identified priority sectors of education, medical and dental, ICT, electrical household goods, cotton products, agriculture and agro-processing industries, mining, tourism, air cargo hub, and streamlining the Government machinery through e-governance.

Under investment promotion, a seventeen-person Malaysian business delegation from eleven organizations belonging to the Malaysian Industrial Development Authority (MIDA) and the Malaysian South-South Association (MASSA) led by Tan Sri Dato' Soong Siew Hoong visited Zambia in March

2007. This was followed by a visit from a delegation of Indian businessmen in April 2007.

Among the initial programmes and projects promoted and planned under the SAIED were the mobile phone assembly factory on Lumumba Road, the rehabilitation of township roads in Kitwe, Livingstone, Lusaka, and Ndola, the Livingstone/Victoria Falls Road, a by-pass road connecting Nakatindi and Lusaka Roads, a state-of-the-art medical centre, Kazungula Bridge, a regional fertiliser manufacturing plant, and a private vocational and technical college.

Under the SAIED/ToH, it was decided to establish a Multi-Facility Economic Zone (MFEZ) somewhere within Lusaka Province in close proximity to the international airport. I had intense negotiations with both President Mwanawasa and Minister Kabinga Pande for the release of 2000 hectares of land from the Lusaka South Forest Reserve on which the MFEZ is located.

The forest reserve was earmarked for a game sanctuary and the Zambia Wildlife Authority (ZAWA) had already received Presidential consent to develop the wildlife project. The President was an ardent conservationist and he put it to me strongly in a letter that he would not allow his Ministers to destroy the environment.

It was a coincidence that at the time, the Zambian Government was embroiled in controversy on two very large development projects that could change Zambia's economy. In both Livingstone and Lusaka, conservationists were having an upper hand in stopping the creation of modern infrastructure that was to generate employment for thousands of Zambians.

Part of my persuasive argument, which made President Mwanawasa approve the degazetting of part of the forest reserve was that,

"In view of the role Japanese investment played in turning Asia into the 'Asian Miracle and Tigers', I cannot doubt the sincerity of one of the latecomers into our development effort to show a difference. I am in an upbeat mood at the prospect of turning Zambia into a 'Roaring Lion of Africa'.

Somehow, someone wants us to continue to conserve and preserve the natural environment of wild animals and trees but does not tell us how we will discard the degrading title of being called poor. We have the largest number of game parks in Africa and yet Zambia is still called a poor country. I plead that Your Excellency facilitates the development of these two rather ambitious but doable projects."

During a tete-a-tete, I reminded the President that on the land where the thirty-eight-story UN Building currently stands in New York, hundreds of bisons (buffaloes) used to roam, carefully managed for centuries by the Red Indians for food and household articles. The animals were annihilated by European migrants, who have never apologized but instead boast of the 'modern' building.

One of the pillars of Malaysian development was the strong political will shown by the Prime Minister. Jegasothy Jegathesan confirmed that President Mwanawasa demonstrated strong political will by re-introducing national planning, which embraced both public and private sector development plans. The three ingredients of a successful ToH were the 'political will and integrity', 'civil service efficiency and integrity', and 'private sector dynamism and integrity'.

I was happy that the MFEZ with the support of experts from Kulim High Tech Park (KHTP) of Malaysia and the game park were both given space to develop. I hope that a way will be found to position the entrance to the MFEZ away from that into the game park, as the ZAWA guards at the western gate in military uniforms are too intimidating for many civilians going to the MFEZ.

On 27 July 2007, I was invited to a farewell dinner for Masaaki Miyashita, the outgoing Japanese Ambassador at the Ambassador's Residence. I had a long chat with the Ambassador, who assured me that his government would honour its commitments on developing all the projects under the ToH. He challenged me to work hard so that when he visits Zambia in fifteen years' time, he should find a changed and modernized Zambia.

On Tuesday 4 September 2007, Professor Kenichi Ohno, who was invited by JICA to visit Zambia, paid a courtesy call on me. I had a very educative discussion with the professor who was the guiding light for the phenomenal development of South Vietnam during a twenty-year period. Professor Ohno gave lectures to audiences of selected economic participants on the development experiences of Asian countries and their applicability in Zambia. He advised that the East Asian experience cannot be directly transferred to Africa. The professor emphasized the necessity for a "powerful and economically literate leader, development as a supreme national goal, ideology, and obsession and an elite technocrat group to support the leader".

My additional reading on the economic take-off of East Asia led me to the live debate on authoritarian and democratic developmentalisms as possible paths to development. I was enlightened on the difference between the two and that East Asia had chosen the former development path against the other, which was propagated by western aid donors.

For even the best inventions, innovations, and revolutions, there are always renegades that oppose because of the fear of the unknown future. Among the thousands of civil servants in the Zambian public service, there were many who did not believe that Zambia could attain development equal to some of the East Asian countries under the ToH.

One of the victims of these negative thoughts was the high-tech medical centre of excellence for keyhole surgery and a college proposed by the LifeLine Group of India. After the change of administration in November 2008, the building which was being renovated and designated for this important health project, was repossessed and reassigned by the ministry of works to be used as a social club for civil servants.

After the demise of President Mwanawasa and my being out of Government, Jegasothy Jegathesan,, the JICA Consultant briefed me that he received a lukewarm reception when he visited Zambia. He briefed me that there was limited political will by the new administration and this led to reduced enthusiasm by Japan, the sponsoring country for the Triangle of Hope.

The Millennium Challenge Account: A test for Zambia's governance probity
Zambia had been a beneficiary of development aid from the United States of America Government through the office of the United States Agency for International Development (USAID) formed in 1961. I had cultivated very productive working relationships with the USAID staff after the establishment of the Lusaka Mission in 1977. The Mission Directors John Patterson and Leslie A. Dean were readily available to exchange views on the role of the USAID in Zambia's development effort in agriculture.

I only differed with Patterson when he insisted that his government was more interested in being involved in the poorest regions of Zambia such as the Northern and North-Western Provinces. My efforts to teach him economies of agglomeration and cluster development failed, and so did his country's efforts to develop the northern region. Zambia was a recipient of wheat from the USA government under its aid programme. And yet, with minimum support of the USA, most food needs of Zambia could have been produced by the farmers in areas with suitable soils.

By 2003 when I became governor for Zambia on the AfDB board, the USA was one of the oldest non-regional members. With no member state of the AfDB with a name starting with letters between 'U' and 'Z', the governors of the USA and Zambia sat next to each other during ADB meetings. While I provided a buffer between the warring USA and Zimbabwean Governors, I also seized the opportunity to engage in very useful conversations with the treasury officials of the largest economy in the world.

I cultivated a close relationship with Bobby J. Pittman of the USA Treasury with whom I shared many light moments. I recall a supporter of a losing candidate accusing me of conspiring with the USA ADB Governor to vote for a particular candidate during the elections for the ADB President in Abuja in May 2005.

In January 2004, a new bilateral foreign aid agency, the Millennium Challenge Corporation (MCC) was established by the USA administration, with a principle of applying a new philosophy toward foreign aid. The MCC was independent and separate from the USAID, which was "thought to suffer from many different and sometimes conflicting goals, which often are a result of political pressures, and for not delivering long-term economic improvements". Selection for participation under the MCC was strict with seventeen indicators to be fulfilled by the applicant country.

In November 2004, Zambia was selected as being eligible to receive MCC

Threshold program assistance. This required the Zambian Government to prepare and submit a Threshold Country Plan, which was submitted to the MCC board. During the ADB Annual Meetings in Ouagadougou in May 2006, we had fruitful discussions with the USA Government delegation led by Ahmed Saeed, Deputy Assistant Secretary of Treasury for Africa and the Middle East. He informed us that the funding under the Millennium Challenge Corporation (MCC) had been approved and the agreement was ready for signing in Washington DC.

I, therefore, travelled from Burkina Faso directly to the USA. On Monday 22 May 2006, I and Lloyd Pierson, Assistant Administrator for the Bureau for Africa (USAID) signed an agreement for a grant of US $24.3 million under the MCC Threshold Program Assistance.

The objective of the Country Plan was 'to strengthen the capacity of the Government to build and promote stronger partnerships amongst the government, private sector, and civil society by tackling administrative barriers that stall trade and investment and remove opportunities for graft by key government ministries'.

Corruption was recognized as a major impediment to the country's transition to a stable democracy with a market-driven economy. President Mwanawasa promulgated and implemented a policy of Zero Tolerance for Corruption in Zambia. The agreement signed in May 2006 for a three-year programme had a strategic objective of reducing corruption and improving Government effectiveness by, promoting greater transparency and thereby reducing opportunities for corruption; establishing the ZDA and PACRA offices in the provinces; and improving border management of trade.

The Threshold Programme was an interim arrangement meant to create an environment for implementation of a project in a specified sector of concern. In order to qualify for the next stage of the MCC assistance, Zambia had to fulfill seventeen benchmarks. The Threshold Programme addressed issues of corruption prevention in the DEC, ZRA, and PACRA by assisting with improvements in their operational systems and procedures.

By June 2008, Zambia was assessed as having met fifteen out of seventeen eligibility benchmarks and qualified for an MCC Compact project. The Zambian Government in 2009 chose a project in water, sanitation and sewerage management in the Lusaka City as the beneficiary of the US $355 million. Having lived in Lusaka since 1964, I was aware of the significant deterioration in the standards of personal and public hygiene in not only Lusaka City, but in all urban areas. The citizens do not take care of public infrastructure such as buildings and water systems and they dump rubbish anywhere, resulting in blocked sewer lines.

Applying such a large amount of donor funds to fixing leaking taps and drainage trenches in Lusaka townships, will not solve a serious national problem of indifference to personal hygiene. A national project in some soft infrastructure such as land policy reform, ICT training, youth empowerment or hygiene education in schools would have been more appropriate and productive.

During the IMF/World Bank Spring meetings in April 2007, my delegation, which included the Zambian Ambassador to the USA, held meetings with the Deputy Assistant Secretary of Treasury (DAST), William Larry MacDonald.

Our discussions centred on an earlier request for technical assistance towards the establishment of a treasury unit in my ministry. The DAST indicated that his department was willing to provide assistance in view of the visible evidence of prudent financial management exhibited by the current Zambian Government. An officer of the USA Treasury Department was seconded to the Ministry of Finance and National Planning to assist in establishing the treasury unit.

CHAPTER 35

An Epitaph For Zambia's Mining Industry

The mining industry has been a kingpin for the economy of Zambia and the forerunner Northern Rhodesia before independence. Much of the urban area along the line of rail from Livingstone to Chililabombwe was established and developed when opening up the mines on the Copperbelt. The major roads and the railway lines were established in order to facilitate the movement of equipment to the mines and in return, facilitate the movement of the minerals to the outside markets. No value addition was ever tried until after Zambia's independence when the Metal Fabricators of Zambia (ZAMEFA) Company Limited was established in Luanshya on the Copperbelt in 1968 to process some copper into rods.

In the Central African region, an experiment at regional integration was tried by forming the Federation of Rhodesia and Nyasaland in 1953, which brought together, under one government, the territories of Northern Rhodesia, Southern

Rhodesia, and Nyasaland. The economic motive behind the amalgamation was to share the abundant copper deposits in Zambia. Zambia "was the wealthiest of the three and actually contributed more to the overall building of the infrastructure in the Federation".

In 1964, when Zambia became an independent state with its own black government, the mines continued to belong to foreign-owned companies. In 1969, President Kaunda announced the part-nationalization of the mining companies during the Matero reforms declaration. The mining operations were put under two companies, namely, Nchanga Consolidated Copper Mines (NCCM) and Roan Consolidated Copper Mines (RCCM) under the management of indigenous Zambian managers, namely Francis H. Kaunda and David Phiri respectively.

The Copperbelt was an enclave of well-to-do and well-paid workers in the midst of the majority poor Zambians. In fact, President Kenneth Kaunda referred to the unsatisfactory dual situation as 'two nations in one'. One nation was enjoying a lavish meal, while the other nation was picking crumbs from under the dining table!

As early as 1971 when I joined the Zambian Government Civil Service, I started hearing complaints about the raw deal the Zambians were getting from the mining companies. When I was an Assistant Development Officer in the Office of the Cabinet Minister for Southern Province in 1971, I visited the Mapatizya amethyst mining area in Kalomo District to familiarize myself with mining operations there. Since I did not find the white boss of the amethyst mine and the mine was guarded by vicious Alsatian dogs, I could not tour the mine.

The security guards informed me that the purple stones were loaded into timber boxes and taken to an airstrip near Kalomo Town. From there, the stones were flown to an unknown destination out of Zambia by the white owners. A check at the Department of Mines revealed that no declarations were made by the exporters of the amethyst.

After discovering that the boreholes we were sinking for drinking water between Munyumbwe and Chipepo yielded red water, I enquired with the Water Affairs Department at head office. I was informed that there was an occurrence of uranium, a poisonous but an important industrial mineral in the area. To mine uranium, there must be a clear protocol as to its marketing and disposal. When one foreign investor tried to mine the uranium discreetly, some of the workers were poisoned and the mining operations were exposed. The amethyst and uranium issues became part of my subjects of interest later during my public service.

Ten years later in 1981, when I rose to the strategic position of Director of the National Budget, I decided to bring the mining revenues into government coffers, so that the rest of the country would benefit.

It was a known fact that the extractive mining industry would exhaust the mineral ore bodies and close down at some point in the future. Additionally, it was a known fact that the prices of minerals and revenues from the mines were unreliable and volatile since they were determined through the London Metal Exchange (LME), an organization over which Zambia had no control.

We decided in 1982 that the tax rate on agricultural income be reduced to fifteen per cent in order to encourage investment in the sector in an effort to diversify the economy. In further support of this plan, I also proposed the introduction of a Mineral Export Tax (MET) and the creation of a Diversification Fund to hold revenues from this source. The Fund was to be used to develop agricultural projects such as the proposed large irrigation projects and infrastructure in other sectors.

In 1982, the Zambia Consolidated Copper Mines (ZCCM) Limited was created by the amalgamation of the two mining companies. The new conglomerate was placed under Francis Kaunda as chief executive officer. I was advised by Special Assistant to the President (Economics) Dominic Mulaisho, to discuss the proposed mineral tax with the Chief Executive Officer of ZCCM as the tax was to mainly affect the mining company.

After a few pleadings, I was given an audience. I actually walked across for the meeting as the Ministry of Finance offices were close to the Anglo American building housing the ZCCM. It took a lot of pluck to visit the CEO of ZCCM, running the richest company in Zambia. We regarded him as the most powerful public officer in the country's economic sector. His status was equated to Mark Chona, who wielded enormous influence in the political arena. The two public officers were rarely seen in public. Luckily, I was introduced to Chona by his spouse Victoria Chona, nee Kalimina, who was a director of the foreign exchange department at the Bank of Zambia. In later years, I became a close functional relative, who was rarely missed at their family functions. I regarded my appointment with Kaunda of ZCCM as a breakthrough in my efforts to relate the country's enormous natural mineral resources to its national development efforts.

My discussions at Anglo American House were not encouraging. The CEO stated that his company was capable of organizing settlement schemes for farmers and there was no need for his company to pay a tax to the Zambian Government. I argued that agriculture and mining were big industries with specialized requirements and it was unwise to put them under one institution. I had been a planner of agriculture for nearly ten years and I knew that agriculture was totally different from mining and not many countries operated the two industries under one management structure.

In spite of the negative reaction to my proposal, we included the proposal for a MET in the 1983 Budget Memorandum to the Cabinet. Before the Cabinet meeting, I had a long briefing session with His Honour Nalumino Mundia, Prime Minister and Minister of Finance, during which I convinced him on the need for a special tax on the mines. After some heated debate by the Cabinet, the new tax was approved. This meant that the management of the mining company was required to disclose the financial status of the company to the Government.

The MET was collected during the financial year 1983 and deposited in the Diversification Fund account at the Bank of Zambia. In August 1983, I was transferred from the Ministry of Finance to the Ministry of Commerce, Trade, and Industry (MCTI). In the following year, the MET Act was revoked and the special account at BOZ was closed. The money in the special account was transferred to the general expenses account of the Zambian Government.

I could not understand the reversal of the tax measures as they were meant to benefit the Zambian owners of the mineral resources. For me, the proposed mining tax regime was a means for the Zambian Government to take control of the large revenues from a very important industry. President Kaunda had advocated for control of the mining industry as early as 1967 when through his lobbying, the Intergovernmental Council of Copper Exporting Countries (CIPEC) was formed in Lusaka. The cartel with membership of Zambia, Zaire, Chile, and Peru, the four major copper producers had a noble objective of controlling the production and marketing of copper so as to influence the prices offered on the LME.

The ZCCM went ahead and established a unit to run agricultural settlement schemes for the retired miners. Some land was acquired in Kabwe for the new scheme. The company also started a huge crop irrigation project in Mpongwe next to the Government's Munkumpu Farm. I politely declined an invitation with attractive conditions to join the ZCCM as an officer in its new agricultural unit.

In 1971, the amethyst at Mapatizya was safeguarded by the foreign operators against Zambians by vicious Alsatian dogs. Not many Zambians knew how much was being realized by the foreign miners. In 1983, efforts to disclose and share the revenues earned by the government-owned ZCCM were also resisted and thwarted. I presume the Zambian managers of ZCCM were also using dogs of the ferocious Alsatian breed to guard the minerals against trespassing fellow Zambians at Nampundwe and on the Copperbelt.

Even as the mines went into a crisis in the late nineties, vital information on the operations of the mines was not readily available within the government system. Due to this state of affairs, doubts were raised as to the amount of money needed by the Zambian Government to maintain the mines during the ZCCM privatization impasse.

I was out of the country between July 1996 and March 2000, the period when the mines were privatized. I am among many Zambians who did not fully understand the meaning of the conditions of the sale of the mines. Many foreigners with whom I interacted with in my overseas job enquired about the deal but I was unable to give an acceptable answer.

At the end of January 2002, the Anglo American Corporation (AAC) that bought the mines in 1999 pulled out of the Zambian mining scene. They gave low copper prices as the reason. Such action could have left an additional 18,000 miners without a livelihood if the Zambian Government of the day had not intervened.

As a reaction to the AAC decision, the newly elected President Mwanawasa was determined to find a solution and stated that, "The decision by Anglo American to withdraw has put Zambia and the lives of its people at risk. Our short-term measure is to renationalize the mines until we get a strategic partner".

With the crisis at hand, the Mwanawasa Government decided to take over KCM as an interim measure to keep the mines running, while a partner was being sought to manage the operations. A Task Force headed by the Director of Mines in Government was appointed to examine options presented by KCM, so as to prevent what many of us believed was an impending national catastrophe.

The World Bank and the IMF showed solidarity with Zambia as they were party to the perceived muddled privatization of the mines. In May 2002, Calisto Madavo, Vice President for the Africa Region visited Zambia and promised to stand by Zambia during the time of the mining crisis.

The Deputy Managing Director of the IMF, Shigemitsu Sugisaki also visited Zambia on a fact-finding mission. He openly conceded that ten years of structural adjustment had left Zambia poorer than it had been before. He indicated that Zambia's annual foreign debt service would reach US $420 million in 2003.

The Minister of Finance, Emmanuel Kasonde assured that funding would be provided if the need arose and declared that, "The solution for KCM lies in the private sector". In June 2002, the Minister announced that he had found adequate money to run the mines until May 2003, when a new partner would take over. This was followed by a statement by President Mwanawasa in July 2002 that negotiations with prospective bidders for the mines were progressing well. By the time I joined the Mwanawasa Administration in June 2003, the privatization of the mines was at its tail-end.

I received stacks of documents for signing from the Zambia Privatization Agency (ZDA) on the privatization of the mines in 2004. Large teams of technically qualified Zambian professionals with foreign advisors sat for months to negotiate the agreements.

On 6 November 2004, I flew into Livingstone Town and signed the agreement by the serene waters of the Zambezi River with Nivan Argawal, Vice Chairman of Vedanta Resources for the acquisition of KCM shares. Fifty-one per cent shares in KCM were sold to Vedanta for a cash payment of US $25 million and $23 million in deferred payment.

As I got involved in the finalization of the privatization of the mines, I then wondered how many Zambians could get it right when even AAC with decades of operating the mines could not get the price dynamics right. As an economist, I preferred that Zambia had sold the accurately valued mining assets, including mineral deposits underground. But then, which Zambian or foreign mining professional was capable of determining the value of these mineral assets lying nearly two kilometres in the ground?

Questions arose on the profitability of the KCM when the new owners announced their profitable first accounts on the operations of the mine. The MMD Administrations under Presidents Chiluba and Mwanawasa sold shares of the mining companies including Konkola Copper Mines (KCM) and not the assets. The balance sheet of ZCCM or KCM never showed the value of the buried copper ore bodies.

On 10 August 2005, a group of ministers accompanied President Mwanawasa to Solwezi for the official opening of Kansanshi Mine owned by First Quantum Minerals. I looked forward to the visit because earlier in 2004 I'd had a surprise encounter with a member of staff of the Canadian High Commission. The high-ranking officer accused me of 'harassing our companies operating in Zambia over taxes'.

The conversation ended in an undiplomatic fashion with the officer bragging that, 'this is the reason we are closing our Mission in Zambia'. I retorted that God had a good reason for putting copper in Zambia and that the officer was free to leave Zambia and its copper. This was the only diplomat I ever had an undiplomatic conversation with.

As we started off early in the morning from Lusaka, we had breakfast at the mine in Solwezi. While Joyce Muwo was apologizing to the president for the delayed breakfast due to the eggs that had to be imported from the Copperbelt, Philip Pascal pulled me into his office. With a comment that I looked strange, he offered me a necktie as I did not have one on me. I had ignored my spouse's advice in the morning that it is always better to be overdressed than to feel out of place. I realized that the Canadian diplomat's arrogance was not shared by the investors.

During the tour of the mining area, the two brothers, Philip and Matt gave a detailed explanation of the operations and future plans. We were amazed at the amount of advanced technology being used, which facilitated young people including females to control sophisticated machines such as huge dump trucks. In the control room, a young female controller impressed us greatly when she boasted that she could shut down the whole mine within seconds. I was more encouraged to learn that she was trained at one of our local colleges.

Among the mining industries started during President Mwanawasa's reign was the mining of nickel and platinum at the Munali Hill in the Mazabuka District by Albidon Limited, an Australian company. I was privy to a detailed brief on the mine project by Dr Sixtus Mulenga, the General Manager (Operations). I was excited with the plans presented by Mulenga a Zambian mining stalwart of over thirty years' experience.

The mine was situated in an agriculturally-active area and in my home area. Since my childhood, I had been hearing of the presence of lubulo (iron) in the area. I was, therefore, looking forward to experiencing the role of mining in developing rural areas. I took time to read the proposed development agreement and made certain that the issues of social responsibility and the participation of the local people in providing transport and health facilities were incorporated.

On Tuesday, 3 April 2007, I was among the guests who were invited to the ceremonial opening of the nickel mine by President Mwanawasa. It was a grand occasion attended by hundreds of people from within the province, who had never seen a large-scale underground mine before. I was lucky that I had the opportunity to go underground at the Broken Hill Mine in Kabwe in 1984 when I was PS for the Central Province.

We were taken on a conducted tour of a new settlement, where displaced villagers were allocated new houses constructed by Albidon Mine. The villagers were also given some cattle and assisted with maize seed and fertilisers for the first crop season. We were informed of plans to expand the local primary school and construction of houses for the four chiefs. I was approached by local small-scale businessmen who expressed gratitude to the Government for the opportunity to be suppliers of services and goods to the mines. All these plans and developments gave me hope on the positive multiplier effects of mining.

In March 2007, the price for nickel had hit US $50,000 per tonne, while platinum was selling for US $30,000 per tonne. I implored the investor to set up a smelting plant on site instead of shipping the ore all the way to China. On Tuesday, 26 June 2007, Board Member Valentine Chitalu and Mulenga gave me a lot of hope in a meeting at my office that plans were on board to establish a smelter once the production had increased to a higher level.

The Munali Nickel Mine proved the unreliability of mining for long-term national development as the mine stopped operations in 2009, a few months after the first sale of minerals. The price of nickel had slumped to US $14,400 per tonne in July 2009. The mine was put under care and maintenance. All the high hopes for a rapid development of the Mazabuka District were shattered. The local people reverted to their ancient but reliable occupation of farming.

President Mwanawasa convened a meeting of the officials of the mining companies to discuss the operations of the mining industry. The meeting held on 30 March 2006 was attended by officials of ten mining companies. They were accompanied by Emmanuel Mutati and Frederick Bantubonse, officials of the Chamber of Mines. Other Zambians in the meeting were John Chongo of Ndola Lime, Valentine Chitalu of Albidon, and Wilbur Simuusa of Maamba Mine. The President informed the mine officials that the Government was considering amending the mining tax regime in order to raise more revenues from the sector.

As Minister of Finance, I wanted to have a second bite at the cherry with another attempt to improve the contribution of the mining sector to government revenues and hence benefits to the country. Fearing another failure like that of 1983, I asked the IMF to fund a study specifically to look at the mining tax regime. A two-person team of consultants undertook a comprehensive study and concluded that the current tax provisions were more in favour of the mining investors to the disadvantage of the country.

Having received adequate information from the IMF consultants, I gave a thorough brief to President Mwanawasa who decided to dialogue with the mining companies again. President Mwanawasa decided to share the results of the consultancy with the senior officials of Lumwana Mine, Mopani, Kansanshi, Konkola Copper Mines, NFC Chibuluma, Albidon, and Chambishi in separate meetings between 2 and 18 May 2007 at State House in Lusaka

The companies were advised that only senior management or shareholders should attend the meetings with the President. Most of the companies were represented by senior managers and the shareholders, many who travelled from their bases abroad. No officials of the Chamber of Mines were present in these meetings as they were neither shareholders nor managers of the mines.

During the meetings, the Secretary to the Treasury gave details of the findings and recommendations of the consultants on mining operations and taxation in Zambia. The President informed the mining executives that the Government would share the report of the IMF consultants with them and this was done. The President went further to state that his administration had decided to renegotiate the Mining Development Agreements (DA's) and he expected to receive maximum cooperation from them.

At about the same period, concern was raised on the operations of the emerald mining industry. The government sent a mission led by Kaunda Lembalemba, Minister of Mines to Botswana to study the operations of the diamond mining industry as this was the nearest successful similar industry. The team toured the diamond mines in Botswana and collected valuable information.

One peculiar aspect learnt was that the diamond industry in Botswana was placed in the security sector with attendant security treatment to safeguard the diamonds. Any trespasser in the diamond mining area was dealt with the highest severity as a security breach.

During the discussions on the team's report, a few of us proposed that the area with emeralds in Ndola Rural District be accorded security protection. I offered to seek funds for a platoon of security personnel to guard and secure the area. My argument was that any expenditure on such security would be easily recovered from the earnings from the sale of Zambia's renowned emeralds. It was estimated that the country was losing over US $600 million from the precious minerals sector each year.

I narrated a story of my visit in the company of my wife to Antwerp in Belgium, which is considered the world centre of jewellery, when we lived in Brussels in the nineties. We asked the shopkeeper for the origins of the bright green emeralds on an artistically-designed and expensive necklace in a tightly secured locker. He told us that it came from an African country called Zambia and asked us if we knew the country.

When we proudly informed him that we were Zambians, he remarked that we should then not admire the necklace as we already owned some expensive jewellery of the highest quality emeralds in the world. I felt very embarrassed that a foreigner was attributing such opulence to me and my spouse and yet we had never even seen a rough emerald in Zambia. A few times, some cunning young men had tried to make deals with me, but their merchandise turned out to be green broken traffic glass.

Back in Zambia in those days, the emeralds, once mined, were securely stored. Not even the Managing Director of the Reserved Minerals Corporation (RMC), Winner Matongo, a long-time family friend, had the courtesy to tell us when he was visiting Ndola rural, the home of the best emeralds in the world. His trips to collect the 'stones' and the flights to the Geneva auctions were guarded secrets.

My consolation was that the proceeds of the auctions found their way into a government bank account, as Matongo was of the highest religious calling and integrity. Of course, the story of emerald mining and auctioning quickly changed after the takeover by the MMD party in 1991.

The protracted debate in the Cabinet in 2007, reminded me of another incident while I was on a trip to Dakar in Senegal in 1999. We had just completed our tour of Dakar's crowded market when my Senegalese escort insisted that I should visit a township called Zambia. After some resistance, I obliged and as we drove along a well-maintained boulevard, my attention was attracted to the many large posh houses.

My escort explained that we were in Zambia Township, where the opulent Senegalese have built heavenly homes. He went on to say that many of them made money from trading in Zambian emeralds and that is how the township got its name.

I could not hide my shame when I recalled that in present-day Zambia, many of the townships named Zambia are unplanned shanty townships, where the poor and the destitute live. Instead of safe-guarding Zambia's name and its natural wealth, the Zambians abuse it by associating it with unplanned settlements with dark alleys and heaps of uncollected garbage. The precious emeralds are acquired by foreigners for a pittance that cannot even be used to erect a decent house.

The Cabinet discussions on emerald mining were inconclusive as there were too many opposing views to the proposed security arrangements under the guise of human rights. Thereafter, I refused to indulge in futile discussions on emeralds as I came to know some black sheep amongst us. The precious emeralds remain unprotected and are given away to make foreigners rich and comfortable, while Zambians continue to wallow in abject poverty.

By 2007, copper prices had risen to record prices above US $3.50 per pound (US $8,000 per tonne) from US $0.81 per pound at the end of the 20th Century. Zambia's copper is sold at the LME price plus a premium for quality. Due to the abnormally high mineral prices, it was decided to constitute a team of local technocrats from various departments under the leadership of the Secretary to the Treasury to study the whole mining industry with a view to renegotiating the Development Agreements.

The DAs signed in the nineties had appropriately allowed long periods of tax relief as incentives in view of the very low copper prices at the time. The Zambian Government had been advised by international organisations that the low prices will continue for a long time.

We asked some foreign governments to host the team and explain the applicable tax regimes on their extractive industries. The team visited many mining countries in both Africa and Europe to study the relationships between the private mining investors and the host governments.

In Europe, the team was hosted by the Norwegian Government, which has a developed and reputable tax system for its crude oil extractive industry. We even organized a seminar in Lusaka for the Norwegians to explain their oil mining tax regime. When visiting some African countries, the team included Zambian traditional rulers in whose land some minerals are situated.

Equipped with appropriate data from around the world and the earlier IMF report, the fifteen-person team went on a retreat in Livingstone to finalize their recommendations on the way forward on the mining tax regime. After a week of simulating each large mine in Zambia, using information submitted at the time of investing, the team concluded that the DAs in their current form were lopsided. The team, therefore, recommended the establishment of a new fiscal and regulatory framework for the mining sector and the renegotiation of the DAs.

In December 2007, while on a Presidential delegation to Lisbon, Portugal, to attend the second EU-Africa Summit, I took the opportunity to brief the President on a number of budget issues. I had carried with me copies of the final report produced by the team of technocrats on the mining tax regime proposed by my Ministry. Due to the sensitivity and technical nature of the matter, I decided to have a witness during my discussions with the President.

I gave a copy of the report to Mutati and asked him to study the report so that he could assist me in briefing the President. As a competent accountant, I expected Mutati to find some faults even minor ones in the calculations of the finances but he was fully satisfied with the numbers.

We agreed that the inner feeling of patriotism should come out fully during the presentation. The minerals being a patrimony from our ancestors should not be taken away without adequate recompense. The two of us then rehearsed on the format of the presentation we were going to make to the President. We even went further to rehearse how the President should present the part of his speech on this issue when he opened Parliament.

It took us just under three hours to discuss the matter of the new mining tax regime with President Mwanawasa. Once convinced, the president stated that he was prepared to personally defend the decision of the Zambian Government anywhere in any properly-constituted court of law. I proposed a novel format of presenting the Presidential speech in Parliament, which would require the President to take a short break just before discussing the mining tax issue.

We were then instructed to draft the part of the speech to Parliament on this matter. President Mwanawasa advised us to consult the Clerk of the National Assembly on our proposed presentation format. I recall the President looking exhausted by the time we were leaving his hotel room at about 2330 hours, but I was pleased that he had finally appreciated the importance of the issue we had discussed.

During the Summit, I signed a funding agreement with the EU. When asked about the mining tax regime, I stated that Zambia would soon not need any aid from Europe as we would be generating enough from the mines.

On our return to Zambia, I briefed my officers and they were excited with the news on the President's reaction to the proposed mining tax regime. We all saw a historic opportunity for Zambia to be independent of donors by raising adequate revenues from our own abundant natural resources.

My officers and I schemed about a radical 'Plan B' that would kick in should the mining companies refuse to cooperate. A few officers from other departments including Zambia Police and immigration were co-opted into our Plan B. The President featured in the alternative plan of action as the Commander-in-Chief of the security services.

I repeated the rehearsal of the presentation of the budget proposals to the Cabinet on many occasions in January 2008, so as to have many converts amongst my colleagues. With the involvement of the President, we carefully crafted the paragraphs on the mining sector. All the time, I was aware that the Chairman of the Cabinet was already a converted disciple and was prepared to defend the new mining taxation system. The Clerk of the National Assembly agreed on our proposed novel format of presenting the Presidential Speech.

On Friday, 11 January 2008, President Mwanawasa delivered his speech at the ceremonial opening of the Second Session of the Tenth National Assembly. In his introductory remarks, he stated that:

Mr Speaker, I believe that all the Members of Parliament have been informed that I intend to break my speech this morning into two parts. When I reach this stage, where I am about to make a very important policy statement I will ask for an adjournment of fifteen minutes to enable me to reconstitute myself and to enable you to come back rejuvenated because it is important that you should be able to understand very well the purpose of this policy statement.

The opening remarks were delivered in the manner befitting the Commander-in-Chief. The tone threw the House into a state of anxiety as "to reconstitute myself" was a grave statement. At 1130 hours, the President called for an adjournment. For the first time in the history of the Zambian Parliament, the House took a historic break of fifteen minutes during the official opening speech. As only the Speaker, the Clerk, I, Mutati and my officers were aware of the unprecedented adjournment, there was speculation that perhaps President Mwanawasa was not feeling well enough to continue with his speech.

I was approached by many Members of Parliament, including some ministers enquiring on what was going on. But I did not give any hint that I knew the reason for the break. At 1145 hours, the President walked into a House full to capacity but dead silent. Everyone was waiting anxiously for the President to resume his speech. In a composed manner, he continued to say:

'Mr Speaker, in my last address to this House in October 2006, I made an undertaking that my Government would introduce measures that would result in increased benefits to the economy and people of Zambia from the mining sector. These measures include the review of the mineral royalties, production of more geological maps and introduction of the mining cadastral surveys, formulation of a Mines Health and Safety Policy, and the empowerment of citizens to participate in the mining sector.'

I would now like to address this Honourable House on the matter of the mining industry and the inadequacy of its contribution to the welfare of the Zambian people.

The President gave an elaborate explanation of the work that had been done in order to arrive at the decision of introducing a windfall tax on the mining industry. He informed the Nation that the DAs were unfair and unbalanced and no longer met their intended purpose of providing maximum benefits to the Zambian people and an appropriate return to the mining companies. As a consequence, it was decided that a new fiscal and regulatory framework for the mining sector would be put in place.

The President stated that the price of copper on the international market had increased by 400 per cent to historic levels. The implication of such a sharp rise in prices was that the mining companies had recouped their initial capital investments and made huge profits within a short period of time. President Mwanawasa elaborated that in spite of the 400 per cent increase in copper prices, the stability periods contained in the development agreements were premised on low prices remaining unchanged and the mining companies were continuing to pay taxes at the concessional rates.

The President concluded that the effect of mining companies paying taxes at concessional rates had resulted in the mining companies paying a paltry US$ 142 million in company taxes and mineral royalty to the Treasury from total earnings of US$ 4.7 billion in the 2005 and 2006 financial years. The taxes were only three per cent of the total earnings. Even assuming operational costs of US$ 2 Billion, the tax was still about five per cent of net income.

It was evident from the reactions of both sides of the House that the message on mining taxation was most welcome. I was delighted that even the opposition Members of Parliament were in full support of the proposals announced by the President.

As a follow-up to the announcement by the President on the new mining taxation regime, I gave the following details in the 2008 budget speech:

CHANGES TO THE MINING FISCAL AND REGULATORY REGIME

Mr Speaker, in my 2007 Budget Address to this august House, I proposed new tax measures for the mining sector. I also informed the nation that the Government would engage mining companies, with whom we had signed Development Agreements, as part of the process of introducing the new tax regime for the mining sector.

Sir, given the complexity of the mining sector, a team of experts was appointed to study this matter in great detail. The findings of the study show that:

(a)   the Development Agreements in their current form are lopsided; and

(b)   even if mining companies were to move to the 2007 tax regime, the country would still not get a fair share from its mineral resources.

Sir, the Government has, therefore, decided to introduce a new fiscal and regulatory regime in order to bring about an equitable distribution of the mineral wealth between the Government and the mining companies.

Mr Speaker, effective 1st April 2008, the new fiscal regime for the mining sector will include the following:

(a)   The corporate tax rate will be thirty per cent;

(b)   Mineral royalty rate on base metals will be three per cent of gross value;

(c)   Withholding tax on interest, royalties, management fees, and payments to affiliates or subcontractors in the mining sector will be at the rate of fifteen per cent;

(d)   Withholding tax on dividend will be at zero per cent;

(e)   A variable profit tax of up to fifteen per cent on taxable income, which is above eight per cent of the gross income, will be introduced;

(f)   A windfall tax will be introduced to be triggered at different price levels for different base metals. For copper, the windfall tax shall be twenty-five per cent at the copper price of US $2.50 per pound but below US $3.00 per pound, fifty per cent at price for the next fifty cents increase in price and seventy-five per cent for price above US $3.50 per pound;

(g)   Hedging as a risk management mechanism shall be treated as a separate activity from mining;

(h)   Capital allowance, that is a depreciation of capital equipment, shall be reduced from 100 per cent to 25 per cent per year;

(i)   A reference price, which shall be the deemed arms-length price, shall be introduced for the purposes of assessing mineral royalties and any transaction for the sale of base metals, gemstones, or precious metals between related or associated parties. The reference price shall be the price tenable at the London Metal Exchange, metal Bulletin or any other commodity exchange market recognized by the Commissioner General; and

(j)   Capital expenditures on new projects shall be ring-fenced and only become deductible when the projects start production.

Mr Speaker, the new mining regulatory framework will be provided for in the Mines and Minerals Act. The framework will also have a modern licensing system based on transparent procedures.

Sir, these measures are competitive, reasonable, and balanced. The expected additional revenues, in 2008, as a result of these new measures are estimated at US $415 million.

The Mines and Minerals Development Act 2008 revoked the Minerals Development Agreements on which privatization was based. It established a legal framework based on international good practice and made provisions for creating a favourable environment for foreign investment.

The new mining law of 2008 also provided for the sharing of mineral revenues with the local communities where minerals are extracted from, with a view to creating synergy with their social and physical development. A formal benefit-sharing framework with procedures for mining company contributions to social development of the local communities was to be enacted by the legislature.

While the parliamentarians were in full support, we realized that unless the mining investors understood the calculations on the windfall tax, they would raise some objections. We, therefore, organized a series of meetings with individual mining owners and managements to discuss the details as they affected each company.

I took charge and my team met officials from Mopani Mines, NFC Africa Mines, Chibuluma Mines, and KCM between 2 and 20 March 2008 in our conference room. My team included all the officers who had participated in the study tours and in the simulations in Livingstone. This time, it was the real situations as presented by the mining investors and not simulations that we discussed in detail.

We went through the initial investment proposals for each mine to appreciate the prices of copper, the production costs, the breakeven prices and the projected rates of return at the time of presenting their investment plans. Everyone in attendance including me was armed with a pocket calculator and each one of us calculated the various ratios, which we compared amongst the group. In all cases, it was clear that the effective tax rate of forty-seven per cent would leave enough revenue for each mine to continue operating profitably.

One financial controller of a big mining company could not add forty-five and two per cent. To our amazement and the embarrassment of the Chairman of his company, who had travelled a long way to come and argue his company's case, the officer who was using a modern pocket calculator, kept saying that the total was forty-nine per cent!

I was informed later that the officer was dismissed immediately the team reached their hotel in Lusaka. He was directed to rush to the Copperbelt to collect his belongings and to leave Zambia by the earliest flight from Ndola.

Apart from this sad incident concerning one of the meeting participants, the meetings were held in a cordial atmosphere. At one point, a Chinese executive jokingly asked for a higher retained profit margin for Chinese investors since investors from other countries had already extracted 16 million tonnes of copper since 1906. According to him, they had therefore long recovered their investments. My comment was that the Zambians expected the Chinese not to adopt the bad habits of the western investors, who had tyrannical intentions behind their actions. I stated that the Chinese should instead equitably share the mineral revenues with the Zambians.

By these elaborate and technical discussions, it became obvious that some of the resident mine managers were feeding the head offices with wrong information. Some senior officials of mining companies were reluctant to come for meetings with us because they discovered that they had been fed wrong information by their representatives.

Soon after our meetings, the price of Zambian copper rose to prices of above US $4.00 per pound! What became of concern was the percentage of the windfall tax collected by the Zambian Government when copper prices rose above US $4.00 per pound or US $10,000 per tonne, which had not been anticipated in our projected prices. At such prices, the Government would collect nearly 100 per cent of the surplus income above the maximum threshold of US $3.50 per pound in the month of revenue collection. The companies would be short of funds for operations before they were paid for exported minerals as deliveries were made but paid for in arrears. This had not been the intended objective of the new windfall tax.

After discussions with the Zambia Revenue Authority, it was decided that the windfall tax would be collected on the provisional basis of monthly copper prices. The effective tax amount would be confirmed at the end of the year after reconciliation. Such a procedure was normal for the revenue collecting authorities so as to allow some revenue to be used for the operations of the taxpayers.

On 25 June 2008, I wrote to President Mwanawasa recommending modifications to the method of collecting the windfall tax in order to level the revenue flows of the mining companies on a monthly basis during the year.

I proposed that (i) the technical team re-examines the whole new mining tax regime, particularly with regard to the windfall tax, taking into consideration the escalating costs of production and the abnormal price of copper and (ii) the Commissioner General of ZRA collects the windfall tax as a provisional tax at the lowest rate of twenty-five per cent, so that the mining companies operations are not adversely affected during the year.

The effect of proposal (ii) was that the effective tax rate would be calculated at the end of the operating year and the windfall tax would then be adjusted accordingly to a maximum of forty-seven per cent. The balancing at the end of the year was in order to align the tax with the Government's policy of preserving the viability of the mining environment, while at the same time getting a fair share of the country's mineral resource.

The contents of my letter were discussed with President Mwanawasa during our telephone conversation of 25 June 2008 before I left for the AU Summit in Egypt. His Excellency accepted my recommendation, which I communicated to the Commissioner General of Zambia Revenue Authority (ZRA), whom I instructed to hold a meeting with the financial directors of mining companies to explain the new payment procedure.

When I returned from Egypt in early July, I was briefed by the management of the ZRA that they had held a successful meeting with Financial Controllers of mining companies in Chingola on 30 June 2008. The meeting discussed the proposed amendment in the collection of the new windfall tax for the mining companies. At the meeting, the amendment on the collection system was agreed to by those present.

Due to policy consistency and adequate consultations within the government and with the mining industry, there was mutual understanding between the mine owners and the Government of President Mwanawasa. After these consultations, I never heard any mining investor threatening to close their operations. The windfall tax was accepted by all mining investors with a provision that at very high copper prices the threshold and government share would be adjusted using an agreed formula.

I had personally briefed Vice President Banda on the amendments to the mining tax regime. His new Minister of Finance had participated in the various discussions on the proposals as economic advisor to President Mwanawasa.

It was shocking to hear later from the secretariat of the Chamber of Mines that the mining investors were not consulted on the new tax regime. Meetings were held not only with the ZRA, the tax collector, but with me and my staff and with President Mwanawasa, who took a bold and nationalistic stance to appropriately tax the extractive mining sector.

Using the new taxation system, an amount of US $485 million in windfall tax was collected in the financial year 2008 and deposited in a special account at the Bank of Zambia. I was left out of the Cabinet appointed on 14 November 2008 by President Rupiah Bwezani Banda after the presidential by-elections of October 2008.

Laws to improve tax revenue collections had been passed with my personal involvement in 1981 and 2008. But these were revoked. The actions of revoking the laws on the taxing of the mines, which have deprived Zambians of large quantities of revenue from the God-given natural mineral resources, were taken by human and political actions. It is not for lack of technically-competent Zambian civil servants that the Zambians are getting a raw deal from the exploitation of their natural mineral resources.

President Mwanawasa understood and accepted our recommendations and announced a more progressive tax regime for the mining industry in his speech in January 2008.

In 2009, the progressive tax regime was revoked by President Banda "in order to ensure that we do not kill the goose that lays the golden egg". The special account was closed without an explanation and the money in the special account transferred to the main account for government ordinary operations. I was even more baffled when an audit query was raised by the office of the Auditor General asking me to explain why I had opened a special account for the safe custody of the mineral revenues.

For the miners that have produced over twenty million tonnes of copper since 1906, and to the millions of Zambians who wallow in poverty, and those who died without benefitting from the mineral resources, President Banda's words are a forlorn dirge for the goose that has long left the nest.

CHAPTER 36

The Fight Against Hiv/Aids And Other Diseases

Zambia's health care system, like those of other countries in Sub-Saharan Africa, are ill-equipped to combat a scourge of the magnitude of the HIV/AIDS pandemic, as they lack the financial and material resources required. The pandemic ravaged the sub-region, decimating the productive workforce, and causing untold human suffering towards the end of the 20th Century. Other long-term effects of the pandemic include reduced food security due to reduced agricultural activity and the plummeting life expectancy of forty-two years for Zambians.

In July 2001, I led a two-person team of consultants that developed the United Nations Development Assistance Framework (UNDAF) for Zambia, which was a framework for collaboration among the thirteen UN agencies and with the Government of Zambia. The UNDAF process entailed us identifying the key development challenges and priorities of the Zambian Government and the harmonization of the support and strategies of the UN agencies based in Zambia towards achievable common development goals.

We identified three strategic areas of intervention and they were employment, social services, and governance along with three cross-cutting issues of HIV/AIDS, gender, and regional integration.

In June 2002, I coordinated four teams of thematic specialists in preparing the GRZ/UNDP Second Country Cooperation Framework (CCF) that identified common objectives and activities for cross-project linkages. Projects were prepared in the areas of environmental protection and natural resource management, and the cross-cutting areas of gender, HIV/AIDS, and information and communication technology.

The projects' strategy supported the Zambian Government's governance programme for poverty reduction as articulated in both the Poverty Reduction Strategy Paper (PRSP) and the Transitional National Development Plan (TNDP) while taking cognizance of the Millennium Development Goals (MDGs) of the international development community.

As team coordinator, I went through the draft reports and moderated the various workshops where the consultants presented their draft reports to GRZ and UNDP officers. This exposure provided me with valuable and detailed situational information on HIV/AIDS, which I used when advising the various ministries on intervention programmes.

President Mwanawasa committed himself to providing free antiretroviral (ARV) drugs in his May Labour Day Speech in 2003. During his visit to Washington DC in June 2003, the President in his discussions with the President of the World Bank again committed to providing leadership in the fight against HIV/AIDS. This encouraged the international community, which pledged to help raise the needed funds for the ARVs. In August 2003, Zambia became the first country in Sub-Saharan Africa to receive a grant of US $42 million from the World Bank for the fight against HIV/AIDS.

In December 2003, I hosted a regional meeting that considered a survey report on the business community's response to HIV/AIDS in Zambia, Kenya, Tanzania, and Uganda. AIDS had grown to pandemic proportions and was the single most serious threat to life and prosperity in the developing world. A global effort was on through UNAIDS, the United Nations agency, which estimated that a staggering forty million people were already infected with HIV worldwide. In Zambia, a survey had estimated that sixteen per cent of all persons between fifteen and forty-nine years of age were infected with HIV.

One of the benchmarks for reaching the HIPC Completion Point, which had not been attained by 2003, was on the fight against HIV/AIDS. As a follow-up to his promise in 2003 to lead the fight against HIV/AIDS, President Mwanawasa instructed the Ministerial AIDS Council to effectively supervise the National HIV/AIDS/STI/TB Council. As a member, this gave me the opportunity to push for the implementation of all the actions required to meet the HIPC target.

Apart from adequately staffing the Council, HIV/AIDS awareness and prevention programmes were mainstreamed in ten ministries. Programmes were worked out and supervised through the Zambia National Response to HIV/AIDS (ZANARA) and the Community Response to AIDS (CRAIDS) project unit in my ministry.

In early December 2004, I accompanied Dr Brian Chituwo to Abuja, Nigeria, for a donors' meeting on coordinated funding of HIV/AIDS programs. The participating donors were highly impressed to see practical cooperation between the Minister of Finance and the Minister of Health and this led to a promise to upscale the funding to Zambia. During the meeting, Zambia was nominated to chair the meeting and also to be the rapporteur.

In 2004, President Mwanawasa declared HIV/AIDS a national emergency and promised to provide ARVs drugs to 10,000 people by the end of the year. Having exceeded this target, he set another target to provide free treatment for 100,000 by the end of 2005. During the year, Zambia received US $254 million from the Global Fund against HIV/AIDS. The leadership of President Mwanawasa against the HIV/AIDS attracted many donors among them the

USA President, whose Emergency Plan for AIDS Relief (PEPFAR) gave a grant of US $149 million in 2006.

President Mwanawasa directed that all Government senior officials must include HIV/AIDS issues in their official speeches at all functions. Some of my family members and friends fell victim to the pandemic and due to self-denial, treatment was late. I adopted the HIV/AIDS pin as part of my permanent dress code in memory of the departed and to remind those I met that there was danger looming in the community.

On Friday, 4 January 2008, a few Ministers and I were invited to Mfuwe for consultations with the President who was on a working holiday. I was among the ministers who were booked at Chimfule Lodge owned by the Mataka family. I seized the opportunity to discuss with my hostess Mrs Elizabeth Mataka on how Zambia could access more funds from the Global Fund to fight HIV/AIDS, TB, and Malaria.

At the time, Mataka of the Zambia National AIDS Network was the Vice Chairperson of the Global Fund based in Geneva and a UN Special Envoy on HIV/AIDS in Africa. The Global Fund was a specialized institution created to mobilize funds for the fight against the AIDS pandemic, TB, and Malaria.

I was aware that Mataka had a lot of influence on the decisions made by the Global Fund. Being a citizen of Botswana and a resident of Zambia, the two countries most affected by HIV/AIDS in the region, she was strategically positioned to help in resource mobilization. The Mfuwe outing provided a conducive environment for me to exchange valuable information and strategies with her.

In the fight against Malaria, Zambia was implementing an ambitious National Malaria Strategic Plan 2006 – 2010. By April 2009, it was reported that Malaria deaths from health facilities in Zambia had declined by sixty-six per cent. This positive result, along with other supporting data, indicated that Zambia had reached the 2010 Roll Back Malaria target of more than fifty per cent reduction in malaria mortality compared to the 2000 results. The programme included the distribution of insecticide-treated mosquito nets, although no Zambian knew what insecticide was being used and its residual effect on humans.

I was aware that funding from the Global Fund was up-scaled because of a strong political will shown by President Mwanawasa to fight the pandemic. The President showed a keen interest in the Sondashi Formula 2000 (SF2000) as a traditional and alternative remedy against AIDS. In 2004, in spite of the Presidential instructions to the Ministry of Health to adequately fund the investigations, no budgetary provision was made by the ministry. We released funds directly from the Ministry of Finance, which were used in carrying out further clinical observations on the herbal medicine in 2005 and 2006.

The remarkable achievements in the fight against HIV/AIDS and malaria were due to the combined and concerted efforts of the Zambian Government, civil society organizations and many unsung heroes and heroines. However, it is anomalous that the Zambian Government, which was the first African government to adopt coartem made from Artemisia, a herb grown by Chinese villagers, has failed to financially support the development of traditional medicines such as SF2000.

In his address to the Third Session of the Ninth National Assembly on Friday, 16 January 2004, President Mwanawasa stated that,

"Mr Speaker, in order to ensure equity of access to the treatment of cancer and cardiac ailments, Government embarked on a program to localize the treatment of the two diseases at the University Teaching Hospital. To this effect, open heart surgery is now being undertaken at the University Teaching Hospital, while at the same time, work on the establishment of a cancer diseases hospital has commenced".

True to his word, President Mwanawasa worked hard on this project supported by the International Atomic Energy Agency (IAEA). The OPEC Fund for Technical Corporation provided a soft loan to the Zambian Government. On Thursday, 19 July 2007, the nation rejoiced and joined the President at the commissioning of the first cancer disease hospital in Zambia and Southern Africa on the UTH grounds. The hospital reduced the agony of cancer patients having to wait for a long period before being attended to and of enduring the odious journey to South Africa and Zimbabwe for treatment.

After joining the Mwanawasa Government in June 2003, I became aware that specialized medical and laboratory services were not available in Zambia. In September 2003, a close friend of mine was evacuated to South Africa for medical attention. I was informed by the health authorities that many other Zambians were in various hospitals in South Africa. I was further informed that medical specimens had to be sent to South Africa for laboratory analysis. This was not only costly, but it delayed the administration of treatments to the patients.

My enquiries revealed that a good number of doctors attending to evacuated Zambian patients in South Africa were Zambian professionals. Some had been in the group of 200 doctors dismissed by the Chiluba Administration in 1998. The specialist who was providing laboratory diagnostic services in the whole Southern Africa region was Professor Neil Nkanza, a Zambian based in South Africa.

Nkanza and I had known each other since our days at the University of Zambia in the sixties. After his graduation, Neil worked for a while at the University Teaching Hospital and later did postgraduate studies in the United Kingdom before migrating to South Africa.

During one of my trips transiting through South Africa, I asked the Zambian High Commissioner to RSA to arrange for a meeting with Neil. Because of time limitations, I requested that Neil be allowed into the VIP Lounge at the OR Tambo International Airport for our discussions. After getting details on his practice, I asked Neil to consider establishing a branch of his medical laboratory in Zambia. He asked for time to consult on my request. During two more meetings at the same venue, we discussed all aspects of such a project.

On 9 May 2006, Nkanza visited my office in Lusaka and informed me that my request had been granted and that he was working on establishing a medical laboratory in Lusaka. I was excited about the good news and promised Neil that I would lobby the Minister of Health to instruct all his medical institutions to use the modern laboratory in Lusaka.

I then informed him that under the Japanese-assisted ToH, an Indian investor was considering establishing a state-of-the-art hospital with a capability to carry out modern keyhole surgery. I invited Neil to participate in the hospital project as well. By coincidence, President Mwanawasa had a meeting with the Resident Doctors' Association of Zambia earlier at 10.00 hours on the same day to brief them on the proposed modern hospital project.

Professor Nkanza honoured his word and established the Lancet-Nkanza Laboratories along Longolongo Road opposite the Levy Junction Mall in Lusaka in 2008. With specialist modern laboratory equipment at this facility in Lusaka, it became possible for Zambian patients to get their medical specimens analysed within hours and the illnesses identified and treated on time.

Sometime in 2007, Cabinet appointed a committee of four ministers to deliberate and make recommendations on the utilization of the money and goods recovered by the Task Force on Corruption. I was appointed Chairman since the committee was to deal with Government assets. After consultations, the committee concluded its deliberations in January 2008 and recommended that some of the goods be sold by public tender. An amount of K13 billion was raised through auctions of various goods plus cash recoveries.

My committee recommended that the money be utilized to construct maternal annexes in rural hospitals as part of the Government's concerted effort towards improving maternal health. Cabinet approved the recommendation and directed that maternal wings be constructed at thirty-four rural hospitals spread throughout Zambia.

In June 2007, I accompanied the First Family to the AU Summit in Accra, Ghana. On our return flight, President Mwanawasa gave a lift to Mundia Sikatana, Minister of Agriculture who was not feeling well. Although this restricted my choice of subjects, I seized the opportunity to persuade the Minister of Agriculture to introduce Artemisia annua (sweet wormwood) as one of the crops for growing by small-scale farmers in view of its importance as a source of coartem, the malaria drug.

I explained to the First Family and the Minister the advantages that would accrue to Zambia health-wise and financially as the price of the plant had skyrocketed because of the acceptance of coartem by the World Health Organization (WHO) as a drug of choice for fighting malaria. I gave an example of the economic value of the medicinal pyrethrum crop to the small-scale farmers in Kenya and Tanzania.

I mentioned that I had already discussed the matter with the Minister of Health, who had shown some interest. In spite of my heavy prodding at the two Ministers, nothing was done and Zambia was beaten by Kenya and Tanzania where small-scale farmers have become important producers of Artemisia for coartem manufacturing in the developed countries.

CHAPTER 37

Planning Zambia's Future Development

As Chief National Planner for the country, I had to keep abreast with all the above development programmes and supervise their coordinated implementation. I had also to come up with innovative plans, projects and programs. Having scored highly in the political arena in 2006 with peaceful elections, the country was ready to embark on the economic path with audacious medium and long-term plans.

The preparation of the Fifth National Development Plan was marshalled by PS James Shamilimo Mulungushi of twenty years' experience in the Ministry. The Plan was finalized by an inclusive conference that brought together Zambians from all corners of the country. The launch of the Fifth Plan by President Mwanawasa on 16 January 2007 was the herald of the restoration of national long-term planning in Zambia. This particular Plan was to provide an umbrella for all the programs and projects during the period 2006 to 2010.

The dissemination of the planning instruments took an important novel aspect in terms of accommodating every stakeholder. For the first time in the planning history of the country, the Vision 2030 and the executive summary of the Fifth National Development Plan 2006-2010 were translated into seven local languages. In alphabetical order, these were ciBemba, ciNyanja, ciTonga, Kaonde, Lozi, Luvale, and Lunda. The production of official documents only in English in the past had marginalized those who could not write nor read in the foreign language of English.

In addition, my Ministry transcribed the Vision 2030 and the executive summary of the Fifth National Development Plan in Braille for the blind to fully participate in the development agenda of the country. It was also decided that major functions should include sign language interpretation. This innovation, which was included in all national events, was greatly appreciated by the stakeholders with disabilities.

Having achieved macroeconomic and political stability, it was time to refocus the energies of citizens into wealth creation and job creation. The overwhelming vote for President Mwanawasa in the 2006 elections was an indicator of the trust the people had in his policies. Many citizens were beginning to feel the positive impact of the projects and programmes by the 'New Deal Administration'. To accelerate the involvement of the citizens in development, the theme of the FNDP was, 'Broad-based wealth and job creation through citizenry participation and technological advancement'.

The theme underlined the aspect that economic growth stimulation should be complemented by distributive measures that have a direct and positive impact on the people. In the Foreword to the FNDP by President Mwanawasa, 'poverty reduction' and 'poverty' were mentioned only once each. I had given instructions to the ministry's officers that the Ministry's documents and my speeches should not focus on 'poverty' nor 'poverty reduction'.

The Ministry officials took a stand that we should aim for wealth creation, which was visionary and inspirational and not on poverty reduction, which was a deficiency symptom. Since there is no limit to richness or wealth, we took the view that even the not-so-poor would need government facilitation for them to consolidate and improve their status. Through such programmes, more secure opportunities would be created for the vulnerable.

While wealth is visible and can be shared, poverty is only a manifestation of a state of being of an affected individual and can never be shared. No one can feel the depth of the impact of another individual's poverty. It is, therefore, the responsibility of the poor to articulate their poverty and a desire to create wealth as a means of alleviating the impact of poverty on them. Each one of the adult Zambians must articulate their own path towards a better future life for themselves and their offsprings.

We had conceptualized a vision for the state of the country at some future date. The United Nations Development Programme earlier offered to develop Vision 2025. After a lot of consultations, it was decided to take a span of twenty-five years. This was to allow a child born in 2005 to go through a deliberate and structured learning program from pre-school through primary and secondary school to tertiary education.

The curriculum was to be reformed to include character formation, culture, the three Rs (reading, 'riting, and 'rithmetic), and skills acquisition to support human capital formation and survival. Efforts were to be made to impart relevant knowledge for dealing with local endowment and resources. A child in an area with fishing potential was to learn fishing skills and the making of fishing equipment. Thus 2030 was coined as the target for the country's long-term development perspective.

Vision 2030 reflected the collective understanding, aspirations, and determination of the Zambian people to be a prosperous middle-income country. It reflected what the Zambian people aspired to be by 2030 and the options they felt would realistically get them there. The Vision was to be operationalized through five-year medium-term instruments, which were to contain specific policies, programmes, and projects towards wealth creation through broad-based growth.

Having physically traversed the world and through my readings, I had become aware of the various paths taken by a number of countries towards development. I became convinced that it would not be feasible for Zambia to follow the path of the many European countries and most of the Americas. These countries had capitalized on low-cost skilled and abundant labour, commonly known as slave labour and the abundant raw materials from the colonies to jump-start their development.

Zambia could not follow the path of the countries that had benefitted from the era of massive inventions as most useful inventions had already been made. What were required were innovations to make the existing inventions relevant to Zambia's particular development situation.

During the negotiations for debt relief and the discussions on the Direct Budget Support, my delegation was often asked as to what new ways of financial management and development we intended to introduce in order to consolidate the country's development path. I got the impression that even those who had poured billions of donor funds into our country were frustrated as they could not see any sustained development.

Dambisa Moyo succinctly stated that "Statistical records from the 1960s are scant, and estimates of the miles of tarred road and railway track, the numbers of bridges and airports, that aid helped build, remain unclear". This was the origin of the term, 'donor fatigue' by development practitioners. It was therefore heartening to hear the Japanese Government proposing a new path for development assistance different from that followed by the Western donor countries and multilateral financial institutions during Zambia's life of five decades.

The behaviour of the entrepreneurial class in Europe with the work ethic that believed in progress, technology, and hard work propelled the industrial revolution during the 19th Century. The invention of the Spinning Jenny in 1764 had a profound impact in the processing of cotton into yarn in Europe. The invention of the sewing machine by Elias Howe and its introduction in American homes in 1887 transformed social patterns and lifestyles. The machine's time-saving character led to economic benefits for families, as many housewives were able to engage in paying jobs outside their homes.

Zambia's special long-thread white cotton had continued to find its way to sewing machines in distant foreign countries after the dismemberment of LINTCO and the closure of textile mills under the privatization exercise.

A small group of Zambian ministers and senior civil servants were sold to a new way of doing things. We coined and openly and loudly voiced the term, 'Brain Re-engineering'. There was a need for a philosophical and ideological change that would lead to a process of rationalization and transformation. The change was to focus on wealth creation and not only growth. The introduction of the concepts of the Vision 2030, ToH, the CEEC, MFEZ, Culture Remodeling, and ICT Policy were efforts towards rationalization and transformation that would result in innovations in social behaviour, technology and economic management.

For the accelerated development of Zambia, we planned to change the mind-set of the majority of Zambians, so that they could easily accommodate innovation and turn negatives into positives. At the September 2005 meeting of ZIBAC in Livingstone, Ashank Desai, one of the advisors, had encouraged Zambians to regard Zambia's geographical situation as that of being 'Landlinked' instead of 'Landlocked'.

He urged the Zambians to produce agricultural commodities for food and industrial raw materials for the 200 million people in the eight surrounding countries. Such trade would not require a seaport, which appears in the archaic definition of landlocked countries by the United Nations as a sign of being a disadvantaged country. In the modern age of the internet, a lot of trade in services goes through invisible channels.

Since the culture of a community is embedded in the mind-set of the individuals, we wanted to remodel the attitudes, activities and relationships of the Zambians. Ashank Desai advised that 'Brain Drain' equals to 'Brain Gain' and that it was the responsibility of the government to provide a conducive environment to attract back and gain from the Zambian nationals in the diaspora.

We conceived a program entitled, 'Culture Remodelling', in which through the use of the print media, radio, and television, the Ministry of Finance and National Planning would expose a number of the major and innovative activities in the country. By sharing this information, we believed that every Zambian would be inspired and aspire to play their part in driving the change and innovation agenda forward. The CEEC was to facilitate the exploitation of the country's great potential by supporting individuals with projects that would overcome the challenges.

For remodelling to succeed, there must be (i) a compelling reason for change, (ii) a clear vision for the future and (iii) a coherent plan for getting to destined futre.

I launched the Culture Remodelling program on Tuesday, 23 October 2007 at the Mulungushi International Conference Centre. The program had a special theme song by pupils of Ndole Primary School in rural Katete District of the Eastern Province. The program became very popular as it showcased the various economic activities across the country. We strategized that some of the activities would be aired and televised just before football matches so as to catch the attention of the football-loving Zambians in their best mood.

After showing the new steel plant in Kafue on television, a senior citizen of the Kaunda era of the seventies called me with a message of congratulations. He confidently stated that with available steel in the country, it would be easy to produce the much-needed tools for development. I disclosed to him that the promoters had promised, during the signing of the investment agreement for the steel plant in 2004, to construct a railway line from the iron ore deposit at Sanje Hill in Mumbwa to the steel plant in Kafue Town.

The missing vital element in national planning had been that of the country's population and the inter-relationship between population and various aspects of development. The last population policy had been produced way back in 1991. The TNDP, FNDP and Vision 2030 had not dealt with this matter in spite of the high correlation between the number and quality of the population and development.

During the launch of the FNDP, it was decided that the Ministry should coordinate a discussion on population dynamics and come up with a population policy to guide the sector ministries in their planning of various interventional projects. It was agreed during the discussions that family planning should be regarded as a development and not a health issue. After extensive consultations, a new National Population Policy was launched on 18 January 2008.

By the time of the presentation of the 2008 national budget in January, Zambia's positive and favourable economic parameters had been confirmed. The Introduction to the budget speech presented on Friday 25 January 2008, therefore confidently stated that,

"Mr Speaker, over the past five years, the Nation has achieved macroeconomic stability characterised by growth in the real Gross Domestic Product (GDP) in excess of five per cent per annum, the reduction of inflation to single digit, a stable exchange rate, declining interest rates, a stable financial system, the removal of the external debt burden, and a substantial build-up in foreign exchange reserves. These achievements have resulted in notable successes in the creation of jobs and wealth, and the reduction in poverty levels.

Sir, our cherished and chosen vision is to be a prosperous middle-income country by 2030. This will be achieved by creating a Nation of dynamic, self-confident and vibrant entrepreneurs. Our foremost challenge, this year and in the medium-term, is to create the fiscal space that will allow us to marshal both human and financial resources. This will enable us to accelerate the implementation of the Fifth National Development Plan.

Mr Speaker, to realize this vision, the theme of this year's budget is 'Unlocking Resources for Economic Empowerment and Wealth Creation'".

The country had moved from 'Austerity' in 2004, through 'Steadfastness' in 2005, 'Sacrifice' in 2006, 'Improved Service' in 2007 to 'Unlocking Resources' in 2008. The final results of the Living Conditions Monitoring Survey done in 2006 indicated that poverty levels had dropped by four points from sixty-eight per cent in 2004 to sixty-four per cent in 2006. Of particular significance was the drop of urban poverty by twenty points from fifty-four to thirty-four per cent within two years. This positive trend raised great optimism that indeed poverty could be significantly reduced amongst the vulnerable within a much shorter period with a GDP growth of six per cent per year.

There was a need to accelerate the implementation of the Public Service Management (PSD), Public Expenditure Management and Financial Accountability (PEMFA) Reforms, Financial Sector Development Plan (FSDP), and the Private Sector Development (PSD) initiative to create an enabling environment for citizens' participation in the economy.

The 2008 budget provided funds for specific programmes within the overall reform agenda. Amongst the major ones were the capitalization of the CEE Fund, the facilitation of the development of the Lusaka South Multi-Facility Economic Zone, and the completion of the Chipata-Mchinji railway line. A number of measures to unlock resources for economic empowerment and wealth creation were announced during the budget presentation.

As per tradition, the Ministry officials spent time explaining the budget to various stakeholders. As a departure from the past, we had decided to undertake tours of the provinces in order to explain the programmes provided for each province in the budget.

High copper prices and improved economic management had led to the trebling of the per capita income. Although Zambia experienced significant overall growth between 2002 and 2008, averaging more than 5.6 per cent per annum, the country was a long way from achieving any significant drop in the high poverty levels and inequality in wealth distribution.

CHAPTER 38

Seeking Public Support Through Politics

I had never contemplated joining mainstream politics during most of my adult life as I had wanted to perfect my skills as a technocrat in economic matters. However, in early 1996, I considered the possibility of standing in the Magoye Constituency in Mazabuka District of the Southern Province as the economic situation in Zambia was deteriorating under President Chiluba's reign. The MMD administration was already cracking and weak with resignations by some senior members.

As I was firming up my plans to stand for elections, the Chiluba Administration nominated me as a candidate for the position of Secretary General of the African Caribbean and Pacific (ACP) Group of States. I was unanimously elected by the ACP Council of Ministers and I was away from July 1996 until February 2000. The move to Brussels, therefore, cut short my plans to engage in active politics in the 20th Century.

During my farewell tour to the ACP regions in February 2000, I discussed my future plans with a number of Heads of State and Government. The discussions, which were prompted by their asking if I intended to engage in national politics, always ended up with advice that I should not rush into politics as it was not a clean game.

After my return to Zambia in March 2000, I opted to assist my elder brother Anderson Kambela Mazoka, President of the United Party for National Development (UPND) with his political ambitions as one of his advisors. In spite of this, in July 2003, Republican President Mwanawasa nominated me a Member of Parliament and appointed me Minister of Finance and National Planning. As I was not a Member of Parliament for a constituency, I still foresaw a bright future outside politics.

On Thursday, 13 April 2006, during a meeting, President Mwanawasa raised the matter of a constituency for me for the forthcoming general elections later in the year. I informed the President that I had not chosen a constituency because I did not intend to engage in active politics. He asked me to reflect on the matter since he had brought it up.

When the matter came up again in May 2006, I informed the President that I preferred to return to the private sector as a consultant, since I had achieved the goals we had set at the beginning of my tenure in 2003. President Mwanawasa argued that since the economy had improved under my stewardship, then I could easily win elections in any part of Zambia. He stated that there was no good reason for my leaving Government at that point in time, especially when he was confident of the ruling party winning the forthcoming elections in October due to its good performance.

The issue of my standing in the elections kept on creeping into my conversations with President Mwanawasa. When he mentioned that he needed me for some future plan of his, I gave in and agreed to stand. In my consultations, a lot of supporters advised me to stand in the Magoye Constituency in the Southern Province.

The passing away of Andy on 24 May 2006 created an atmosphere that liberated some of the UPND members to show open hostility to me for having joined Mwanawasa's government. In Parliament, my strongest critics were UPND MPs and in particular those from the Southern Province, where I hailed from. Even the MP I had personally helped to win the Magoye Constituency in 2001 joined the group of my critics.

I was desirous of getting a clarification from Hakainde Hichilema, the new President of UPND, on the confrontational behaviour of UPND Members of Parliament and arranged for a meeting. Unfortunately, the meeting between HH and I arranged for 9 June 2006 did not take place. On account of the continuing hostility, President Mwanawasa objected to my standing in the Southern Province, fearing that the UPND would concentrate their campaign resources in the constituency and I would lose.

The President explained that my winning elections in a constituency outside the Southern Province would also enhance my nationalist character, which was needed for his future plan. After further consultations, I finally accepted to stand in the Chilanga Constituency in the Lusaka Province. The Constituency was a good testing ground for my acceptability because it has both an urban and rural voting population.

By this time, many candidates had mounted vigorous campaigns, a situation I was not aware of since I had not planned to stand. In the Chilanga Constituency, there were some active MMD members who had already made inroads and even started organizing structures at the grassroots. Two of the most active hopefuls, Kelvin Sampa and Chiselwa Chafwa introduced themselves to me and offered to withdraw and help me with the campaign.

I was among a large number of candidates interviewed by a panel made up of Provincial and District Committee members at the Garden Motel, the birthplace of the MMD. The interviews were done professionally as they consisted of the same questions asked to all the candidates. Fortunately for me, a good number of questions were on Zambia's economy and international trade matters.

On Saturday, 10 June 2006, I was adopted by the MMD NEC at a meeting held at State House as the MMD candidate for the Chilanga Constituency. After adoption, I started touring the constituency to familiarize myself and to participate in a number of public functions.

One of these was a ceremony for laying a foundation stone for the new Chilanga Market in late July 2006. I was invited to the ceremony by the PS for Lusaka Province. The plot for the market was under the Kafue District Council, which had a dispute with a Mrs Mwelwa.

I found myself summoned at the High Court as a joint defendant for having attended the ceremony. I was accused of taking away the plot from Mrs Mwelwa to start a market as an appeasement to the marketeers. After a few appearances at the High Court, I was acquitted as I had never dealt with the plot. It transpired that the Patriotic Front Party had assisted Mrs Mwelwa to bring the matter to the courts to derail my campaign.

Between 10 June and 26 July 2006, I divided my time between public office and the party campaign. Sampa took me to some wards and introduced me to his organizers and followers. Chafwa being the Chilanga Constituency Chairman accompanied me on my tours and later was appointed as my campaign manager.

On 28 June 2006, I received a telephone call from Hakainde Hichilema during which we exchanged greetings. He then stated that *"Tulivwide mang'unung'unu"*, meaning 'We are hearing the whispers'. I confirmed with him that I was the adopted MMD Party candidate for the Chilanga Constituency in Lusaka Province. He concluded our conversation by saying that it would be an onerous task for me.

The nomination centre for Chilanga Constituency was at Musamba Primary School near the Lafarge cement factory. The order of appearance was that the United Democratic Alliance (UDA) candidate would be the last, just after me, in the afternoon. The UDA was an alliance formed between UPND, FDD, and UNIP.

There was a large crowd for the UDA candidate with some supporters bussed from outside the constituency. At the conclusion of the nomination program, the UPND President addressed a public rally at the nearby sports grounds, where my name featured in the speeches. Chilanga Constituency was the only one that was personally visited and addressed by the UPND President on nomination day. I then realized why he had said that it would be a big challenge for me.

When I went to the offices of the Electoral Commission of Zambia to pick up some election documents, I was informed by a senior official that the Patriotic Front and UPND had made a pact to target their campaigns on me. I was further informed that the two parties had already agreed to petition the results up to the Supreme Court should I win. I was advised to be extra careful during the campaigns and avoid giving any kind of gifts even sweets to children.

Chilanga Constituency turned out to be much larger than I had thought. It shares boundaries with six constituencies in all directions. The constituency, which covers most of the peri-urban south-western, western, and north-western sides of Lusaka City, is very rich in both human and natural resources, with good soils suitable for agricultural activities.

The population strata constitute of mostly farm and office workers, farmers, retirees, and landlords. One peculiarity of the constituency was the preponderance of prominent retired and serving public and private sector personalities. For example, there were fifteen retired military and security officers of the rank of general who were resident in the constituency and many former senior leaders of UNIP.

A large number of serving and retired ministers, permanent secretaries, and chief executive officers of parastatal and private companies resided in the area. Among them were my former bosses and workmates, whom I knew during my thirty-five years in the public service, who volunteered to assist me in the campaigns.

As it was difficult to bring together these prominent people into formal committees and gatherings, I formed a strategic planning committee. The leader of my consultation team was Dr Chapa Chikamba, a formidable former student political activist during our UNZA days. In the southern area was Josias Songolo. For the working class, I invoked the assistance of Chintu Mulendema to organize meetings at various outing places during the weekends, where we engaged in some technical conversations.

Since the constituency had been lost by the MMD and was regarded as a UPND stronghold, I could not rely on the campaign strategies of the past. I found space to introduce my own campaign strategy, and a number of party officials fell by the wayside as they could not agree with it.

I formed a campaign team outside the party structures, led by Ms Grace Choombe. The councillor candidates, members of the parallel team, and some loyal MMD Party officials, constituted the Constituency Campaign Team. I was the overall leader and provider of both campaign strategies and materials.

I received a lot of cooperation from the various groups and was allowed to address workers on farms separately from the farm owners. This allowed the workers the freedom to freely explain issues affecting them, most of which related to their treatment and working conditions. The working middle class residing in the peri-urban areas were concerned with issues of roads and security. Many were aware of Mwanawasa's plan for an ambitious ring road system in the city, which would solve their mobility problems.

Discussions with retirees centred on their insufficient retirement benefits. Many former high-level personalities owned sizable pieces of land given freely by the UNIP government but they could not productively utilize this precious asset to make a living. Suggestions of subdividing and selling portions were totally rejected as the land was being reserved for their offsprings. The counter suggestion that they now subdivide and give land to their children was also rejected.

At a meeting of landowners, I suggested that they form a public company and employ an agricultural extension officer on a part-time basis to advise on the commercial use of their land. My suggestion that they use their land as security to borrow from financial institutions was not welcome. Some explained that the young people in lending institutions discriminated against them and insurance companies also refuse to cover senior citizens, who were above the threshold age.

This unfavourable environment left the majority of the prominent retirees living in deplorable conditions with disintegrating houses built at the peak of their careers. Many are unable to find money to buy medicines for their 'old age' ailments, such as arthritis, diabetes, gout, and high blood pressure. They reminded me of a law passed some years back on free medicines for the elderly for specific ailments, which was not being observed. By the end of the campaign period, I realized the great neglect of the old retired workers.

The two main opposition parties divided the constituency between them. The PF adopted the southern part, while the UDA took the northern segment. The presidents of the two parties made frequent sallies using public transport to the designated parts of the constituency, right up to the voting day.

On the afternoon of Wednesday, 27 September 2006, the day before the elections, the ECZ suddenly replaced the returning officer and most of the election officers and voting assistants in the Chilanga Constituency with new officers. A senior officer from the ECZ head office was appointed as the new returning officer. He put in extra efforts to deliver all voting materials during the night and all stations were ready for voting by daybreak.

There was peace on the voting day in the whole constituency. I toured most polling stations from north to the southern tip and found enthusiastic voters in long queues. At the conclusion of the election exercise, I was declared the winner followed by Captain Moono of UPND and Priscila Kamanga of PF in third position.

I was proud that I was accepted and had won elections in a constituency outside the Southern Province, my place of birth. By this time, politics had degenerated into tribal affiliations with candidates seeking votes from the electorate because 'I am your child'. Others appealed for support claiming their umbilical cords were buried in the constituency in which they were standing. I was a Member of Parliament on the basis of the voters' assessment of my contribution to their well-being and not on the basis of my origins or future promises.

The petition against my election

Sometime in October 2006, President Mwanawasa summoned me to his office and informed me that a petition had been lodged in the High Court against me by the two losing candidates from the UPND and the PF parties. I then revealed to the President what I was told by the ECZ official in July 2006 on the intentions of the two opposition parties to fight me up to the Supreme Court.

President Mwanawasa jokingly wondered why the UPND should petition me when "we have implemented most of their plans and the Zambian people are happy". He was least concerned as to whose plans we were implementing, as long as they helped to resolve Zambia's economic problems.

When asked if I had a lawyer to represent me, I told the President that since the matter was new to me I had not thought of any legal representation. The President then informed me that he had arranged for one of Zambia's best legal minds on constitutional law, Mr Steven Caution Mwaba Malama, State Counsel of Messrs Jacques & Partners to represent me in the matter.

Malama was a former Member of Parliament for Wusakile Constituency in Kitwe between 1974 and 1978 under UNIP. He was a member of the legal team that had represented President Mwanawasa during the petition on the 2001 elections. The name was familiar to me, but I had not had the opportunity to know him closely.

I received the petition documents on 27 October 2006 with sixty-two allegations. At our first meeting, Malama assured me that he would handle the matter to the best of his abilities and would expect me to give him the latitude to proceed in his own way. He emphasized that the alleged malpractices were too simple and would not lead to any serious conclusions.

According to him, the petition was a political ploy to tarnish my name and curtail my future political advancement and to weaken President Mwanawasa's administration. The two petitioners were represented by counsels Mulilo Kabesha and Edgar Chagwa Lungu, who later became President of Zambia.

The petition was heard by a panel of judges of the High Court led by Justice Mr Marvin Mwanamwambwa. During the early stages of the hearing, the plaintiffs amended their plea to include a recount of the votes to which my lawyer agreed. The court was also informed that only one petitioner, Captain Moono would be present during most of the time. The case hearing went on for most of 2007 as the judges had a lot of other election petitions to handle.

After the court hearings showed that the allegations could not be corroborated and some were trumpery, the petitioners were banking on the recount to reveal different vote numbers. Unfortunately for the petitioners, the recount conducted by the Registrar of the High Court even improved my score. The recount showed a clear division of the constituency by the two parties. I was number two to Captain Moono in the northern part of the constituency and number two to Priscilla Kamanga in the southern part.

In his four-hour judgement, made on Monday, 30 July 2007, Judge Marvin Mwanamwambwa stated that he did not find any acts of bribery nor corruption as defined by the Electoral Act. He further said that the proven non-compliances with the Act did not warrant nullifying the election result. He gave details that out of 17,883 valid votes cast, I got 6,478 votes and this was less than fifty per cent of the total valid votes cast. The opposition candidates shared among themselves 11,405 votes. His conclusion was that I would have lost if the opposition had not split the votes.

I was delighted to have been cleared of all the sixty-two allegations brought against me. However, having been forewarned by my lawyer and the ECZ official on the political nature of the petition case, I suspected that the battle would be shifted to another arena. I was therefore not surprised to be informed a few weeks later by my lawyer that Ms Kamanga of PF had appealed to the Supreme Court.

As I was not familiar with court procedures, I accepted the advice of my lawyer that we wait for the hearing of the appeal, especially since the appellant was a lawyer herself. The petition, which took its own course, was decided in my favour on 19 August 2008, the day President Mwanawasa passed on at Percy Military Hospital in France.

While the petition was being processed through the courts, I was busy liaising with the community in my constituency on their development needs. A few weeks after the elections, I requested the Ward Committees to nominate candidates for membership to the Constituency Development Committee (CDC), which was responsible for supervising the utilization of the Constituency Development Fund (CDF).

Together with the officers of the Kafue District Council, we selected six members. I then proposed Moses Nawa, residing in Namalombwe Ward, as chairman of the CDC to the Council. The six plus a Chief's Representative, the Director of Works, and the District Planning Officer and I constituted the ten-member Committee.

With Moses Nawa, an experienced Lozi banker as chairman, the CDF was properly managed and resulted in the completion of fifty-six community projects in the areas of agriculture, education, human and livestock health, manufacturing, security, roads, and water between 2007 and 2010. Apart from giving technical advice during the selection of the projects, I was not involved in the choice of the projects that benefitted from the CDF. These were submitted by the ward committees to the CDC Secretariat in the council and selected by the CDF Committee using strictly laid down criteria.

Payments to contractors were by cheques, which were drawn by the Secretary and signed by the CDF Chairman and one other member but not the Member of Parliament. I only saw the cheques when the Chairman requested to sign them during the meetings of the CDF Committee. I was therefore surprised to hear so many stories of embezzlement of CDF money by some Members of Parliament. It became evident that Members of Parliament were conniving with Council staff to misapply the CDF funds. I requested the Minister of Local Government to design new operational procedures for the

CDF, so as to seal the loopholes.

CHAPTER 39

Winning President Mwanawasa's Trust And Respect

I had left public service in May 1994 as a Group Investment Director at ZIMCO Limited responsible for the Agribusiness Directorate consisting of twenty-one companies in the agriculture and agro-processing subsectors. The Group Investment Directors were mere observers during the negotiations between potential buyers of parastatal companies and specially-constituted teams by the Zambia Privatization Agency.

I was frustrated with the Chiluba Administration's 'no sacred cow' privatization programme, after all that I had done to create, operationalize, and develop many of the parastatal institutions during my twenty-three years of public service. For example, I did not see any good reason for privatizing or liquidating the Lima Bank, an action that deprived the farming community of a source of focused financing for their operations.

I was an active member of the Economics Association of Zambia (EAZ) taking part in discussions on many economic issues. One of the topical issues was the Structural Adjustment Programme (SAPs) agreed between the Zambian Government and the IMF based upon the principles of wholesome economic liberalisation and privatization.

A Zambian student, Gerry Nkombo Muuka doing PhD studies at the Edinburgh University in the United Kingdom organized a seminar in Kitwe in July 1994 to discuss the Structural Adjustment Programme in Zambia in view of the strong criticism made against the programme all over the developing world due to its 'one size fits all' principle.

At the seminar, I was introduced to Levy Patrick Mwanawasa, Vice President of Zambia who was attending on behalf of the Zambian Government. This was my first meeting with the man who later in the 21st century ascended to the Presidency of the Republic of Zambia.

My views were at great variance to those of the Vice President who defended the Government's blind loyalty to the IMF-instigated SAPs. I was aware of many developing countries in Asia and South America that had ignored the advice of the IMF to privatize all parastatal companies.

The implementation of the SAP failed as the Zambian Government did not meet the SAP performance criteria in 1995 and 1999. By 2000, President Chiluba was criticizing the IMF for the failed reforms that caused great poverty among the Zambians. In 2001, only three out of fifteen benchmarks of the HIPC Initiative were met. There was no policy consistency and a lack of good governance. By 2003, the Zambian economy was in total disarray with a huge budget overrun and high inflation due to unbudgeted and unplanned expenditures.

During our second meeting nine years later on 8 June 2003, President Mwanawasa informed me that he was thinking of appointing me to the position of Minister of Finance and National Planning (MFNP) as soon as I accepted the offer. The position had been vacant since March 2003 when Minister Emmanuel Kasonde was relieved of his duties.

President Mwanawasa admitted that he did not personally know me. In fact, I had to remind him that we had met in 1994. He stated that he was relying on information from a lot of people who interacted with me and who vouched for my integrity. The President stated that he was aware of my membership of the United Party for National Development (UPND) and of my role as economic advisor to Anderson Mazoka, the Party President. He continued to say that this did not matter as I was not even going to work for him but for the Zambian people who were affected by the poor economy.

As a gesture of a good host, the President offered a drink and I asked for some fruit juice. As he was persuading me to get a glass of wine, I told him that I had stopped taking alcohol in the eighties. "Oh, I did not know that", he exclaimed. I was pleased that the President at least knew one important aspect of my social behaviour.

Since 2000, when I came back from the ACP Secretariat, no senior official of the MMD Government had spoken to me. I was once more with another dilemma as I could not believe that an MMD President could make a genuine offer of employment.

President Mwanawasa accepted my request to consult on his offer. This was the first time in my working life that I exercised some personal authority on a Head of State. Previously, I had obeyed orders by Presidents Kaunda and Chiluba without any hesitation as an obedient civil servant.

During my employment under KK's Administration, I learnt of my promotions or transfers during presidential press conferences. FTJ tried to do better by sending emissaries to inform me of his desire to appoint me in his administration in 1991. However, when we met at Government House, President Chiluba assigned me to a totally different position, which I took up even when many people felt that it was subordinate to my experience.

President Mwanawasa did not feel jilted with my reaction. Instead, he requested me to prepare to leave for Washington DC USA to join a Zambian Government team to the IMF as a consultant. In respect of the   President, I accepted the offer of a consultancy and left Zambia on Friday 13 June via Johannesburg and London and joined the team in Washington DC the following day.

My assignment during the team's discussions was easy as I was relegated to a silent back row observer. I concluded that the cause of the cool relationship with the team leader was a lack of clarity on my role. I heartily welcomed the opportunity of knowing and sizing up the officers of the IMF and World Bank, who were dealing with Zambia. On 18 June 2003, I was directed to stay on in Washington DC and await the arrival of President Mwanawasa on 22 June 2003.

By the time President Mwanawasa arrived on Sunday 22 June 2003, I was on top of things with vital information from the IMF and World Bank officers. Using the information I had gathered, I helped Moses Banda, Special Advisor (Economics), to prepare a detailed brief for the 'President's eyes only'. In our long briefing meeting, the President gave us time to explain the pertinent issues that were likely to come up in the meetings with the various officials. Being my first technical meeting with President Mwanawasa, I put up my best show to prove my credentials and to turn him from a lawyer into an economist.

President Mwanawasa's patience to listen attentively made me feel comfortable that he was a supervisor I could work with. As a lawyer, he had one attribute similar to mine of writing copious notes during discussions. This helped us later when reviewing our conclusions of meetings and the status of follow-up actions on various issues.

During the meetings with the heads of the IMF and World Bank, the President was clear as to his mission. He did not only know what to say, but he knew how to say things in the financial and economic jargon. A senior officer of the IMF even mentioned to me that he had never met such a humble African Head of State.

In his round-up meeting with the President of the World Bank on 24 June 2003, President Mwanawasa promised "a strong economic team, participatory management of the State, privatization that is beneficial to the Zambians, and presidential leadership on the fight against HIV/AIDS and corruption". He then requested President Wolfensohn to, "help the new Minister of Finance, who is here with me to do the correct things for the benefit of the country". I acknowledged the gesture pointing in my direction with a low bow and I reckoned then that I had passed the litmus test.

At a dinner hosted by the Human Resources Development Institute, the subject of Genetically Modified Organisms (GMOs) in food was raised. President Mwanawasa was categorical in his rejection of GMO maize, as there was no proven research on their long-term effects on human health. This strong stance took centre stage in international circles heralding a caring African President of a small country, who could rebuff an offer of free food.

While in Washington DC, I found time to discuss with President

Mwanawasa some issues that required immediate attention. I left Washington DC on Friday 27 June 2003 after being paid the consultant's fee at my minimum fee rate of US $500 per day at the time.

The long period without a Minister of Finance invited heavy criticism by the opposition parties, including the UPND. In reply, President Mwanawasa stated that he would "take as much time as was required to find a suitable and committed Zambian to appoint in the position".

When I arrived in Lusaka on Sunday, 29 June 2003, I found a message that my seventy-nine-year-old father was very sick at Nkonkola Village. I left for the village on Wednesday, 2 July 2003. On Thursday 3 July 2003, while I was at the village, an announcement was made in Lusaka on my appointment as Minister of Finance and National Planning.

On Friday 4 July 2003, I was sworn-in at State House by President Mwanawasa as the new Minister of Finance and National Planning. In his swearing-in comments, the President stated that although he did not know me personally, he was appointing me to the lofty position of great trust only because I was a Zambian of considerable competence, experience, and patriotism. I felt greatly honoured that President Mwanawasa considered me one of the committed and suited Zambians amongst the millions of citizens.

He hoped that I would be loyal to him and to the Zambian people. The President mentioned a few problems, including the budget deficit and inflation, which had beset the Zambian economy and hoped that I would use my immense experience and skills to solve them. I was happy that President Mwanawasa remembered some of the notes we had prepared for him while in Washington DC.

I had long discussions with Mazoka, the President of the UNDP on 3 June at his Taba Farms in Kabwe and on 10 June at my residence to discuss the offer by President Mwanawasa. We finally concluded that I should accept the offer and Mazoka gave me his blessings.

Once President Mwanawasa had made clear his intentions to appoint me, I asked him to write a detailed letter of appointment with clear terms of reference. As a listening boss, President Mwanawasa did as I requested and my detailed letter of nomination as a Member of Parliament and appointment as Minister of Finance and National Planning dated 3 July 2003 was delivered to me on 4 July 2003.

In the letter, I was informed of the importance of my new position as follows;

"The position of Minister of Finance and National Planning is a very important one, and particularly given our current economic status, and requires that you must be aggressive, hardworking, and display a high sense of integrity. In this connection, it is important that you must help me to project and uphold that which advances the interests of this country forward".

The President directed that I should keep all our cooperating partners, particularly the IMF, World Bank, and EU fully engaged so that we derive maximum benefit from our association with them.

The President went further to state that,

The position of Minister of Finance and National Planning is one which builds or destroys this Administration in that Government will depend on you to mobilize the resources and to advise on how best those resources can be used for the benefit of the Nation. I want you to keep me fully and timely informed and advised. I have no doubt, given your wide experience, that you will live up to my expectation.

I expected a lot of comments on my appointment and I was encouraged that even leaders of some opposition political parties welcomed it. Amongst them was Michael Chilufya Sata, President of the Patriotic Front who recalled having known me as a hardworking man with immense experience and knowledge in economics. "I hope Magande will help President Mwanawasa rectify the Budget overrun", Michael Sata told a Times of Zambia reporter on 4 July 2003.

President Mwanawasa had forewarned me of the likely hostility from fellow cabinet ministers, especially as I was coming from another political party. Since part of my assignment was to eliminate the budget deficit by prudent financial management, some civil servants saw me as an obstacle in achieving their intentions. I, therefore, decided to focus my energies on fulfilling the mandate given to me in writing by the Appointing Authority.

Luckily, I acquired a copy of President Mwanawasa's Mission Statement, which he had adopted in 2001 after his election to guide his conduct and action in the highest Office of President. This was the first time for me to come across a Head of State with a written down statement on his Mission. The Statement read as follows,

I will provide continuity with change. In the interest of our Nation, Zambia and the common good, sacrificing all and expecting little in return, I wholeheartedly commit myself with God's help and guidance, to serve Zambia and Zambians to the best of my ability with loyalty, honour and integrity, with all my heart and strength, with love and justice, with consideration and compassion, with commitment and dedication and in collaboration with all stakeholders, women and men of goodwill, to give fresh hope to our people, to create opportunities for all and bring honour, dignity and prosperity to our country, through honest selfless hard work above and beyond the normal call of duty.

The statement was pertinent to my duties and I, therefore, adopted it as my own. One of my major immediate preoccupations was to get a program with the IMF, which would open up doors for continued foreign financial assistance. A program with the IMF was also one of the conditions for qualifying to the Completion Point of the HIPC Initiative.

During our Ministry management meetings, we had agreed that the Cabinet must be fully engaged and involved in whatever we were planning and this meant holding frequent briefing meetings. I advised the President to revive the Economic Reconstruction and Development Committee (ERDC) of Cabinet. Apart from taking my advice, he made himself available to chair meetings of the Committee, which were held every fortnight.

In early September 2003, I attended the Second Zambia International Business Advisory Council (ZIBAC) meeting in Livingstone, Southern Province. The original concept by the Commonwealth Secretariat for these high-powered councils was for them to advise only the Heads of State and Government. However, President Mwanawasa decided instead to open participation in the ZIBAC meetings to ministers and private sector executives.

As we were about to begin a Cabinet meeting sometime in October 2003, President Mwanawasa asked me to pray, which was a normal habit for starting the meetings. I declined and replied that I did not pray loudly and in public. This was the last time President Mwanawasa and I discussed the matter of religion. We kept our religious beliefs a long distance away from our work relationship.

In 2005, I only came to know of the President's baptism some two days later. This important event in the personal life of President Mwanawasa never featured in any Cabinet discussions. I feel strongly that my relationship with my God or Creator should be a personal thing and not be the subject of public display or debate.

In October 2003, while I was busy with the preparations of the 2004 budget, I was directed to accompany the President on a state visit to the Peoples' Republic of China. The trip was undertaken between on 5 and 12 November 2003.

My request not to travel due to the preparation of the 2004 budget was turned down by the President, who explained that the documents to be signed in Beijing were on financial assistance and only the Minister of Finance could sign. I was happy to be in China having last visited the country in 1980.

During President Mwanawasa's State visit to China, a number of protocols were signed between the two countries. I was honoured to sign on behalf of the Republic of Zambia under the watchful eyes of Presidents Mwanawasa and Hu Jintao of China. Before the signing ceremony, I had a meeting with the President during which he asked me if I was personally happy with the contents in the memoranda I was to sign. I was getting to understand what level of confidence President Mwanawasa had in me.

In his address when opening the Third Session of the Ninth National Assembly on Friday, 16 January 2004, President Mwanawasa declared that,

Notwithstanding these developments, my administration is determined to ensure that Zambia attains the Completion Point this year. I am therefore directing the Ministry of Finance and National Planning to ensure that mechanisms are put in place to monitor the budget performance. Mr Speaker, good budgetary execution is not only about remaining within the budget. Importantly also it is about quality expenditure or spending public money on the top priorities as defined in the budget.

The President also covered issues of the sovereign debt and the need for a debt policy and strategy. Having received the Presidential instructions through his Parliamentary speech, we quickly completed the drafting of the 2004 budget proposals, which we presented to the Cabinet on 19 January 2004.

The closure of Luanshya Mine had caused a lot of hostility against the MMD administration. Luanshya Town had become a 'no go' area for MMD Government officials. On Saturday 24 January 2004, President Mwanawasa made his first visit to Luanshya Town. Although the security wings had been put on alert, in anticipation of trouble, we were peacefully received by an enthusiastic large crowd that filled the football stadium.

The President promised the former mine workers payment of their terminal benefits once the 2004 budget was approved. He informed the people that a new investor would soon open the Luanshya mine and create jobs for the people. I was elated when he lavishly introduced me to the crowd as a patriot who would resolve their outstanding financial problems. As per the President's promise, the payments were made during the year.

We left the Copperbelt for Lusaka at 1230 hours on Sunday, 25 January 2004 and resumed the cabinet meeting on the budget at 1500 hours. At 1900 hours, the President passed over the Chairmanship of the Cabinet meeting to me. We adjourned the meeting at 2400 hours and resumed at 1000 hours on Monday morning. At 1800 hours, the President resumed his chairing of the meeting and the Cabinet approved the 2004 National Budget at 1900 hours.

The experience of guiding Cabinet colleagues on discussions of sharing the nation's resources, although over a short period, was awesome and educative. Not many Cabinet Ministers were given the opportunity to chair Cabinet meetings. This meant that I had to own all the decisions in the budget as I had provided the conclusions on each subject.

On Wednesday, 28 January 2004, the President held a reception at State House with the Diplomats accredited to Zambia. After introducing me, he appealed to the donors to support the 2004 budget with funds, while inviting the other diplomats to explain the 'New Deal' Administration's plans to their governments. This was President Mwanawasa's interpretation of economic diplomacy.

On Sunday, 1 February 2004, the President was the guest of honour at a festival by the Muslim Community at the Makeni Islamic Centre. I was among the ministers who had been invited to accompany him to the function.

As per tradition, I read the draft budget speech to the Cabinet on the evening of Thursday, 5 February 2004. In concluding the evenings' agenda, President Mwanawasa gave instructions to members of the Cabinet to fully support me and defend the 2004 budget at all fora.

I delivered the 2004 budget speech with verve on the afternoon of Friday, 6 February 2004, to an anxious Parliament presided over by the Honourable Mr Speaker Amusaa Mwanamwambwa and the first female clerk of the National Assembly Doris K. Mwiinga. I had consultations with both of them on Parliamentary etiquette and I followed the rules as advised.

At the Monday meeting of the Cabinet, I reported the happenings at Parliament and the various meetings held over the weekend on the budget. President Mwanawasa was very happy and openly expressed his gratitude for my budget presentation and defence of the various proposals. He reminded us of what had happened to the 2003 budget and hoped that nothing of the sort would happen again.

On Saturday, 14 February 2004 the President invited a small group of Cabinet Ministers at the State Lodge to discuss how to handle the opposition to the budget arising from both the opposition politicians and the trade unions. My proposal to engage the opposition parties was approved by the President and I was given the leeway to meet anyone or any organization for face-to-face discussions.

I arranged for meetings between my ministry and members of the opposition parties who proposed fifty-two amendments to the budget. After each discussion, I held sessions with President Mwanawasa to explain to him my proposed replies to the proposed amendments. Finally, we agreed with the opposition on twelve amendments, which I was mandated to present during the budget debates in the House. The budget was quickly approved by parliament taking into account the meaningful amendments.

In May 2004, I attended the Annual Meetings of the AfDB Group in Kampala, Uganda as Governor for Zambia. By the time I returned to Zambia after a seven days' absence, I found that my opponents had been at work to disorganize the Ministry. Amongst others, two letters I had written to the President just before our departure for Kampala on the Task Force on Corruption and on staff transfers had not reached the President's desk.

On 2 June 2004, I addressed and hand-delivered a long letter to the President in which I tried to explain how the actions and many other things done by other Ministers were undermining my work. It was such uncoordinated decisions within the Government that had led to the budget overrun of 2003.

On 1 and 2 June 2004, there were bomb scares at the KCM and ZRA offices respectively. I was fully briefed on the two incidents by the security wings as they concerned two important institutions in the economy.

In spite of the bomb scares, the President and the First Lady left Zambia for Mozambique on 3 June 2004. I was invited to join the two and indulge in the comfort of the Presidential Challenger jet as one of the passengers. Among other issues, the President brought up the matter of the letter I had presented on the actions of some of my colleagues.

I informed him that my enquiry on the staff transfers with the Secretary to the Cabinet had been interpreted as interference of a politician in civil service matters. I told the President that without the cooperation of the civil servants, I would not be able to attain our set goals. He assured me that he would take some action once he was back at base.

In Maputo, the President had a busy schedule with meetings with NEPAD staff and with the Norwegian Minister of International Development, Ms Hilde Johnsonn, whom I had known for some time. He participated in discussion panels on the role of the private sector in national development, and on governance.

On the second day, President Mwanawasa left Maputo for Dar as Salaam to attend a Summit of Heads of State and Government on the Great Lakes Region. During our flight from Lusaka, we had discussed the matter of the secretariat for the new regional body and the imperative to get a Zambian to lead the organization. At the Summit, President Mwanawasa managed to get the approval of his colleagues to the appointment of Dr Siteke Mwale to head the Secretariat.

President Mwanawasa held a Press Conference on 15 June 2004, at which he announced staff reshuffles, which included the replacement of the Secretary to the Cabinet, Mr Leslie Mbula by Joshua Kanganja. On the morning of Wednesday 16th June 2004, I was in a celebratory mood when I addressed a Press Conference to announce the approval of a new Poverty Reduction and Growth Facility (PRGF) by the International Monetary Fund (IMF). I promised that in view of the President's encouragement and support expressed publicly during his press conference the previous day, Zambia would reach the Completion Point within six months.

President Mwanawasa had some difficulties in his relations with former President Chiluba. He managed to get Parliament to lift Chiluba's immunity in 2002 in order to pursue prosecution on the basis of the alleged corruption. From advice from various sources, President Mwanawasa had accepted to pursue another channel of settling the matter outside the courts of law.

In June 2004, President Mwanawasa invited the former President of Nigeria, General Olusegun Obasanjo to assist in resolving some of the issues concerning the corruption allegations. I had the opportunity of sitting next to former President Obasanjo at a State banquet on 17th June 2004. During our conversation, I learnt a lot from a General who had preferred to be a chicken farmer instead of fighting to be president of a country!

On 29th June 2004, I was privileged to attend a dinner at State House for Jonathan Oppenheimer, a member of the Anglo American Corporation dynasty, the mining company that had ditched Zambia in January 2002. The AAC Executive apologized to President Mwanawasa for the action taken by AAC of abruptly abandoning their mining operations in Zambia. He explained that his company was interested in coming back to Zambia to engage in oil exploration in the North-Western Province.

Without showing any animosity, President Mwanawasa told Oppenheimer that AAC was welcome as no one had chased them away from Zambia. The President's friendly reaction dazed me and I could have choked if we were still on the main course. I had expected President Mwanawasa to show some anger to someone who had left a monumental economic problem for his administration.

In July 2004, I informed the President by letter that we were beginning to build a family home in the Lilayi area of Lusaka Province. During some light moments, he asked why I had informed him of the construction of our house. I told him that I was keeping the pact and felt obliged to brief him on developments in our asset base in view of the high sensitivity of my current public assignment.

On 30 July 2004, President General Yoweri Kaguta Museveni of Uganda arrived in Zambia to officiate at the annual Agricultural and Commercial Show in Lusaka. I attended the bilateral talks that were held at State House. The visiting President explained his Government's development programs in agriculture and how science and technology were playing a major role in the Ugandan economy.

President Museveni explained that due to research, Ugandan agricultural scientists had developed coffee varieties with a yield potential of five times the current varieties. He briefed us on a programme of establishing coffee cafes owned by Ugandans in foreign countries to sell Ugandan coffee instead of selling raw coffee beans. The price differential between the two products was fourteen times and the Ugandan leader felt that the coffee producers would benefit more than the middlemen.

The visiting President suggested to his counterpart that Uganda, Congo DR, and Zambia, the three largest producers of cobalt in the world, should establish a cobalt value-addition plant in Zambia. The three countries should then ask the USA Government to assist with technology for the manufacture of cobalt products that are required by the American aeronautical industry. He stated that such a sophisticated industry could be manned by scientists from the three countries, many of whom were working in the USA. He stated that he was a strong believer in value addition.

He then enquired on the status of ZamCapital Limited, a specialized manufacturing company that had been started in the seventies under former President Kaunda. He recalled having met a brilliant Zambian scientist, who was the head of the company at the time. Luckily, I was aware of the company from my work at the Ministry of Defence in the eighties. After getting permission to intervene, I explained that the scientist, Joseph Nyaywa had passed on.

When I commented that I had attended Makerere University in Uganda in the seventies, President Museveni remarked that he remembered meeting me at the ACP Secretariat. Listening to a conversation between two members of the new generation of African leaders on Africa's technological and innovative capabilities gave me great hope for the future of Mother Africa.

On Tuesday, 21 December 2004, we held a joint meeting of cabinet ministers and officials at which we discussed the Medium-Term Expenditure Framework (MTEF) and the 2005 budget proposals. During the discussions, President Mwanawasa brought up the matter of the role of DMs in the administration of the State.

He directed the cabinet ministers to fully involve their juniors as there were a lot of new policies, programmes, and procedures that were being introduced. He warned that cabinet ministers would be held responsible if their deputies brought up matters, which were contrary to agreed Government policy on finance management during their contributions in Parliament. This was one of the strongest messages of support for me.

As per tradition, the end of the year came with so many parties by various institutions. I was directed by the President to stand in for him at the Zambia Air Force Annual Ball at the Chamba Valley Mess on the evening of 24 December 2004. Although this was at short notice, I could not refuse the privilege of representing the Commander-in-Chief who had delegated his responsibility.

Although I was addressed only as 'Honourable' by General Singogo, I relished the highest protocol close to that reserved for their Commander-in-Chief. Joyce and I had an enjoyable Christmas evening with General Singogo and his team who looked after us very well.

The directive on the annual ball included an invitation for me to be in Mfuwe over the weekend for consultations with the President who was on a Christmas working holiday. I briefed the President on my conversation with the JICA Mission during my trip to Denmark earlier in the month. I was delighted when he showed interest in the proposed program for what became known as the Triangle of Hope.

Between 10 and 13 January 2005, the Cabinet considered the detailed budget proposals together with the President's speech to Parliament, which was officially opened on Friday 14 January 2005. On Saturday, 15 January 2005, the Cabinet convened to finalize the budget and synchronize it with the President's speech delivered the day before.

At thirty minutes past midnight on Sunday morning, the Cabinet approved the 2005 budget. I was then informed that I was to be on the Presidential delegation leaving for Japan on the same day, as the major assignment of the budget preparation had been completed.

The Cabinet met on the evening of 27 January 2005 to listen to and approve my budget speech. The budget speech was read to the full Cabinet on the evening before its presentation to Parliament. This gives a last-minute opportunity for the Cabinet members to thrash out any policies and measures for the following year.

During the discussions, some contentious policy issues came up for debate. In his comments, President Mwanawasa stated that I should always consult my Cabinet colleagues on issues concerning their Ministries and not take arbitrary decisions. By the tone of the President's voice, I felt that the comment was too harsh and felt hurt. I apologized but continued to read the speech.

When I reached home late in the night, I explained to my spouse what had happened. I told her that I was not going to Parliament to present the budget the following afternoon. Early in the morning, I rushed to Parliament and had a discussion with the Clerk of the National Assembly on what had happened the night before. I sought advice as to what would happen if I failed to attend Parliament that afternoon.

The Clerk advised me that I should present the budget as it would be a bad precedent since nothing of the sort has ever happened in the history of the country. As a *mulamu,* she joked that she was looking forward to another ovation after I had read the 2005 budget. I was under pressure from the family to fulfil my role as our fifteen-year-old granddaughter, Amanda Munkombwe Kiboyo-Kisoro, had come from South Africa to escort me into the Parliament building for the occasion.

I finally succumbed to advice and presented the 2005 budget on the afternoon of Friday, 28 January 2005, escorted by our granddaughter, who regarded the occasion as one of her lifetime achievements. I then requested for and had an appointment with President Mwanawasa during the weekend.

After apologizing for the Cabinet incident, I asked that I be dropped or be allowed to resign if he felt that I had not delivered on my responsibilities. I explained that I'd had prior discussions with the concerned Minister on the issue discussed by the Cabinet. I told the President that I did not expect him to generalize the debate as it concerned only one Minister, who I suspected of not supporting me.

President Mwanawasa indicated that he was just being frank as he did not fully support the policy proposed in the budget. He informed me that he still had faith in me and wanted me to continue being in his team.

This was the only time that I and President Mwanawasa had a confrontation that led me to threaten to resign from the Cabinet during my long service with him. From this early nasty encounter, President Mwanawasa realized how frank I could be and I also was on guard not to be misunderstood by thoroughly briefing him on most issues.

President Mwanawasa and I started building a strong relationship by engaging in frank discussions, exchanging and sharing ideas on both personal and national issues, and in fashioning and selling a common vision for the country. He started delegating me with assignments that were not on financial matters.

The budget preparation system had evolved under President Mwanawasa to include the publication of the Green Paper. There was advance disclosure of the following year's revenue estimates and expenditure proposals on which the public were solicited to make comments.

One of President Mwanawasa's momentous reforms was the involvement of non-state actors in national planning, which he had revived in 2002. The budget was one of the most important development instruments in which the stakeholders were involved through the Sector Advisory Groups (SAGs).

My experience of the initial eighteen months at the Ministry convinced me then that much of the corruption and 'dirt' in the management of Government public resources could be cleaned up. But this would require me developing a thick skin to all innuendoes that would be flying in my face. I realized that whatever good I may do for my country, my opponents would still find faults and fabricate stories just to tarnish my name. For example, I was surprised when the Post newspaper wrote an article alleging that I was part of President Mwanawasa's family tree.

On Sunday, 17 April 2005, I left Washington DC for Jakarta, Indonesia, to represent the President at the Asian-African Summit to commemorate the Bandung Conference of 1955. The ultra long-haul flight of twenty-eight hours via Los Angeles and Tokyo was made longer and more tiring by the time difference between the two cities of fifteen hours and an emergency landing in Japan to drop off a passenger, who had become very sick. We arrived in Jakarta at 2300 hours on Tuesday, 19 April 2005.

I had the honour of addressing the Summit and reading a speech on behalf of President Mwanawasa. The celebrations were held in Jakarta and Bandung in West Java. A new agreement, the New Asian-African Strategic Partnership (NAASP) to rekindle the Bandung Spirit was signed at the end of the conference.

Each head of delegation planted an Asia-Africa tree on the grounds of the Tegala Gardens in Bandung. I hope that the tree I planted has thrived and one day, I will have the opportunity to visit it and enjoy its fruit.

In July 2005, I accompanied President Mwanawasa to London where he had been invited to address a seminar by the Commonwealth Business Council. The meeting held on 5 and 6 July coincided with the G8 Summit, which was being held in Gleneagles, Scotland during the same time.

Early on Tuesday, 5 July 2005, I was awakened by a hotel porter who delivered a beautiful large bouquet of flowers. The nicely decorated card that accompanied the bouquet was signed by the First Lady Maureen Kakubo Mwanawasa, who had accompanied her husband to London. The gift reminded me that the day was my 58th Birthday.

In the evening of the same day, President Mwanawasa introduced me to Patrick, his son, who was studying in the United Kingdom. I felt highly privileged to be remembered by the First Family on such an occasion and to get to know another member of the First Family. Patrick was the only child of

President Mwanawasa that I came to know well as the others were young and we had no common issues to discuss.

The President and some officials left London for Lusaka on the evening of 6 July 2005 at the close of the seminar. On the morning of Thursday, 7 July 2005, during the rush hour, three bombs were detonated aboard the London underground trains across the city and, later, a fourth on a double-decker bus.

I received a number of telephone calls from my family, State House, and friends enquiring on my safety and that of the First Family. I assured all the callers that I was safe and that the President and the First Lady were also safe as they had travelled during the night, long before the morning bomb attacks.

Early in 2005, President Mwanawasa indicated that he preferred the Cabinet Ministers to be members of the National Executive Committee (NEC) of the MMD Party. Such a situation would facilitate the implementation of Party policies by the Government. He advised us that those who had intentions of standing in the 2006 general elections and aspired to be appointed to Ministerial positions should stand for NEC positions at the MMD Party Convention.

The MMD Party calendar required that a convention shall be held every five years and this should be the year before the general elections. This was to allow for healing amongst the winners and losers before the nominations and campaigns for Members of Parliament. A convention was held at the Mulungushi Rock of Authority near Nkrumah Teachers' Training College in the Kabwe District between 13 and 17 July 2005.

I had already decided that I was not going to stand in the 2006 general elections for a political office as I wanted to return to the private sector as a consultant. At the time, I had no position in any political party and was invited to the convention to give a brief on the state of the Zambian economy. I, therefore, arrived at the Mulungushi Rock on 14 July, when others had arrived much earlier to campaign.

An hour before the deadline for nominations on 15 July, President Mwanawasa summoned me to his villa. He asked me if I had filed my nomination and I informed him that I had not done so as I did not intend to continue as a party functionary beyond 2006. The President directed me to rush to the nomination centre and file documents for the position of Chairman for the Committee on Finance and Economic Affairs.

I arrived at the nomination centre at Nkrumah Teachers' College, across the stream, only ten minutes before the closing time. The female electoral officer even thought that I was joking until when I produced the nomination fee and she gave me a receipt. She informed me that the only candidate who had filed for the position was Mbita Chitala, my deputy minister. When I reported to the President that I had managed to file my nomination, he summoned Mrs Margaret Kaemba to lead a team to assist me with the campaign.

My campaign was greatly helped by the powerful presentation I gave to the convention on the state of the Zambian economy. It was relatively easy to talk of 'Mr HIPC' and the improving economy. Later in the evening, more people joined my campaign team and we went into full swing until 23.30 hours when I left for Lusaka to prepare some campaign material.

I arrived back at the Mulungushi Rock early on Saturday, 16 July 2005 and was one of the early voters because I had to leave Zambia for Senegal on the same day. The following day, while in Dakar, I received a telephone call from President Mwanawasa informing me of my election as Chairman of the NEC Committee on Finance and Economic Affairs.

When I returned to Zambia, I was directed by the Secretary General of the MMD Party to present a list of the members of my committee. I ignored the directive until President Mwanawasa got involved and asked me why I had not complied with the Secretary's instruction. I explained to the President that in the economics area of my operations, I consult many leaders of both public and private financial and institutions and these are my shadow committee members. I requested that I be excused from submitting any list as most of my advisors were technocrats who work behind closed doors and not political activists.

My understanding president accepted my reasoning and instructed the secretary general to stop harassing me. I take this opportunity to permanently record my profound gratitude to all those who accepted the onerous responsibility of giving me advice on the many issues that propelled Zambia's economy forward.

On Wednesday, 10 August 2005, I and a few ministers accompanied President Mwanawasa to Solwezi for the official opening of Kansanshi Mine owned by First Quantum Minerals.

In early September 2005, I led a delegation to India for a meeting of the Joint Permanent Commission. While in India, I received a message that I should proceed to London to join the President, who had a special appointment with the British Prime Minister, Tony Blair I arrived in London on Sunday 11 September 2005. The following day on Monday 12 September 2005, I joined the President at a special breakfast meeting with the British Prime Minister and his Foreign Affairs Minister.

The British PM expressed his admiration for the good governance of Zambia by President Mwanawasa and his government. He promised to do everything in his power to assist in the development of the country. President Mwanawasa informed the Prime Minister that he was lucky that he had a good team, especially in public finance management and introduced me to the Prime Minister as the leader of the financial team.

The year 2005 would close by an unexpected and eventful happening. President Mwanawasa travelled to the DRC early on Tuesday, 20 December 2005 for a Joint Permanent Commission Meeting. At about 10.00 hours, I received a telephone call from the Secretary to the Cabinet Joshua Kanganja enquiring if I had a trip out of Lusaka during the week. I informed him that I had a number of meetings in Lusaka and would be around.

In the afternoon, I received a letter written by the Secretary to Cabinet accompanying a document duly signed by the President. The document dated 20 December 2005 was an Instrument in which the President had under Article 39(1) of the constitution directed and authorized me, 'to discharge all the functions and exercise all powers of President'.

A chat with the Secretary to the Cabinet ended up with laughter when the SC, a former classmate, said, 'Now you are my boss'. Telephone calls to the members of the Defence Council assured me that they were all aware of the absence of their Commander-In-Chief and would make certain that the country's peace was not disturbed. Reflecting on the gravity of my new responsibility, I felt like someone had put a tonne-load of stones on my shoulders.

In the evening, I attended a cocktail reception at the Intercontinental Hotel. Although I had my usual protocol officers from our Ministry, I became aware of a few guests who spent time chatting with so many other guests. I inferred that they were part of my wider security detail as Acting Head of State.

When President Mwanawasa returned on Thursday 22 December 2005, I was at the airport to 'hand over' the country to him. As the first public official to greet the President when he stepped foot onto Zambia's ground, I shook hands with him and whispered, 'Welcome back to Zambia, Mr President'. I then assured him that the country was at peace and everything was all right.

I was lucky that during the period when I was acting, there were no crises or emergencies, which required the Zambia Air Force to scramble. The experience of being given such a heavy responsibility without any preparation or notice was most humbling.

On Tuesday, 27 December 2005, I was among a few officers who were invited by the President to his Palabana Farm. We spent some time touring the farm under the guidance of the farm manager, who was ably assisted by President Mwanawasa. The President seemed to know everything going on, although he claimed that it was the First Lady, who supervised the operations as he was too busy with State matters.

The farm had a variety of crops under irrigation including cabbage, tomatoes, onions, green maize and many types of poultry including ducks, layer chickens, and quails. The farm was supplying large quantities of fresh vegetables and eggs to the Soweto Market in Lusaka. Surplus exotic quails were being exported. A new big incubator had just been installed and the President offered the facility for my use, as our incubator was too small for eggs from large poultry such as geese.

We had a sumptuous meal of fresh foods from the President's farm. The discussions under such a friendly environment were frank and open. I felt that the occasion was meant for the President to know more about me as I was subject to a lot of personal queries. Some Ministers were asked questions about me and they had to openly answer in my presence.

I realized that for the first time in the history of Zambia, the positions of President, Minister of Finance, and Minister of Agriculture were occupied by ardent commercial farmers. Ben Kapita, who was the Minister of Agriculture, was a large-scale poultry farmer on the Copperbelt. I was a national medal-winning commercial tobacco farmer and accomplished cattle rancher.

I was convinced that there was no way Zambian agriculture could fail under the guidance of the three of us. I challenged the Minister of Agriculture to produce an ambitious agricultural plan, knowing well that any such plan would get the President's full support. But no plan was produced and it was business as usual, which left the majority of Zambians living in the rural areas as paupers.

President Mwanawasa recognized my style of management and my tutoring of my DMs by promoting two of them to cabinet minister posts. He mentioned that I was the only cabinet minister who had produced cabinet ministers out of my juniors.

The two Deputy Ministers who had been promoted were Felix Mutati, a professional accountant, and Kapemba Simbao, an electronics engineer, both of whom appreciated my role in supporting and guiding them. One of them wrote to me after his promotion that,

Minister, you created a platform for me that enabled me to confront issues in a more substantive and holistic manner. The experience that I gained under your tutelage will no doubt stand me in good stead as I now face the challenges that now confront me as Minister.

The year 2006 began in an atmosphere of high exuberance and great relief following the country's qualification in 2005 for debt write-off under the HIPC and MDR Initiatives. The positive change in the management of public resources by the New Deal Government of President Levy Patrick Mwanawasa had won the confidence and trust of both the Zambian citizens and the international community.

President Mwanawasa acknowledged the support of the citizens on the path to this recognition in his speech when opening Parliament on Friday, 13 January 2006. As a follow-up to the President's policy announcements, I presented the 2006 Budget on Friday, 3 February 2006 with the theme, 'From Sacrifice to Equitable Wealth Creation'.

The Mwanawasa Administration was determined to raise the economic growth rate to over six per cent in order to reduce the stubborn poverty levels, which were above fifty per cent. In order to position development in a medium-term framework, it was decided to prepare a Fifth National Development Plan (FNDP) to cover a five-year period. As the preparation of the Plan was already advanced, the 2006 budget marked the beginning of the implementation of the Plan.

President Mwanawasa was desirous of having a comprehensive development plan, which would be implemented by any new government that would be formed after the 2006 elections. As part of his consensual planning process, he convened a Consultative Stakeholders Meeting in July 2006 to consider and finalize the Fifth National Development Plan and Vision 2030. The meeting held between 24 and 27 July 2006 at the Mulungushi International Conference Centre was attended by hundreds of stakeholders from all the districts of Zambia, many of whom had participated in evolving the seventy-two District Plans.

On Friday, 30 March 2007, I was among a group of officers who accompanied President Mwanawasa to the Western Province for the Kuomboka Ceremony. On Sunday, 1 April 2007, we flew into Ndola City, where the President officiated at an international Golf Tournament at the Ndola Golf Club.

On Saturday, 30 June 2007, I was once more privileged to fly with President Mwanawasa and the First Lady to Accra Ghana for an AU Summit of Heads of State and Government. The flight by the Presidential Challenger was rather long as we had to make a number of detours due to bad weather along the normal route. However, I took the opportunity to brief the First Family on a number of development programmes and projects and some of my ideas for accelerating the development of Zambia's economy.

I looked forward to touring some of the small-scale programmes funded by the Ghanaian Government from HIPC savings. I had made contact with my Ghanaian counterpart to arrange some tours for me. The President had indicated his desire to get information on the currency rebasing exercise that Ghana had recently undertaken.

One of the agenda items at the Summit was the adoption of the establishment of a Unity Government for Africa. Debate on the subject at previous AU Summits had been inconclusive and the proponents of the idea led by President Colonel Muammar Gaddafi of Libya expected a positive final decision in Accra.

President Mwanawasa suggested that such a political idea should be discussed and voted upon by citizens of each member country. The President went on to propose that while waiting for an African Union Government, the African governments with surplus money should pool the resources into an African fund for infrastructure such as roads, railways, and telecommunications across the African continent towards economic integration.

The proposal upset President Gaddafi so much that he concluded his speech by informing the Summit that he would never bring up the idea again. As per his own prediction, the idea of a United States of Africa with a unity government seems to have died with Colonel Muammar Gaddafi in 2011.

President Mwanawasa's curiosity on currency rebasing was adequately dealt with by a thorough presentation by Ms Margaret Mwanakatwe, a Zambian banker working for Barclays Bank in Ghana. I and some officials visited a few markets and interrogated some marketers and ordinary shoppers, who confirmed that they did not see much benefit from the rebasing exercise.

We observed that there was no major economic benefit apart from that of reducing the quantity of the currency to carry. During our flight back to Zambia, the President and I discussed the currency rebasing issue and concluded that more attention be given to the Kwacha parity with other currencies as the levels affected the prices of services and goods exchanged.

On 7 December 2007, I was a member of the President's delegation to Lisbon, Portugal to attend the Second EU-Africa Summit. The Summit's main agenda item was the Economic Partnership Agreements (EPAs) of the Cotonou Agreement of which I was an expert, having been Secretary General of the ACP Secretariat.

The invitations to the Summit caused a lot of controversy as President Mugabe of Zimbabwe was under a travel ban to EU countries because of governance issues in Zimbabwe. President Mwanawasa, who was Chairman of SADC and some other African Heads of State threatened not to attend the Summit if President Mugabe was not invited. Finally, President Mugabe was invited by the Portuguese Government, who held the rotating presidency of the European Union. This caused British Prime Minister Gordon Brown to boycott the Summit.

During the Mfuwe retreat at the beginning of the year, the President had directed me to spend more time in 2008 touring the country to inspect the various developmental projects that we had funded in the various sectors. On Sunday, 13 January 2008, I visited Ndola and inspected the works at the Ndola Technical School for Girls and the Military Northern Hospital.

We also visited the Dag Hammarskjold Memorial. I was shocked with the state of neglect of the site dedicated to the former Secretary General of the United Nations who had died in a plane crash on 18 September 1961 while on a peace mission to the Congo. I concluded that the young officers were not aware of the important role played by the Swede author, economist, and diplomat in averting a human catastrophe in the region.

On Thursday, 17 January 2008, I accompanied President Mwanawasa on an aerial tour of the areas inundated by the heavy rains in the Mazabuka and Monze Districts of the Southern Province. The tour by helicopter took us to the Mbiya, Hakunkula, and Bweengwa areas, where some crop fields had been submerged by the floods.

Fortunately, by the time of our tour, the water levels had receded to the normal river courses. During a lunch break in Monze, the President addressed a closed meeting of four traditional chiefs and a large number of village headmen and took the opportunity to introduce me.

On Wednesday, 26 March 2008, Kabinga Pande, Patrick Mwanawasa, and

I accompanied President Mwanawasa to Gaborone, Botswana for a two-day visit. The President had been invited to witness the handing-over of the presidency from outgoing President Festus Mogae to incoming President Lt. General Ian Khama.

After settling down in the Challenger plane, President Mwanawasa introduced us to his son, giving a short biodata of each one of us. He then gave a short brief of Patrick, emphasizing that he was busy with his studies, but was interested in politics.

The flight seemed shorter than usual because the President was busy talking about his plans for when he retired from politics. He passionately talked about farming. At one point, he sounded like this was to be his last trip as President of Zambia. Patrick gathered courage and asked his father as to when he planned to retire. To our amazement, he gave a straight answer, "anytime soon". He then lamented the lack of provisions in the Zambian Constitution that would facilitate a seamless change of state leaders like they do in Botswana.

We were met at the airport by President Mogae, Vice President Lt General Mompati Merafhe, and the Zambian High Commissioner to Botswana. The President took the opportunity to introduce the three of us to the two leaders. He had finished introducing Pande and Patrick when he was about to introduce me but was interrupted by VP Merafhe. The Botswana VP stated that I was well-known to them as we had been working together on many regional issues. President Mwanawasa retorted, "Anyway, for the time being, he is our Minister of Finance".

The celebrations were very colourful and full of pomp, dance, and laughter. They included a banquet and a solemn hand-over ceremony the following day. The opposition party members, civic leaders, academia, and captains of industry were all present enjoying the occasion. I was among familiar faces.

Daniel Moroka the new Minister of Trade and Industry was a former MD of BP (Zambia) and I had known him when he lived in Lusaka in the nineties. Baledzi Goalathe was the long-serving Minister of Finance and Development Planning. Both were renowned cattle ranchers and we spent most of the evening discussing cattle ranching and put aside the issues of inflation and exchange rates.

President Mwanawasa seized the opportunity to discuss with his counterpart the Kazungula Bridge project, which had stalled due to some boundary dispute with Zimbabwe. The project was on his list of top priorities and he was seeking a way to implement the project. He proposed the relocation of the route of the bridge further north in order to avoid the area under dispute. He informed his counterpart of the willingness of the Japanese Government to assist if there was agreement amongst the leaders of the affected countries. President Mwanawasa did not want another disappointment like that on the Chembe Bridge.

The Botswana President agreed with the relocation idea and asked

President Mwanawasa to speak to the Namibian President as the new route was to pass over an island in Namibia.

On Sunday, 18 May 2008, I was among the officials who accompanied the President on a tour of parts of the Eastern Province. We visited Vubwi and Chadiza Districts before proceeding to Chama and back with a stopover in Lundazi. At the rally at Vubwi, the President paraded me and informed the people that if they did not get enough fertiliser during the coming season, I was to blame as I had the ability to source the required additional funds.

Later during the trip, the President instructed me to source funds so that the number of beneficiaries and the fertiliser subsidy level would be increased. He further directed that once the funds were available, I should arrange to visit the Eastern Province to announce the good news from there.

On Monday, 16 June 2008, we held a cabinet meeting at State House to discuss a number of issues on the economy. We felt satisfied with the progress made in a number of sectors but the members felt that the agricultural sector was not achieving satisfactory results in spite of the large amounts of money spent. It was therefore decided to have a special meeting for all the relevant Ministers.

In winding up the meeting, President Mwanawasa introduced the issue of succession. He openly stated that he would prefer to be succeeded by a younger person, who would be able to continue with many of the programmes and projects he had started. He mentioned that once he returned from the AU Summit in Egypt, he would make some adjustments to his team.

On 18 June 2008, I went back to State House to brief the President on the funding to the agricultural sector. Before discussing the subject of my visit, the President resumed the issue of succession. He had earlier on informed me that I was among the list of ministers he was considering to succeed him. This time, he informed me that he had narrowed his search for a successor to only three cabinet ministers and that I was amongst the three candidates.

I thanked the President wholeheartedly for including me on his shortlist. I asked as to when he would reduce the list further. He answered that from three he would go down to one as having two people could lead to a division amongst his supporters.

On Saturday, 21 June 2008, I was among the officials who converged at the State Lodge to discuss financing and strategies for the agricultural sector and the fuel issue. We concluded that the Ministry of Agriculture should produce a comprehensive medium-term plan on the development of the sector. In view of the unsatisfactory operations of the Fertiliser Input Support Programme (FISP), it was decided to modify the programme to make it more beneficial to all farmers and the country.

We also agreed that fuel prices should be reduced for the consumers to benefit from the reduced prices for crude oil on the international market. The President was in a jovial mood and made a lot of jokes during our lunch. At some point, I was a subject of some philosophical jokes between the President and some of my Lozi cousins.

At the end of our meeting, the President announced that he would be travelling to the Eastern Province to campaign in the by-elections in one of the constituencies. I was told by the President that I should prepare to leave on 26 June 2008 for the AU Summit in Egypt as a member of the advance party.

The President travelled to Chipata as indicated. When I telephoned Chipata to find out when he would be back in Lusaka, I was informed by the special assistant that he had decided to stay on in Chipata to meet the Vice President who had lost his mother. The special assistant went further to say that the President wished to speak to me before I leave for Egypt and that they would telephone me later in the afternoon.

At 1700 hours on 25th June 2008, I received a telephone call from Chipata informing me that President Mwanawasa was on the line to speak to me. Our farewell conversation must have lasted nearly two hours as we covered so many subjects.

Among the subjects we discussed were my election court petition, the campaign in the by-elections, the Zambian Airways issue, funds for increased fertiliser subsidies, ZRA scanners, a reduction in fuel prices due to a global price fall, the new mining windfall tax, and the earth-moving equipment. I informed the President that I would be writing letters on some of the subjects to him and to the appropriate Ministers before my departure the following day.

By way of concluding our conversation, President Mwanawasa brought in an unexpected subject. He informed me that he had heard a rumour that I would be one of the presidential candidates during the forthcoming elections. I was most puzzled and I asked as to which elections as there would be no presidential elections until 2011.

I stated that since Presidential rumours are credible stories, I believed him and asked as to what I should do in preparation. President Mwanawasa stated that I must start touring the rural areas to get closer to the people. He revealed that from the many foreign trips we had made together, he was satisfied that I was well-known by his counterparts in many countries. This is when I realized the purpose of the numerous trips on which I had been invited to accompany the President.

When I asked him why I could not be spared from the Egypt trip so that I could start the local tours, the President answered that it was very important that I was in the delegation. We ended our conversation by wishing each other safe trips. President Mwanawasa was travelling to the AU Summit in Egypt on 28 June 2008.

I took some more time in the office to draft letters and notes on the issues I had discussed with the President. As usual, I left a computer diskette on my personal assistant's desk with instructions that she should finalize the letters for my signature before my departure the following day.

When I arrived home, I asked Mrs Magande to join me while I was having my late dinner and briefed her on my long conversation with President Mwanawasa. She commented that perhaps the President would explain the election issue while we were in Egypt and hence his insistence that I make the trip.

CHAPTER 40

The Tragedy Of Sharm El-Sheikh

S ome Ministers and I left Lusaka for Egypt at 13.30 hours on 26 June 2008 and the trip took us through Johannesburg, Dubai, Paris, and Cairo. We arrived in Sharm el-Sheikh in the early hours of Saturday 28 June 2008. The Zambian delegation, which included George Kunda, State Counsel and Minister of Justice, a long-time friend of President Mwanawasa, and others who had gone earlier, was large and we had to share vehicles. I shared a vehicle with Kunda right from the airport until the end of our trip.

My partner and I decided to have an early breakfast on Saturday as we planned to leave for the Conference Centre, which was a long distance away from our hotel. As we were having our breakfast, Kunda asked me for the purpose of my being on the trip. Since the question had never crossed my mind, I had to find a befitting answer. I told Kunda that I was to contribute to the debate on the financing of water and tourism projects under the New Economic Partnership for African Development (NEPAD) of the AU.

I saw that Kunda was not satisfied with my technical answer. At this point, he shared some startling and detailed information on a discussion he'd had with President Mwanawasa. He informed me that the President was going to make an important announcement during our stay in Sham El Sheikh on a succession plan, in which I would be the main actor. It was for this reason that I had to be at this particular AU meeting.

The Minister drew my attention to the large Zambian delegation, which included seven cabinet and deputy ministers. Usually, the Presidential delegations were small with no more than two cabinet ministers. Kunda went further to say that a number of ministers had already been briefed on the plan and instructed on their roles to assist me once we returned home.

This was when I knew that President Mwanawasa had concluded his search for a successor and had settled for me. I connected the information to the many conversations with the President, including the one while he was in Chipata when he mentioned that I would be a presidential candidate. But Kunda did not explain how President Mwanawasa was to constitutionally cause a presidential election, as he had another three years to rule.

Kunda and I were at the Conference Centre until 1100 hours when we left for the airport to receive the President and his entourage. My remark on the President's weak appearance was answered by Kunda, who conjectured that this might be due to the long flight over the hot desert skies and the Chipata campaign. The absence of some presidential senior medical personnel reassured me of the good health of President Mwanawasa, otherwise they would have been in the delegation.

Early on the morning of Sunday 29 June 2008, Kunda, Masebo, Pande, and I had breakfast together to share notes on the issues on the AU Summit agenda. Masebo, Minister of Local Government and Housing, had arrived much earlier in Egypt with Kabinga Pande, Minister of Foreign Affairs, to participate in the ministerial preparatory meetings on water and sanitation provision, which was the theme of this particular AU Summit.

All the members of the Zambian delegation attended a meeting at 1000 hours to brief the President at his lodge on the items on the summit agenda. During the meeting, the President who was active and alert gave instructions to the Ministers of Local Government and Tourism to spend a lot of their time learning how the Egyptians were able to develop the tourist resort of Sharm el-Sheikh in the desert. In 2008, the town had facilities to receive four million tourists in a year.

The President directed the two Ministers to come up with a master plan to develop Livingstone City into a modern holiday resort. He directed me to accompany the ministers on their tour of the city and assured them of my capability to raise the required resources. By 11.45 hours, we had covered a lot of topics and Pande suggested that we give time to the President to prepare for the day's meetings. I enjoyed a casual conversation with the President as I was leaving his lodge.

Kunda and I spent the afternoon of Sunday 29 June 2008 attending a Ministerial meeting on Reforms of the United Nations System and only left the Centre at around 17.30 hours. On arrival at our hotel at 18.30 hours after a day's hard work, we agreed to quickly change our working attire and proceed for a deserved dinner.

As I was changing into casual attire, I received a telephone call from Michael Kaingu, Minister of Tourism and Environment, who informed me that President Mwanawasa was very sick and had been admitted to the National Hospital. The minister mentioned that Kunda and I were the only ministers not at the hospital.

I telephoned Kunda and broke the sad news. We abandoned our dinner plans and left for the hospital immediately. Luckily, our driver was still chatting with his friends in the car park and had not left for his home. We gave him instructions to rush to the National Hospital as we had to visit a patient who we did not disclose.

As we did not tell the driver as to who was the patient, he could not negotiate his passage with the heavy security along the roads. At one roadblock, the driver got out of the car to negotiate with some senior officers. When he came back to the car, he informed us that the Zambian President had been taken ill and President Hosni Mubarak had rushed to the hospital. He further stated that he was advised to inform the security personnel on the roads that he was carrying Zambian Ministers going to see their sick President.

In spite of being cleared through the heavy traffic, we reached the hospital after more than an hour's agonizing drive. We found a doctor at the entrance, who seemed to have been assigned to receive and brief us. The doctor's brief was elaborate and we immediately realized the gravity of the situation. When the doctor mentioned the word 'stroke', I recalled a conversation with President Mwanawasa during which he stated that the doctors advised him to avoid situations that could cause another stroke as that would be fatal. I pondered on whether this was the fatal stroke that the President had been warned about.

The doctor then led us into the lift for the second floor, where the President was in the Intensive Care Unit (ICU). He directed me to proceed to the bed behind a curtain, while Kunda was asked to wait nearby. As I stood by the side of the bed with a healthy-looking but unconscious President Mwanawasa on it, the doctor gave a graphic explanation of the treatment being administered using a maze of medical equipment.

The doctor ended by saying, 'We will try our best'. As I drew nearer to the bed to bid farewell, I saw that President Mwanawasa was not breathing and even the modern machines were not showing the slightest movement to indicate any sign of life. At that moment, my eyes gave up and I could not hold my tears as they rolled down my cheeks. Even as I said, "Get well soon" in a distraught and dejected voice, I concluded that the fatal stroke had come and taken President Mwanawasa's life.

The First Lady, who was with Masebo in an adjoining room, narrated to me what had happened and what the doctors explained. I stayed with the two ladies until Kunda came over and the two of us went to speak to Pande, who also narrated the events from about noon until they arrived at the hospital. He informed us that President Mwanawasa was being briefed by a delegate from one of Zambia's neighbouring countries when he suddenly slumped over and collapsed. President Mwanawasa's footprints were buried by the sands of the Sahara Desert at Sharm el Sheikh and no one could find his path to eternity.

CHAPTER 41

The Consequences Of Mwanawasa's Abrupt Absence

President Mwanawasa suffered a stroke in the afternoon of 29th June 2008 within the Conference Centre in Sharm el Sheikh as he was going to attend a side meeting. By 22.00 hours, all except two members of the Zambian Delegation to the AU Summit were at the hospital. The stroke had affected the left side of the President's brain and he was not in a position to speak or move.

The delegation discussed a number of issues including arrangements for attending to both the sick President and also the AU meetings. We took some time to agree on the wording of the message, which was sent to the Vice President due to medical ethics and legal implications. We agreed that a senior member of the delegation should be available at the hospital to meet any dignitaries, who might want to visit the President. We agreed that Pande, Minister of Foreign Affairs should lead the Zambian delegation at the AU Summit.

By the time we were leaving the hospital, it was in the early hours of Monday, 30 June 2008. Luckily, the hospital had arranged some food for us all. On the way to the hotel, I was privy to some legal interpretations by the Minister of Legal Affairs, George Kunda of the Constitutional provisions in case of incapacitation of the President of Zambia. He advised me that since I had been mentioned by the President in his succession plan, I should be calm and wait for the evolution of events.

When we reached our hotel, I telephoned a member of the Defence Council in Zambia. After apologizing for waking up the General, I briefed him of the tragedy that had befallen our delegation and asked him to keep the country at peace. I suspected that the Defence Forces had been briefed by President Mwanawasa about his plans to change the team after his trip to Egypt.

I, Kunda and Masebo were having breakfast on the following morning, when the Permanent Secretary for Foreign Affairs came over and informed us that Pande had preferred to stay at the hospital for protocol duties instead of being at the AU meetings. The PS went on to say that his Minister had suggested that I lead the delegation to the AU Summit.

Against my objection, the two Ministers persuaded me to accept Pande's suggestion. I wondered if Masebo had also been aware of the purpose of my inclusion on the trip. I informed the PS of my acceptance and asked him to give me all the necessary documentation for the Summit. Since the subjects of water and sanitation were under Masebo's portfolio, she had a draft copy of the President's speech, which she gave me immediately.

I then gave a television interview to one of the Zambian media. The interview, which was broadcast in Zambia, reassured the Nation that the Zambian delegation was still capable of representing the country effectively in spite of what had happened to the Commander-in-Chief. From then on, I coordinated the activities of the Zambian delegation.

When the Summit opened at 10.30 hours, I was in the seat of the delegation leader, next to Zimbabwean President Robert Mugabe. I made an off the cuff opening remarks informing the delegates of the ill health of President Mwanawasa before delivering his speech. As I was the last speaker, immediately I finished, many dignitaries came over to convey their sympathies to the delegation and congratulate me for showing such strong will and character in delivering the speech in spite of the calamity that had befallen our delegation.

The medical team attending to President Mwanawasa determined that he had to be evacuated to France for specialist treatment. On the evening of Tuesday 1st July 2008, the whole Zambian delegation was at the airport to witness the evacuation. The manner the lifeless body was being tossed about aroused sorrowful emotions such that many officers wept uncontrollably. I had the unenviable responsibility of consoling the wailing officers. The First Lady and some State House staff had left for France earlier to await the arrival of the patient.

I felt disconsolate as the chief pilot of the presidential challenger plane and some ministers persuaded me to sit in the seat usually occupied by the president as we took-off for Zambia on 2nd July 2008. Since there were six ministers on the plane, we discussed many issues including the format of presenting our consolidated report to the Vice President and the rest of the Cabinet. We agreed that all the ministers who were on the trip should together go to see the Vice President the following morning. When we arrived in Lusaka at 20.10 hours and as I disembarked, I took the salute by the military crew.

On the morning of Thursday, 3 July 2008, exactly five years since I had rejoined the government of Mwanawasa, I called a meeting of the senior staff at the Ministry of Finance and briefed them on the events in Egypt. I assured them that the doctors in France were doing their best to resuscitate President Mwanawasa.

When I telephoned the office of the Vice President to ask for an appointment for our team to brief him, I was told that he had not reported at the office and that he was operating from Government House, his official residence. I presumed that he was still receiving sympathizers on the loss of his mother.

My telephone calls to Kunda and Pande went unanswered. When I called the Government House at 11.00 hours, I was informed that in fact, both ministers had already seen the Vice President, but separately. This greatly puzzled me as we had agreed to act as a team. I had been designated as the leader of the Zambian Delegation to the AU Summit and I had effectively played this role since the hospitalization of President Mwanawasa.

After lunch, I went straight to Government House to see the Vice President. We had a short conversation about the trip to Egypt and the illness of President Mwanawasa. From his comments, I concluded that he already had all the information on the events in Egypt from the two ministers who had seen him earlier. Both of them were close to President Mwanawasa and were among the ministers who had been informed of President Mwanawasa's succession plans. I wondered if they had shared information on this subject with the Vice President. This was my last meeting on a one-to-one basis with Vice President Banda.

The two senior ministers were party to the decision made on my coordinating role. Why were they acting individually and in an unpredictable manner? It was difficult for me to call a meeting of the delegation to write a report on the tour to Egypt. This was the first time I failed to submit a report after an official trip.

A few days after our return from Egypt, I learnt that President Mwanawasa had engaged in a fruitful discourse with a large gathering of bishops at the Regional Conference of Catholic Bishops in Lusaka the morning before he left for Egypt. His speech touched many issues on state governance including his reconciliation with Sata. He had then left for the airport straight from the conference venue. This was as if to signal that he did not want the profound and holy words he had exchanged with the men of God to be diluted before his going on to his eternal home.

A number of cabinet ministers and ordinary people visited my home and informed me of their parting conversations with President Mwanawasa before he left for Egypt. Most of them talked of a succession plan and my involvement in the plan. Their versions were the same as I had been informed by Kunda during our breakfast in Sharm el-Sheikh, Egypt.

Kunda and I had spent a lot of time discussing a number of issues during our flight to Egypt. After our return, I visited Kunda at their new home in Lusaka East. The two of us discussed the illness of President Mwanawasa and hoped that he would recover fully in spite of what the doctors had told us about the devastating effect of a stroke. We somewhat banked our hopes of his recovery on improvements in medical care. Kunda once more advised me to remain calm as the matter of succession was to be dealt with according to the constitution. He did not volunteer any information on his conversations with the Vice President.

Kunda and Chituwo visited Percy Military Hospital in France. The Minister of Health tabled a report in Parliament on the President's illness and the report attracted active discussion by the public. The Minister of Legal Affairs did not make any report to Parliament or the public. It became difficult for me to meet the Minister of Justice, even after the presidential by-elections in October 2008, when he was appointed the Vice President of the Republic of Zambia by President Banda.

By the time of the by-election in the Chilanga Constituency after my expulsion from the MMD Party in September 2010, Vice President Kunda was a faithful proselyte to the vulgar political language. He wittingly denounced and made malicious allegations against me. At a campaign rally at Mt Makulu Research Station, the Chief Government legal advisor even announced that he knew much about my activities while in the government and that he was prepared to divulge the same if I continued to criticize the government. I publicly confirmed that indeed the two of us had shared a lot of confidential information and state secrets. My offer of a public debate with the Vice President, which he did not take-up, eased our permanent parting of the ways with my legal advisor of Sham el-Sheikh.

On Friday 4th July 2008, a false story circulated in the media emanating from South Africa that President Mwanawasa had passed away in France. I contacted the Bank of Zambia and requested that an officer monitors the exchange rate from morning to late afternoon to gauge the reaction of the capital markets.

By 17.30 hours when I checked with Denny Kalyalya, the deputy governor since the Governor was out of the country, the sad news had registered a huge negative impact on the Kwacha. The local currency had lost 13 percent of its parity with the US Dollar. The anxiety on the health of President Mwanawasa was beginning to undo our hard-earned macroeconomic stability achievements and I decided to avert a crisis.

The actors in the monetary sector met with the Central Bank. I and Governor Fundanga discussed and agreed that we come out and calm the capital markets. We both gave interviews to the reputable global news media 'Reuters'. We stated that President Mwanawasa had established systems and procedures that will not break easily because of his ill health. We told the whole world that President Mwanawasa gave space to his juniors to implement government policies and these juniors were available to continue the good work in his absence.

Governor Fundanga announced that Zambia had foreign reserves of 5.6 months import cover. We vowed to continue with prudent fiscal and monetary management. It also transpired that the death story was not true, although the President was still in a coma. Our efforts paid dividends as the Kwacha stabilized around K3.20 per US dollar.

Beginning on Saturday, 12 July 2008, the National Assembly (NA) of

Zambia was to host over 300 members of the Commonwealth Parliamentary Association (CPA), Africa Region, in Livingstone for four days. Late on Monday afternoon, I received a telephone call from the Clerk of the NA Doris Mwiinga concerning the conference.

The Clerk informed me that although they made adequate preparations, she had received information that the National Airport Corporation (NAC) planned to ground Zambian Airways (ZA) on Tuesday 15 July 2008 due to outstanding fees. The Zambian Parliament had arranged to showcase Zambia's economic successes on this day by ferrying the delegates to various development projects in the country with planes chartered from Zambian Airways.

I immediately telephoned Robinson Misitala, the Managing Director of NAC, who confirmed that the story was true and that notice had been given to the airline some weeks back. I reasoned with him that the timing was poor because of the CPA delegates from all over Africa who were anxious to see the results of Zambia's development efforts. When he could not make a favourable reply, I decided to speak to Minister of Transport and Communications Dora Siliya.

When I was told that the Minister was out of the country and unreachable, I called back the MD of NAC and threatened that he would be dismissed if Zambian Airways did not fulfill its obligation to the NA. I reminded him of the irreparable damage that would be done to the country's image at this particular moment in time. In my mind was the thirteen per cent loss in the value of the Kwacha in one day on 6 July 2008 due to misinformation on the hospitalized President. I presumed that any further negative information would be spread to the whole Commonwealth by the frustrated delegates.

I then raised Acting President Banda at about 2345 hours and informed him of my conversation with the MD of NAC, including my threat to dismiss the MD if he disobeyed my instruction. I requested for the President's intervention with the MD. I learnt later that no intervention was made, although the story had a happy ending as the NAC did not take the intended action against Zambian Airways.

The CPA delegates were conveyed to various places of their interest according to plan. Articles in praise of Zambia's economic achievements appeared in the newspapers from the groups that visited Kansanshi Mine in Solwezi and Nakambala Sugar Estates in Mazabuka.

I brought the good news to the attention of the MD of NAC and invited him to own the praise showered on Zambia by the foreign visitors. To my utter surprise, my efforts to preserve the country's restored good image at a critical period in its history were construed by my enemies to be part of my schemes to save the Zambian Airways. However, the gracious Speaker of the National Assembly, Amusaa Mwanamwambwa wrote me a 'thank you' letter to me for assisting in the smooth organization of a successful CPA Conference.

On Monday, 21 July 2008, the Vice President was travelling to Livingstone by a ZAF plane. Since he was flying out from the City Airport, I decided to go and see him off and expected other officials to be there. I was shocked and puzzled to be alone apart from the military officers at the airport. There were no other passengers on the plane apart from the Vice President. When I returned to my office, I telephoned the SC to find out why there were no officials at the airport. He replied that even he was not aware of the Vice President's trip to Livingstone. The normal procedure was to announce such trips and purpose in a cabinet meeting.

I soon learnt from my officers that my advice to the Minister of Communications and Transport to allow the deferment of the paying of outstanding fees by Zambian Airways to NAC had been rejected. I learnt that some of the earth-moving equipment had arrived in Lusaka and my proposal for new mode of utilization was rejected. I learnt that an additional much higher subsidy on fuel was being proposed to cabinet. I learnt that a larger number of scanners were being planned for purchasing from China.

As a number of decisions being made by the higher authority had financial implications, I sought a way of distancing myself from direct involvement in managing public finances during the unsure situation. I and Evans Chibiliti, Secretary to the Treasury went to propose stringent measures to the Acting President in order to safeguard Government assets. We suggested that no Minister or politician should be involved in any dealings to do with Government funds and property. I was delighted when the Acting President bought into my proposal.

The Secretary to the Treasury convened a meeting of all Controlling Officers at the MICC and explained the new procedure early in August 2008. He followed up the meeting with a Circular to all Ministers and Controlling Officers banning us from being involved in all matters concerning financial dealings of Government. At our Ministry, the Secretary to the Treasury became the decision maker and would only brief me at his pleasure. I was not involved in releasing funds not even those for the bills for Percy Hospital in France.

On Monday 11th August 2008, I was in Chipata as a Guest of Honor at the official opening of the Indo Zambia Bank branch office. As instructed by President Mwanawasa on 19th May during our visit to Vubwi, I seized the opportunity to announce the increase of the fertilizer subsidy from 60 to 75 percent and an increase in the number of beneficiaries from 125,000 to 200,000. Being topical and important issues, the news on the two subjects was widely covered by the media all over the country.

I returned from Chipata on the same day. On the morning of Tuesday 12th August 2008, the Secretary to the Treasury (ST) came over to my office and informed me that he had been called to a meeting by the Acting President the previous day. The Acting President wanted a written press release on the fertilizer subsidies, so that he could announce the new levels. I immediately telephoned the Acting President and informed him that I had already announced the fertilizer subsidy and the number of beneficiaries while I was in Chipata the previous day.

The Vice President expressed his strong displeasure and told me that such an important issue should have been announced to the Nation by him. I was taken aback as I recalled President Mwanawasa in his report to Cabinet on the tour of Eastern Province mentioning that the Minister of Finance and National Planning will scout for additional money and will announce the subsidy level. Our telephone conversation with the Vice President ended by a reminder to me that things had changed.

On 12th August 2008, I went to South Africa to attend a meeting of SADC Ministers of Finance to discuss regional integration. While in the meeting the following day, a message came through from my Personal Assistant that the Vice President was not happy with my trip. I asked my protocol officer to make immediate arrangements for my return to Zambia on the earliest flight. I was back in Lusaka by 09.00 hours the following day.

When explaining my trip, I reminded the Vice President that I had mentioned the trip during our conversation on the Chipata fertilizer trip. I was told that I should have written a request letter and waited for his reaction.

On 16th August 2008, I was a guest speaker at the first-ever teen conference at the Mulungushi International Conference Centre, organised by Chibamba Kanyama and his associates. The invitation for my attendance had been delivered much earlier. I had accepted as I saw an opportunity to entice the youth to embrace national planning and Vision 2030 and give them hope for a prosperous future. At a cabinet meeting the following day, a cabinet colleague jokingly reminded me that I was not the Minister responsible for the youth portfolio. In explaining his remark, he told me that there was a view that the Vice President should have opened the conference.

After consultations, a decision was made to use part of the concessional loan from China to acquire a fleet of heavy earth-moving equipment from China. The loan was the first to be contracted after the HIPC Initiative debt write-off. President Mwanawasa promised the Zambian people improved feeder roads by the time of harvesting crops in 2009. He instructed me and the Minister of Works and Supply to make sure that the equipment arrived on time.

In early August 2008, the equipment arrived in Tanzania, but could not proceed to Zambia due to its abnormal weight, which was above the allowable axle limit on Tanzanian roads. After negotiations, the Tanzanian Government graciously allowed the equipment to be moved.

The equipment was received by the Acting President Rupiah B Banda at a ceremony held at 08.30 hours at the Independence Stadium on 19 August 2008 at 08.30 hours, at which CATIC, the Chinese suppliers handed-over the equipment.

To mortify me, the equipment was divided into nine units, one for each province and further subdivided into district units. Some districts were given only road-forming machines without diggers or water bowsers, while some received earth movers without diggers. In Solwezi, the equipment delivered from Lusaka by hired drivers was parked under trees and remained immobile for lack of competent drivers. The expensive equipment was vandalized and rendered unusable even before it made a single road.

The new mode of managing the equipment, that I and President Mwanawasa had agreed upon, and the establishment of a spare parts manufacturing factory in Zambia after three years, were not mentioned. The omissions were brought to my attention by the suppliers of the equipment. But I could not do anything as I was not consulted on the issue.

After the speeches, we had the opportunity to admire the brand new equipment specially made to open up Zambia's countryside for development. As I was going around, I received a call from an MMD cadre informing me that the election appeal case was on the agenda of the Supreme Court sitting that morning. I immediately rushed to the Supreme Court and found that the judgement was being read by the Chief Justice. The judgment was not very long and soon it was all over with the Court's decision to uphold the decision of the High Court on my innocence.

I was then driven across Independence Avenue to the Ministry of Finance and National Planning. As I was alighting from the vehicle, I telephoned Phesto Musonda, Chairman of the Zambia International Trade Fair, to confirm a lunch appointment to celebrate my court victory and to discuss his emerald exchange project. Immediately after Musonda's conversation, I received a call from Jack Kalala informing me that President Mwanawasa had passed on that morning at Percy Military Hospital in France.

Musonda insisted on having the lunch in spite of the sad news. He advised me to take extra care in view of the demise of my boss as some people would try to destroy me, even physically, since I would be the carrier of President Mwanawasa's legacy. He advised that should there be any slightest hint of the Acting President wishing to contest the by-elections, I should back off.

I informed Musonda that Vice President Banda had assured both President Mwanawasa on many occasions that he did not intend to contest for any political position. I proposed to my associate that I would see the Acting President and raise the by-election issue with him. In spite of me reassuring Musonda that I'd had good relations with the Vice President since 2004, he rejected my plan of any discussions and described my proposal as preposterous and called me naïve.

Early in the morning of Tuesday 19 August 2008, I lost my supervisor-turned friend, His Excellency Dr Levy Patrick Mwanawasa, State Counsel, the third President of the Republic of Zambia. About mid-morning of the same day, the election appeal was determined in my favour by the Supreme Court chaired by His Lordship Chief Justice Ernest Sakala.

CHAPTER 42

My Reflections On President Levy Patrick Mwanawasa

I do spend some quiet moments reflecting on the coincidental heaven-sent judgment on the election appeal and the untimely demise of President Mwanawasa on the same day of 19 August 2008. I rejoined the Zambian Government on 3 July 2003 at the invitation of President Mwanawasa having resigned from the public service in May 1994 after twenty-three years of service. At the time, Mwanawasa and I had met only once. We, therefore, did not know each other.

During my swearing-in, President Mwanawasa stated that I was to serve the Zambian people and save Zambia, my country, from the ignominious name of Heavily Indebted Poor Country (HIPC). By my active participation in various fora, I also contributed to the development of many other countries. My interaction with the peoples of these foreign countries provided me with a rare opportunity to enhance my understanding of development challenges in many parts of the world.

I entered the parliamentary election race in 2006 and won on the prodding and support of President Mwanawasa. By the time of his death, Mwanawasa and I had become close workmates openly sharing our inner thoughts on how to improve the livelihoods of our families and those of the Zambian people.

At a political campaign rally held on Tuesday 19th September 2006 at Kalundu Basic School to support my candidature as Member of Parliament for Chilanga Constituency, President Mwanawasa used the analogy of a ship, the captain, and the compass to explain his leadership of the country.

He informed the large gathering that when he became President of Zambia, he identified the country's challenges and the direction to take in confronting them. He went on to say that as the captain, he charted a route and managed to steer the ship called Zambia across the turbulent waters because of a reliable compass that helped him to maintain the correct readings.

Turning and pointing at me he said, "This gentleman standing next to me is the compass I have used. I ask you to vote for him so that Zambia continues to move in the correct direction". For me, President Levy Patrick Mwanawasa was an inspiring leader of integrity, who trusted me and made me reach the great heights of brinkmanship and success in a difficult assignment. I worked hard to achieve his vision and our shared mission because he believed in my capabilities.

On Thursday, 11 September 2008, I gave an extensive interview to the editor of 'The African Economy' magazine highlighting the positive environment created by President Mwanawasa during his seven-year rule. The magazine, under Chairman Ikechi Emenike, followed and covered Zambia's journey from 2005 under President Mwanawasa, with extensive annual surveys of the economy by a dedicated team of economic reporters, who included Charity Chukwuma, Chichi Mung'omba, and Emmanuel Okafor.

Special editions of the magazine were produced and distributed at the annual meetings of the AfDB, IMF, and the World Bank from 2005 to 2007. The exposure of Zambia's positive changes built confidence in the economic management team, of which I was the compass, to entrench the winning processes and systems in support of shared national policies and a vision. As a cheerleader, I helped in getting many people to believe in and share President Mwanawasa's vision for Zambia's prosperous future.

In my interview, I declared that "Zambia's economic policies are irreversible" and my full interview was reproduced in the October-December 2008 issue of the magazine. Editor Kelechi Anyanwu stated in the particular edition that, 'Zambia seems to give observers a modicum of repose when the question of stability in the aftermath of this transition comes to the mind. Talking of political stability, Zambia shines as a model of democracy with over sixteen years of peaceful change of power in a multiparty setting.

But observers have some reasons to be restive about the state of Zambia's economy, which is believed to have been transformed by the good policies and projects implemented by the team of late President Levy Mwanawasa, the renowned anti-corruption campaigner".

I am aware that the subsequent MMD and PF administrations changed some of the policies and plans, but this has been to the detriment of the future well-being and prosperity of the Zambians.

Mwanawasa had a list of priorities that he wanted to accomplish before the end of his second term in 2010. Among these was the Chembe Bridge on the Luapula River between the DRC and Zambia. His efforts to get the cooperation of the neighbour to construct the bridge did not succeed. The donors could not give financial assistance without a cooperation agreement between Congo and Zambia, the two neighbouring countries. Finally, Zambia footed the bill for the bridge alone.

A trip was organized for me and some ministers to visit the Chembe Bridge on Sunday, 14 September 2008, eleven days after Mwanawasa's burial. I recalled my comment to Danny Musenge in 1969 when we were on the Chembe pontoon as UNZA students on the need for a bridge. My vision and the mission of late Mwanawasa were being fulfilled at the time of his death. When the bridge was completed, it was named Levy Mwanawasa Bridge in recognition of the efforts made by the late President for the bridge to exist.

Another project on President Mwanawasa's list of priorities was the restoration of the status of President Kaunda as a founding father of the Nation of Zambia. President Chiluba had revoked KK's protocol and withheld his benefits and accused him of being a foreigner to be deported to Malawi, the origins of his family. President Mwanawasa achieved his goal of restoring the deserved respect of President Kaunda and I always feel the warmth of the company of one of the founding fathers of Zambia.

As per his Presidential Mission Statement adopted after winning the elections in 2001, President Levy Patrick Mwanawasa, State Counsel, brought honour, dignity and prosperity to Zambia through his honest and selfless hard work.

CHAPTER 43

Learning How To Mourn A President

The Zambian Cabinet was convened immediately at Cabinet Office to share the sad news of the death of President Mwanawasa on 19 August 2008. The event was a new thing for everyone as nothing of the sort had happened before in the Nation. The incident tested the State machinery in organization and protocols, which also involved the family of the late President.

By the end of the working day, I had received many visitors at my office and many telephone calls offering condolences on the passing away of my boss.

I had no personal experience of losing a boss during my nearly four decades of employment. During funerals of my senior family members such as grandparents, uncles, and my parents, I had never been given any prominent role. In our tradition, the clan members decide the conduct of the funeral. However, having witnessed many funerals in my life, I accepted death as part of God's hidden plan. Death is a consequence of birth. I decided years back not to indulge in the ritual of body-viewing as it has no meaning to me.

The Cabinet took some time to discuss the protocols to be followed. Cabinet became some kind of Presidential Funeral Committee, with meetings being called whenever some issue arose. Some of the meetings involved consultations with the family members of the late President and therefore, protocols on meetings of Cabinet were not strictly followed.

Questions arose as to who was the Chief Mourner between the Acting President and the widow? Where was the funeral gathering to be? Was it to be in State House or somewhere else? The debate on the site of the funeral gathering was concluded and the decision was that both State House and the Agricultural Show Grounds would be used. Individual mourners could decide where to go.

At some point, President Mwanawasa had insisted that Cabinet produces a manual on funeral proceedings and procedures for mourning both private and public leaders. As far as he was concerned, some private citizens contributed more than many public workers to the well-being of Zambians. Due to some opposition to the President's wish to include private citizens in the funeral protocols, the specific regulations and rules that we finally agreed upon were only for public leaders minus the president. This meant that funeral procedures for lower-ranking officers would not be at the whims of individuals.

With President Mwanawasa having died outside the country, it was not known when his remains would arrive in Zambia. We, therefore, decided to allow for seven days of national mourning as per existing regulations with a provision for change when other details became available.

Cabinet decided that I lead a team of four ministers to France to accompany the remains of the late president on the journey to Zambia. As final arrangements were being made on the logistics, we were informed that the French President had offered to shoulder the entire responsibility. My team was ready to depart for France when I was informed that I should not travel on the objections of the family of the deceased.

From that point onwards, I was not consulted on the travel and many other arrangements. I learnt that some other ministers travelled to France, but I was not privy to what the team did in France as no report was made to the Cabinet.

I had not spoken to the former First Lady since July 2008 in Sharm el-Sheikh, Egypt. My efforts to contact her in France during the hospitalization of President Mwanawasa had not succeeded. My resort to sending text messages did not achieve much as the messages were also not acknowledged.

I was at the airport on 23 August 2008 when the body of the late president arrived. There was a large crowd at the airport and an overwhelming outpouring of grief. I had an opportunity to speak for a moment to the former First Lady, to express my condolences. As the cortege was leaving the airport, Sylvia Masebo reminded me that no Zambian Government official had greeted the military crew that brought the late president's body to Zambia. She asked me to do something about this show of ingratitude.

I went over and asked the French Ambassador to Zambia if it was permissible for me to enter the military aircraft. When she said it was alright, I asked her to accompany me into the aircraft. As we were climbing the ramp, we met the senior officer and informed him that I wanted to greet the crew. He quickly organized the crew into a saluting formation. I shook hands with them and thanked them for the commendable job they had done of safely conveying the remains of late President Mwanawasa to Zambia.

The French Ambassador followed suit and thanked me as we walked away from the plane. We joined Masebo and walked to the car park, which was by this time nearly empty as most of the people had left for the Mulungushi International Conference Centre, where the body of the late president lay in state.

One of the issues, which could not be concluded quickly by the Cabinet and the family, was the burial place for the late president. It was revealed that President Mwanawasa had wished to be buried at his Palabana Farm in Chongwe, east of Lusaka City.

On 30 August 2008, some family members and a lawyer came over to my residence to inform me that the common law provides that the living may ignore the wishes of the dead if such a wish inconvenienced the living. It was argued that burying late President Mwanawasa at Palabana Farm would inconvenience the living who might want to visit the grave to pay their respects. The proposal was to designate the Diplomatic Triangle outside Cabinet Office as a Presidential burial ground.

I was among those who supported the view that we follow the wishes of the deceased, as selecting a VIP burial ground in a hurry might not be good planning. My question on the inadequacy of the designated area as a Presidential burial ground was not soberly dealt with. My proposal to design a layout for at least ten mausoleums in a chronological order of service was totally ignored as the focus was on burying one dead president. When Zambians are in mourning mood and discussing funeral matters, they throw caution to the winds to the neglect of future orderly conduct. A final decision was made to bury late President Mwanawasa at the new burial grounds.

By 2015, when a third president was being buried, no credible answers were given to curious relatives who quipped about the locations and sizes of the mausoleums. The mausoleum for President Mwanawasa who was the youngest and third president occupies the prominent site right in front of the cenotaph.

A decision was made to take the late president's body to all the provincial capitals to lay in state for body-viewing. The mourning period was therefore extended in order to accommodate the period the body would be taken throughout the country by the Zambia Air Force. The burial was set by the family for 3 September 2008, the birthday anniversary of the late president.

CHAPTER 44

Stabbed In The Back By Political Allies

The tour of the provinces began on Monday, 25 August 2008 in Chipata, Eastern Province. Early in the morning of that day, I was informed that I should accompany the body on the tour. As the tour group had already left for Chipata, I was advised to charter a plane to catch up with the group in Chipata.

I contacted people in the aviation industry and soon a trusted pilot with his plane was ready to take me to Chipata. On my way to the airport, I was informed that Lucy Changwe, a deputy minister would accompany me on the flight.

As our plane approached the Luangwa Valley, we were informed by the pilot that the tour group had left Chipata for Kasama in the Northern Province. The pilot offered to take us to Kasama, so long as we refuelled at Mfuwe Airport. After refuelling at Mfuwe, we flew straight to Kasama, where we joined the tour party.

In the evening, the MMD provincial leaders from the Northern Province, who included ministers and Members of Parliament, held their meeting to work out logistics for body-viewing. They also discussed the issue concerning the selection of the MMD presidential candidate for the by-election. I was informed that at some point, potential candidates, including me were discussed.

Among those who were vehemently opposed to my candidature were some ministers, who had been close to me for a long time. In fact, I had known some of them since the 1990s and I even played a part in their appointments as President Mwanawasa consulted me and I advised in their favour. I was informed that there were also strong tribal overtones when discussing my candidature by the province's leaders.

At the Kasama Stadium, the venue for body-viewing, I sat alone with empty chairs on both sides until a junior MMD Party official came over to keep me company. I was consoled by the loud ovation I was given when my name was called out during the body-viewing, as many shouted my given nickname of 'Mr HIPC'.

We then flew to Mansa, Luapula Province, where there was an even larger crowd of mourners and I was given a louder ovation. I was informed that my name was well-received at the meeting of the provincial MMD Party leaders. Some Party officials suggested that I find time to visit the bridge, which was under construction between Zambia and the DRC on the Luapula River at Chembe. According to their understanding, I was instrumental in sourcing funds to construct the long-awaited bridge.

From Mansa, we flew to Ndola City for a night stop. The body-viewing at Ndola was allocated the whole day of Wednesday, 27 August 2008, to accommodate people from all the towns on the Copperbelt. The MMD Party leaders were divided on the issue of an MMD presidential candidate, with some favouring the convening of a full Convention. Others, including the provincial chairman, pronounced themselves as being totally opposed to my candidature.

The following day as the tour group was about to depart for Solwezi Town in the North-Western Province, I was informed by Alfred Chipoya, Principal Private Secretary to the late President that I was wanted in Lusaka urgently. He handed me a plane ticket and asked me to take out my bag from the plane's luggage hold. I remained at the airport until after all the military departure formalities had been completed and the cortege left for Solwezi. I then took my flight to Lusaka at 0900 hours.

On arrival at home, I found a letter written by Acting President Banda, in which he charged me with an offence of leaving Lusaka for Kasama without his permission. An enquiry with the Secretary to the Cabinet established that this was the first such letter ever written to a cabinet minister by a president. Normally, erring ministers were reminded of the standing instruction of not leaving Lusaka by the assistants to the president.

The Acting President denied that he was the one who had stopped my continuing with the provincial tour. I requested that I be given time until after the burial to reply. I, therefore, had no answer at the time, to the many people who enquired on why I dropped out from the tour of the provinces, which made news headlines.

From Solwezi, the funeral group went to Mongu and the party officials held a meeting after body-viewing. At some point after midnight, a faithful supporter of mine put his cellular phone on voice and I followed the rowdy discussions. There was a near punch-up between my supporters and one of the senior MMD Party leaders, who was against me. It was only then that I knew the member of the Mwanawasa family who was working hard to reduce my visibility.

My request to the Acting President to proceed to Livingstone Town for the Southern Province body-viewing ceremony was approved and I urgently organized a plane ticket and left for Livingstone.

Although I was warmly welcomed by the crowd gathered at the Livingstone airport, some of the MMD provincial officials were already in the campaign mood. The provincial minster, who was a senior party official, publicly denounced young people who were vying to stand for the presidency even when they have no capacity to lead the nation. He stated that the Province would support the acting president as the party's candidate as he was old and mature. I was sixty-one years old at the time and had been a cabinet minister for five-and-a-half years. Former President Kaunda had become President of Zambia in a more challenging environment at the age of forty years, a fact well-known by the senior party official.

Many people, including the traditional chiefs, were surprised with the stance taken by the MMD senior party officials in the Southern Province. The Party official was the first one in the country to talk about the elections during the mourning period. I was advised not to attend the provincial meeting of the MMD Party officials in view of the hostility that was targeted at me.

About the same time, an elderly Tonga 'king maker', my Oondela, publicly declared his support for the acting president. There was also talk that it was not time for Tongas to rule. Up to that point in time, I had not been aware of the existence of a roster indicating when each tribe would rule Zambia. I was aware of a proposal for a roster indicating rotational times, when each province and not tribe was to nominate presidential candidates. The proposal, which was meant to reduce competition amongst the provinces, for the position of republican president, was rejected by one of the Constitutional Commissions of Enquiry.

I now had opposition from the Northern and Southern Provinces, both with large numbers of voters, even in NEC, and the Eastern Province, who were told to vote for "mwana wanu", meaning "your child'. For fear of being labeled tribalists, no Tonga called me their child.

Cabinet Ministers were assigned to play host to the foreign Heads of State and Governments coming to the burial ceremony on 3 September 2008. As a senior minister, I was delegated to play host to Zimbabwean President Mugabe, the longest serving Head in SADC. I looked forward to interacting with President Mugabe as I had worked with him when I was at the ACP Secretariat and his country was the president of the ACP council of ministers. To my surprise, President Mugabe arrived at the Parliament Buildings accompanied by a Zambian permanent secretary. On enquiry, it was claimed that the protocol officers could not find me to take me to the airport to play my role as minister-in-waiting.

As Cabinet was discussing late President Mwanawasa's will in connection with the burial, the matter of a video of a farewell message surfaced. The lawyer for late President Mwanawasa revealed that the President had recorded a farewell message in March 2005 to be broadcast to Zambians after his death. It was decided that the farewell message to the Zambians be handled by the Government, while the will be dealt with by the family.

Some ministers were panicky that the late president might have mentioned a succession plan and my name in the recorded message. It was also feared that the recording might contain messages that could be inimical to State interests.

Therefore, a preview of the message by a few government officials was arranged before airing it to the general public. I was not among the selected few officials who enjoyed the privilege of listening to the original message.

On 4 September 2008, a day after the burial, the Cabinet met at Government House to listen to the farewell message. It was weird to sit and listen attentively to a voice of a dead person thanking us for attending his funeral! This was Levy Patrick Mwanawasa, 'Loya wa ma-loya', doing something never done or heard of before. Everyone was attentive as speculation was rife on the issue of a successor.

At the end of listening to the message, there was relief on the faces of a number of ministers. One of those who was close to President Mwanawasa, but hostile to me shouted excitedly, "He did not mention anyone!' I wondered as to the reason for ministers rejoicing at listening to the voice of a dead person.

The living ignored the wish of the late president on his preferred burial grounds. The living were on safe ground if they erased the part of the message talking about a successor, if they considered such a thing as inconvenient to themselves. After all, this would be acceptable according to common law.

The things that the living do to the dead and at funerals are just to appease themselves as the dead have no feelings in their gravely state. In any case, even if all the wishes of late President Mwanawasa were completely ignored, he would not resurrect to punish the disobedient former junior officials, who were now in control of his lifeless body.

CHAPTER 45

Aspiring To Be MMD Party Presidential Candidate

The National Executive Committee (NEC) of the MMD Party met on 22 August 2008 to share the bereavement that had befallen the Party and the Nation. The NEC decided that Members of Parliament, cabinet ministers, and NEC members should be available in their provinces for body-viewing. They may also take the opportunity of their gatherings to discuss with the local party officials the process of selecting a presidential candidate for the party for the impending by-elections.

After acrimonious debate within the Party, the NEC decided to hold a mini-convention on 5 September 2008 to be attended by NEC members only, who would elect a presidential candidate.

The Secretariat worked out a programme and when they invited applicants, I was the first to announce my candidature on 25 August 2008. My declaration was regardless of the mode to be used to select the candidate, be it by a full convention or by NEC members only. Having been close to President Mwanawasa, I was convinced that I could carry forward his legacy and complete his mission 'to give fresh hope to our people, and to create opportunities for all'.

I received telephone calls from traditional leaders from six provinces conveying their condolences and encouraging me to stand for election at the NEC meeting. On 28 August 2008, I was called to a meeting at a home of an opposition leader to discuss the political situation with a group of chiefs. Their Royal Highnesses assured me that they would speak to leaders of all opposition parties to discourage them from contesting the elections, if I won at the NEC meeting, as the MMD Party presidential candidate.

On 31 August 2008, the Post newspaper carried a headline from an interview they'd had with the former First Lady during which she disclosed that the late President Mwanawasa had preferred me to succeed him. She stated that there were many ministers who knew about the President's preference as he had spoken to them and she called upon them to speak out.

When the media approached me on the succession story, I told them that I was aware that the late President was in the process of choosing a preferred successor but that he did not personally inform me of his final decision. I went further to say that a number of ministers had confirmed to me that they'd had conversations with late President Mwanawasa during which he'd asked them to help me with the campaign.

Following on from the statements by the former First Lady and me, only Masebo came out in the open to confirm that she had been told about me by the late President. Some ministers, who spoke to me just after my return from Egypt, denied knowledge of President Mwanawasa's preference and some refused to comment on the matter when asked.

Many foreign delegates who came for the funeral of President Mwanawasa visited my office or residence to pay courtesy calls and to convey their condolences. Some expressed anxiety on what would follow in the absence of President Mwanawasa. The cooperating partners were worried that all the achievements made during the previous four years in financial management discipline would be destroyed.

Some visitors voiced their fears of political instability, as had happened elsewhere in Africa. A few of them disclosed their conversations with President Mwanawasa about me but advised that if I should lose at the NEC elections, I should not pursue the matter any further.

I assured them that Zambia had reached cruising speed and only a reckless new president would destroy the solid foundation laid by President Mwanawasa's Administration. I supported my stance by giving examples of the many laws, regulations, systems, procedures, plans, Vision 2030, and reforms that had been enshrined in the governance system of the country, which would assist in steering and stabilizing its development. I also assured them that I would respect the decision of the MMD NEC voters.

After the burial ceremony on 3 September 2008, all the MMD NEC members were accommodated at the Chrismar Hotel opposite the Government House, the residence of the Vice President. I expected that we the candidates would be allowed to visit them at the hotel and campaign. Instead, they were provided with special escorts up to the day of the vote, who thoroughly intimidated them and told them not to vote for me.

As the MMD Party members dithered on the choice of a candidate, the other political parties waited anxiously before they could announce their presidential candidates. During this period, senior members of both the PF and the UPND approached me with a gesture of patriotism.

They proposed that if I won the MMD Party's election, they would withdraw from the elections. This was in line with my discussions with the Chiefs. This would give me a chance of being unopposed and consequently no elections would be held and the country will save a lot of money. I would then be the successor to late President Mwanawasa and this would allow for continuity of his legacy for the three years before the next general elections in 2011. The opposition parties felt that I had played a pivotal role in actualizing the late President's mission and plans.

I followed the generous offer by the opposition by checking on the projected cost of the by-elections. The budget officers indicated an estimated cost of K350 billion, which could be saved. I assured the patriotic opposition members that in such a situation, I would invite them to decide collectively on the use of the savings on a memorial project demonstrative of President Mwanawasa's mission and their magnanimity.

I took the opposition parties' offer to the Secretary General of the MMD Party, who embraced the idea. Surprisingly, the strongest opposition to the noble idea and to my candidacy came from some ministers and senior members of the ruling MMD Party. They demanded that regardless of the quality of the MMD Party's candidate, the costly general elections should be held. A leader of an opposition party, whom I met in the company of chiefs also joined the clamour for holding general elections and even announced his candidature two days before the MMD Party NEC elections.

Mbita Chitala, a northerner and a former deputy minister in President Mwanawasa's administration, even internationalized the debate on a successor by giving an interview to the Voice of America (VOA). In his interview, he was dismissive of the roles of late President Mwanawasa and me in Zambia's economic revival. He attributed the country's economic revival, during President Mwanawasa's reign, to the work of a previous administration, when Zambians were buying their staple food, mealie meal, by the roadside in one-kilogram packs nicknamed 'Pamela'. Chitala was among the ministers, who resigned early from Chiluba's government, alleging corruption and mismanagement in the government.

When I visited Washington DC for the 2008 IMF Annual Meetings in October, I became aware of the contents of the whole interview, as I listened to it on *YouTube*. I was asked by the reporter to rebut the claim by my former junior officer, but I politely declined to make a comment on the disparaging interview.

On 5 September 2008, the day of the MMD elections, there was a large number of us vying for the position of MMD Party presidential candidate. The elections at the NEC meeting were not transparent as there were a lot of anomalies. Our request to be afforded some time to address the NEC voters was rejected by the MMD Electoral Commission. However, the campaign against me that was waged by ordinary MMD members, especially those on the Copperbelt, spilled over into the NEC meeting and was allowed by the commission.

Catherine Namugala, a northerner and the National Chairperson of the MMD Women's Committee distributed copies of a tabloid to all NEC members except me, which had an article that alleged my collusion with Zambian Airways to evade meeting their financial obligations to various government institutions. With a show of fervent hostility, she stated that I should not be voted for in view of my support to the local airline. I was not allowed to answer the allegations or to address the NEC meeting.

I was taken aback by the behaviour of the chairperson towards me, as I had enjoyed a friendly relationship for a long time. As privatization was unfolding in 1991, she was among the early business people to engage the parastatal companies by supplying commodities. She was among those who sought my intervention in resolving a contract issue with a parastatal under my supervision. My intervention in the ZA-NAC relationship was no different from what I did during my long public service when Namugala and many others sought my assistance for their companies or on personal basis.

As we were about to vote, I discovered that my name was not even on the printed ballot papers. The secretariat officials reported that the reason was that I had not paid the required amount of the nomination fee. Having paid the shortfall instantly, the elections officials proposed to write my name at the bottom of the ballot papers. I objected to the proposal and after heated protestations from a number of NEC members, the elections were postponed to the afternoon to allow for printing of new ballot papers. This gave me the opportunity to campaign to the NEC members.

The new ballot papers, done during lunch break, put my name at the bottom of the list and not in the correct position by alphabet. Exuding with confidence after my lunch hour campaign, I allowed the voting to go ahead. Candidates were not allowed to witness the counting of the votes in a backroom. After the counting of the votes, it was announced that the Acting President had received forty-three votes against eleven votes for me out of fifty-six voters.

As I walked out of the hall, full of security personnel, I was supported by Masebo, who doubted the correctness of the announced vote numbers for RB and me. When we passed through the crowd of women and youths, clad in MMD Party regalia, they sang praise songs on the economic improvements brought about by President Mwanawasa and me. A sizable group of youths even escorted us up to our vehicles. Some recounted my visionary speech during the youth conference at the same venue a month before.

When I got home, I gave a thorough brief to my spouse on the happenings at the Mulungushi Conference Centre. Joyce expressed admiration for me for exhibiting so much courage in a highly charged environment. She then asked if in my opinion, I expected Acting President Banda to help with my campaign using the State machinery had I beaten him in the NEC elections. I did not give an intelligent and convincing answer to my wife's searching and loaded question. My spouse was well aware of the strained relations between the Acting President and me.

Some years later, a former senior MMD official, who had taken part in organizing the NEC elections and the counting of the votes, called me naïve for not observing the counting of the votes at the NEC meeting. The official advised me to quit politics as I did not understand the game. Although I had heard of the swapping of vote numbers in the political arena, I could not do anything about the matter, as the 'winner' was already in control of all the state institutions.

I was not included in the campaign programme except when the MMD candidate held a rally in Kafue Town, when as Member of Parliament for Chilanga Constituency, I assisted Bradford Machila, the local Member of Parliament in organizing the meeting. At the rally, the leaders of the opposition parties supporting the MMD candidate, took centre stage in addressing the gathered MMD members. They invited the MMD cadres to vote for RB this time and to vote for them in 2011 as the MMD party had no capable leaders.

I appeared on Television Zambia on Sunday 26 October 2008 to explain economic issues as Chairman of the Finance and Economic Committee of the MMD Party. Benny Tetamashimba contacted me the following day from the Copperbelt inviting me to join the campaign team. He claimed that a lot of people were happy with my television appearance and wanted to hear and see me at the rallies. I declined to join the campaign team at the last minute as there had been no explanation why I had been left out since the beginning of the campaign.

The elections, which were held on Thursday, 30 October 2008, were won by RB followed in second place by Michael Sata of the Patriotic Front.

CHAPTER 46

The New President Disdains My Public Service

Although RB and I had last met in July 2004 when he visited my office, seeking some assistance, President Mwanawasa made us meet in some unplanned circumstances in 2006. During his campaign tours for the 2006 elections, President Mwanawasa challenged the people of the Eastern Province that if they voted for him and the MMD Members of Parliament, he would reward them with a senior appointment. In a meeting attended by a select few, he instructed the MMD Party Provincial Chairman Alfred Chioza, a former member of parliament for Kapoche constituency and a personal friend of mine, to supervise the election campaigns effectively.

With the President's carrot dangling in his face, Chioza mobilized all the prominent people in the province to campaign for the MMD Party. Two days before the elections, Chioza informed me in a telephone conversation that President Mwanawasa would be very happy with the election results as he had convinced even prominent opposition members including RB to join the MMD campaign.

Chioza went further to say that RB at some point had expressed very kind words about me and he wanted to know what I had done for him. I did not disclose anything that had happened between RB and me in 2004. Chioza did also not answer my question on whether RB had joined MMD after what he said about his lifetime UNIP membership a few days earlier.

The MMD Party scooped the majority seats in the Eastern Province in the elections. Against the expectations of many of us, who felt that MMD Party Provincial Chairman Chioza had carried out the President's directives and therefore deserved to be appointed into the promised high position, instead, RB got the appointment.

When I visited RB at his office at Cabinet Office in 2006 to welcome him, he reminded me of his visit to my office in 2004. He again expressed emotive words of gratitude and told me that his family was appreciative of my assistance. He stated that President Mwanawasa and I were kind, young people, who deserved his full support. The Vice President praised me for winning the nickname of 'Mr HIPC' by getting Zambia out of its debt trap in 2005.

Whenever I visited RB at his office at Parliament or Cabinet Office to brief him, I enjoyed my favourite cup of tea with organic honey and some evocative stories from Vice President Banda's long-lived life.

Once when I asked him about his future plans after 2011, the Vice President talked of his imminent retirement to his Chipata farm as he had no intention of standing for any political office again. *"Ivi nivanu, ba-Magande. Imwe mukali baana"*, meaning, "These issues are yours Mr Magande, as you are still young" he said. The message which I'd thought was for my ears only was repeated to President Mwanawasa, who wholeheartedly believed it and informed me.

RB and I worked together cordially until in 2008, when President Mwanawasa fell ill in June and subsequently passed on in August 2008. The disappearance of President Mwanawasa brought out a succession of events that resulted in a whole new dimension to my close relationship with RB. The privilege of having a cup of tea vanished instantly as if the tea maker had taken an indefinite leave on hearing of Mwanawasa's illness.

As early as 3rd July 2008, I realised that I had to tread carefully, when the Vice President did not summon me, as leader of the Zambian delegation to the AU Summit in Sharm el Sheikh to brief him on the happenings, which included the hospitalisation of President Mwanawasa. RB and I had created a lot of shared friends under President Mwanawasa, who freely informed me of what was being said and done, where and when I was not present. I had also been in public service for a long period and had accumulated various skills of self-survival.

At the ceremony to receive the earth-moving equipment from China at the Independence Stadium on 19 August 2008, the day President Mwanawasa passed on in France, Acting President Banda forgot to shake my hand. Seven days later on 26 August 2008, Acting President Banda, using his newly acquired presidential red pen, signed a letter charging me with indiscipline thereby becoming the first boss in my thirty-seven years of public service to charge me with an offence of insubordination.

The offence was that of, "leaving Lusaka for Kasama without my permission" when I escorted the body of the late president on the tour of the provinces. My exculpatory letter written after the funeral was never replied to and therefore, the matter not concluded, thereby leaving the only record of indiscipline in my staff file throughout my employment life.

Immediately when President Mwanawasa won the elections in 2001, he made public pronouncements that due respect, protocol, and benefits must be accorded to former President Kaunda. One of the retirement benefits was a house. The Minister of Works and I worked as instructed and the house was completed in June 2008.

After all the effort I made to fulfill President Mwanawasa's mission to restore the dignity of former President Kaunda, I was not invited to the handing-over ceremony officiated by Acting President Banda on 16 September

2008. I only saw the final result of my work exactly four years later in September 2012 when I went to convey my condolences to the old man on the demise of Mama Betty Kaunda.

President Mwanawasa held fruitful discussions with the management of Lafarge during the laying of the foundation stone for the new cement factory at Chilanga in 2006. The proprietors of the company made a covenant to support the local people with building materials and services. This was one of the flagship projects I was proud of, as it was established by the foreign investors under government's prodding when I was the Member of Parliament for Chilanga.

The ceremony for commissioning the new factory was held on the morning of 14 November 2008, with Vice President Banda as the guest of honour and I was a co-host as the Member of Parliament. The Vice President once again did not shake my hand. He also did not inspect the new factory as he was rushing for a press conference at State House. I came to know of the press conference by a telephone call from my special assistant after the factory function.

As I passed through the office on my way to the press conference, I was made aware of a lot of speculation on my future as a new cabinet was to be announced. A number of officers, presumably including the young officer who sat in my meeting with RB in June 2004, were busy comforting my special assistant that I would be included in the new cabinet in consideration of what I had done for RB. I let the young people indulge in speculation, although my action of clearing my office of all personal effects, before hand, must have convinced Brigid Siakalenge that I knew my fate.

At the press conference, where he announced a new Cabinet, newly elected President Rupiah Bwezani Banda did not only leave me out of the cabinet, but he did not even find space or a moment to mention my name in any connection.

Two weeks after the cabinet reshuffle, I received a letter signed by President Banda and dated 28 November 2008, terminating my appointment with immediate effect. As if on President Banda's orders, I received only five letters from Zambians to thank me for the service I rendered to the republic of Zambia for five and a half years.

I was comforted by the fact that after serving as Minister of Finance and National Planning for Zambia, a developing country, for such a long period, the only case my enemies could condemn me for, was that of advising another Minister to support Zambian Airways, a Zambian-owned company, on how to survive the temporal global high fuel prices. This was not the only case in which I used my delegated authority as public officer to assist a Zambian against the excess use of power by a government institution.

As I chatted with the immaculately-dressed lady in my office, tears suddenly roared on her cheek onto her dress. Within sobs, she explained that these were tears of joy, as her company, which had been blacklisted for a long time, had been allocated some foreign exchange.

It was a tearful site when this old man wobbled into my office to thank me for having been paid some long outstanding money owed by the government. He told me that I had saved him from the indignity of failing to provide for his family. I went into a reflective mood in the middle of the night, when I received a telephone call from an officer of the IMF, who informed me that Zambia's foreign debt had been reduced to US $500 million from US $ 7.2 billion.

As I went round the modern facilities of the Livingstone SOS Village, an officer thanked me for having negotiated with the Livingstone Council and the Ministry of Environment and Natural Resources for the land on which the village stands. She showed me twins, who had been brought into the SOS village a few days earlier, as their mother did not survive childbirth. The officer told me that it was my personal intervention that gave hope for a life to the orphaned twins. I failed to get a plot from the council for personal use.

No Zambian or foreigner alleged any corruption, nepotism or theft of public funds against me during my service. I did not maintain a foreign account and even my accounts in Zambia with various local banks had no suspicious deposits. I had retired all the millions of kwacha of imprest I got for the numerous travels I made locally and to foreign countries. I was contented that my assistance to many Zambians, who were not my relatives and whom I did not know personally, resulted in positive benefits and prosperity.

Among the many messages that I received from foreigners, whom I interacted with when carrying out my public duties, was one which summed up my work as Minister of Finance and National Planning for Zambia and it read as follows:

"Let me take this opportunity to thank you for the service and support you provided to this office during your tenure as Minister of Finance and National Planning. I shall remember your clear and excellent grasp of issues, devotion to work, and interest in the common good of the Africa Group.

Your achievements can clearly be demonstrated in your contribution towards Zambia's economic performance. The resurgence in the country's economy has been anchored on improved economic management and continued implementation of prudent macroeconomic and structural policies. The slowdown in the global economy and declining oil and commodity prices now impose new challenges for the country. I am encouraged that you will remain in Parliament from where the country would continue to benefit from your experience.

Let me thank you once more for your services and wish you success in your new endeavours".

CHAPTER 47

Life As A Backbencher In The Zambian Parliament

While I lost my Ministerial position on 14th November 2008, I did retain my Parliamentary seat as a Member of Parliament for the Chilanga Constituency. When Parliament resumed its sitting on 16th January 2009, I was a backbencher and had to learn a few issues of protocol. Sitting at the back and observing the happenings in the House, I wondered as to what will keep me busy to continue with the busy rhythm I was used to while in the ministerial office.

The Speaker at one time advised that the role of a Member of Parliament was to speak in the House on any issue concerning the people. What issues will keep me busy? I contemplated resigning as a Member of Parliament. I imagined that I will be kept busy if I reverted to private practice as a consultant.

Suddenly, enemies surfaced within the MMD ranks and peddled stories that I got an international job and was about to forsake my country for money. At that time, I really did not want a fulltime job outside the country, although openings were available in some international organizations. In Zambia, which was declared a Christian Nation, it was easy for me to be consoled by the Scriptures as Jesus said in Luke 4: verse 24, "No prophet is accepted in his own country".

The majority of those I consulted advised me against resigning from Parliament, because I was elected by the people and that I should not be seen not to care about their welfare. Others argued that since RB was only completing the balance of late Mwanawasa's term as he clearly stated during the campaign, the MMD Party mighty need me as a presidential candidate in 2011. Others stated that since I cared so much about proper use of public funds, it will be in bad taste for me to allow the use of money on a meaningless bye-election.

I finally decided to stay on as a Parliamentarian until the end of the term in 2011. Little did I imagine that the future will be hazardous as the MMD Party cadres will be unleashed upon me. After the demise of President Mwanawasa, I became enemy number one, who was to be physically eliminated or hounded out of the party. Having won the court battles against the opposition PF and UPND parties, which were waged over a two year period, now the battle for recognition was within the MMD Party.

On 30th November 2008, my family vacated the government house on Gore Brown Close. Instead of relocating to the farm in Choma, we shifted to a small lodge next to our plot in the Chilanga area to supervise the construction of a new house on a plot we bought from farmer Chindindiindi.

As a Backbencher, I presumed that I will be appointed a member of some Parliamentary Committees. I requested the Clerk that I be put into Committees, which did not deal with financial matters. My feeling was that my presence in any Committee dealing with public finance will be intimidating to the witnesses, many of whom I supervised for so many years.

I was appointed to the Health, Community Development and Social Welfare and the Communications, Transport, Works and Supply Committees. During the Committee elections, I was voted Chairman of the Communications Committee. Later in 2010, I was elected Chairman of the Joint Committee on Energy, Environment, Tourism, Health, Community Development and Social Welfare. I was also appointed to serve on the Parliamentary Select Committee to scrutinize the Presidential Appointments of Puisne Judges.

When interviewing the candidates, a member of the Committee joked that this was the only chance to interrogate the learned justices, who become so intimidating and hide in those fearful wigs once they are on the bench. I later learnt that the archaic dress code of wigs was introduced in order to hide the identities of the justices in view of the fear of revenge by the relatives of those found guilty and sentenced to prison terms.

Among the candidates scrutinized by our Parliamentary Committee was Counsel Patrick Matibini, who continued to hide behind a fearful wig when he became Speaker of the National Assembly of Zambia in October 2011. The wig was discarded in 1992 by Speakers of the British Parliament, the colonial master of Zambia, when the first female Speaker Betty Boothryod refused to wear one.

I continued to be a member of the National Constitutional Conference (NCC), which was constituted by President Mwanawasa to look at the Mung'omba Draft Constitution. The NCC of 500 members met at the Mulungushi International Conference Centre, when Parliament was not in session. I suddenly found myself very busy with the work of the Parliamentary Committees and the Constitutional Conference.

Due to the timetables of the Parliament and the NCC, I adjusted my travel time from Chilanga to Parliament buildings and Mulungushi Conference Centre through the busy town centre. In spite of the heavy traffic, I maintained my strict time-keeping habit and never arrived late for any meeting.

The first sitting of Parliament in 2009 was preoccupied with the budget discussions. Since I was familiar with the government financial systems, I added my voice to the debates on the various budget proposals. Strangely enough, most often my contributions were not welcome by the MMD front bench. The MMD Party strategized to take advantage of any opportunity to attack me both inside and outside Parliament.

When Parliament adjourned sine die on Friday 27th March 2009, I took the opportunity to visit my constituency to check on the progress of the on-going projects started under the Constituency Development Fund and other funding sources.

After Parliament resumed sitting in June 2009, the Parliamentary Committee on Health, Community Services and Social Welfare undertook tours of the Southern, Central and Copperbelt Provinces to inspect health facilities. The tour of Southern Province ended on Monday 15th June 2009 and we resumed the tours of the other two provinces on Saturday 20th June 2009.

In August 2009, the Committee on Communications toured sector related infrastructure in Southern and Western Provinces, which included the Chirundu One-Stop-Border Center, Choma-Chitongo Road, Zimba-Livingstone Road, Livingstone weighbridge and the Sesheke One-Stop-Border Centre, which were under construction.

Everywhere we went, people easily recognized me and thanked me for the work I had done at the Ministry of Finance and National Planning. The recognition and intimate conversations I had with the fish mongers at the Magoye Bridge and at the Mwandi market and the sellers of sweet potatoes near Kapiri Mposhi town amazed the other Patriotic Front members of the Committee.

We had stopped for refreshments at a restaurant in Kapiri Mposhi Town, when a young man cried uncontrollably when he was introduced to me. He kept on shouting repeatedly, "I have seen Mwanawasa, drawing the attention of more people who surrounded me. In those good days even a sizable crowd of people could not lead to an arrest under the Public Order Act. In my address, I encouraged the young man and the others to soldier on with hope for a better future.

At Mkushi Town, we had a rest and a tasty lunch at the Shalom Lodge owned by the MMD Member of Parliament. My rest while, watching a football game between Zambia and Algeria, was interrupted by a request to address a kitchen party being held on the same premises. Of course I had to part with some of my travel imprest to 'tayila' the dancers.

At both Kitwe and Ndola Shoprite supermarkets, business came to a standstill, when I was spotted in the shops. At a small shop named JK in rural Lufwanyama, the shopkeeper offered me an additional packet of biscuits for our lunch, after recognizing me by my voice.

On Wednesday 7th April 2010, the Parliamentary Committee on Communications started a tour of seven days covering the Central, Copperbelt and North Western Provinces. Parliament was considering the proposed regulations as a follow-up to the enactment of the Information and

Communications Technologies (ICT) Act of 2009. The Committee wanted to appreciate the extent of the availability of these modern facilities even in the remotest areas of the country.

In Ndola and Kitwe, we had extensive tours of the telecommunication facilities. We made a strong recommendation that the PTC College in Ndola be retained by the Zambian Government and be turned into an ICT university. President Banda took exception to this recommendation and singled me for an attack at the KKIA. In spite of the president's objection, I am happy that the college was not sold and is being upgraded into a university. In Solwezi, we met the former Permanent Secretary for the Ministry of Communications and Transport, who gave us a thorough briefing on what happened at his former Ministry and why and how he found himself in Solwezi.

The public hearings in Solwezi, Kabompo, Zambezi and Chavuma Towns were well-attended. In Zambezi, I had the pleasure of having conversations with freedom fighters and senior citizens Rodgers Sakuhuka and John Njapau. At Chavuma, I visited the Angola-Zambia border post, where I was given a dignitary's reception by the Angolan Government officials. For the night we stayed at the scenic 'God Is Great' Lodge owned by a local citizen and located on the banks of the Zambezi River.

We departed from Zambezi for Lusaka at 0600 hours on 14th April 2010 through the Watopa Pontoon, Lukulu, Kaoma and Mumbwa. At the pontoon, we were in the hands of a lively coxswain, Mukuka who took great interest in my future plans. One of the passengers on the pontoon was Kumesa Kumesa, a young historian and a resident of the nearby village, who amazed me with his knowledge of my life story.

At Lukulu Shopping Centre, I was moved to tears when a deranged pretty young mother, with a baby strapped on her back and scavenging for food in a dustbin called out my name as the Committee members past her. She politely asked me for food for her young baby. She explained that she recognised my voice as she knew it while at a secondary school before she had a misfortune, which led to her unfortunate situation.

As I wiped off tears from my face, a Lozi lady, just about my age, shouted, "Why are you crying, when it is you Tonga bulls who cause problems to young girls because of your insatiable desires. That baby is your product". The below-the-belt assault on me by one of my traditional cousins sent the crowd into a hilarious laughter.

When I took the young mother into a shop, she insisted that she wanted only food for her baby. However, the owners of the shop, the Soma brothers, whom I had never met before, offered to give the young lady whatever she wanted on my behalf for free. I remembered the 'God Is Great' Lodge we stayed in Chavuma and connected the gesture by the Soma brothers as a gift from God. One of the Soma brothers explained that they were thanking me for the work I did as a minister.

Spiced by tours into the country-side and a trip to Uganda to learn of the ICT developments, Parliamentary work was enjoyable and I fully participated in the debates on most bills brought into the House. Among the bills were those on the subjects of national interest, such as agricultural credits and marketing, animal health and veterinary, anti-corruption, company registration, consumer protection, dairy industry, disaster management, engineering institution, financial intelligence, health, ICT, immigration, non-governmental organizations, protection of whistleblowers and public-private partnerships.

Many of the Acts passed on these subjects have my personal input. I am as familiar with them as I was with the Public Finance Act No. 15 of 2004 and the Financial Regulations of 2006, which were my daily reference laws at the Ministry of Finance and National Planning. By the time I left Parliament in 2010, I had earned and deserved the life-long distinguished title of 'Honorable'.

During the meetings of the National Constitutional Conference (NCC) in 2009 and 2010, I was a reference point when dealing with matters of public finance management. While a lot had been done during the previous five years to establish financial management systems, there was still room for improvements and we were instructed by President Mwanawasa to support all progressive proposals by the NCC.

Of particular interest to President Mwanawasa was the loan contraction legal provisions. He directed that national loan contraction should be covered by a specific provision in the new Constitution, which will spell out the involvement of Parliament. The ministry proposed and members agreed that national planning be embedded in the Constitution, so that the country's future development will be in a more predictable and coordinated fashion and not on haphazard basis by the whims of whoever was in power.

CHAPTER 48

The MMD Party Schemes Against Me

While I was busy with work at Parliament and the National Constitutional Conference to maintain my name and share valuable experiences, my enemies in the MMD were working hard to discredit me and reduce my visibility. Every so often, a group or individuals in the MMD were covered by the public media with allegations of my insubordination and a call for my expulsion from the party.

In September 2008, a group of party cadres led by Benton Chewe, Provincial Youth Chairman for Lusaka Province were organized and given space in the government media to attack and malign me. The malicious campaign was fomented by some Cabinet Ministers who were not happy with my strict control of public funds and did not want me to succeed late President Mwanawasa to continue with such financial discipline.

On Wednesday 21st January 2009, the Minister of Communications and Transport, Dora Siliya made a ministerial statement in Parliament on the matter of Zambian Airways, stating that the matter was political. The same minister had earlier on 8th August 2008, while President Mwanawasa was alive, replied to the request from Zambian Airways. She refused to consider the request by the airline for deferment of some financial obligations for lack of a business plan and because she had rejected requests from other foreign airlines.

In early February 2009, Kaande, the Deputy National Secretary of the MMD Party organized a group of cadres to march to State House to show solidarity with the President. Some cadres displayed placards again calling for my expulsion from the Party.

In his reply to the chanting supporters, President Banda, while waving a file, shouted that he had correspondence in which I had promised to write-off the debts of Zambian Airways to the various government departments, if I won the presidential elections. A challenge to substantiate the allegation was never answered.

On Monday 2nd March 2009, Chewe and other praise singers appeared on Television Zambia and after publicly denouncing me, they called on the MMD NEC to discipline me for 'abuse of office' when I was minister. On 10th March 2009, a senior member of the MMD Party and a Member of Parliament supported the cadres in a speech in Parliament.

He stated that I did not deserve to be called 'Mr. HIPC' because others including him worked hard to bring Zambia into the HIPC Initiative. And yet, the MMD Party even used the nickname during the successful 2006 election campaigns without any objectors. I found it strange that someone was claiming to be called by the same nickname. In most cultures, they do not give one praise nickname to two different people.

I reacted to Chewe's allegations by writing a letter to him, requesting that he brings evidence within fourteen days or else I will resort to courts of law. Unfortunately, Chewe passed-on soon after the correspondence and his pack of lies were buried with his cold corpse.

As there was no party cadre to trumpet the allegations against me after Chewe's death, the MMD Party under the Chairmanship of Republican President Banda turned to using the state machinery to intimidate me. On 17th June 2009, I was summoned by the Drug Enforcement Commission (DEC) to answer charges of, 'Abuse of office by stopping the National Airports Corporation from closing the Zambian Airways to recover unpaid fees'. At my level and former status, the President would have approved the investigations by the DEC especially that he claimed to have some evidence.

During the interview at the DEC offices, I was referred to the events of July 2008 and my discussions with the MD of NAC. I informed my interviewers that what I did in 2008 was within my authority as Chief Economic Advisor and 'owner' of all Zambian Government assets including NAC. I emphasized that as Minister of Finance, I never encouraged parastatals to take such negative and punitive measures against any active participant in the Zambian economy as development was a collective responsibility between public and private stakeholders.

I went further to state that I will again do what I did if similar circumstances arose that threatened to tarnish the good name of Zambia, which President Mwanawasa worked hard to restore. I became aware of the establishment of Zambezi Airlines in 2008, which also ceased operations in 2012 due to debts owed to NAC.

The work of Parliamentary Committees, which included tours to the provinces, brought me face-to-face with those who benefitted from my ministerial work. They encouraged me to focus on the pending MMD Party convention, which was to elect the candidate for the 2011 general elections.

By December 2009, the fight was taken to my constituency by the Lusaka Provincial Chairman, William Banda, who claimed that I had not started any projects during my term as Member of Parliament. He made this claim while sitting on one of the comfortable new desks donated to Chilanga Basic School, by a private company at my request. He went on to say that RB had already been endorsed as the only candidate. On the Copperbelt my supporters were being identified and chased away from MMD Party functions.

By the beginning of 2010, the debate in the MMD Party on whether or not to hold a convention to elect a presidential candidate for the 2011 elections heightened. The voices favouring the holding of the convention seemed to be winning. I was busy consulting on my chances of winning at such a convention, since RB was not going to stand in 2011, if he kept his earlier word.

During President Banda's visit to Chief Mwanachingwala of the Tonga people in Mazabuka District on 14th February 2010, Daniel Munkombwe, a senior party official assured the President that, 'all delegates from the Southern Province are for you and any competitor will be suffocated and will not be allowed to speak to the people'. This was when I realized that some MMD members had been campaigning for President Banda to stand in the 2011 elections.

At that time, I had been identified as the strongest contender vying for the position of MMD Presidential candidate should a convention be convened. I recalled that the strongest opposition to my appointment by President Mwanawasa was from my tribesmen. In 2008, most of those who dissuaded me from standing in the presidential by-elections were also my tribesmen. I could not understand why politicians from the Southern Province, my region of birth, were opposed to my ascending to the highest public office in the land and openly campaigned against me. I had planned development projects in the province as early as 1971 when I was an assistant development officer at the provincial office.

On 13th March 2010, the MMD Party organized a Party Card renewal function at the Mulungushi Conference Centre, which I also attended. Michael Mabenga, Party Chairman, when introducing the members of the National Executive Committee, mentioned my name last and without any title.

As Mabenga continued with his speech, a group of youths entered the hall and while rushing towards the front rows where I sat, chanted 'Magande Out, Magande Out'. I looked at the Party Chairman, who had stopped speaking, for some reaction, but none was forthcoming. I turned to the high table trying to invite the attention of the senior officials, including the President. They were all laughing and enjoying the disgusting spectacle.

Recalling my father's teaching on courage as a virtue of a leader, I stood up, against the advice of Kaunda Lembalemba, who sat next to me. I faced the advancing youths and commanded in an authoritative manner, 'Be quiet and sit down'.

Suddenly, the advancing youths 'melted' into the crowd and there was dead silence in the packed huge conference hall. I realized that even the dignitaries on the high table who were laughing obeyed my command to keep quiet. I, Mabenga and security personnel were the only people standing. I turned and looked at the high table and sat down.

It was one awesome moment in my life, when I felt so proud of myself-belief for being so courageous, as to take control of a gathering of thousands of people, who included the Commander-in-Chief of the Armed Forces of Zambia.

Mabenga cut short his speech without any reference to what had happened. As the card renewal exercise commenced, William Banda came over to me and advised me to immediately leave the hall through the back door as, 'Youths could beat you up'. I refused to take his advise and I stayed on until after I had renewed my party card.

On Friday 16th April 2010, the Catholic Church was receiving Saint Patrick's Primary School situated along the Chilanga-Kafue Road in the Chilanga Constituency from a volunteer organization from Ireland. The Guest of Honour was the First Lady, Thandiwe Banda and the host was His Grace Archbishop Terence Mpundu. I invited myself to the function as Member of Parliament for Chilanga Constituency.

As the formalities were coming to an end, there were frantic consultations amongst the invited guests to which I was not privy. Then the master of ceremony came over to me and invited me to speak. I resisted as I could see that my inclusion was a last minute afterthought. But finally I accepted the late invitation to address the gathering.

I informed the gathering of my campaign meeting in the unplanned settlement during the 2006 elections. At the meeting, there was a group of children whom I had a separate meeting with. When I asked them what they wanted, one of the older girls stated that they wanted a school. She said that it might be too late for her as she was already old. But she stated that other young people will benefit from the school. '*Ba-Magande, tinanvela zamene munacita. Muzakatiletela sikulu kuno*', she said. It was after this moving request that I promised to work hard to bring a school to the area.

I told the gathering that it was faith that made it possible for me to get volunteers from Ireland to construct Saint Patrick's Primary School. As we were inspecting the new classrooms, First Lady Thandiwe Banda came closer and whispered, 'So, you believe a lot in faith?', to which I replied in the affirmative.

I thought that my first meeting with the First Lady will bring good tidings and peace with the first family. Unfortunately, it made my situation complicated. Two days later on Sunday, the MMD Party Chairman, Mabenga took his turn in attacking me for advocating for a convention and demanded that I should leave the MMD Party.

On 20th April, RB made me a subject of his address to the party cadres in Kitwe, calling me a puppet of the Post newspaper. He bragged that he defeated me during the MMD NEC elections and that he will do the same during the convention. This was the first affirmation that President Banda intended to stand during the 2011 general elections.

On Sunday 23rd May 2010, I was being interviewed by Frank Mutubila at a hotel in Northmead, when a group of MMD cadres led by the MMD

Provincial Chairman came to disrupt the function. They shouted insults at me publicly in the presence of so many people.

The interview was cut short by the rowdy mob. As we left the hotel car park, occupants of two cars, brandishing hand guns and threatening bloodshed, chased us in the Rhodes Park residential area. The incident was reminiscent of those of the James Bond films. Fines Mulunda, our driver, a retired police officer, used his skills to evade the pursuing vehicles. My report to the Police headquarters nearby did not achieve much.

Unlike during President Mwanawasa's time, when discipline was observed both in the civil service and the party, this time, the MMD party cadres were in total control and the Zambia Police could not take any action against them.

On Sunday 25th July 2010, I hosted an associate at home who shared some useful political information with me. He informed me that he was close to the Patriotic Front leadership and knew most of their plans. He advised me to join the PF as I will add great value to the organization in economic management. He informed me that as at that point in time, the PF was ahead of the MMD in voter preference and will win the elections.

I asked him for the shadow cabinet of the PF and the backgrounds of the members. He startled me when he stated that Sata, the president of PF did not believe in such details and is not willing to discuss the government structures even with his closest party members. When I asked about the integrity of the PF leadership, he stated that the Zambians just wanted to remove the MMD Government and were not interested in integrity.

I asked if his group, with its strong stance on integrity and their concerted fight against corruption had also given up their fight because of the general public mood. He replied that they will go along with the public in order to remove the MMD from power, but being 'king makers', they will influence appointments by the President to get the right people in important government positions.

I informed my visitor that with the constitutional powers vested in the President of Zambia, they will be ignored by their chosen 'king'. I told him that I was surprised with his assertion that Zambians did not care to choose leaders of integrity. He promised to come back after the elections to persuade me to join the new PF Government.

On 12th August 2010, I went to the funeral house of late Lameck Chibombamillimo in the company of Sylvia Masebo. A group of MMD cadres openly assaulted me. They tripped me and ripped off the pocket of the jacket of my suit. As I fell down, they grabbed my cellular phone from one of the pockets.

I reported the incident at the Woodlands Zambia Police, only after a lot of persuasion from friends, as I was aware of the incompetence of the Police in the face of intimidation from the MMD cadres. A few days later, some of my contacts whose numbers were in the phone started received threatening and abusive calls for supporting me. My request to the Zambia Police to trace the callers through the phone service providers did not achieve any positive results.

The MMD officials tried to implicate me in a case of a bouncing cheque we had issued to a security firm providing security to the family. They then hatched the story of an unpaid Tanzanian trader, claiming that he had supplied thousands of tons of rice through my agent in Mbala. The news made headlines in one of the government newspapers. Our daughter working in the civil service was denied confirmation and promotion, in spite of her good performance. I was lucky that I was fully briefed on all these happenings by some government officers and I knew who was behind all these schemes.

In spite of all this harassment, I was still determined to stand at the MMD Party convention, whenever it was convened. With the overwhelming support and welcome I received during the tours of the Parliamentary Committees to the provinces, I was convinced of victory. My supporters were also campaigning and the party membership was divided between RB and me. Some of the vocal supporters of RB during the 2008 by-elections had turned against him for not being appointed to government positions.

In the midst of the tension, I was invited by some opposition parties to resign from the MMD and join their parties. However, many within the MMD were of the view that I should remain in the party and challenge President Banda at the convention. By this time, the President had changed his earlier statements and was openly declaring his intentions to stand, not only at the convention, but during the 2011 general elections.

My opponents realized that all their schemes to stop me from advancing my political ambitions failed. Malicious allegations and physical attacks by MMD Party cadres and senior officials did not achieve their intended objectives. Neither did the use of the state institutions work, as they did not find a case against me.

On Saturday 4th September 2010, while I was reading Michael Porter's 'The Competitive Advantage of Nations' in our lounge at home, I received a telephone call from Bates Namuyamba, a senior MMD NEC member asking me why I was not at the NEC meeting going on at State House. I informed him that I was not aware of the meeting as I did not receive any notice.

He then informed me that I had been expelled from the MMD Party by the NEC meeting being chaired by President Banda. When he came home after the meeting, he gave me some details of the debate at the NEC meeting. I was surprised with the opposition to my standing, which was supported by some ministers, who I had regarded as friends.

I received the letter of expulsion on 5th September 2010. The opposition PF and UPND failed to remove me from Parliament since 2006 through the courts of law. President Banda terminated my appointment as a minister and I became a backbencher. The MMD NEC chaired by President Banda finally expelled me from the MMD Party in order for me to lose my membership of

Parliament. By his unprecedented manoeuvres, President Banda managed to block all my important sources of income.

No member of parliament who won election petitions in courts of law against opposition parties was removed from parliament by their own party. The general conclusion was that I was expelled so that I did not have an opportunity to attend the MMD Party convention and challenge President Banda. I made history of fighting two opposition parties and a governing party within a period of three years.

Realising how President Banda used his powers as President of both the MMD Party and the Republic of Zambia to disadvantage me, I accepted the decision of NEC, as I did not expect to win against the mighty Commander-in-Chief of the armed forces of Zambia.

I wrote to Mr. Speaker that he could declare the Chilanga Constituency seat vacant. Mr. Speaker wrote back a memorable letter wishing me best wishes for the future. I was approached by senior officials from both the Patriotic Front and the United Party for National Development, the two parties that had colluded for over two years to remove me from Parliament to stand on their tickets. Now they wanted me to stand as their candidate in the same constituency. Having won the battles against the PF and UPND parties in the courts, I decided to have nothing to do with them as I suspected them of having ulterior motives in their invitations.

At a campaign rally near Mount Makulu Research Station for the by-elections in Chilanga constituency, both President Banda and Vice President Kunda made me a subject of their speeches. The large crowd in attendance was drawn from the community that benefitted from a dip tank, maternity ward, Saint Patrick's Primary School, a market, a repainted and furnished Chilanga Primary School and the Larfage Expansion Project during my tenure as Member of Parliament.

In reply to many questions on my expulsion, the president stated that I had become a difficulty member of the party. I was listening attentively and anxious to hear more from him about my transgressions. Suddenly, his speech was cut short by a strong whirlwind, that blew-off the tent and the gathering scampered for safety. With my great faith, I concluded that the Creator could not allow the beneficiaries of my developmental work to listen to falsehoods.

As per my prediction, the by-election held on 25th October 2010 in the Chilanga Constituency was won by the UPND candidate and not the governing MMD Party candidate. This was an early pointer of what was to befall the MMD Party in the 2011 general elections.

CHAPTER 49

Formation Of The National Movement For Progress Party

On 30 August 2010, Logan Shemena of Solwezi came to Lusaka and ended up at Parliament where he asked to see me. I willingly accepted to see him as I had known him when he was the Secretary General of the United Party for National Development under President Mazoka.

In Shemena's view, I could still play an active part in the politics of the country through another route as I had integrity, which I exhibited during my public service. In reaction, I answered that I had a lot of misgivings on the future of Zambian politics as it was becoming money-centred. I told him that instead, I planned to form a nongovernmental organization (NGO) as a vehicle for lobbying the government in development matters. Shemena embraced my idea and agreed to assist in establishing the organization.

On Saturday, 25 September 2010, I was summoned to travel to Choma to appear before a Council of Traditional Chiefs. Without disclosure of the agenda, although I suspected that it was to do with my future political plans, I declined to make an extempore trip.

The following day, I received a written message that some Chiefs would travel to Lusaka for discussions with me on Monday 27 September 2010. As notified, Their Royal Highnesses, Senior Chief Monze, Chief Macha and Chief Hanjalika arrived at our residence in Chilanga at 09.30 hours.

I had frank discussions with their Royal Highnesses on a number of issues. I explained the circumstances that had led to my expulsion from the MMD Party. I briefed them on an earlier meeting I'd had with other chiefs in August 2008, at which some of the issues being discussed were dealt with. The earlier meeting had been convened to discuss issues pertaining to the presidential by-elections after the demise of President Mwanawasa. Their Royal Highnesses fully comprehended and appreciated my explanations and requested that I should continue to brief them on my plans for the future.

I assigned Shemena with the responsibility of recruiting founding members, who were to apply for registration of the organization. Shemena had no difficulties in getting individuals willing to join and to be founding members. Of course, most of them were ordinary citizens as the prominent people were not prepared to come out into the open to support my plans.

In concluding my consultations on my future role in Zambia's development, I, and supporters firmed our plans to form an NGO called the National Movement for Progress (NMP). The ten applicants were interviewed by panels of eight officers from the security wings over a three-week period. The final interviews were concluded on 20 October 2010, and due security clearance were given for the registration of the non-political organization.

All the registration formalities were completed and application forms submitted to the Registrar of Societies on 5 November 2010. We were advised that the Movement could start operations while waiting for a printed certificate of registration. The executive committee was formed and met to agree on operational modalities. The committee appointed me the patron of the organization.

The NMP started forming branches and allowed the members to elect office bearers at the district level. Everything seemed smooth going as I was getting calls of support from all over the country.

On 31 January 2011, we received a letter from the Registrar of Societies, which confused us on the status of the organization. The letter in part read as follows;

"I wish to inform you that your application can only be considered for registration if you clearly state that this is a political party rather than using a name of a pressure group as a front for political activities.

You are therefore advised to henceforth stop carrying out activities of your organization until it is registered as a political party."

Intensive consultations on the new stand taken by the registrar did not resolve the matter as members insisted that our organization was not for political activities, as advocacy in favour of a cause does not need to be always done on a political basis. While the consultations were going on, I was visited by Elias Chipimo Junior and his spouse, who enquired on whether I had made up my mind to join politics.

I informed him of my plans of forming an NGO and that I was instead being pushed into politics. He then informed me that he had just registered a political party and was keen in getting me to join. He explained in detail the background to his entering the political arena. We then agreed to continue meeting to find a way of working together.

I also had a meeting with Charles Milupi, during which we discussed politics. He also informed me that he had registered a political party and was inviting me to join. I informed him that I had registered an NGO and wished to approach advocacy from another angle. I did not give him a conclusive answer and we agreed to maintain active contact as we moved on.

I then started consulting individuals that I thought would constitute a good team to run an effective political party. Many of them were technocrats, who preferred working and complaining behind closed doors. I had behaved in a similar manner working behind late Anderson Mazoka until late President Levy

Mwanawasa had removed my veil and exposed me to the public.

A Zambian who had passed by the ACP Secretariat in Brussels, Belgium revealed to me how he had to be convinced by a staff member that one of the portraits in the corridors of the Secretariat was that of me as I had been the Secretary General of the global institution. He said that this was because there was little talk in Zambia of my appointment to such a lofty international position.

CHAPTER 50

Negotiating A Political Alliance

After the registration of a political party, I was visited by many people including a number of senior citizens giving various proposals and all shades of advice. Most of them encouraged me to have discussions with the leaders of other parties in order to form an alliance that would field one presidential candidate.

The belief by many of my visitors was that there were other leaders of political parties with similar characters to mine, in terms of integrity. It was felt that we could provide a formidable alternative to the ruling party during the elections due in September 2011, despite the advice that Zambians did not care about integrity. I was advised that it would be easier to discuss with the leaders of parties that did not have any Members of Parliament.

After visiting Livingstone and the Copperbelt for consultations, I approached Elias Chipimo, Charles Milupi, General Godfrey Miyanda, and Fred Mtesa for discussions on forming an alliance amongst our parties. The first three embraced the idea and attended a series of meetings. We made a lot of progress and agreed to constitute a team of our members to study all the manifestos and come up with a consolidated one. We agreed that once we had sold the alliance idea, we would then discuss the modalities for choosing a presidential candidate for the alliance.

We finally agreed to meet to give instructions to our juniors to draft a press statement for an announcement the following day. In anticipation of the important assignment, a large number of senior members of our parties turned up for the meeting at my residence, and the car park was full of friendly and lively chat.

After the usual opening formalities, I asked if any of my colleagues had any special issues to raise. The one who asked for the floor stated that at the meeting of their national executive committee the previous night, they had decided that their party should not join the alliance. The main reason given was that the issues covered in their manifesto were new and progressive and would be diluted if incorporated into a consolidated one under the alliance. It was claimed that only the members of that new party would sell the ideas in the manifesto to the people of Zambia and win the elections.

One of the other leaders asked whether there was any room for negotiating this new stance with the opposing NEC members. We were told that the decision was final. As some comfort, we were informed that this particular party would not attack any of the other parties that had engaged in this futile exercise during the campaign for the coming elections.

In closing the meeting, I stated that even without attacking one another, none of our four parties would win the September 2011 elections. I concluded that I would not be available in the foreseeable future to engage in any discussions on political party alliances. Since there was not going to be an alliance statement, we agreed that each one of us was responsible for transmitting the sad end of our discussions to their party members.

CHAPTER 51

Campaign Malpractices And Corruption In Zambia

The NMP party officials and I refocused our campaign message. We became technical in our presentations and promised the continuation of the policies that had been implemented under late President Mwanawasa. By this time, the new MMD administration had abandoned many policies and procedures, which had been developed by the late president, including the windfall tax on the mines. Having worked in four parastatals and six ministries, I was conversant with the operations of the Zambian public service and the NMP party's manifesto was on the real problems of the people.

Our party's campaign became more focused and members of the NMP Party appearing on public media carried copies of the party manifesto and referred to specific provisions when debating the chosen subjects. The manifesto was also put on the party's website and any literate enquirer was sent a copy through the internet. Unfortunately, these strategies exposed some of our bright members who became targets of purchase by other parties.

In Lusaka, one of our members who provided an intelligent discussion on a television programme was waylaid outside the studios and offered a substantial amount of money to defect to another party. Cadres from another party threatened to beat him up if he continued to campaign for the NMPP. I was not sure whether he left the NMPP because of threats or the money.

In some provinces, our members were followed immediately after our meetings and offered large sums for them not to present themselves during nomination day. On the day of nominations, many party members did not turn up, giving all manner of excuses. Bright young candidates joined the gambling game and made themselves available to the highest bidder, as they preferred cash to future national responsibilities.

As per electoral procedures, our party nominated an official to travel to South Africa to observe the printing of the ballot papers. We were convinced that the NMPP representative understood the party's instructions on his responsibilities. We were in touch with him for some time. As the NMPP was often cited as an example in most of the explanations by the printers, we felt that our party official had made a great impact. A few days before the party officials were due to return to Lusaka, we lost contact with our representative as his phone went unanswered permanently.

One young man defected to NMPP from UPND some weeks before nominations and successfully applied as an NMPP candidate. As the printed ballot papers with his name on them were about to be brought to Zambia from South Africa, he defected back to the UPND. After consulting the ECZ, I was advised that there was nothing they could do about the candidate. Such an incident of a candidate defecting when ballot papers have already been printed was the first of its kind in the electoral history of Zambia.

In my former home area in Magoye Constituency, the MMD Party used armed cadres to terrorize the people during the campaigns. When these terror methods failed, they resorted to more vile means. A few days before the elections, Willies Malambo, the NMPP candidate for the Magoye Constituency died from suspected poisoning. The elections for a parliamentarian in the constituency were postponed to a later date but we could not find anyone willing to risk their life.

CHAPTER 52

Recognition By The Global Development Community

The elections were held on Tuesday, 20 September 2011. Joyce and I voted at the Parklands School in Chilanga Township. As usual, the results were announced over a three-day period. At about 04.00 hours on Thursday morning, we were gathered in the lounge when it was announced that I had received seven votes in the Itezhi-Tezhi Constituency in the Namwala District of the Southern Province. All those in the room expressed utter surprise with the result and in an impromptu reaction, Joyce my spouse, a qualified midwife with limited computer literacy, shouted, 'These votes are computer generated".

The remark immediately removed my anxieties, such that from that moment, I never felt any humiliation for my poor showing during the September 2011 elections. In the Magoye Constituency, where I also got poor results, my relatives disputed the results, as they claimed to have voted for me. Since I believed my relatives, I attributed my poor results to malpractices and corruption before, during and after the voting.

President Michael Chilufya Sata of the PF was announced the winner, while nine of us, including Rupiah Banda, the MMD Party candidate and sitting Republican President, lost the elections. Under the provisions of the Zambian Constitution of the time, the winner was the one who got the highest votes even by one vote. Since this formula produced minority winners, the provision in the Constitution was amended to provide that the winner should get 50 per cent plus one vote.

By the end of September 2011, the NMPP inner circle met to review the happenings since the registration of the NMPP as a party in March 2011. The major difficulty was lack of support to the party in either material or monetary terms from the public. We concluded that Zambian politics had been infiltrated by gamblers, who staked all they have in order to win votes, which will place them in positions, where they become masters and not servants of the people.

After the announcement of the cabinet on 29th September 2011, by President Sata, my political associate, who had invited me to join the PF earlier on, came back to admit to me that the 'king' was too powerful to be influenced by the 'kingmakers'. I reminded him that the office of the president of the

Republic of Zambia is vested with so much authority that the occupant can make irreconcilable and irredeemable decisions on any matter.

During the many years of public service and interaction with many heads of state and government all over the world, I had the privilege of intimate conversations with some of them. They shared with me the intricacies of the operations of their offices and how they managed to continue winning elections even under loud public revolt. Most often, they used the immense power of their offices to get what they wanted.

While I was still bewailing my loss in the elections, I was invited, in July 2011, by Todd Moss Chairman of the Centre for Global Development (CGD), a Washington-based think tank, concerned with global poverty and the people of the developing world, to join other development experts in a study of the operations of the International Development Association (IDA) of the World Bank. The Future of IDA Working Group of twenty-three, "brought together serious scholars, practitioners, and policymakers to explore specific options for World Bank management and shareholders to consider".

The invitation to membership of this group, in my personal capacity, was the greatest recognition and honour bestowed on me, by the global development community, for my efforts in proposing various solutions to the eradication of poverty in the world, during my forty years of public service.

IDA was created in 1960 to give concessional funds to poor countries to sort out the problems of their poor citizens. A provision in the IDA conditions states that the countries whose gross domestic income rises above a specified threshold shall graduate to middle-income status. In spite of the intractable poverty in Zambia, the country benefitted from these concessional funds since it became a member in 1965.

Regrettably, most leaders of developing countries, especially in Africa, have failed to utilize the cheap funds in a judicious manner to eradicate the poverty of their citizens due to corruption and poor management. In Asia, a number of countries that put the cheap IDA resources to good use did manage to move millions of their citizens out of poverty. A number of them are graduating into the middle-income status. Once a country graduates and attains the new status, it becomes ineligible for concessional finances.

Most leaders of developing countries still require lessons from Hernando de Soto on "The Mystery of Capital" as "The Other Path" to development. Lack of clarity on capital will mean that most of the world's poor people will still live in middle-income countries, which are no longer eligible for IDA aid in the 21st Century. It is not clear where these vulnerable people will find resources to develop, as much of the local resources will be under the control of the elite, who have personal agendas.

The assignment on IDA, as a member of a global think tank, took me back to what I knew and enjoyed best – the debate on development. With outings to Paris and Washington DC, rubbing shoulders with the likes of Nancy

Birdsall, one of the authors of "The East Asian Miracle: Economic Growth and Public Policy, New York: Oxford University Press, 1993), I was once more assured of enjoying the conversations with those I meet on my continuing journey.

The route I have taken has at times led me deep into the 'jungle' full of many challenges. It has been a remarkable and memorable one that has given me the opportunity to leave deep indelible footprints on the clear path I made, as I continue onto my unknown destination. Having surpassed 65 years, the age of reflection, I can confidently answer and say, **"Yes, it has been okay to have been me."**

Acknowledgements

This book has a lot of information on my ancestry, dating back long before I was born. My thanks go to Grandmother Mizinga her brother Grandfather Matongo Father Simwaale, Aunt Namweemba (bina-Hachiloli) and Uncle Aaron, who were blessed with long lives and were available and willing to assist me in reconstructing my ancestry.

After settling down in the ferry, taking us away from the Robben Island, I informed my spouse, Joyce that I wanted to record my life history. As she hesitated to react, I started to tell her in detail the violent plane incident on our flight to Fiji in 1998, to prove the state of my memory at the age of 65 years. Joyce then agreed with my proposal. I thank her for agreeing to my project and sitting late into the night to assist me, whenever I needed to confirm the details of some of the incidents that occurred in my life.

Dennis Chiwele, Robert Liebenthal and Dennis Wood put aside their work and reviewed the first draft. They assisted in identifying mix-ups between some headings and the write ups, and suggested appropriate headings for some of my thoughts. As a first-time author, only used to writing technical official documents, I was fortunate to get the assistance of Joanna Booth who expertly edited the manuscript. She toned down the technical slant of the book and made it user-friendly to the general readership. I thank the reviewers and any stray technical word is all my fault.

I thank all my children, in particular Nchimunya Namboozi Magande, who read through the draft and assisted in making corrections and designed the format of the book. As we relied on modern communications for e-conferencing, I had a discussion with my grandchildren in America, South Africa, and in Zambia. The subject was the choice of my picture to use on the book. We had four pictures to choose from.

I could hear my granddaughter Zuria arguing with Arieh her young brother, in America in the background. The group discussion went on until the four-year old American, Arieh shouted, "This one, shows grandpa thinking". That was when I realized how much detail each family member was committing, in order to get the best results. My grandchildren give me delight that they already are demonstrating that they have found and are following my footprints.

I am grateful to my friends and relatives, too many to mention, who encouraged me to undertake this project.

Index

J

K

L

T

U

Y

Y2K, 250
Yamado, Kiyoshi, 395
Yaqona Drinking Ceremony, 256
Yeta, Ilute, 70, 107, 108
Yeta, Prince Inyambo, 107
Young Turks, 181
Youth Empowerment Programme, 354
Yoyo, Arthur, 54

Z

ZAF Planes, 274
Zambezi Escarpment, lv
Zambia Agricultural Development Bank
(ZADB), 171
Zambia Agricultural Marketing And
Processing Infrastructure Project
(ZAMPIP), 205
Zambia Airways, 95, 107, 143, 150, 338
Zambia Congress Of Trade Unions
(ZCTU), 291
Zambia Consolidated Copper Mines
(ZCCM), 403
Zambia Financial And Banking Services
Association (ZFBSA), 317
Zambia Had To Be Saved, 281
Zambia Horticultural Products Limited
(ZAMHORT)., 112
Zambia Industrial And Commercial
Association (ZINCOM), 161
Zambia Institute Of Chartered
Accountants (ZICA),, 317
Zambia Institute Of Management
(ZAMIM), 92
Zambia Institute Of Purchasing And
Supply (ZIPS), 306
Zambia National Building Society
(ZNBS), 131, 132

Zambia National Commercial Bank, 155,
179, 191, 193, 200, 310, 311
Zambia National Human Development
Report (ZNHDR), 373
Zambia National Wholesale Corporation
(ZNWC), 95
Zambia Privatisation Agency (ZPA), 179
Zambia Privatization Agency (ZPA)., 204
Zambia Procurement And Purchasing
Authority (ZPPA)., 306
Zambia Revenue Authority (ZRA), 239,
294, 295, 301, 417
Zambia Safaris Limited, 162
Zambia Union Of Financial And Allied
Workers (ZUFIAW), 319
Zambia Wildlife Authority (ZAWA), 397
Zambian Airways, 460, 469, 470, 486,
491, 498, 499
Zambian Avocadoes, 118
Zambian Technocrats, 294
ZANACO, 191, 192, 193, 194, 195, 197,
199, 201, 202, 203, 204, 286, 299,
310, 311, 312, 322, 330, 331, 334
ZCCM Settlement Scheme, 164
Zebron, Ernest, 180
ZESCO, 74, 75, 104, 148, 175, 279, 330,
331, 334, 388
Zimbabwe, 28, 50, 71, 75, 109, 157,
187, 235, 242, 245, 264, 365, 366,
422, 457, 458
ZIMCO, 175, 179, 191, 193, 195, 196,
204, 287, 297, 439
Zukas, Simon, 190
Zulu, Alexander, 142
Zulu, Ballard, 205
Zulu, Mary Grace, 298
Zulu, Maureen, 128
Zulu, Sebastian, 312
Zulu,Grey, 144, 145, 147, 148, 149
Zuria, Granddaughter, 93, 515

Made in the USA
Columbia, SC
19 March 2024

33273757R00321